NUMB TO THIS
Memoir of a Mass Shooting

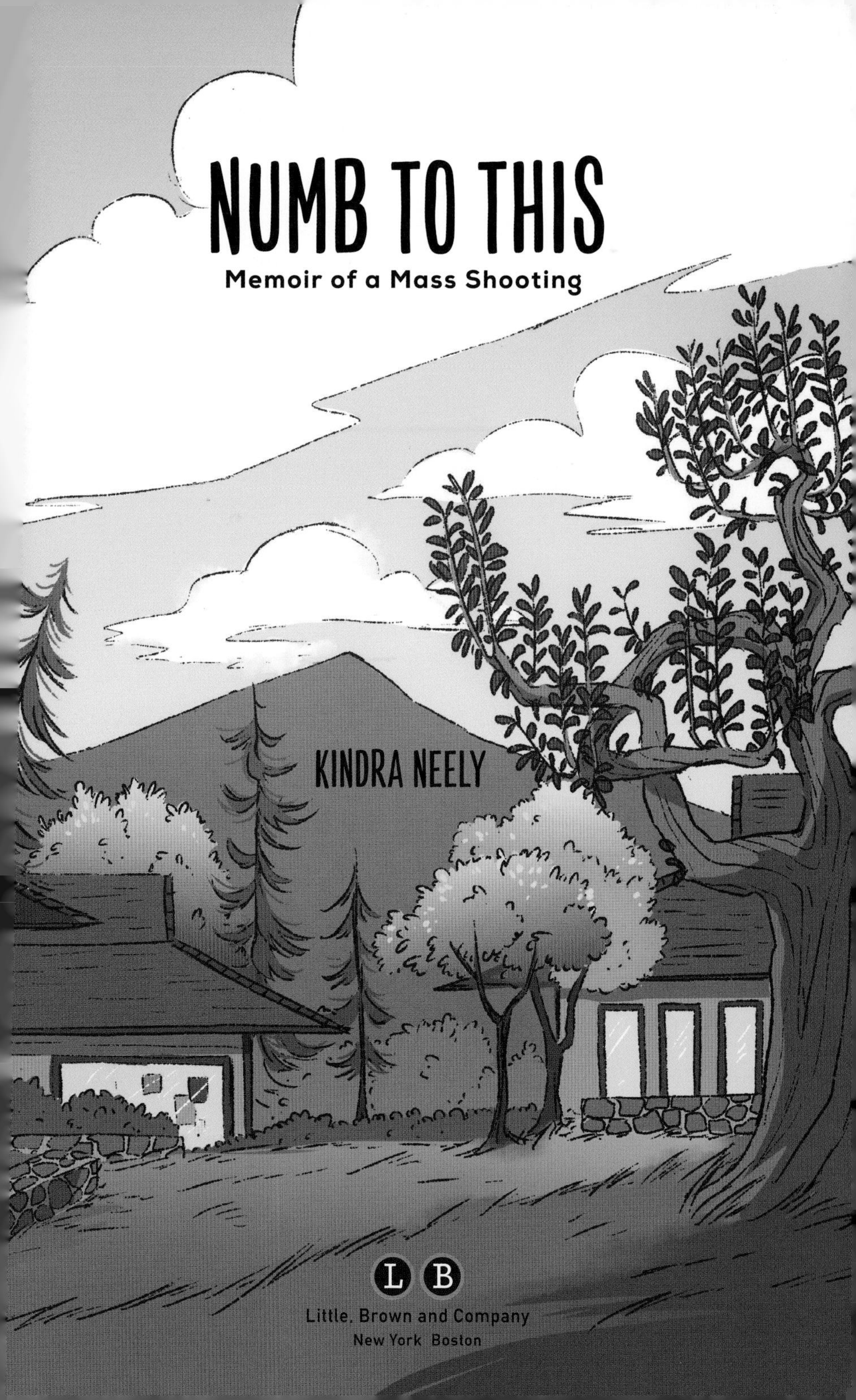

NUMB TO THIS

Memoir of a Mass Shooting

KINDRA NEELY

Little, Brown and Company
New York Boston

ABOUT THIS BOOK

This book was edited by Andrea Colvin and designed by Megan McLaughlin. The production was supervised by Bernadette Flinn, and the production editor was Lindsay Walter-Greaney. The text was set in Action Figure BB and Din and the display type is Colby Compressed and Nexa.

Little, Brown and Company
Hachette Book Group
1290 Avenue of the Americas, New York, NY 10104
Visit us at LBYR.com

First Edition: October 2022

Little, Brown and Company is a division of Hachette Book Group, Inc.
The Little, Brown name and logo are trademarks of Hachette Book Group, Inc.

The publisher is not responsible for websites (or their content) that are not owned by the publisher.

Library of Congress Cataloging-in-Publication Data
Names: Neely, Kindra, author. | Neely, Kindra, illustrator.
Title: Numb to this: memoir of a mass shooting / Kindra Neely.
Description: First edition. | New York : Little, Brown and Company, 2022. | Audience: Ages 14 & up | Summary: "Author Kindra Neely recounts her journey to healing after surviving a mass shooting during her first year of college." —Provided by publisher.
Identifiers: LCCN 2020041822 | ISBN 9780316462082 (hardcover) | ISBN 9780316462099 (trade paperback) | ISBN 9780316462075 (ebook)
Subjects: LCSH: Neely, Kindra—Comic books, strips, etc. | Victims of violent crimes—Oregon—Roseburg—Biography—Comic books, strips, etc. | School shootings—Oregon—Roseburg—Comic books, strips, etc. | Umpqua Community College (Roseburg, Or.)—Comic books, strips, etc. | Graphic novels.
Classification: LCC HV6250.3.U53 R676 2022 | DDC 362.88/293092 [B]—dc23
LC record available at https://lccn.loc.gov/2020041822

ISBNs: 978-0-316-46208-2 (hardcover), 978-0-316-46209-9 (pbk.), 978-0-316-46207-5 (ebook), 978-0-316-28072-3 (ebook), 978-0-316-28082-2 (ebook)

PRINTED IN CHINA

APS

Hardcover: 10 9 8 7 6 5 4 3 2 1
Paperback: 10 9 8 7 6 5 4 3 2 1

This book is dedicated to those who have been taken by gun violence and to the families, loved ones, and first responders who carry on their memories.

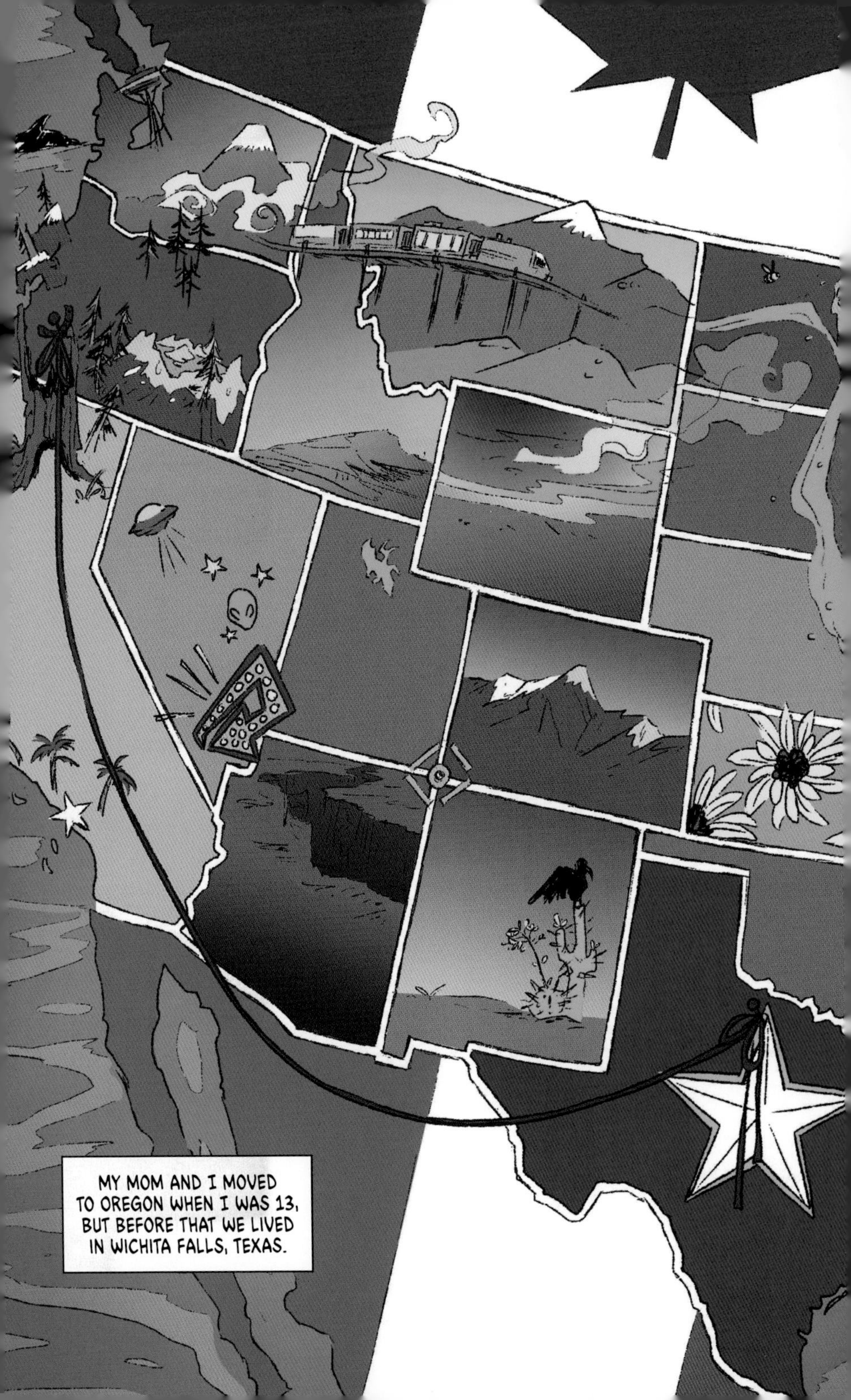
MY MOM AND I MOVED TO OREGON WHEN I WAS 13, BUT BEFORE THAT WE LIVED IN WICHITA FALLS, TEXAS.

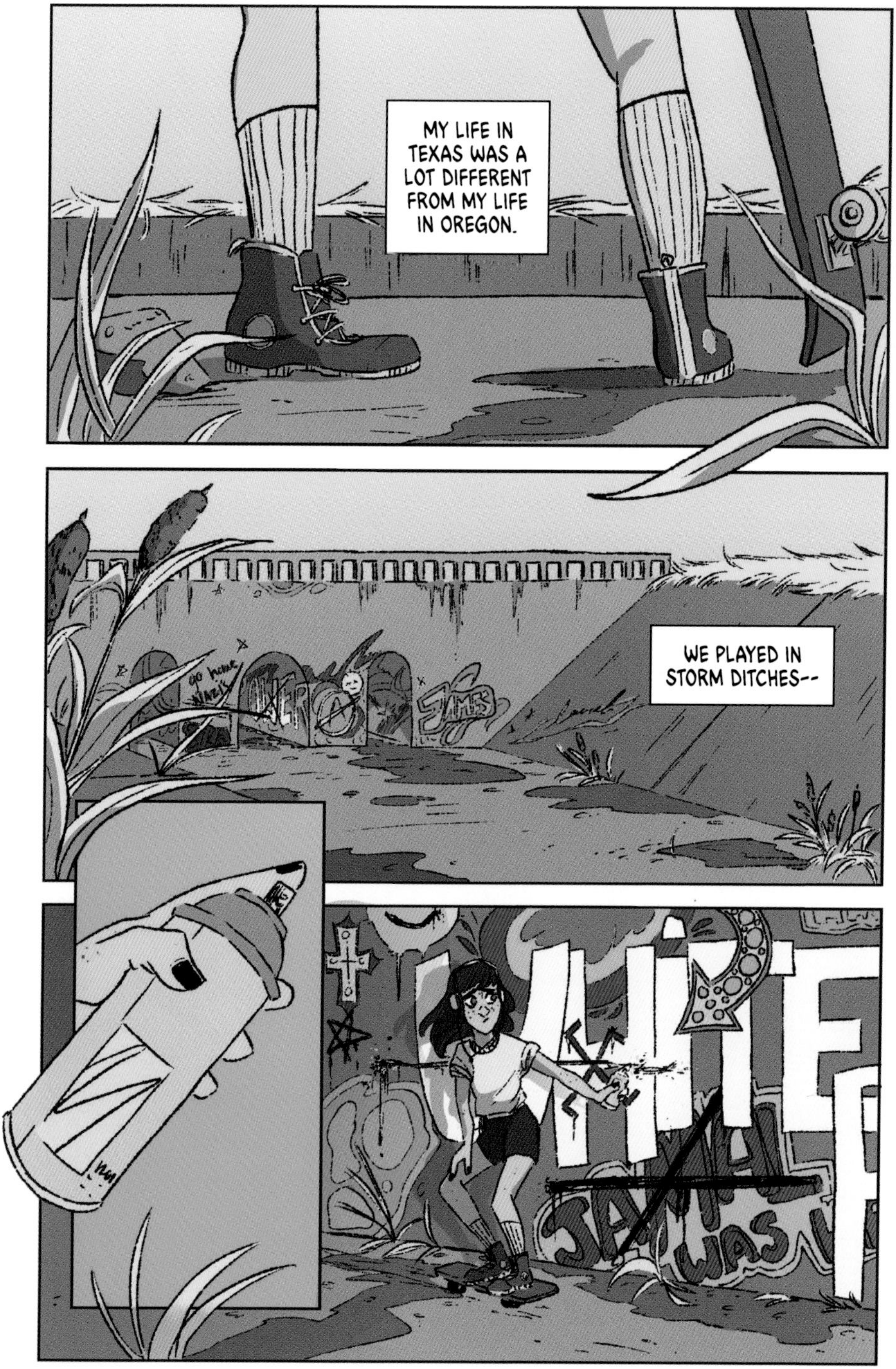
MY LIFE IN TEXAS WAS A LOT DIFFERENT FROM MY LIFE IN OREGON.
WE PLAYED IN STORM DITCHES--

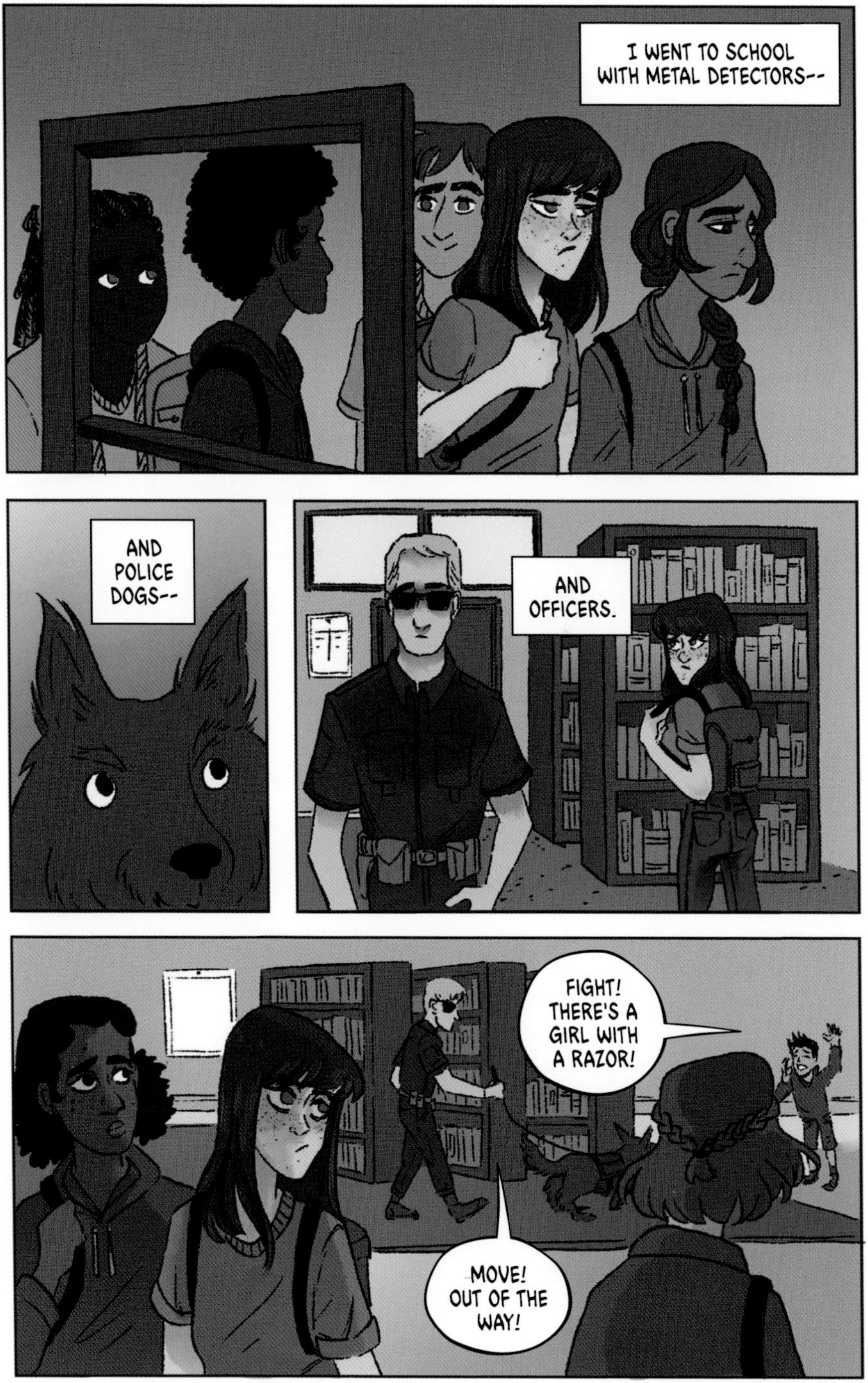
I WENT TO SCHOOL WITH METAL DETECTORS--
AND POLICE DOGS--
AND OFFICERS.
FIGHT! THERE'S A GIRL WITH A RAZOR!
MOVE! OUT OF THE WAY!

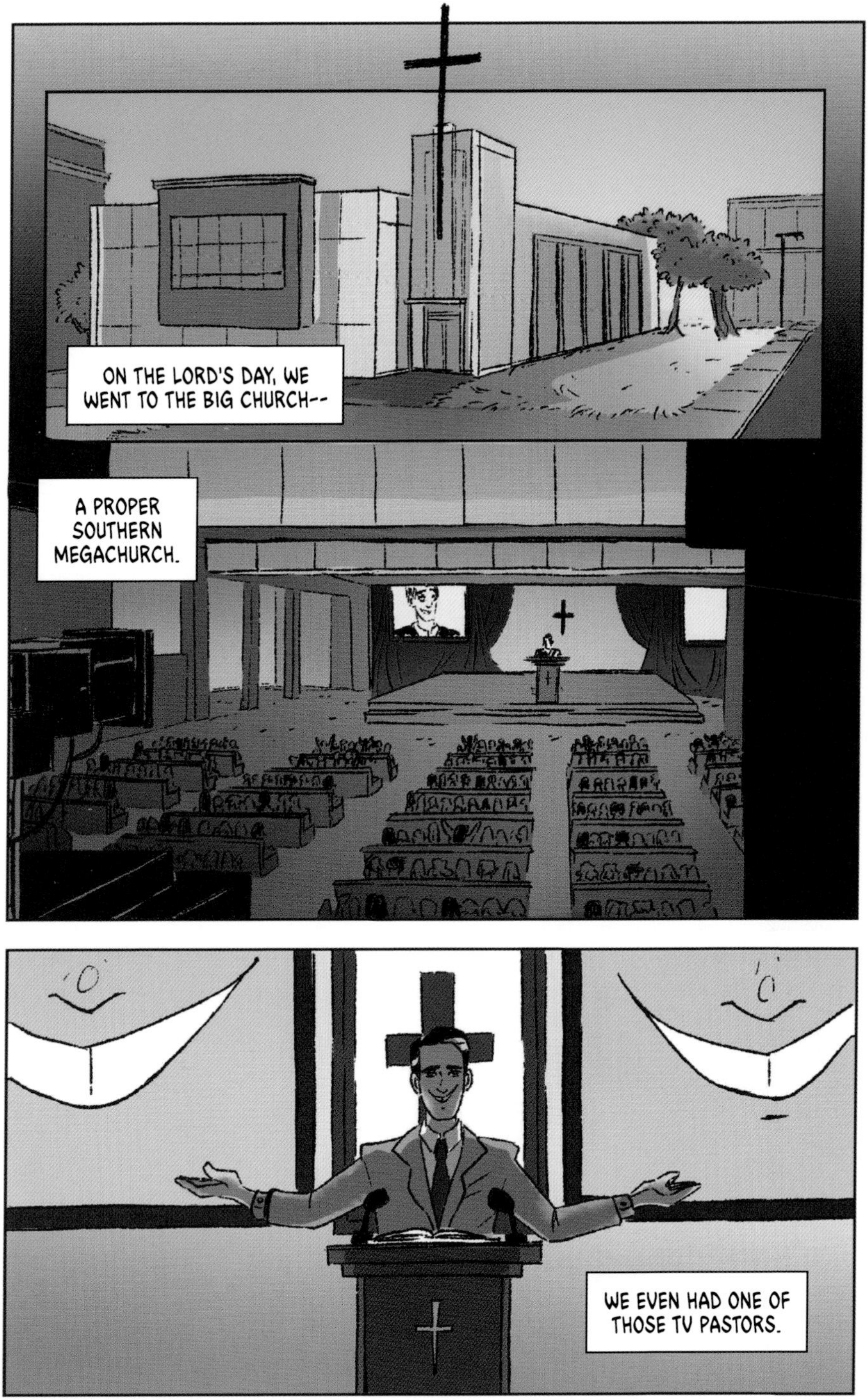
ON THE LORD'S DAY, WE WENT TO THE BIG CHURCH--
A PROPER SOUTHERN MEGACHURCH.
WE EVEN HAD ONE OF THOSE TV PASTORS.

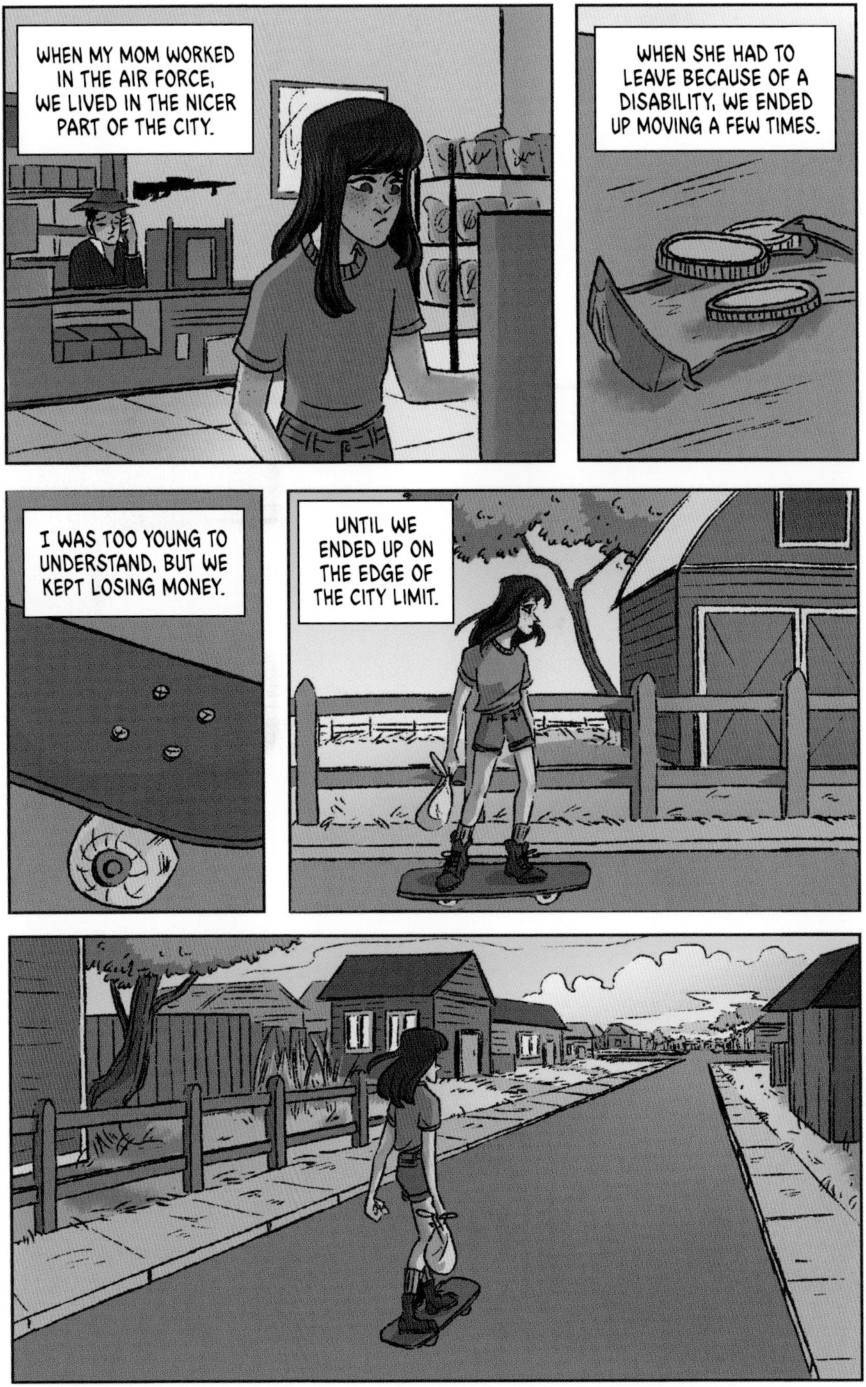
WHEN MY MOM WORKED IN THE AIR FORCE, WE LIVED IN THE NICER PART OF THE CITY.
WHEN SHE HAD TO LEAVE BECAUSE OF A DISABILITY, WE ENDED UP MOVING A FEW TIMES.
I WAS TOO YOUNG TO UNDERSTAND, BUT WE KEPT LOSING MONEY.
UNTIL WE ENDED UP ON THE EDGE OF THE CITY LIMIT.

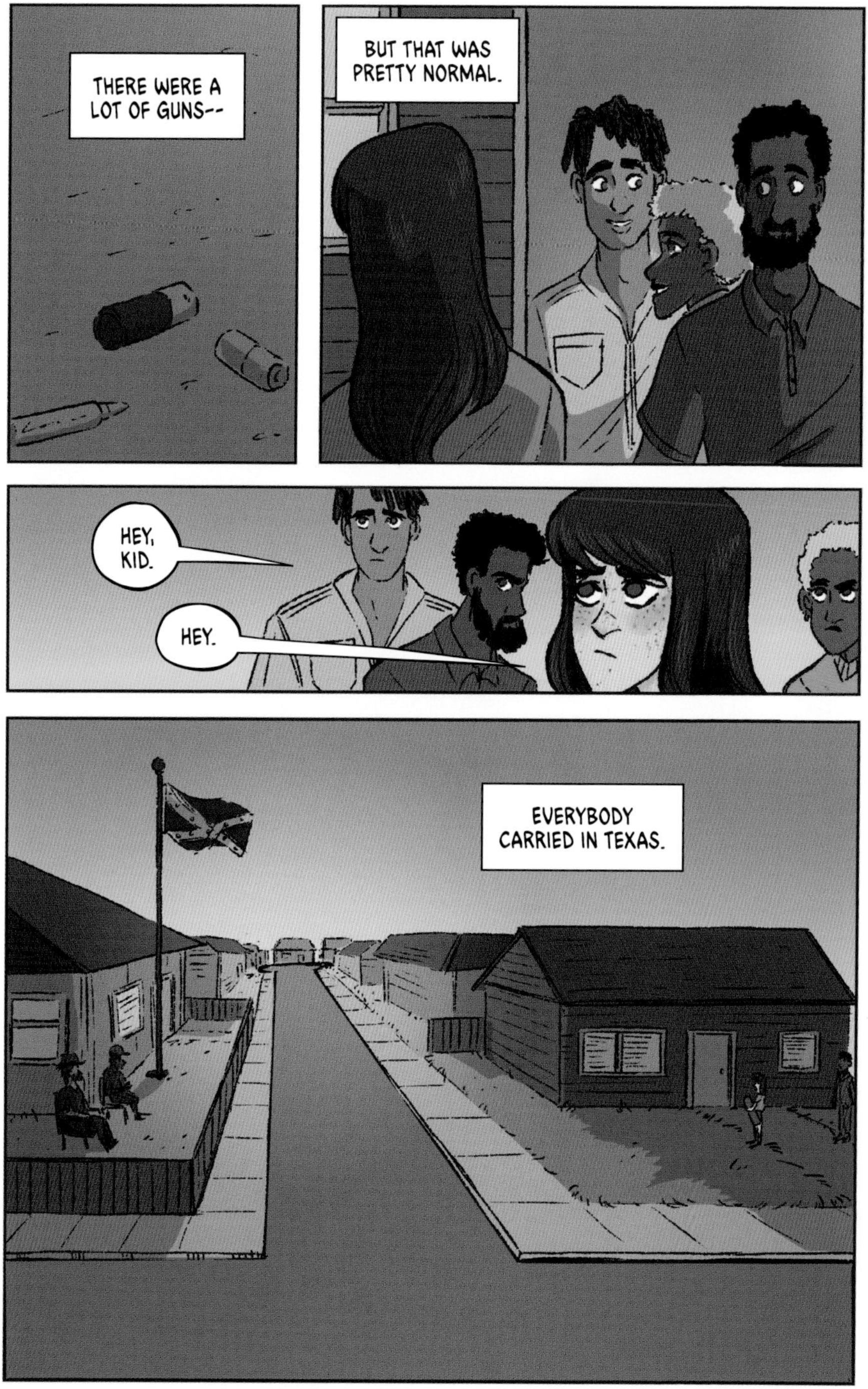
THERE WERE A LOT OF GUNS--
BUT THAT WAS PRETTY NORMAL.
HEY, KID.
HEY.
EVERYBODY CARRIED IN TEXAS.

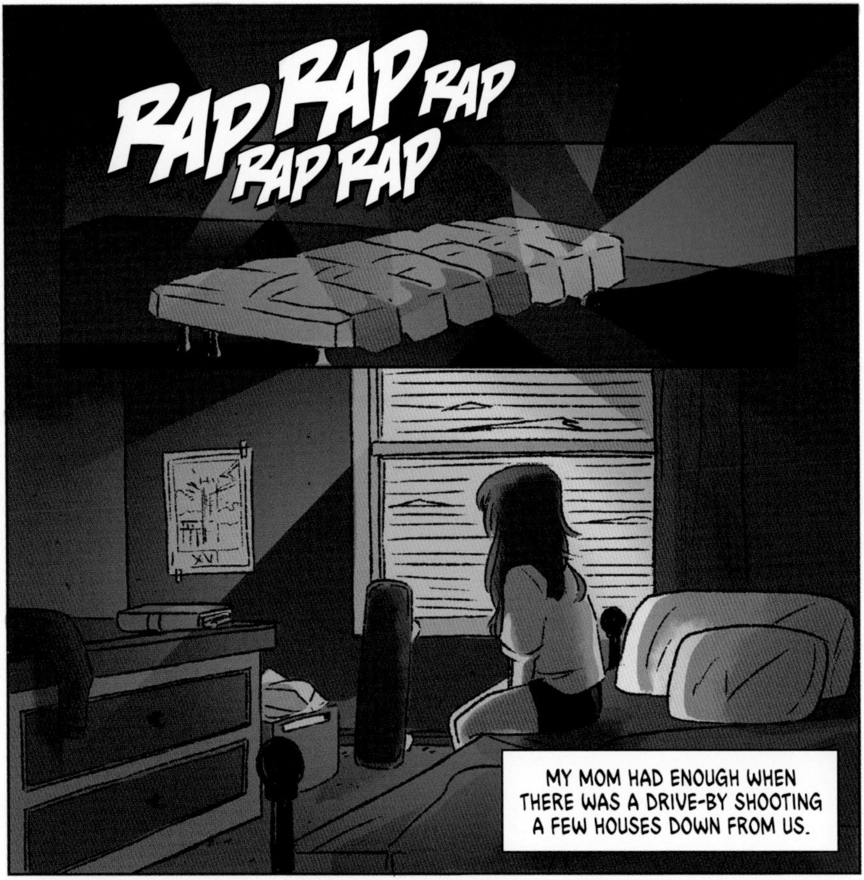
RAP RAP RAP
RAP RAP
MY MOM HAD ENOUGH WHEN THERE WAS A DRIVE-BY SHOOTING A FEW HOUSES DOWN FROM US.

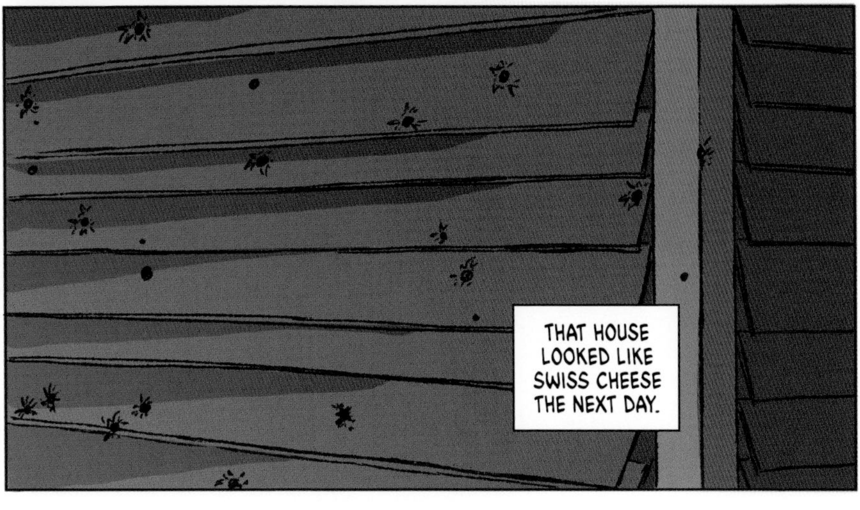
THAT HOUSE LOOKED LIKE SWISS CHEESE THE NEXT DAY.

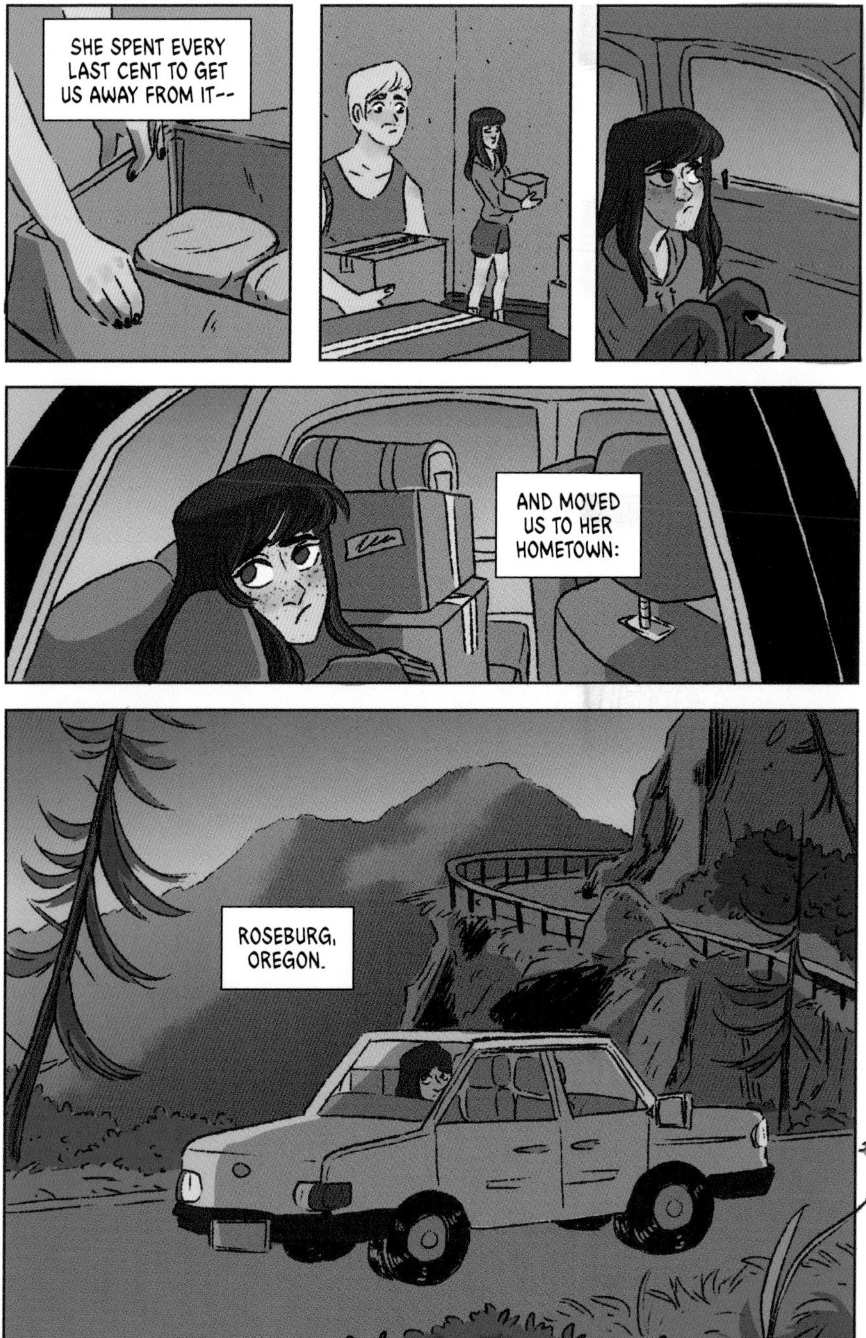
SHE SPENT EVERY LAST CENT TO GET US AWAY FROM IT--
AND MOVED US TO HER HOMETOWN:
ROSEBURG, OREGON.

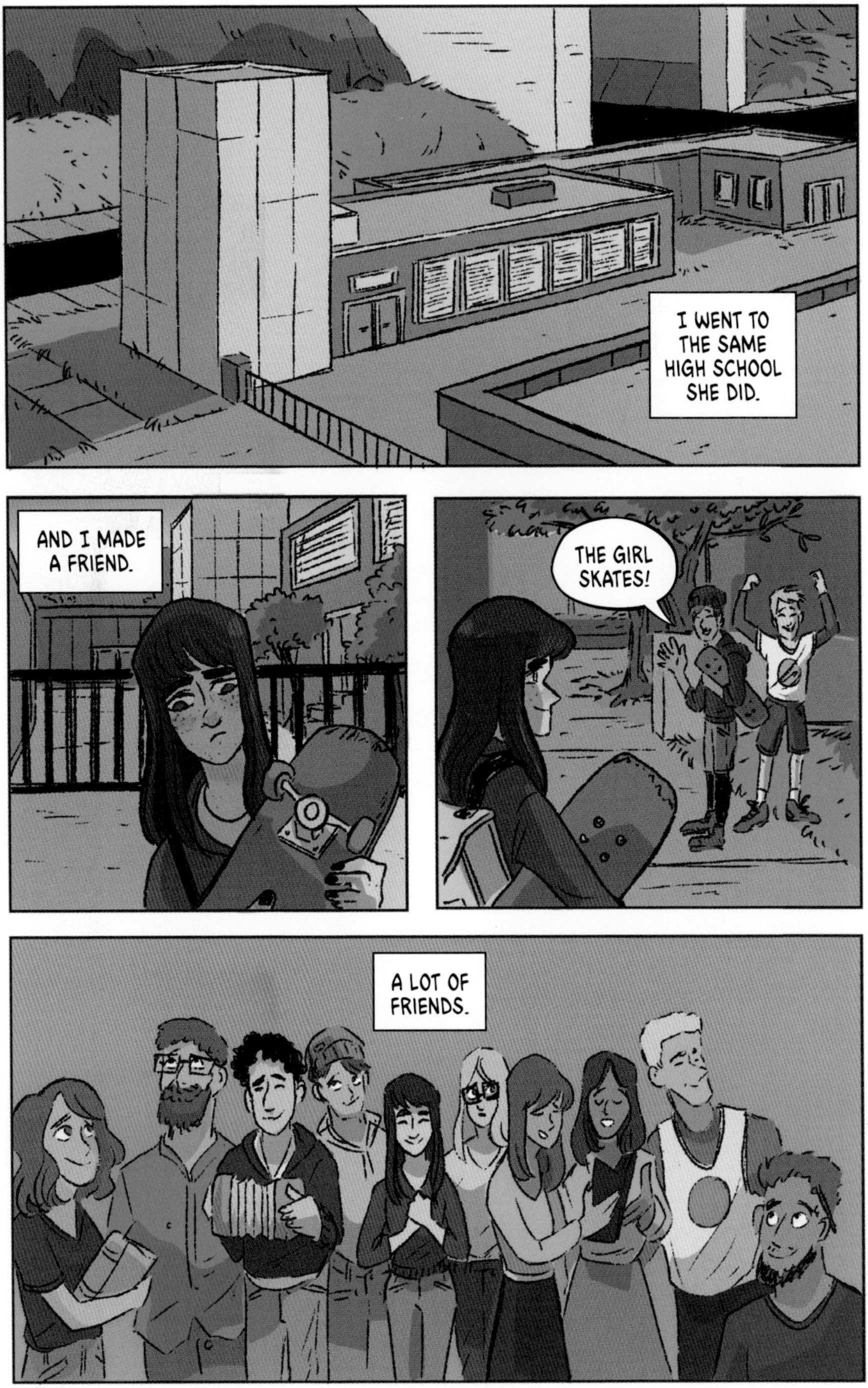
I WENT TO THE SAME HIGH SCHOOL SHE DID.
AND I MADE A FRIEND.
THE GIRL SKATES!
A LOT OF FRIENDS.

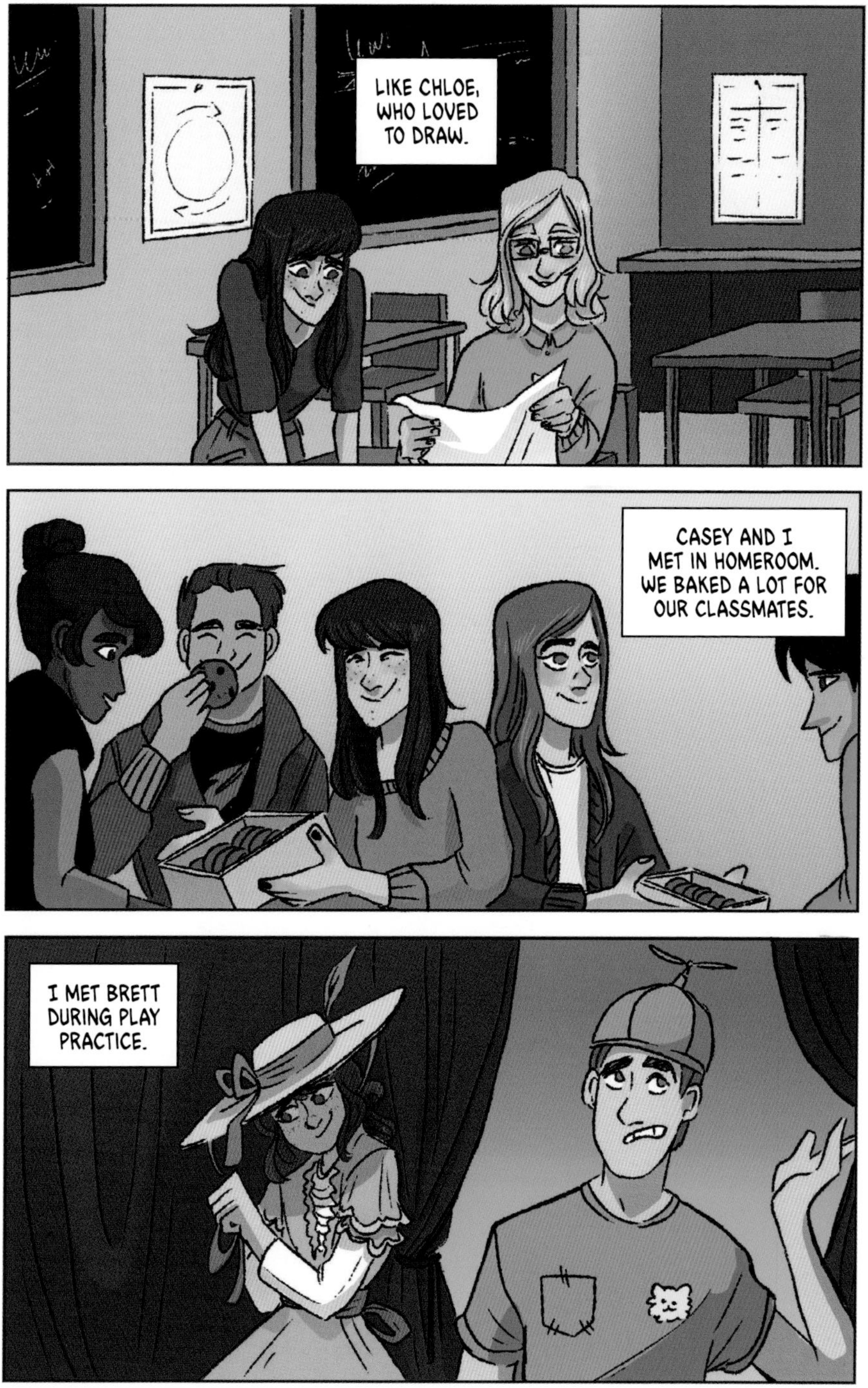
LIKE CHLOE, WHO LOVED TO DRAW.
CASEY AND I MET IN HOMEROOM. WE BAKED A LOT FOR OUR CLASSMATES.
I MET BRETT DURING PLAY PRACTICE.

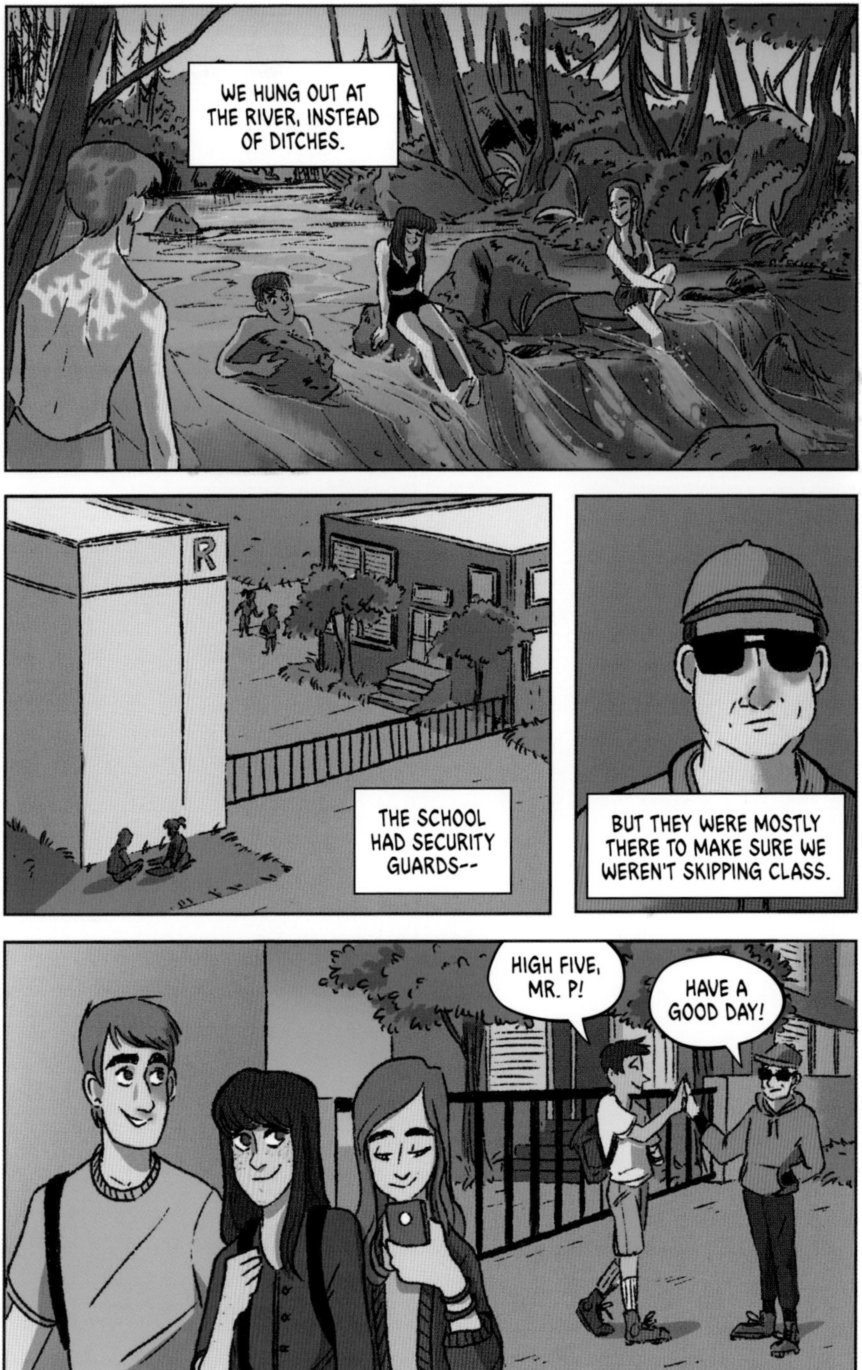
WE HUNG OUT AT THE RIVER, INSTEAD OF DITCHES.
R
THE SCHOOL HAD SECURITY GUARDS--
BUT THEY WERE MOSTLY THERE TO MAKE SURE WE WEREN'T SKIPPING CLASS.
HIGH FIVE, MR. P!
HAVE A GOOD DAY!

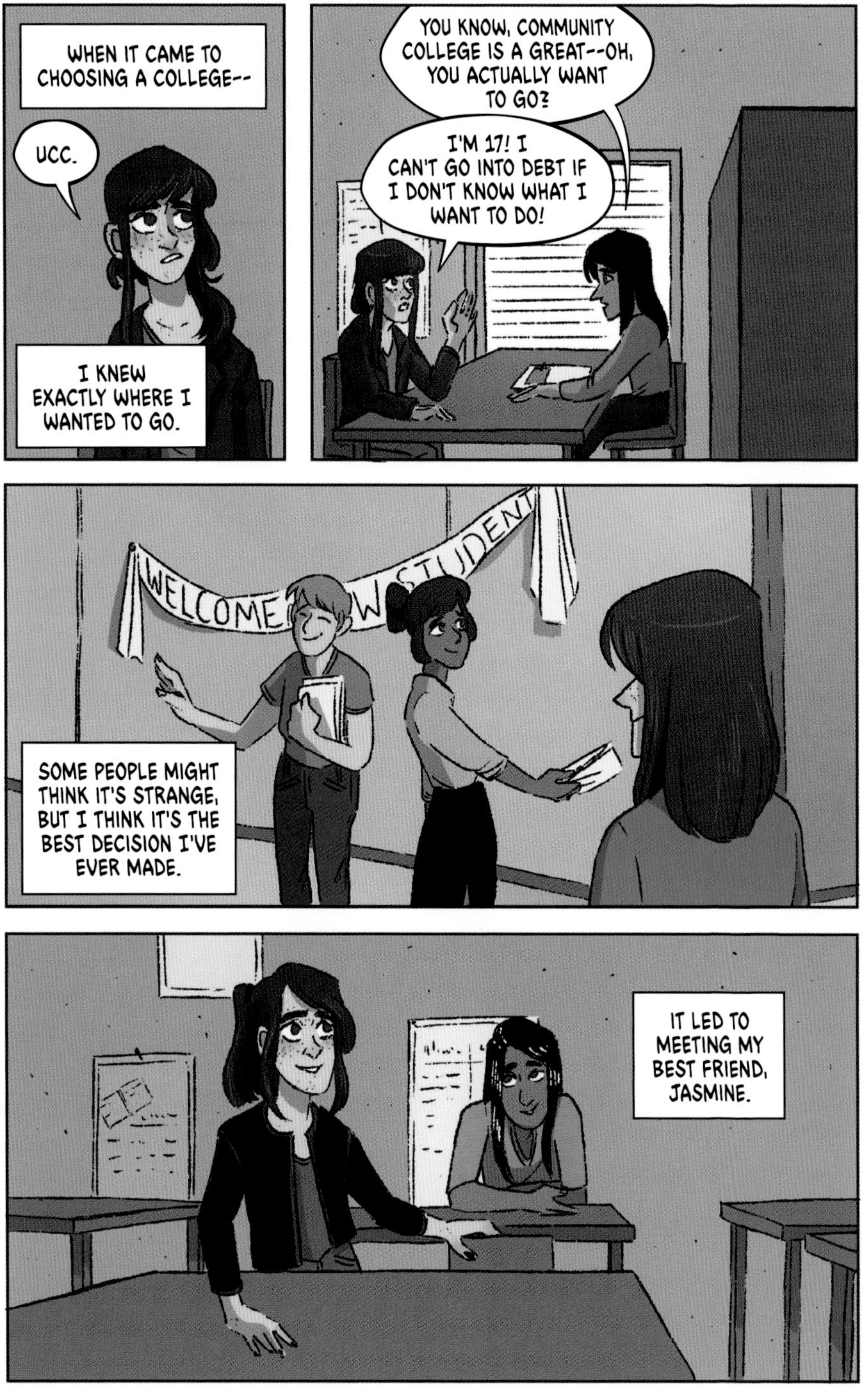
WHEN IT CAME TO CHOOSING A COLLEGE--
UCC.
I KNEW EXACTLY WHERE I WANTED TO GO.
YOU KNOW, COMMUNITY COLLEGE IS A GREAT--OH, YOU ACTUALLY WANT TO GO?
I'M 17! I CAN'T GO INTO DEBT IF I DON'T KNOW WHAT I WANT TO DO!
WELCOME W STUDENT
SOME PEOPLE MIGHT THINK IT'S STRANGE, BUT I THINK IT'S THE BEST DECISION I'VE EVER MADE.
IT LED TO MEETING MY BEST FRIEND, JASMINE.

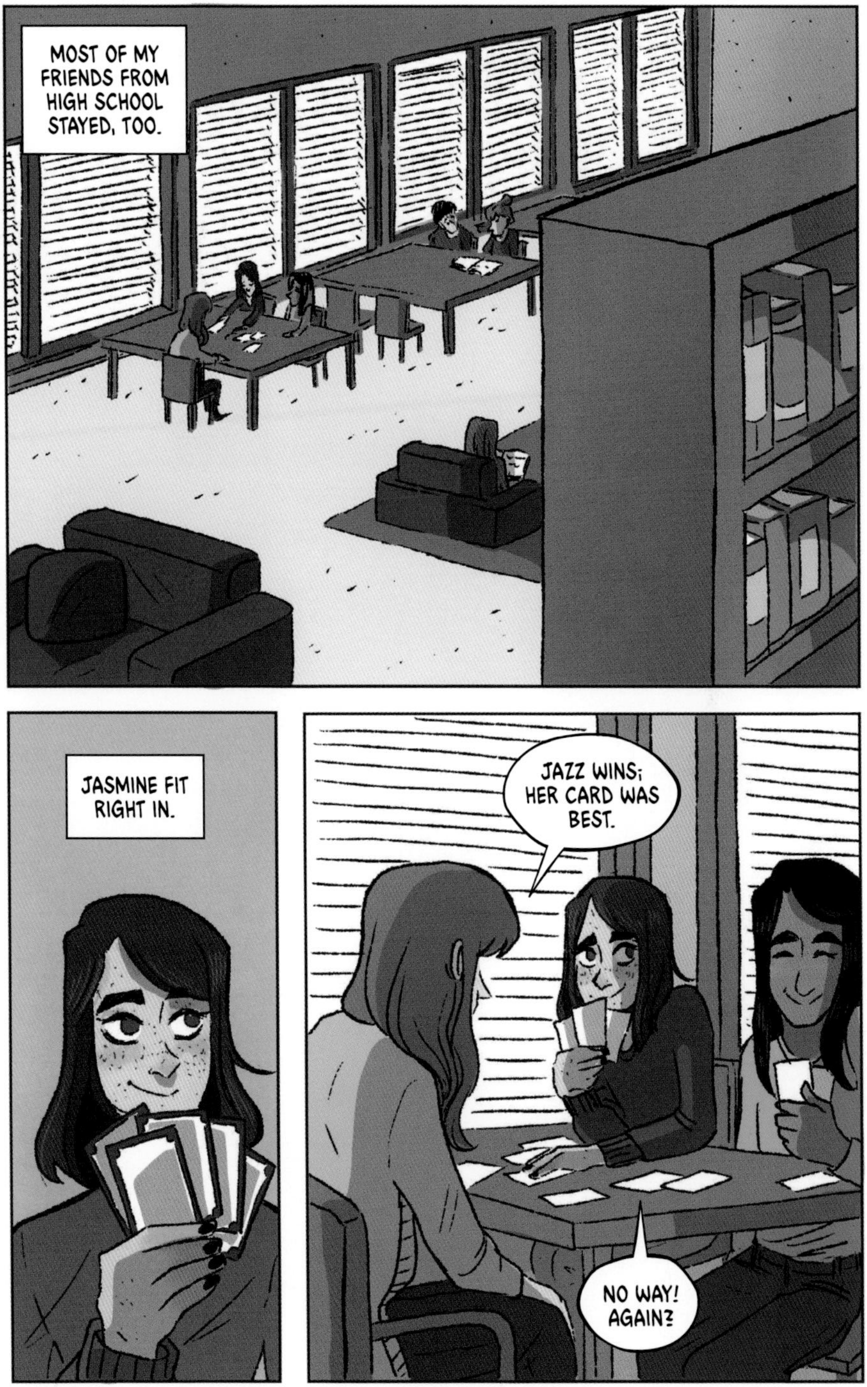
MOST OF MY FRIENDS FROM HIGH SCHOOL STAYED, TOO.
JASMINE FIT RIGHT IN.
JAZZ WINS; HER CARD WAS BEST.
NO WAY! AGAIN?

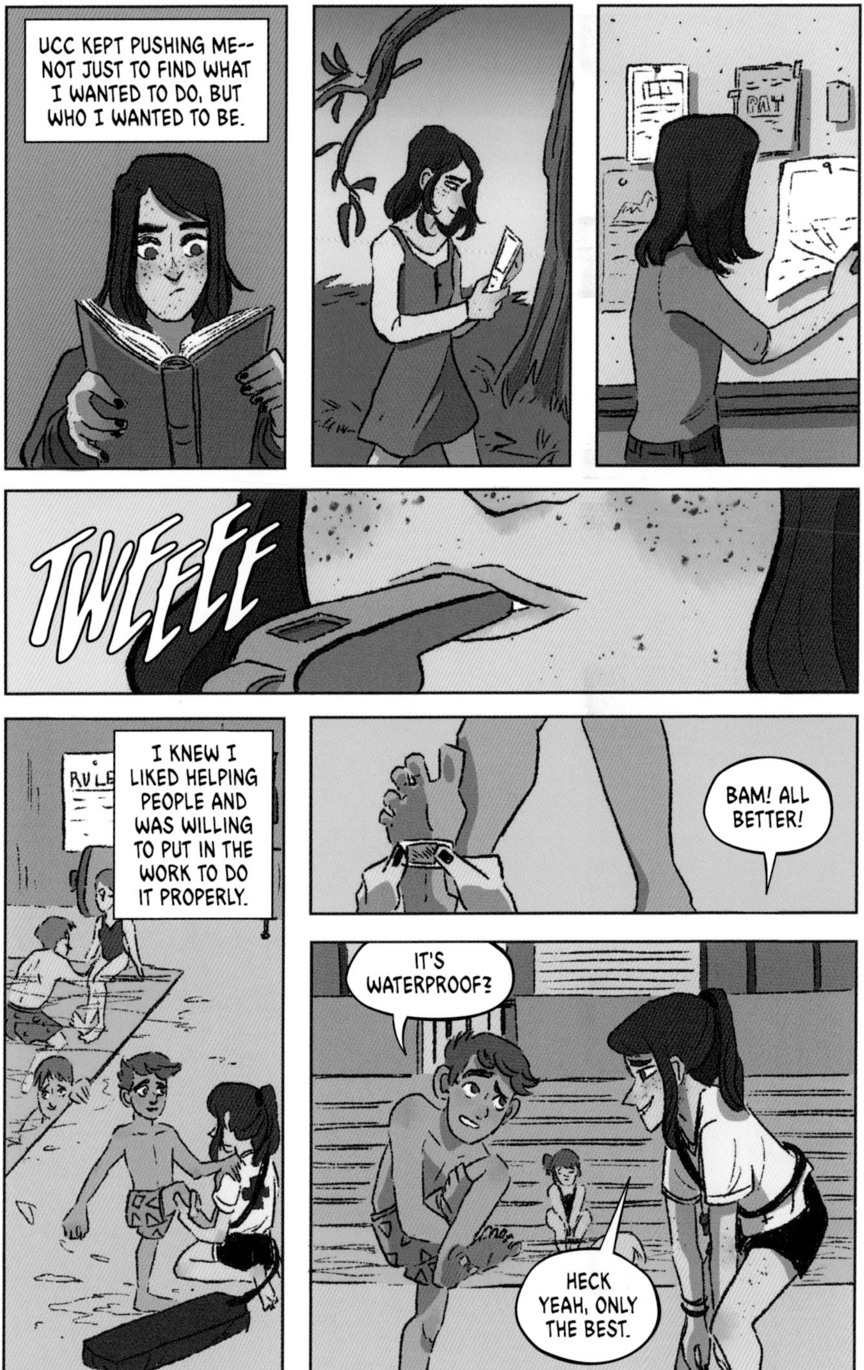
UCC KEPT PUSHING ME--
NOT JUST TO FIND WHAT
I WANTED TO DO, BUT
WHO I WANTED TO BE.
TWEEE
I KNEW I LIKED HELPING PEOPLE AND WAS WILLING TO PUT IN THE WORK TO DO IT PROPERLY.
BAM! ALL BETTER!
IT'S WATERPROOF?
HECK YEAH, ONLY THE BEST.

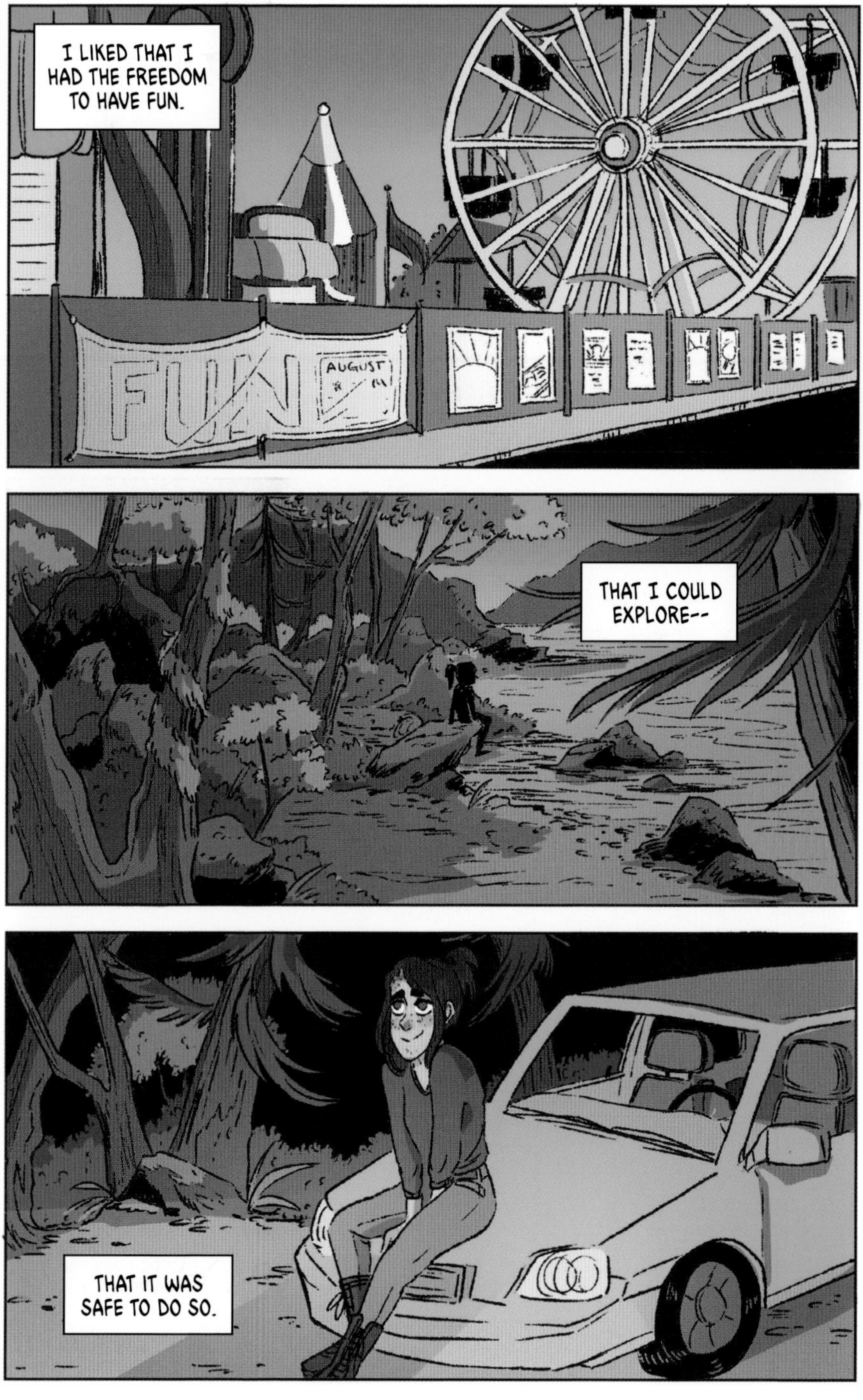
I LIKED THAT I HAD THE FREEDOM TO HAVE FUN.
FUN
AUGUST
THAT I COULD EXPLORE--
THAT IT WAS SAFE TO DO SO.

IT'S NOT THAT EVERYTHING WAS PERFECT IN OREGON--

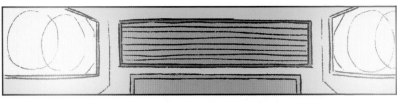

BUT I COULD BE MYSELF--

AND HAVE THE SPACE TO FIGURE OUT WHAT EXACTLY THAT MEANT.

GUN VIOLENCE WASN'T SOMETHING I WAS UNACCUSTOMED TO.

IT JUST WASN'T EXPECTED.

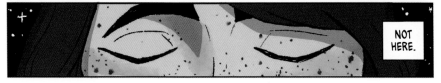

NOT HERE.

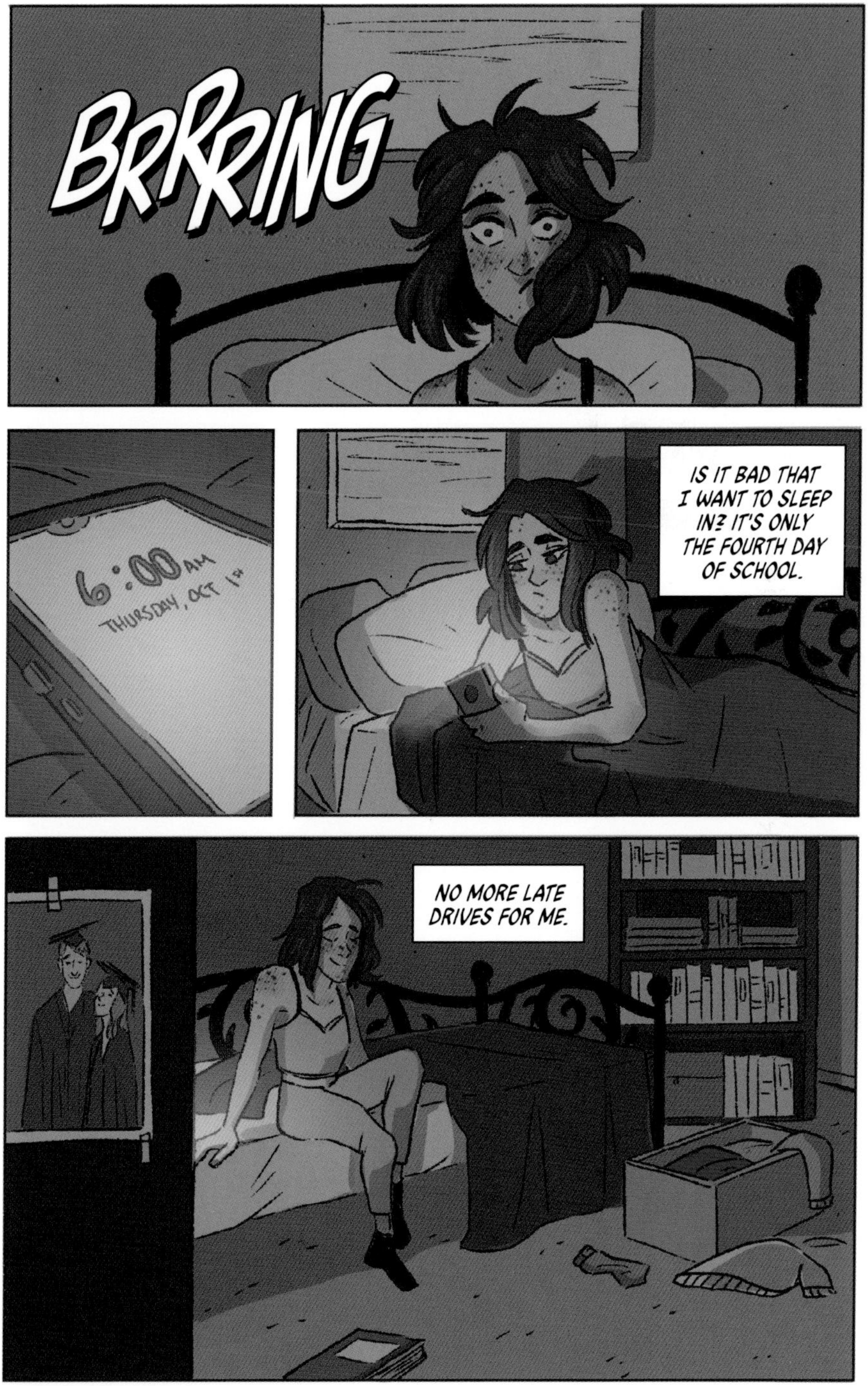
BRRRING
6:00 AM
THURSDAY, OCT 1st
IS IT BAD THAT I WANT TO SLEEP IN? IT'S ONLY THE FOURTH DAY OF SCHOOL.
NO MORE LATE DRIVES FOR ME.

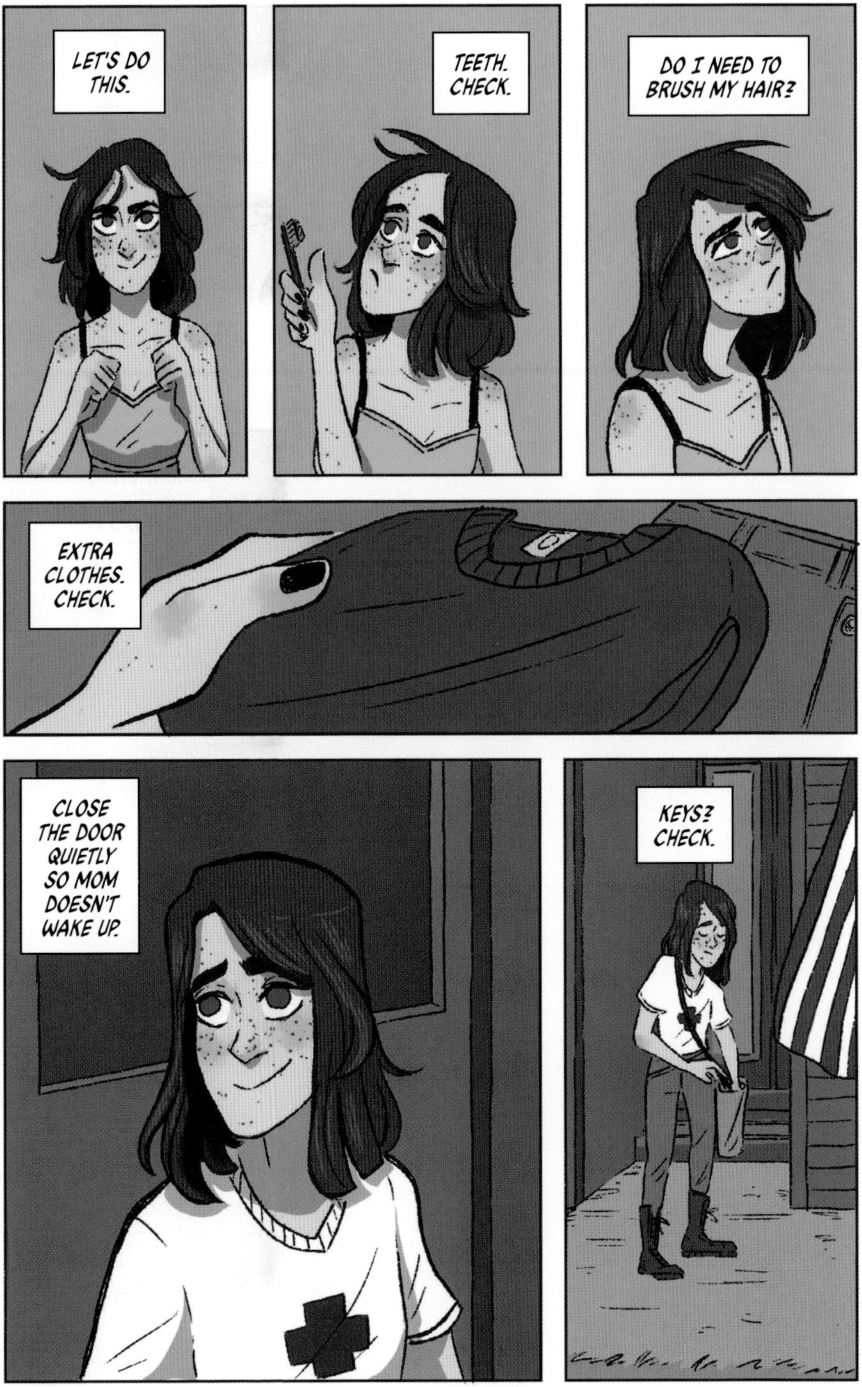
LET'S DO THIS.
TEETH. CHECK.
DO I NEED TO BRUSH MY HAIR?
EXTRA CLOTHES. CHECK.
CLOSE THE DOOR QUIETLY SO MOM DOESN'T WAKE UP.
KEYS? CHECK.

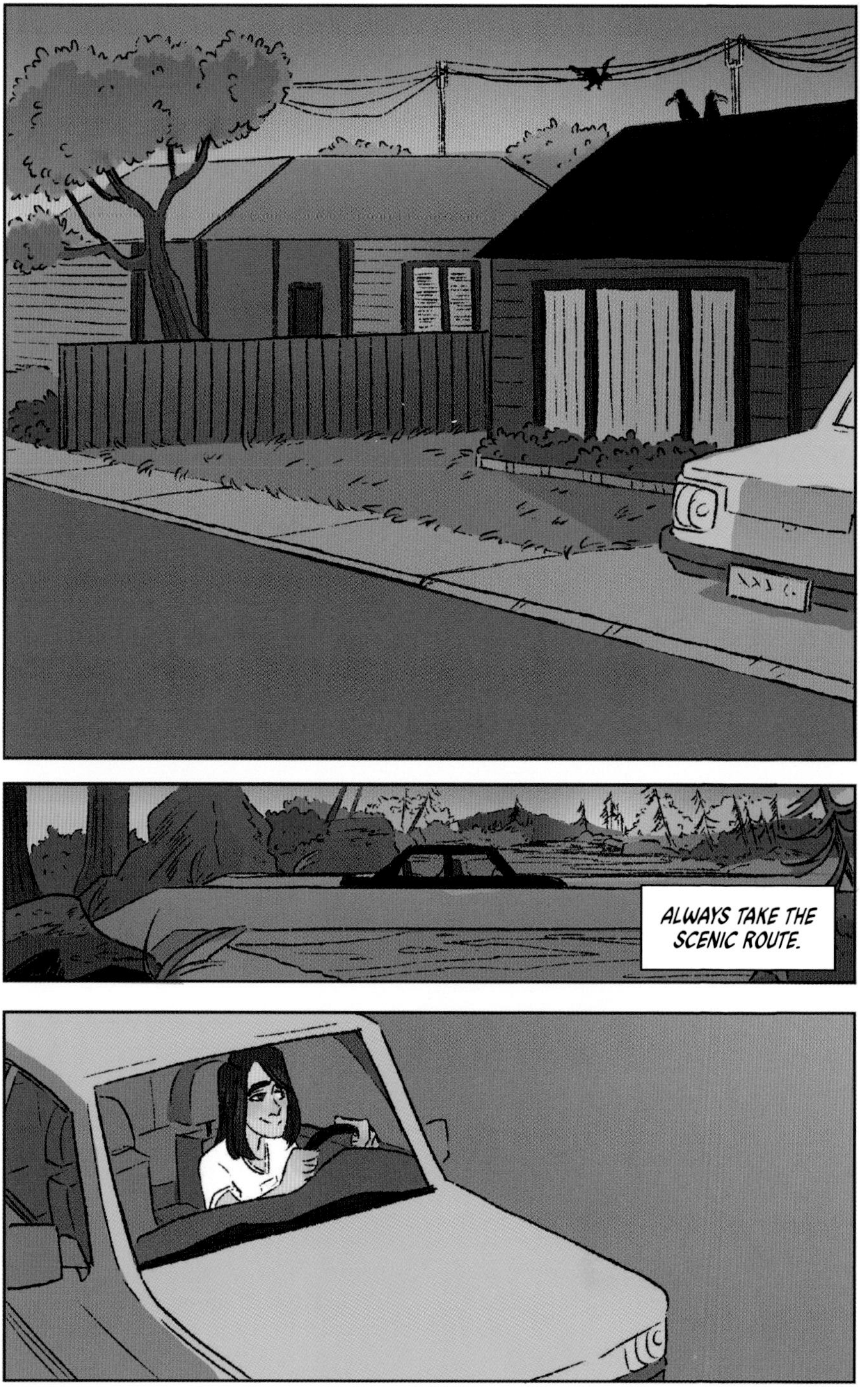
ALWAYS TAKE THE SCENIC ROUTE.

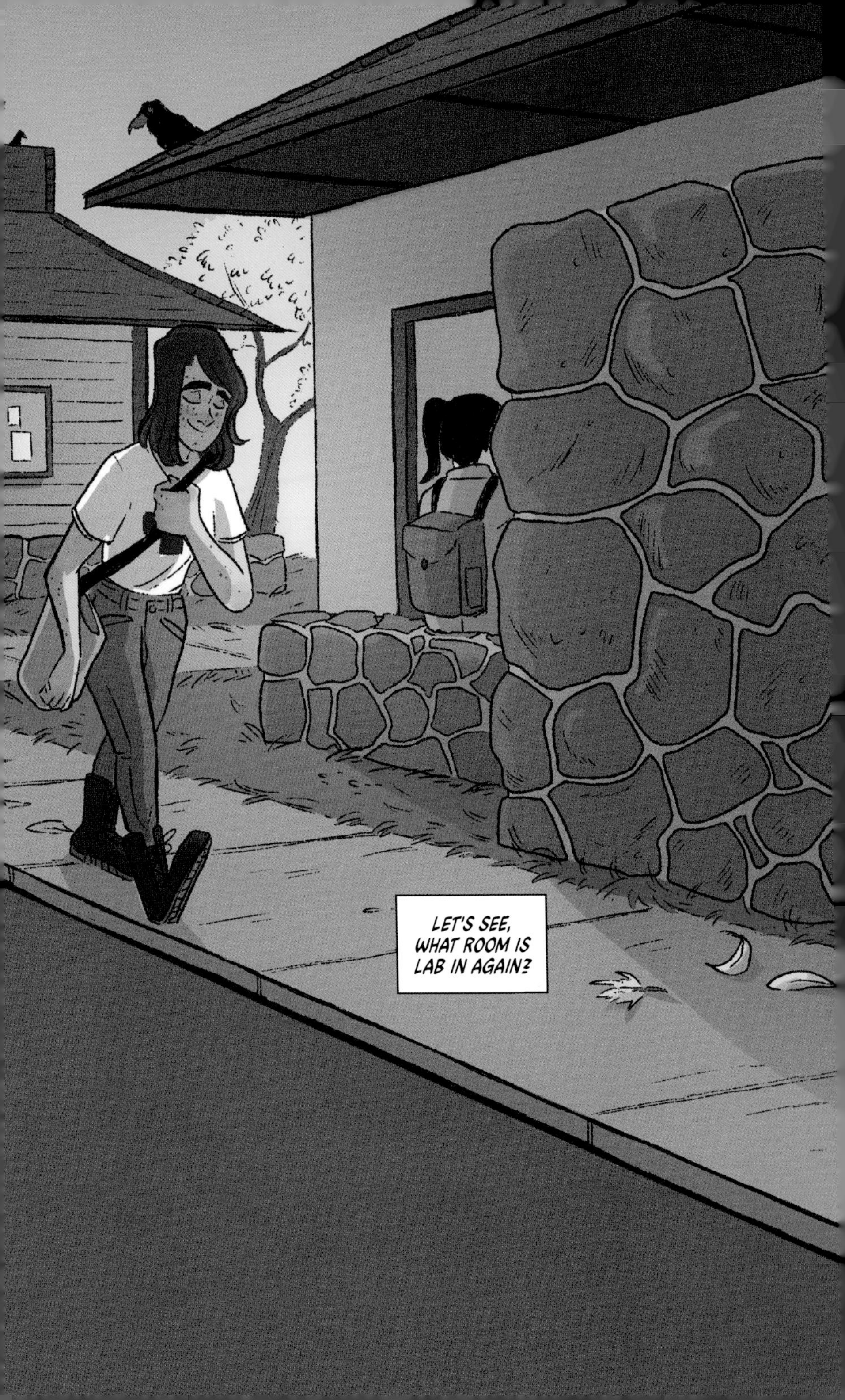
LET'S SEE, WHAT ROOM IS LAB IN AGAIN?

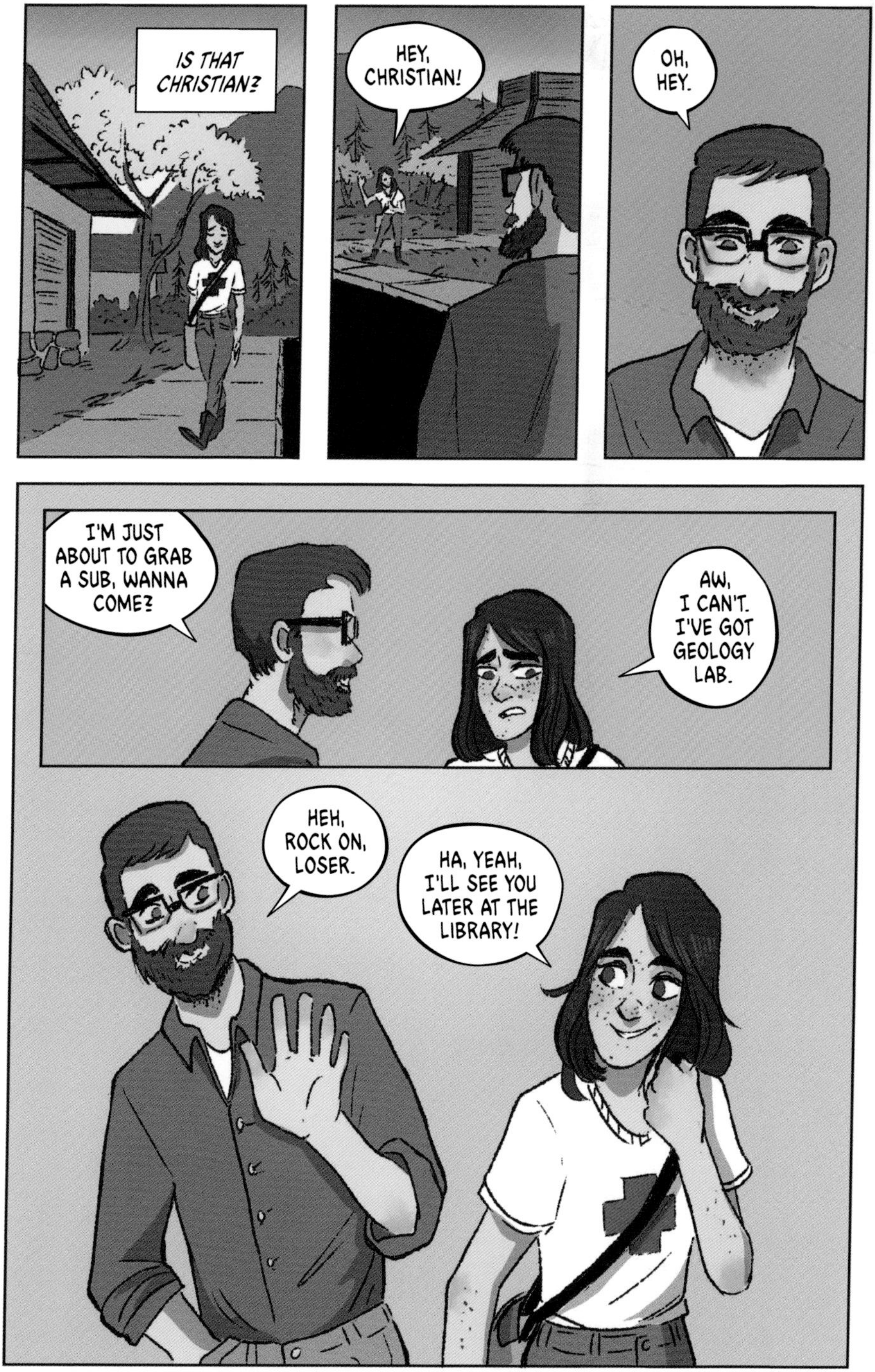
IS THAT CHRISTIAN?
HEY, CHRISTIAN!
OH, HEY.
I'M JUST ABOUT TO GRAB A SUB, WANNA COME?
AW, I CAN'T. I'VE GOT GEOLOGY LAB.
HEH, ROCK ON, LOSER.
HA, YEAH, I'LL SEE YOU LATER AT THE LIBRARY!

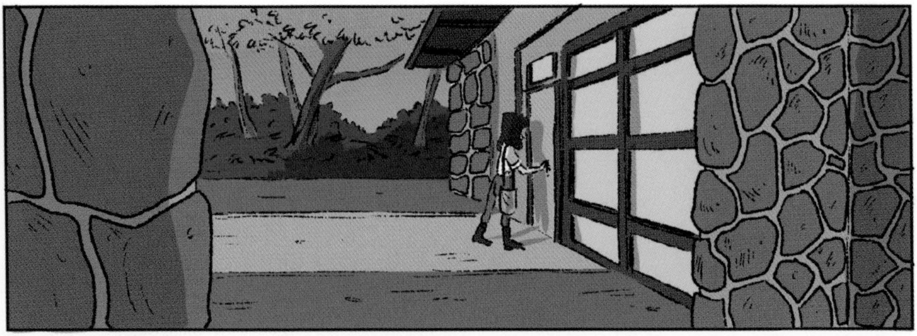

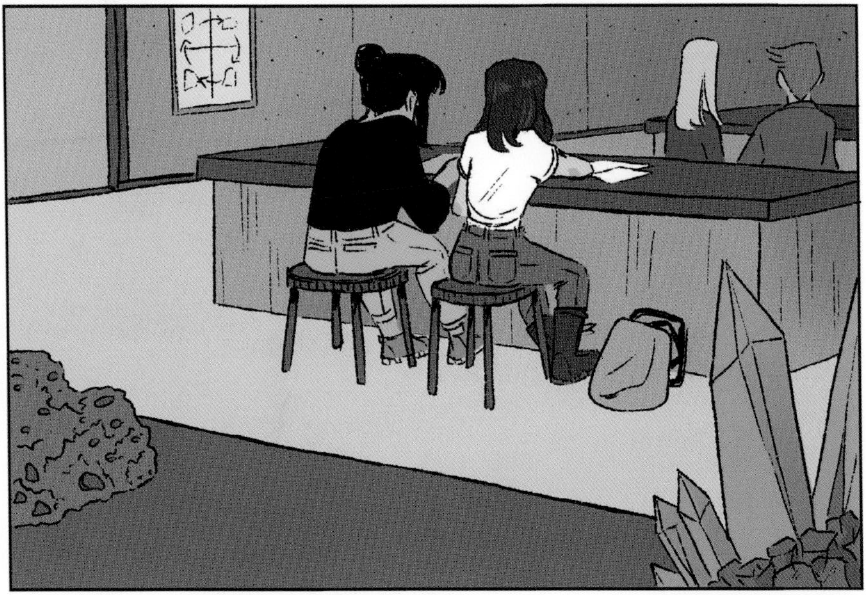

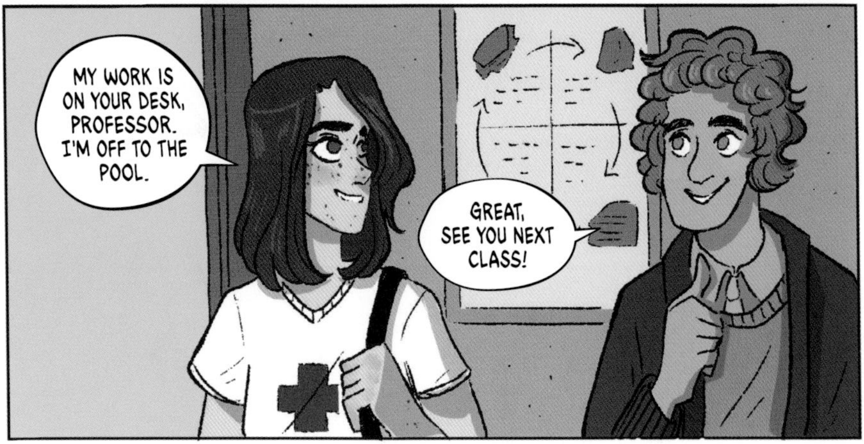
MY WORK IS ON YOUR DESK, PROFESSOR. I'M OFF TO THE POOL.
GREAT, SEE YOU NEXT CLASS!

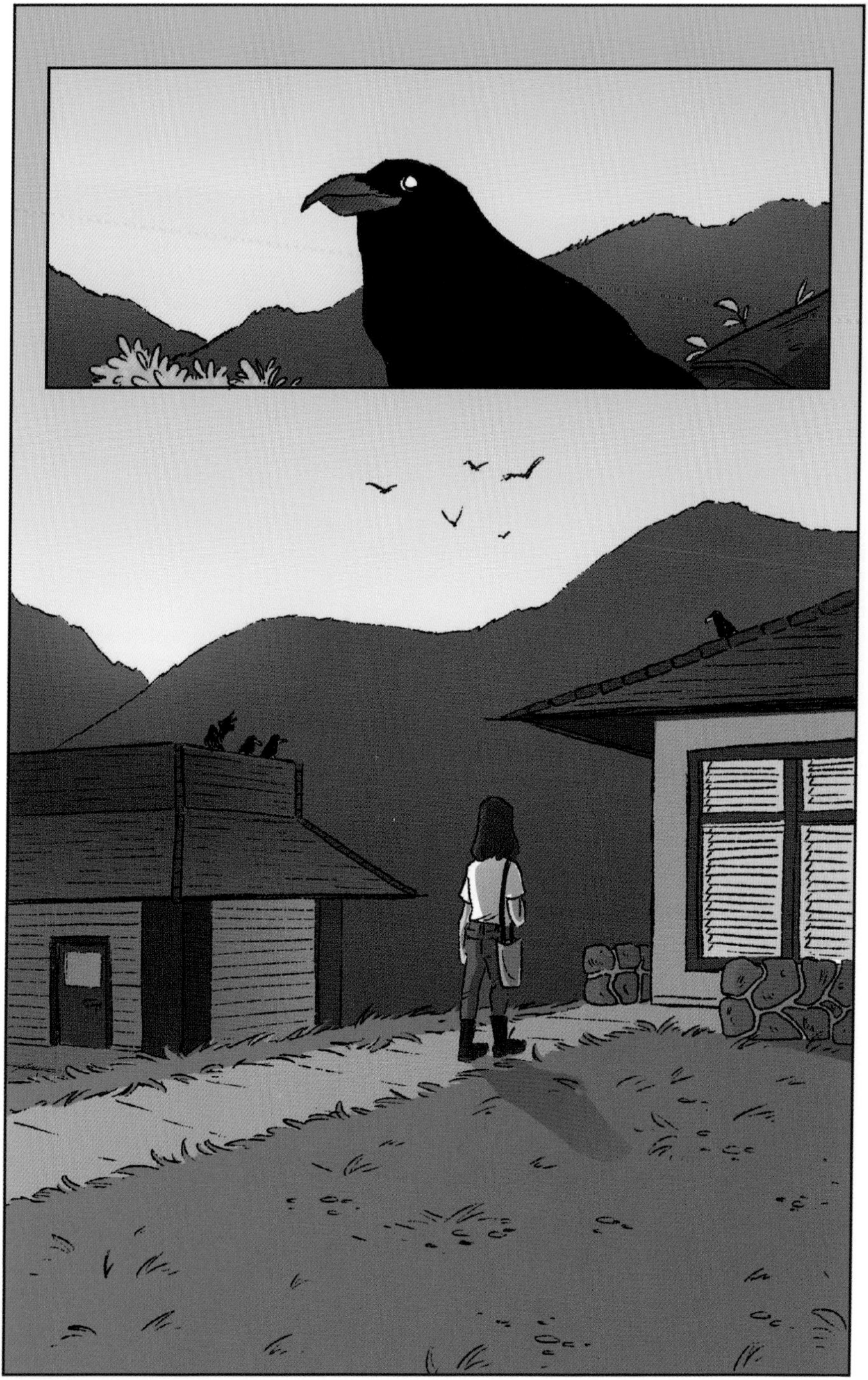

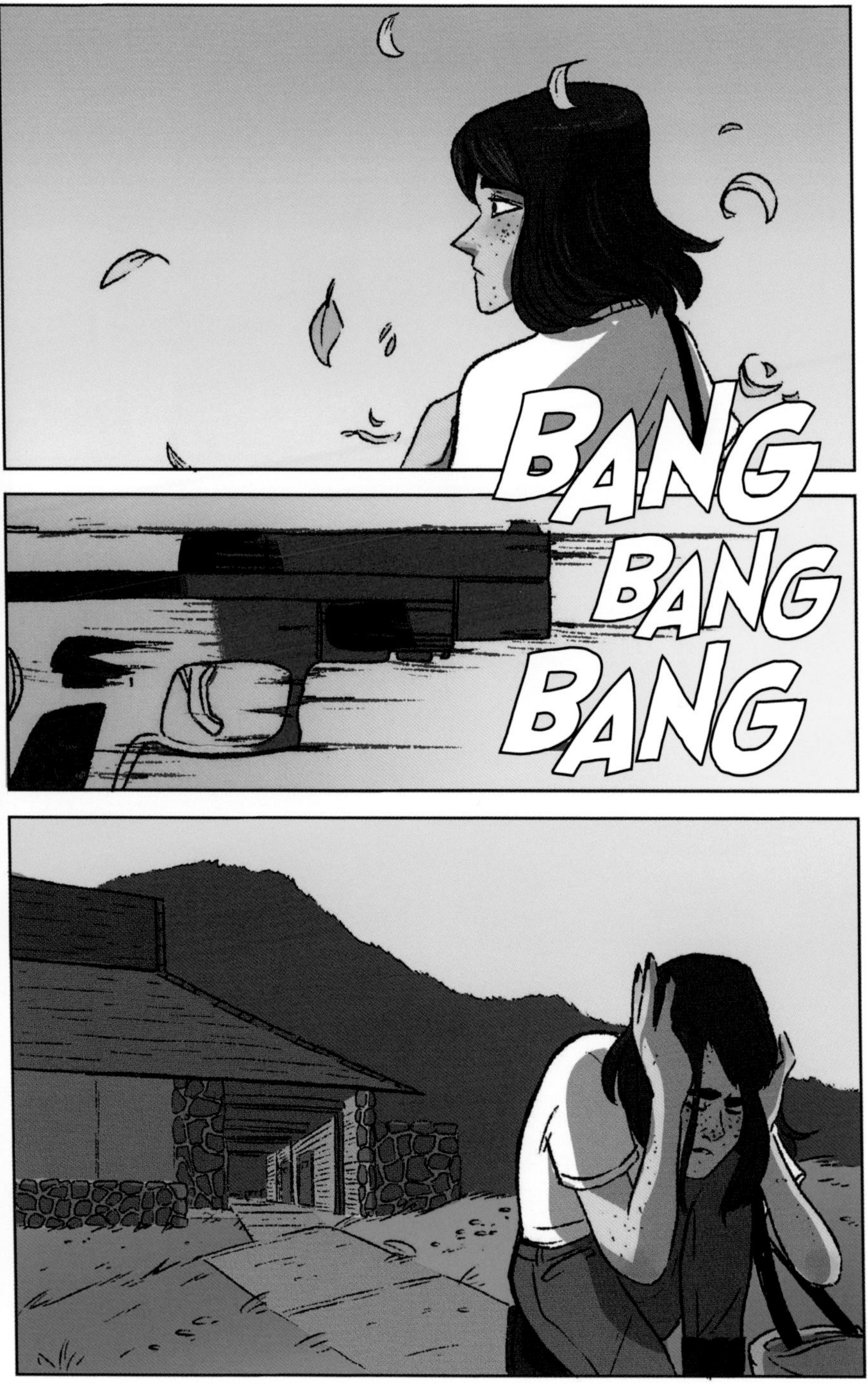
BANG
BANG
BANG

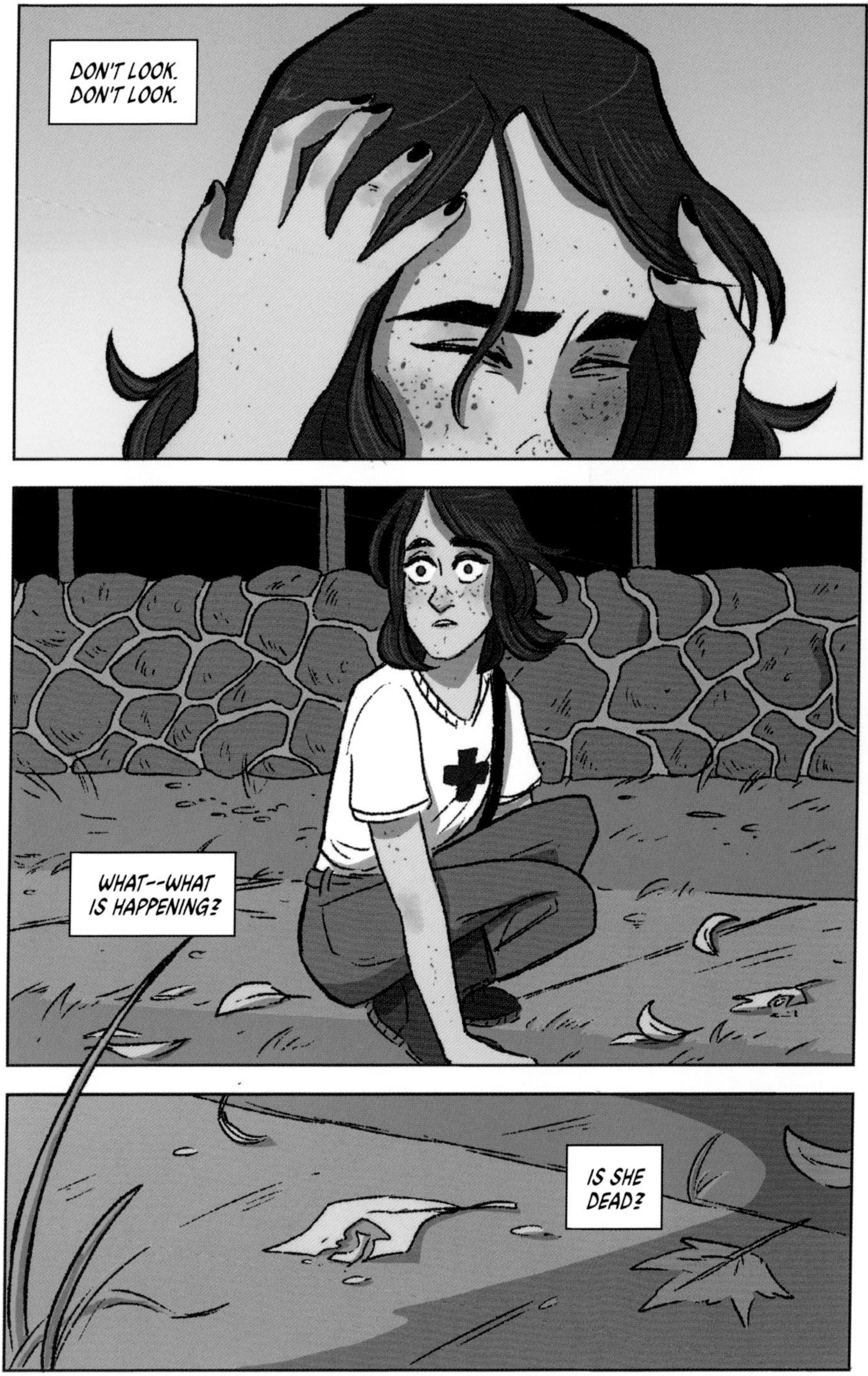
DON'T LOOK.
DON'T LOOK.
WHAT--WHAT
IS HAPPENING?
IS SHE
DEAD?

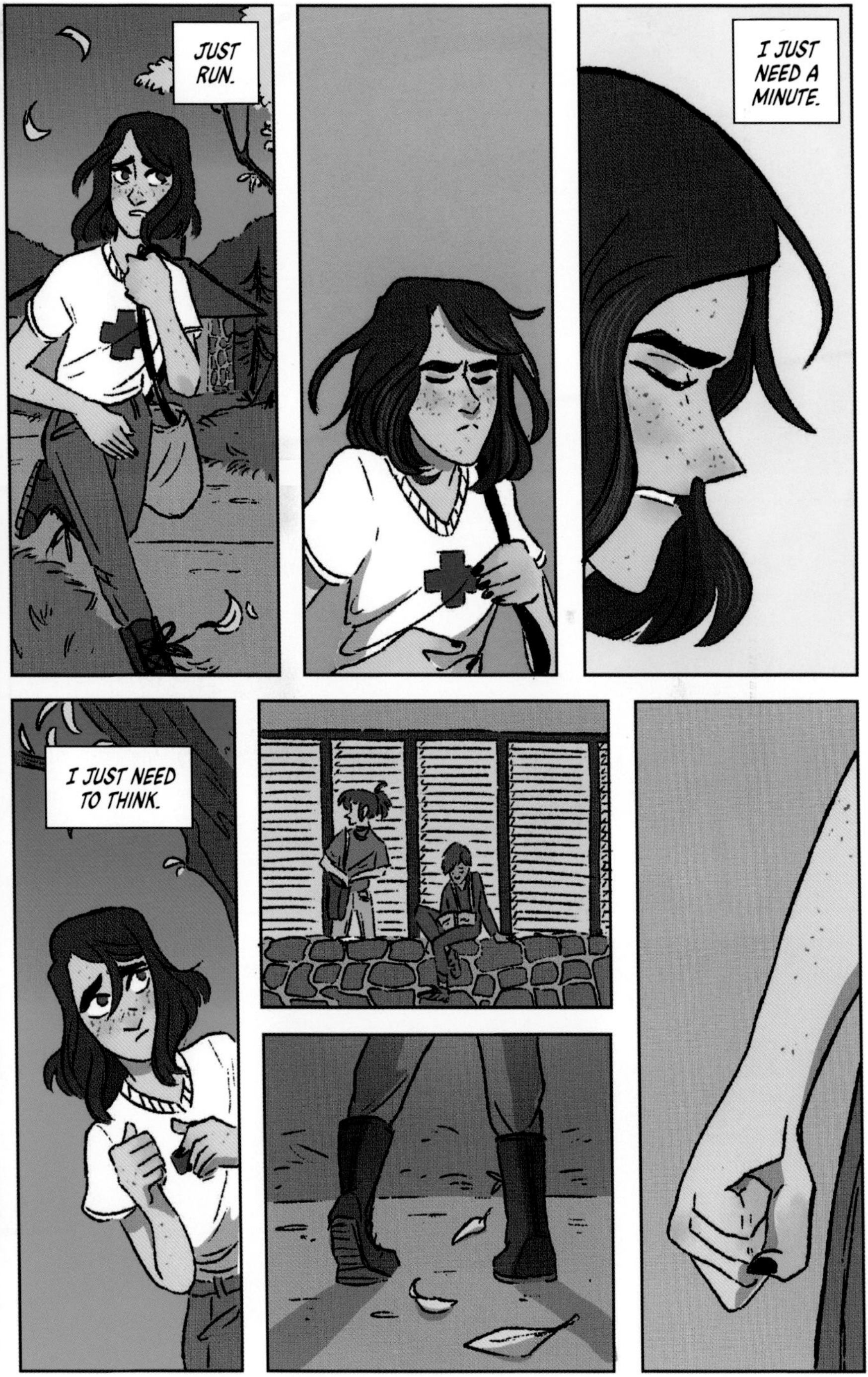
JUST RUN.
I JUST NEED A MINUTE.
I JUST NEED TO THINK.

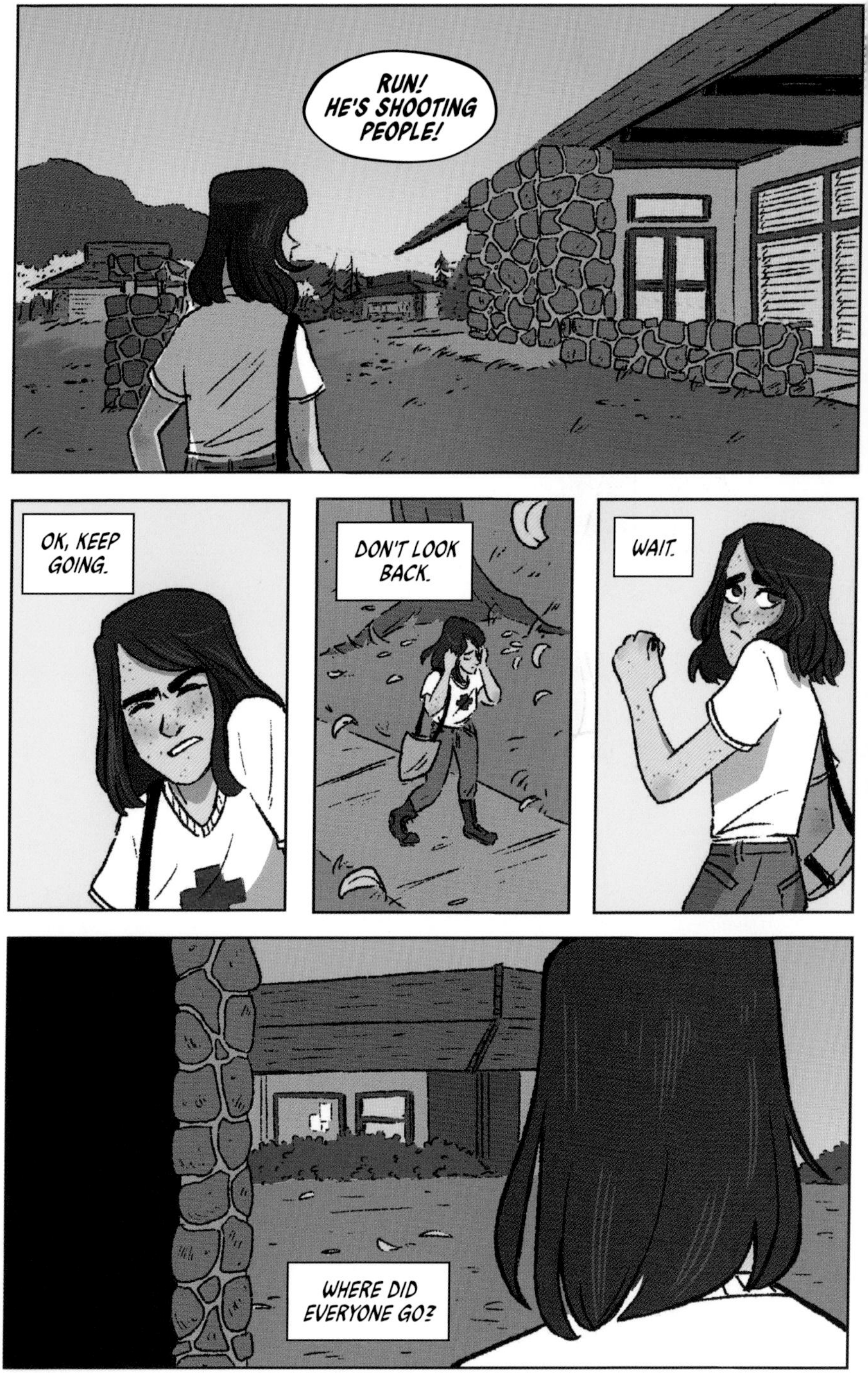
RUN! HE'S SHOOTING PEOPLE!
OK, KEEP GOING.
DON'T LOOK BACK.
WAIT.
WHERE DID EVERYONE GO?

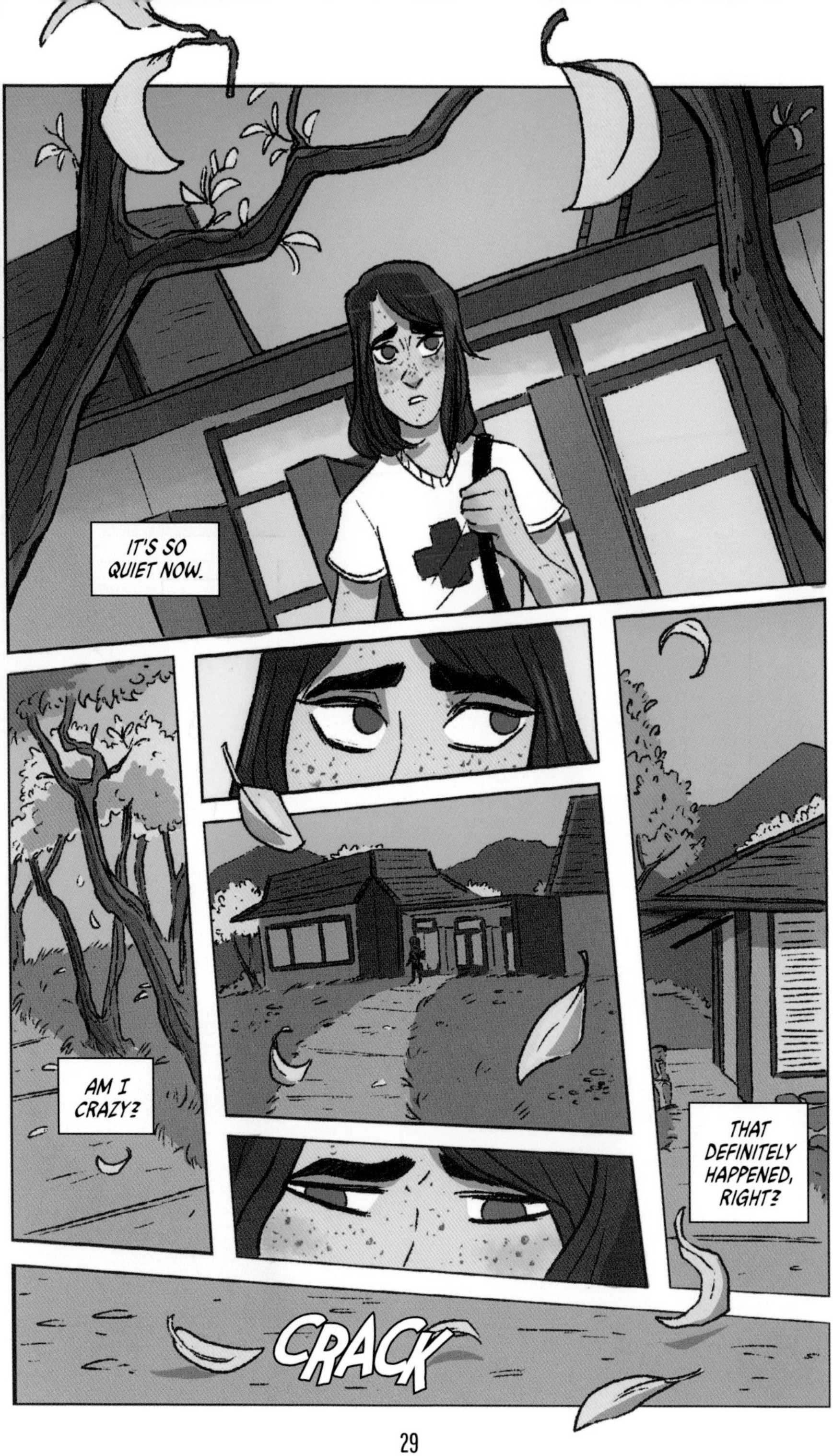
IT'S SO QUIET NOW.
AM I CRAZY?
THAT DEFINITELY HAPPENED, RIGHT?
CRACK

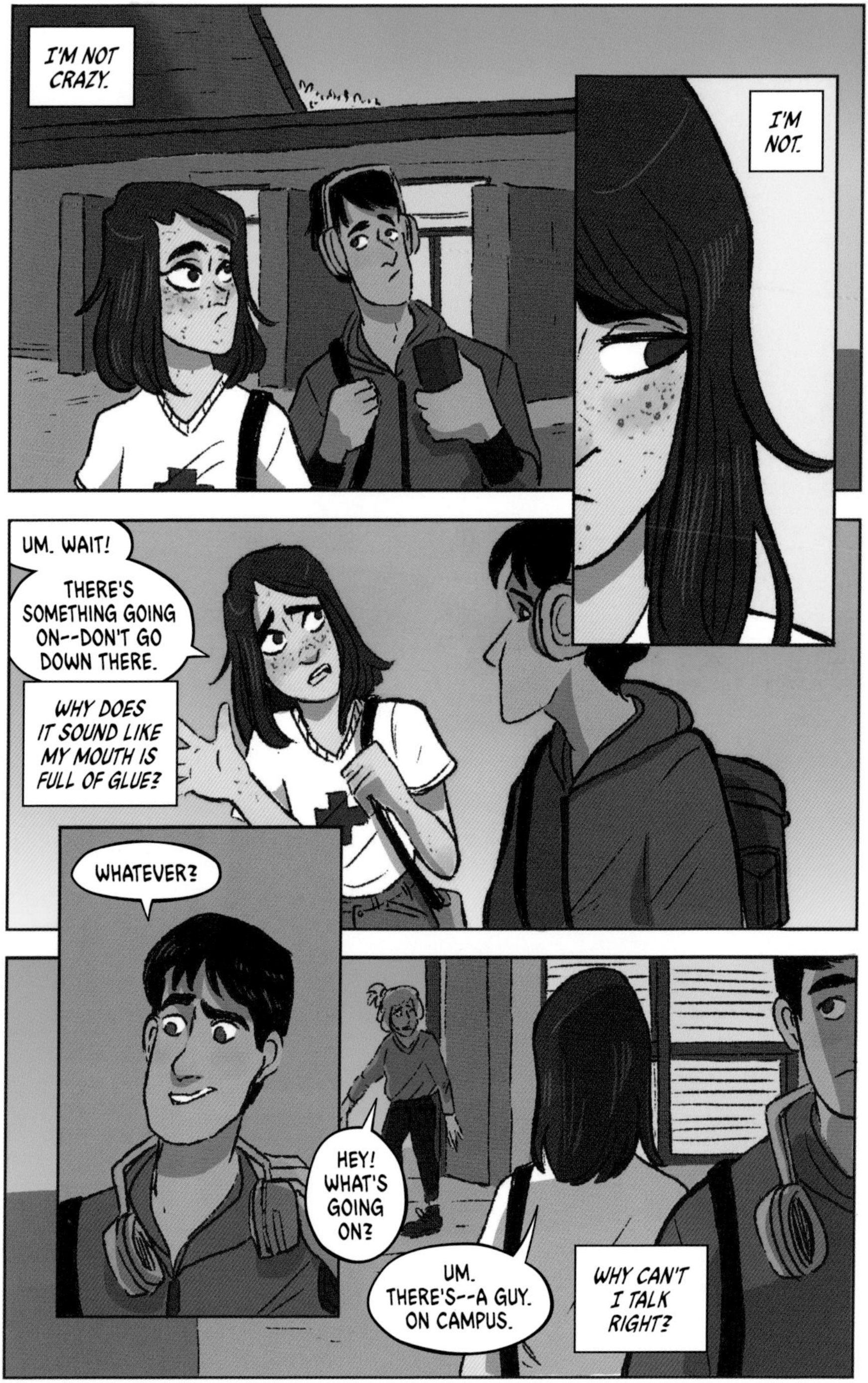

I'M NOT CRAZY.
I'M NOT.
UM. WAIT!
THERE'S SOMETHING GOING ON--DON'T GO DOWN THERE.
WHY DOES IT SOUND LIKE MY MOUTH IS FULL OF GLUE?
WHATEVER?
HEY! WHAT'S GOING ON?
UM. THERE'S--A GUY. ON CAMPUS.
WHY CAN'T I TALK RIGHT?

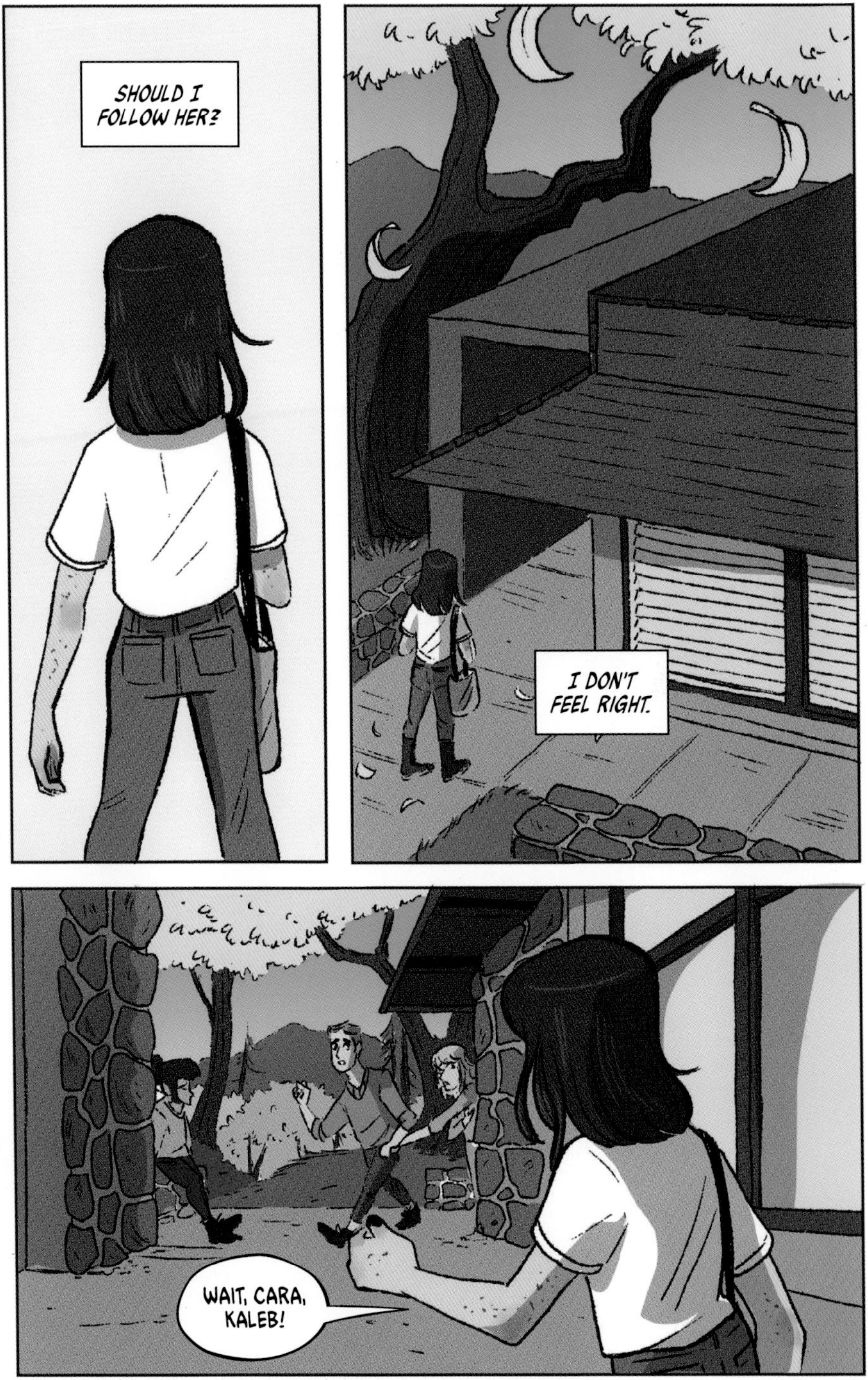
SHOULD I FOLLOW HER?
I DON'T FEEL RIGHT.
WAIT, CARA, KALEB!

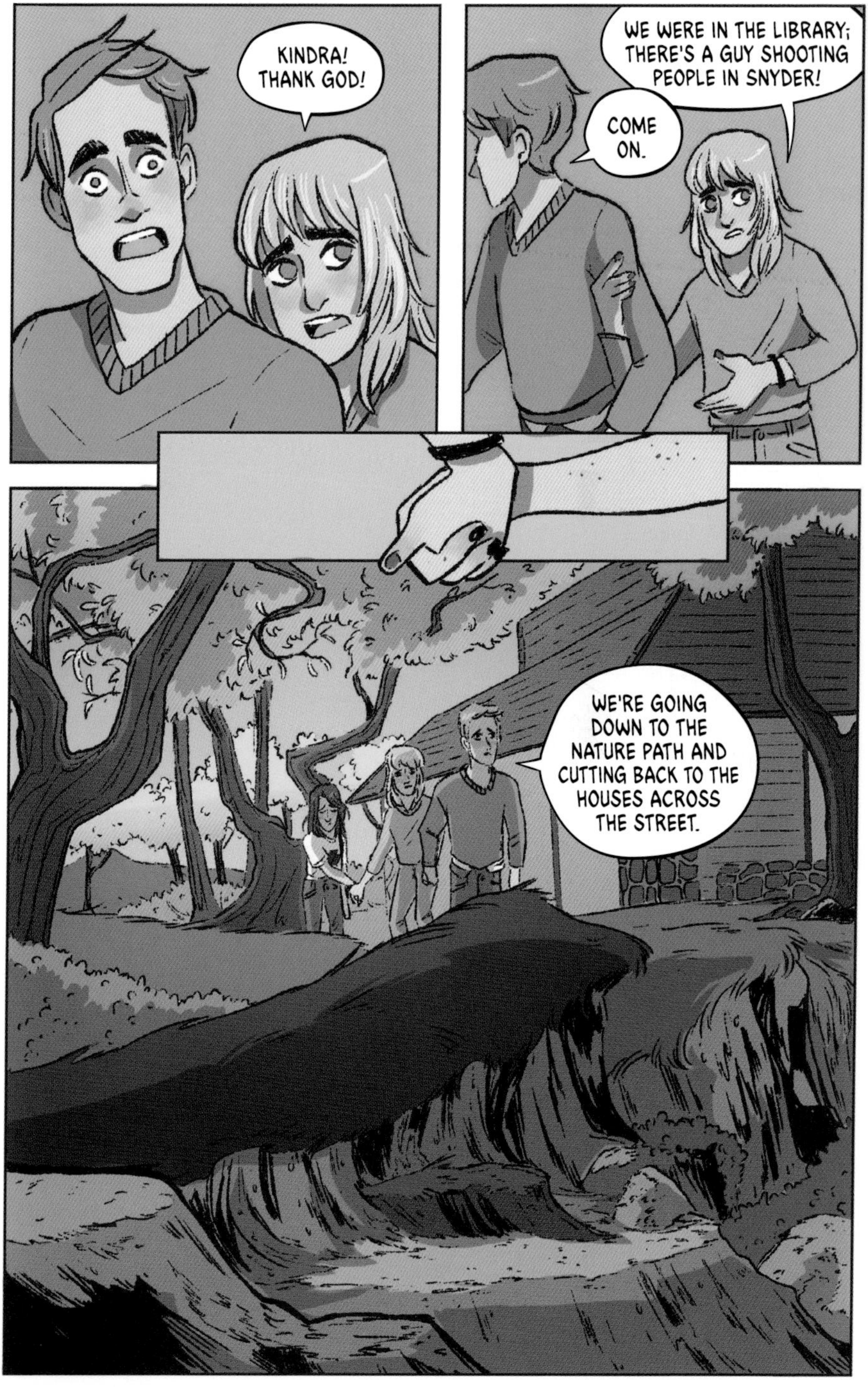
KINDRA! THANK GOD!
WE WERE IN THE LIBRARY; THERE'S A GUY SHOOTING PEOPLE IN SNYDER!
COME ON.
WE'RE GOING DOWN TO THE NATURE PATH AND CUTTING BACK TO THE HOUSES ACROSS THE STREET.

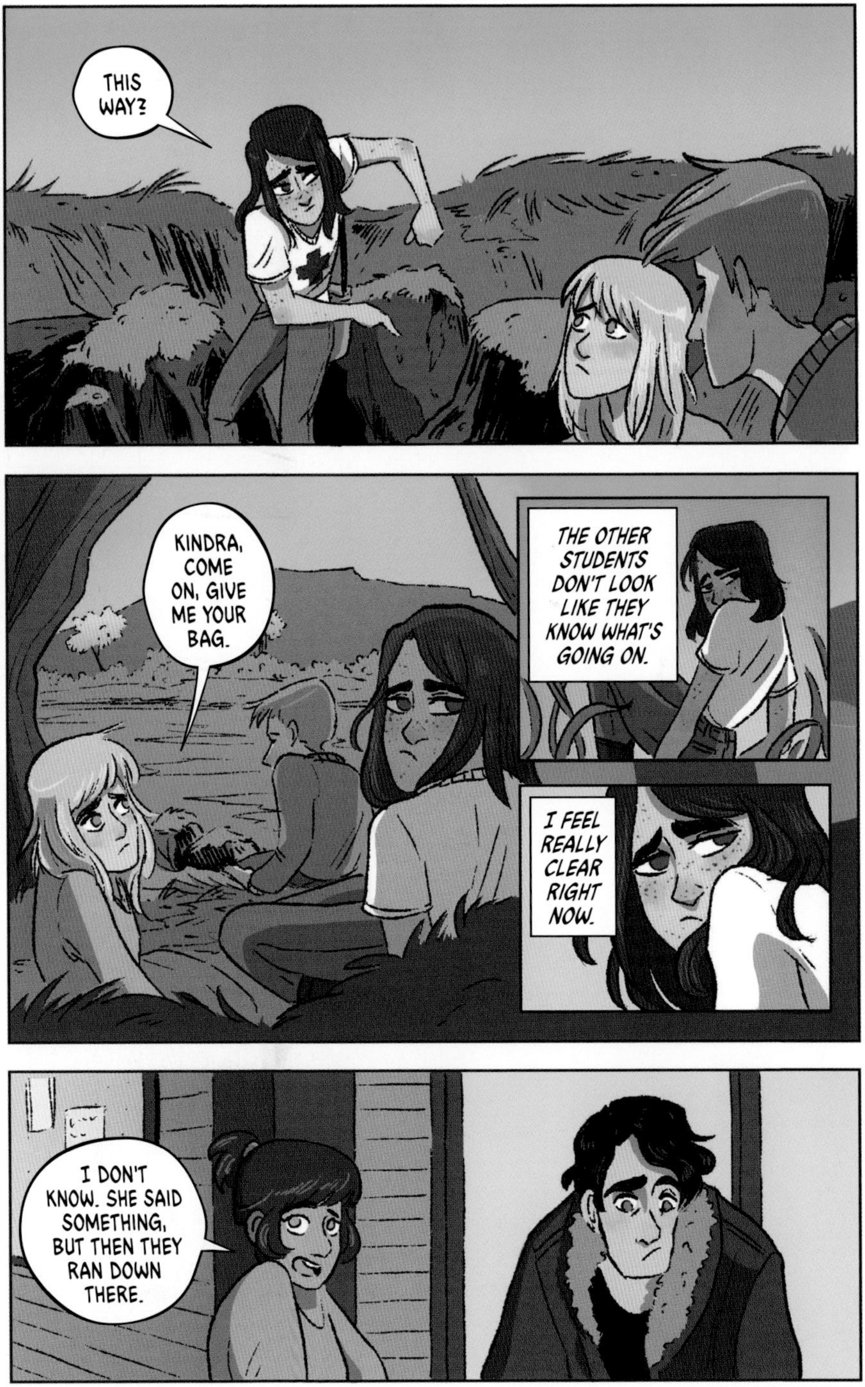
THIS WAY?
KINDRA, COME ON, GIVE ME YOUR BAG.
THE OTHER STUDENTS DON'T LOOK LIKE THEY KNOW WHAT'S GOING ON.
I FEEL REALLY CLEAR RIGHT NOW.
I DON'T KNOW. SHE SAID SOMETHING, BUT THEN THEY RAN DOWN THERE.

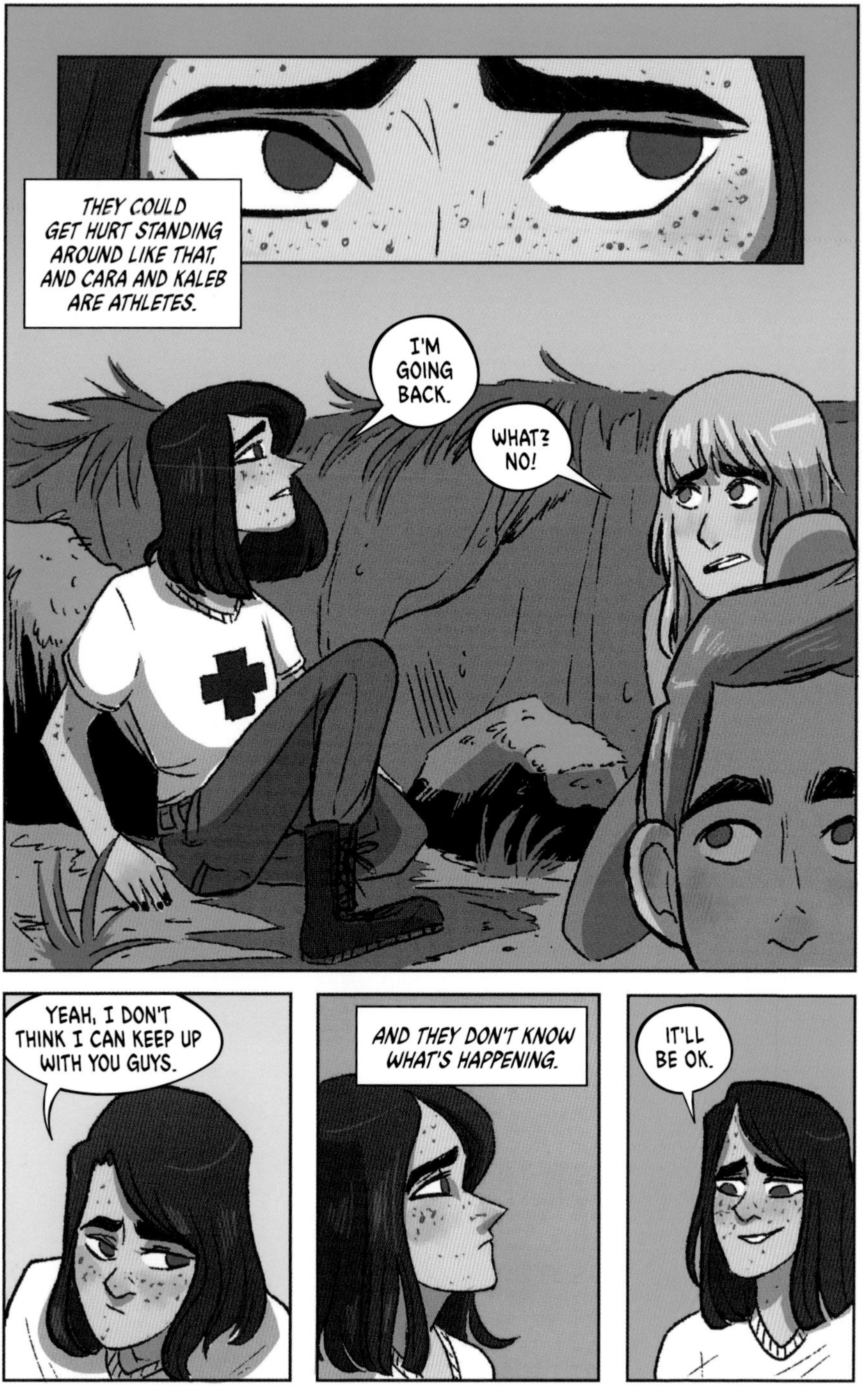
THEY COULD GET HURT STANDING AROUND LIKE THAT, AND CARA AND KALEB ARE ATHLETES.
I'M GOING BACK.
WHAT? NO!
YEAH, I DON'T THINK I CAN KEEP UP WITH YOU GUYS.
AND THEY DON'T KNOW WHAT'S HAPPENING.
IT'LL BE OK.

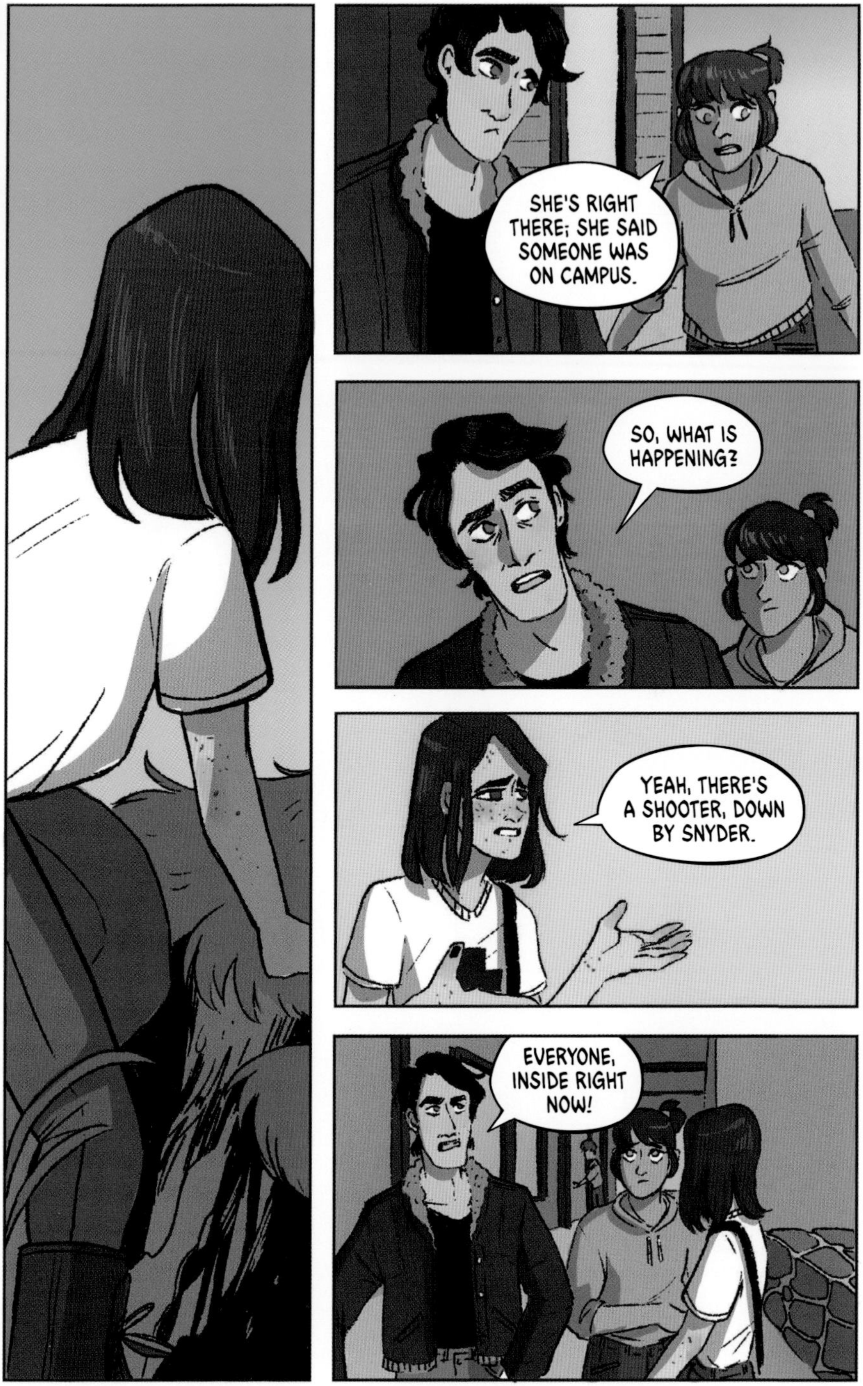
SHE'S RIGHT THERE; SHE SAID SOMEONE WAS ON CAMPUS.
SO, WHAT IS HAPPENING?
YEAH, THERE'S A SHOOTER, DOWN BY SNYDER.
EVERYONE, INSIDE RIGHT NOW!

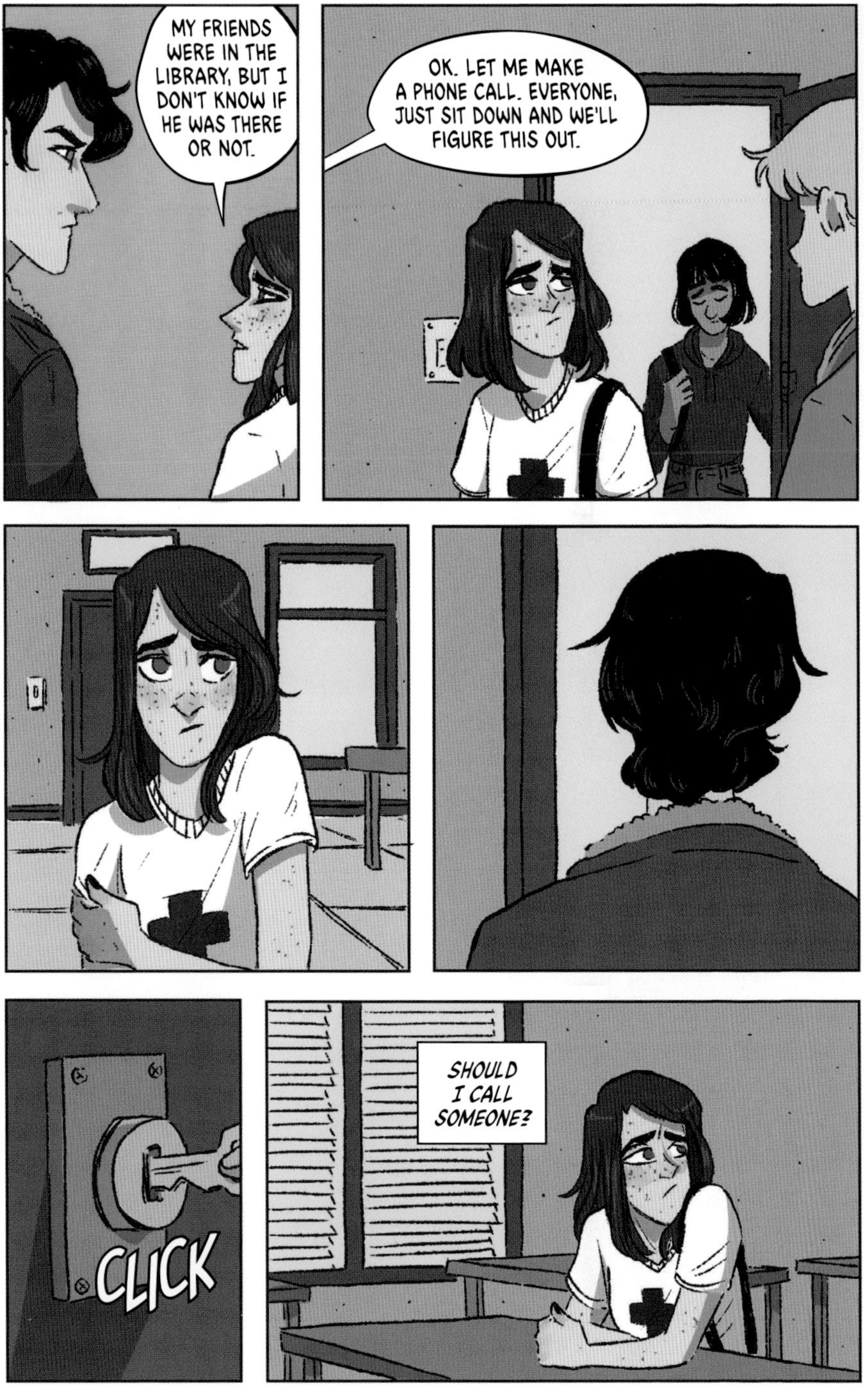

MY FRIENDS WERE IN THE LIBRARY, BUT I DON'T KNOW IF HE WAS THERE OR NOT.
OK. LET ME MAKE A PHONE CALL. EVERYONE, JUST SIT DOWN AND WE'LL FIGURE THIS OUT.
CLICK
SHOULD I CALL SOMEONE?

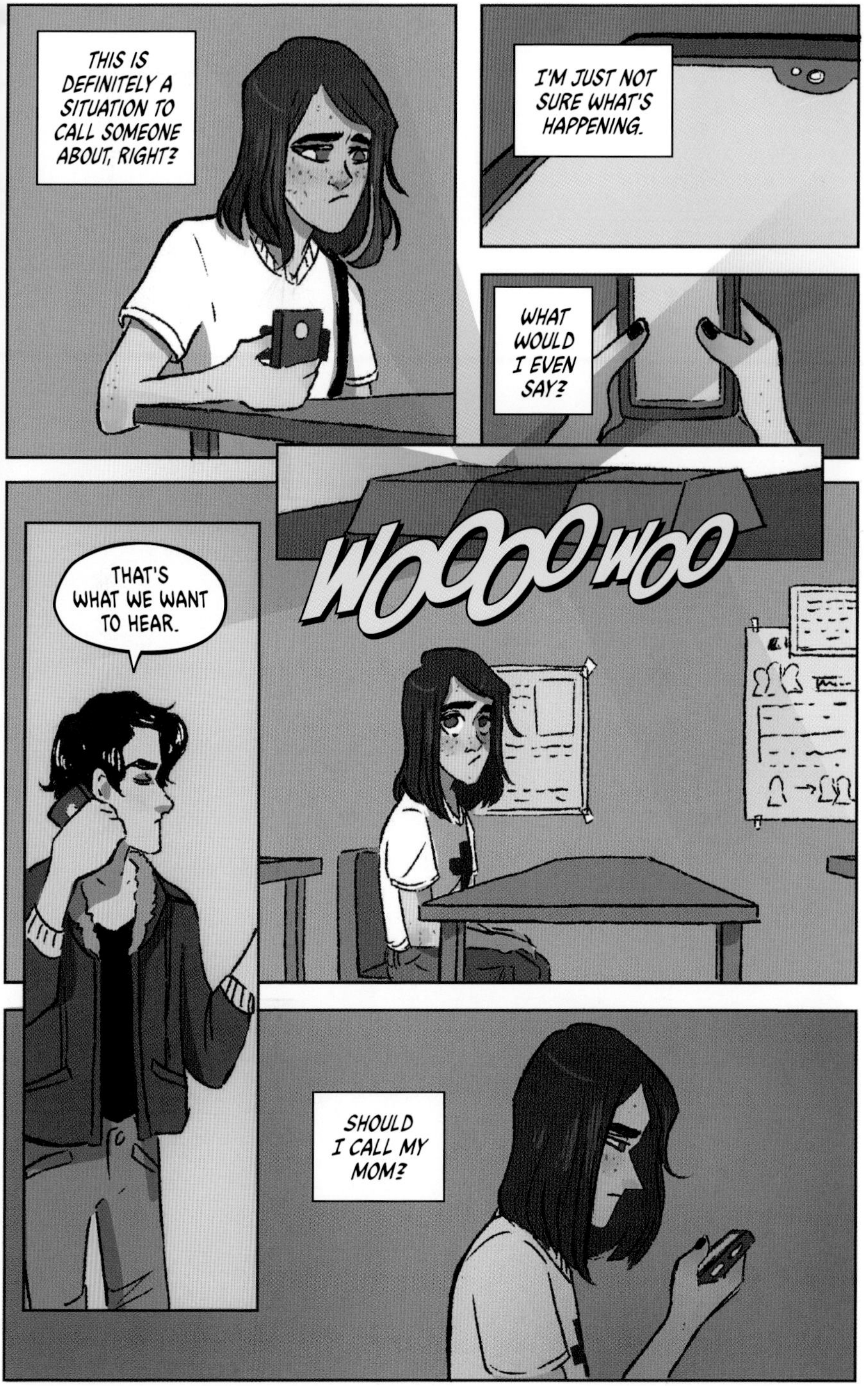
THIS IS DEFINITELY A SITUATION TO CALL SOMEONE ABOUT, RIGHT?
I'M JUST NOT SURE WHAT'S HAPPENING.
WHAT WOULD I EVEN SAY?
WOOOOWOO
THAT'S WHAT WE WANT TO HEAR.
SHOULD I CALL MY MOM?

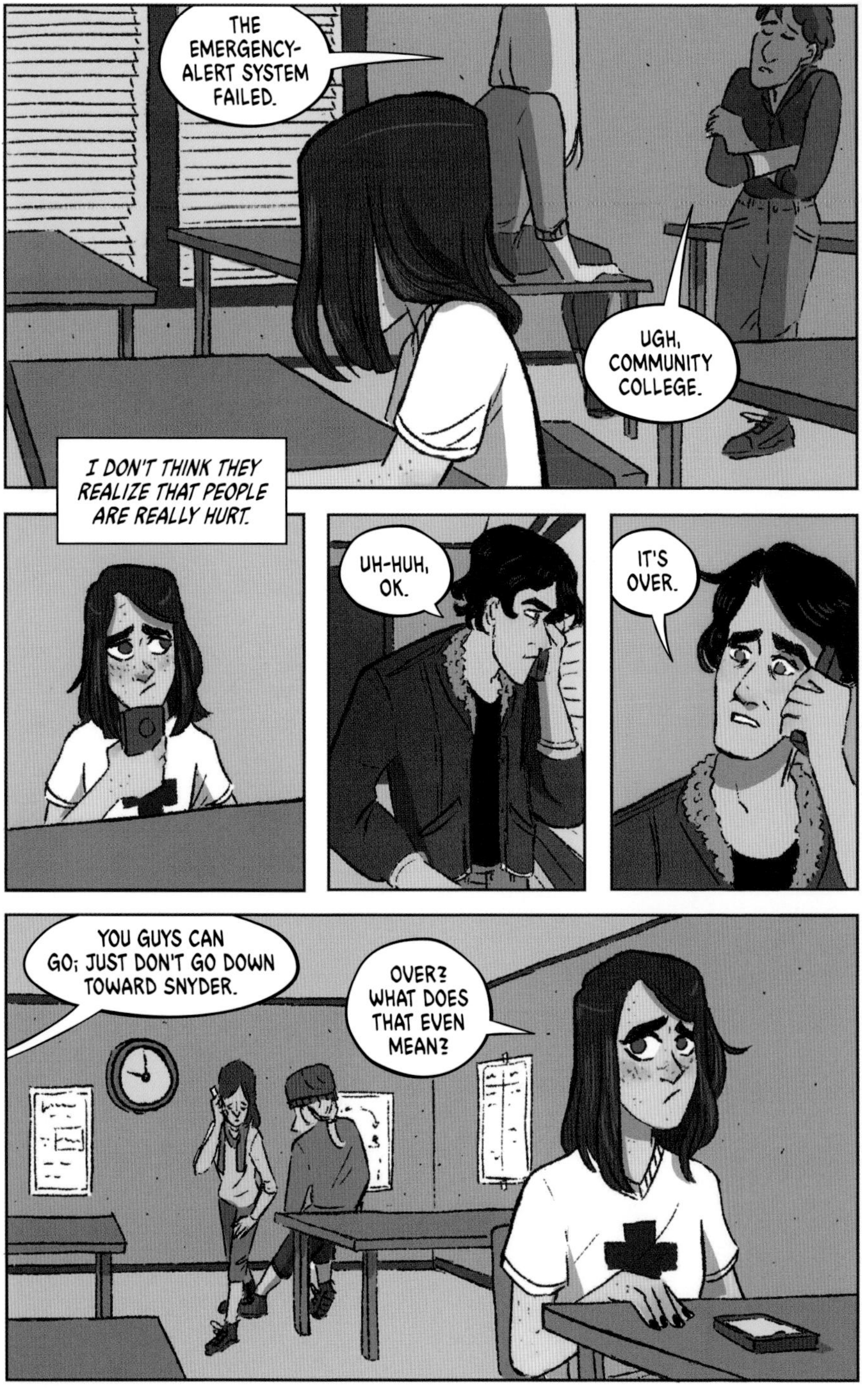
THE EMERGENCY-ALERT SYSTEM FAILED.
UGH, COMMUNITY COLLEGE.
I DON'T THINK THEY REALIZE THAT PEOPLE ARE REALLY HURT.
UH-HUH, OK.
IT'S OVER.
YOU GUYS CAN GO; JUST DON'T GO DOWN TOWARD SNYDER.
OVER? WHAT DOES THAT EVEN MEAN?

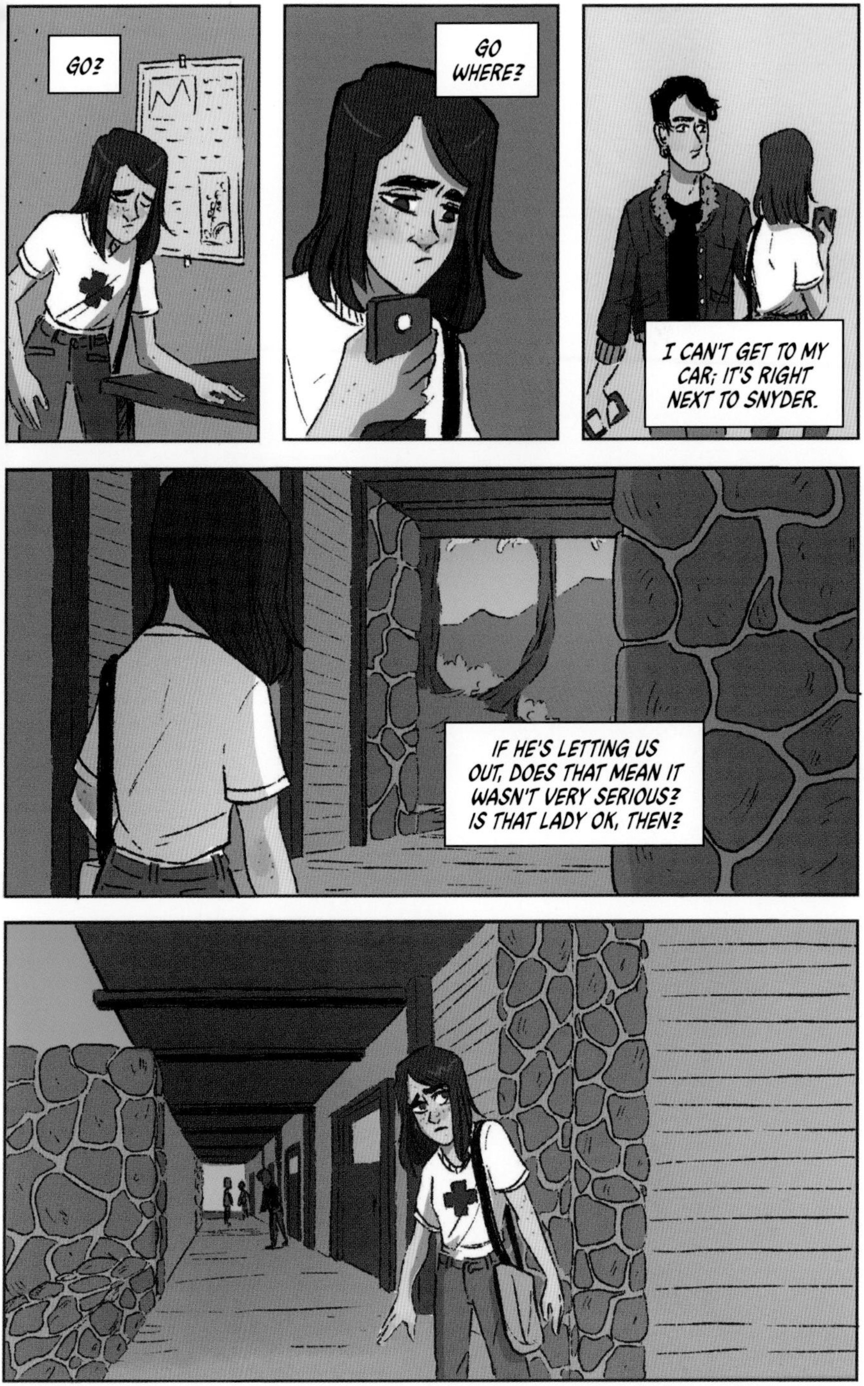
GO?
GO WHERE?
I CAN'T GET TO MY CAR; IT'S RIGHT NEXT TO SNYDER.
IF HE'S LETTING US OUT, DOES THAT MEAN IT WASN'T VERY SERIOUS? IS THAT LADY OK, THEN?

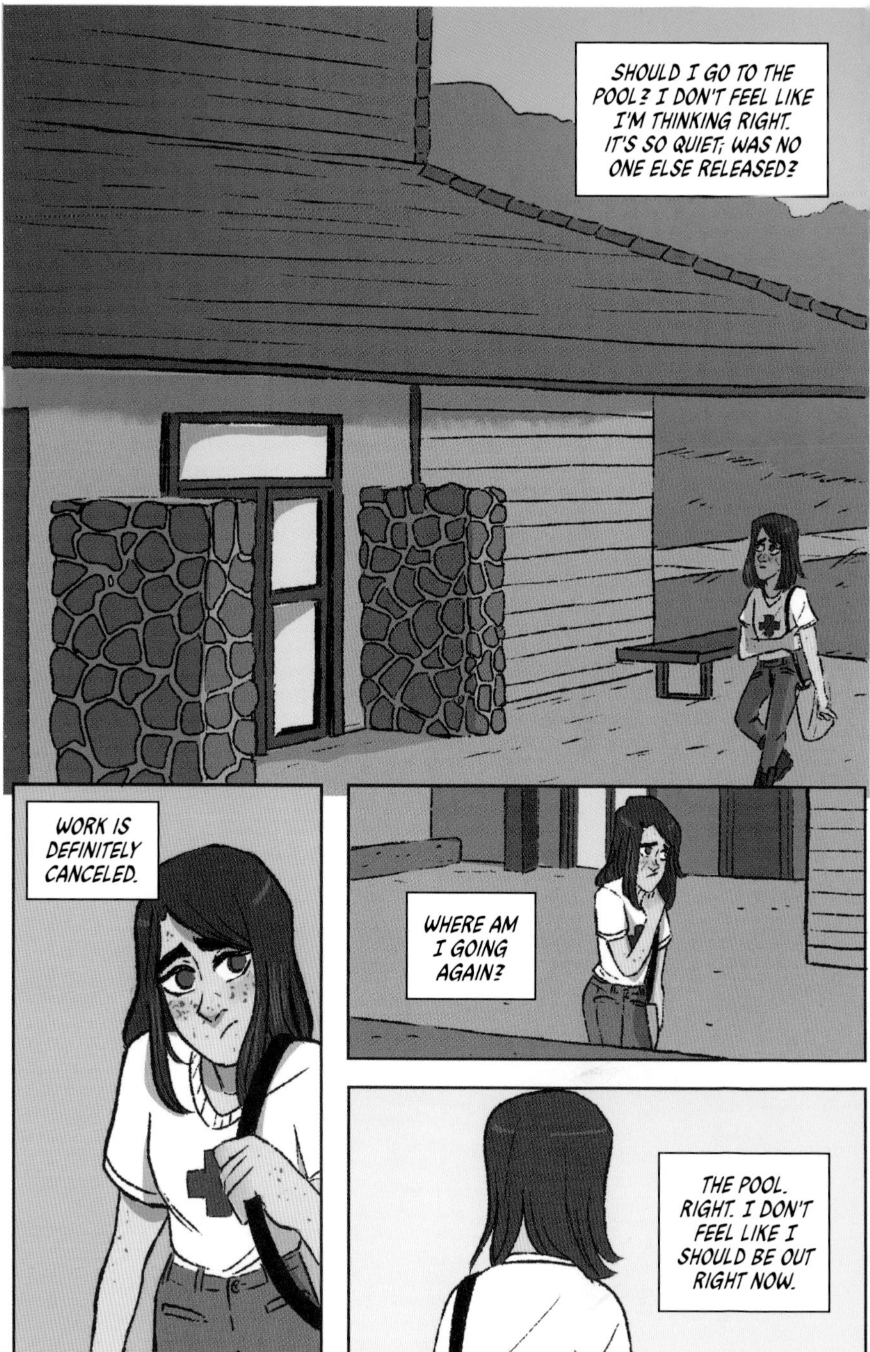
SHOULD I GO TO THE POOL? I DON'T FEEL LIKE I'M THINKING RIGHT. IT'S SO QUIET; WAS NO ONE ELSE RELEASED?
WORK IS DEFINITELY CANCELED.
WHERE AM I GOING AGAIN?
THE POOL. RIGHT. I DON'T FEEL LIKE I SHOULD BE OUT RIGHT NOW.

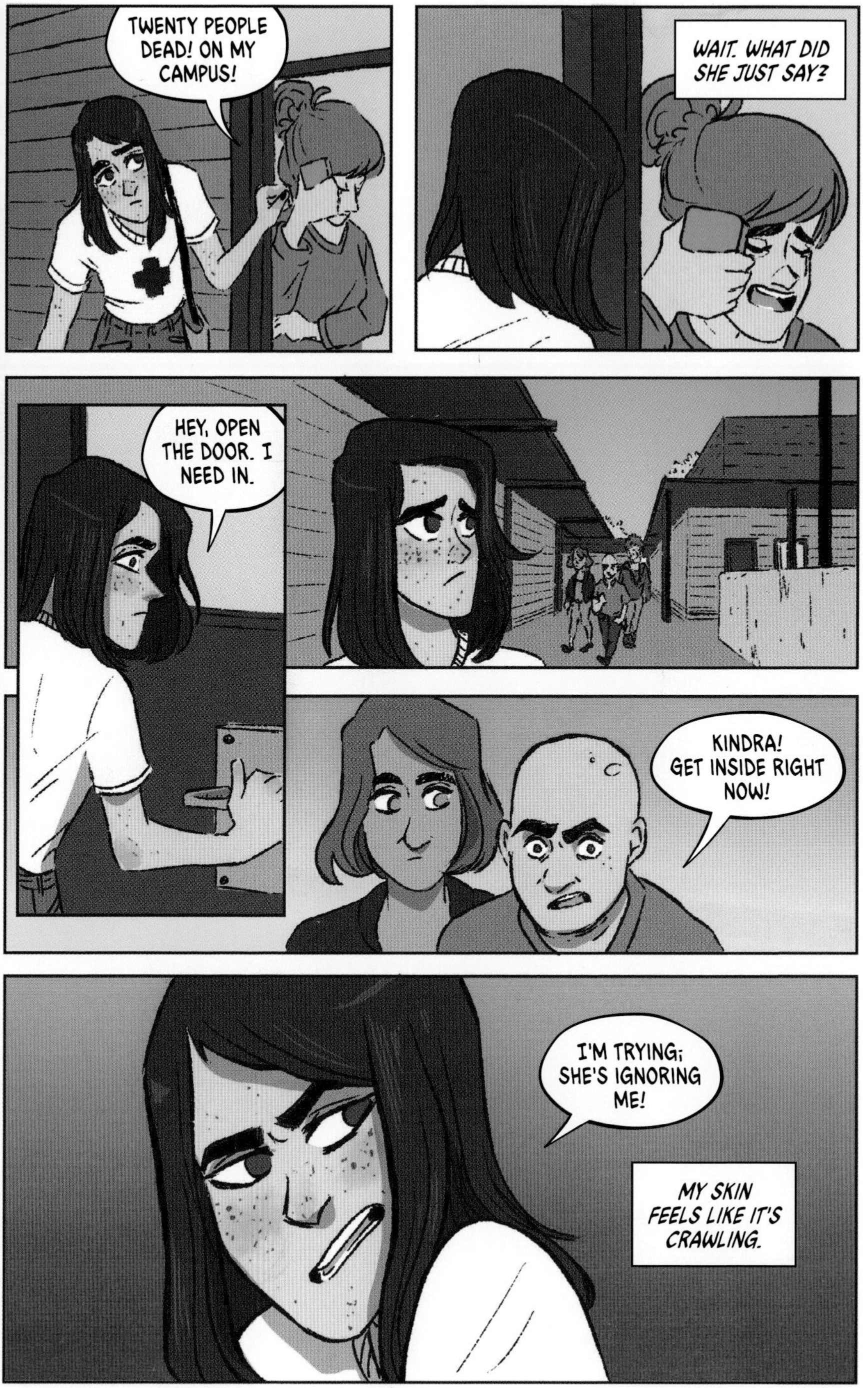
TWENTY PEOPLE DEAD! ON MY CAMPUS!
WAIT. WHAT DID SHE JUST SAY?
HEY, OPEN THE DOOR. I NEED IN.
KINDRA! GET INSIDE RIGHT NOW!
I'M TRYING; SHE'S IGNORING ME!
MY SKIN FEELS LIKE IT'S CRAWLING.

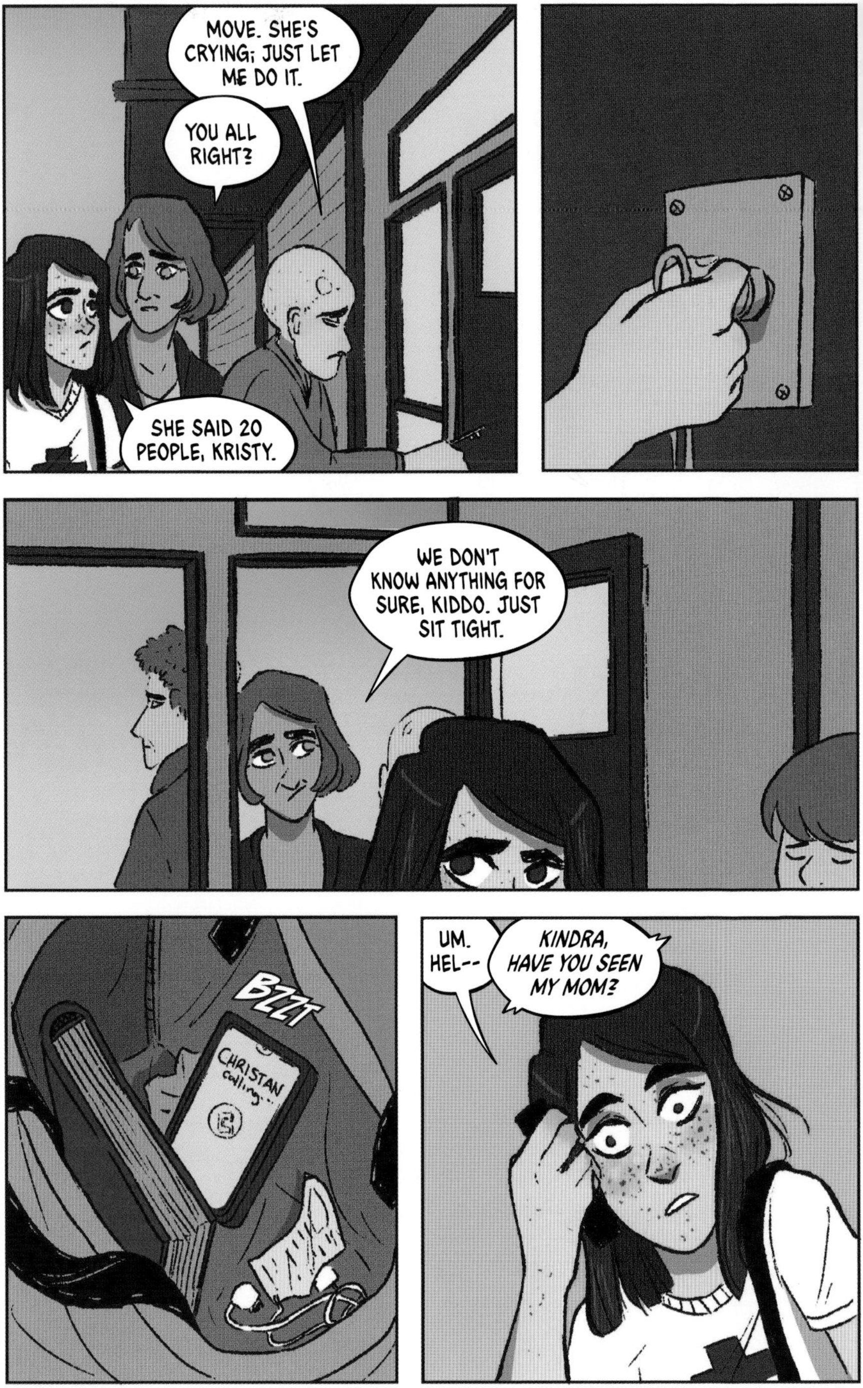
MOVE. SHE'S CRYING; JUST LET ME DO IT.
YOU ALL RIGHT?
SHE SAID 20 PEOPLE, KRISTY.
WE DON'T KNOW ANYTHING FOR SURE, KIDDO. JUST SIT TIGHT.
BZZT
CHRISTAN calling...
UM. HEL--
KINDRA, HAVE YOU SEEN MY MOM?

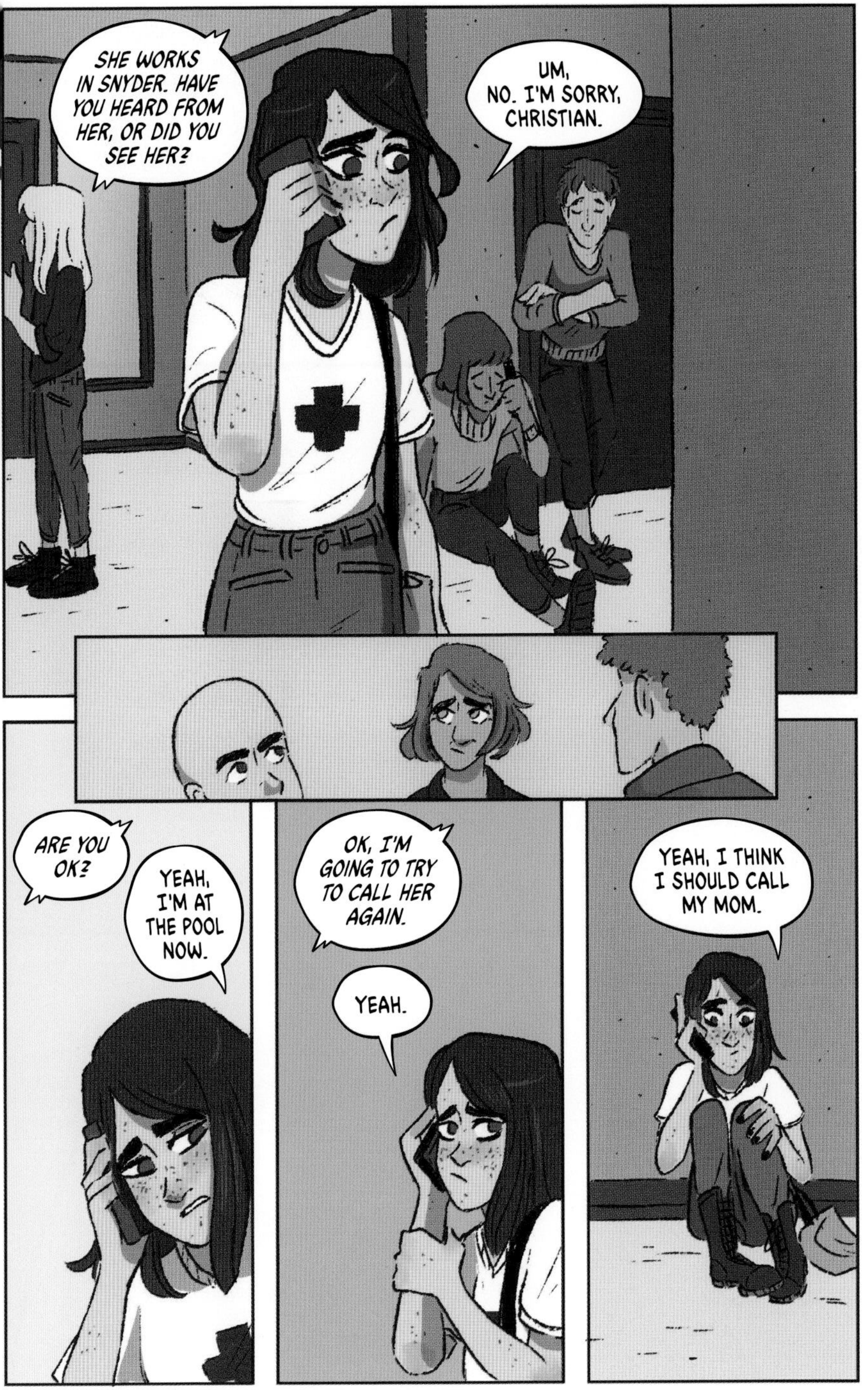
SHE WORKS IN SNYDER. HAVE YOU HEARD FROM HER, OR DID YOU SEE HER?
UM, NO. I'M SORRY, CHRISTIAN.
ARE YOU OK?
YEAH, I'M AT THE POOL NOW.
OK, I'M GOING TO TRY TO CALL HER AGAIN.
YEAH.
YEAH, I THINK I SHOULD CALL MY MOM.

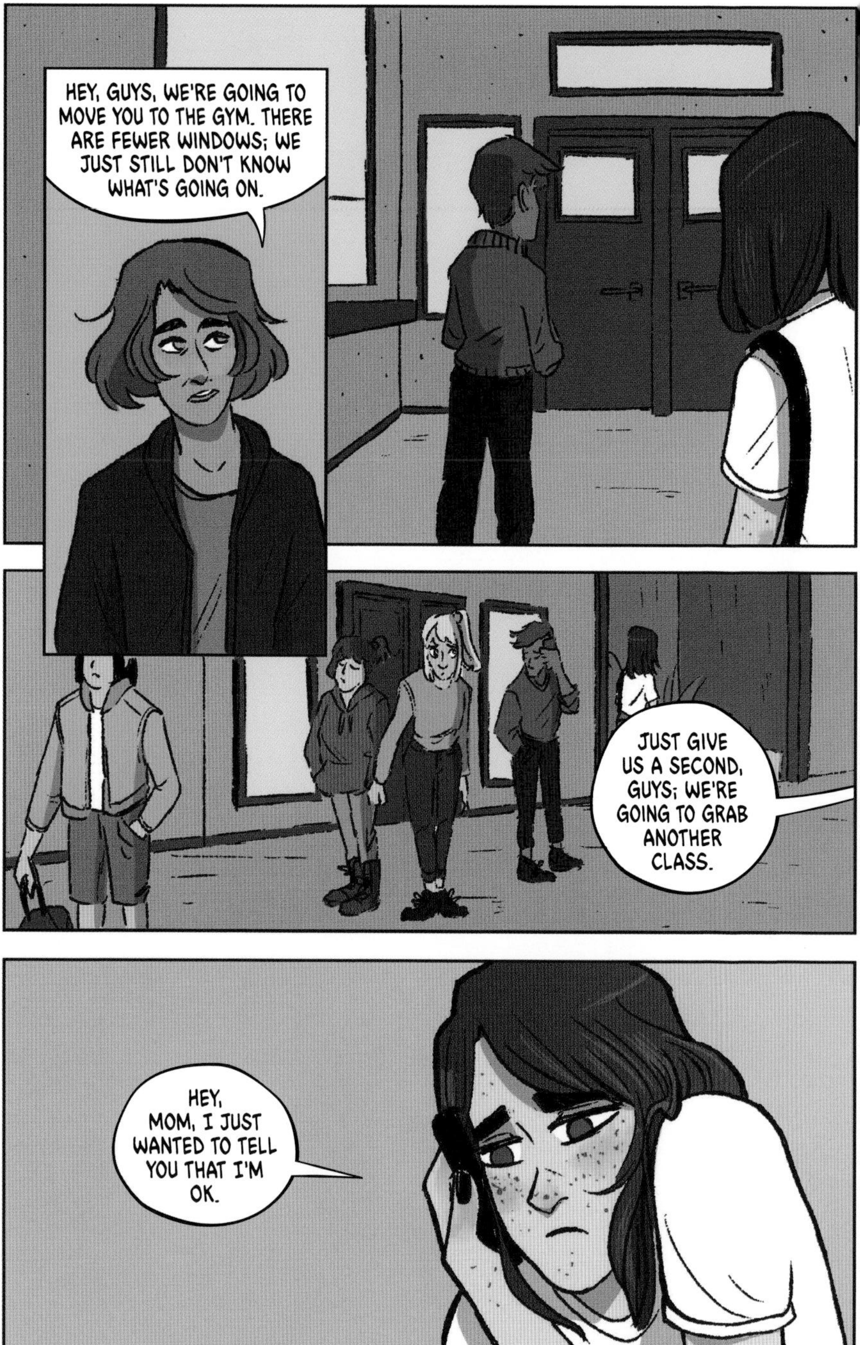
HEY, GUYS, WE'RE GOING TO MOVE YOU TO THE GYM. THERE ARE FEWER WINDOWS; WE JUST STILL DON'T KNOW WHAT'S GOING ON.
JUST GIVE US A SECOND, GUYS; WE'RE GOING TO GRAB ANOTHER CLASS.
HEY, MOM, I JUST WANTED TO TELL YOU THAT I'M OK.

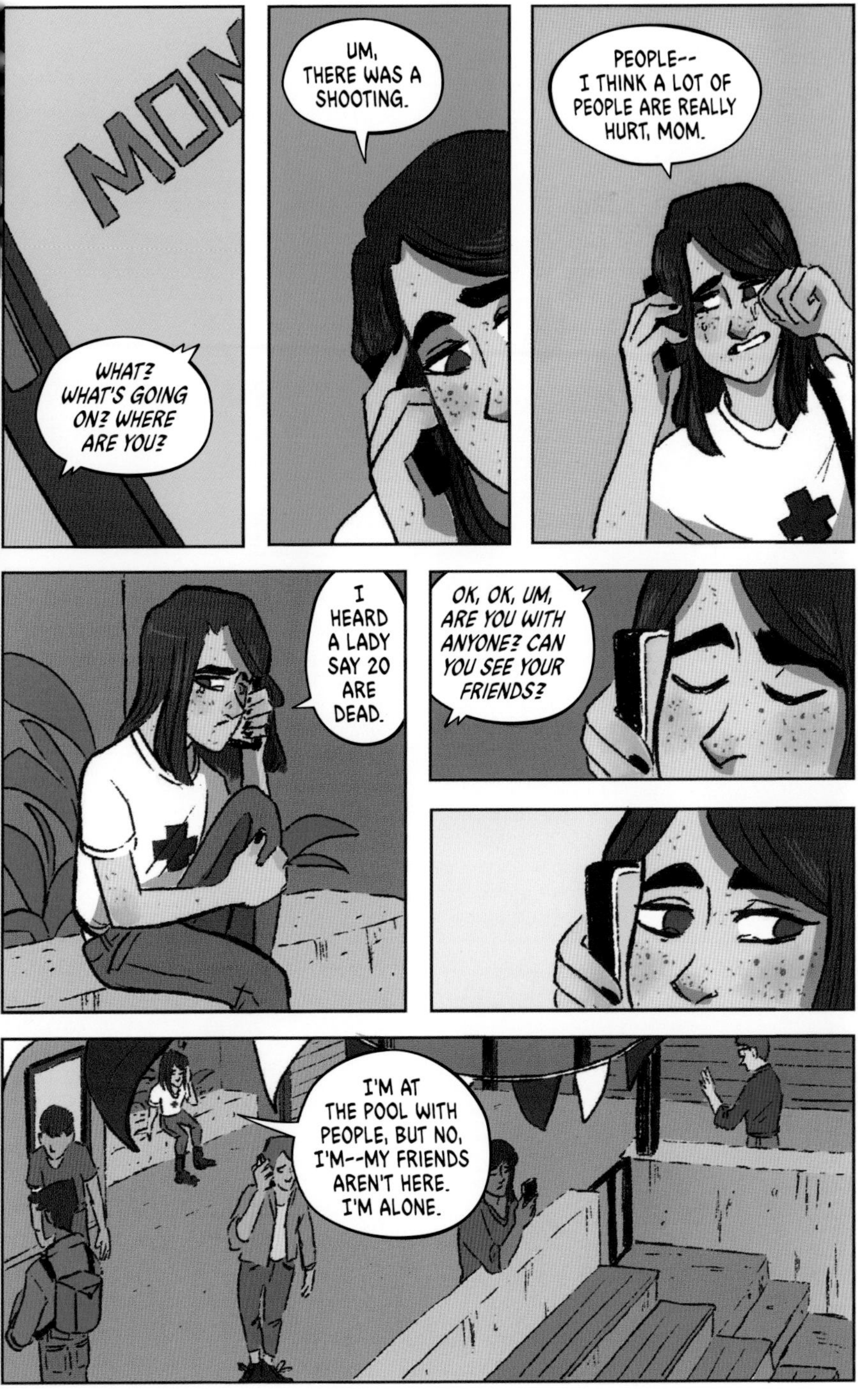
MOM
WHAT? WHAT'S GOING ON? WHERE ARE YOU?
UM, THERE WAS A SHOOTING.
PEOPLE-- I THINK A LOT OF PEOPLE ARE REALLY HURT, MOM.
I HEARD A LADY SAY 20 ARE DEAD.
OK, OK, UM, ARE YOU WITH ANYONE? CAN YOU SEE YOUR FRIENDS?
I'M AT THE POOL WITH PEOPLE, BUT NO, I'M--MY FRIENDS AREN'T HERE. I'M ALONE.

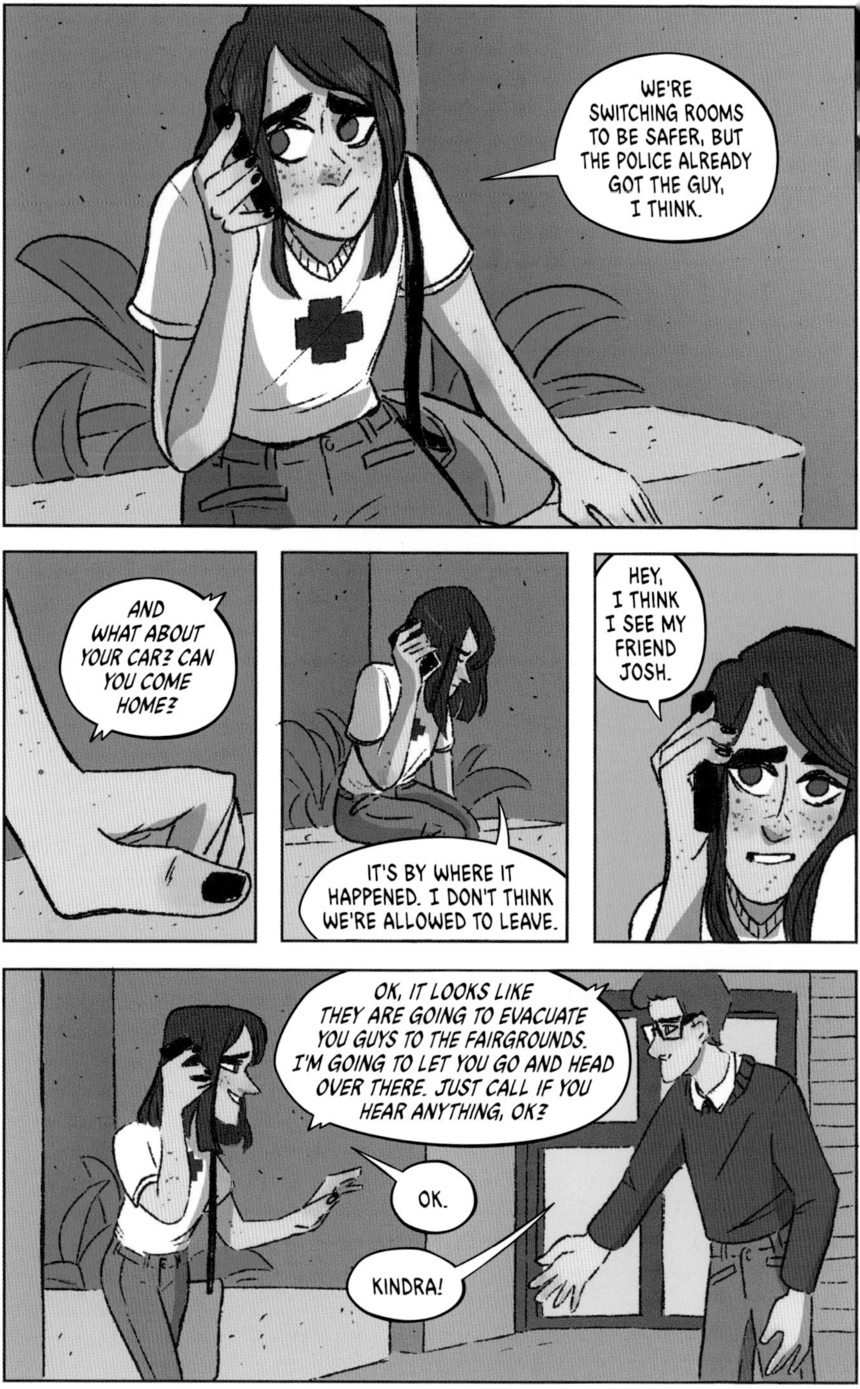
WE'RE SWITCHING ROOMS TO BE SAFER, BUT THE POLICE ALREADY GOT THE GUY, I THINK.
AND WHAT ABOUT YOUR CAR? CAN YOU COME HOME?
IT'S BY WHERE IT HAPPENED. I DON'T THINK WE'RE ALLOWED TO LEAVE.
HEY, I THINK I SEE MY FRIEND JOSH.
OK, IT LOOKS LIKE THEY ARE GOING TO EVACUATE YOU GUYS TO THE FAIRGROUNDS. I'M GOING TO LET YOU GO AND HEAD OVER THERE. JUST CALL IF YOU HEAR ANYTHING, OK?
OK.
KINDRA!

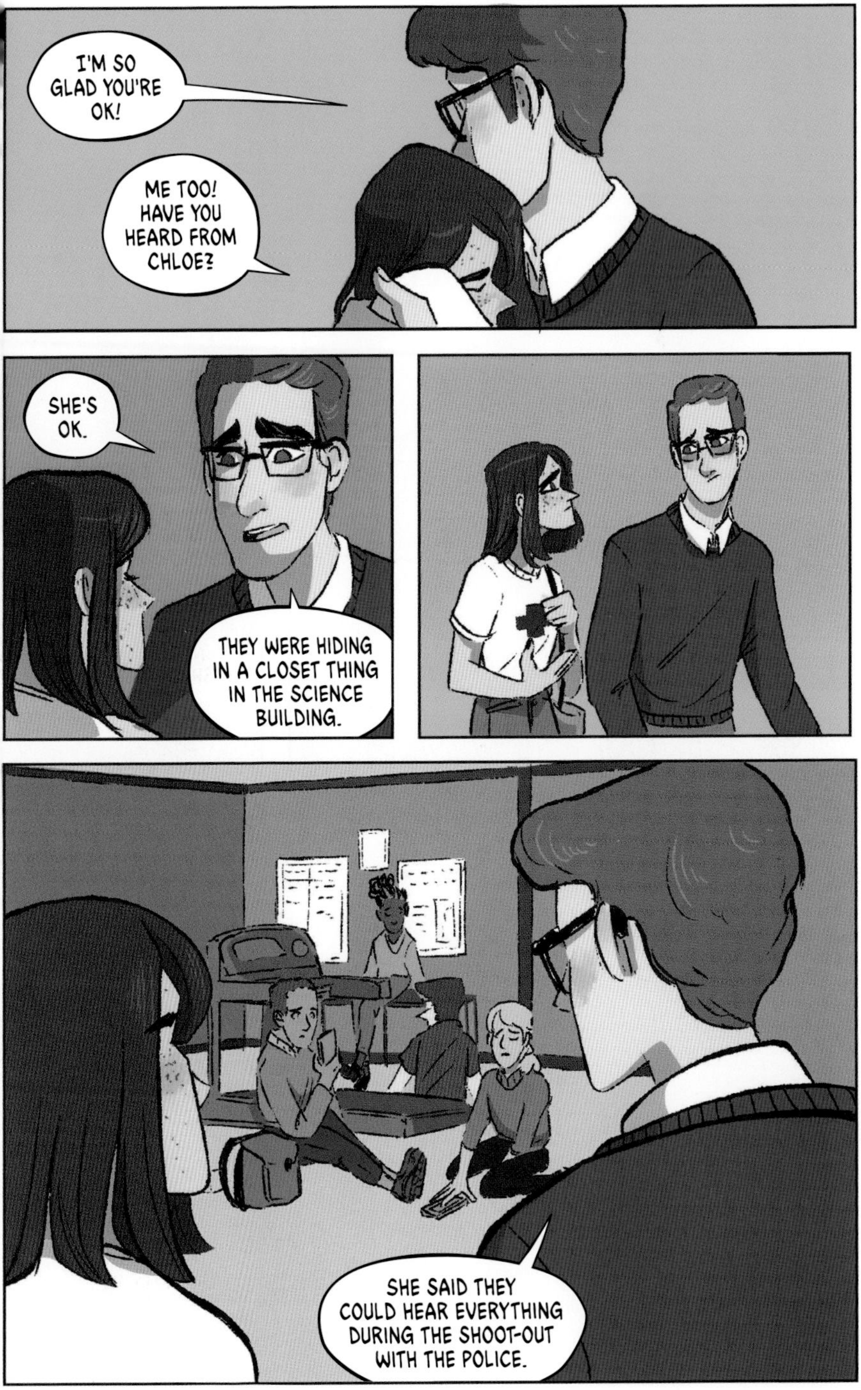
I'M SO GLAD YOU'RE OK!
ME TOO! HAVE YOU HEARD FROM CHLOE?
SHE'S OK.
THEY WERE HIDING IN A CLOSET THING IN THE SCIENCE BUILDING.
SHE SAID THEY COULD HEAR EVERYTHING DURING THE SHOOT-OUT WITH THE POLICE.

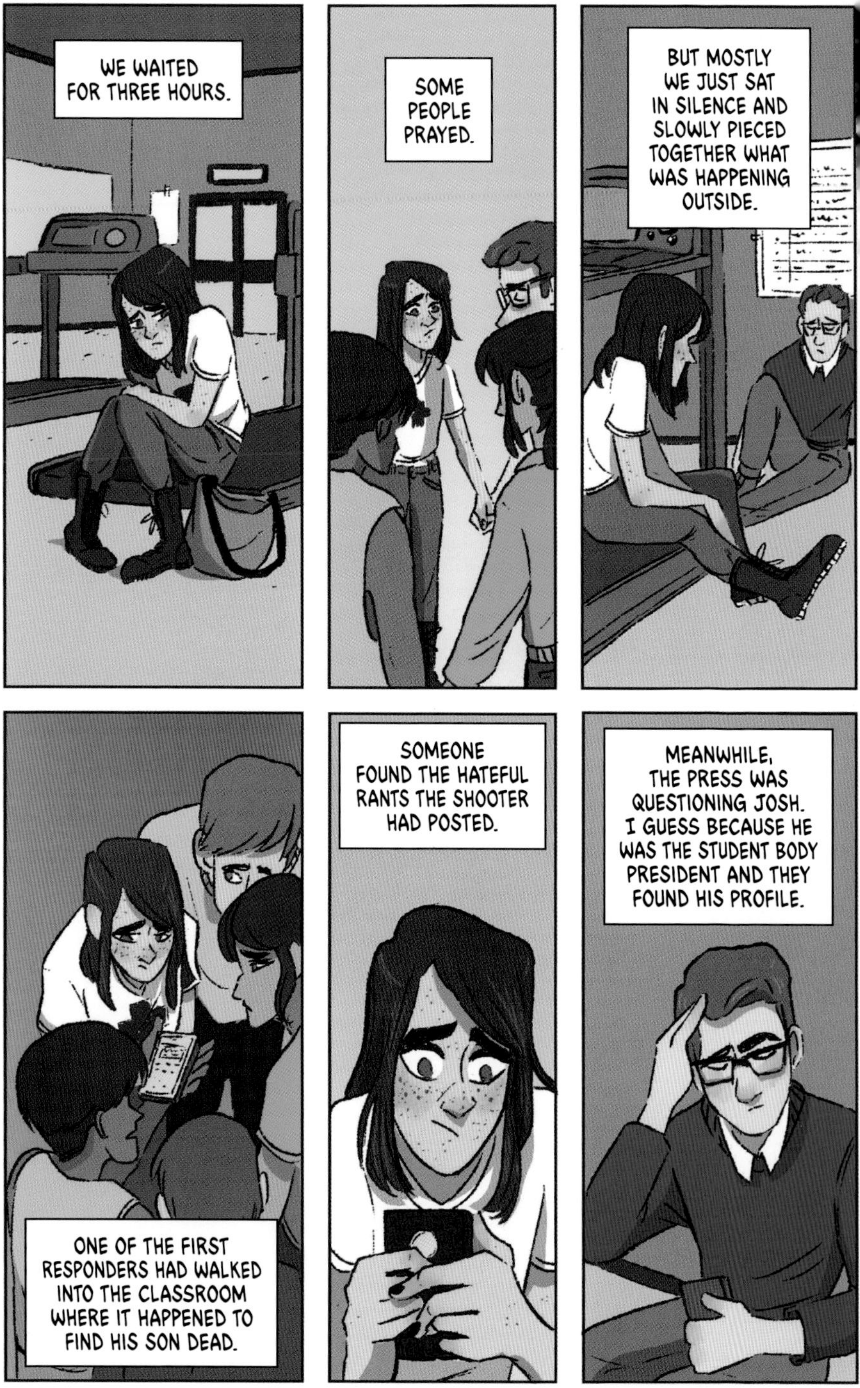
WE WAITED FOR THREE HOURS.
SOME PEOPLE PRAYED.
BUT MOSTLY WE JUST SAT IN SILENCE AND SLOWLY PIECED TOGETHER WHAT WAS HAPPENING OUTSIDE.
ONE OF THE FIRST RESPONDERS HAD WALKED INTO THE CLASSROOM WHERE IT HAPPENED TO FIND HIS SON DEAD.
SOMEONE FOUND THE HATEFUL RANTS THE SHOOTER HAD POSTED.
MEANWHILE, THE PRESS WAS QUESTIONING JOSH. I GUESS BECAUSE HE WAS THE STUDENT BODY PRESIDENT AND THEY FOUND HIS PROFILE.

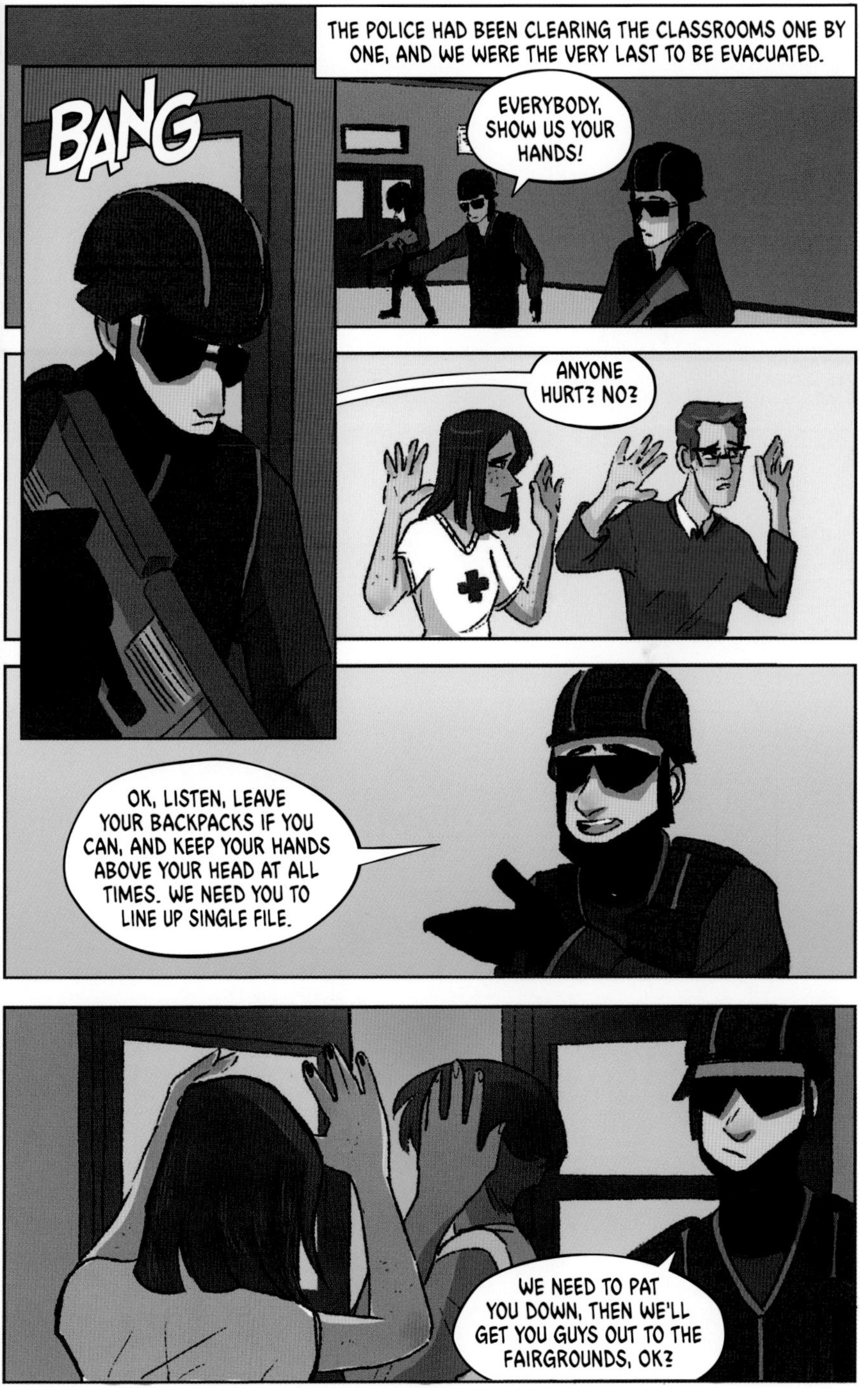

THE POLICE HAD BEEN CLEARING THE CLASSROOMS ONE BY ONE, AND WE WERE THE VERY LAST TO BE EVACUATED.
BANG
EVERYBODY, SHOW US YOUR HANDS!
ANYONE HURT? NO?
OK, LISTEN, LEAVE YOUR BACKPACKS IF YOU CAN, AND KEEP YOUR HANDS ABOVE YOUR HEAD AT ALL TIMES. WE NEED YOU TO LINE UP SINGLE FILE.
WE NEED TO PAT YOU DOWN, THEN WE'LL GET YOU GUYS OUT TO THE FAIRGROUNDS, OK?

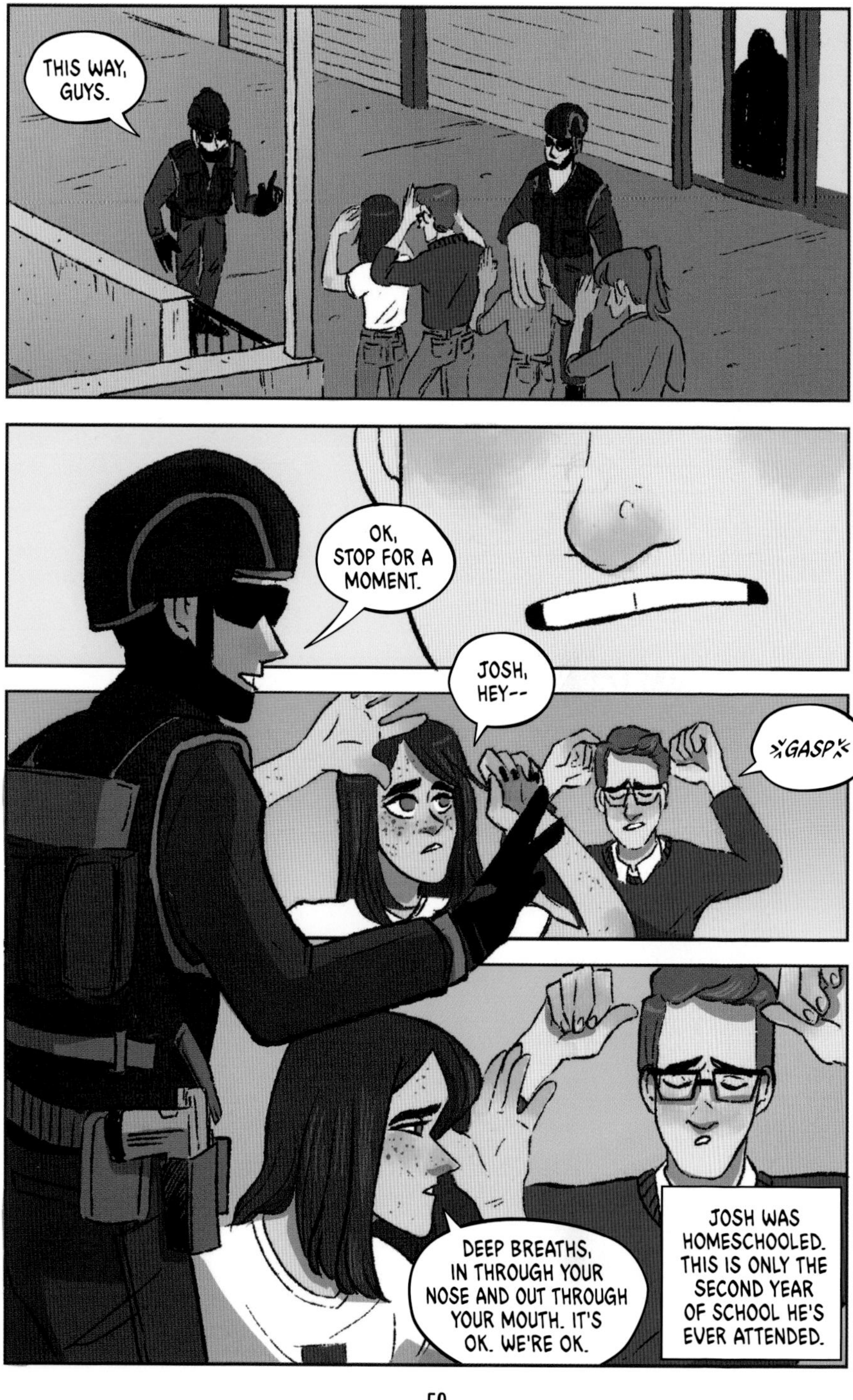
THIS WAY, GUYS.
OK, STOP FOR A MOMENT.
JOSH, HEY--
GASP
DEEP BREATHS, IN THROUGH YOUR NOSE AND OUT THROUGH YOUR MOUTH. IT'S OK. WE'RE OK.
JOSH WAS HOMESCHOOLED. THIS IS ONLY THE SECOND YEAR OF SCHOOL HE'S EVER ATTENDED.

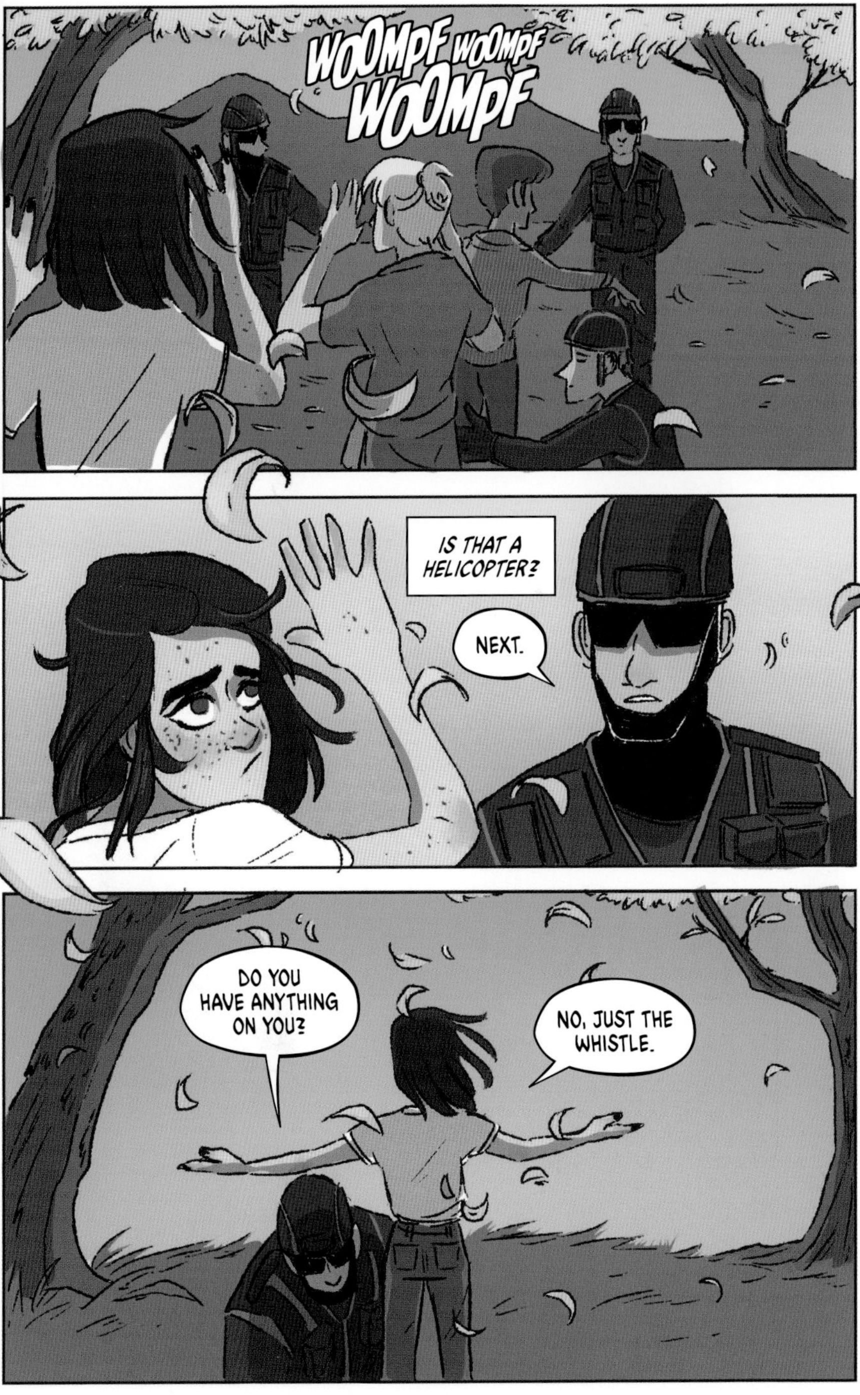
WOOMPF WOOMPF
WOOMPF
IS THAT A HELICOPTER?
NEXT.
DO YOU HAVE ANYTHING ON YOU?
NO, JUST THE WHISTLE.

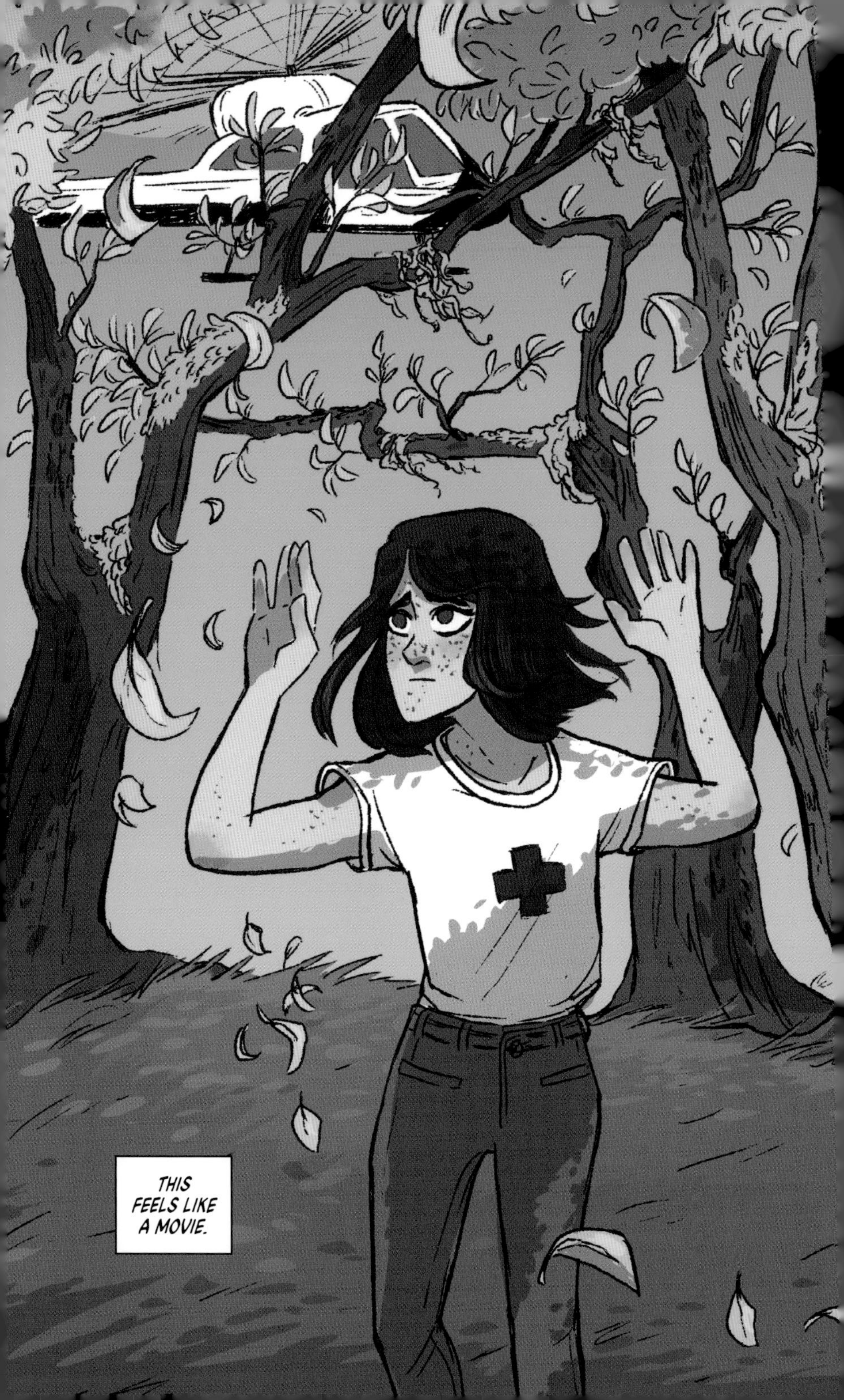
THIS FEELS LIKE A MOVIE.

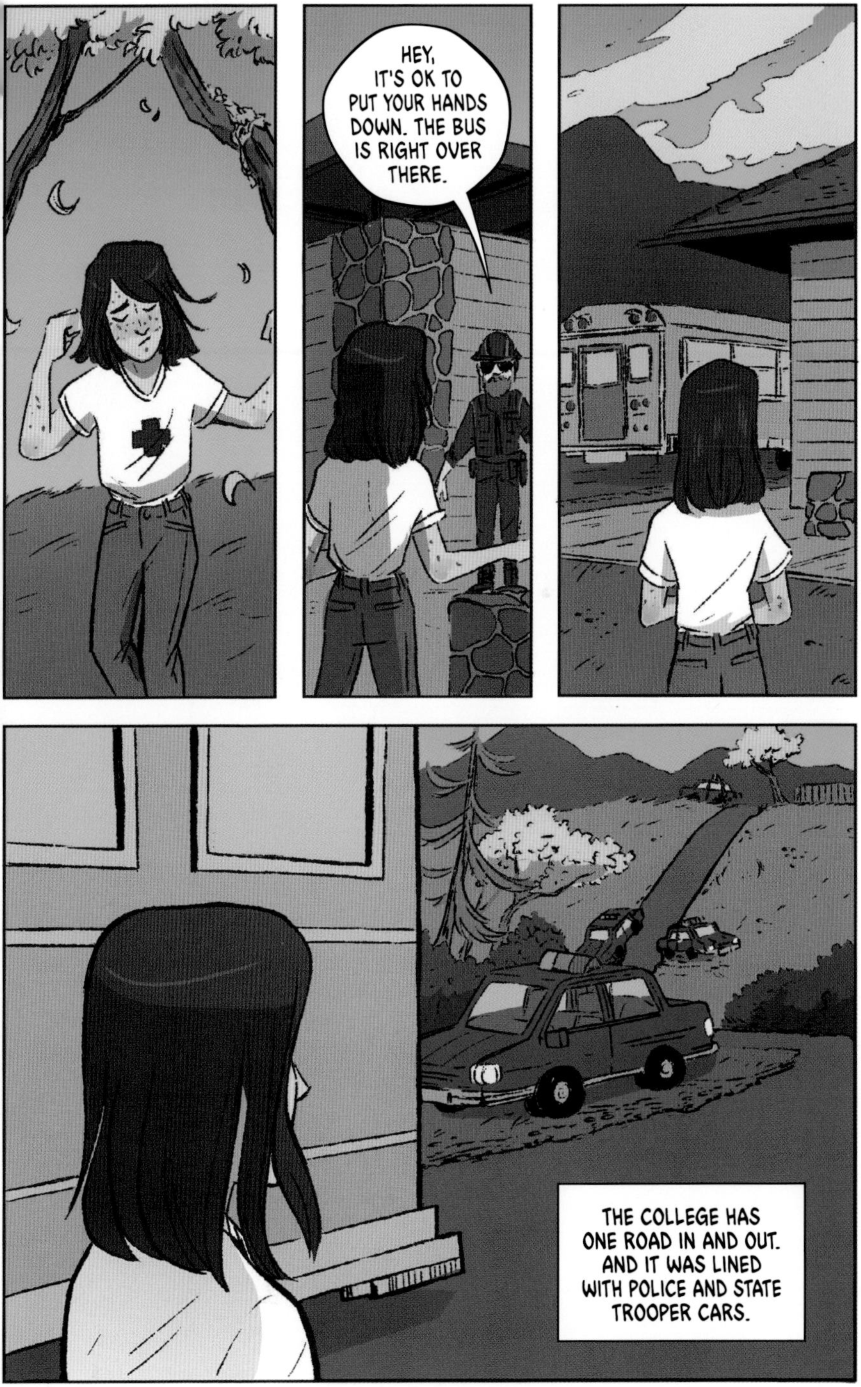
HEY, IT'S OK TO PUT YOUR HANDS DOWN. THE BUS IS RIGHT OVER THERE.
THE COLLEGE HAS ONE ROAD IN AND OUT. AND IT WAS LINED WITH POLICE AND STATE TROOPER CARS.

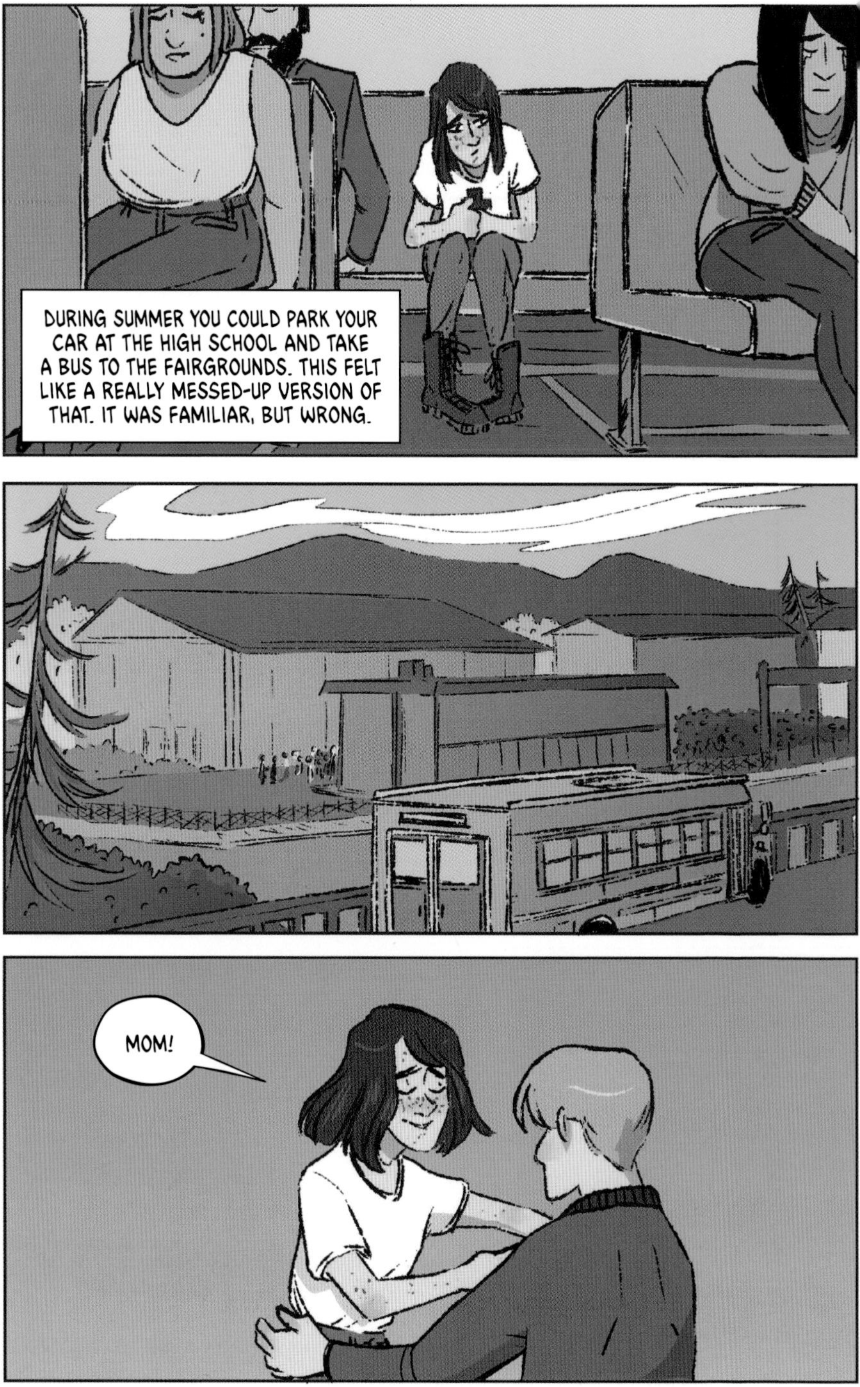
DURING SUMMER YOU COULD PARK YOUR CAR AT THE HIGH SCHOOL AND TAKE A BUS TO THE FAIRGROUNDS. THIS FELT LIKE A REALLY MESSED-UP VERSION OF THAT. IT WAS FAMILIAR, BUT WRONG.
MOM!

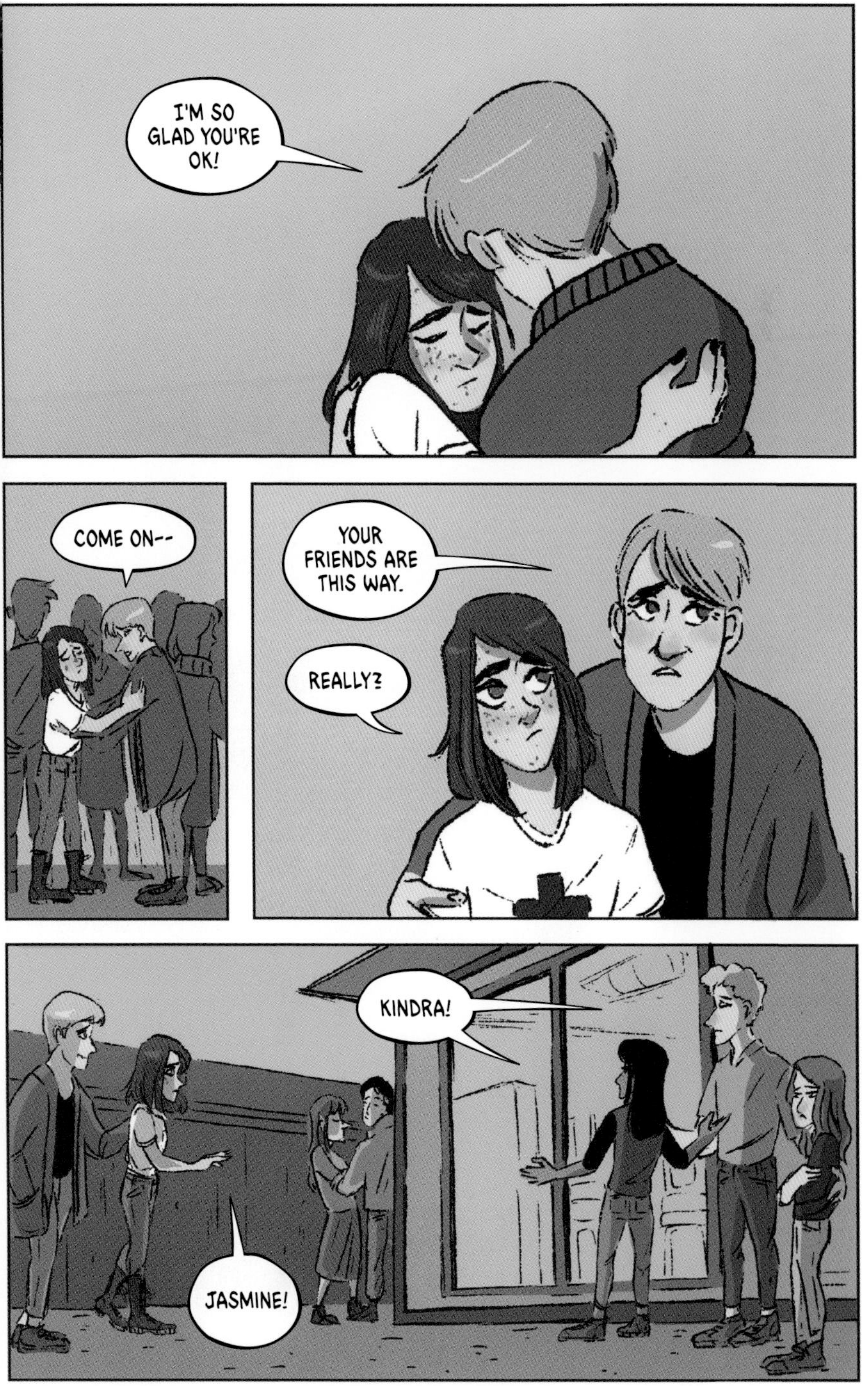
I'M SO GLAD YOU'RE OK!
COME ON--
YOUR FRIENDS ARE THIS WAY.
REALLY?
KINDRA!
JASMINE!

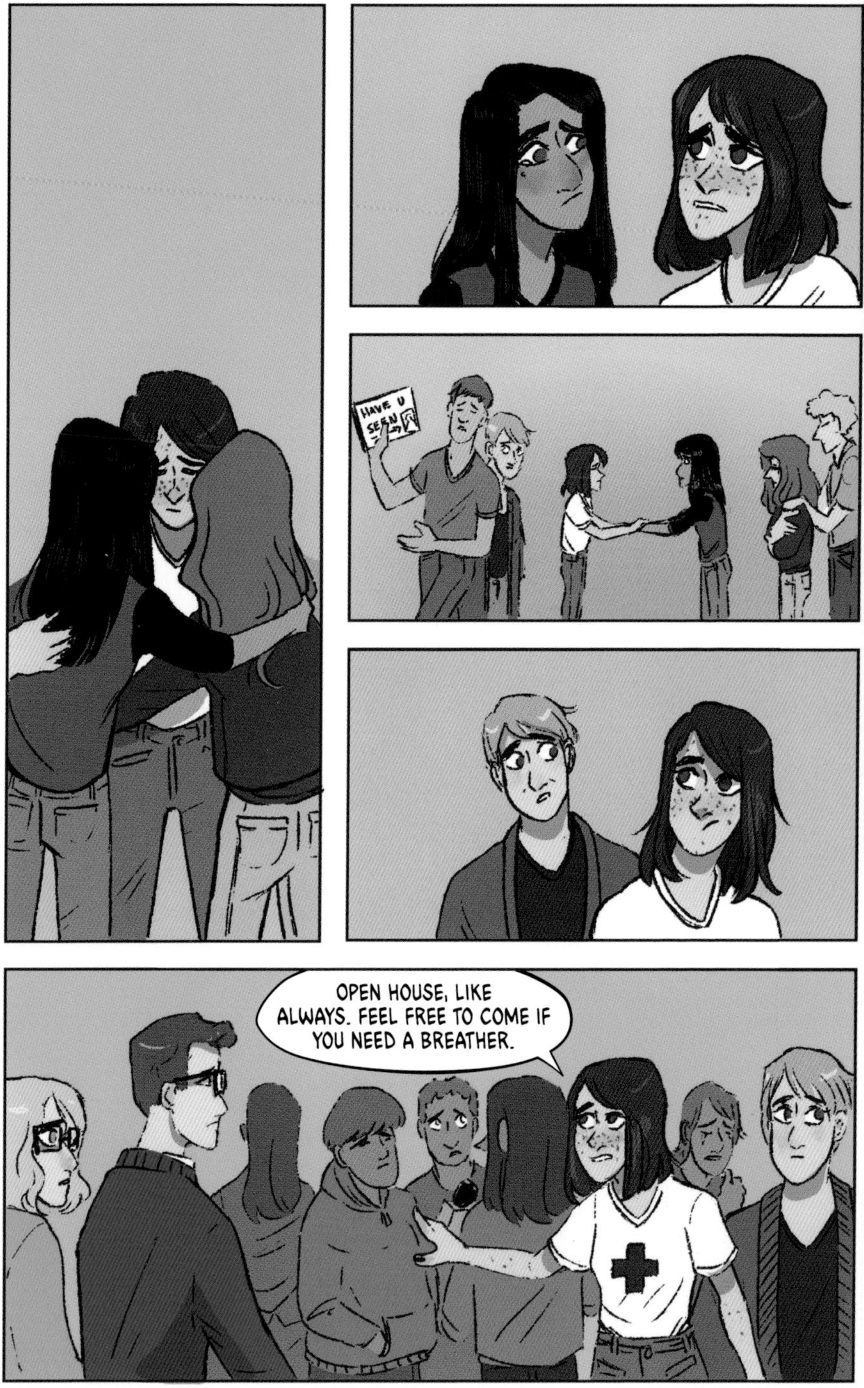
HAVE U SEEN
OPEN HOUSE, LIKE ALWAYS. FEEL FREE TO COME IF YOU NEED A BREATHER.

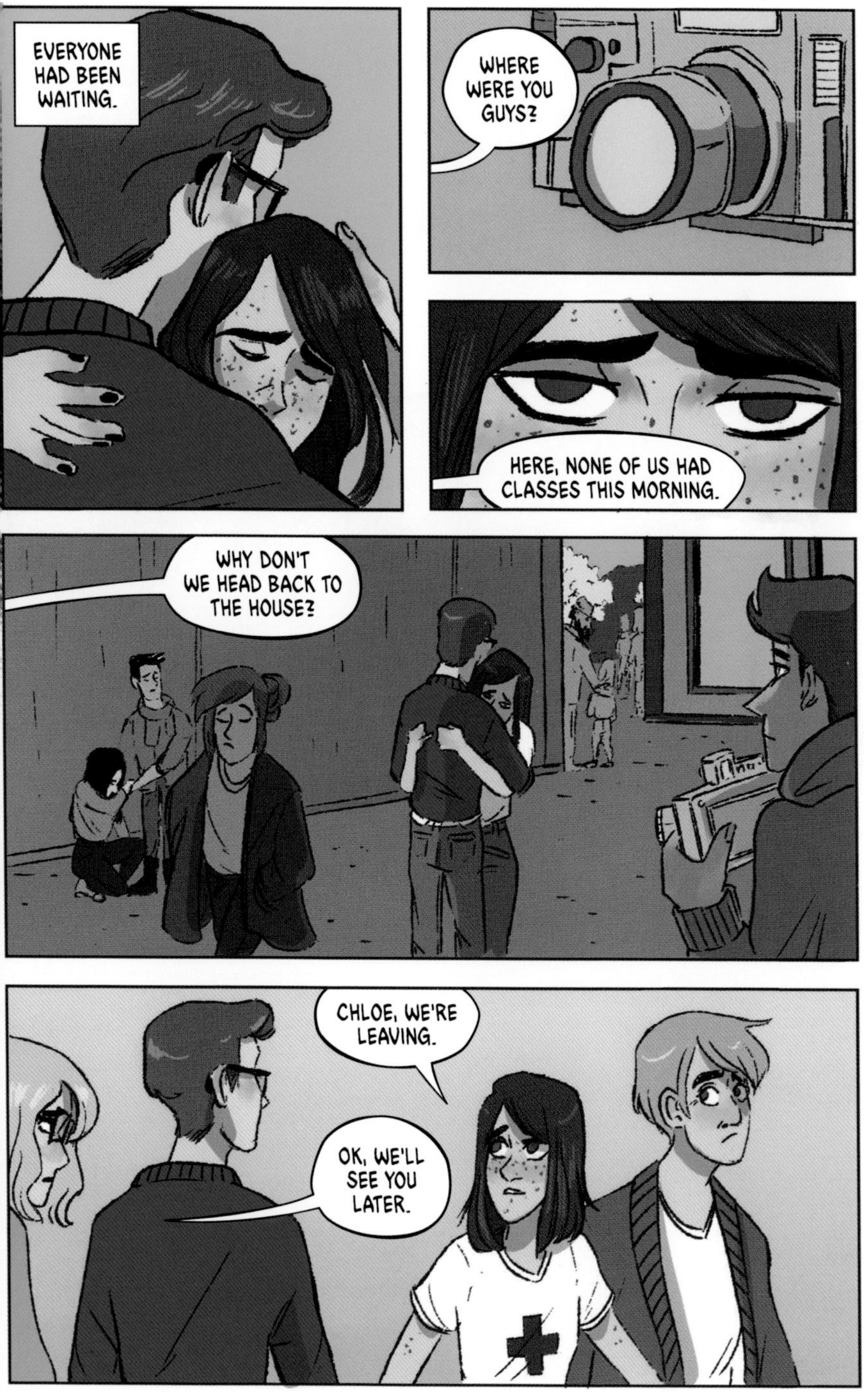
EVERYONE HAD BEEN WAITING.
WHERE WERE YOU GUYS?
HERE, NONE OF US HAD CLASSES THIS MORNING.
WHY DON'T WE HEAD BACK TO THE HOUSE?
CHLOE, WE'RE LEAVING.
OK, WE'LL SEE YOU LATER.

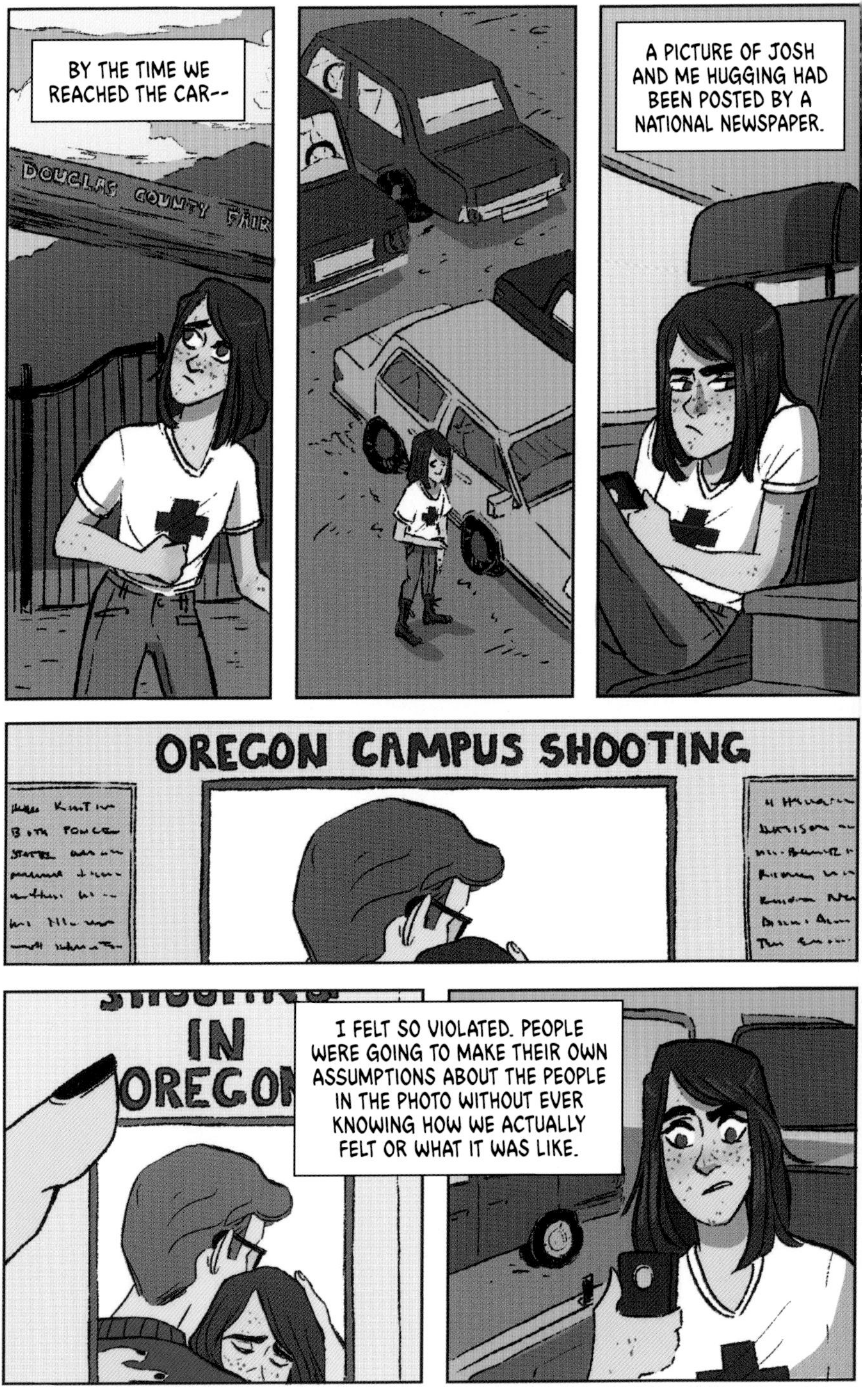
BY THE TIME WE REACHED THE CAR--
DOUGLAS COUNTY FAIR
A PICTURE OF JOSH AND ME HUGGING HAD BEEN POSTED BY A NATIONAL NEWSPAPER.
OREGON CAMPUS SHOOTING
IN OREGON
I FELT SO VIOLATED. PEOPLE WERE GOING TO MAKE THEIR OWN ASSUMPTIONS ABOUT THE PEOPLE IN THE PHOTO WITHOUT EVER KNOWING HOW WE ACTUALLY FELT OR WHAT IT WAS LIKE.

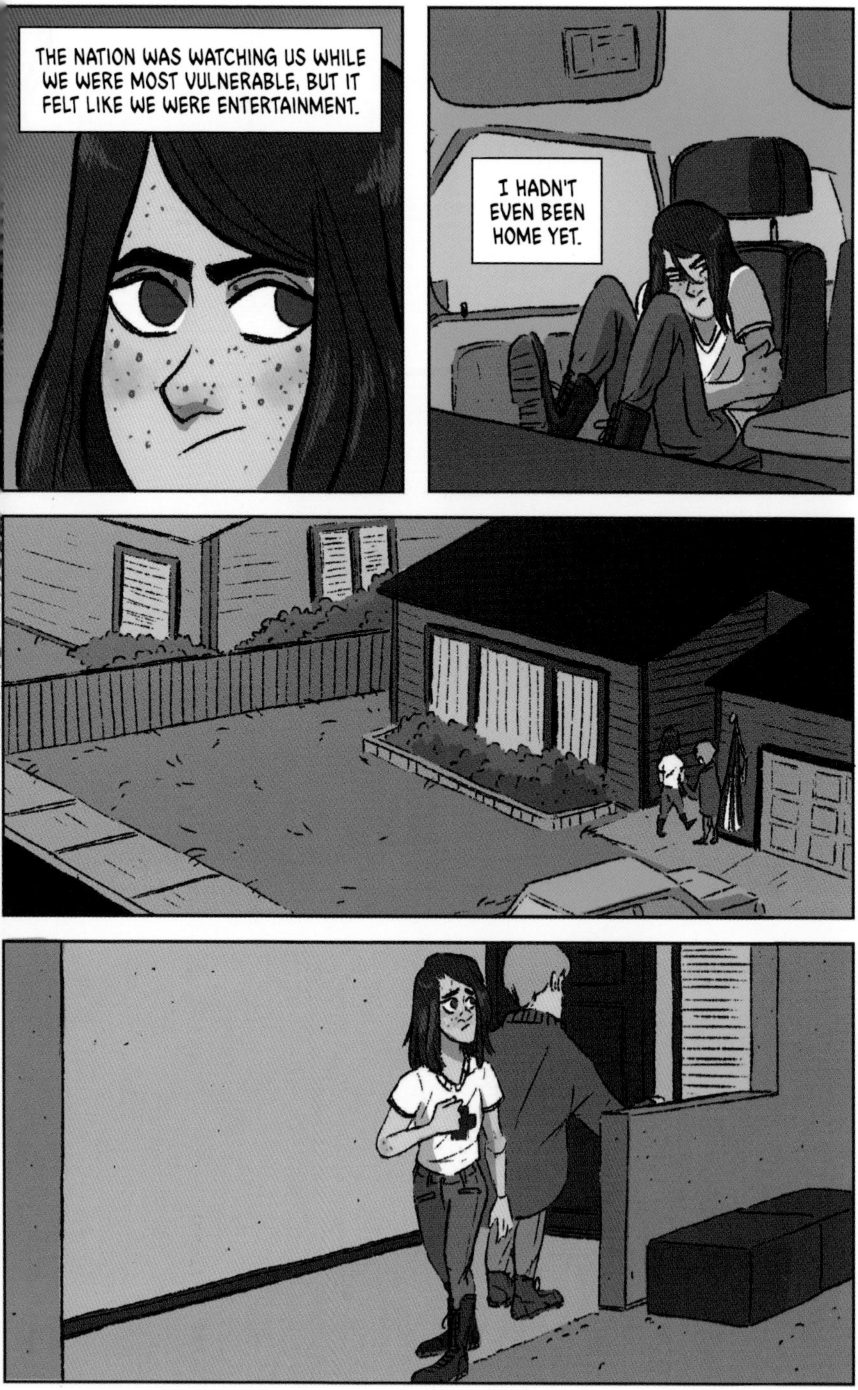
THE NATION WAS WATCHING US WHILE WE WERE MOST VULNERABLE, BUT IT FELT LIKE WE WERE ENTERTAINMENT.
I HADN'T EVEN BEEN HOME YET.

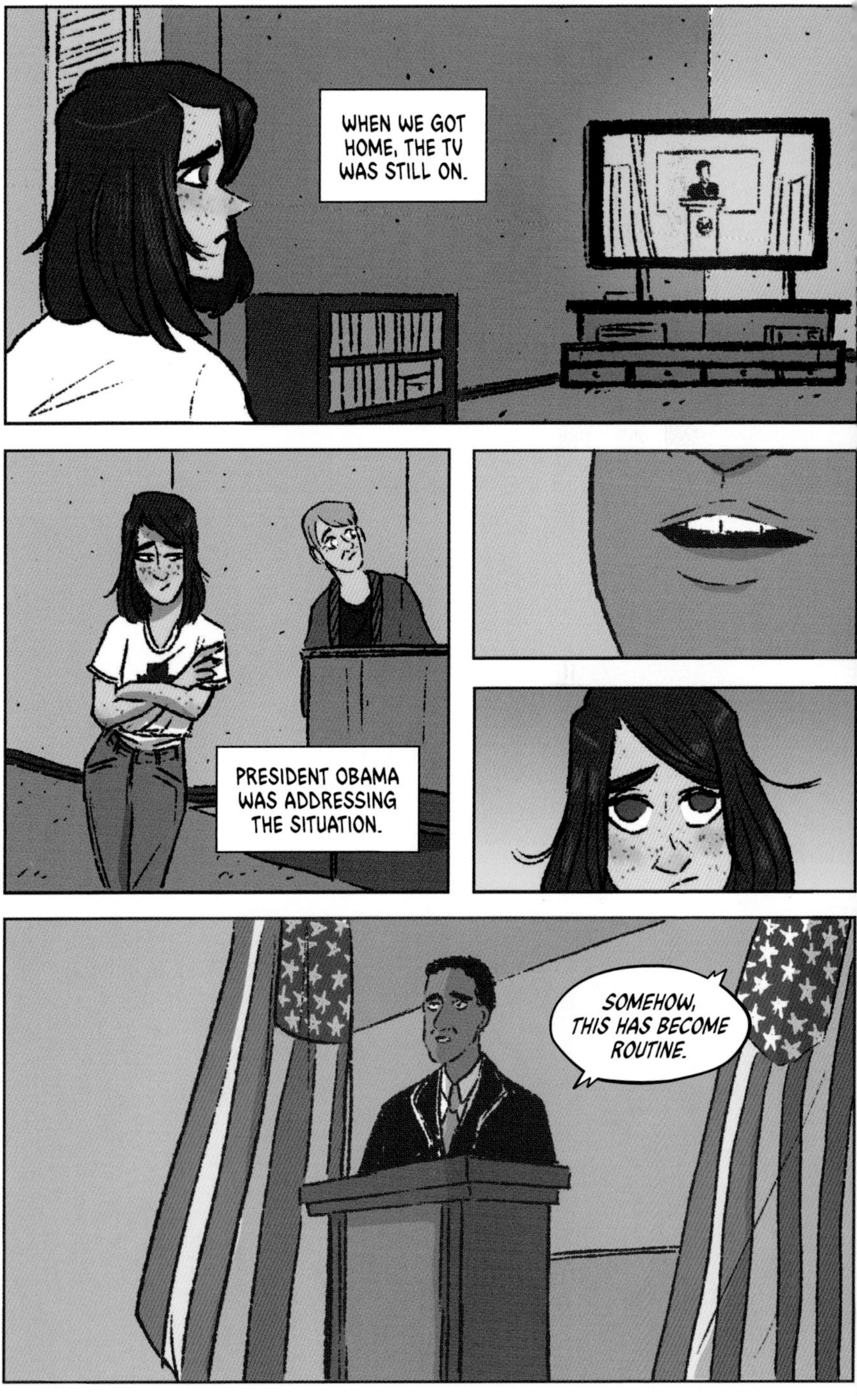
WHEN WE GOT HOME, THE TV WAS STILL ON.
PRESIDENT OBAMA WAS ADDRESSING THE SITUATION.
SOMEHOW, THIS HAS BECOME ROUTINE.

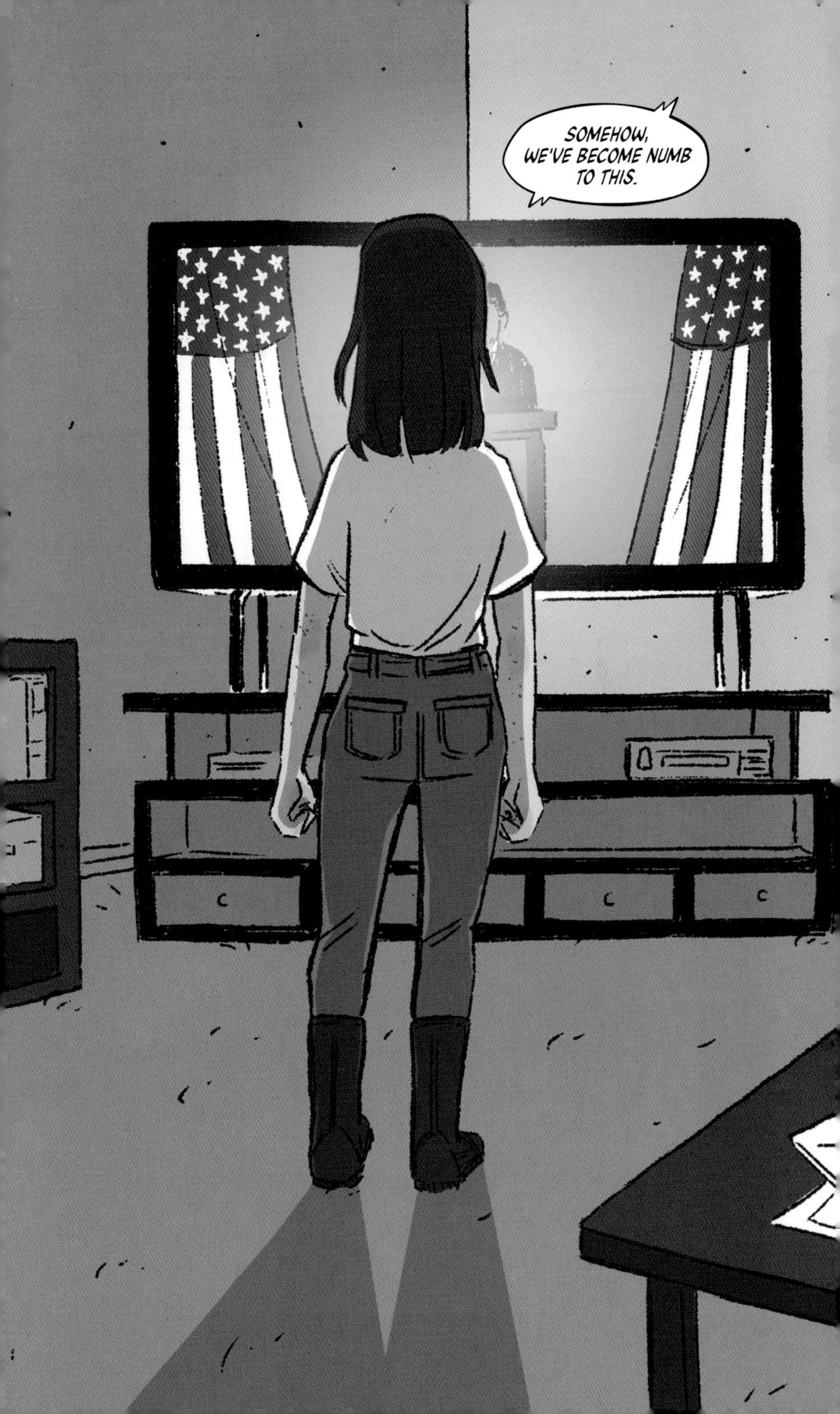
SOMEHOW, WE'VE BECOME NUMB TO THIS.

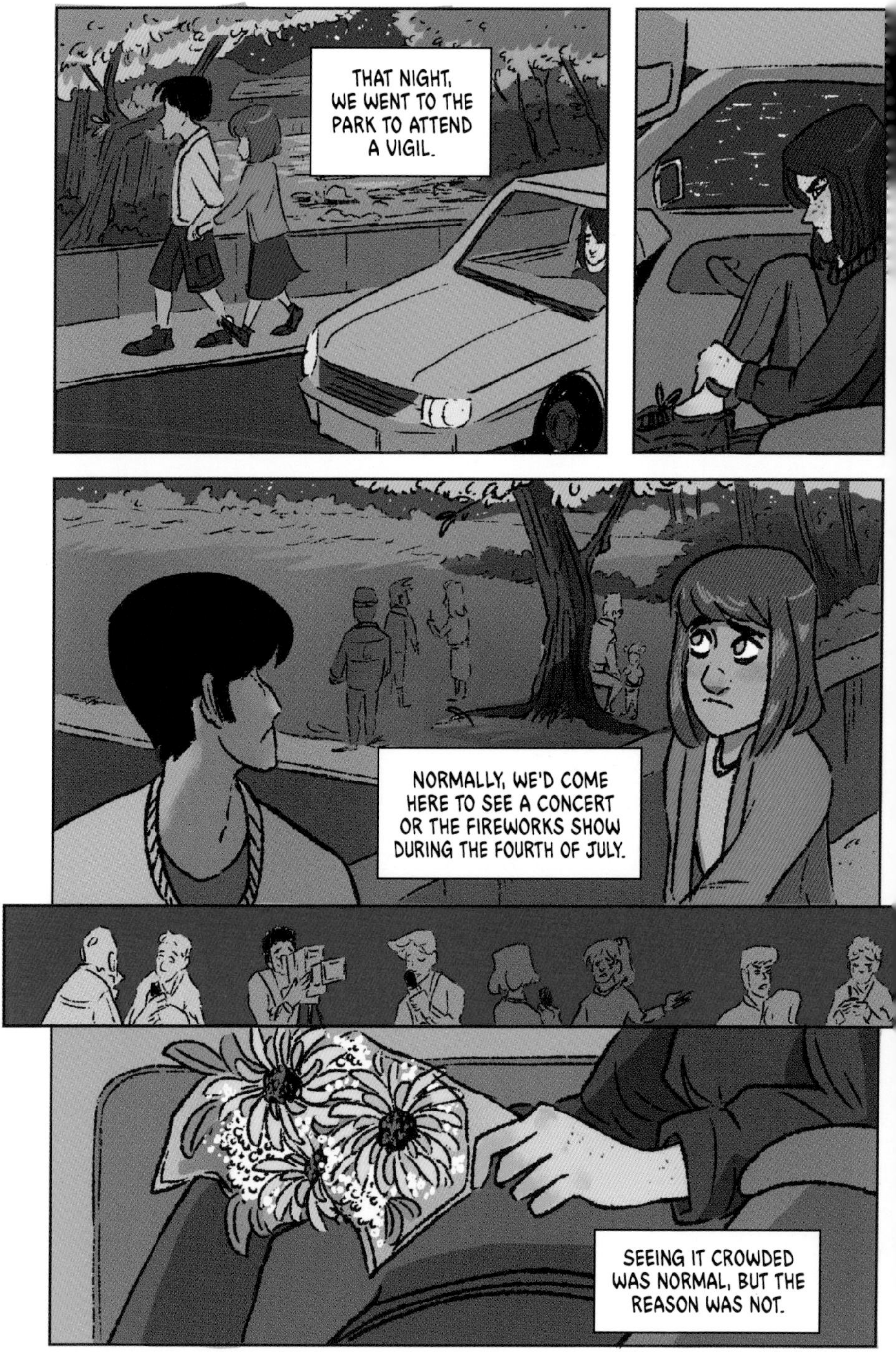
THAT NIGHT, WE WENT TO THE PARK TO ATTEND A VIGIL.
NORMALLY, WE'D COME HERE TO SEE A CONCERT OR THE FIREWORKS SHOW DURING THE FOURTH OF JULY.
SEEING IT CROWDED WAS NORMAL, BUT THE REASON WAS NOT.

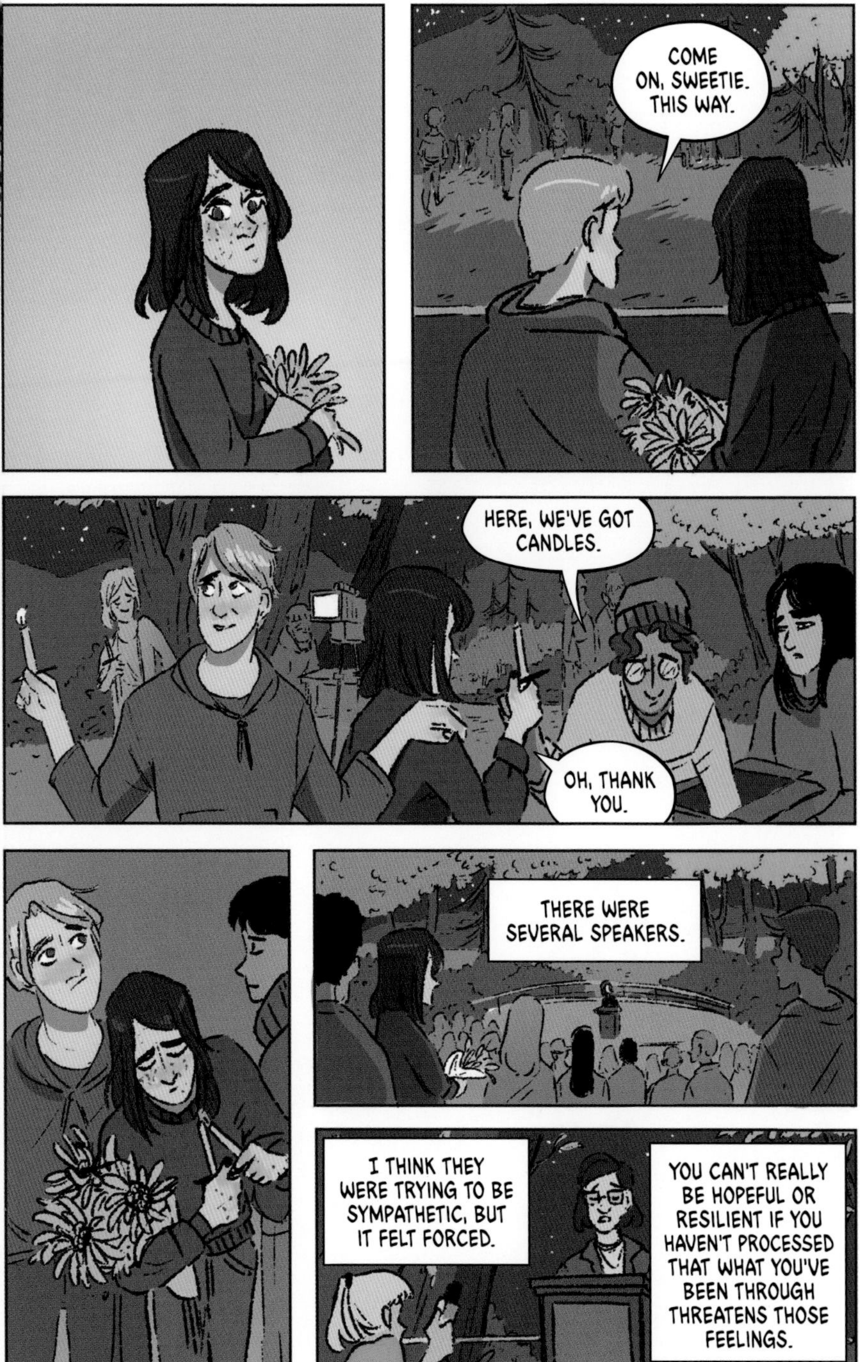
COME ON, SWEETIE. THIS WAY.
HERE, WE'VE GOT CANDLES.
OH, THANK YOU.
THERE WERE SEVERAL SPEAKERS.
I THINK THEY WERE TRYING TO BE SYMPATHETIC, BUT IT FELT FORCED.
YOU CAN'T REALLY BE HOPEFUL OR RESILIENT IF YOU HAVEN'T PROCESSED THAT WHAT YOU'VE BEEN THROUGH THREATENS THOSE FEELINGS.

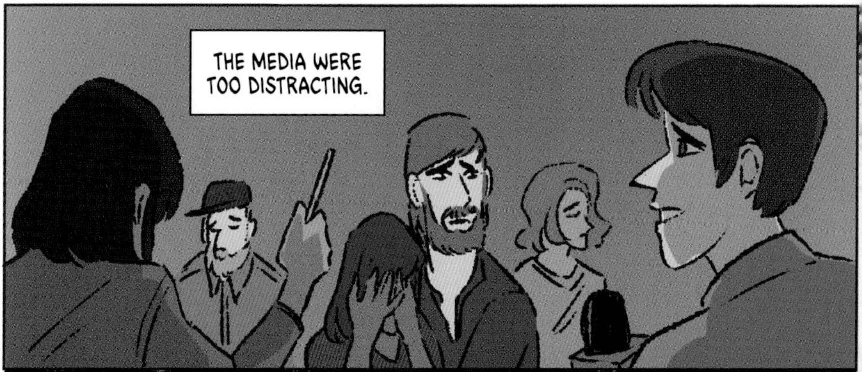
THE MEDIA WERE TOO DISTRACTING.

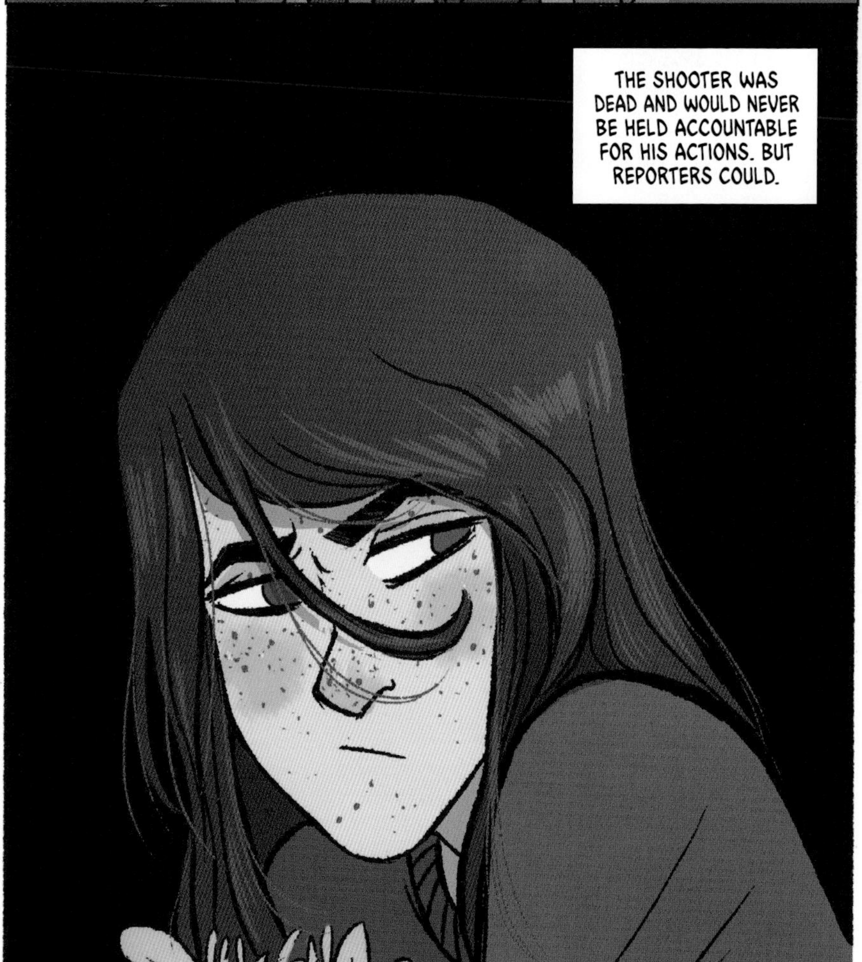
THE SHOOTER WAS DEAD AND WOULD NEVER BE HELD ACCOUNTABLE FOR HIS ACTIONS. BUT REPORTERS COULD.

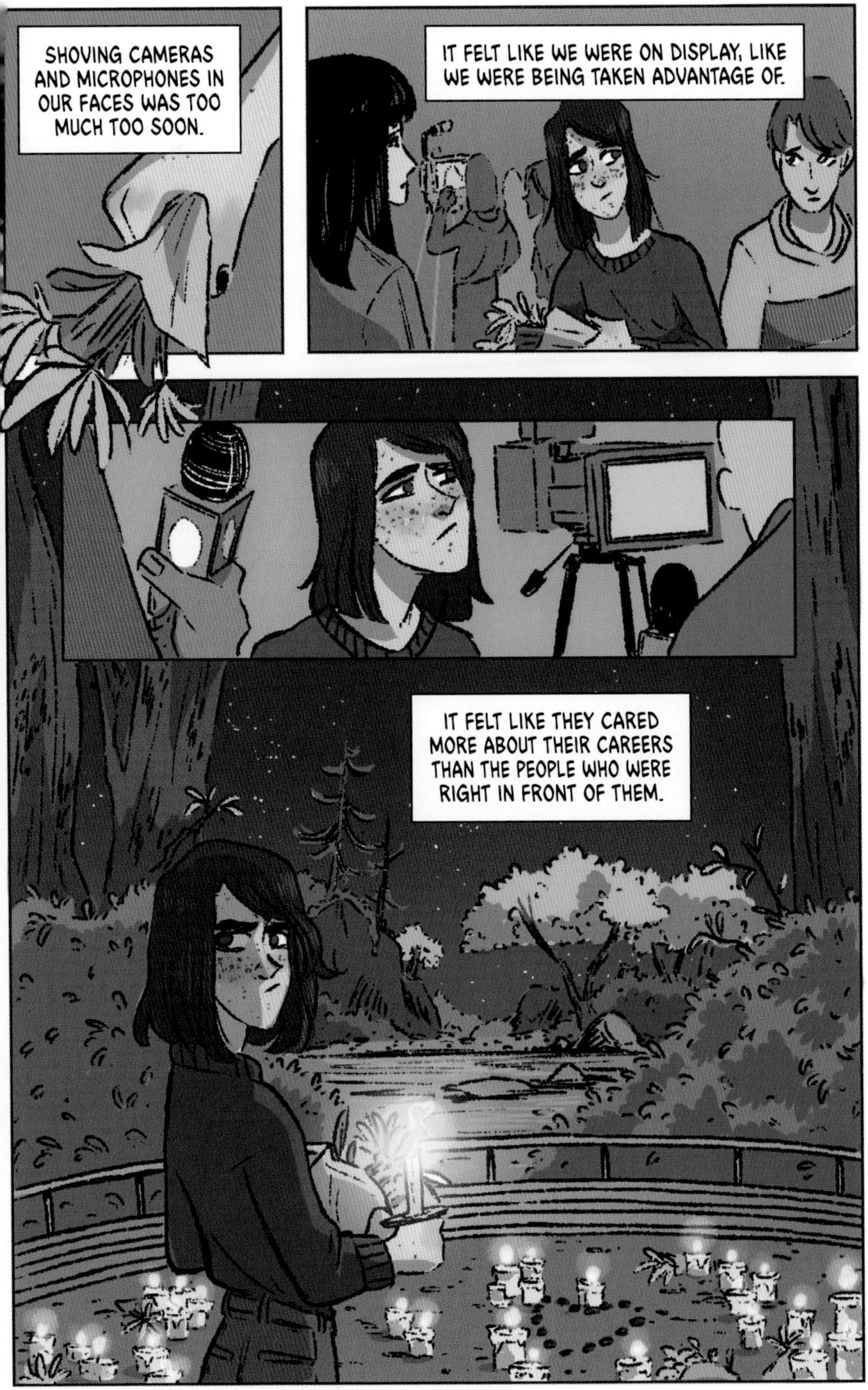
SHOVING CAMERAS AND MICROPHONES IN OUR FACES WAS TOO MUCH TOO SOON.
IT FELT LIKE WE WERE ON DISPLAY, LIKE WE WERE BEING TAKEN ADVANTAGE OF.
IT FELT LIKE THEY CARED MORE ABOUT THEIR CAREERS THAN THE PEOPLE WHO WERE RIGHT IN FRONT OF THEM.

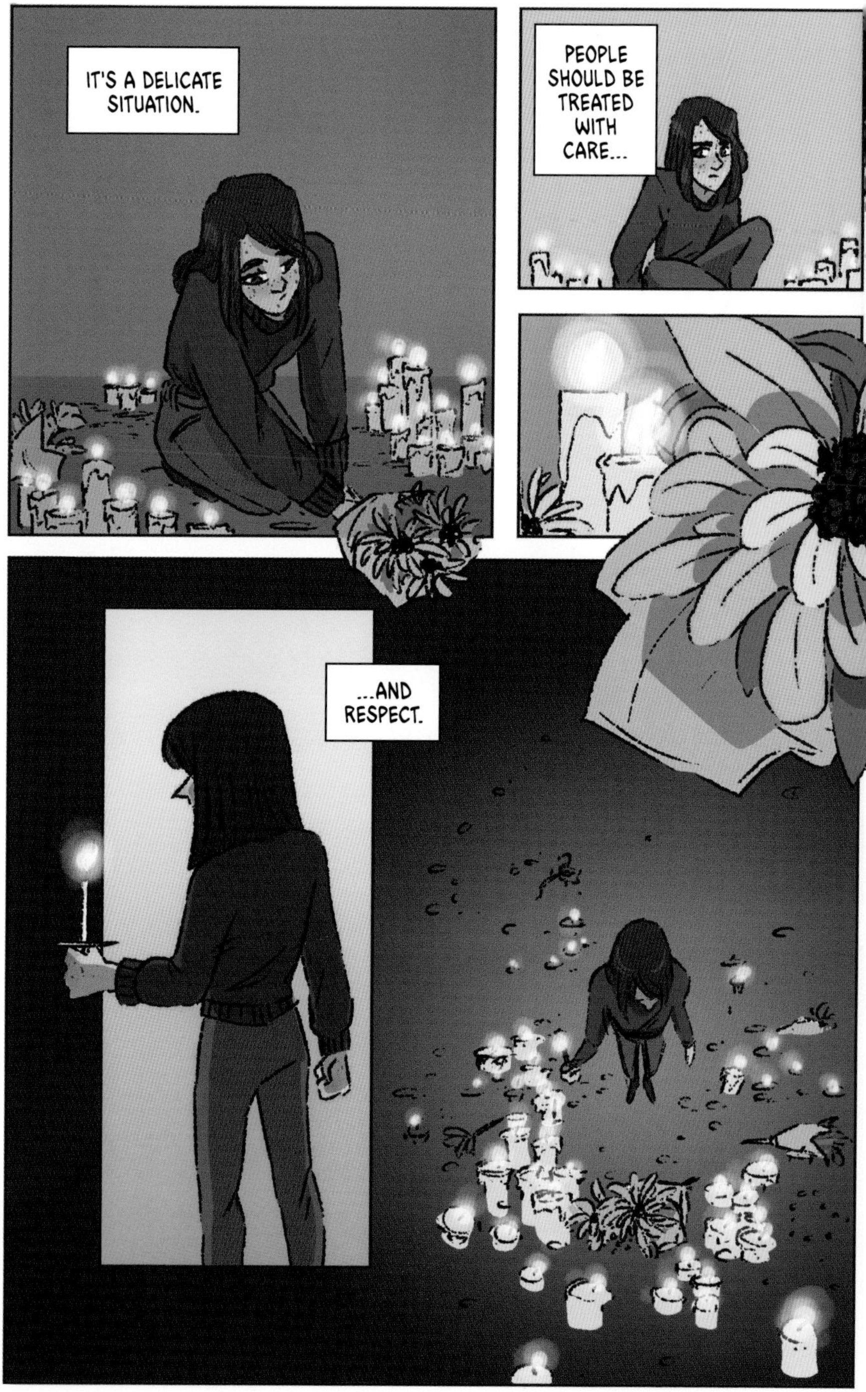
IT'S A DELICATE SITUATION.
PEOPLE SHOULD BE TREATED WITH CARE...
...AND RESPECT.

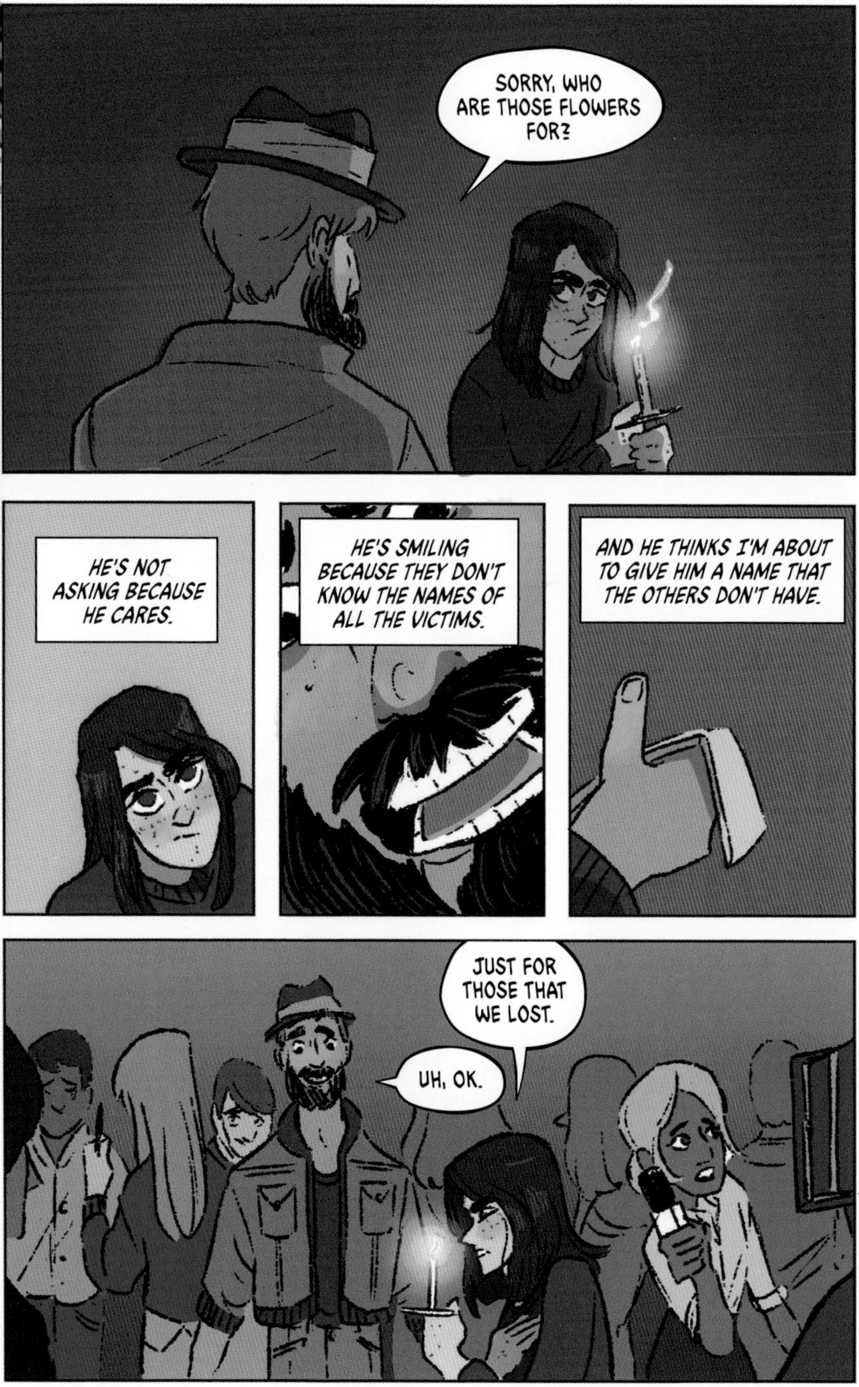
SORRY, WHO ARE THOSE FLOWERS FOR?
HE'S NOT ASKING BECAUSE HE CARES.
HE'S SMILING BECAUSE THEY DON'T KNOW THE NAMES OF ALL THE VICTIMS.
AND HE THINKS I'M ABOUT TO GIVE HIM A NAME THAT THE OTHERS DON'T HAVE.
JUST FOR THOSE THAT WE LOST.
UH, OK.

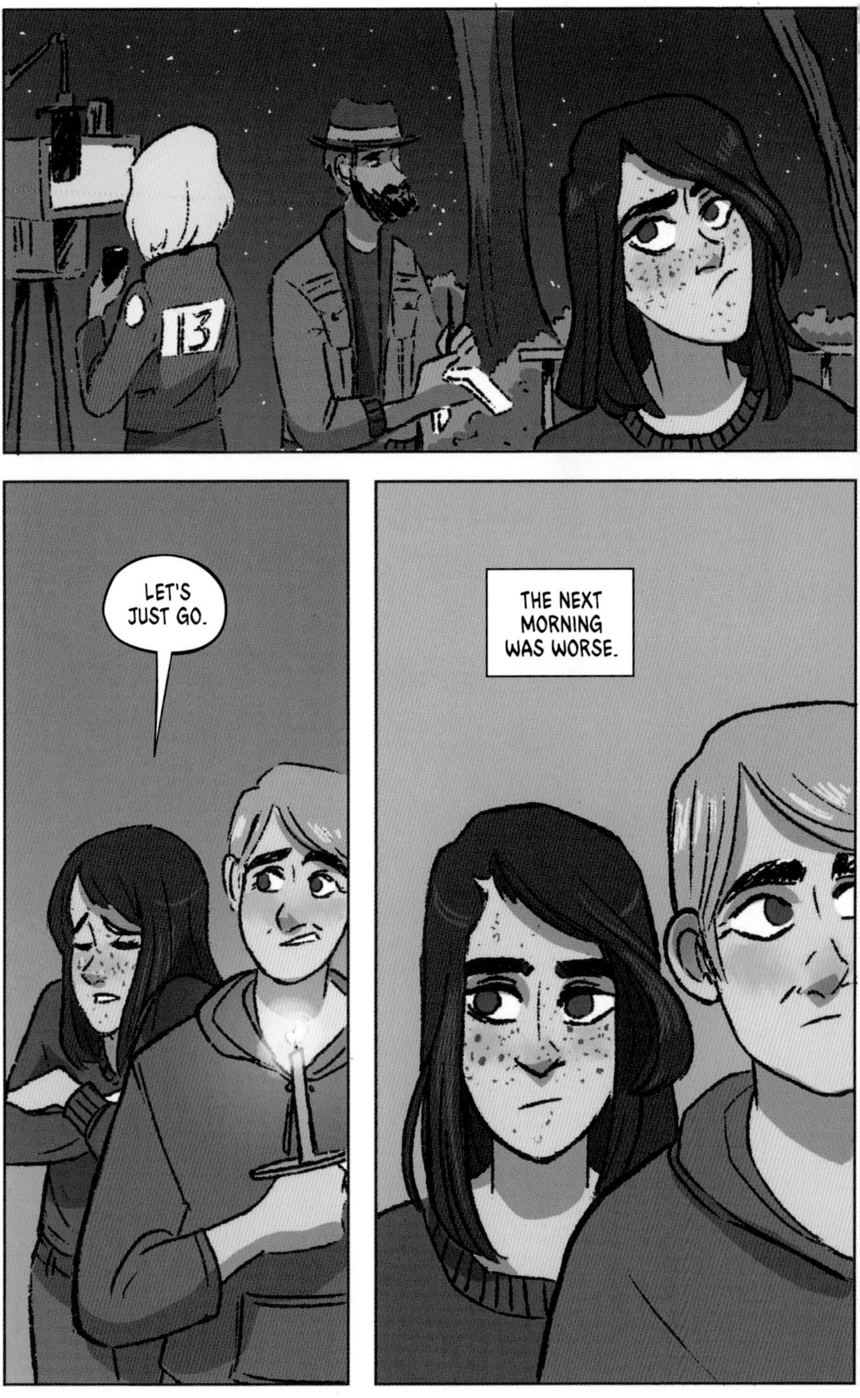
13
LET'S JUST GO.
THE NEXT MORNING WAS WORSE.

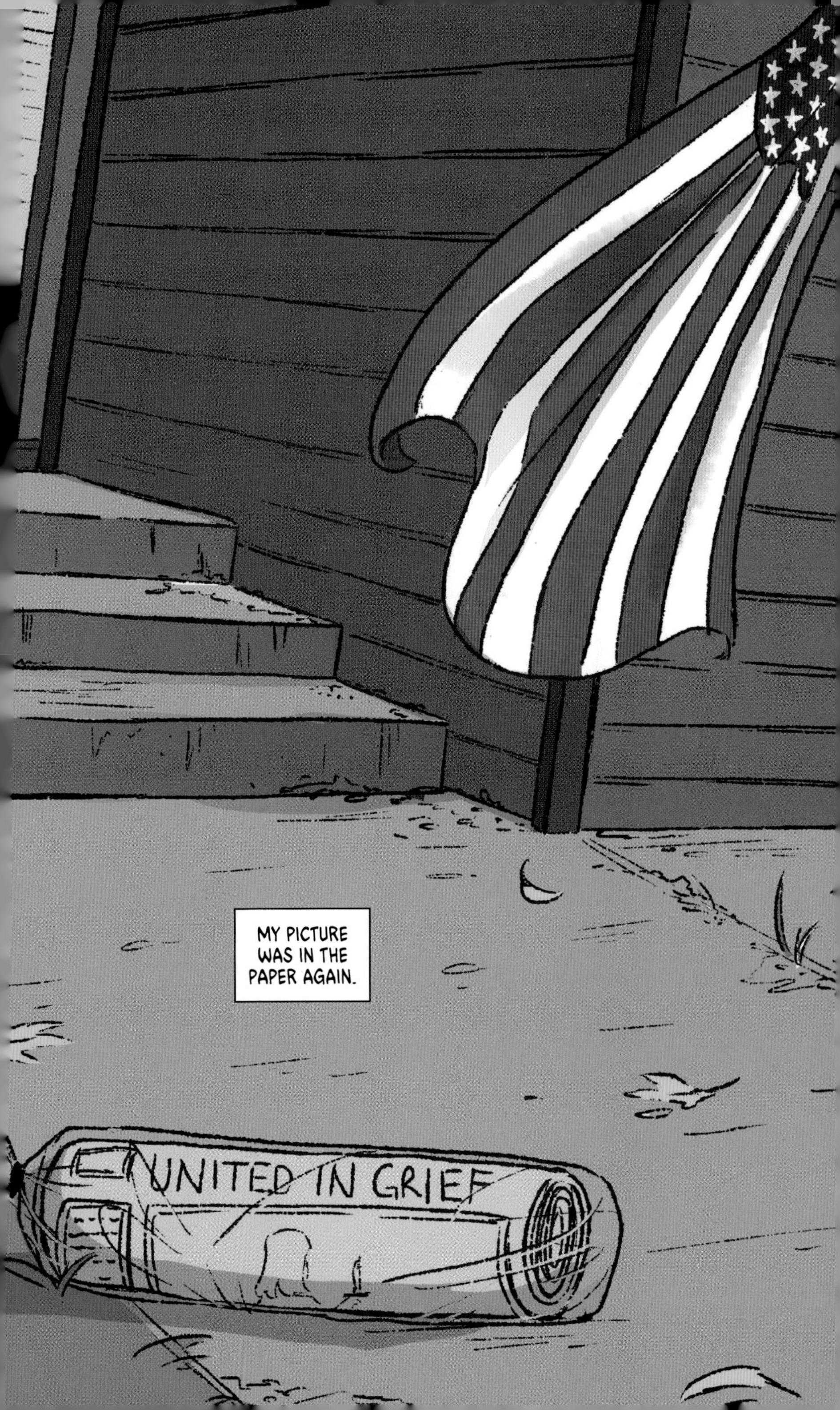
MY PICTURE WAS IN THE PAPER AGAIN.
UNITED IN GRIEF

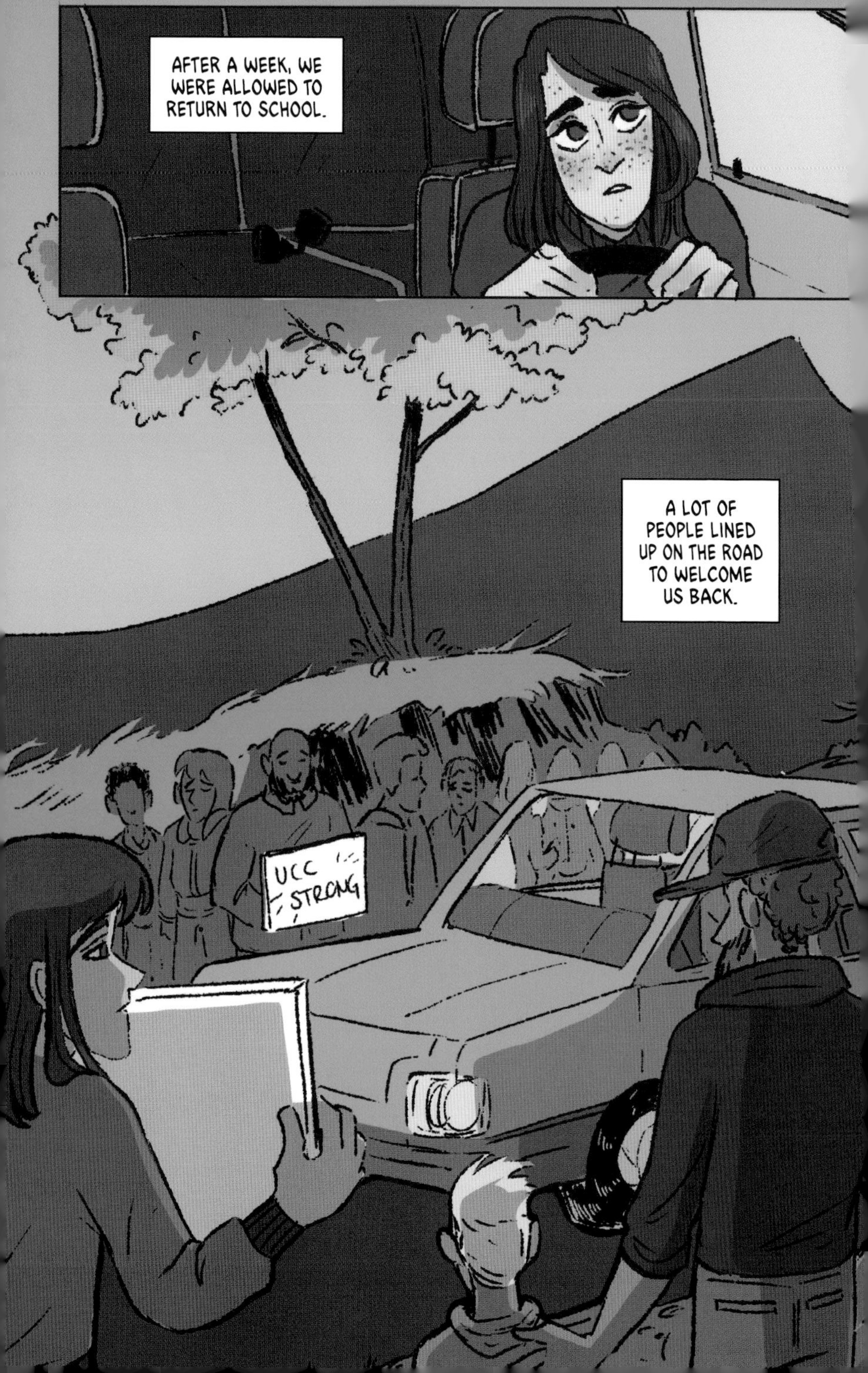

AFTER A WEEK, WE WERE ALLOWED TO RETURN TO SCHOOL.
A LOT OF PEOPLE LINED UP ON THE ROAD TO WELCOME US BACK.
UCC STRONG

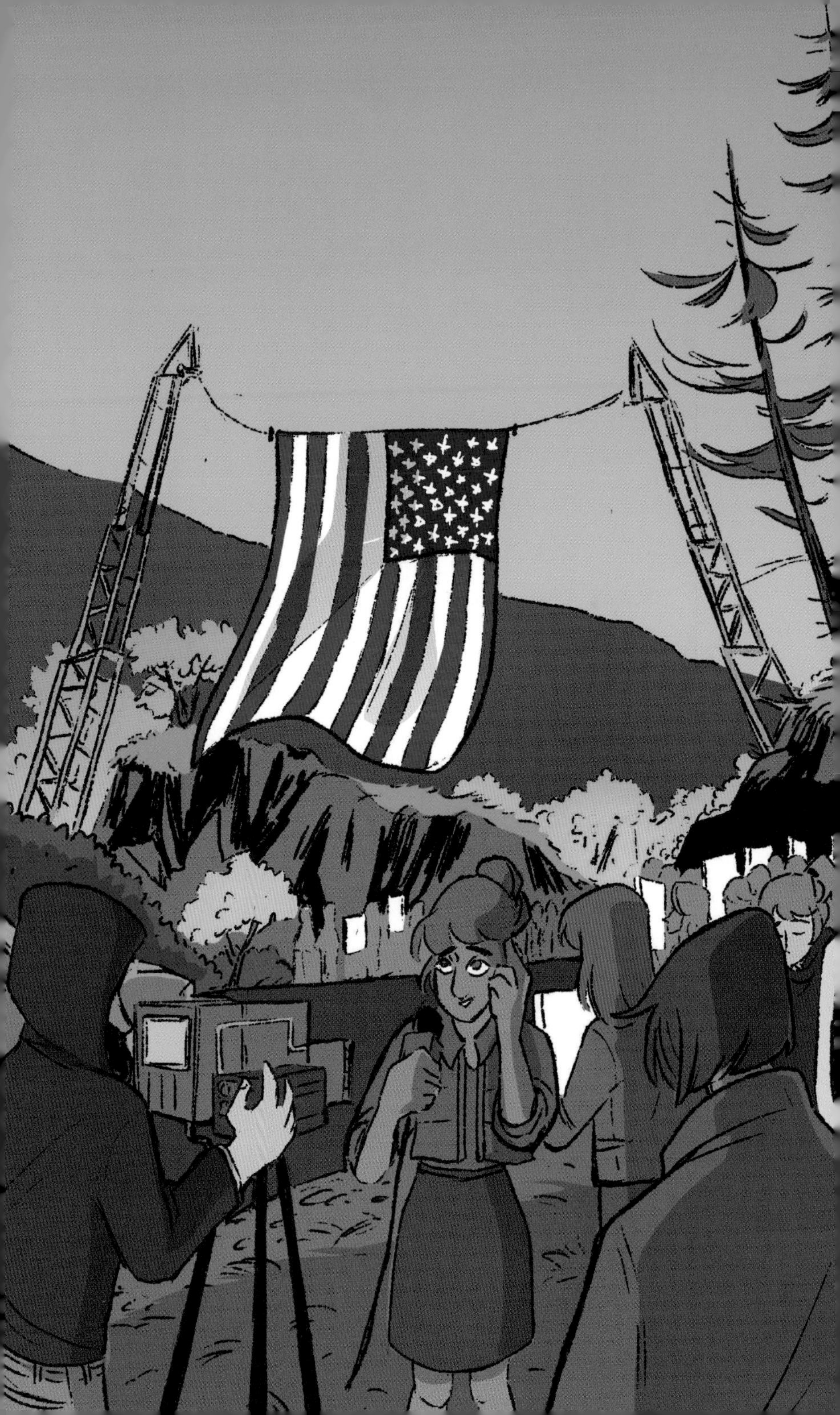

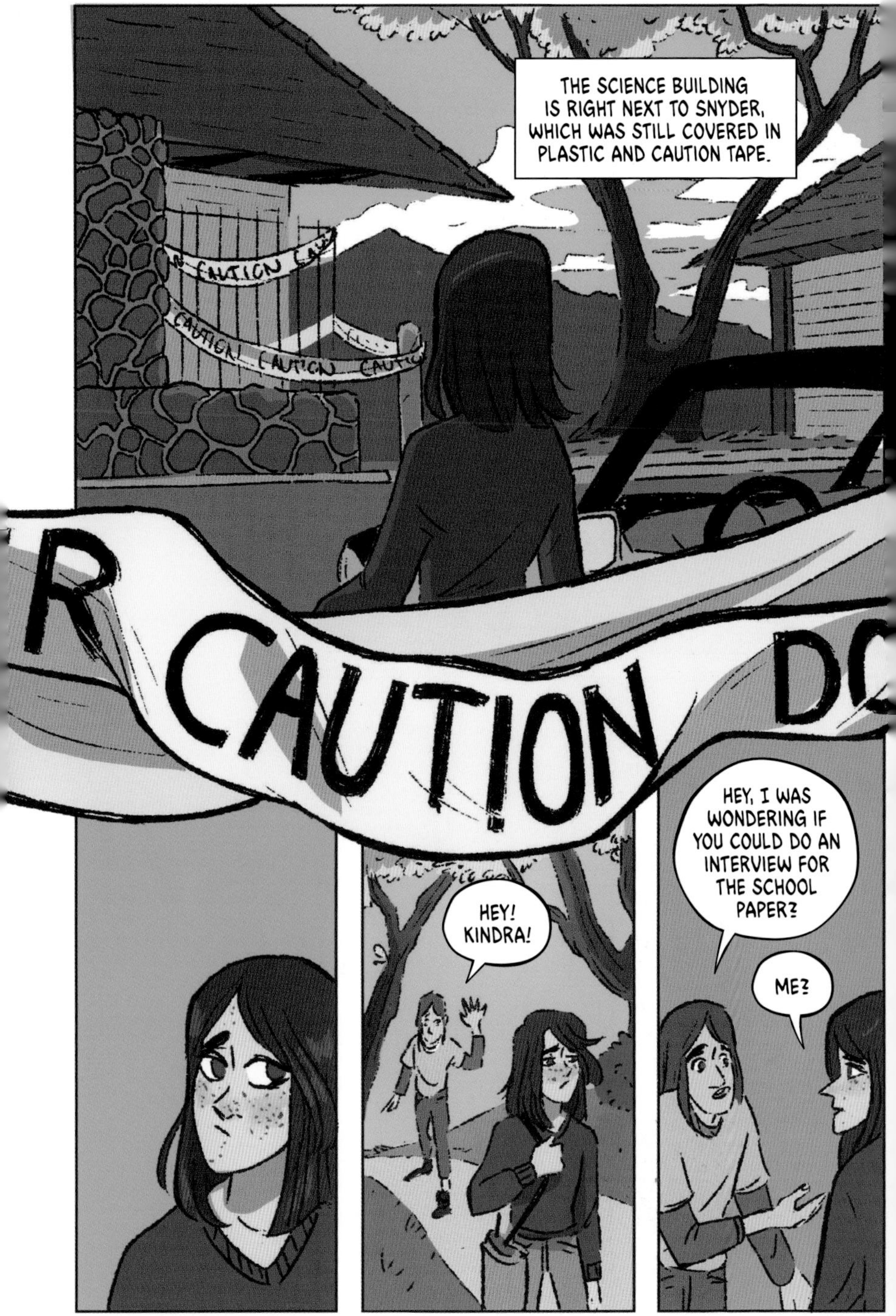
THE SCIENCE BUILDING IS RIGHT NEXT TO SNYDER, WHICH WAS STILL COVERED IN PLASTIC AND CAUTION TAPE.
CAUTION
CAUTION
CAUTION
R CAUTION DO
HEY! KINDRA!
HEY, I WAS WONDERING IF YOU COULD DO AN INTERVIEW FOR THE SCHOOL PAPER?
ME?

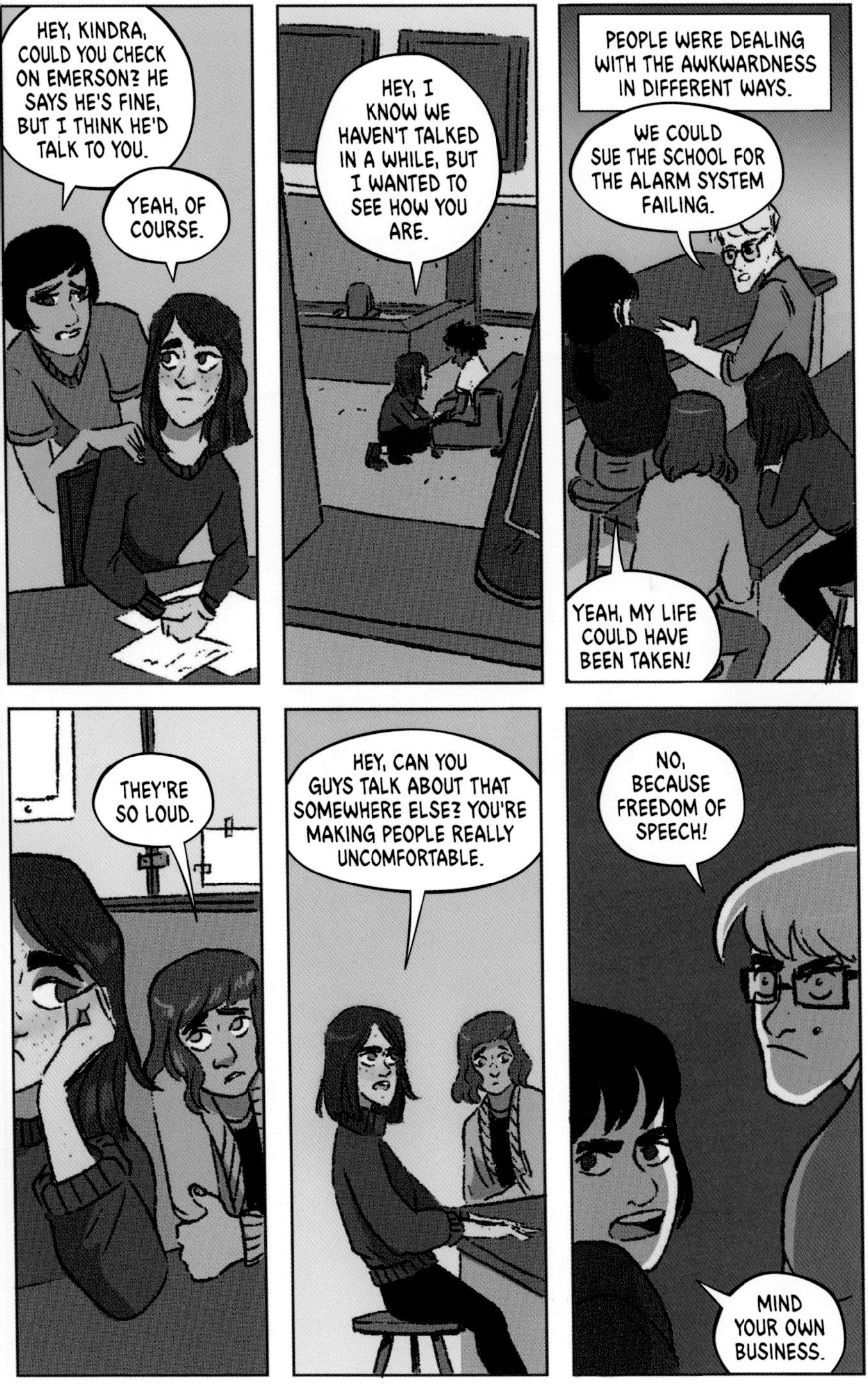
HEY, KINDRA, COULD YOU CHECK ON EMERSON? HE SAYS HE'S FINE, BUT I THINK HE'D TALK TO YOU.
YEAH, OF COURSE.
HEY, I KNOW WE HAVEN'T TALKED IN A WHILE, BUT I WANTED TO SEE HOW YOU ARE.
PEOPLE WERE DEALING WITH THE AWKWARDNESS IN DIFFERENT WAYS.
WE COULD SUE THE SCHOOL FOR THE ALARM SYSTEM FAILING.
YEAH, MY LIFE COULD HAVE BEEN TAKEN!
THEY'RE SO LOUD.
HEY, CAN YOU GUYS TALK ABOUT THAT SOMEWHERE ELSE? YOU'RE MAKING PEOPLE REALLY UNCOMFORTABLE.
NO, BECAUSE FREEDOM OF SPEECH!
MIND YOUR OWN BUSINESS.

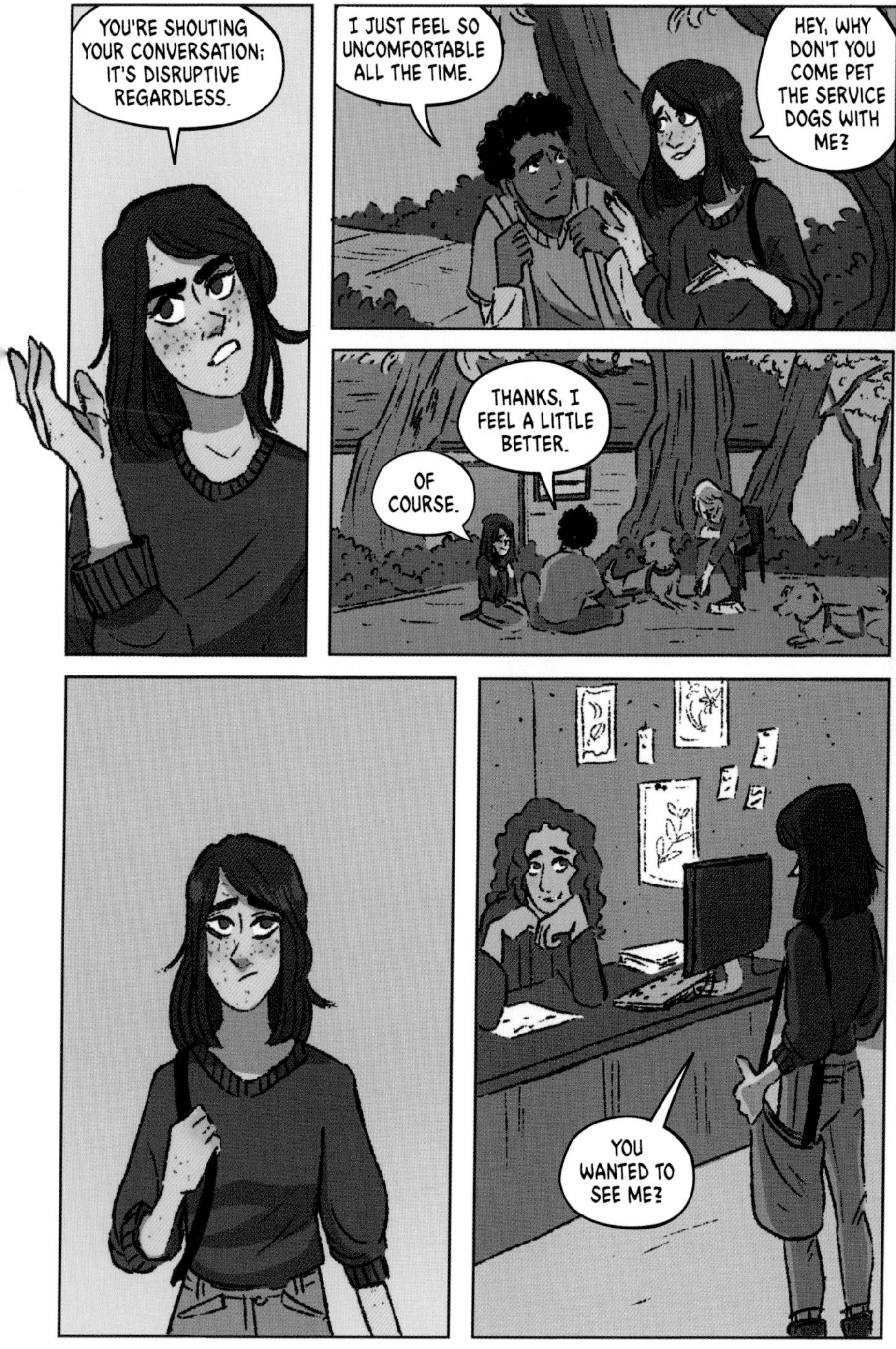
YOU'RE SHOUTING YOUR CONVERSATION; IT'S DISRUPTIVE REGARDLESS.
I JUST FEEL SO UNCOMFORTABLE ALL THE TIME.
HEY, WHY DON'T YOU COME PET THE SERVICE DOGS WITH ME?
THANKS, I FEEL A LITTLE BETTER.
OF COURSE.
YOU WANTED TO SEE ME?

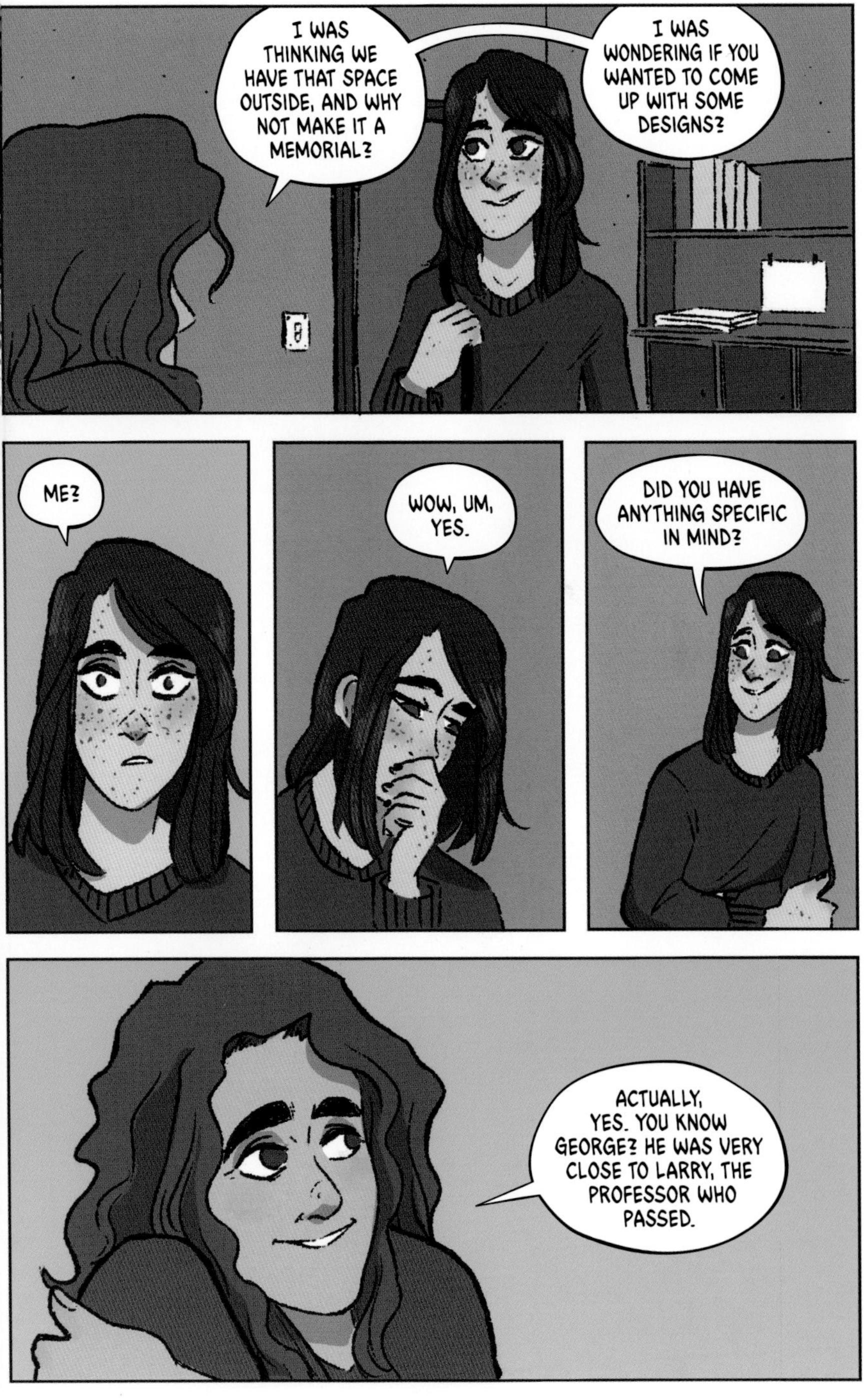
I WAS THINKING WE HAVE THAT SPACE OUTSIDE, AND WHY NOT MAKE IT A MEMORIAL?
I WAS WONDERING IF YOU WANTED TO COME UP WITH SOME DESIGNS?
ME?
WOW, UM, YES.
DID YOU HAVE ANYTHING SPECIFIC IN MIND?
ACTUALLY, YES. YOU KNOW GEORGE? HE WAS VERY CLOSE TO LARRY, THE PROFESSOR WHO PASSED.

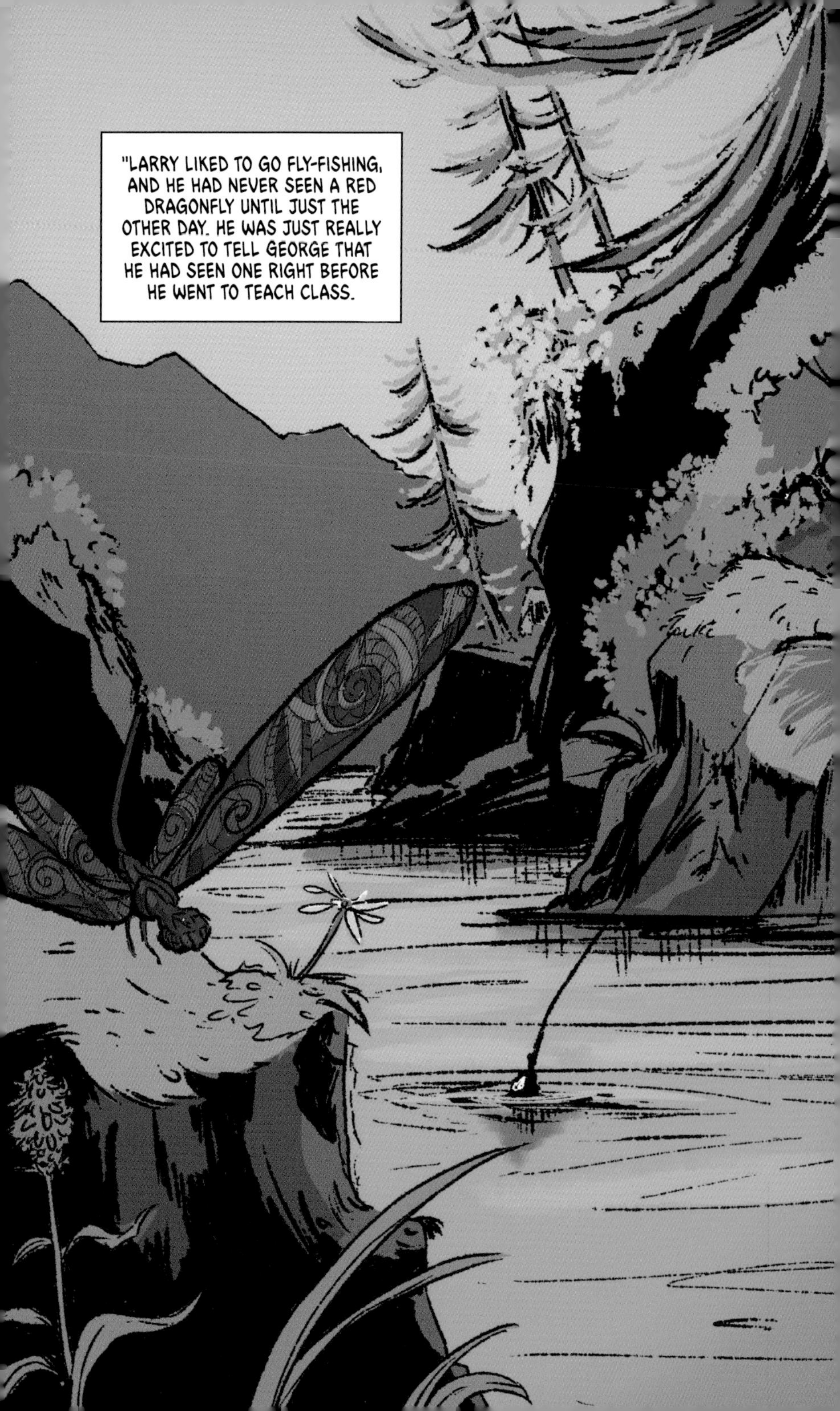
"LARRY LIKED TO GO FLY-FISHING, AND HE HAD NEVER SEEN A RED DRAGONFLY UNTIL JUST THE OTHER DAY. HE WAS JUST REALLY EXCITED TO TELL GEORGE THAT HE HAD SEEN ONE RIGHT BEFORE HE WENT TO TEACH CLASS.

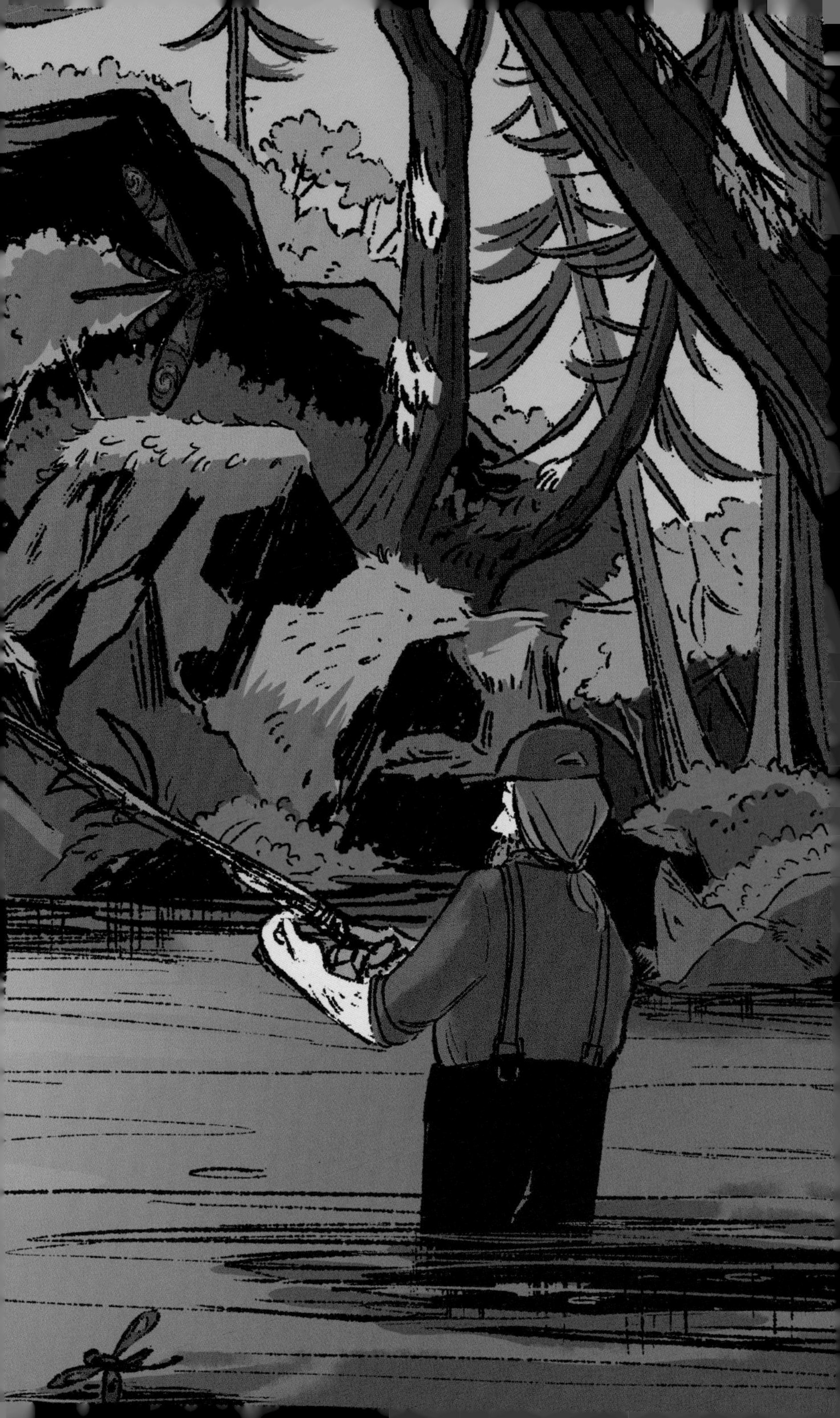

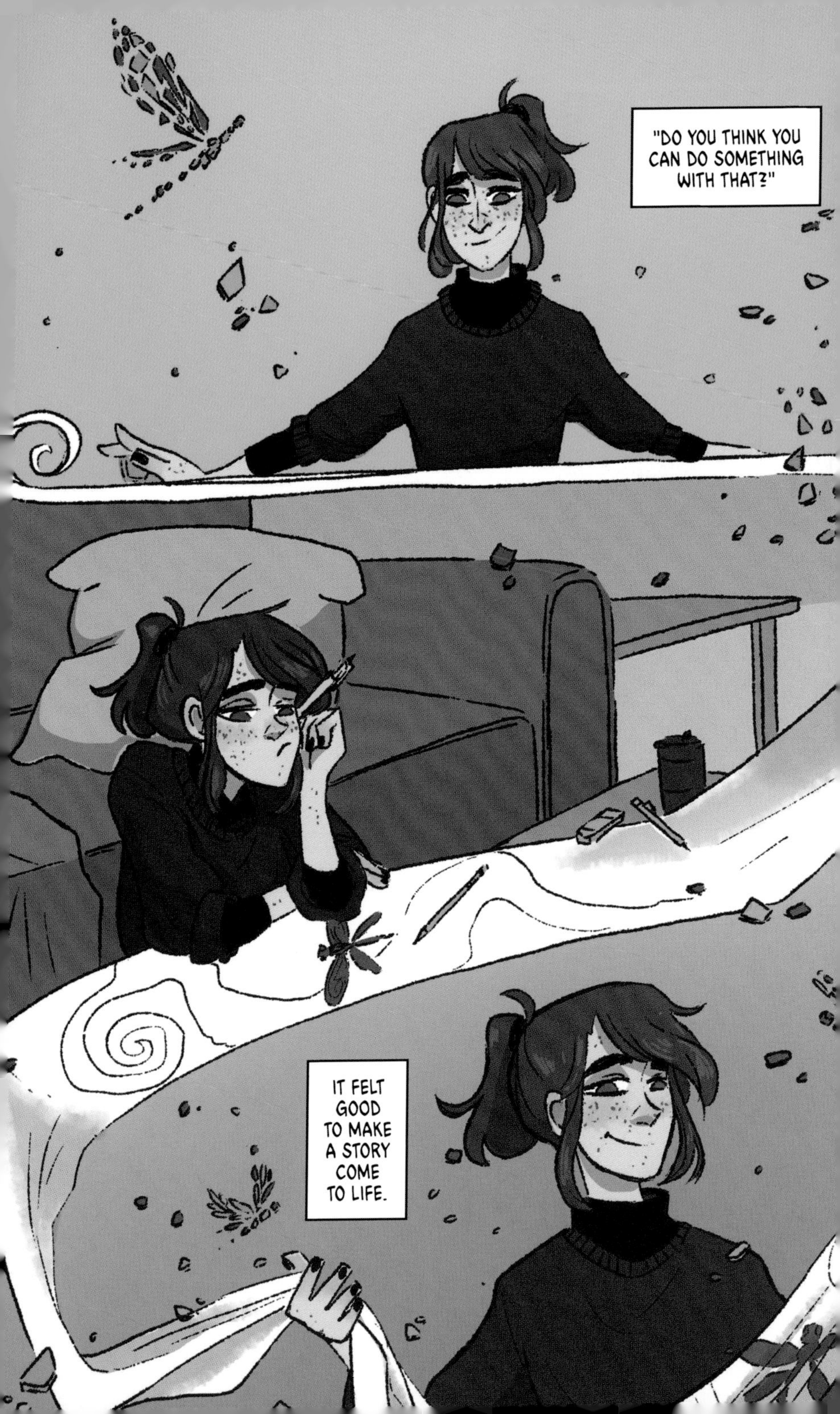
"DO YOU THINK YOU CAN DO SOMETHING WITH THAT?"
IT FELT GOOD TO MAKE A STORY COME TO LIFE.

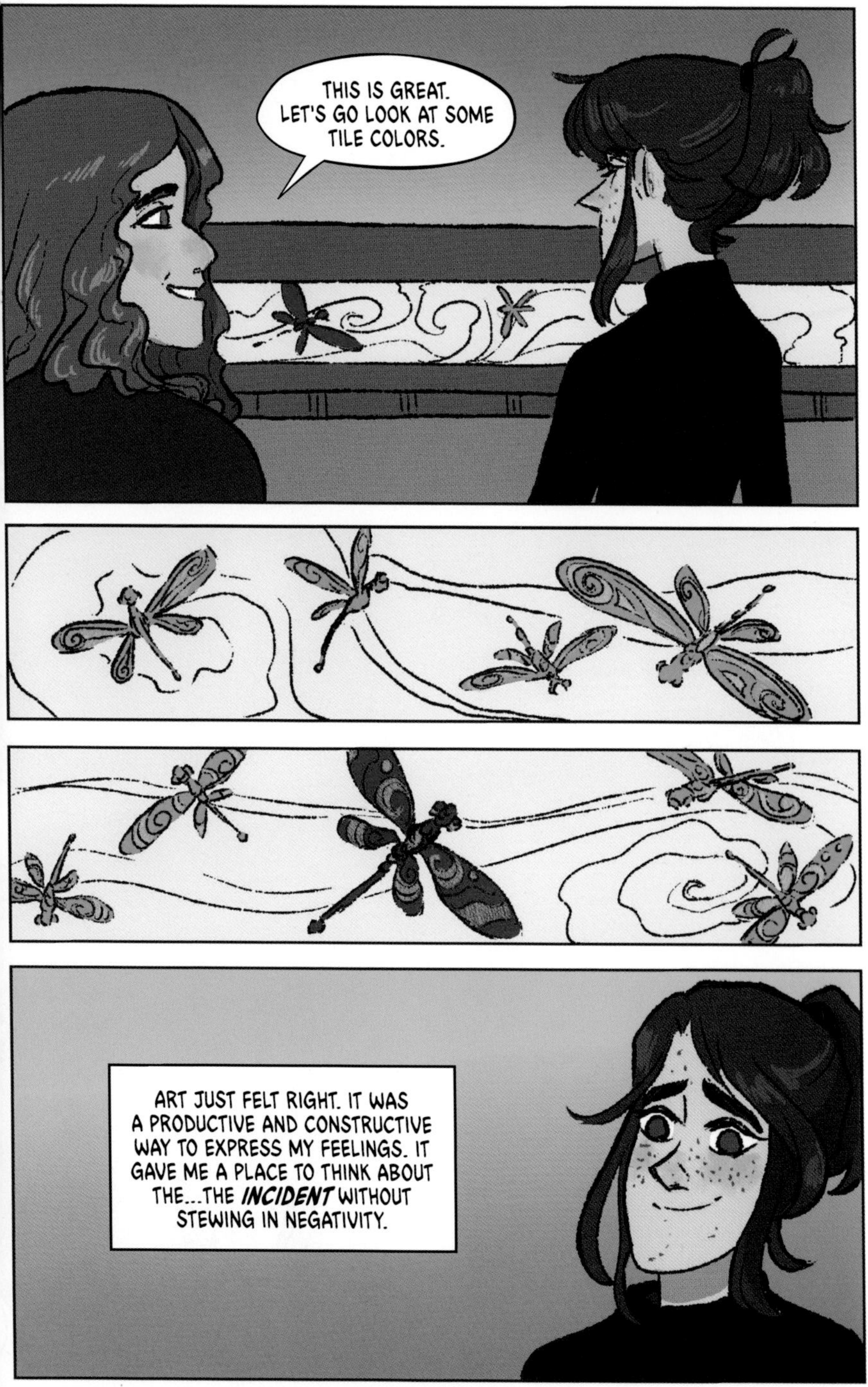
THIS IS GREAT. LET'S GO LOOK AT SOME TILE COLORS.
ART JUST FELT RIGHT. IT WAS A PRODUCTIVE AND CONSTRUCTIVE WAY TO EXPRESS MY FEELINGS. IT GAVE ME A PLACE TO THINK ABOUT THE...THE *INCIDENT* WITHOUT STEWING IN NEGATIVITY.

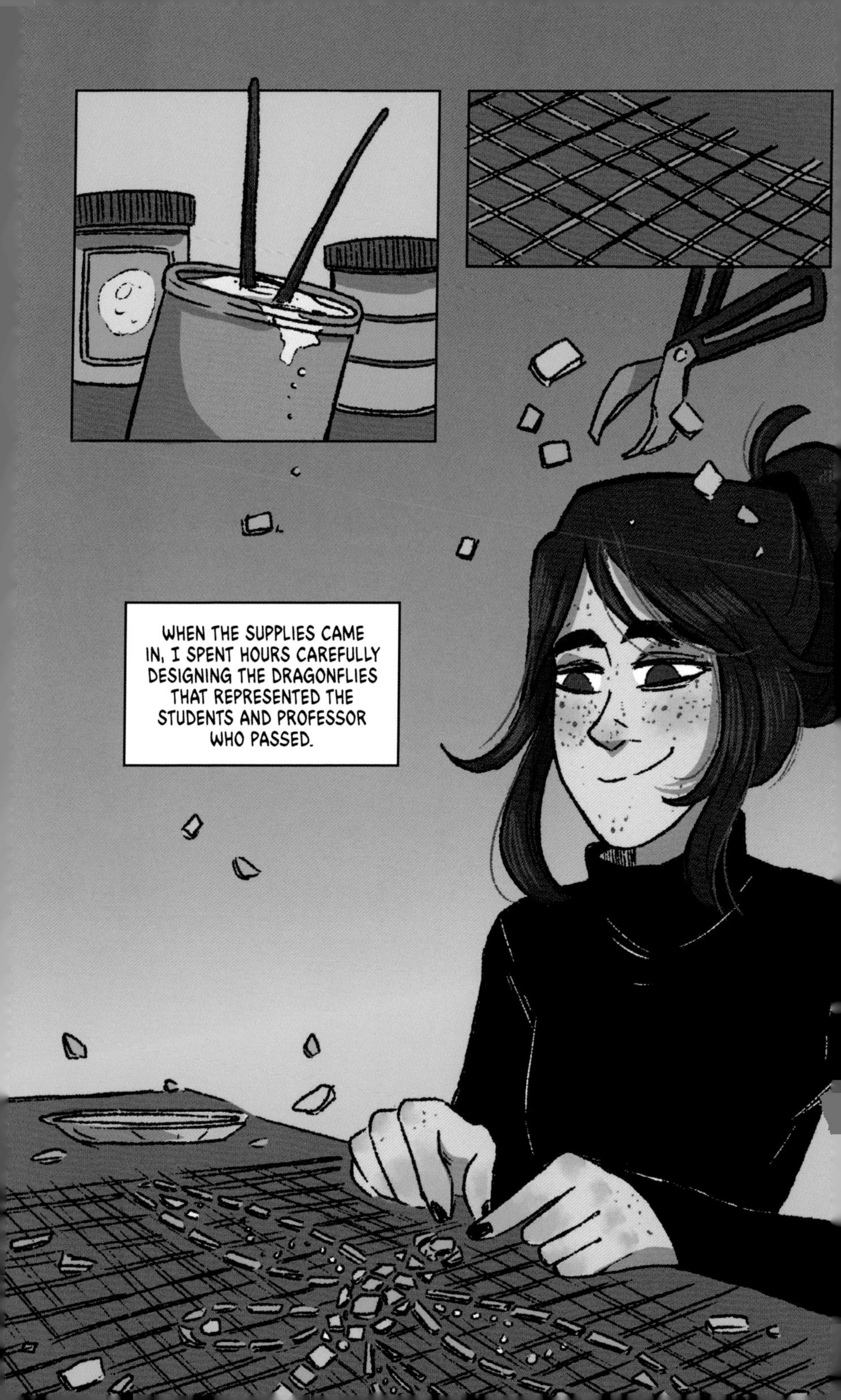
WHEN THE SUPPLIES CAME IN, I SPENT HOURS CAREFULLY DESIGNING THE DRAGONFLIES THAT REPRESENTED THE STUDENTS AND PROFESSOR WHO PASSED.

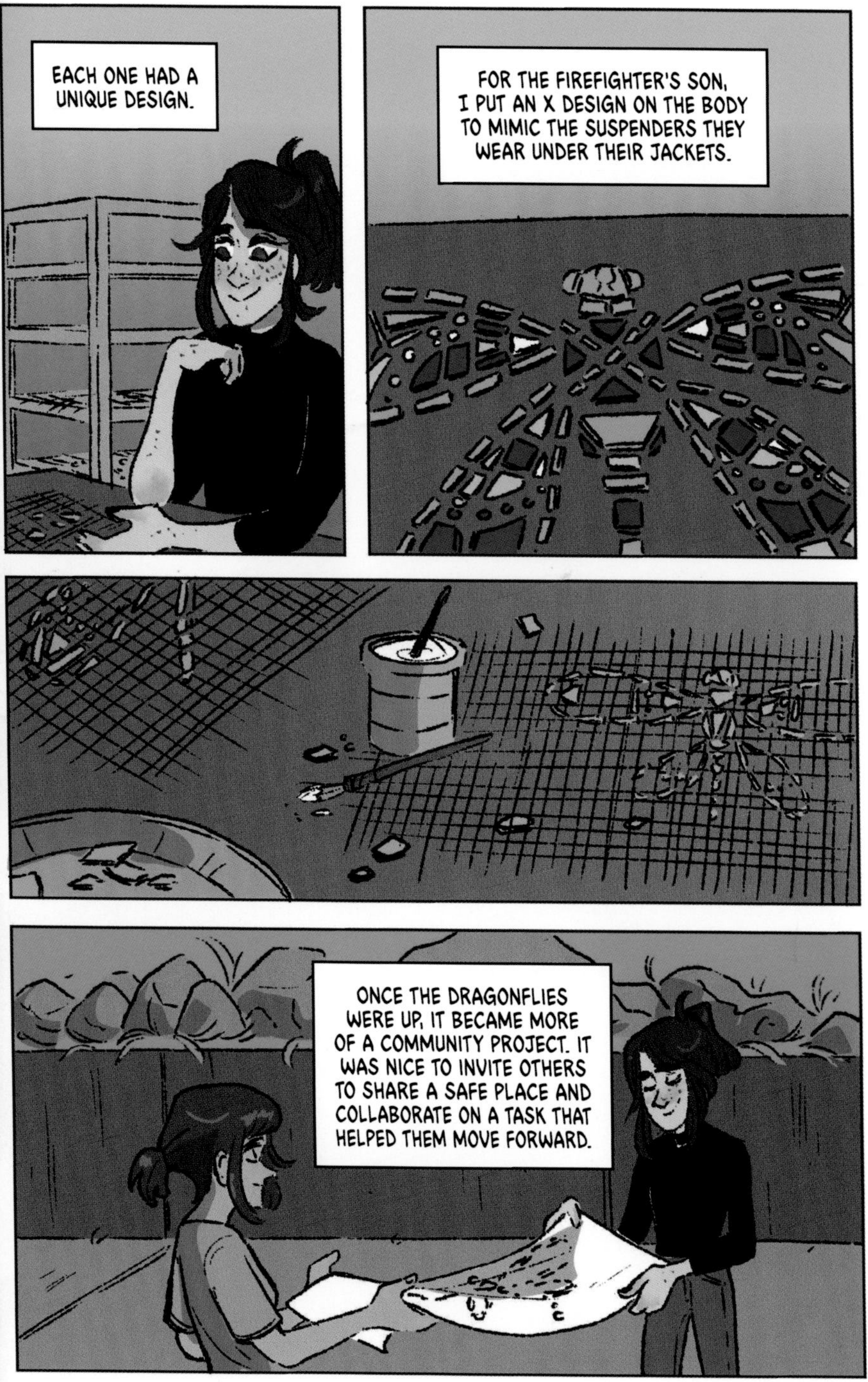
EACH ONE HAD A UNIQUE DESIGN.
FOR THE FIREFIGHTER'S SON, I PUT AN X DESIGN ON THE BODY TO MIMIC THE SUSPENDERS THEY WEAR UNDER THEIR JACKETS.
ONCE THE DRAGONFLIES WERE UP, IT BECAME MORE OF A COMMUNITY PROJECT. IT WAS NICE TO INVITE OTHERS TO SHARE A SAFE PLACE AND COLLABORATE ON A TASK THAT HELPED THEM MOVE FORWARD.

I WAS JUST GLAD I GOT TO CONTRIBUTE SOMETHING MEANINGFUL.

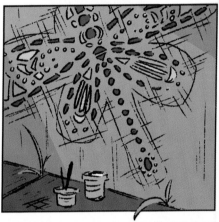

AND IT HELPED ME DECIDE THAT ART WAS THE RIGHT PLACE FOR ME.

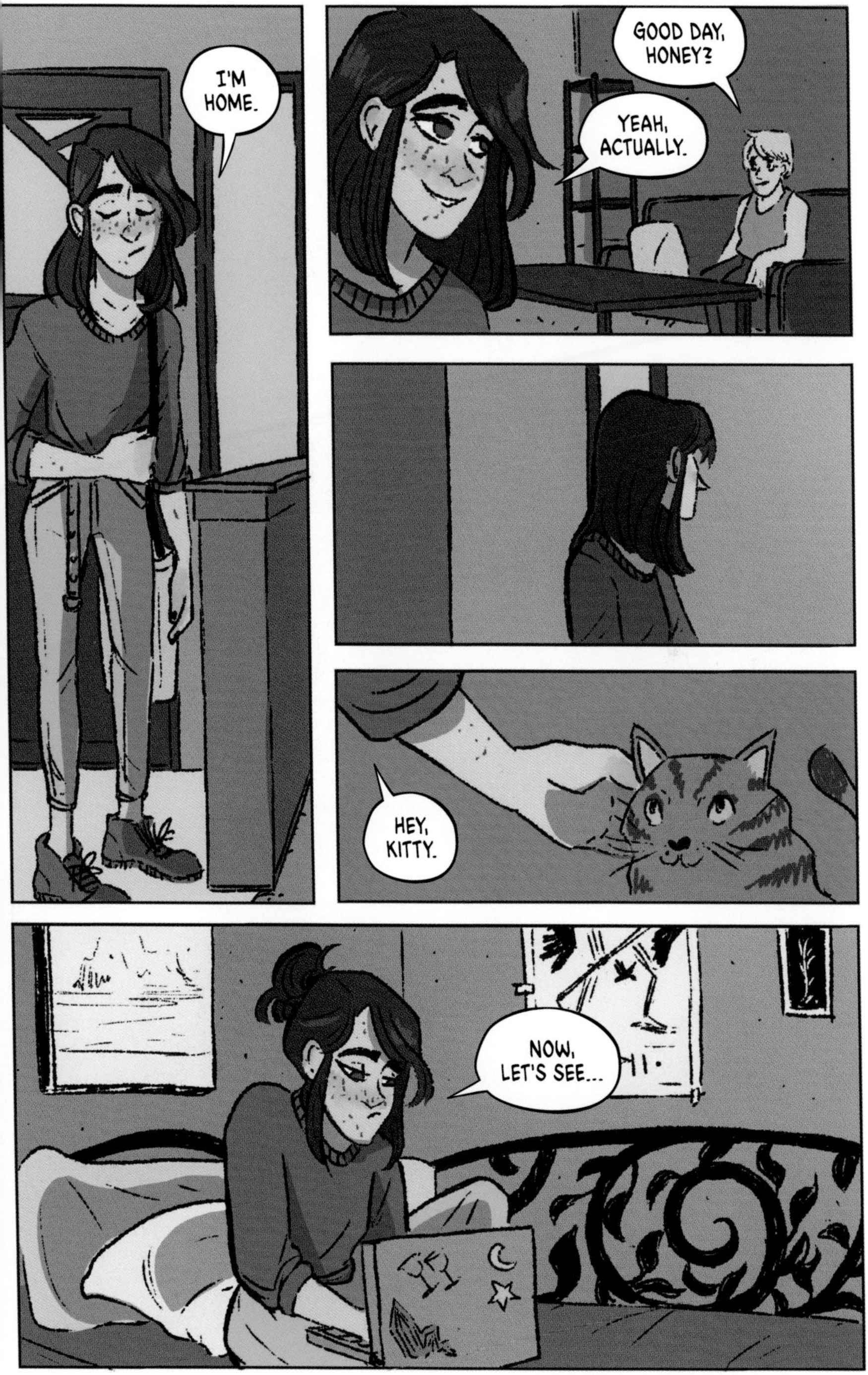
I'M HOME.
GOOD DAY, HONEY?
YEAH, ACTUALLY.
HEY, KITTY.
NOW, LET'S SEE...

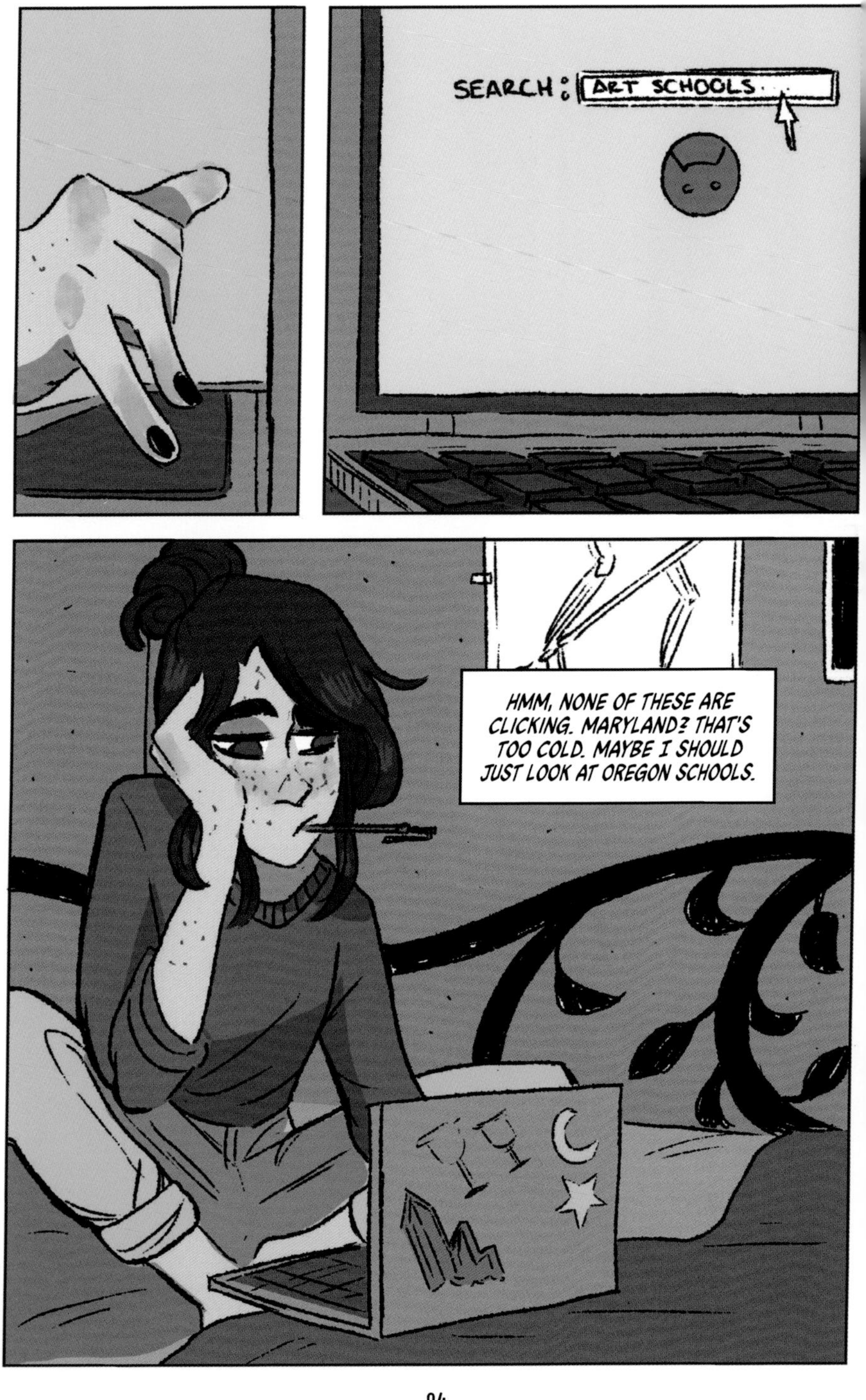
SEARCH: ART SCHOOLS...
HMM, NONE OF THESE ARE CLICKING. MARYLAND? THAT'S TOO COLD. MAYBE I SHOULD JUST LOOK AT OREGON SCHOOLS.

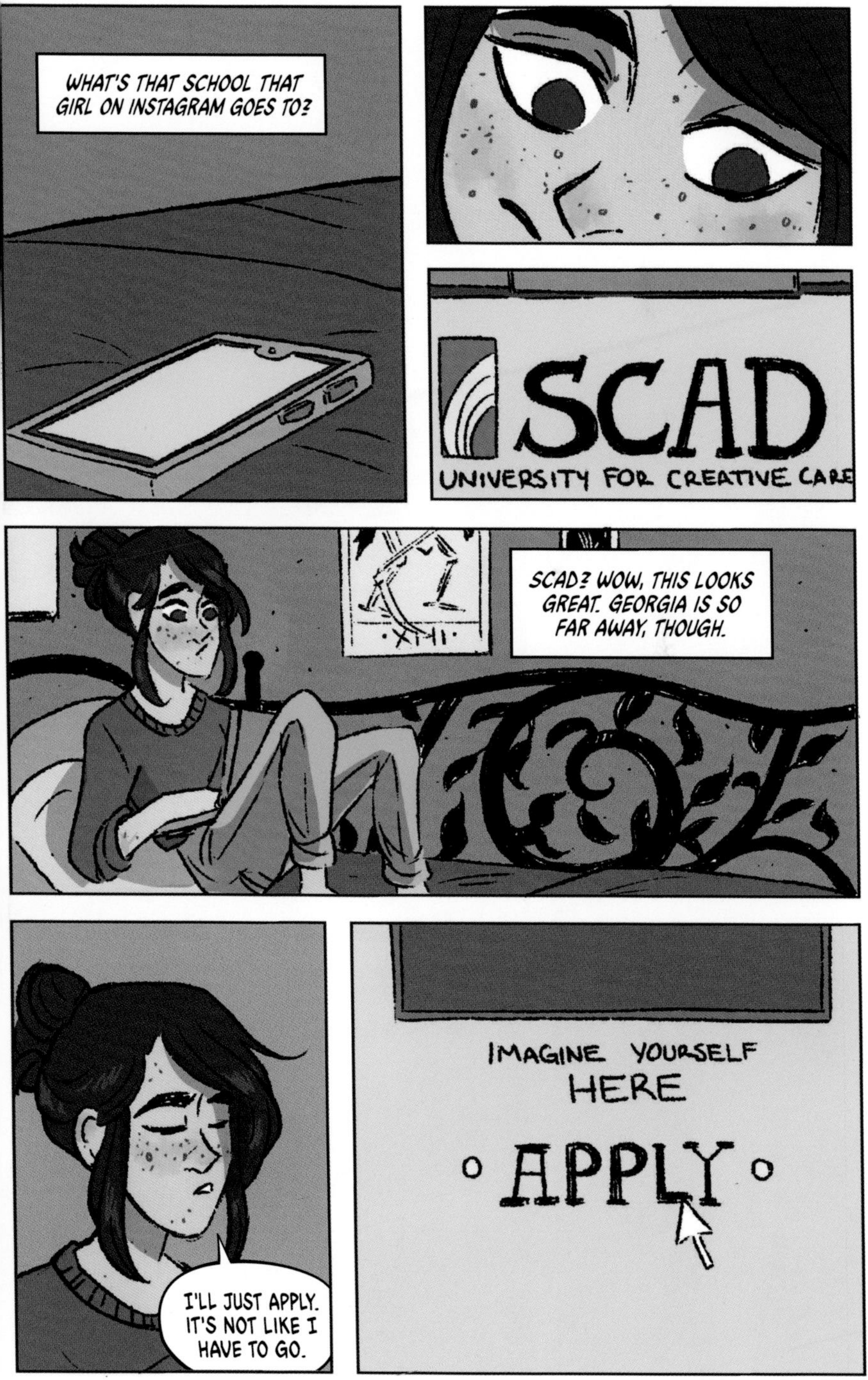
WHAT'S THAT SCHOOL THAT GIRL ON INSTAGRAM GOES TO?
SCAD
UNIVERSITY FOR CREATIVE CARE
SCAD? WOW, THIS LOOKS GREAT. GEORGIA IS SO FAR AWAY, THOUGH.
I'LL JUST APPLY. IT'S NOT LIKE I HAVE TO GO.
IMAGINE YOURSELF HERE
APPLY

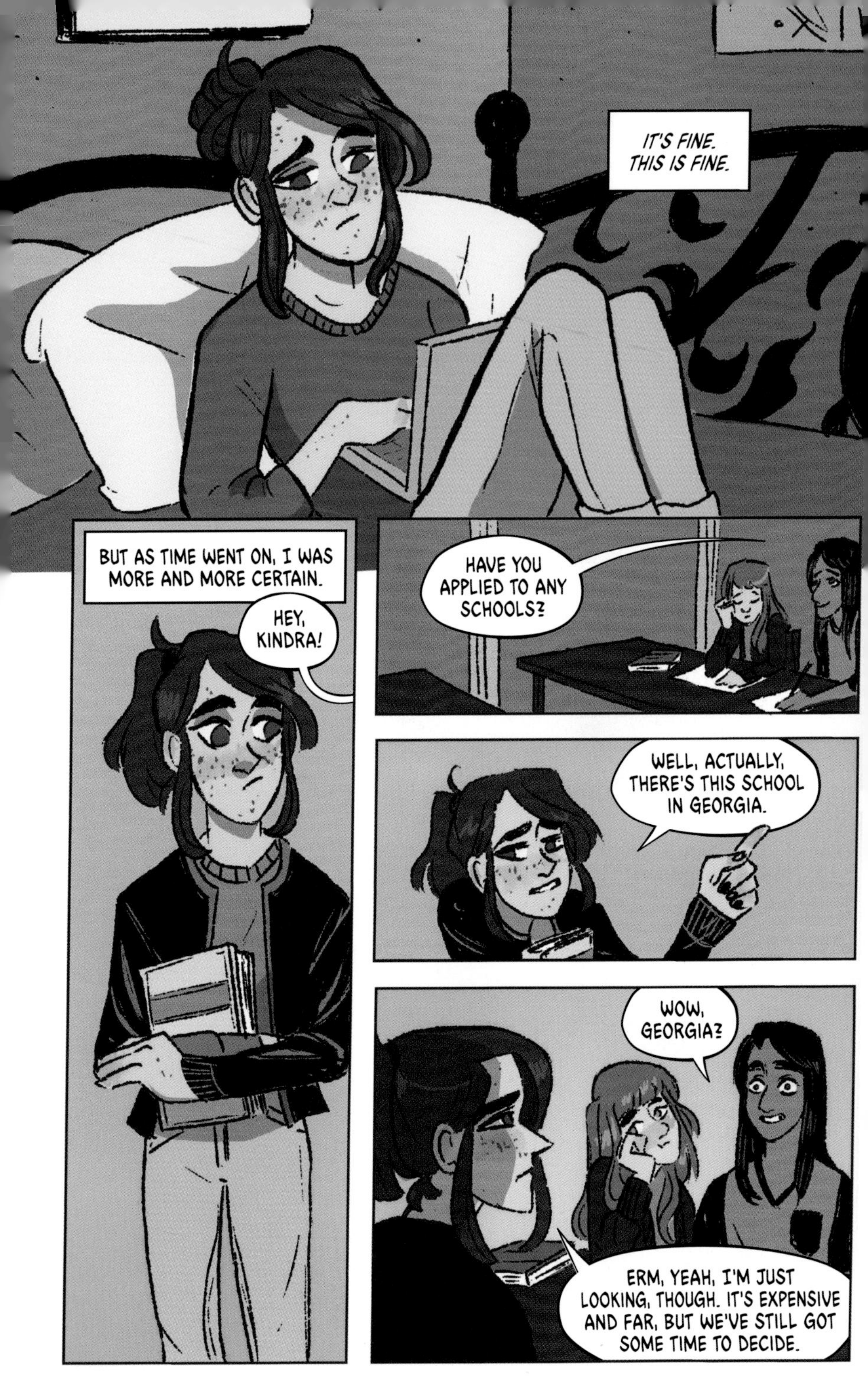

IT'S FINE.
THIS IS FINE.
BUT AS TIME WENT ON, I WAS MORE AND MORE CERTAIN.
HEY, KINDRA!
HAVE YOU APPLIED TO ANY SCHOOLS?
WELL, ACTUALLY, THERE'S THIS SCHOOL IN GEORGIA.
WOW, GEORGIA?
ERM, YEAH, I'M JUST LOOKING, THOUGH. IT'S EXPENSIVE AND FAR, BUT WE'VE STILL GOT SOME TIME TO DECIDE.

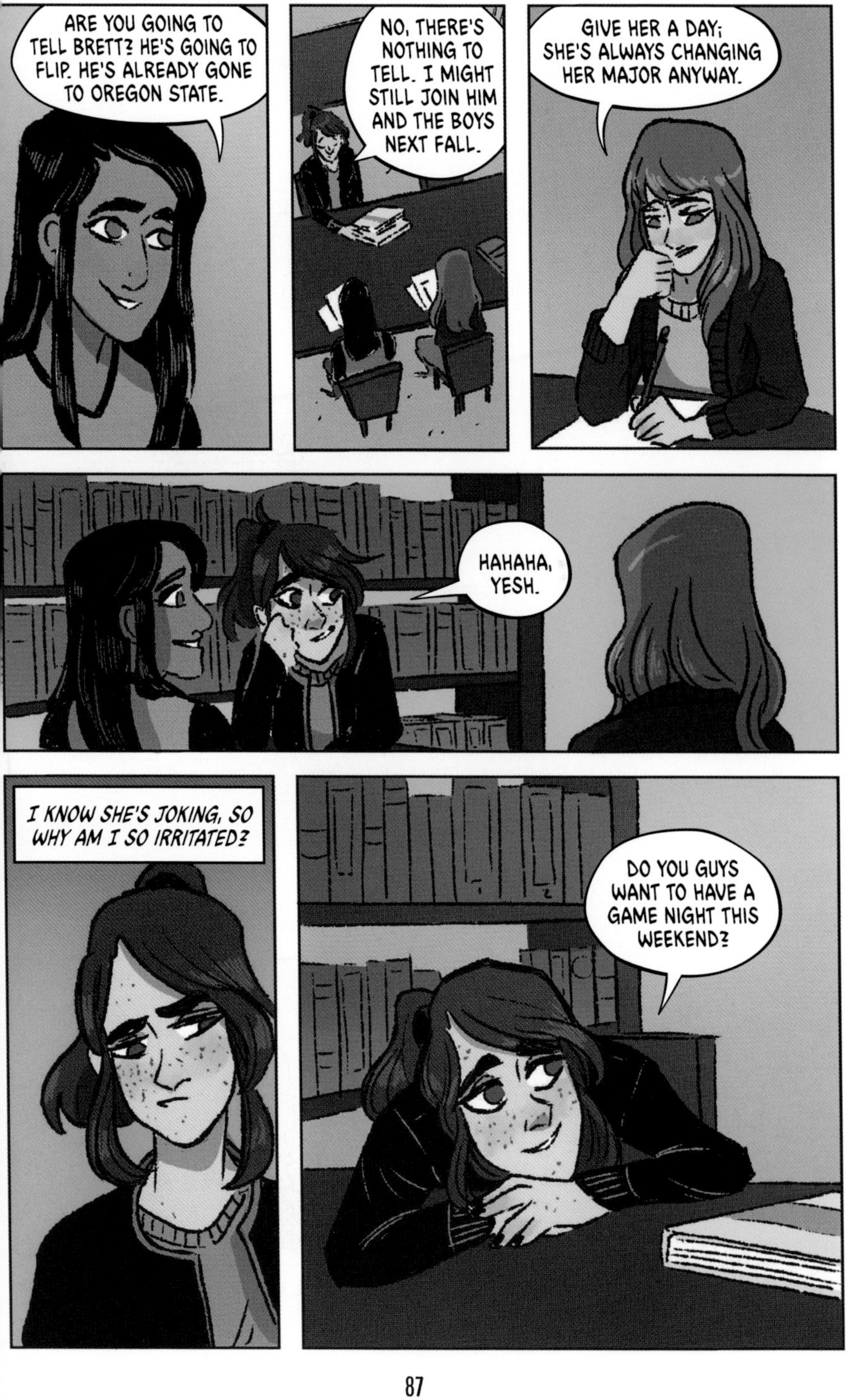
ARE YOU GOING TO TELL BRETT? HE'S GOING TO FLIP. HE'S ALREADY GONE TO OREGON STATE.
NO, THERE'S NOTHING TO TELL. I MIGHT STILL JOIN HIM AND THE BOYS NEXT FALL.
GIVE HER A DAY; SHE'S ALWAYS CHANGING HER MAJOR ANYWAY.
HAHAHA, YESH.
I KNOW SHE'S JOKING, SO WHY AM I SO IRRITATED?
DO YOU GUYS WANT TO HAVE A GAME NIGHT THIS WEEKEND?

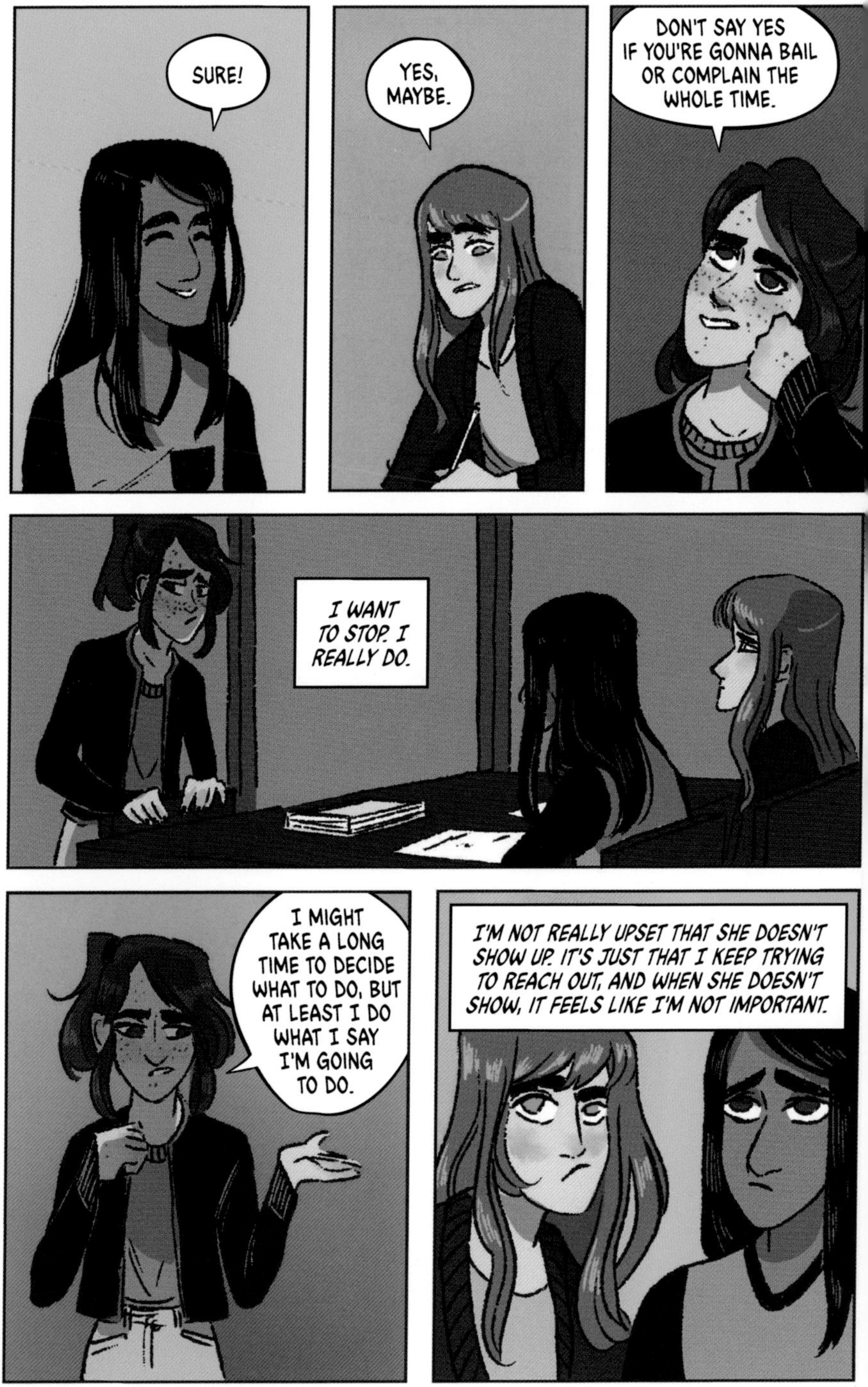
SURE!
YES, MAYBE.
DON'T SAY YES IF YOU'RE GONNA BAIL OR COMPLAIN THE WHOLE TIME.
I WANT TO STOP. I REALLY DO.
I MIGHT TAKE A LONG TIME TO DECIDE WHAT TO DO, BUT AT LEAST I DO WHAT I SAY I'M GOING TO DO.
I'M NOT REALLY UPSET THAT SHE DOESN'T SHOW UP. IT'S JUST THAT I KEEP TRYING TO REACH OUT, AND WHEN SHE DOESN'T SHOW, IT FEELS LIKE I'M NOT IMPORTANT.

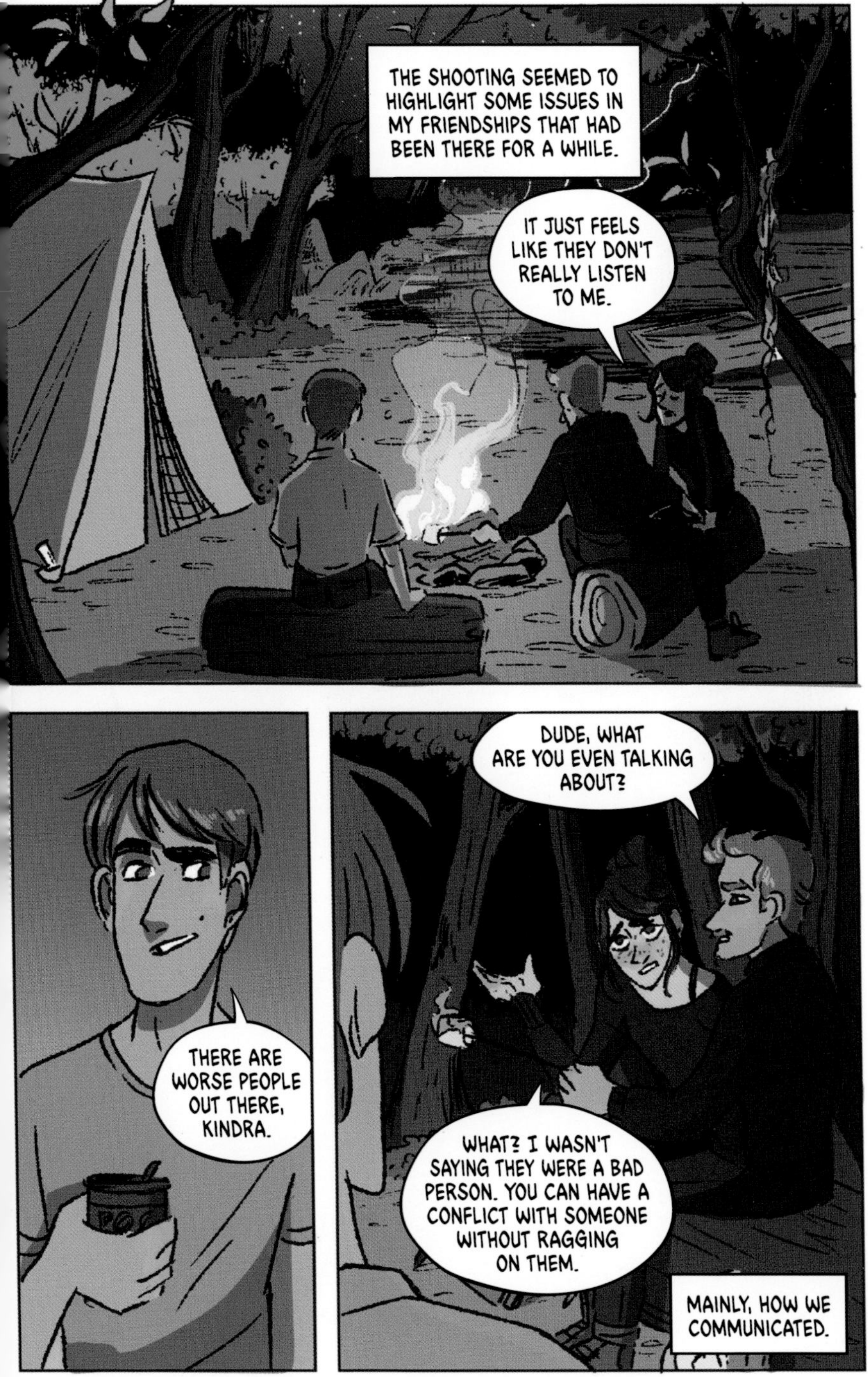
THE SHOOTING SEEMED TO HIGHLIGHT SOME ISSUES IN MY FRIENDSHIPS THAT HAD BEEN THERE FOR A WHILE.
IT JUST FEELS LIKE THEY DON'T REALLY LISTEN TO ME.
THERE ARE WORSE PEOPLE OUT THERE, KINDRA.
DUDE, WHAT ARE YOU EVEN TALKING ABOUT?
WHAT? I WASN'T SAYING THEY WERE A BAD PERSON. YOU CAN HAVE A CONFLICT WITH SOMEONE WITHOUT RAGGING ON THEM.
MAINLY, HOW WE COMMUNICATED.

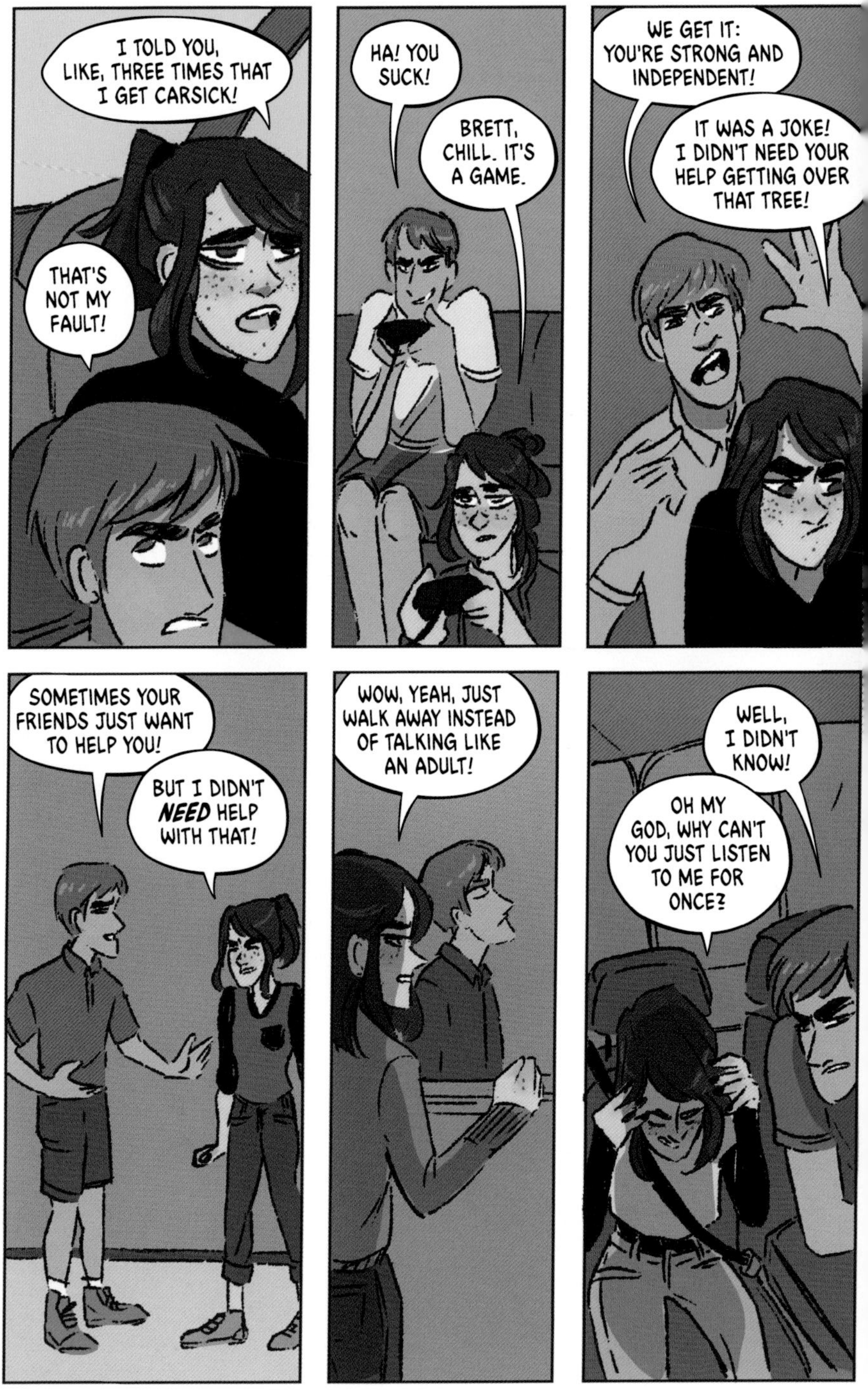
I TOLD YOU, LIKE, THREE TIMES THAT I GET CARSICK!
THAT'S NOT MY FAULT!
HA! YOU SUCK!
BRETT, CHILL. IT'S A GAME.
WE GET IT: YOU'RE STRONG AND INDEPENDENT!
IT WAS A JOKE! I DIDN'T NEED YOUR HELP GETTING OVER THAT TREE!
SOMETIMES YOUR FRIENDS JUST WANT TO HELP YOU!
BUT I DIDN'T *NEED* HELP WITH THAT!
WOW, YEAH, JUST WALK AWAY INSTEAD OF TALKING LIKE AN ADULT!
WELL, I DIDN'T KNOW!
OH MY GOD, WHY CAN'T YOU JUST LISTEN TO ME FOR ONCE?

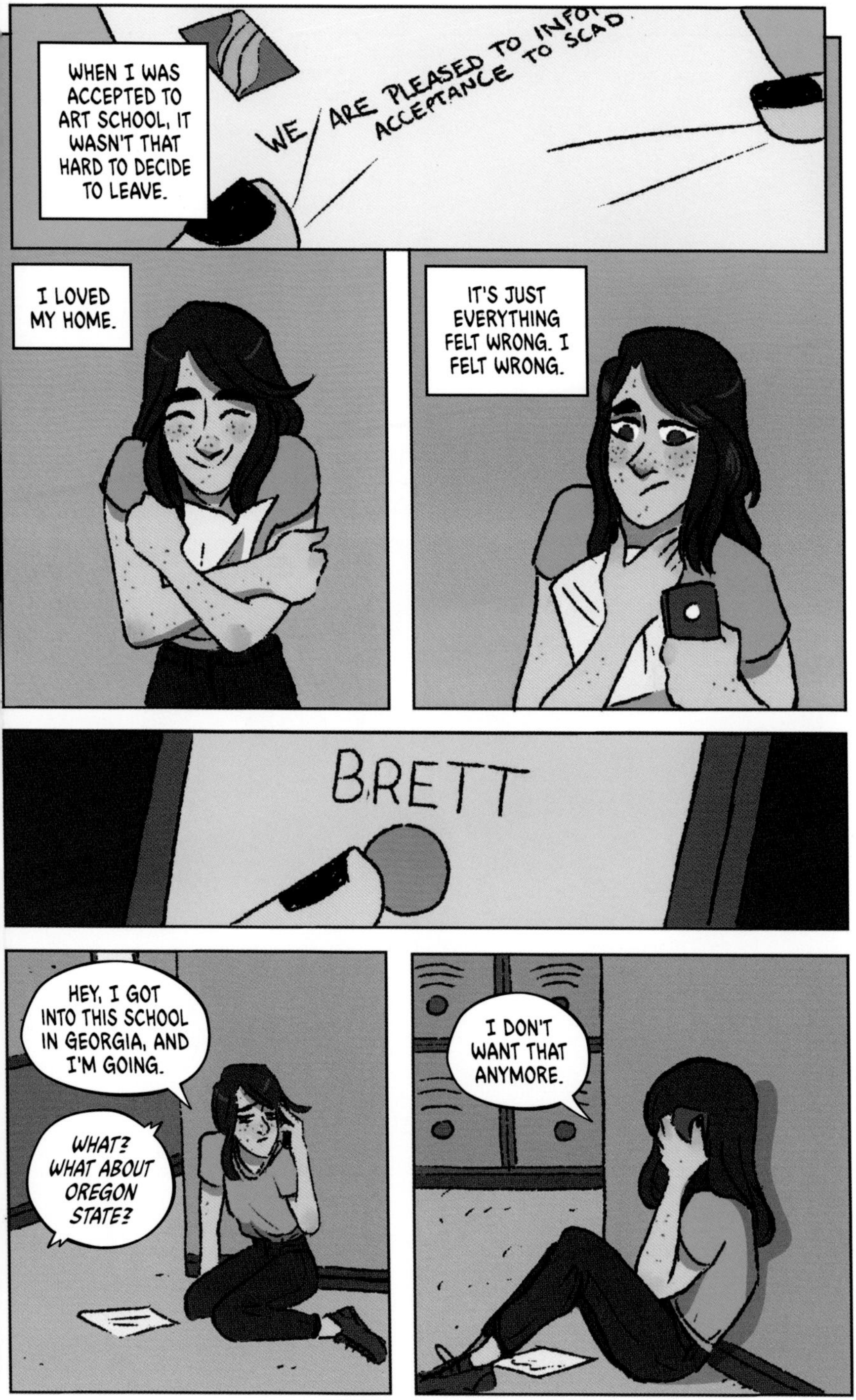
WHEN I WAS ACCEPTED TO ART SCHOOL, IT WASN'T THAT HARD TO DECIDE TO LEAVE.
WE ARE PLEASED TO INFO
ACCEPTANCE TO SCAD
I LOVED MY HOME.
IT'S JUST EVERYTHING FELT WRONG. I FELT WRONG.
BRETT
HEY, I GOT INTO THIS SCHOOL IN GEORGIA, AND I'M GOING.
WHAT? WHAT ABOUT OREGON STATE?
I DON'T WANT THAT ANYMORE.

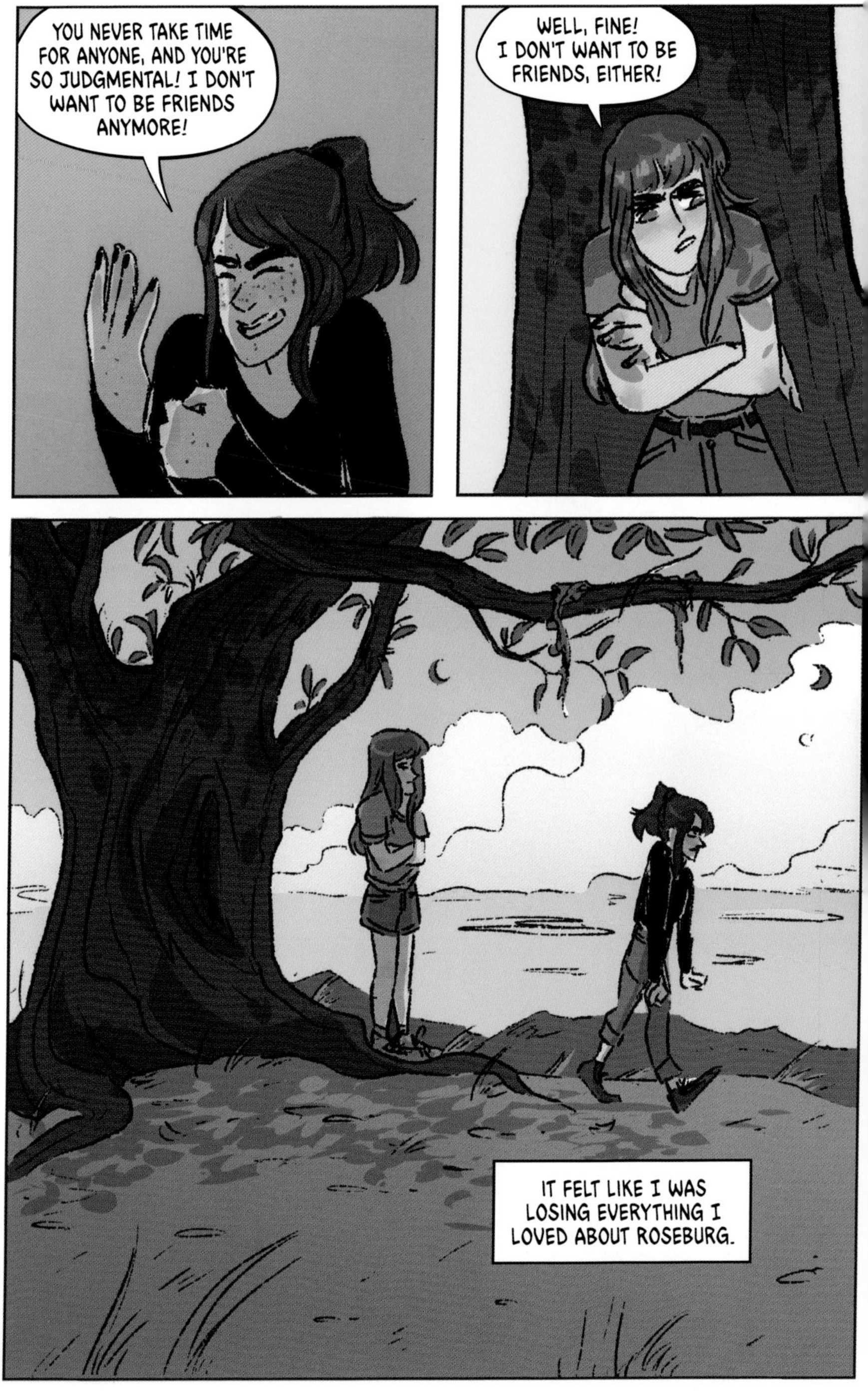
YOU NEVER TAKE TIME FOR ANYONE, AND YOU'RE SO JUDGMENTAL! I DON'T WANT TO BE FRIENDS ANYMORE!
WELL, FINE! I DON'T WANT TO BE FRIENDS, EITHER!
IT FELT LIKE I WAS LOSING EVERYTHING I LOVED ABOUT ROSEBURG.

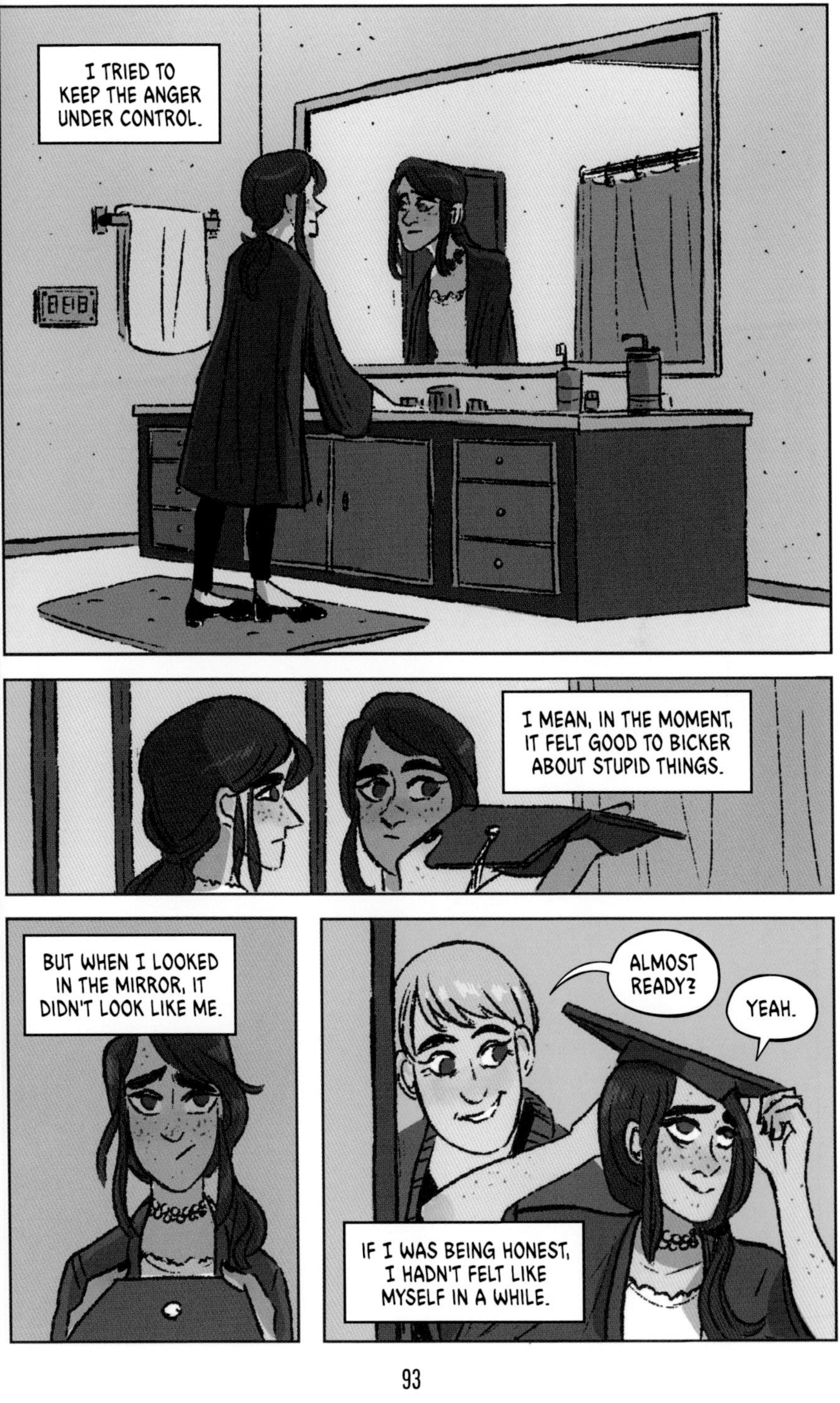
I TRIED TO KEEP THE ANGER UNDER CONTROL.
I MEAN, IN THE MOMENT, IT FELT GOOD TO BICKER ABOUT STUPID THINGS.
BUT WHEN I LOOKED IN THE MIRROR, IT DIDN'T LOOK LIKE ME.
ALMOST READY?
YEAH.
IF I WAS BEING HONEST, I HADN'T FELT LIKE MYSELF IN A WHILE.

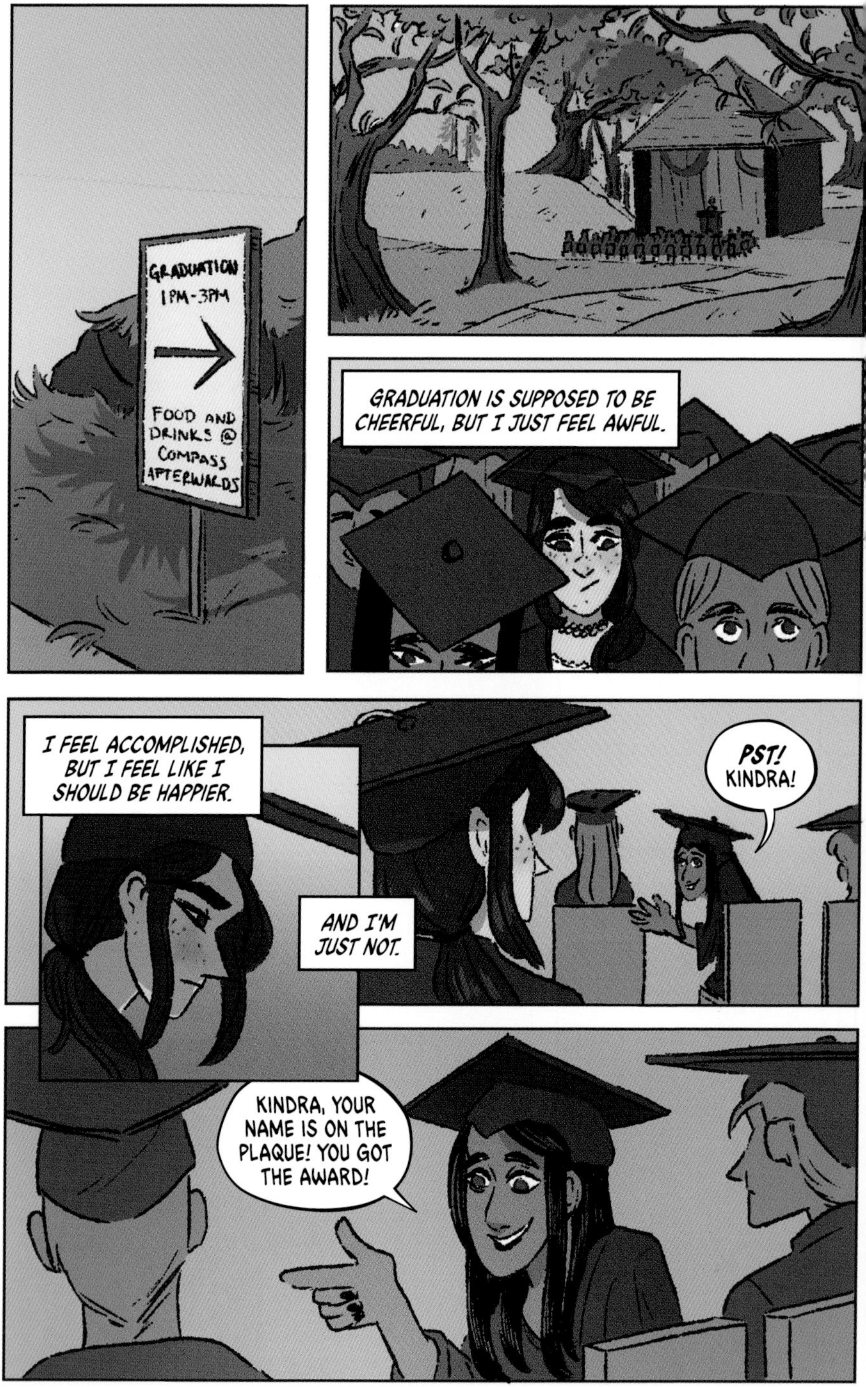
GRADUATION
1PM-3PM
FOOD AND DRINKS @ COMPASS AFTERWARDS
GRADUATION IS SUPPOSED TO BE CHEERFUL, BUT I JUST FEEL AWFUL.
I FEEL ACCOMPLISHED, BUT I FEEL LIKE I SHOULD BE HAPPIER.
AND I'M JUST NOT.
PST! KINDRA!
KINDRA, YOUR NAME IS ON THE PLAQUE! YOU GOT THE AWARD!

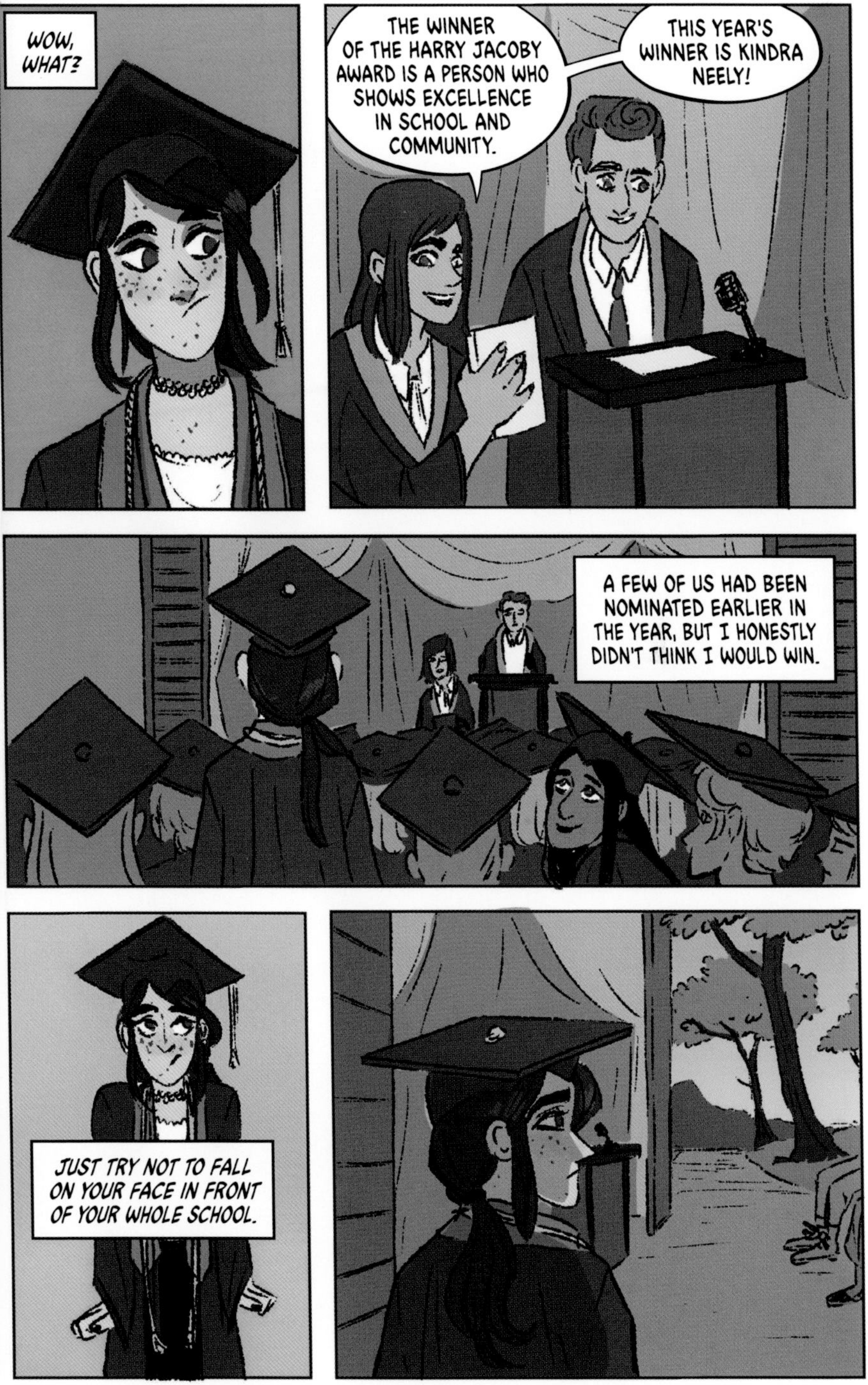

WOW, WHAT?
THE WINNER OF THE HARRY JACOBY AWARD IS A PERSON WHO SHOWS EXCELLENCE IN SCHOOL AND COMMUNITY.
THIS YEAR'S WINNER IS KINDRA NEELY!
A FEW OF US HAD BEEN NOMINATED EARLIER IN THE YEAR, BUT I HONESTLY DIDN'T THINK I WOULD WIN.
JUST TRY NOT TO FALL ON YOUR FACE IN FRONT OF YOUR WHOLE SCHOOL.

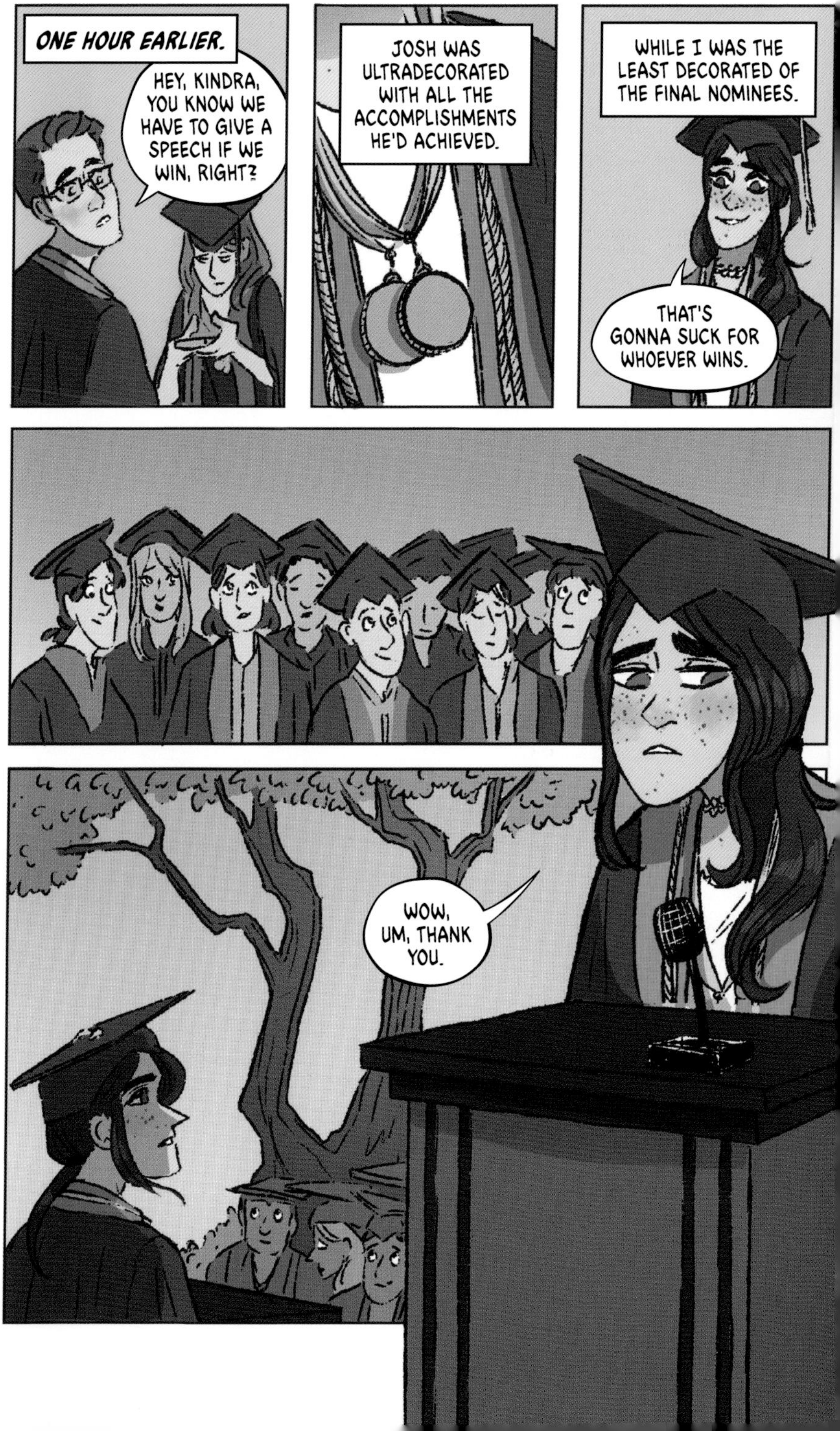
ONE HOUR EARLIER.
HEY, KINDRA, YOU KNOW WE HAVE TO GIVE A SPEECH IF WE WIN, RIGHT?
JOSH WAS ULTRADECORATED WITH ALL THE ACCOMPLISHMENTS HE'D ACHIEVED.
WHILE I WAS THE LEAST DECORATED OF THE FINAL NOMINEES.
THAT'S GONNA SUCK FOR WHOEVER WINS.
WOW, UM, THANK YOU.

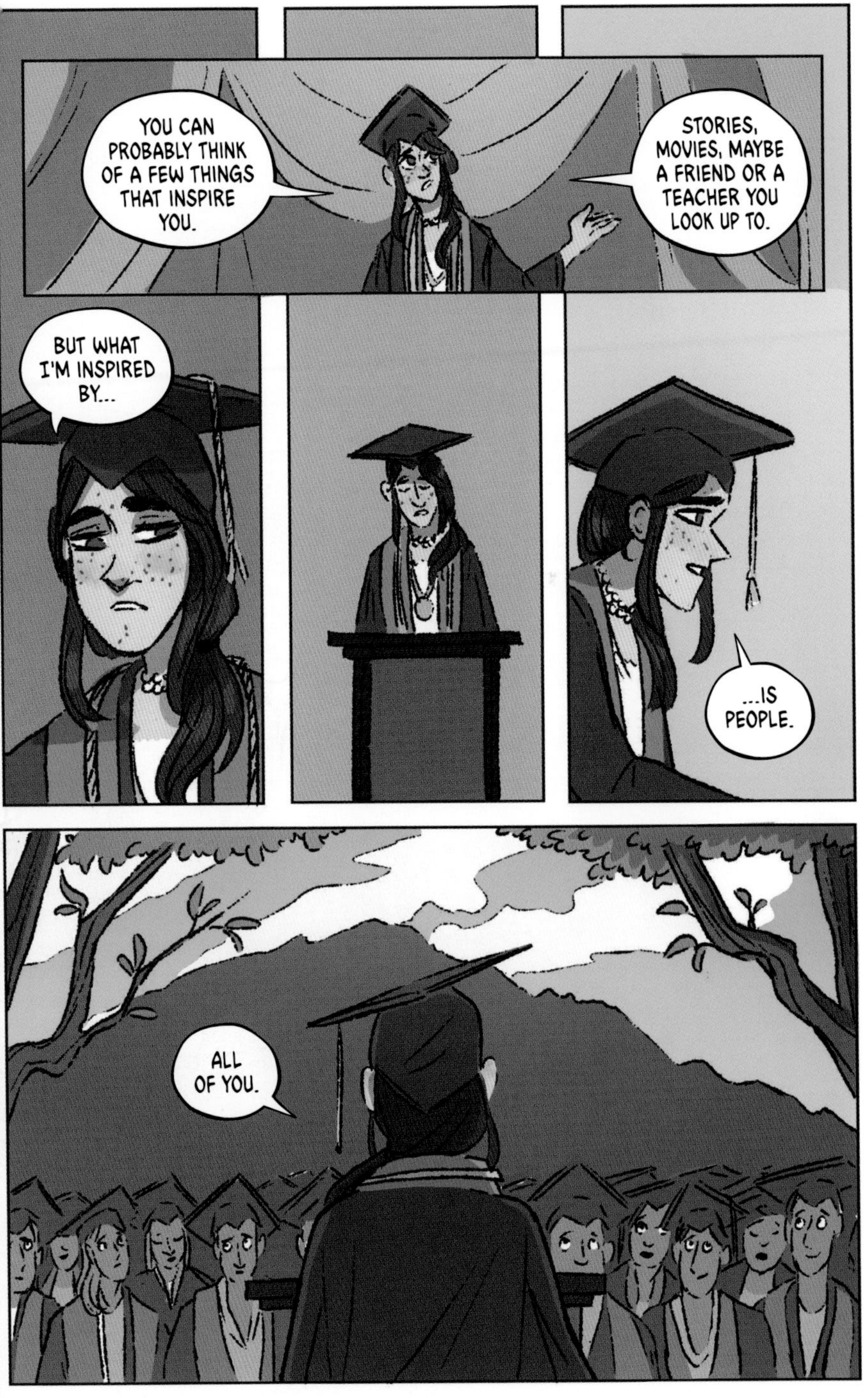
YOU CAN PROBABLY THINK OF A FEW THINGS THAT INSPIRE YOU.
STORIES, MOVIES, MAYBE A FRIEND OR A TEACHER YOU LOOK UP TO.
BUT WHAT I'M INSPIRED BY...
...IS PEOPLE.
ALL OF YOU.

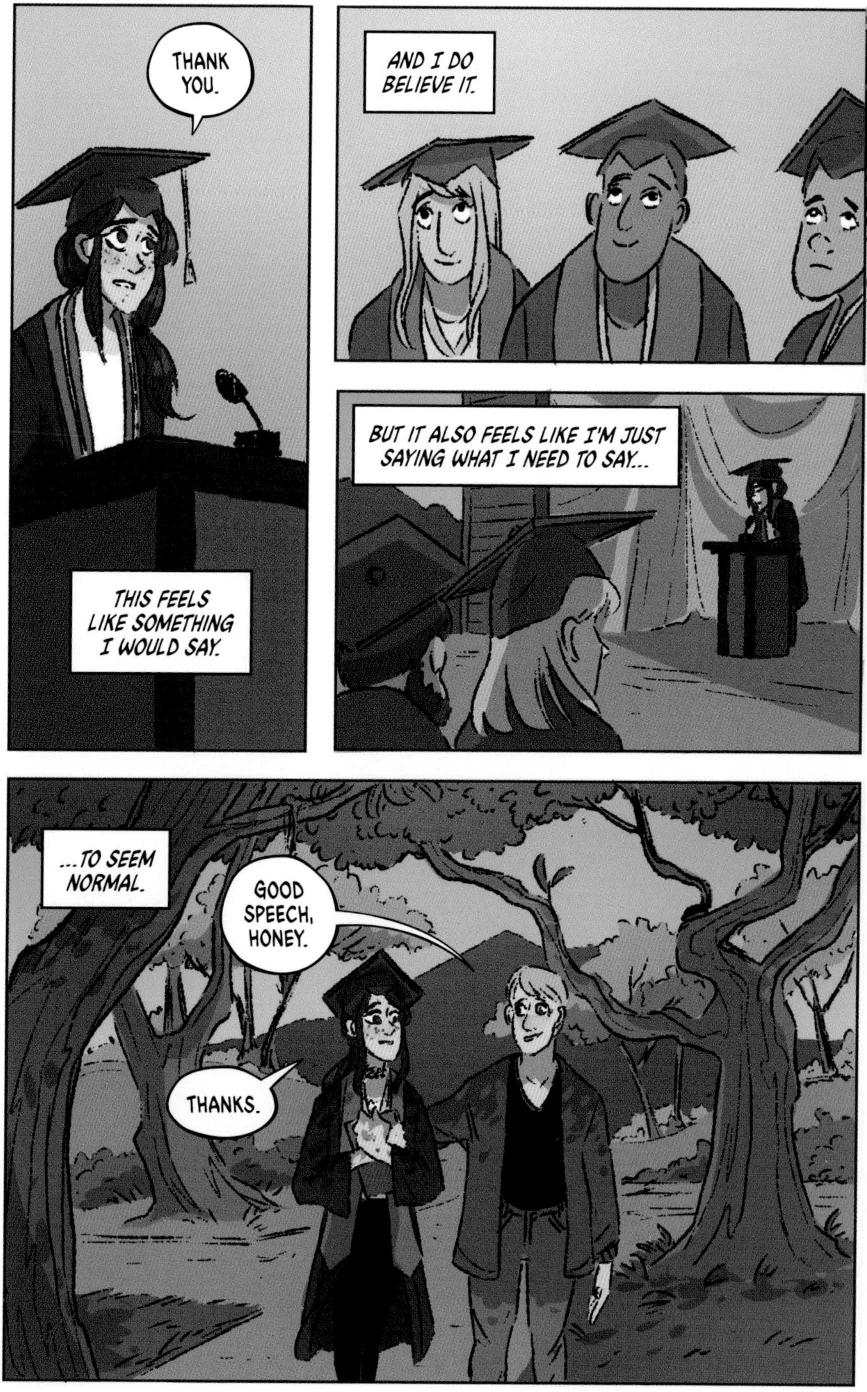
THANK YOU.
THIS FEELS LIKE SOMETHING I WOULD SAY.
AND I DO BELIEVE IT.
BUT IT ALSO FEELS LIKE I'M JUST SAYING WHAT I NEED TO SAY...
...TO SEEM NORMAL.
GOOD SPEECH, HONEY.
THANKS.

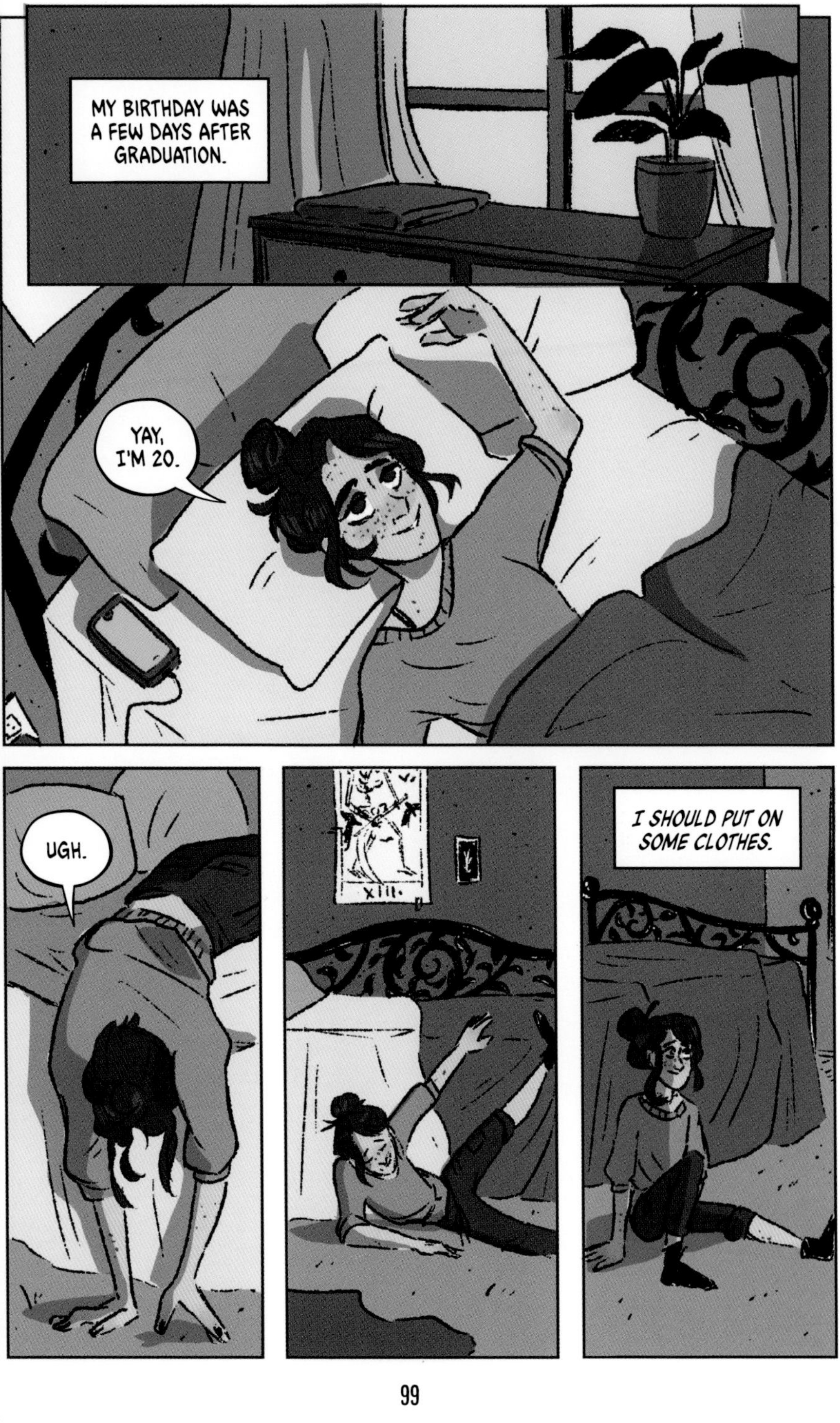
MY BIRTHDAY WAS A FEW DAYS AFTER GRADUATION.
YAY, I'M 20.
UGH.
I SHOULD PUT ON SOME CLOTHES.

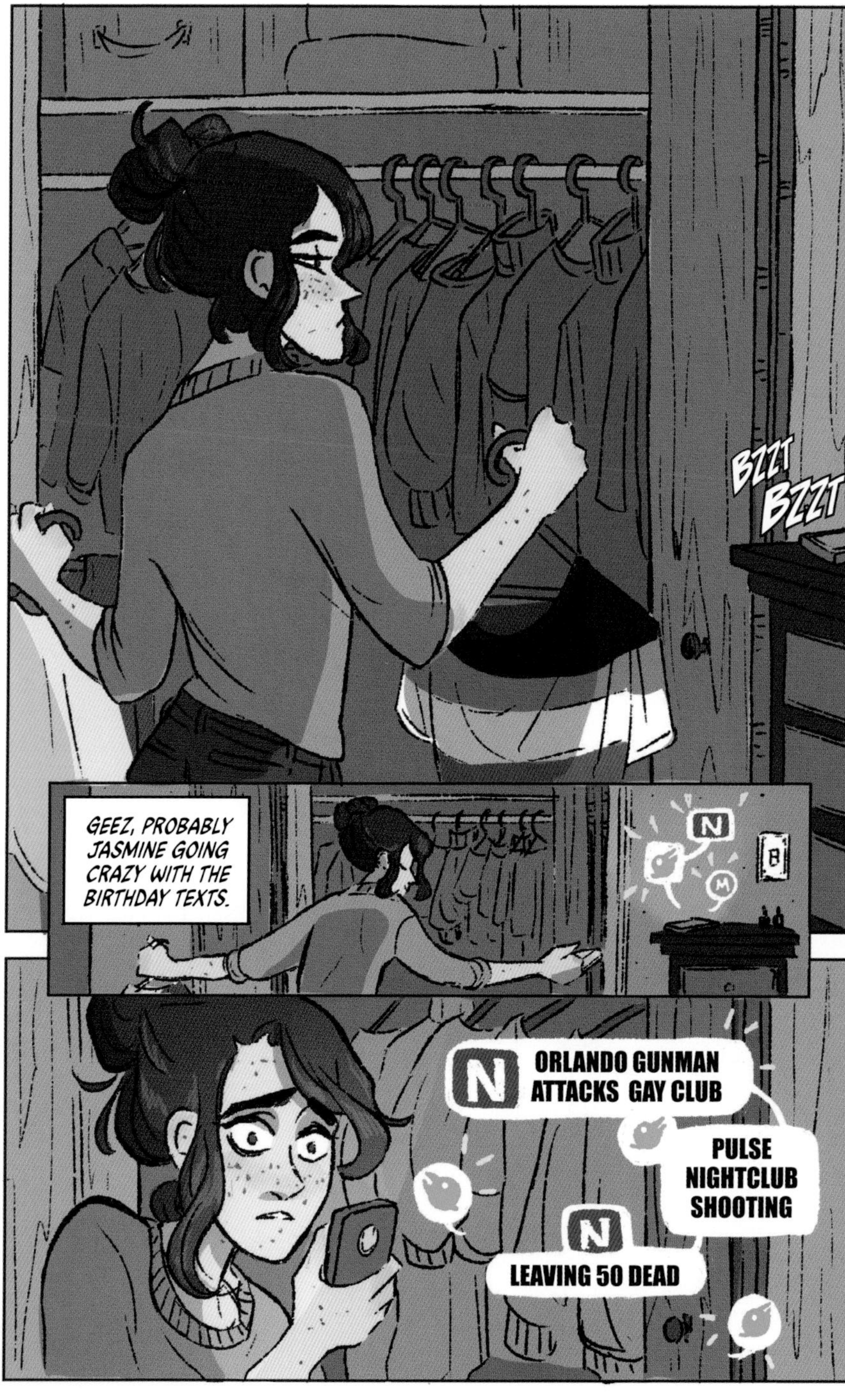
BZZT
BZZT
GEEZ, PROBABLY JASMINE GOING CRAZY WITH THE BIRTHDAY TEXTS.
N
M
N
ORLANDO GUNMAN ATTACKS GAY CLUB
PULSE NIGHTCLUB SHOOTING
N
LEAVING 50 DEAD

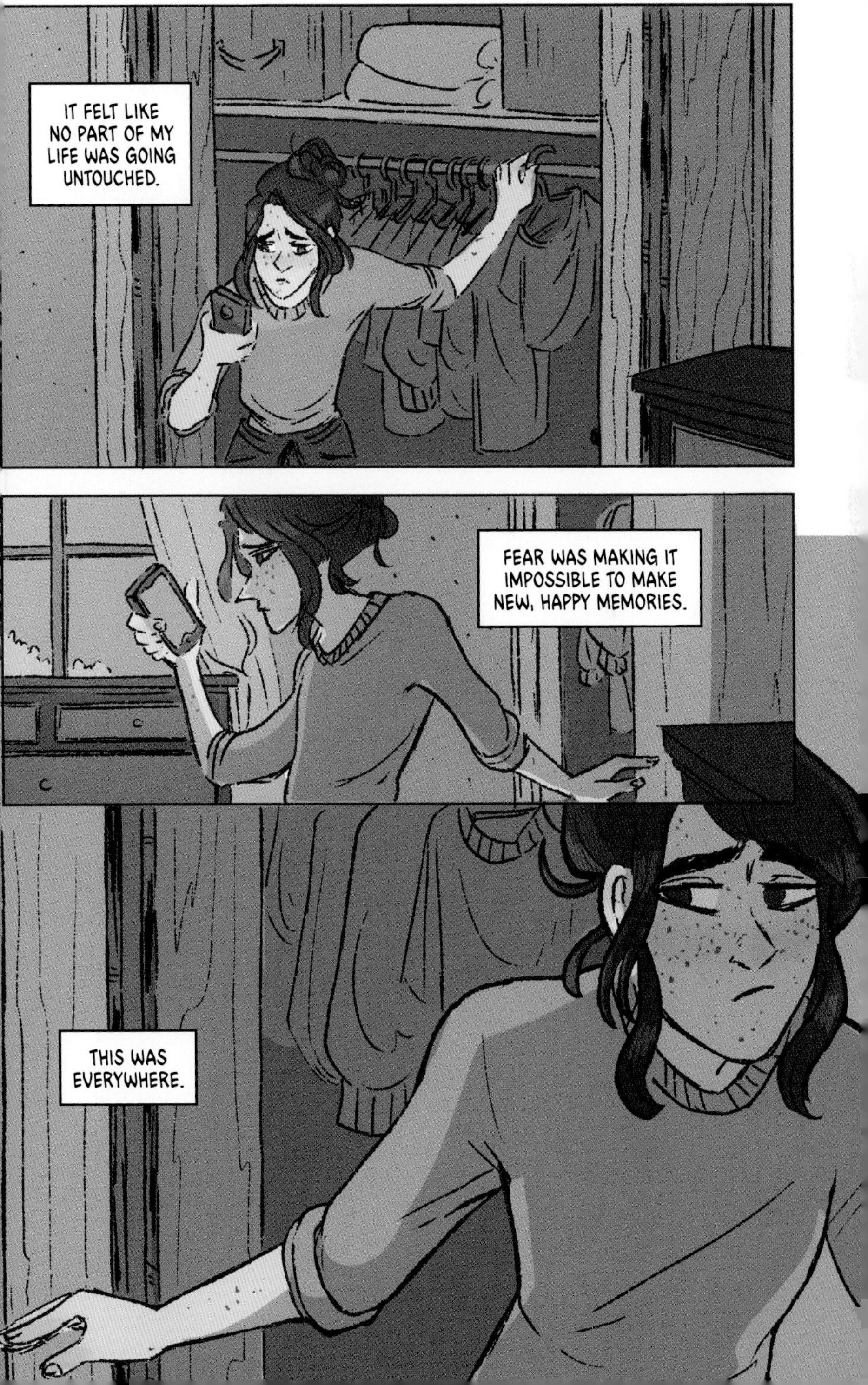
IT FELT LIKE NO PART OF MY LIFE WAS GOING UNTOUCHED.
FEAR WAS MAKING IT IMPOSSIBLE TO MAKE NEW, HAPPY MEMORIES.
THIS WAS EVERYWHERE.

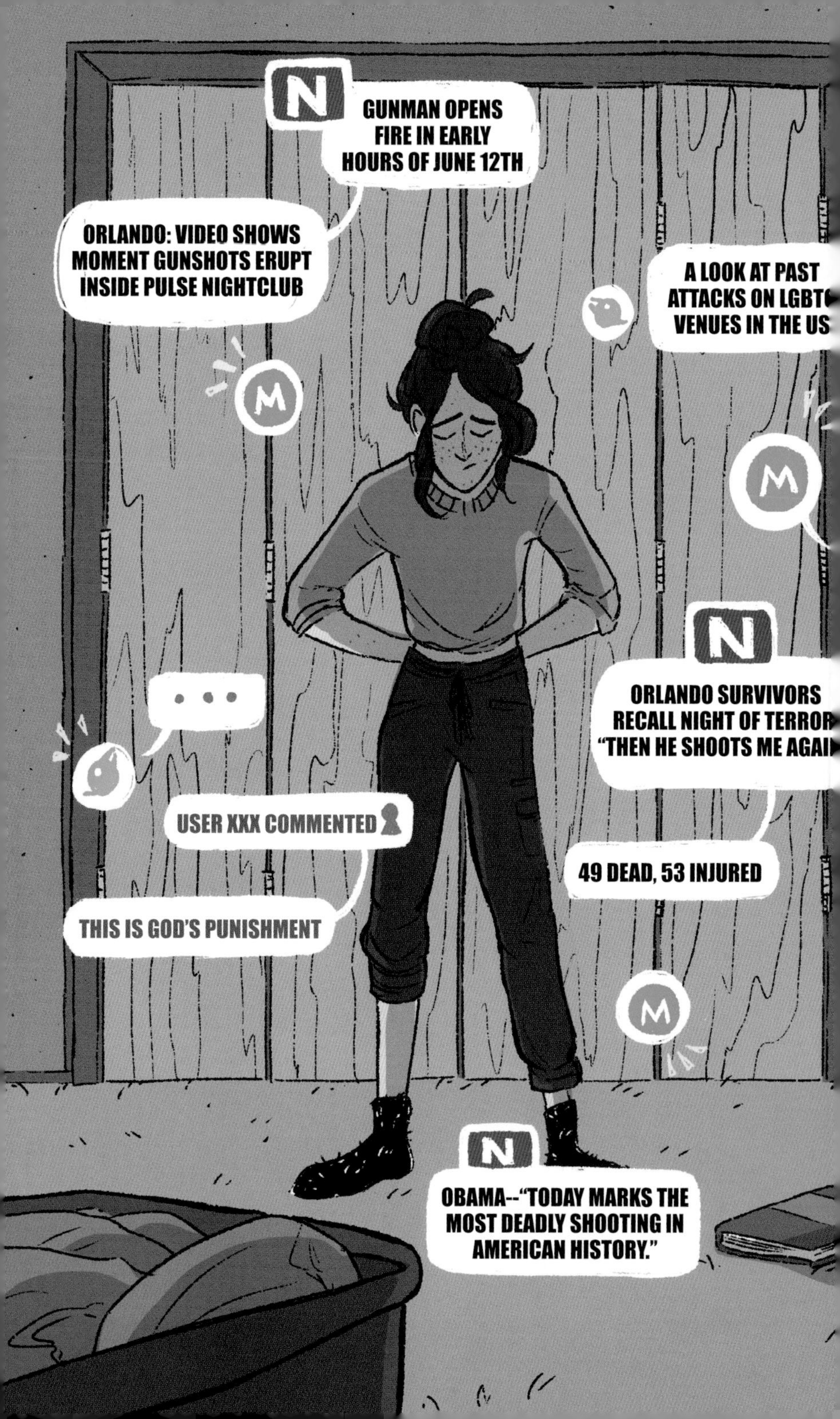
GUNMAN OPENS FIRE IN EARLY HOURS OF JUNE 12TH
ORLANDO: VIDEO SHOWS MOMENT GUNSHOTS ERUPT INSIDE PULSE NIGHTCLUB
A LOOK AT PAST ATTACKS ON LGBT
VENUES IN THE US
...
ORLANDO SURVIVORS RECALL NIGHT OF TERROR
"THEN HE SHOOTS ME AGAI
USER XXX COMMENTED
49 DEAD, 53 INJURED
THIS IS GOD'S PUNISHMENT
OBAMA--"TODAY MARKS THE MOST DEADLY SHOOTING IN AMERICAN HISTORY."

IT'S MY BIRTHDAY.

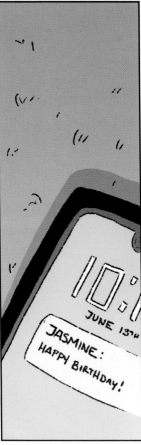

JUNE 13TH

JASMINE:
HAPPY BIRTHDAY!

AND FOR THE FIRST TIME, I DON'T REALLY SEE A POINT IN HAVING ANOTHER.

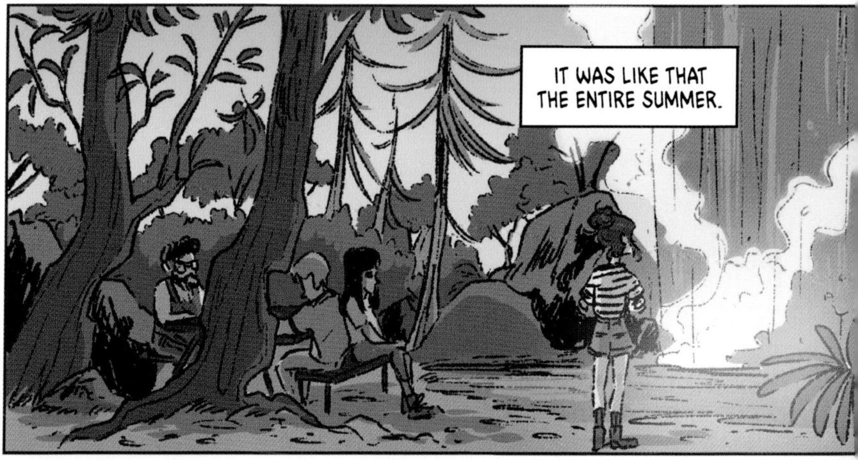
IT WAS LIKE THAT
THE ENTIRE SUMMER.

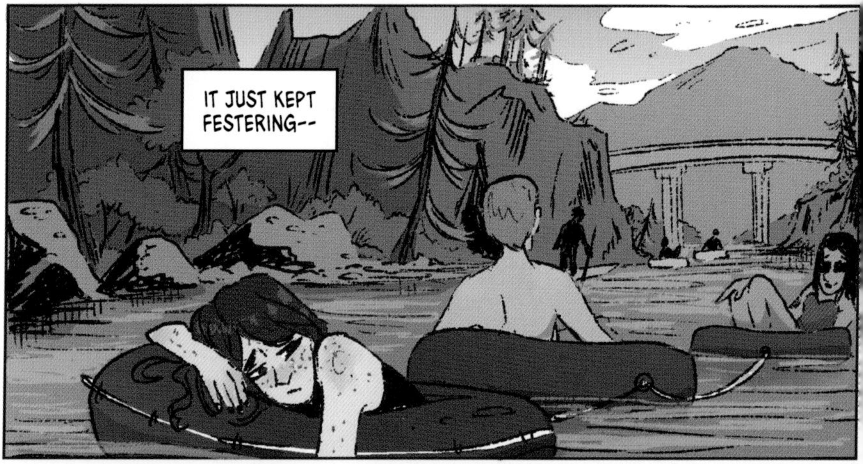
IT JUST KEPT
FESTERING--

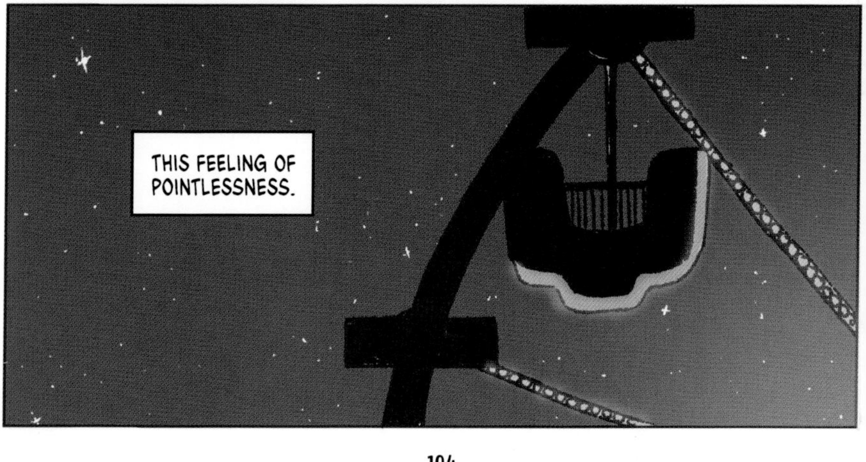
THIS FEELING OF
POINTLESSNESS.

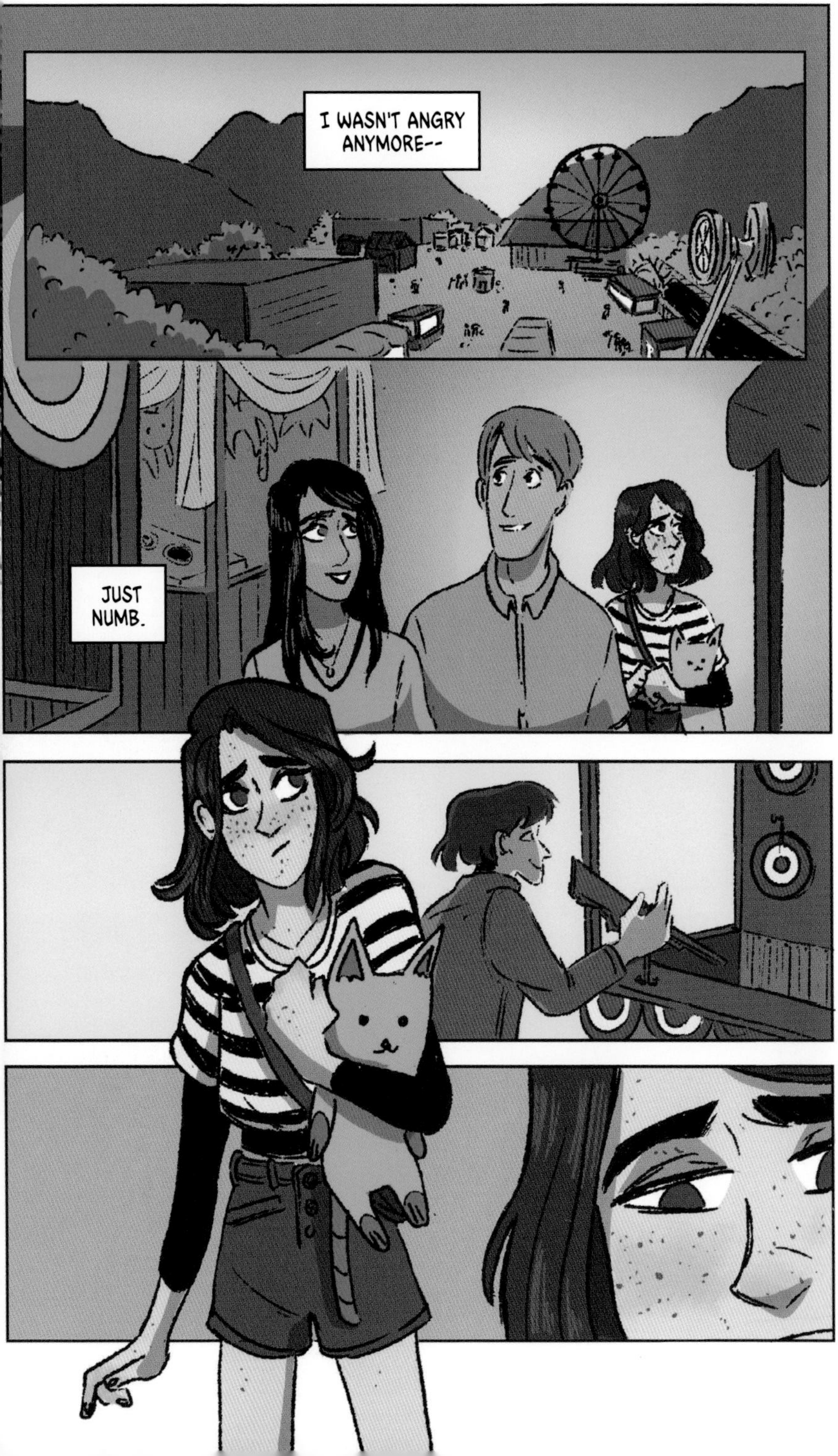
I WASN'T ANGRY ANYMORE--
JUST NUMB.

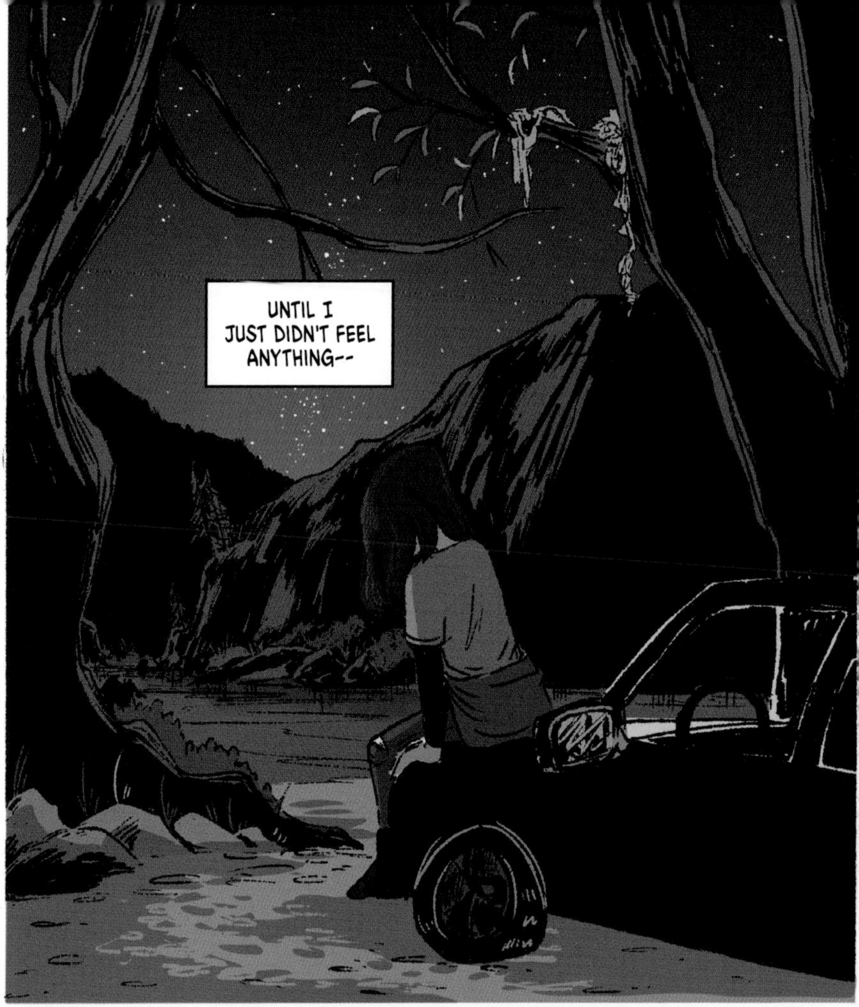
UNTIL I
JUST DIDN'T FEEL
ANYTHING--

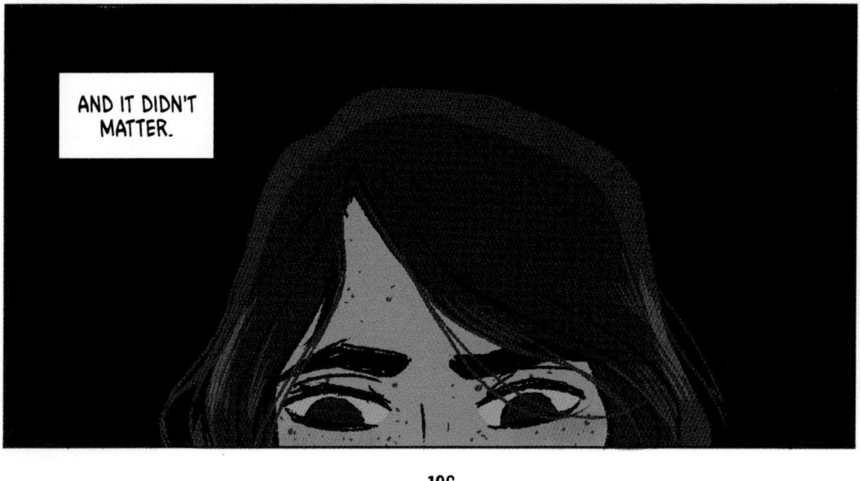
AND IT DIDN'T
MATTER.

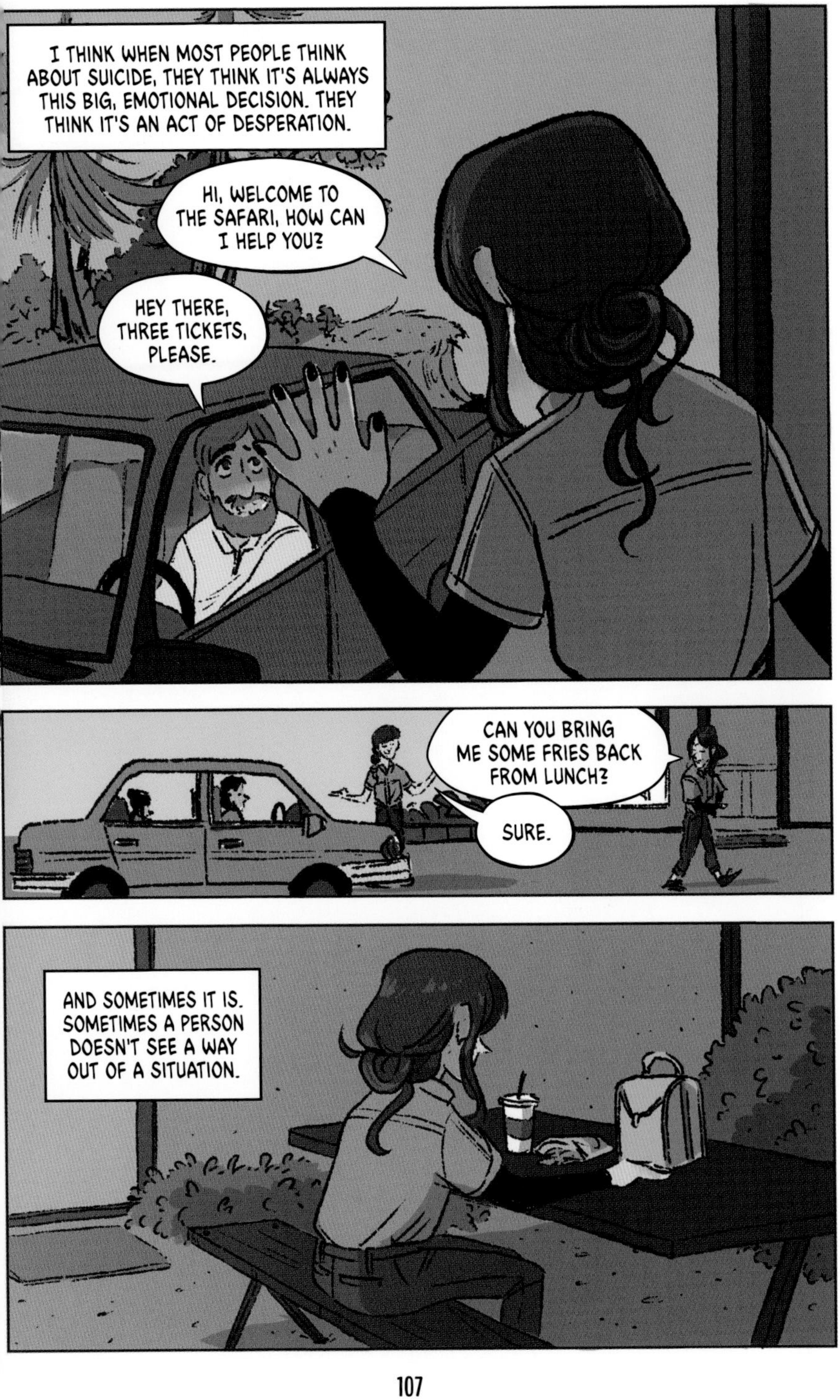
I THINK WHEN MOST PEOPLE THINK ABOUT SUICIDE, THEY THINK IT'S ALWAYS THIS BIG, EMOTIONAL DECISION. THEY THINK IT'S AN ACT OF DESPERATION.
HI, WELCOME TO THE SAFARI, HOW CAN I HELP YOU?
HEY THERE, THREE TICKETS, PLEASE.
CAN YOU BRING ME SOME FRIES BACK FROM LUNCH?
SURE.
AND SOMETIMES IT IS. SOMETIMES A PERSON DOESN'T SEE A WAY OUT OF A SITUATION.

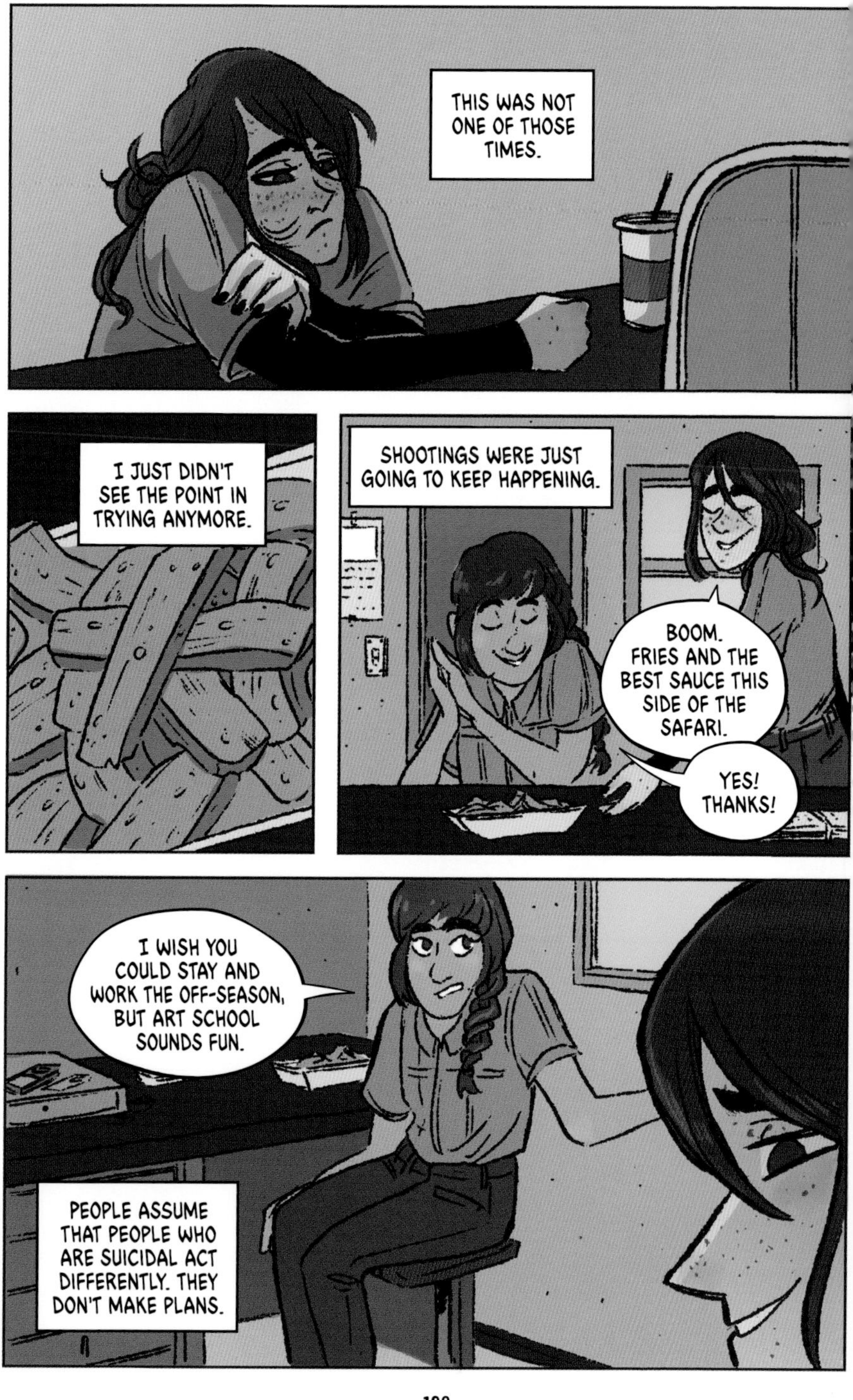
THIS WAS NOT ONE OF THOSE TIMES.
I JUST DIDN'T SEE THE POINT IN TRYING ANYMORE.
SHOOTINGS WERE JUST GOING TO KEEP HAPPENING.
BOOM. FRIES AND THE BEST SAUCE THIS SIDE OF THE SAFARI.
YES! THANKS!
I WISH YOU COULD STAY AND WORK THE OFF-SEASON, BUT ART SCHOOL SOUNDS FUN.
PEOPLE ASSUME THAT PEOPLE WHO ARE SUICIDAL ACT DIFFERENTLY. THEY DON'T MAKE PLANS.

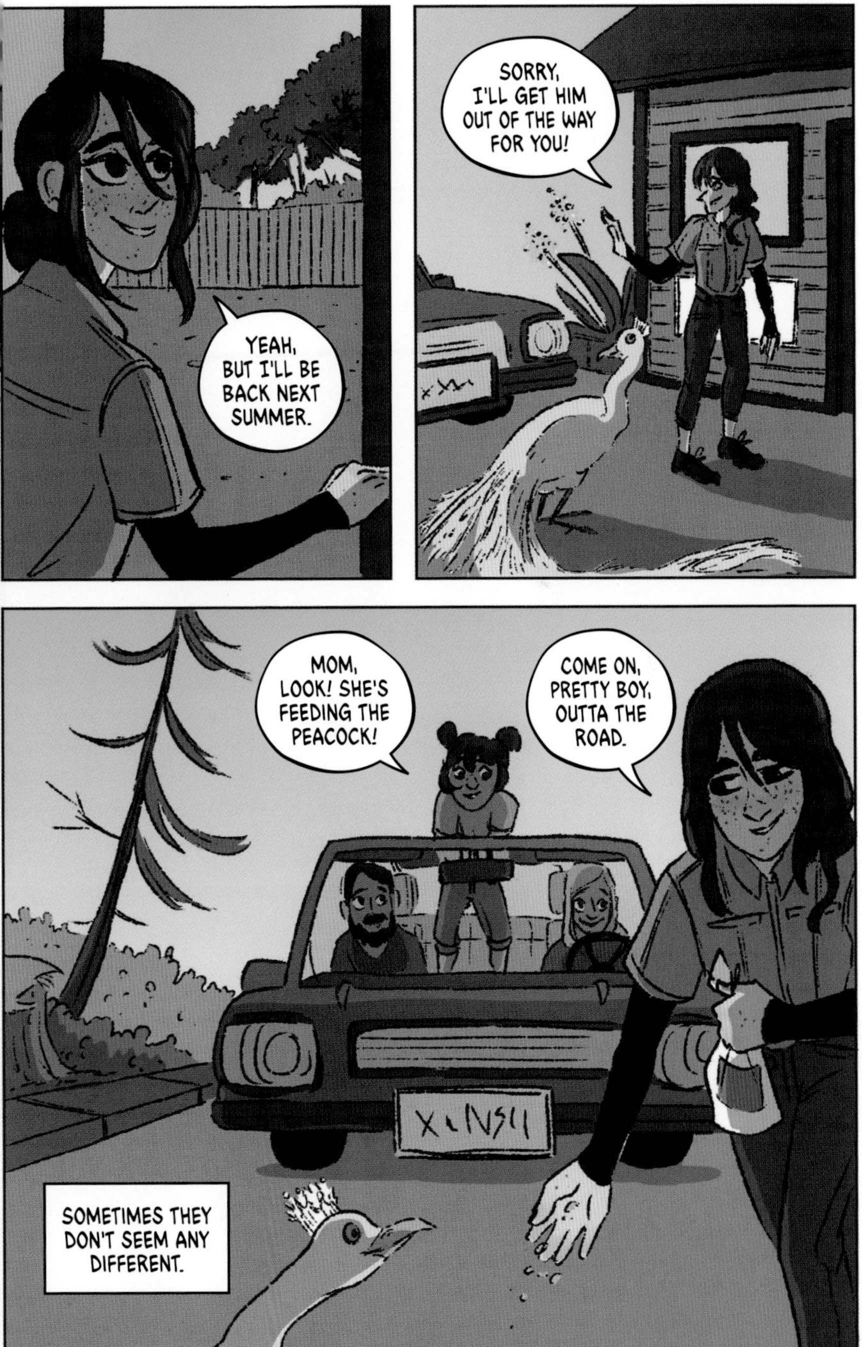
YEAH, BUT I'LL BE BACK NEXT SUMMER.
SORRY, I'LL GET HIM OUT OF THE WAY FOR YOU!
MOM, LOOK! SHE'S FEEDING THE PEACOCK!
COME ON, PRETTY BOY, OUTTA THE ROAD.
SOMETIMES THEY DON'T SEEM ANY DIFFERENT.

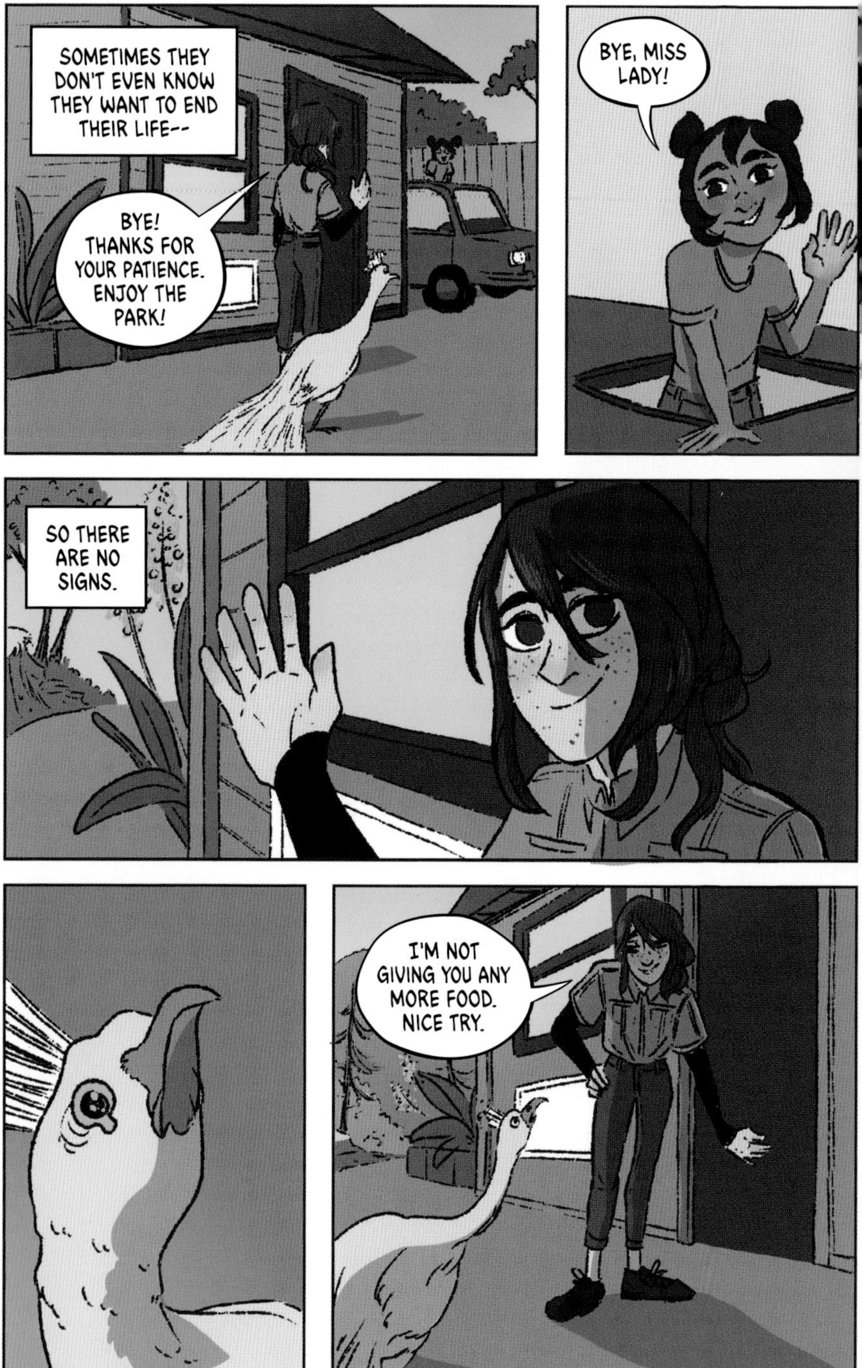
SOMETIMES THEY DON'T EVEN KNOW THEY WANT TO END THEIR LIFE--
BYE! THANKS FOR YOUR PATIENCE. ENJOY THE PARK!
BYE, MISS LADY!
SO THERE ARE NO SIGNS.
I'M NOT GIVING YOU ANY MORE FOOD. NICE TRY.

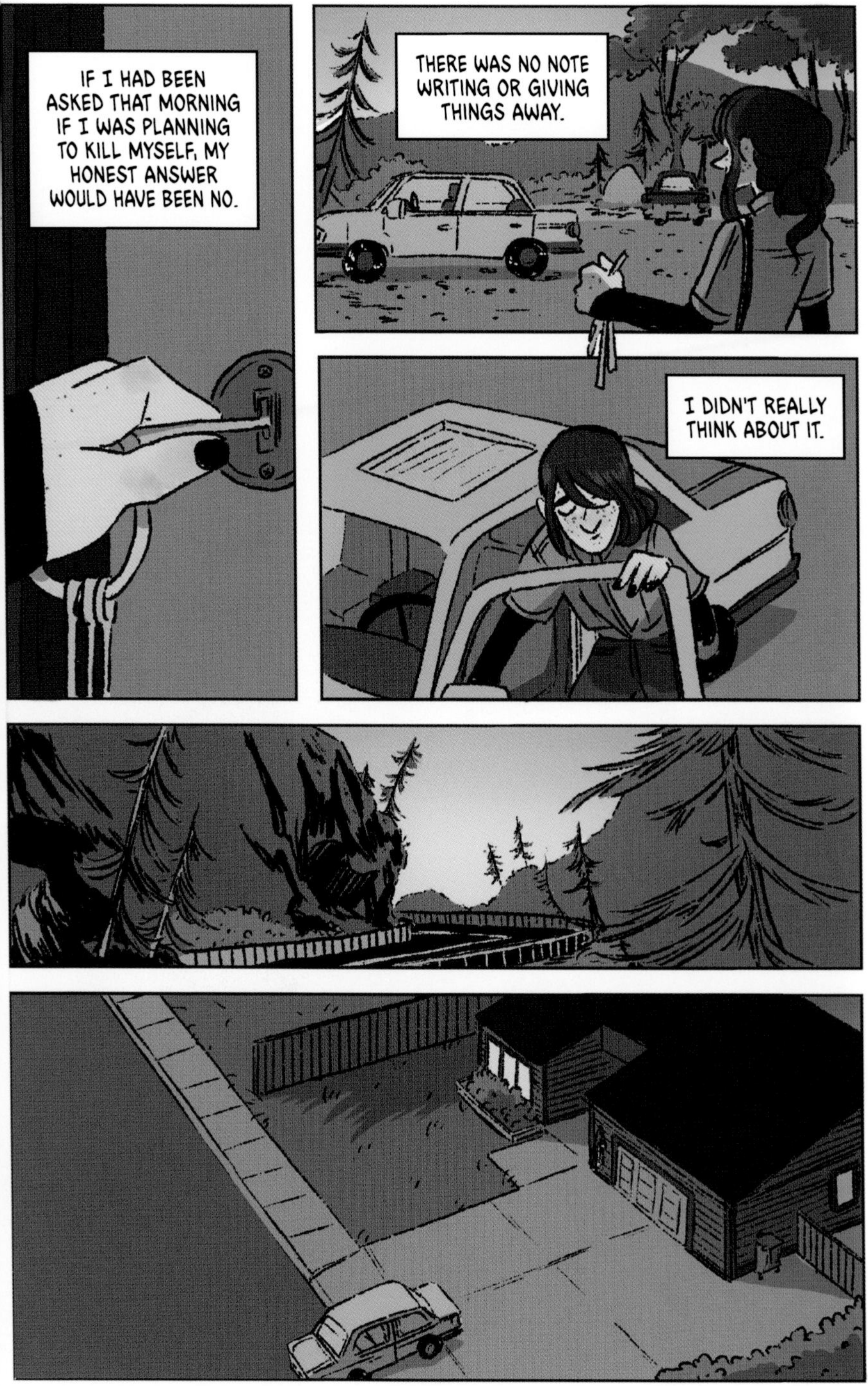
IF I HAD BEEN ASKED THAT MORNING IF I WAS PLANNING TO KILL MYSELF, MY HONEST ANSWER WOULD HAVE BEEN NO.
THERE WAS NO NOTE WRITING OR GIVING THINGS AWAY.
I DIDN'T REALLY THINK ABOUT IT.

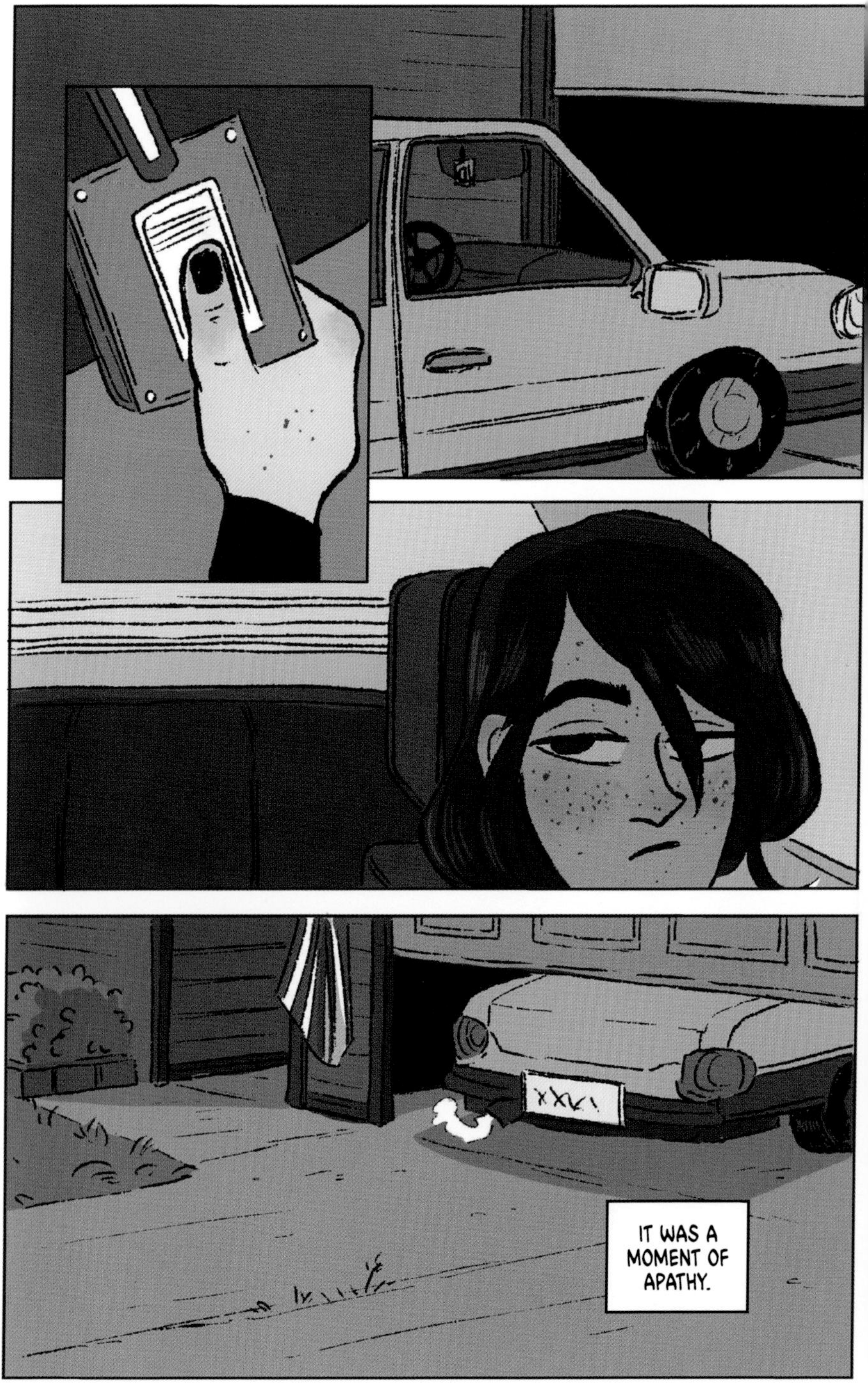
IT WAS A MOMENT OF APATHY.

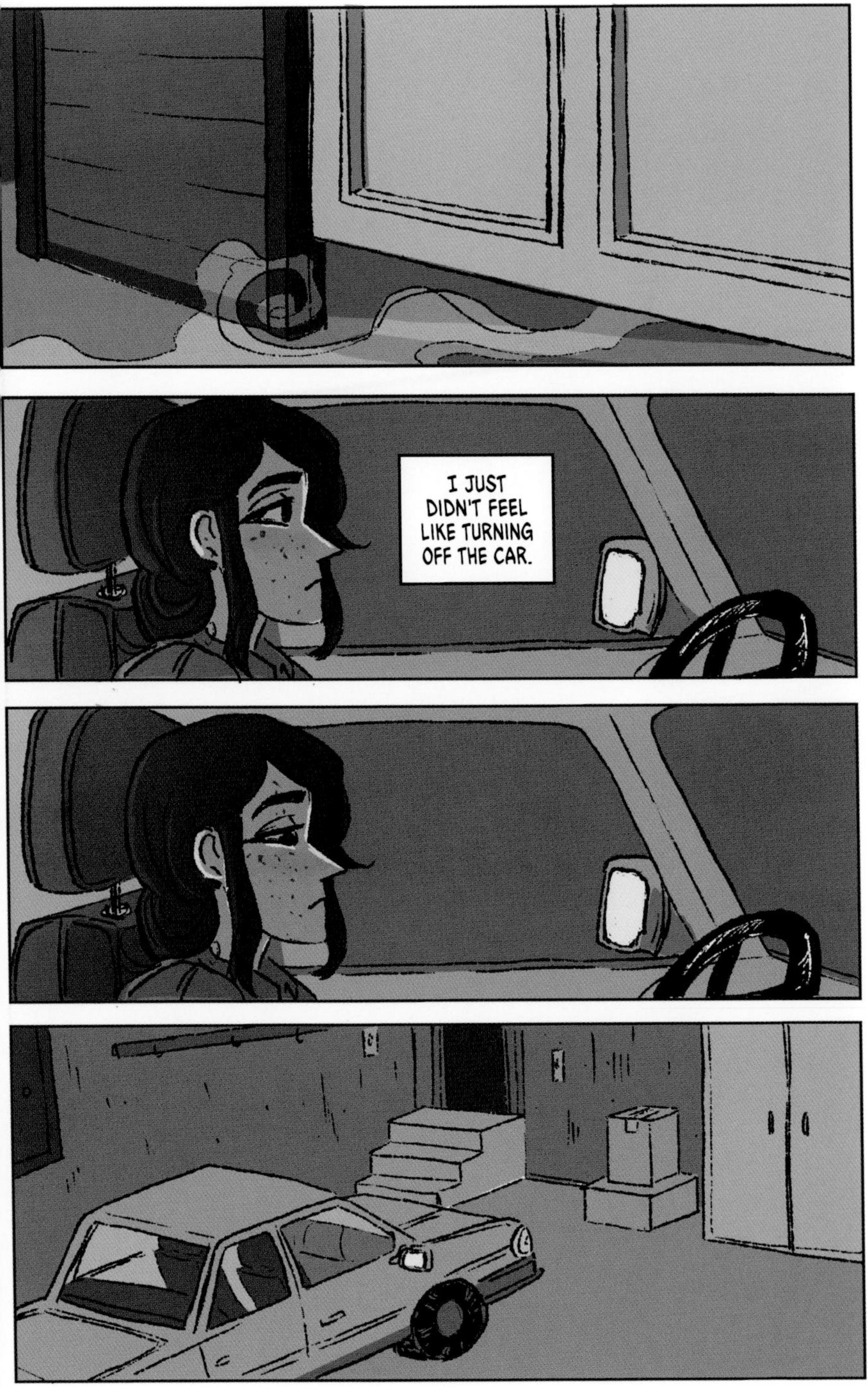
I JUST DIDN'T FEEL LIKE TURNING OFF THE CAR.

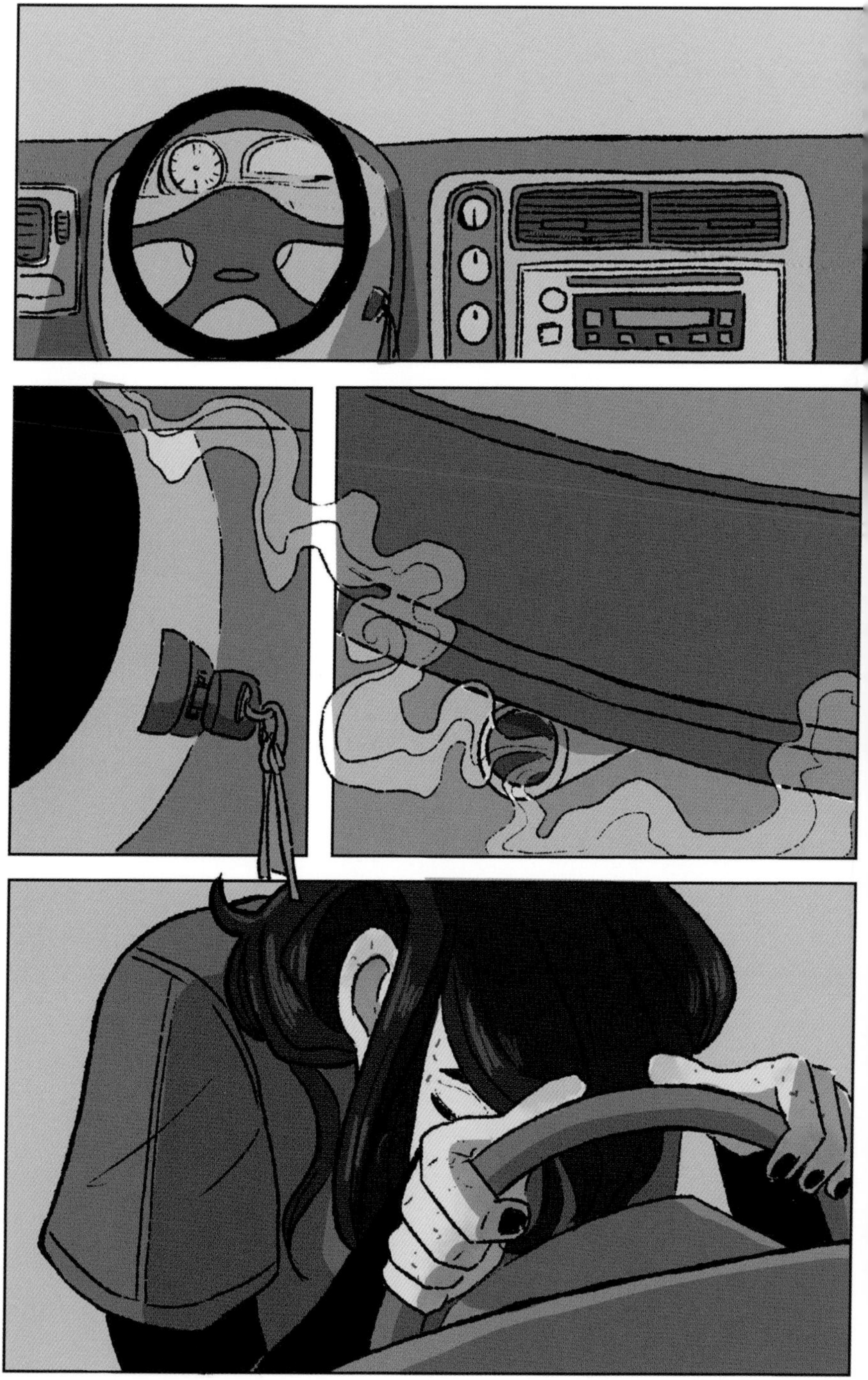

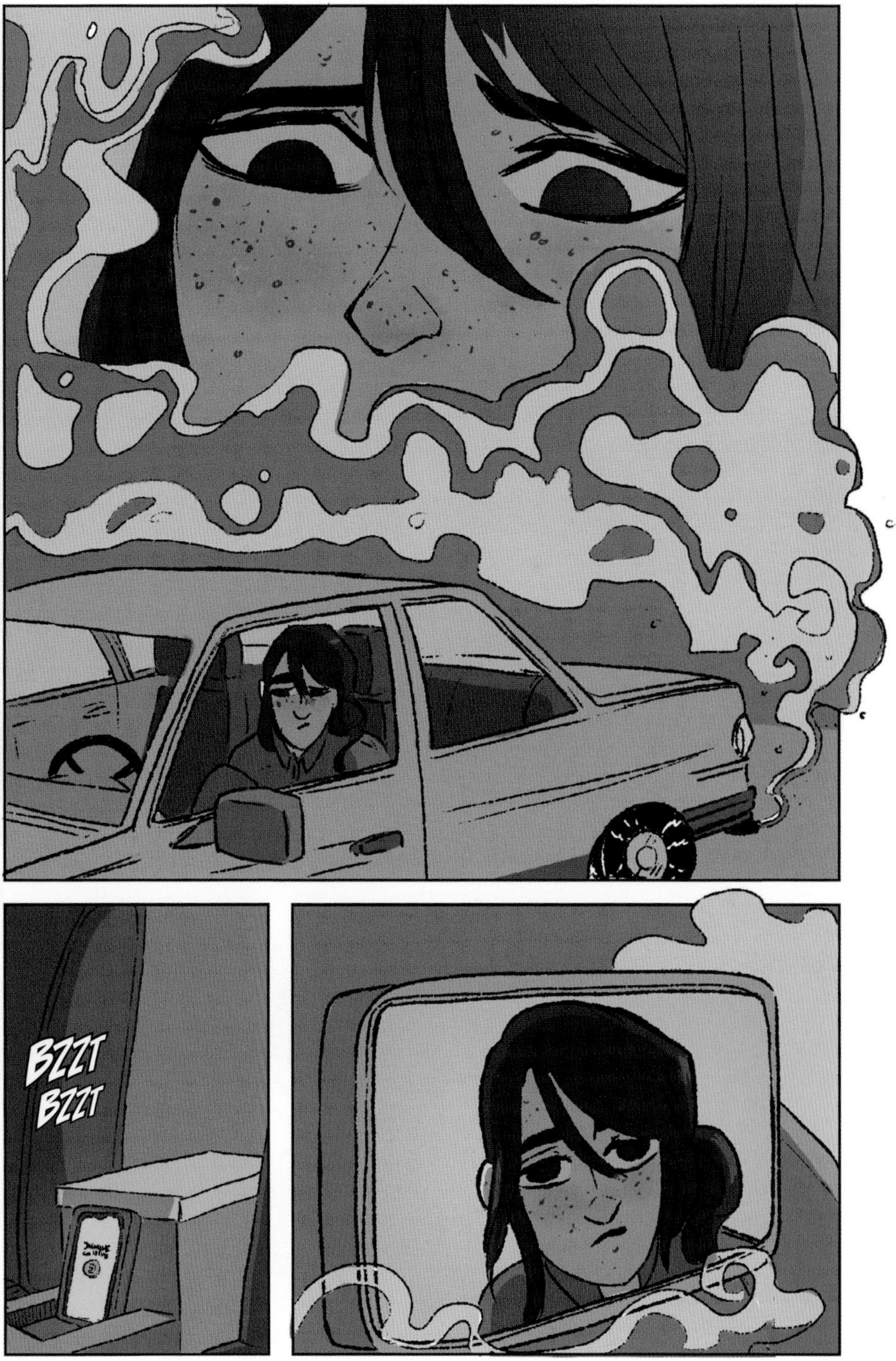
BZZT
BZZT

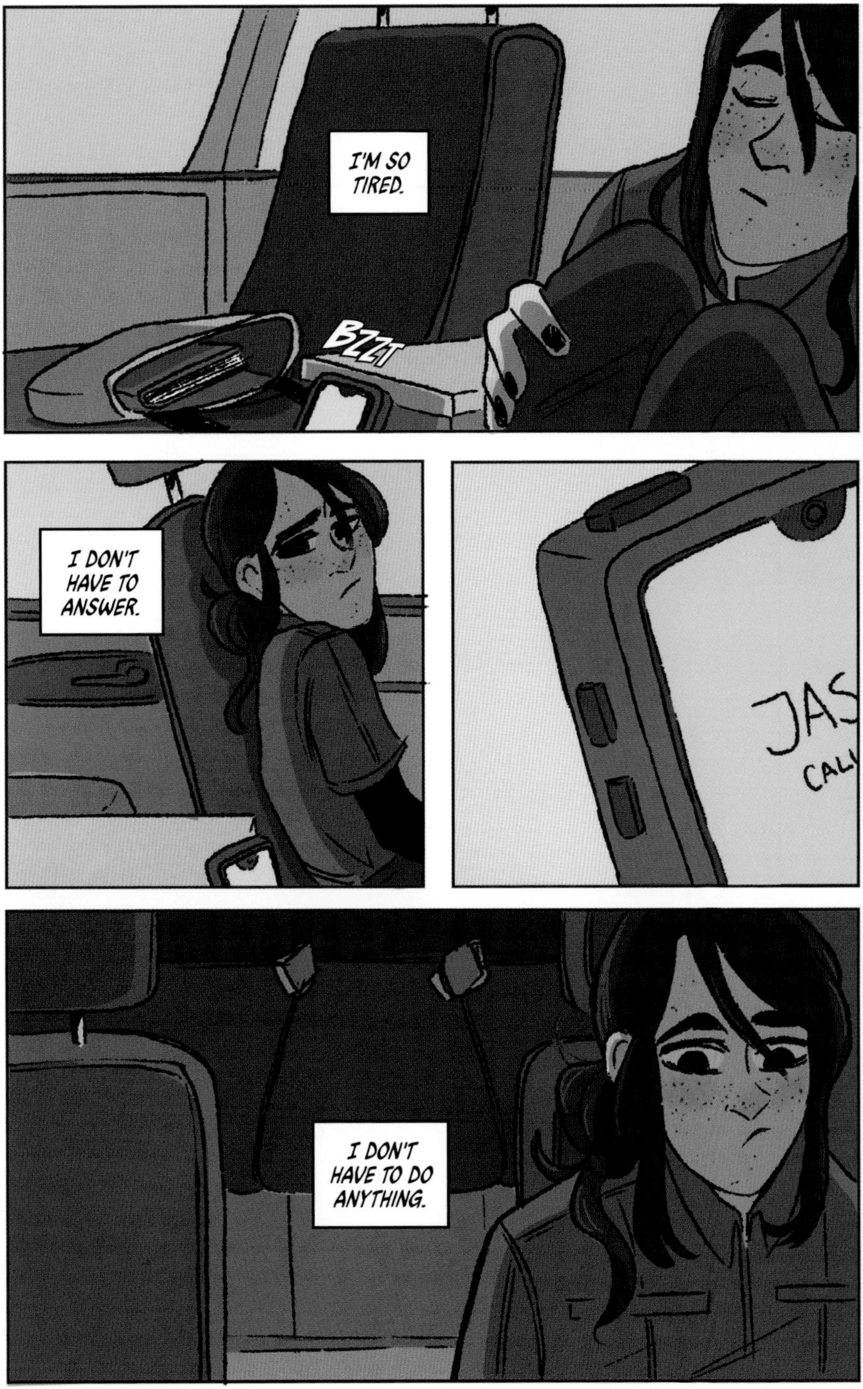
I'M SO TIRED.
BZZT
I DON'T HAVE TO ANSWER.
I DON'T HAVE TO DO ANYTHING.

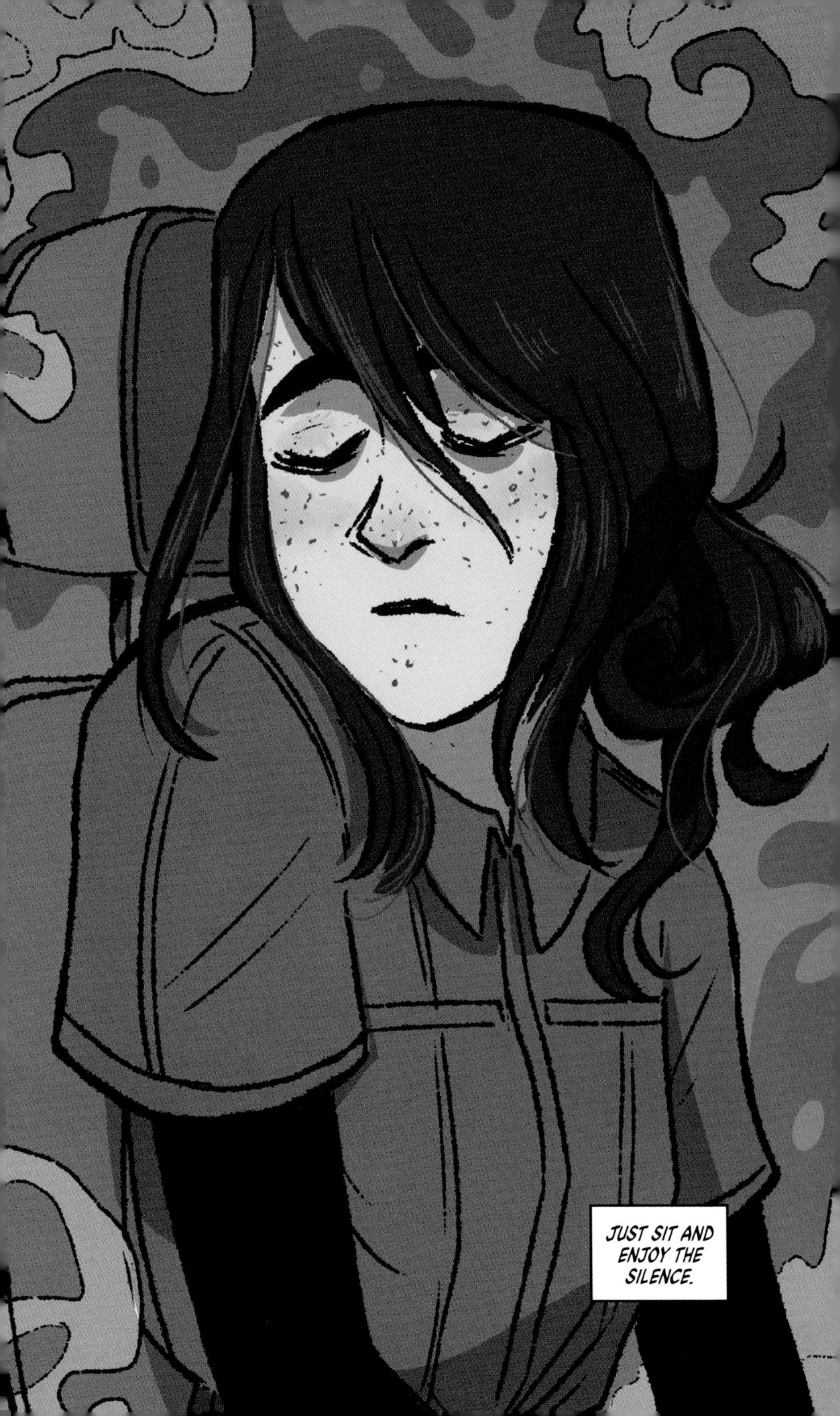
JUST SIT AND ENJOY THE SILENCE.

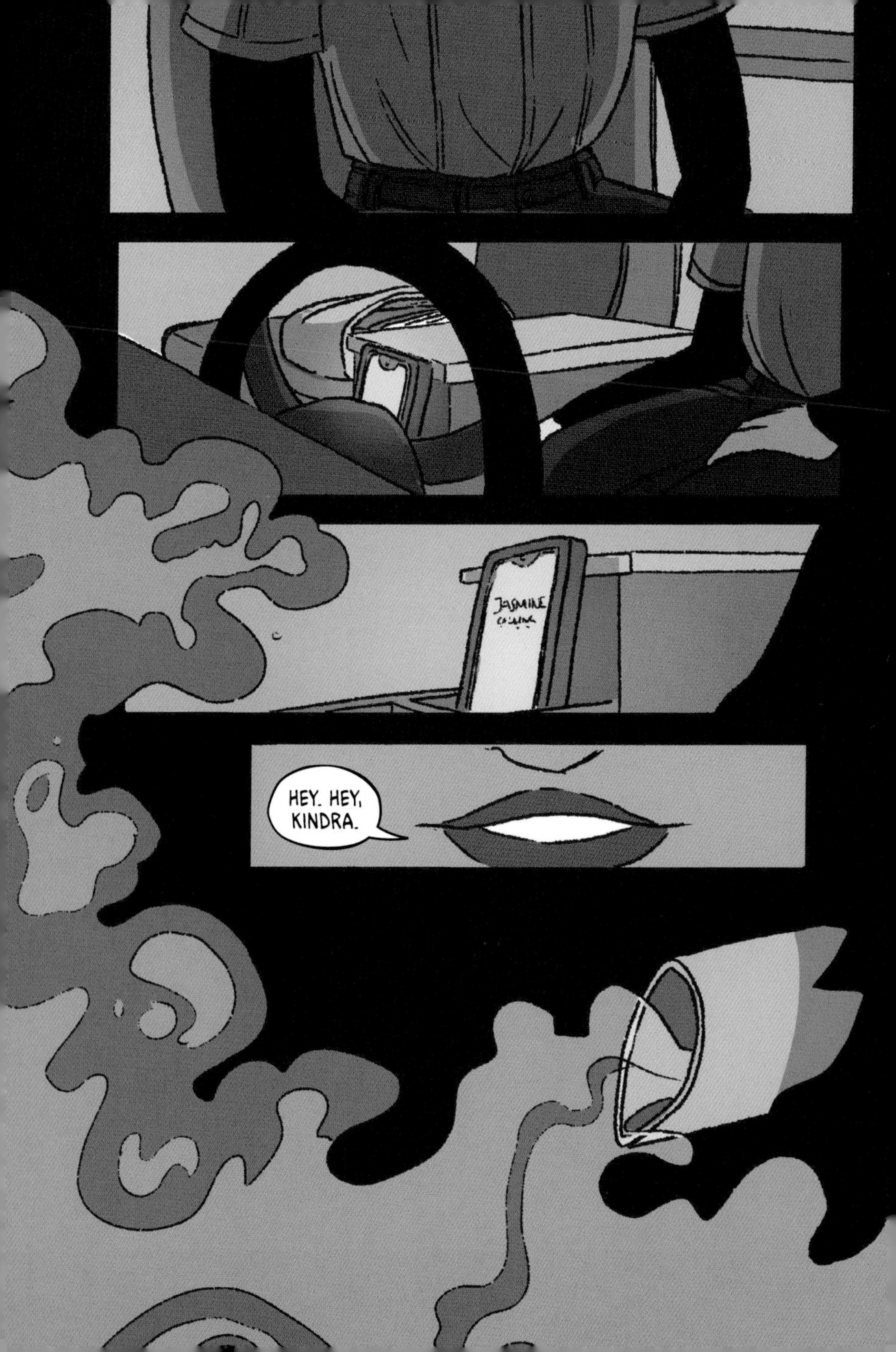
JASMINE
HEY. HEY, KINDRA.

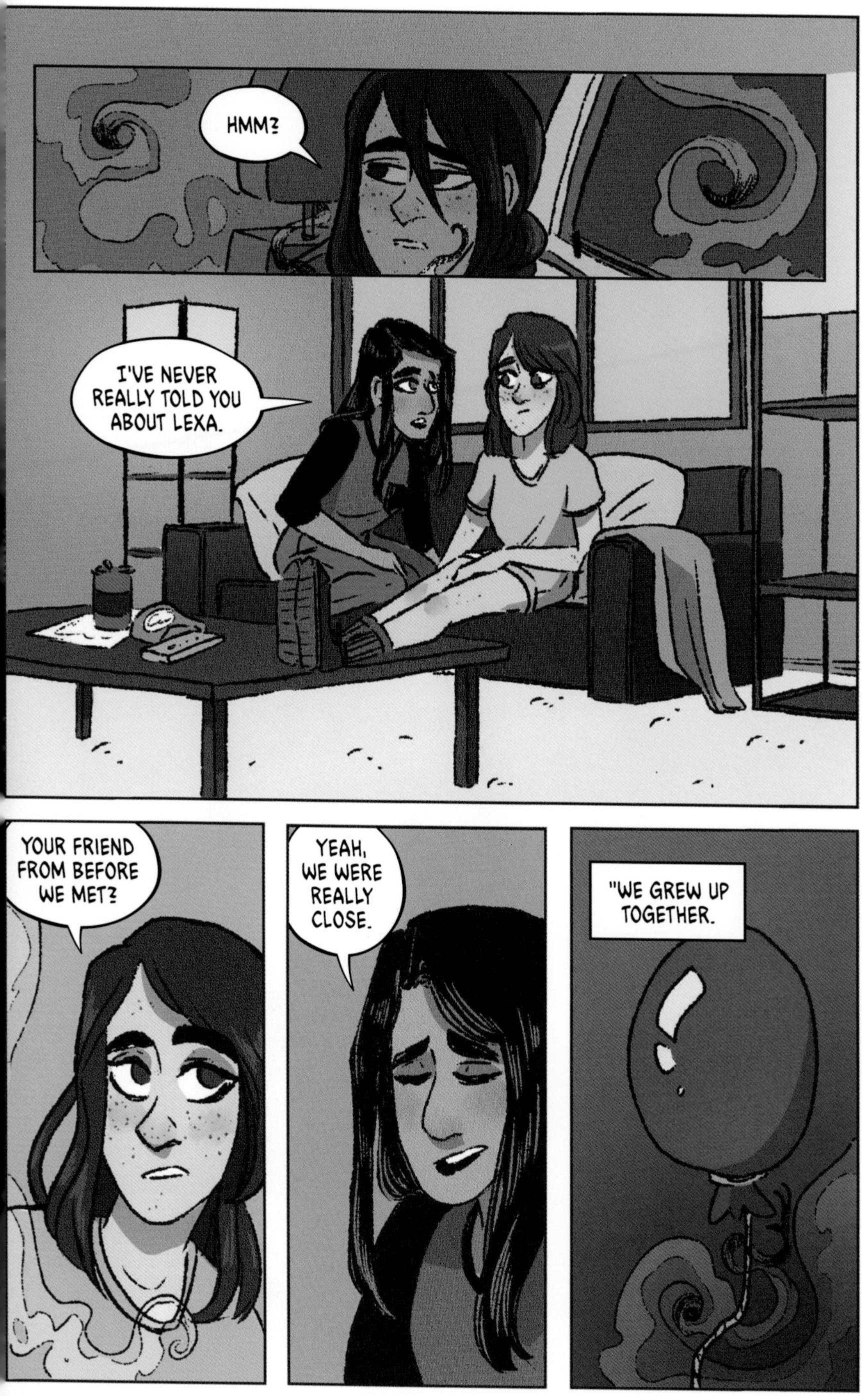
HMM?
I'VE NEVER REALLY TOLD YOU ABOUT LEXA.
YOUR FRIEND FROM BEFORE WE MET?
YEAH, WE WERE REALLY CLOSE.
"WE GREW UP TOGETHER.

"BUT IN HIGH
SCHOOL, SHE WAS
DEPRESSED.

"SHE WAS GOING
THROUGH A
ROUGH TIME.

"I TRIED
TO HELP
HER, BUT...

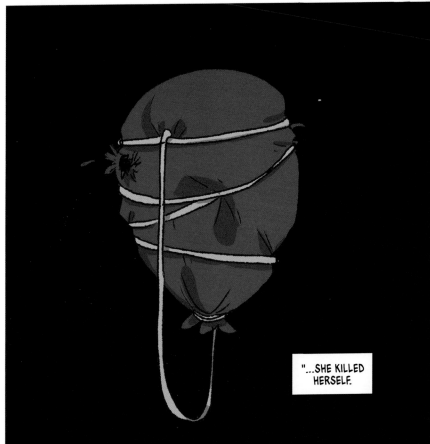

"...SHE KILLED
HERSELF.

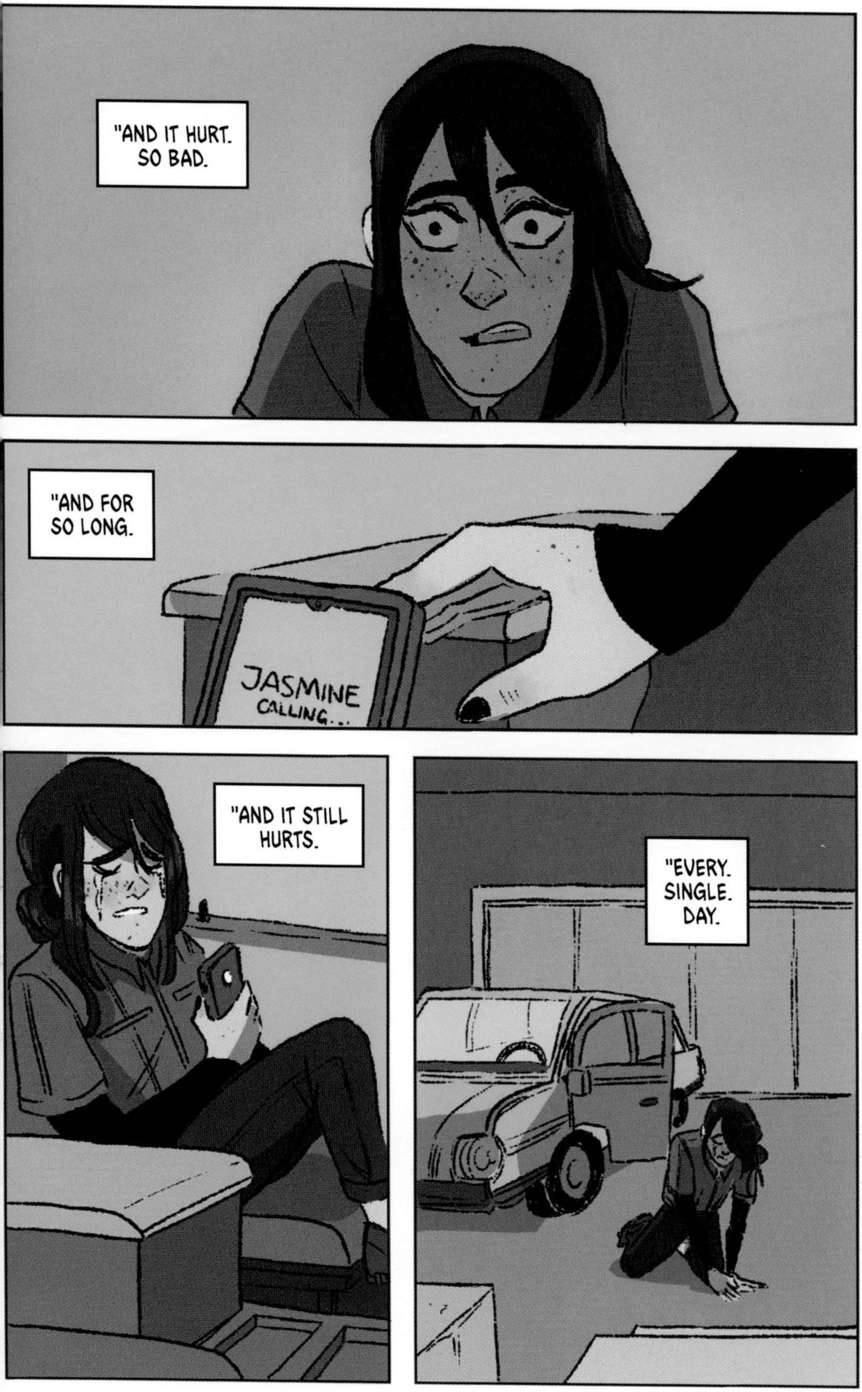
"AND IT HURT. SO BAD.
"AND FOR SO LONG.
JASMINE CALLING...
"AND IT STILL HURTS.
"EVERY. SINGLE. DAY.

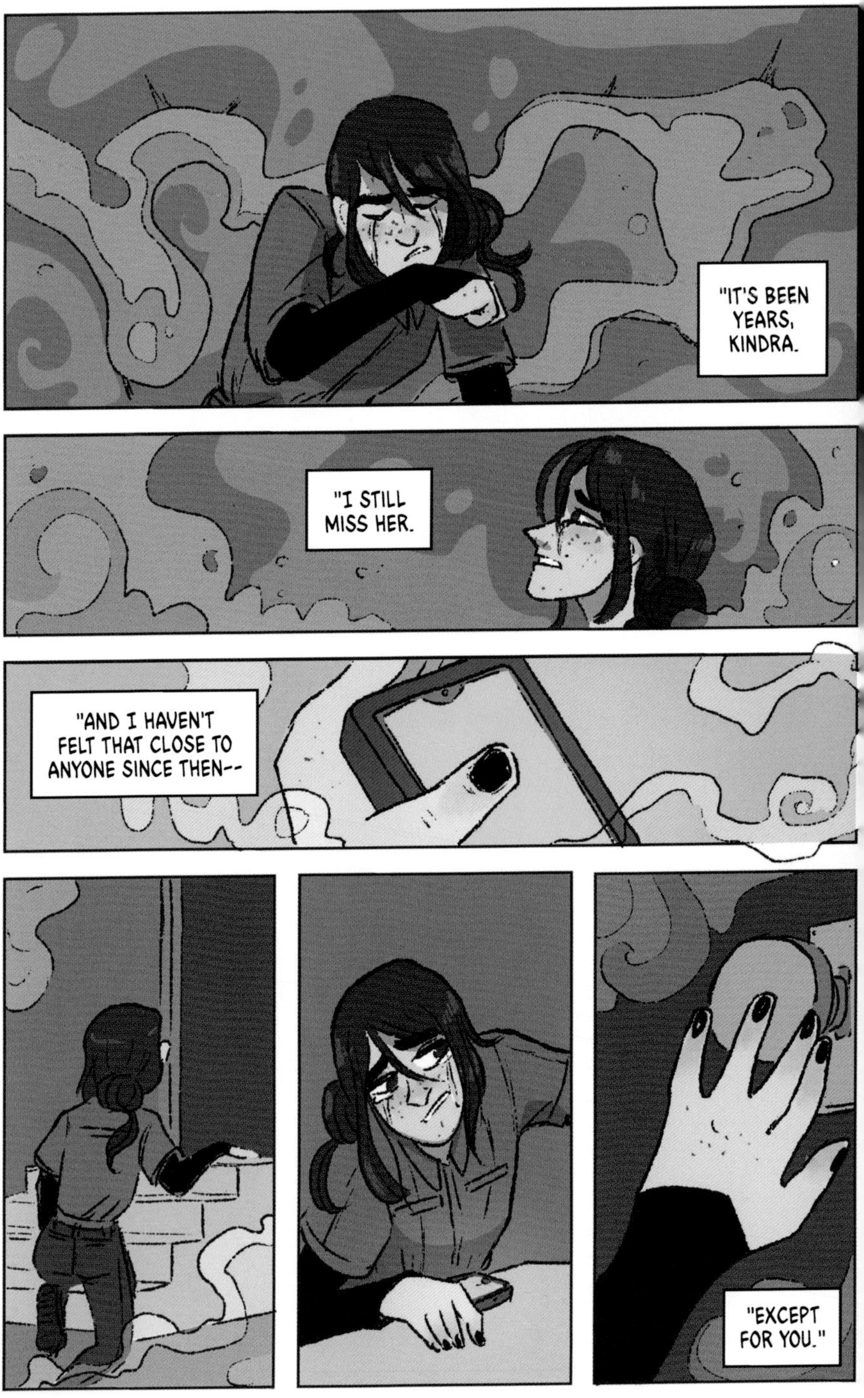
"IT'S BEEN YEARS, KINDRA.
"I STILL MISS HER.
"AND I HAVEN'T FELT THAT CLOSE TO ANYONE SINCE THEN--
"EXCEPT FOR YOU."

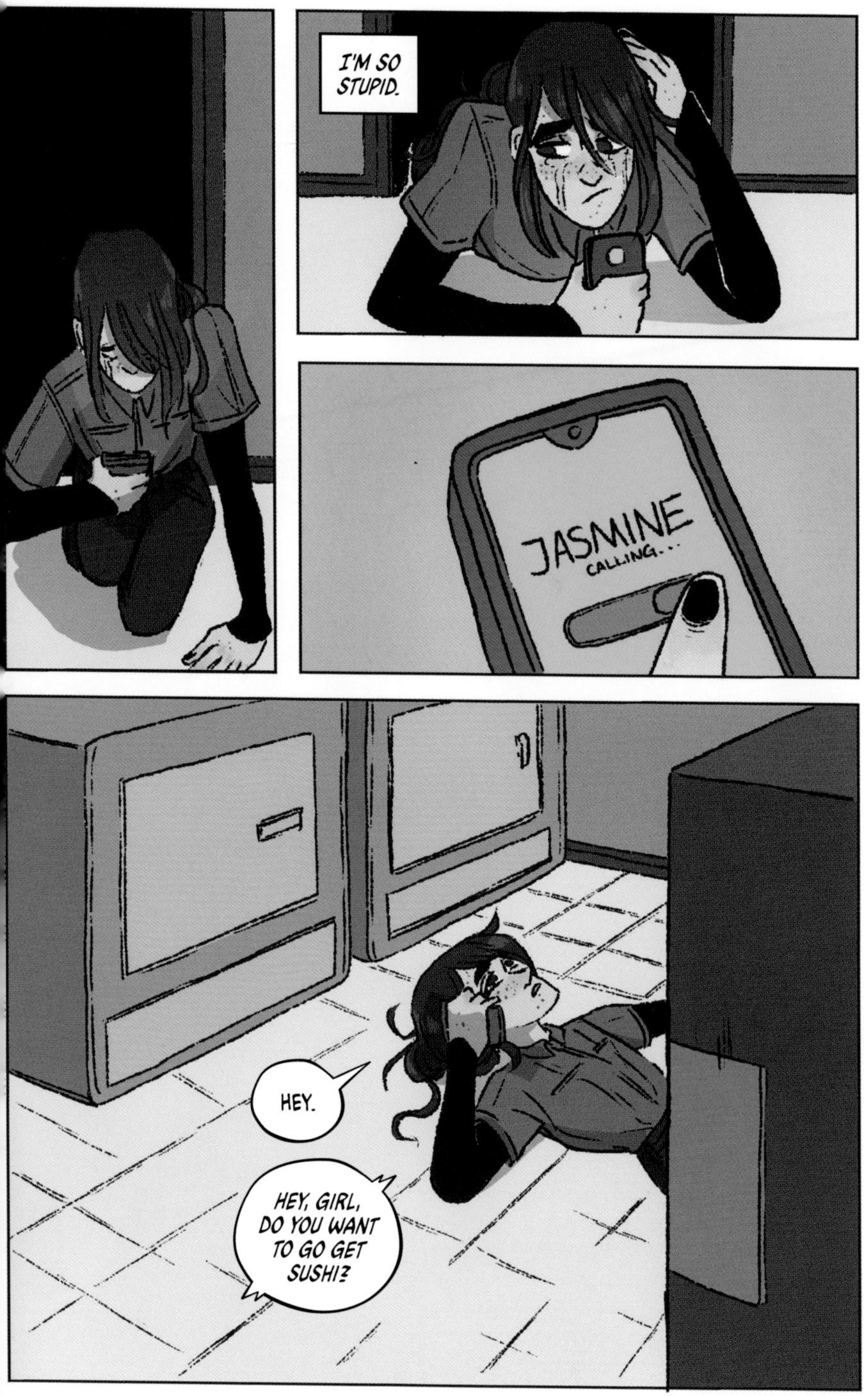
I'M SO STUPID.
JASMINE
CALLING...
HEY.
HEY, GIRL, DO YOU WANT TO GO GET SUSHI?

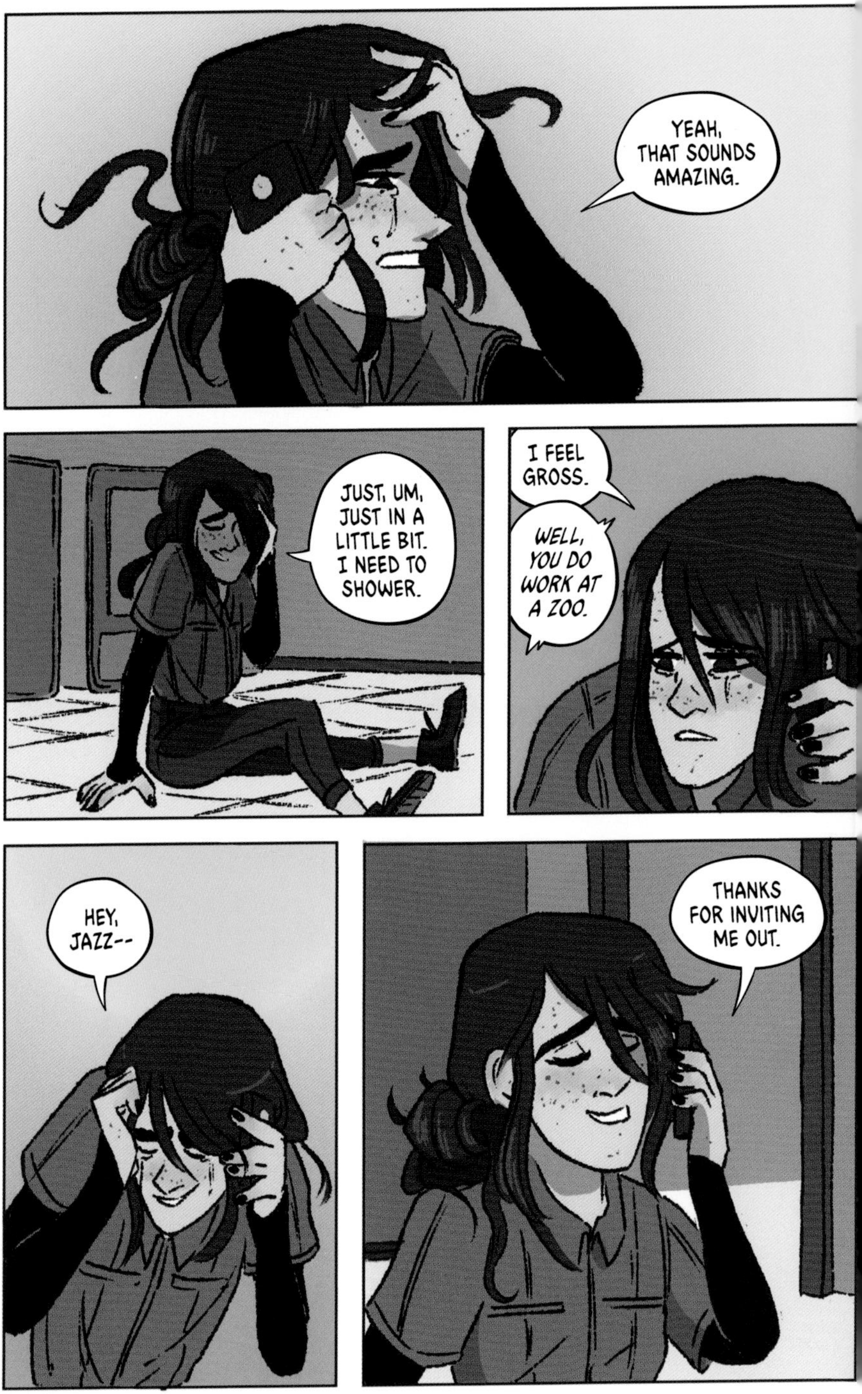
YEAH, THAT SOUNDS AMAZING.
JUST, UM, JUST IN A LITTLE BIT. I NEED TO SHOWER.
I FEEL GROSS.
WELL, YOU DO WORK AT A ZOO.
HEY, JAZZ--
THANKS FOR INVITING ME OUT.

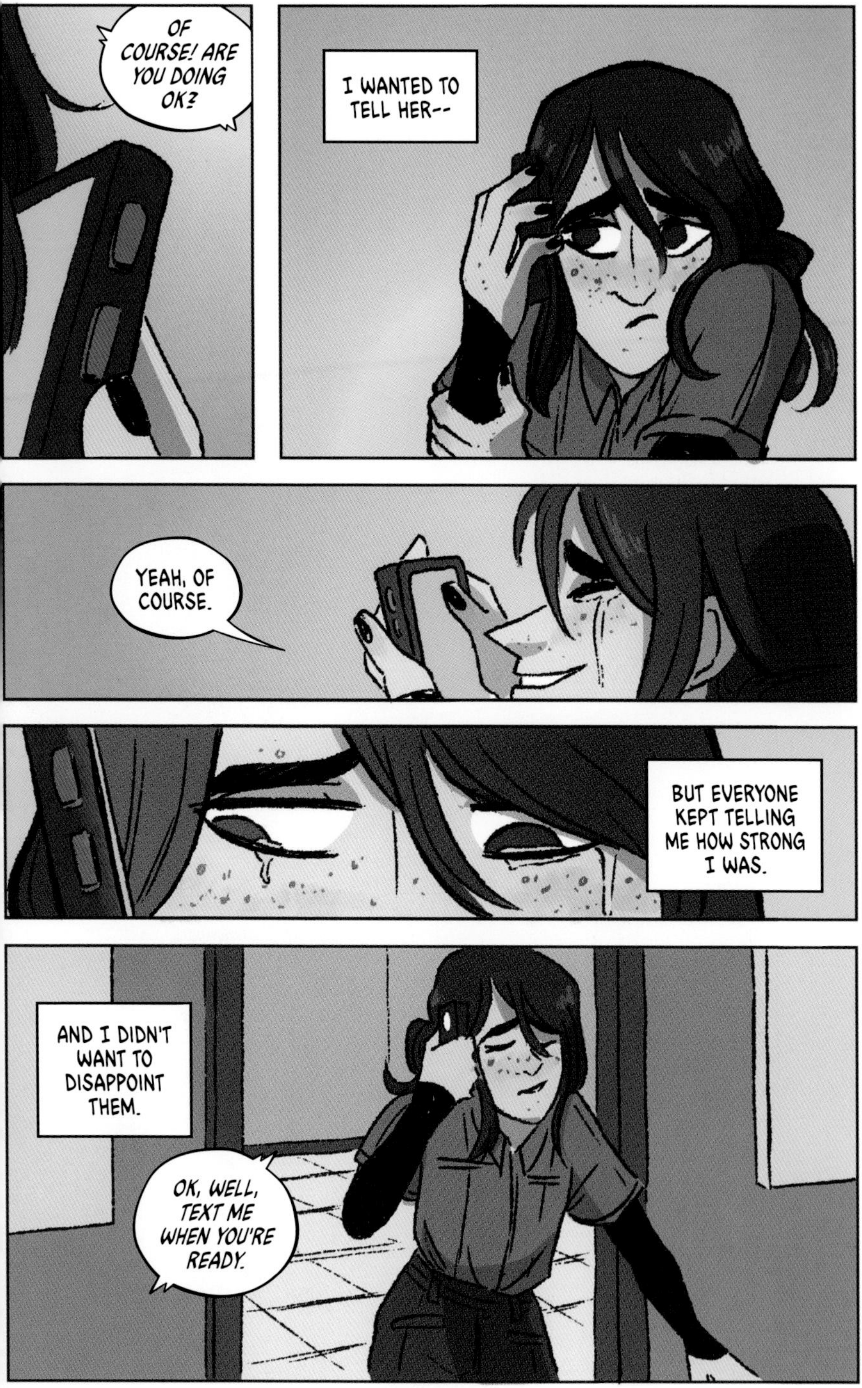
OF COURSE! ARE YOU DOING OK?
I WANTED TO TELL HER--
YEAH, OF COURSE.
BUT EVERYONE KEPT TELLING ME HOW STRONG I WAS.
AND I DIDN'T WANT TO DISAPPOINT THEM.
OK, WELL, TEXT ME WHEN YOU'RE READY.

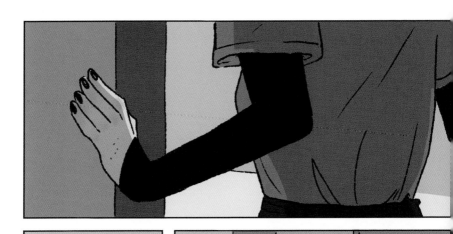

I'M NOT STRONG; LOOK AT WHAT I'VE DONE.

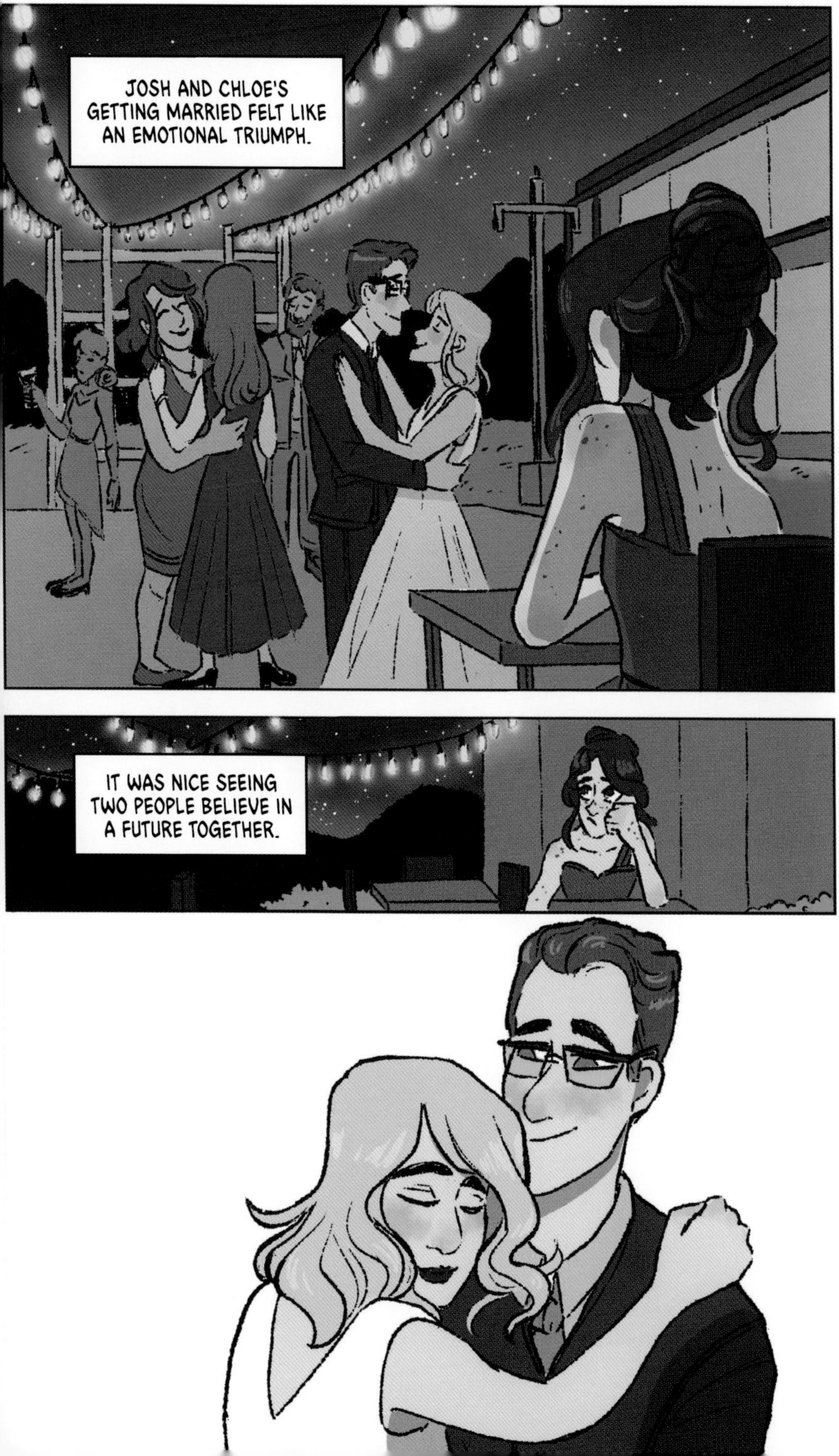
JOSH AND CHLOE'S GETTING MARRIED FELT LIKE AN EMOTIONAL TRIUMPH.
IT WAS NICE SEEING TWO PEOPLE BELIEVE IN A FUTURE TOGETHER.

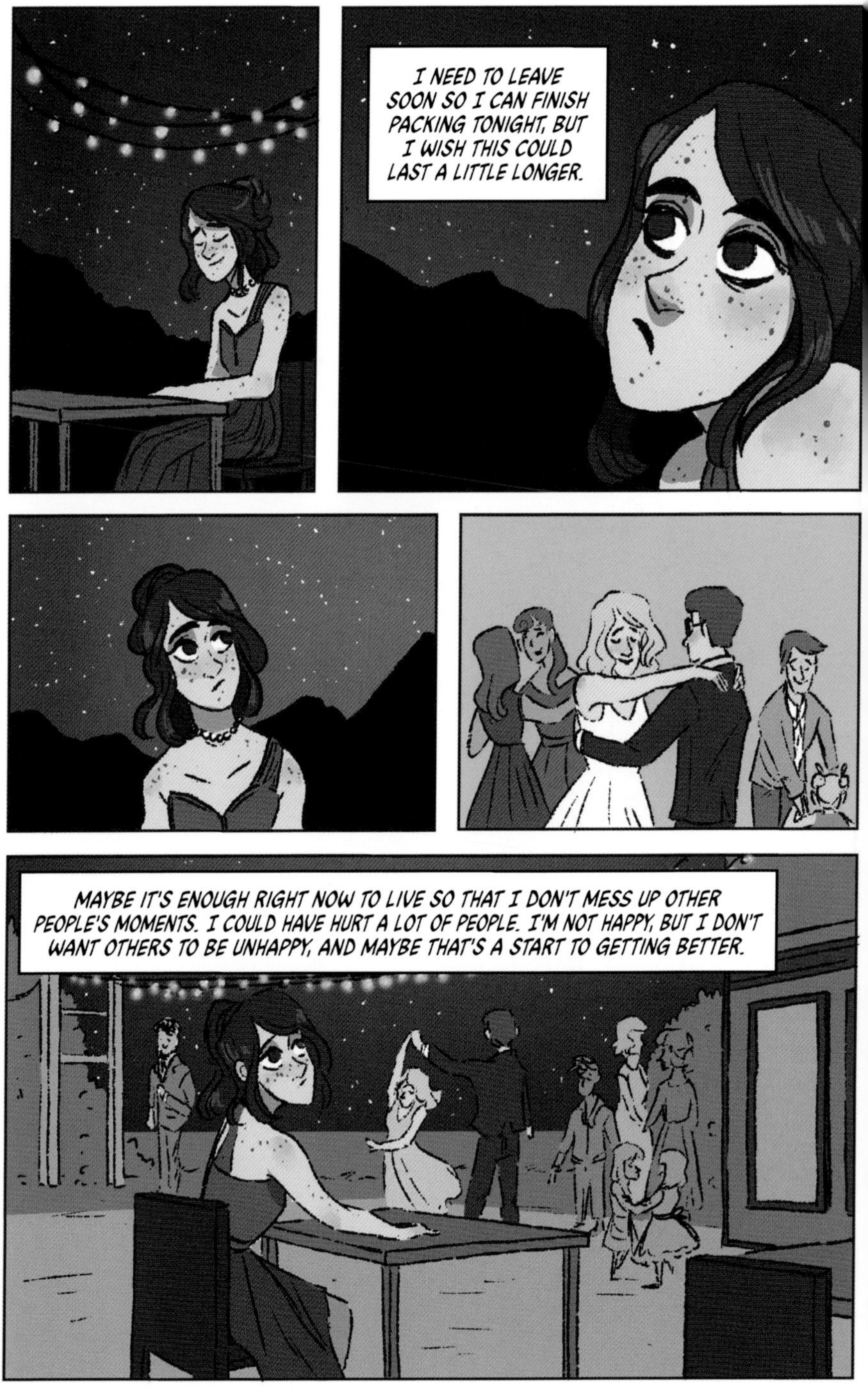
I NEED TO LEAVE SOON SO I CAN FINISH PACKING TONIGHT, BUT I WISH THIS COULD LAST A LITTLE LONGER.
MAYBE IT'S ENOUGH RIGHT NOW TO LIVE SO THAT I DON'T MESS UP OTHER PEOPLE'S MOMENTS. I COULD HAVE HURT A LOT OF PEOPLE. I'M NOT HAPPY, BUT I DON'T WANT OTHERS TO BE UNHAPPY, AND MAYBE THAT'S A START TO GETTING BETTER.

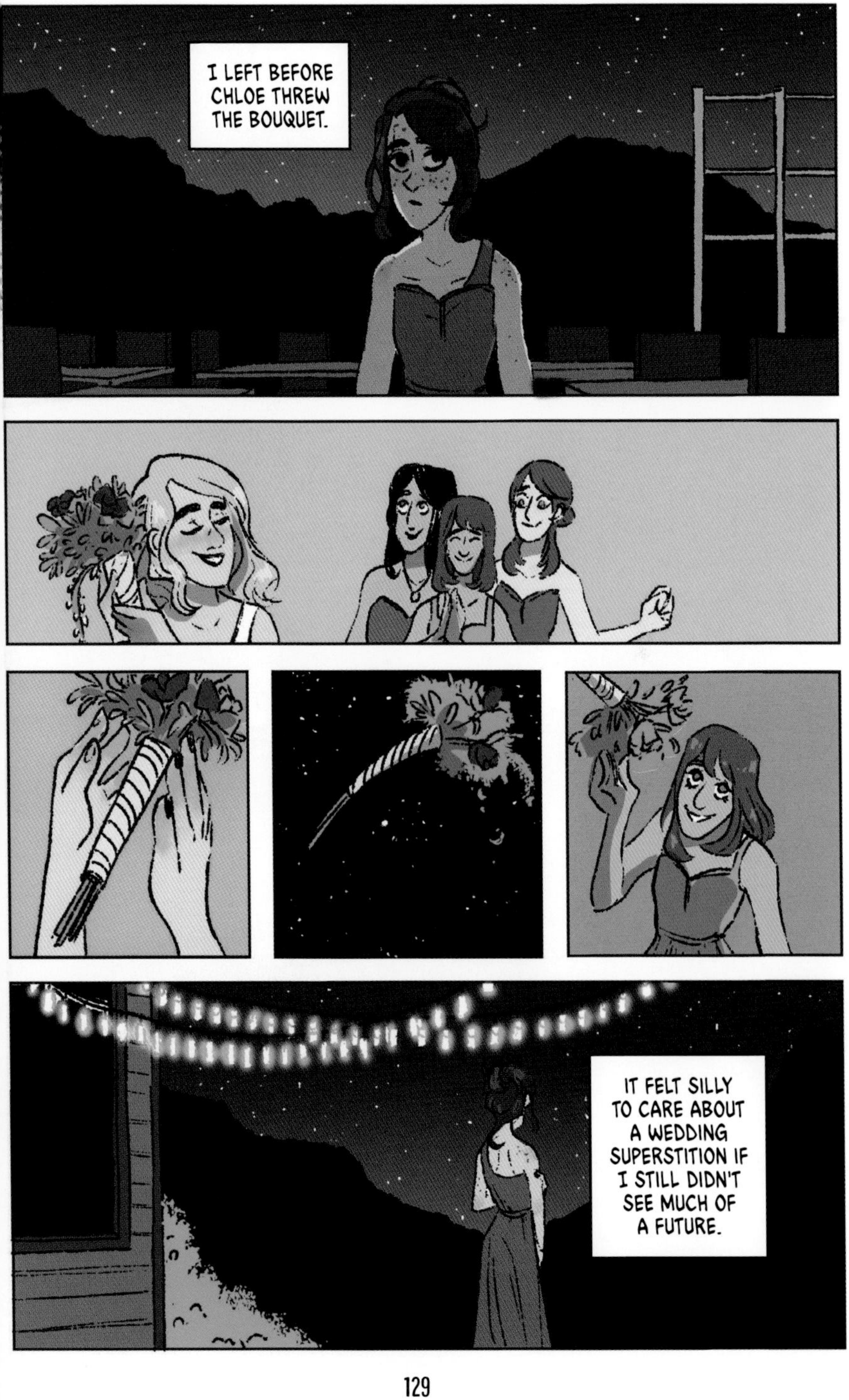
I LEFT BEFORE CHLOE THREW THE BOUQUET.
IT FELT SILLY TO CARE ABOUT A WEDDING SUPERSTITION IF I STILL DIDN'T SEE MUCH OF A FUTURE.

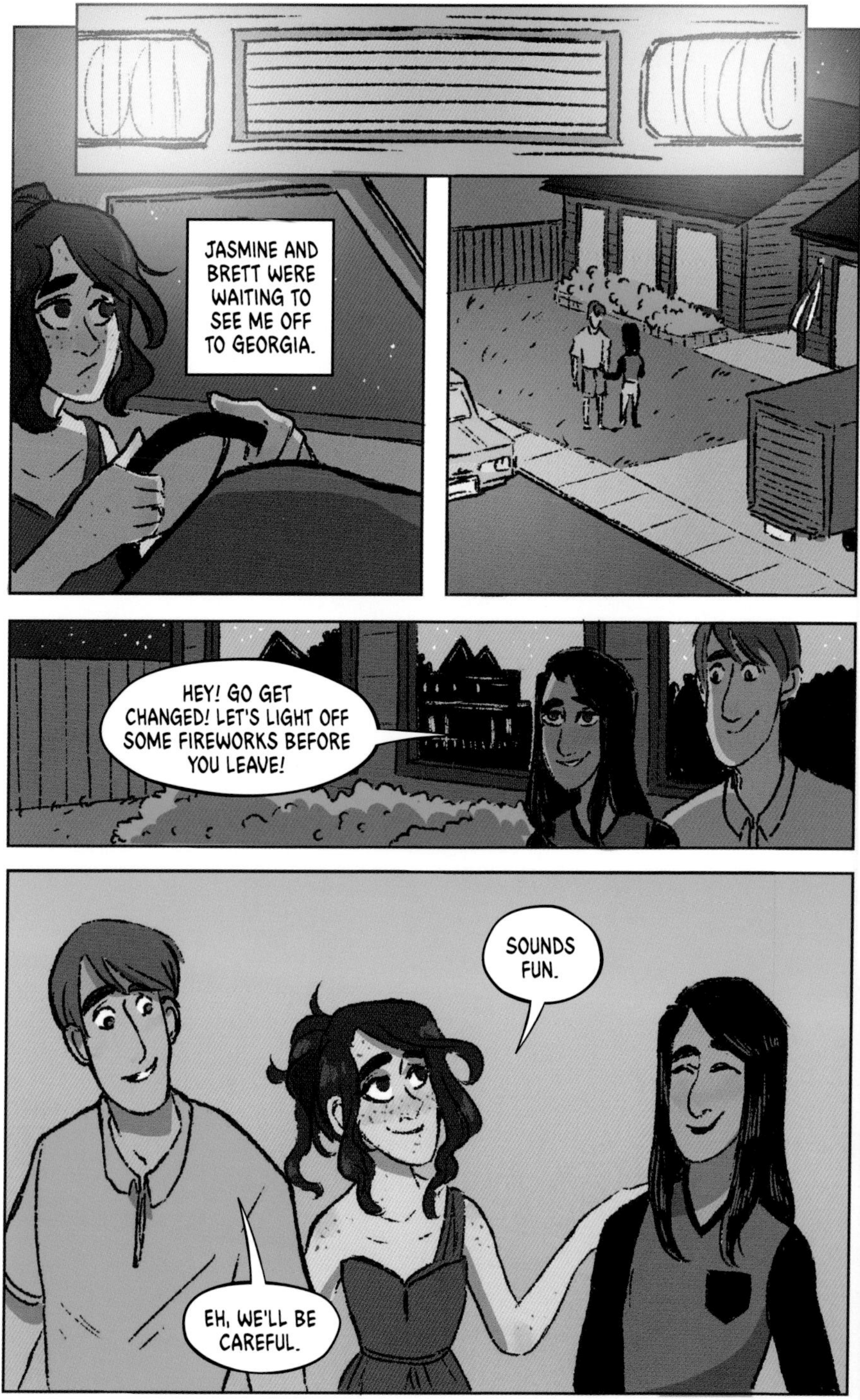
JASMINE AND BRETT WERE WAITING TO SEE ME OFF TO GEORGIA.
HEY! GO GET CHANGED! LET'S LIGHT OFF SOME FIREWORKS BEFORE YOU LEAVE!
SOUNDS FUN.
EH, WE'LL BE CAREFUL.

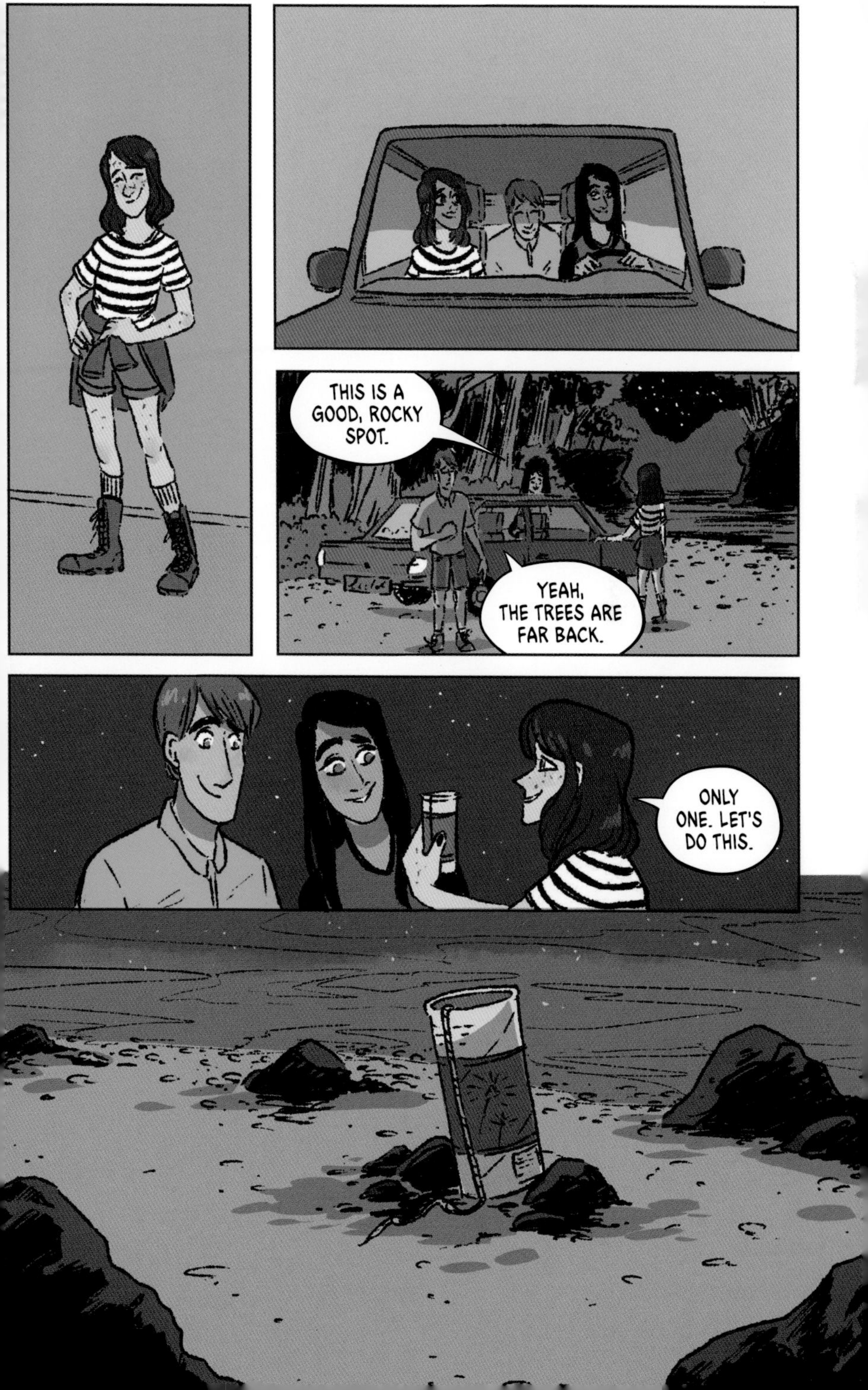
THIS IS A GOOD, ROCKY SPOT.
YEAH, THE TREES ARE FAR BACK.
ONLY ONE. LET'S DO THIS.

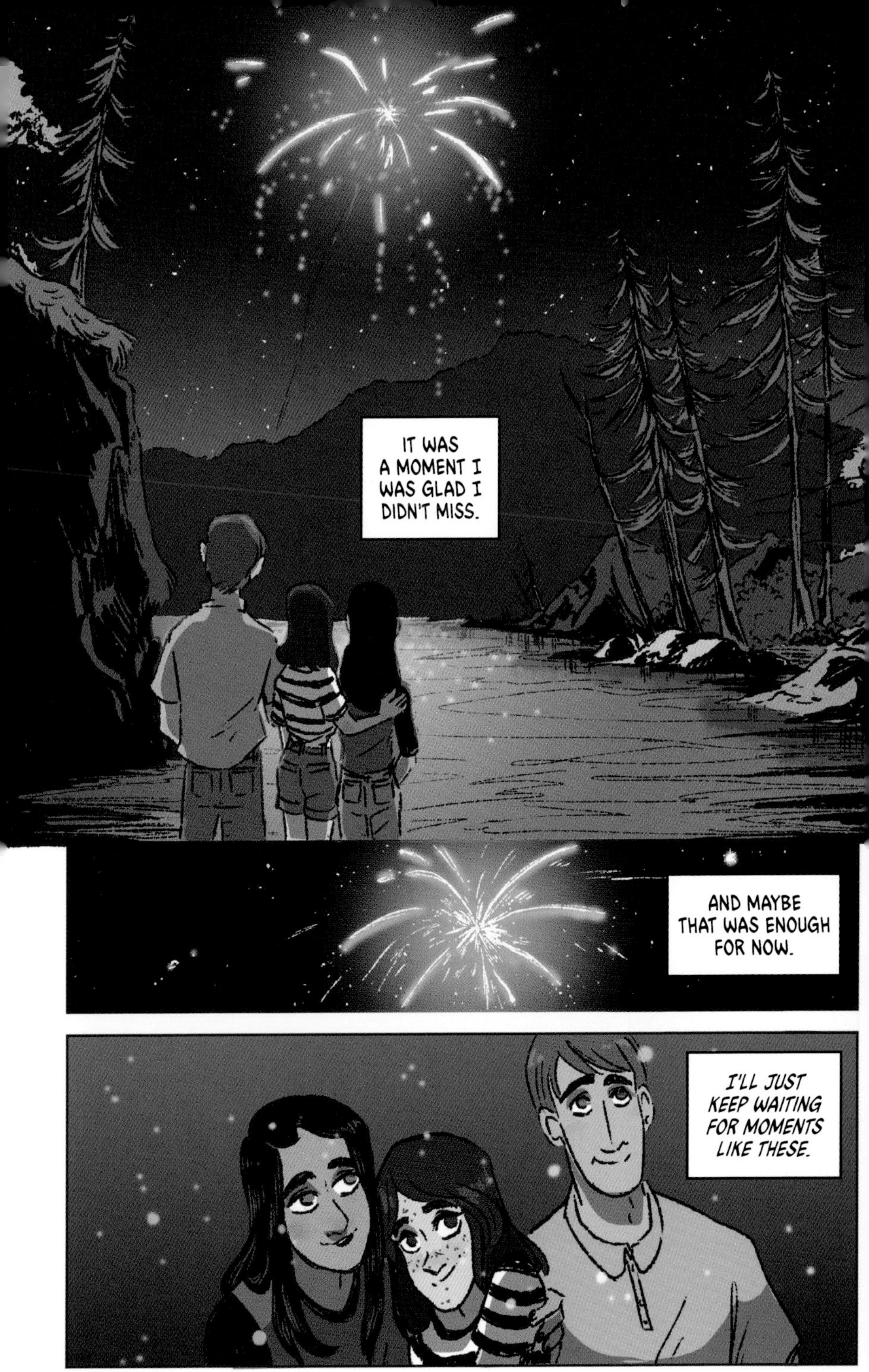
IT WAS A MOMENT I WAS GLAD I DIDN'T MISS.
AND MAYBE THAT WAS ENOUGH FOR NOW.
I'LL JUST KEEP WAITING FOR MOMENTS LIKE THESE.

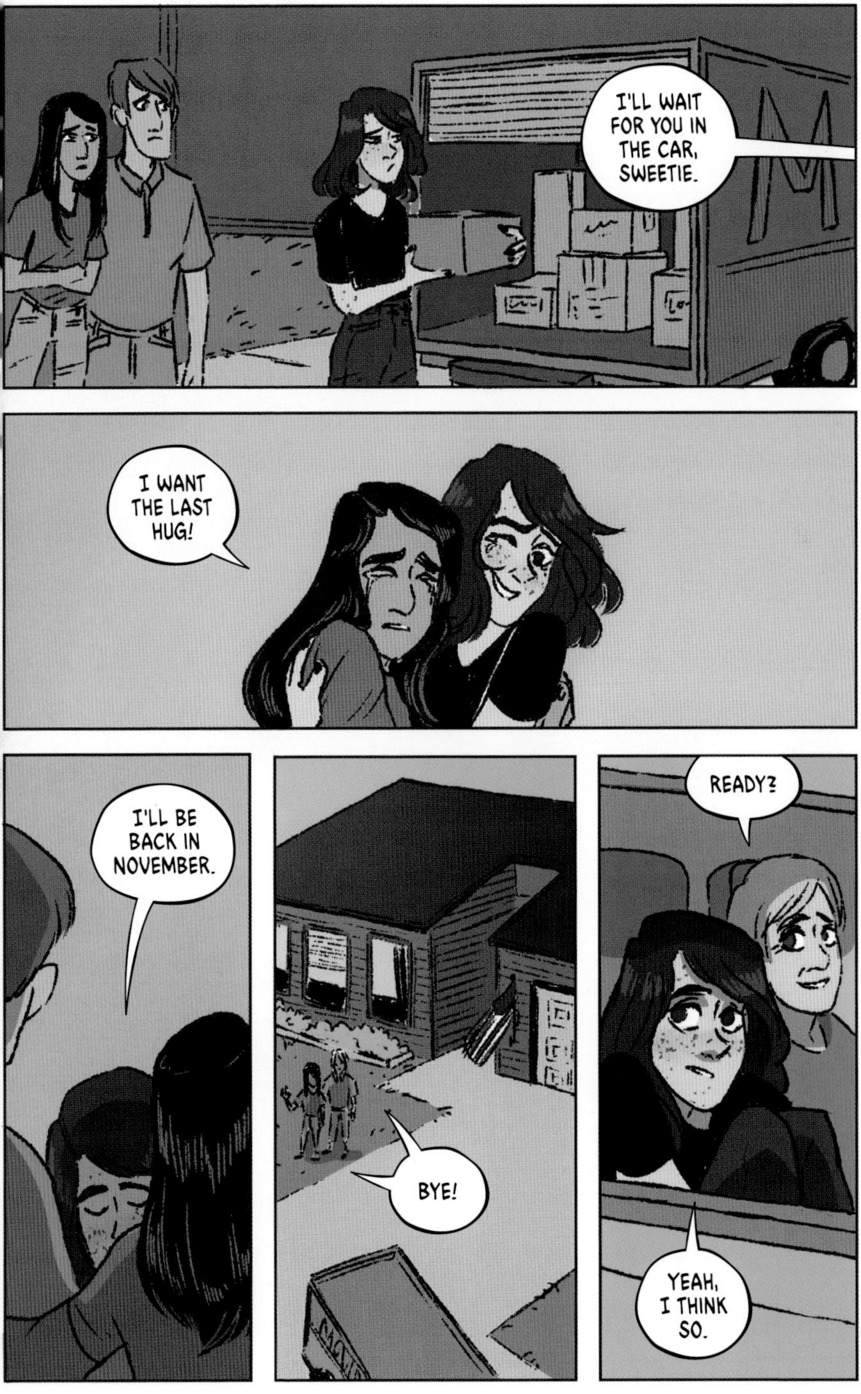
I'LL WAIT FOR YOU IN THE CAR, SWEETIE.
I WANT THE LAST HUG!
I'LL BE BACK IN NOVEMBER.
BYE!
READY?
YEAH, I THINK SO.

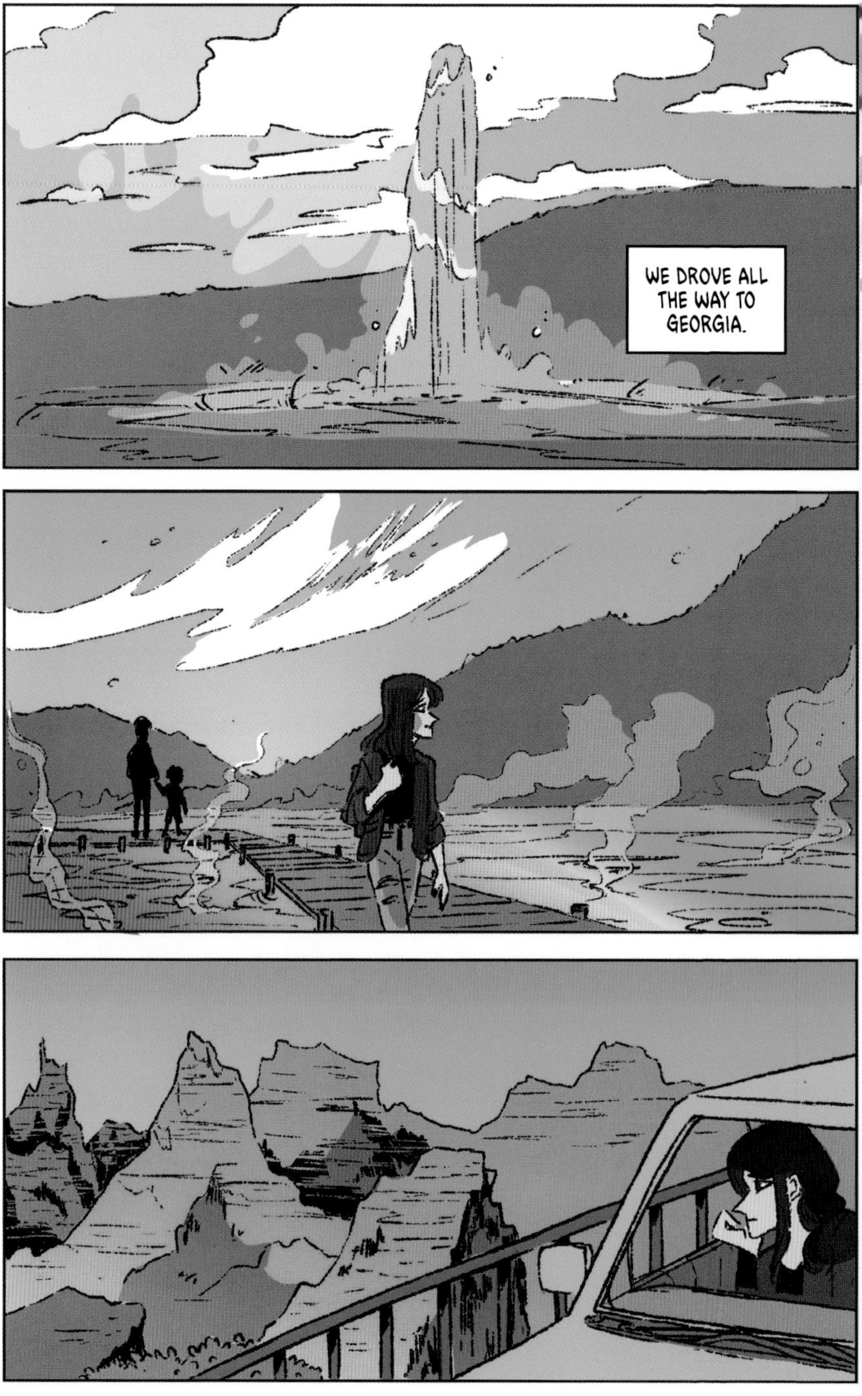
WE DROVE ALL THE WAY TO GEORGIA.

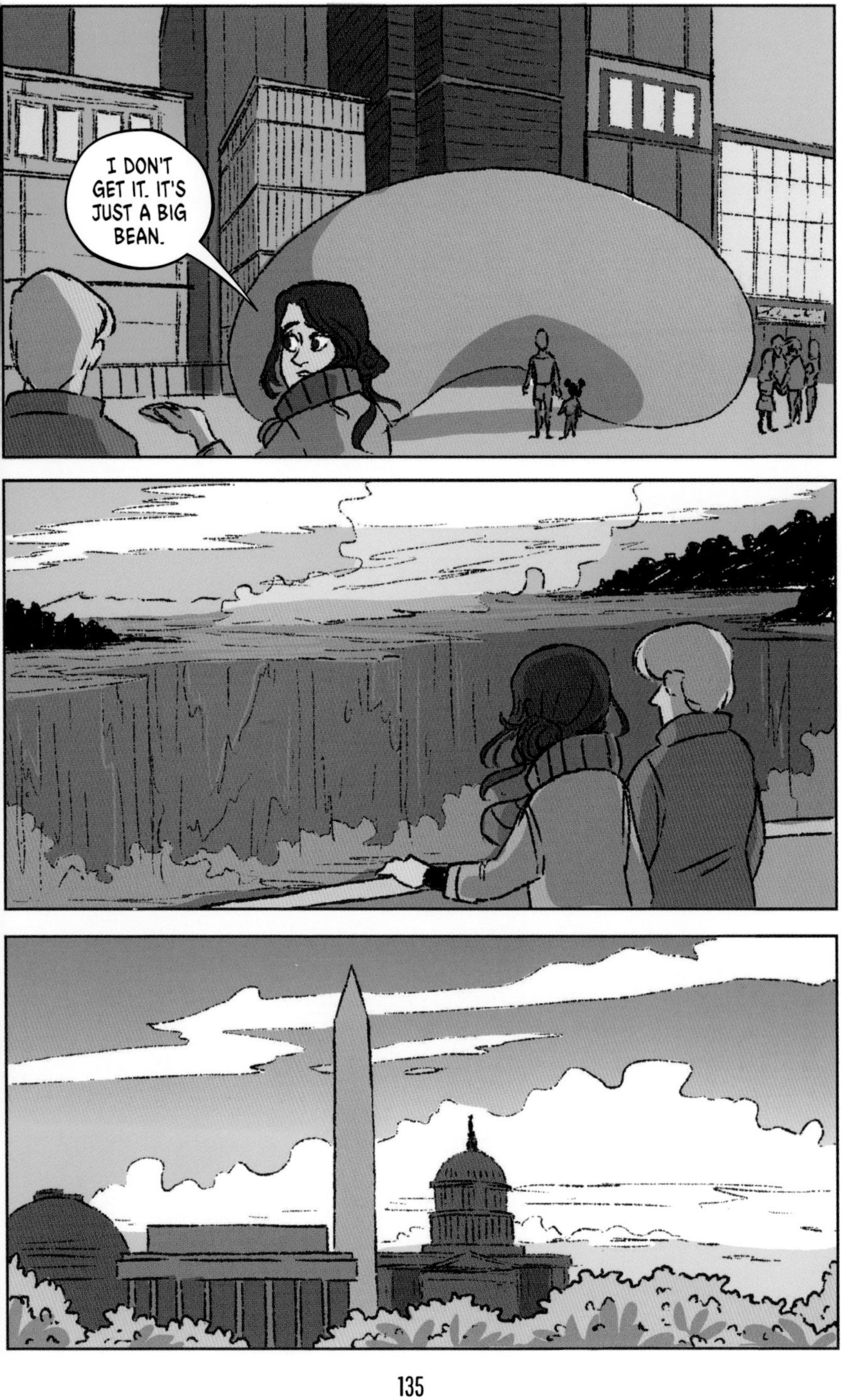
I DON'T GET IT. IT'S JUST A BIG BEAN.

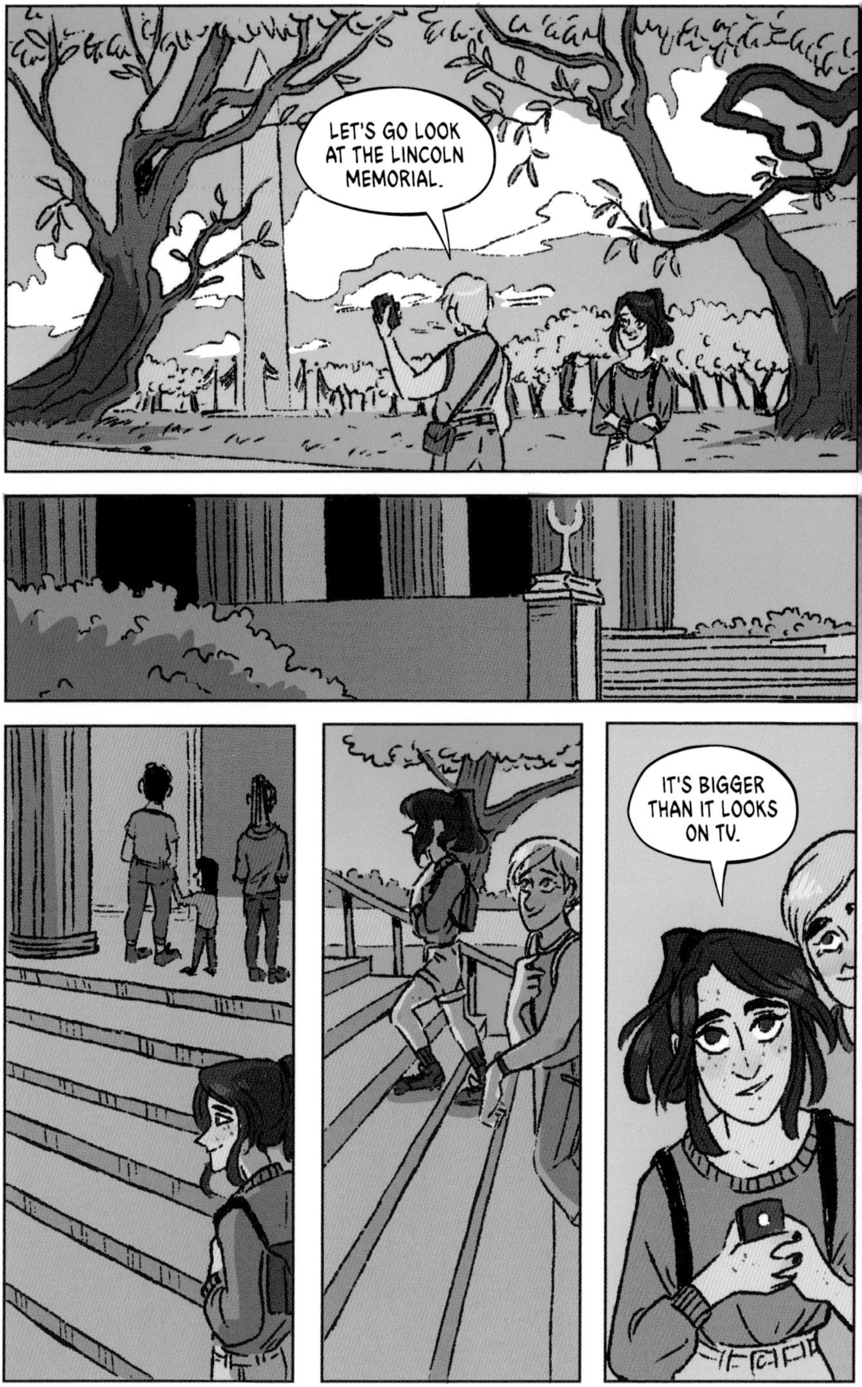
LET'S GO LOOK AT THE LINCOLN MEMORIAL.
IT'S BIGGER THAN IT LOOKS ON TV.

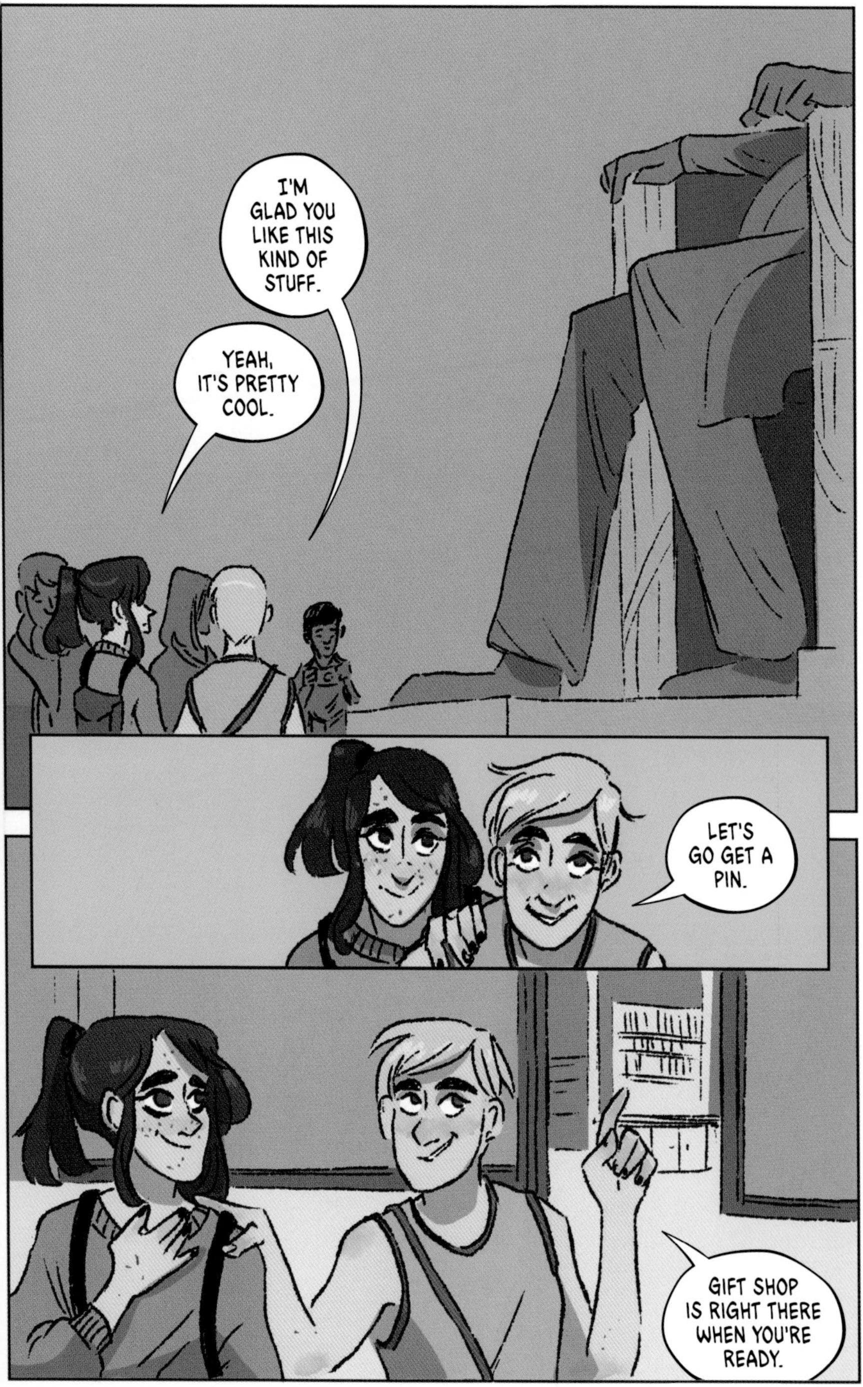
I'M GLAD YOU LIKE THIS KIND OF STUFF.
YEAH, IT'S PRETTY COOL.
LET'S GO GET A PIN.
GIFT SHOP IS RIGHT THERE WHEN YOU'RE READY.

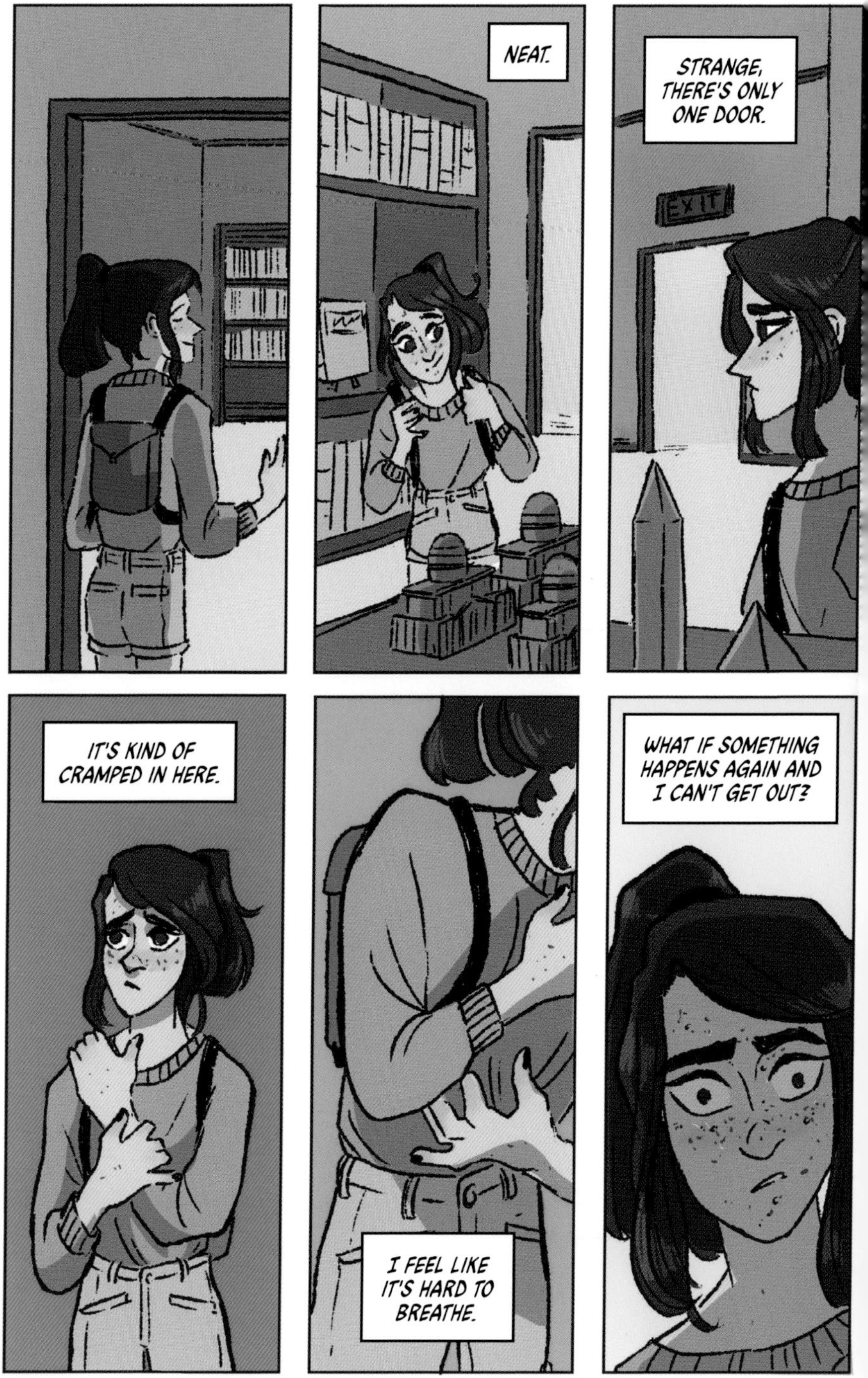
NEAT.
STRANGE, THERE'S ONLY ONE DOOR.
EXIT
IT'S KIND OF CRAMPED IN HERE.
I FEEL LIKE IT'S HARD TO BREATHE.
WHAT IF SOMETHING HAPPENS AGAIN AND I CAN'T GET OUT?

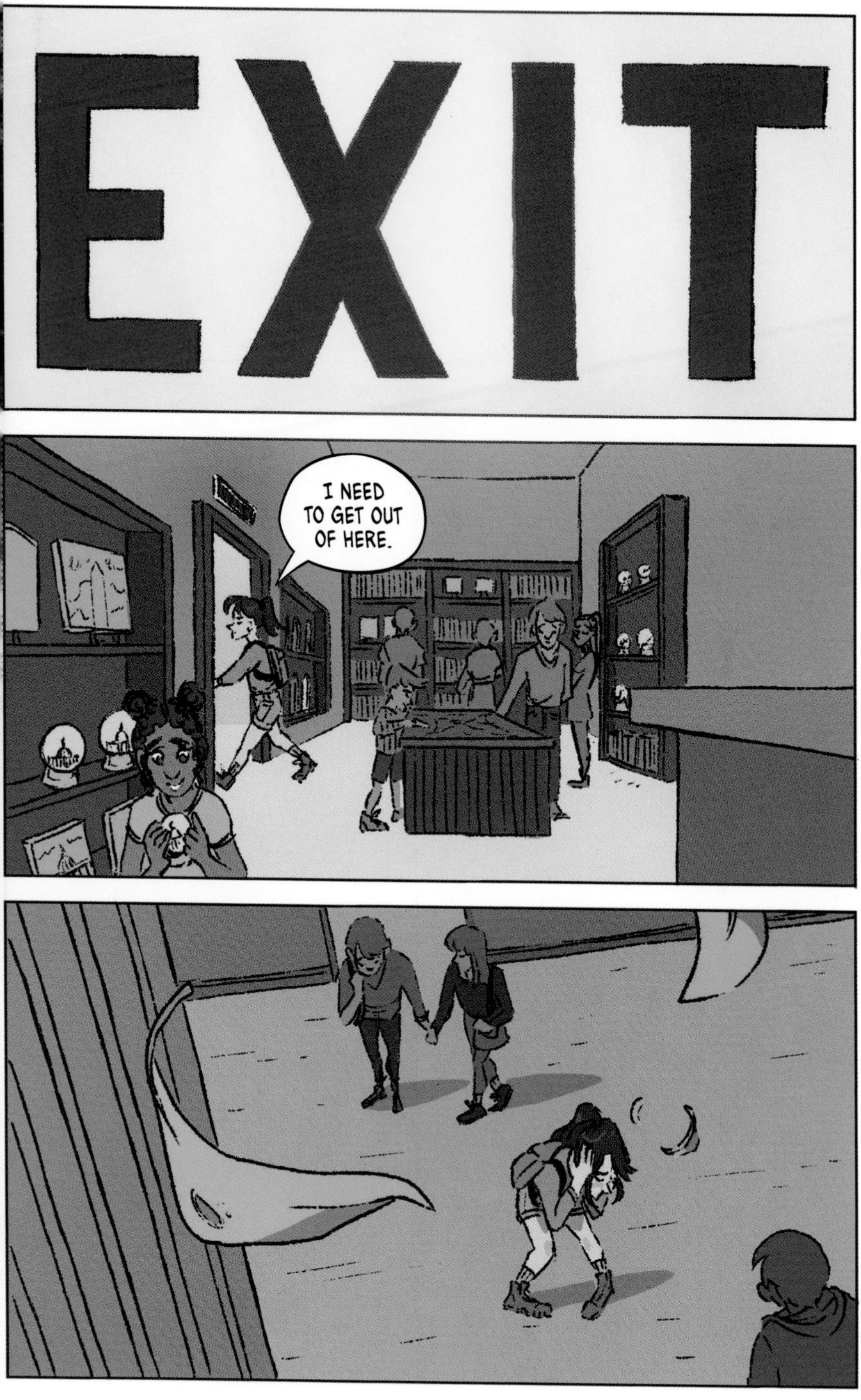
EXIT
I NEED TO GET OUT OF HERE.

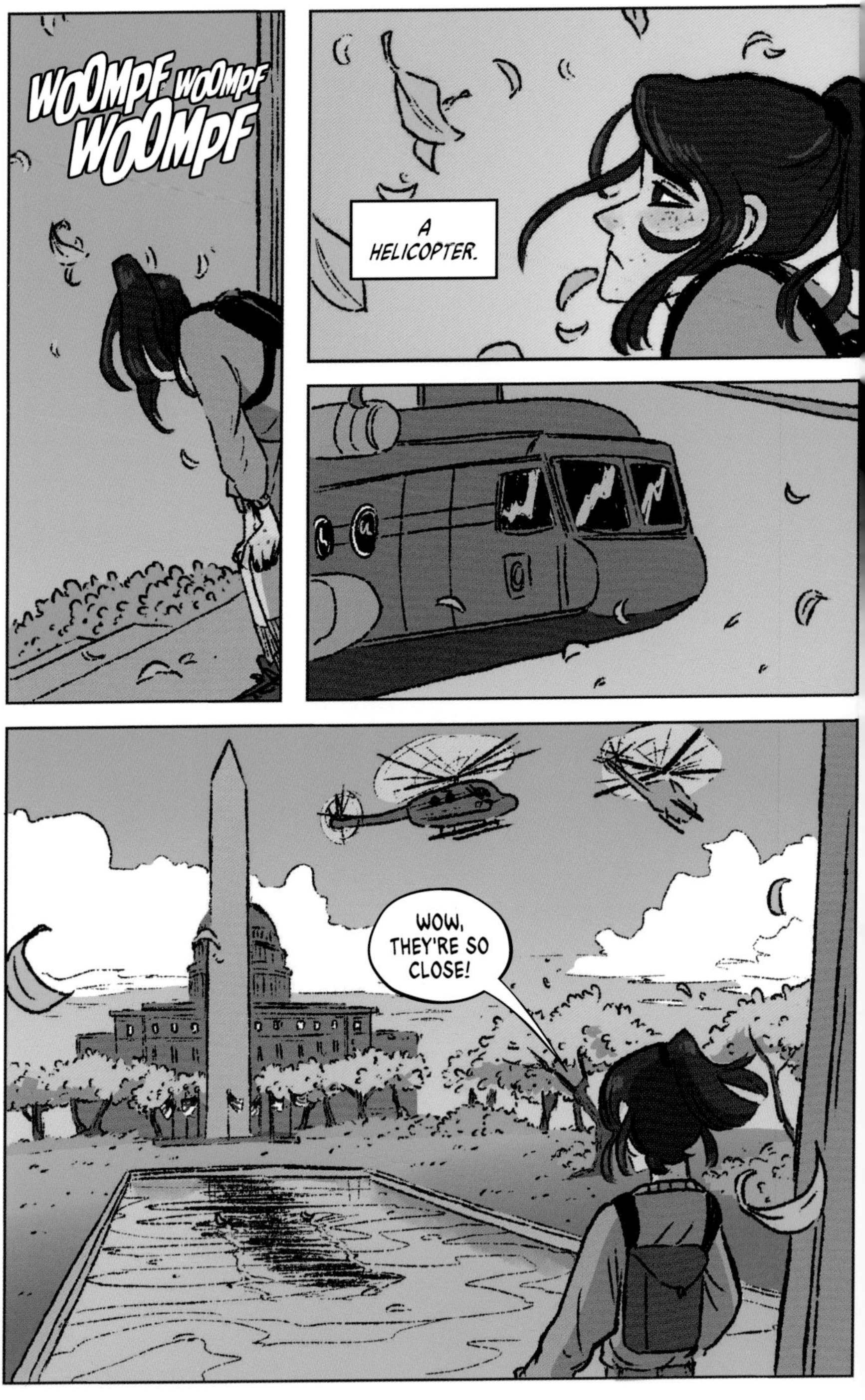
WOOMPF WOOMPF
WOOMPF
A HELICOPTER.
WOW, THEY'RE SO CLOSE!

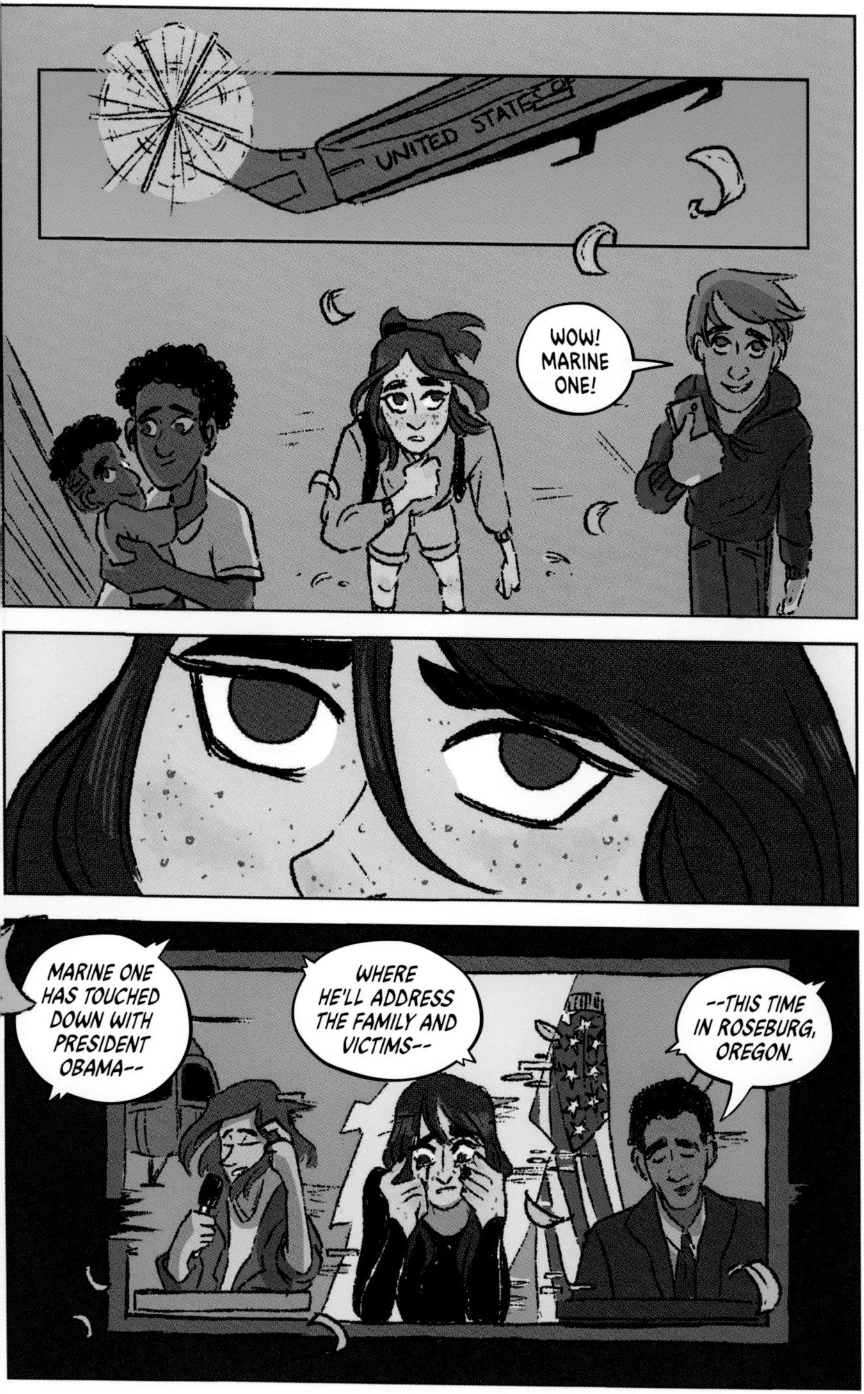
UNITED STATES
WOW! MARINE ONE!
MARINE ONE HAS TOUCHED DOWN WITH PRESIDENT OBAMA--
WHERE HE'LL ADDRESS THE FAMILY AND VICTIMS--
--THIS TIME IN ROSEBURG, OREGON.

SOMEHOW, WE'VE BECOME NUMB TO THIS.

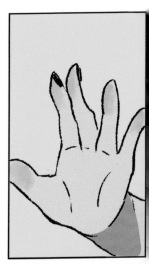

HEY, KIDDO. WOW, MARINE ONE!

WHAT?

OH, UH, YEAH.

LITTLE CROWDED IN THERE?

YEAH.

HEY, DO YOU REMEMBER WHEN OBAMA CAME TO ROSEBURG?

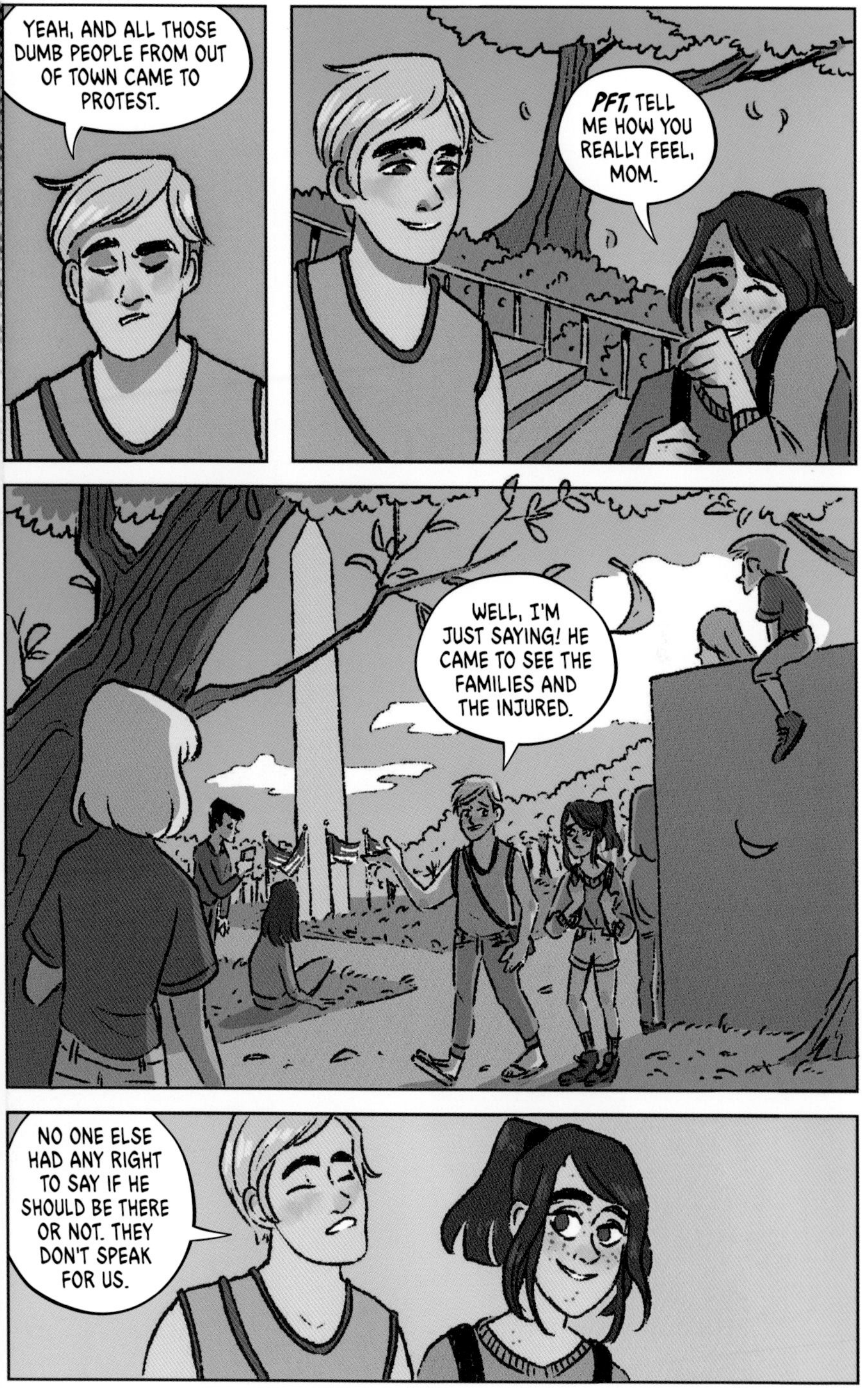
YEAH, AND ALL THOSE DUMB PEOPLE FROM OUT OF TOWN CAME TO PROTEST.
PFT, TELL ME HOW YOU REALLY FEEL, MOM.
WELL, I'M JUST SAYING! HE CAME TO SEE THE FAMILIES AND THE INJURED.
NO ONE ELSE HAD ANY RIGHT TO SAY IF HE SHOULD BE THERE OR NOT. THEY DON'T SPEAK FOR US.

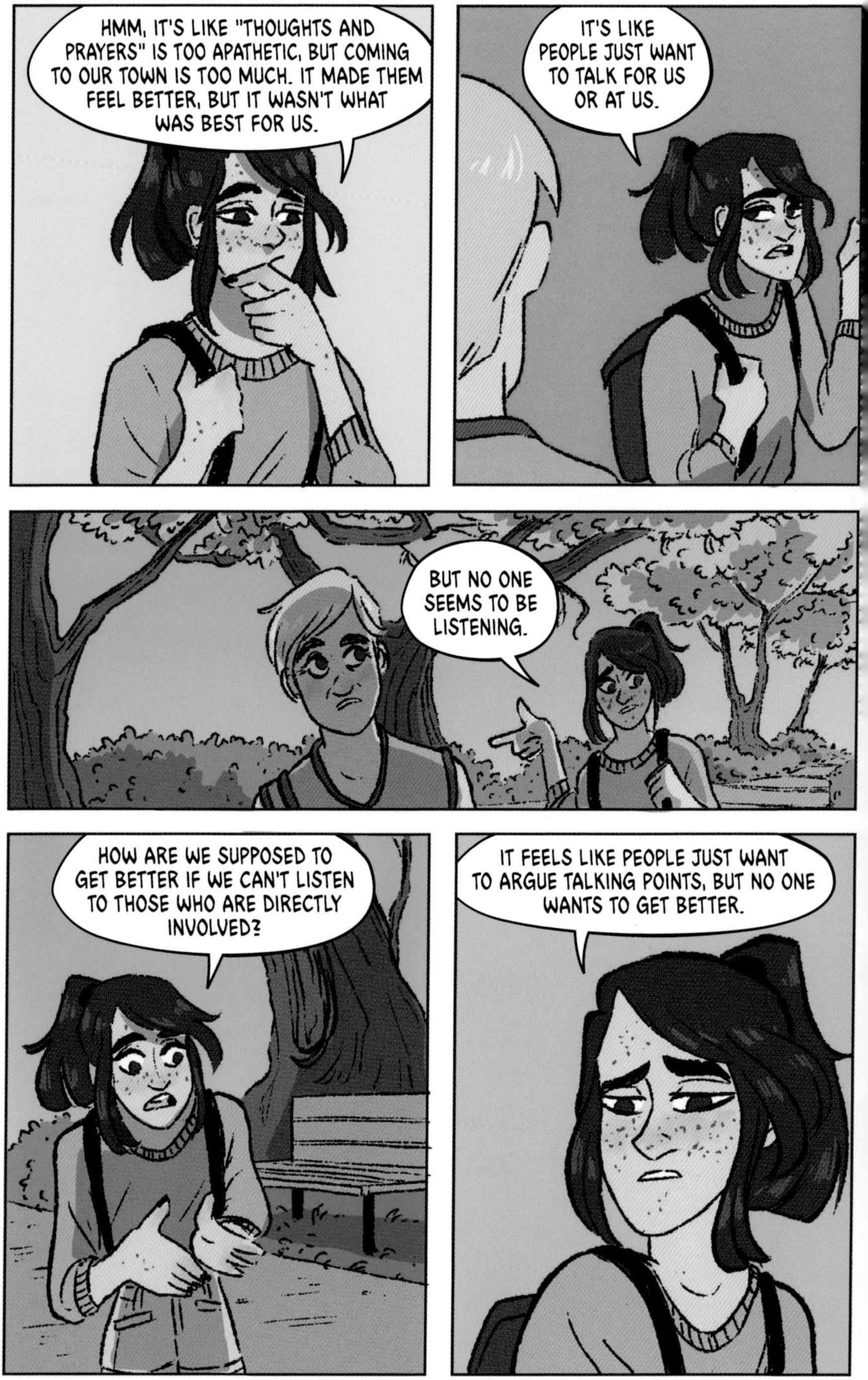
HMM, IT'S LIKE "THOUGHTS AND PRAYERS" IS TOO APATHETIC, BUT COMING TO OUR TOWN IS TOO MUCH. IT MADE THEM FEEL BETTER, BUT IT WASN'T WHAT WAS BEST FOR US.
IT'S LIKE PEOPLE JUST WANT TO TALK FOR US OR AT US.
BUT NO ONE SEEMS TO BE LISTENING.
HOW ARE WE SUPPOSED TO GET BETTER IF WE CAN'T LISTEN TO THOSE WHO ARE DIRECTLY INVOLVED?
IT FEELS LIKE PEOPLE JUST WANT TO ARGUE TALKING POINTS, BUT NO ONE WANTS TO GET BETTER.

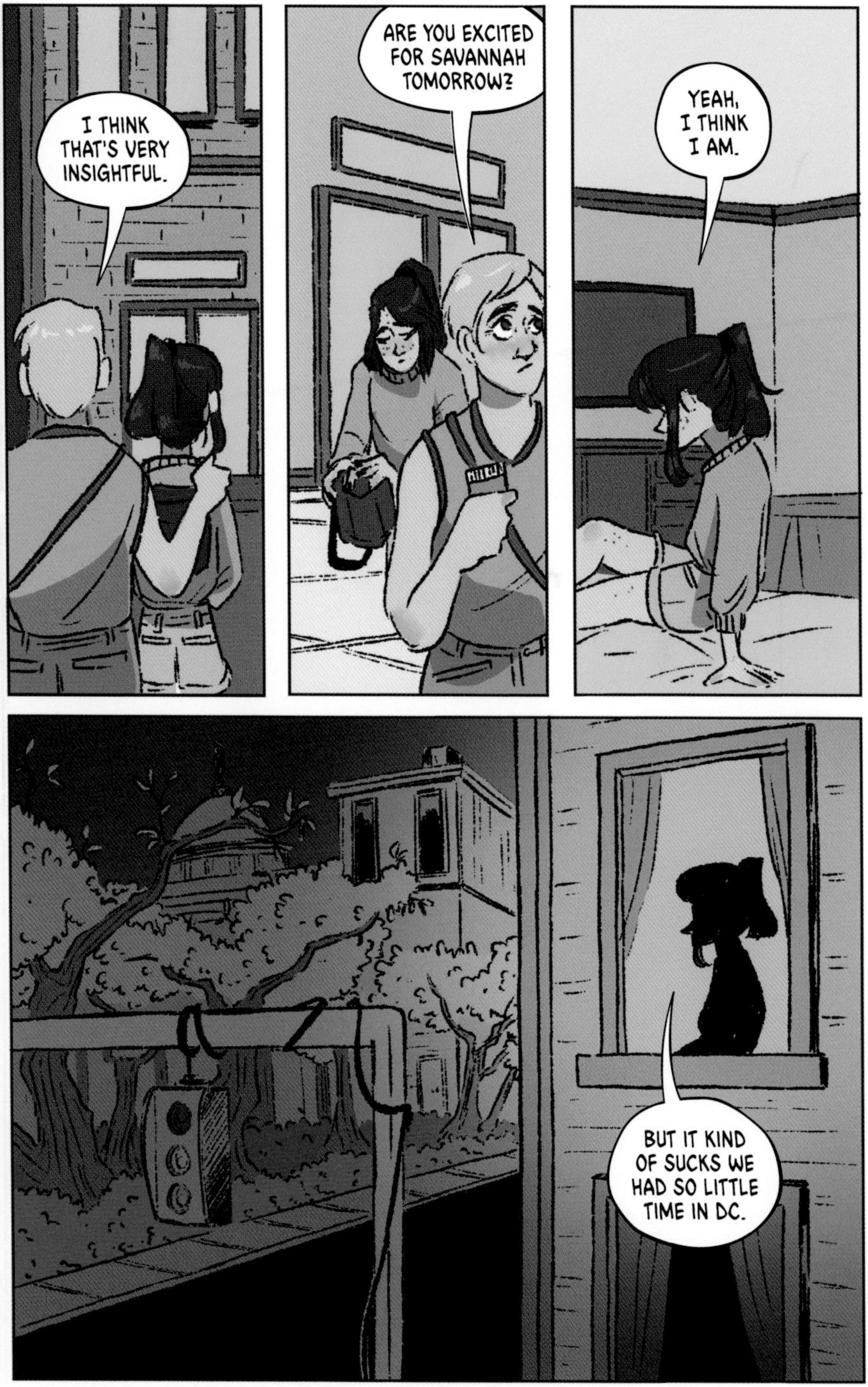
I THINK THAT'S VERY INSIGHTFUL.
ARE YOU EXCITED FOR SAVANNAH TOMORROW?
YEAH, I THINK I AM.
BUT IT KIND OF SUCKS WE HAD SO LITTLE TIME IN DC.

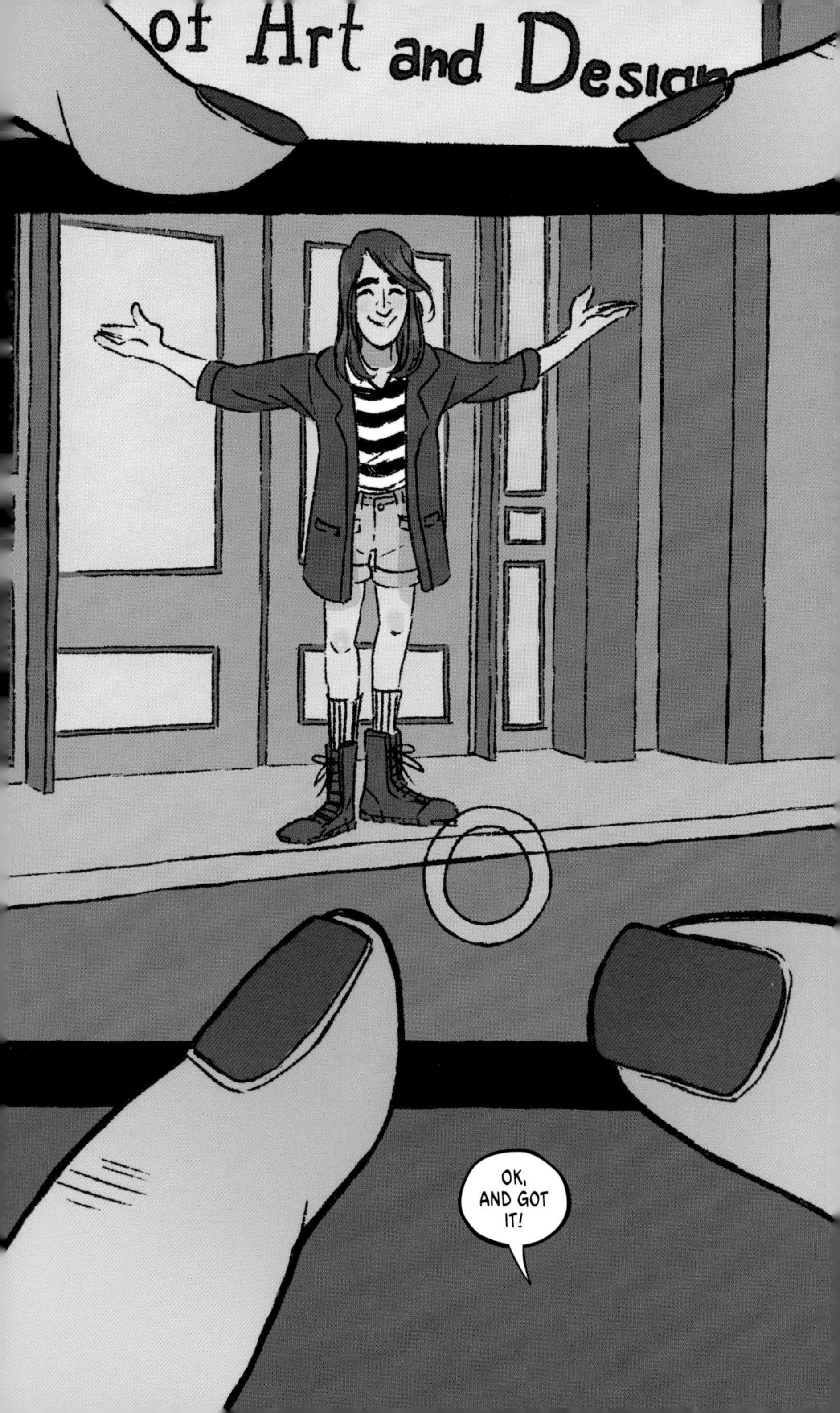
of Art and Design
OK, AND GOT IT!

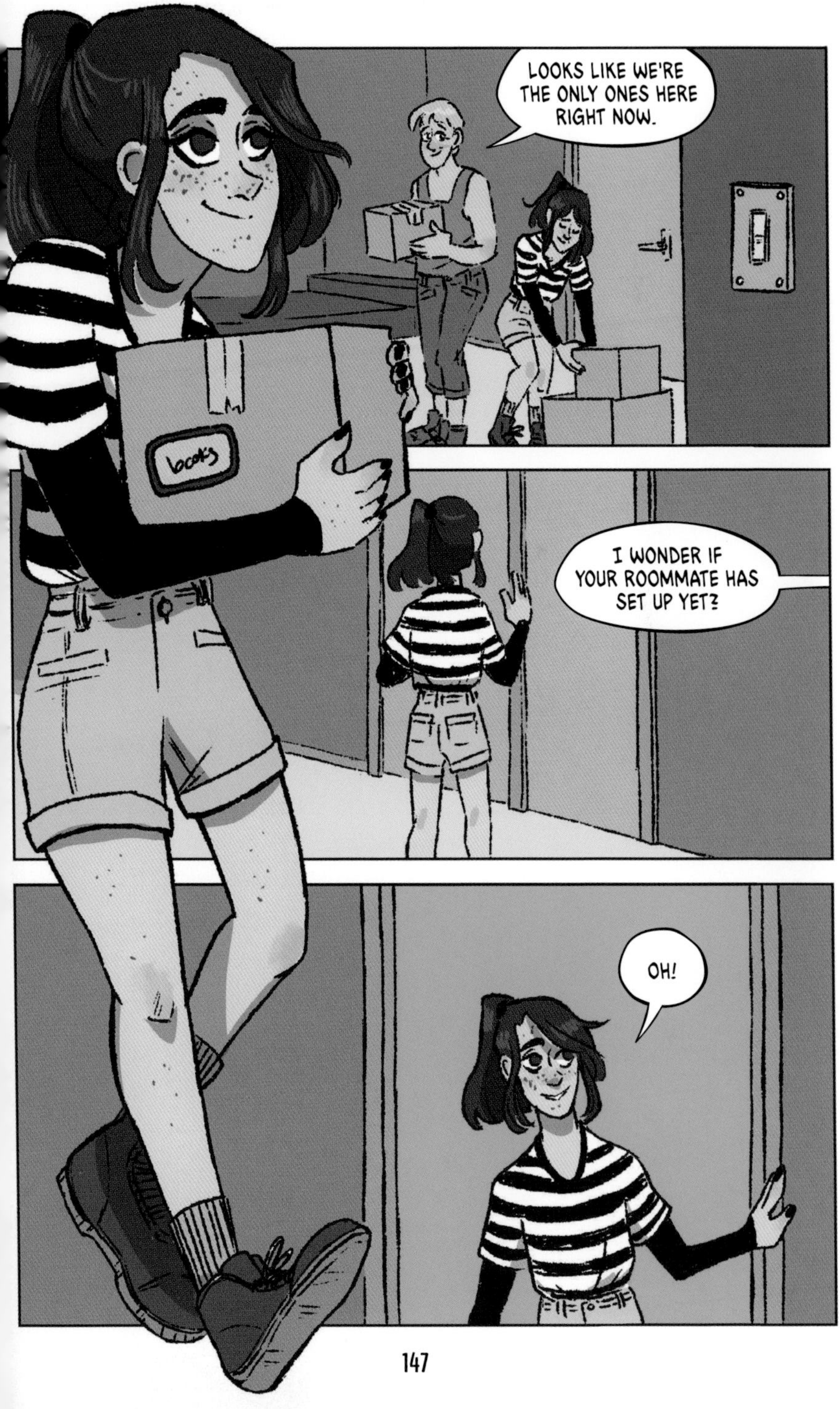
LOOKS LIKE WE'RE THE ONLY ONES HERE RIGHT NOW.
books
I WONDER IF YOUR ROOMMATE HAS SET UP YET?
OH!

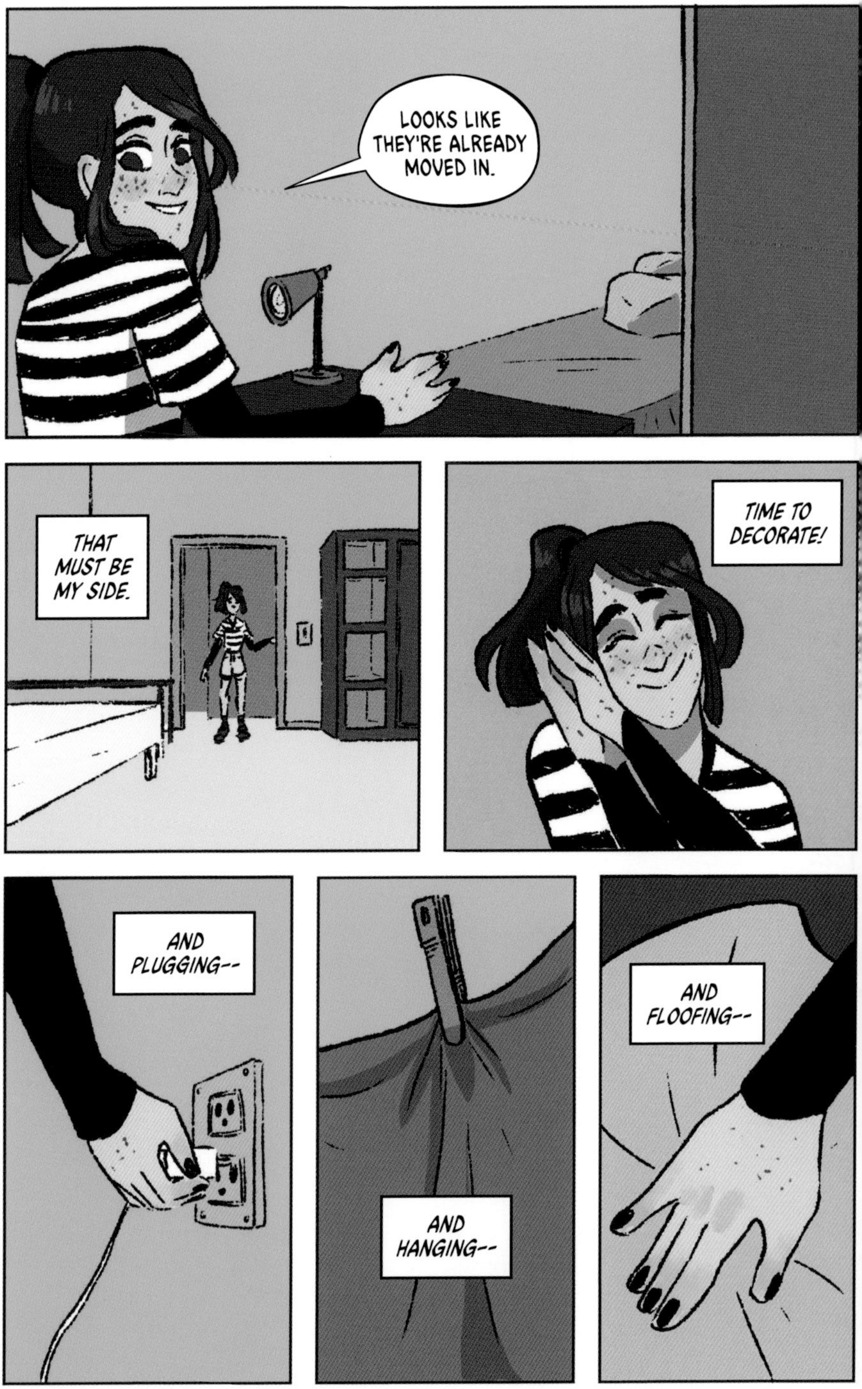
LOOKS LIKE THEY'RE ALREADY MOVED IN.
THAT MUST BE MY SIDE.
TIME TO DECORATE!
AND PLUGGING--
AND HANGING--
AND FLOOFING--

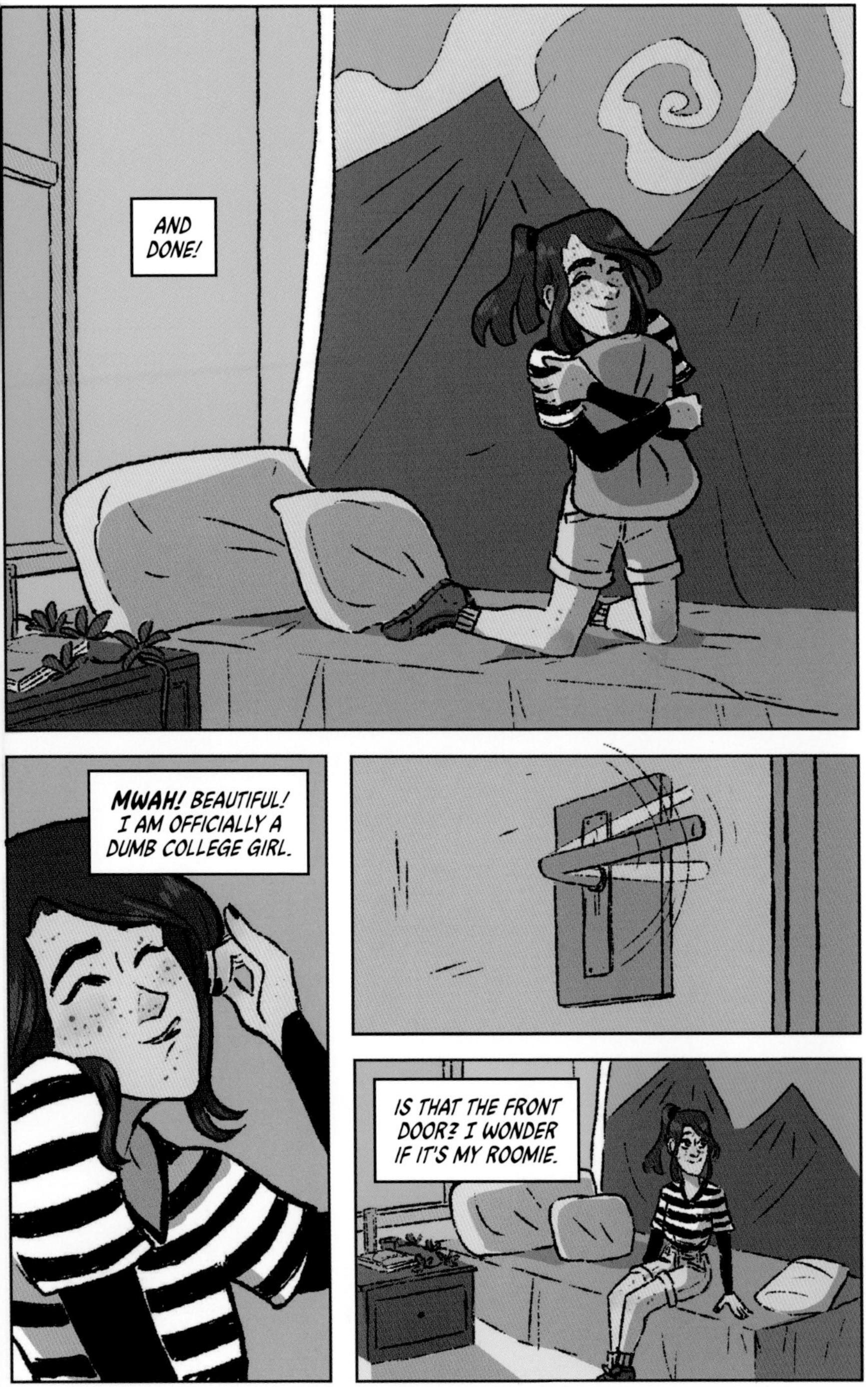
AND DONE!
MWAH! BEAUTIFUL! I AM OFFICIALLY A DUMB COLLEGE GIRL.
IS THAT THE FRONT DOOR? I WONDER IF IT'S MY ROOMIE.

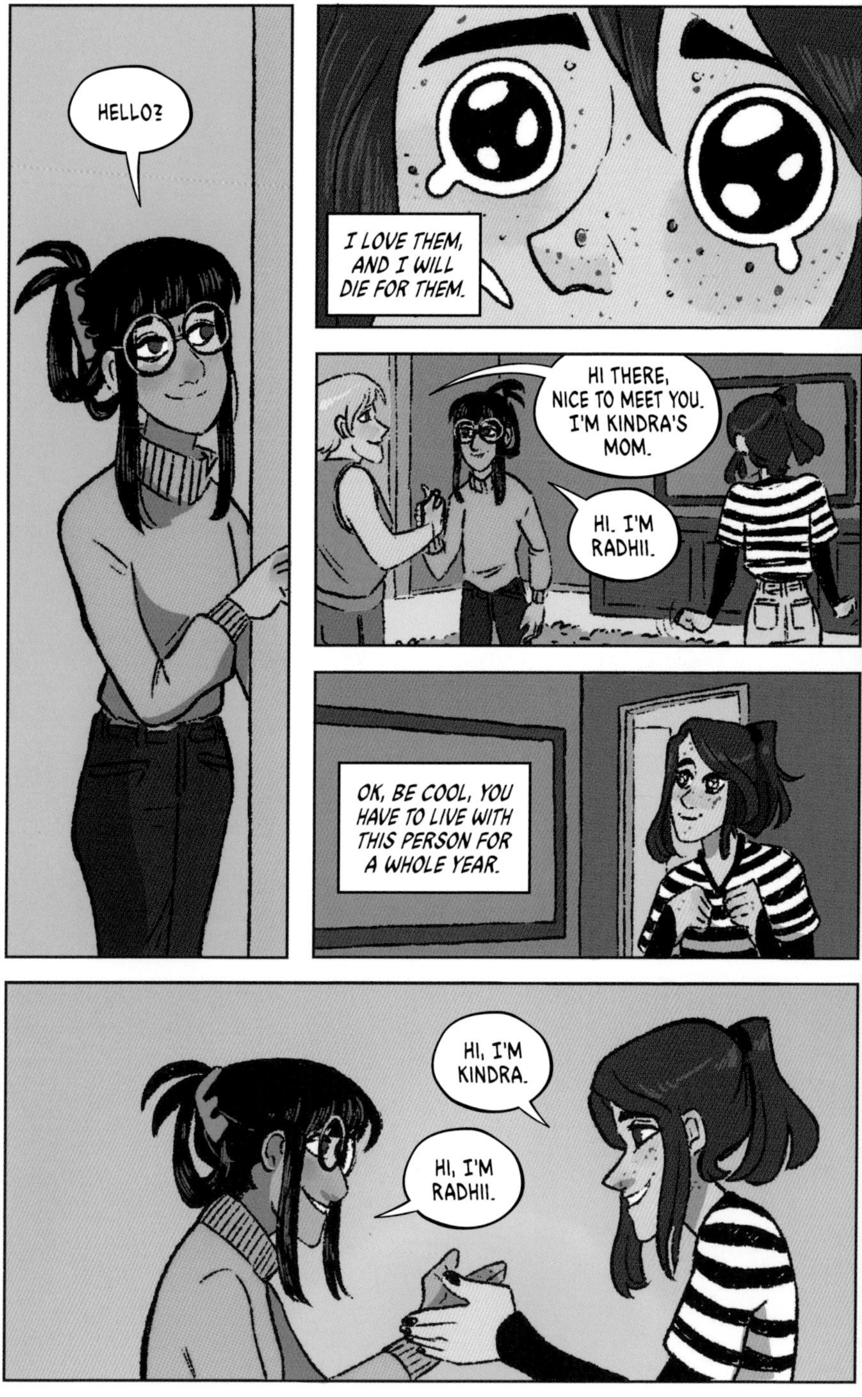
HELLO?
I LOVE THEM, AND I WILL DIE FOR THEM.
HI THERE, NICE TO MEET YOU. I'M KINDRA'S MOM.
HI. I'M RADHII.
OK, BE COOL, YOU HAVE TO LIVE WITH THIS PERSON FOR A WHOLE YEAR.
HI, I'M KINDRA.
HI, I'M RADHII.

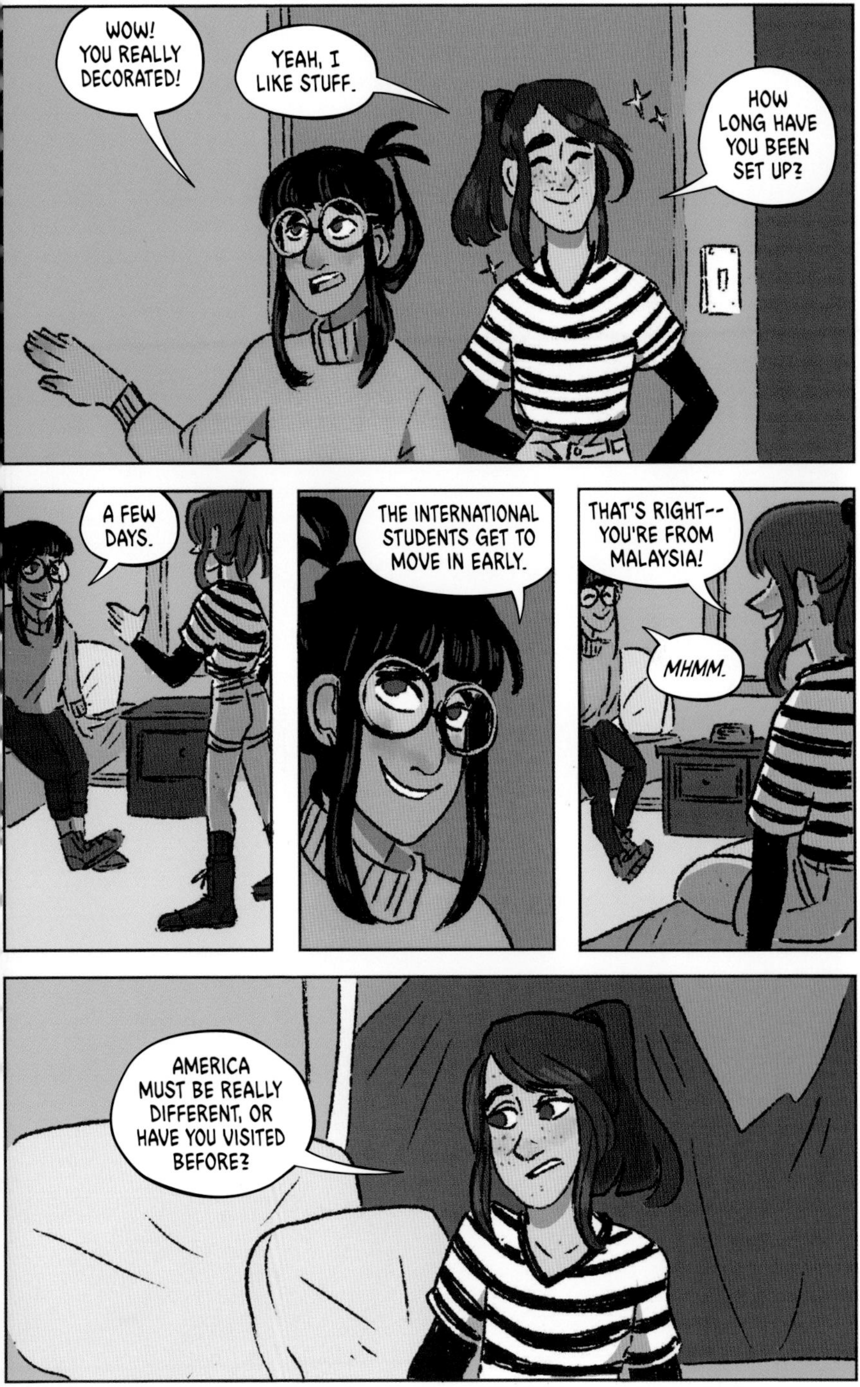
WOW! YOU REALLY DECORATED!
YEAH, I LIKE STUFF.
HOW LONG HAVE YOU BEEN SET UP?
A FEW DAYS.
THE INTERNATIONAL STUDENTS GET TO MOVE IN EARLY.
THAT'S RIGHT-- YOU'RE FROM MALAYSIA!
MHMM.
AMERICA MUST BE REALLY DIFFERENT, OR HAVE YOU VISITED BEFORE?

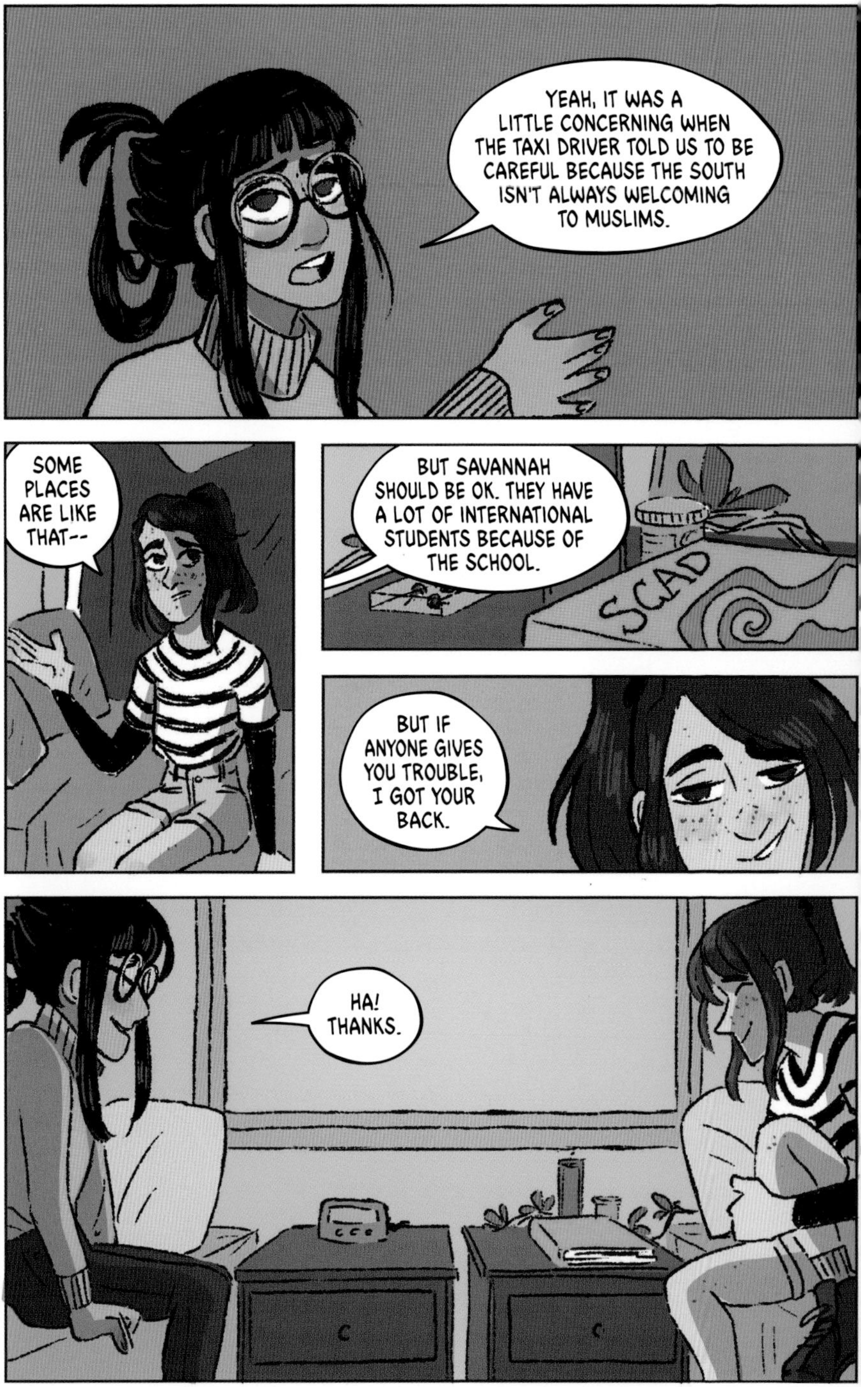
YEAH, IT WAS A LITTLE CONCERNING WHEN THE TAXI DRIVER TOLD US TO BE CAREFUL BECAUSE THE SOUTH ISN'T ALWAYS WELCOMING TO MUSLIMS.
SOME PLACES ARE LIKE THAT--
BUT SAVANNAH SHOULD BE OK. THEY HAVE A LOT OF INTERNATIONAL STUDENTS BECAUSE OF THE SCHOOL.
SCAD
BUT IF ANYONE GIVES YOU TROUBLE, I GOT YOUR BACK.
HA! THANKS.

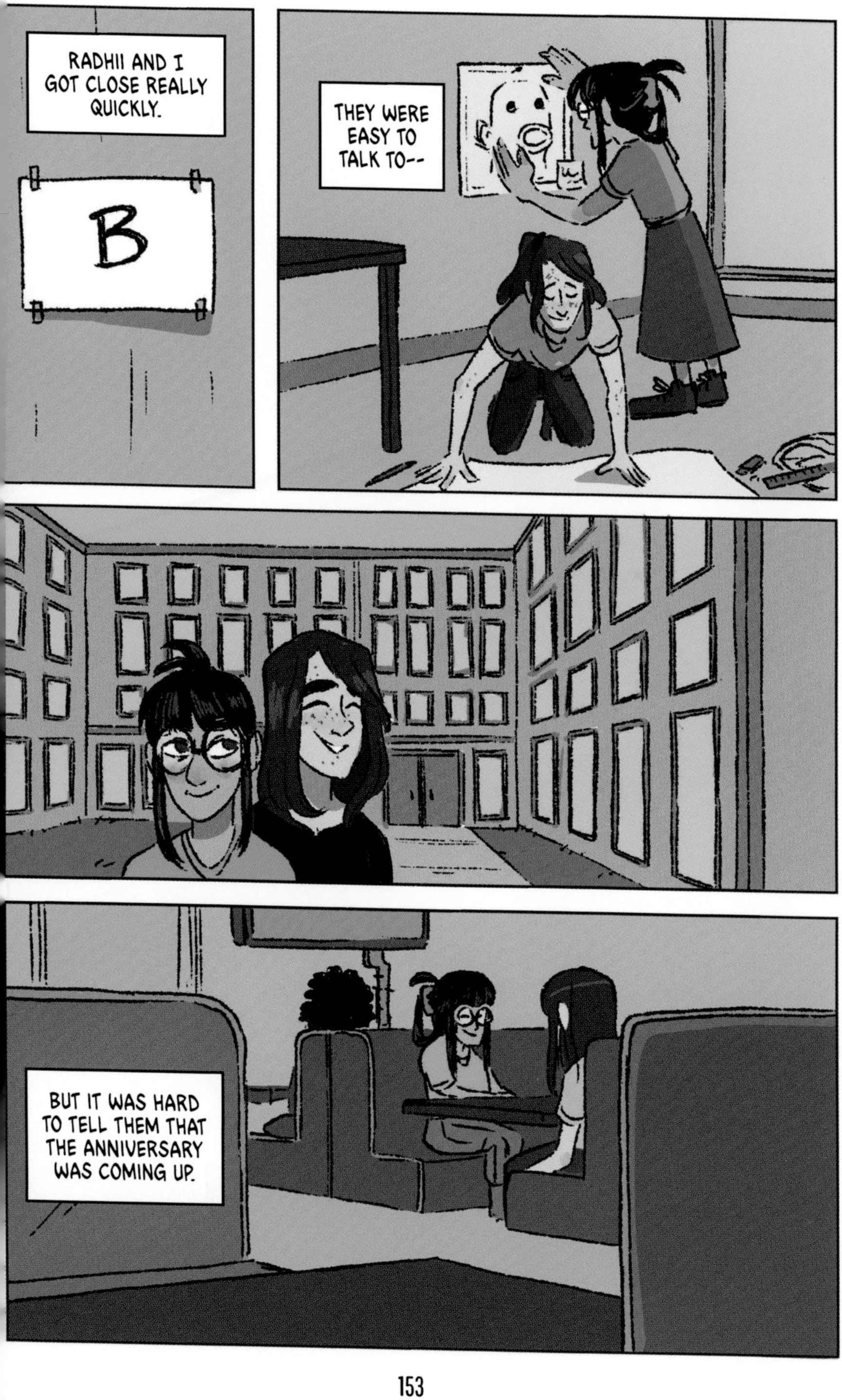
RADHII AND I GOT CLOSE REALLY QUICKLY.
B
THEY WERE EASY TO TALK TO--
BUT IT WAS HARD TO TELL THEM THAT THE ANNIVERSARY WAS COMING UP.

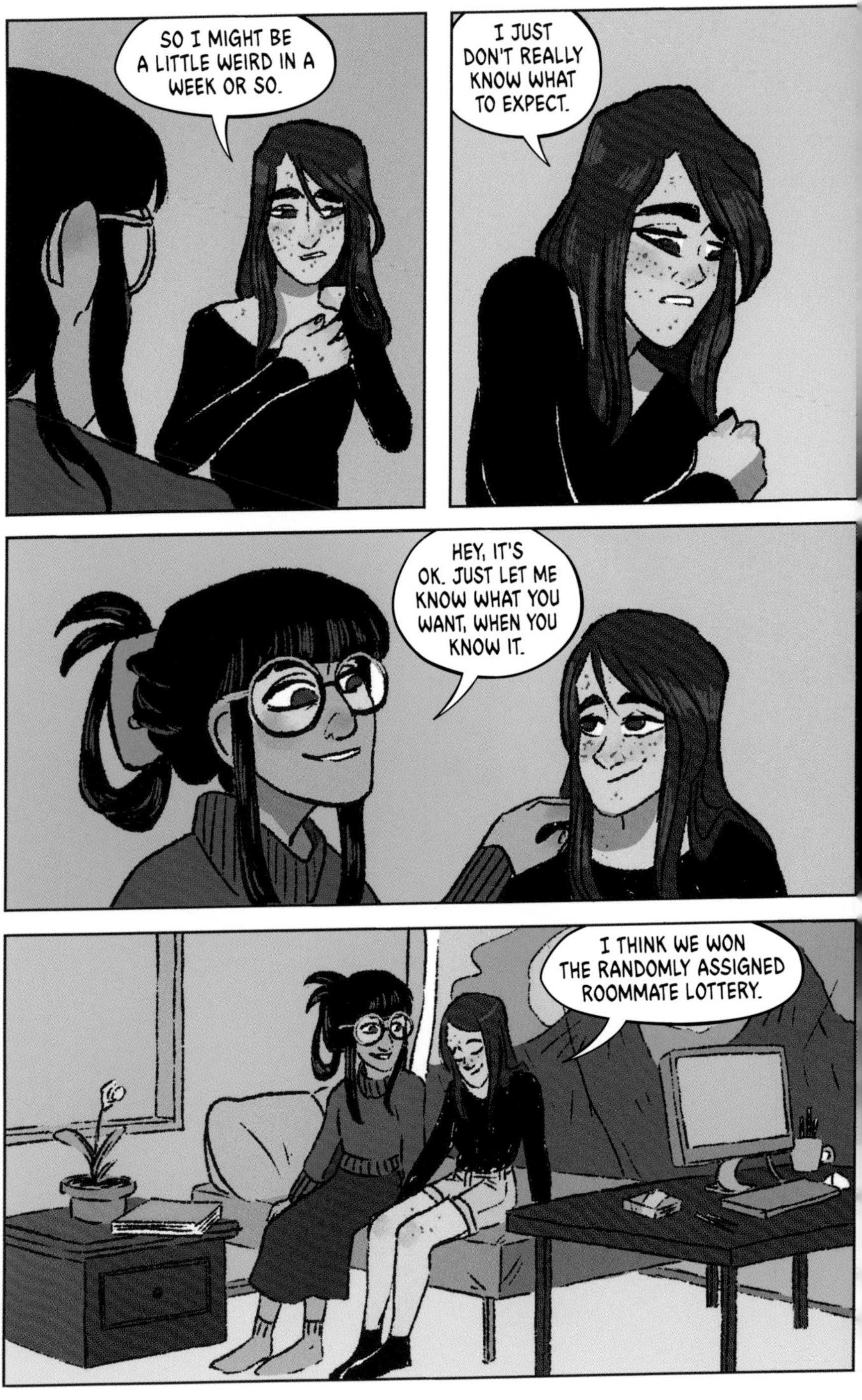
SO I MIGHT BE A LITTLE WEIRD IN A WEEK OR SO.
I JUST DON'T REALLY KNOW WHAT TO EXPECT.
HEY, IT'S OK. JUST LET ME KNOW WHAT YOU WANT, WHEN YOU KNOW IT.
I THINK WE WON THE RANDOMLY ASSIGNED ROOMMATE LOTTERY.

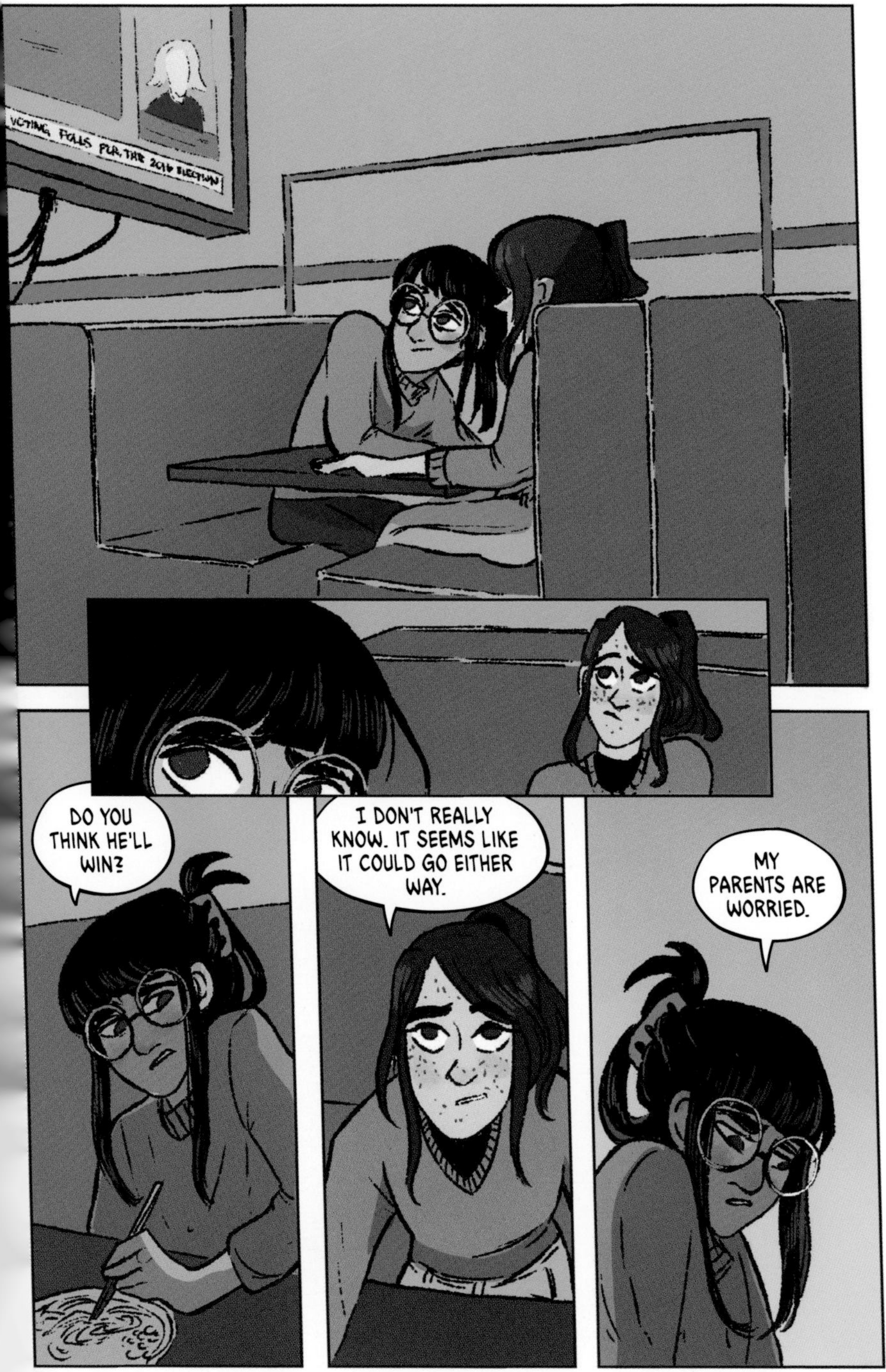
VOTING POLLS FOR THE 2016 ELECTION
DO YOU THINK HE'LL WIN?
I DON'T REALLY KNOW. IT SEEMS LIKE IT COULD GO EITHER WAY.
MY PARENTS ARE WORRIED.

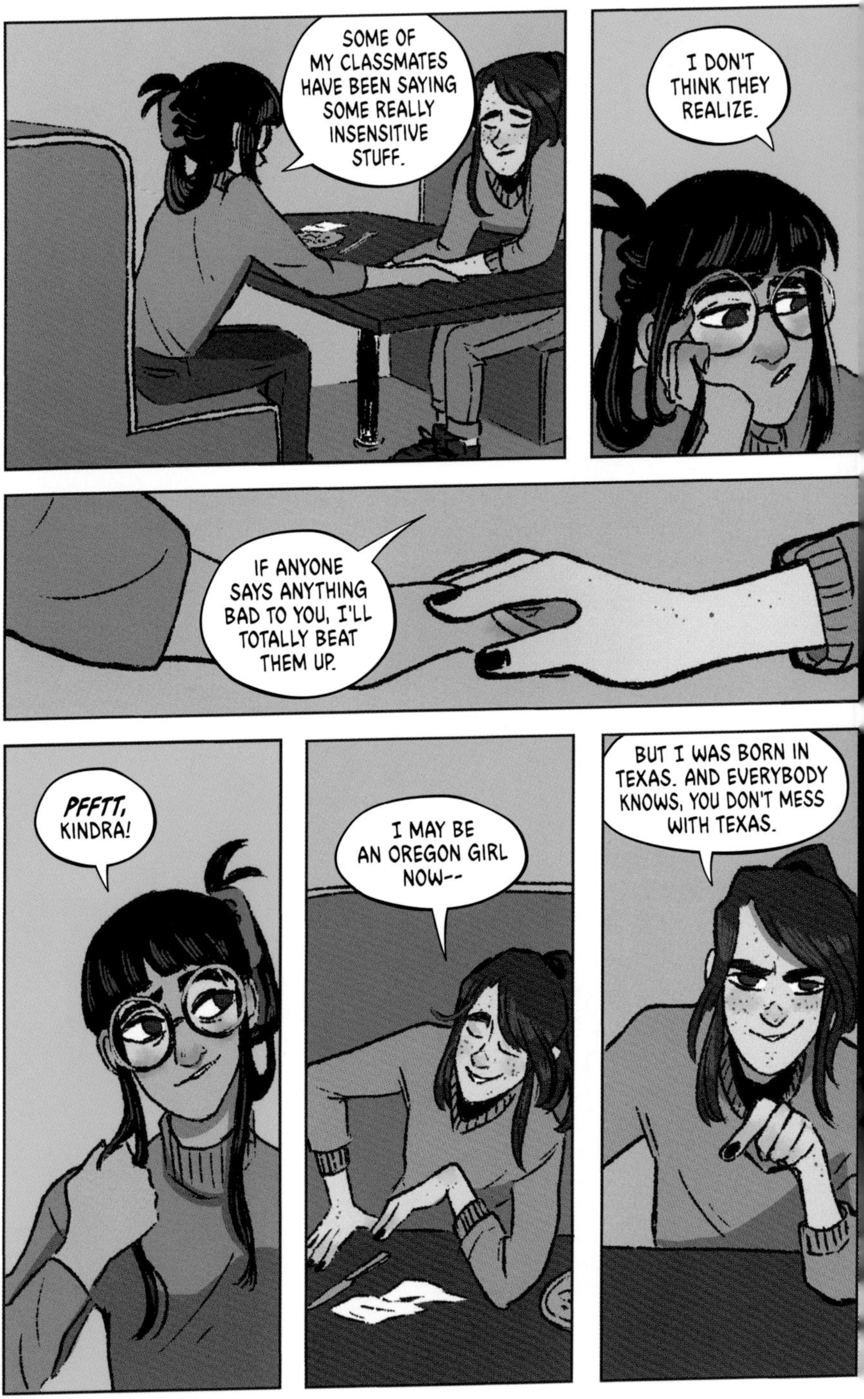
SOME OF MY CLASSMATES HAVE BEEN SAYING SOME REALLY INSENSITIVE STUFF.
I DON'T THINK THEY REALIZE.
IF ANYONE SAYS ANYTHING BAD TO YOU, I'LL TOTALLY BEAT THEM UP.
PFFTT, KINDRA!
I MAY BE AN OREGON GIRL NOW--
BUT I WAS BORN IN TEXAS. AND EVERYBODY KNOWS, YOU DON'T MESS WITH TEXAS.

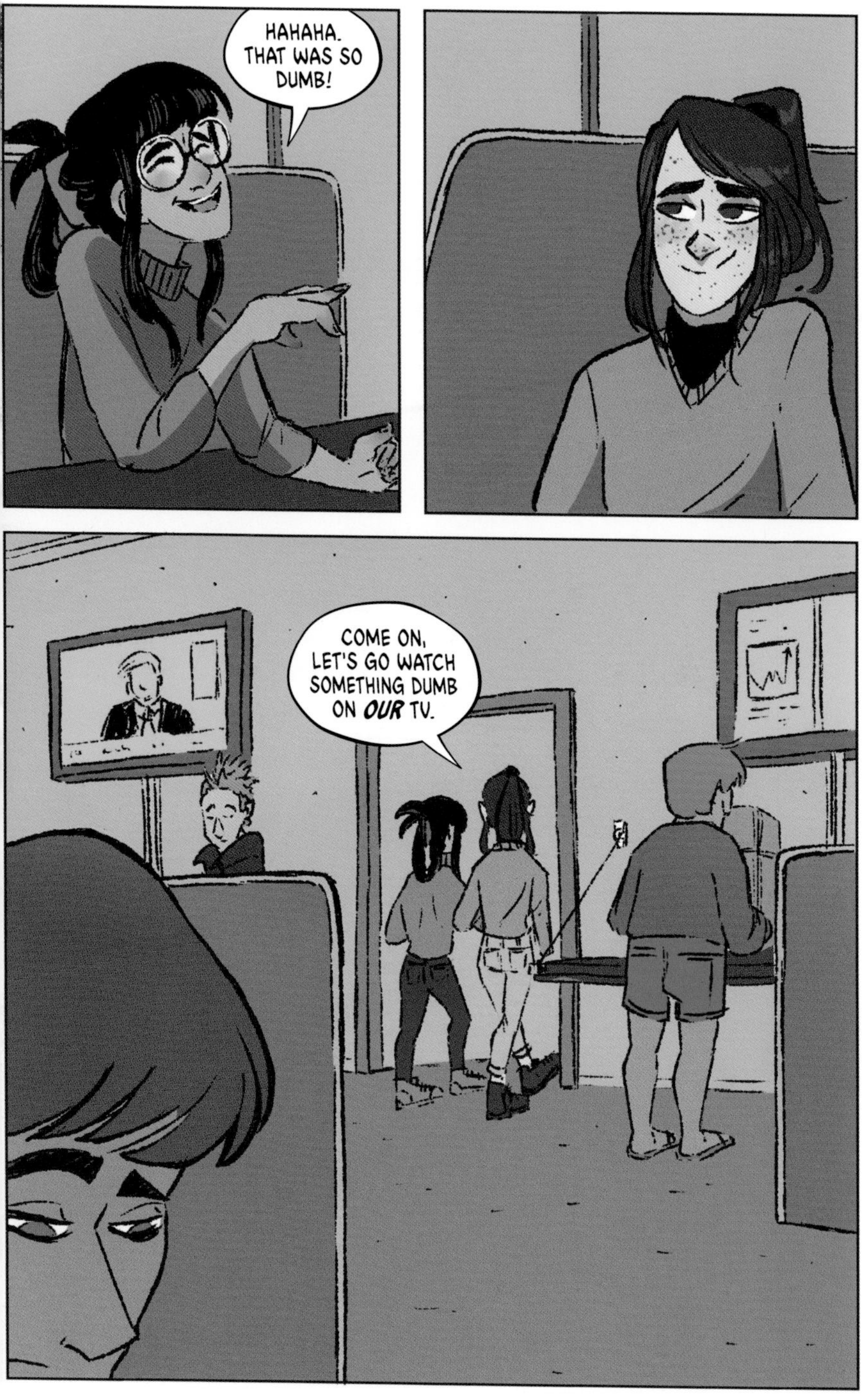
HAHAHA. THAT WAS SO DUMB!
COME ON, LET'S GO WATCH SOMETHING DUMB ON *OUR* TV.

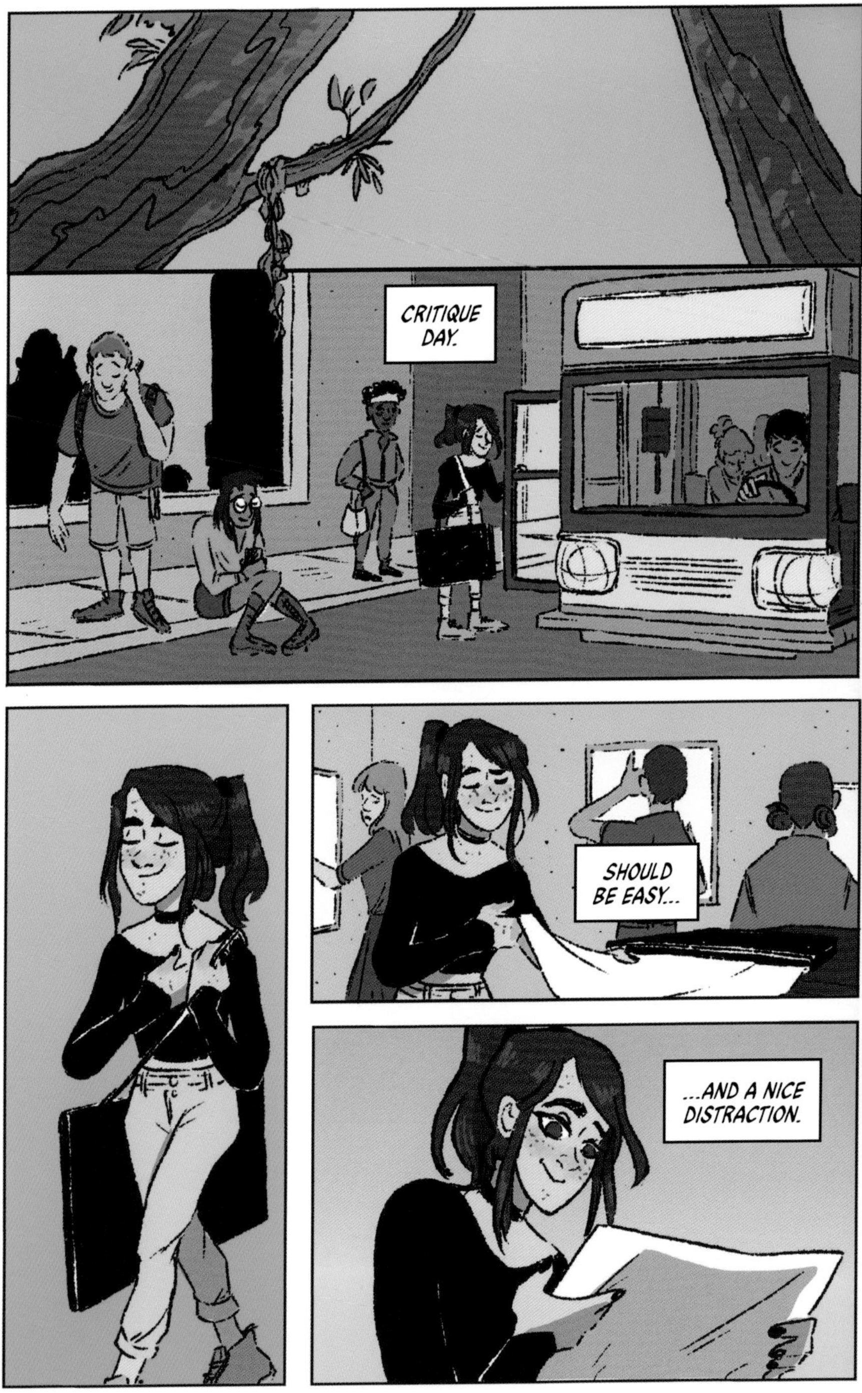
CRITIQUE DAY.
SHOULD BE EASY...
...AND A NICE DISTRACTION.

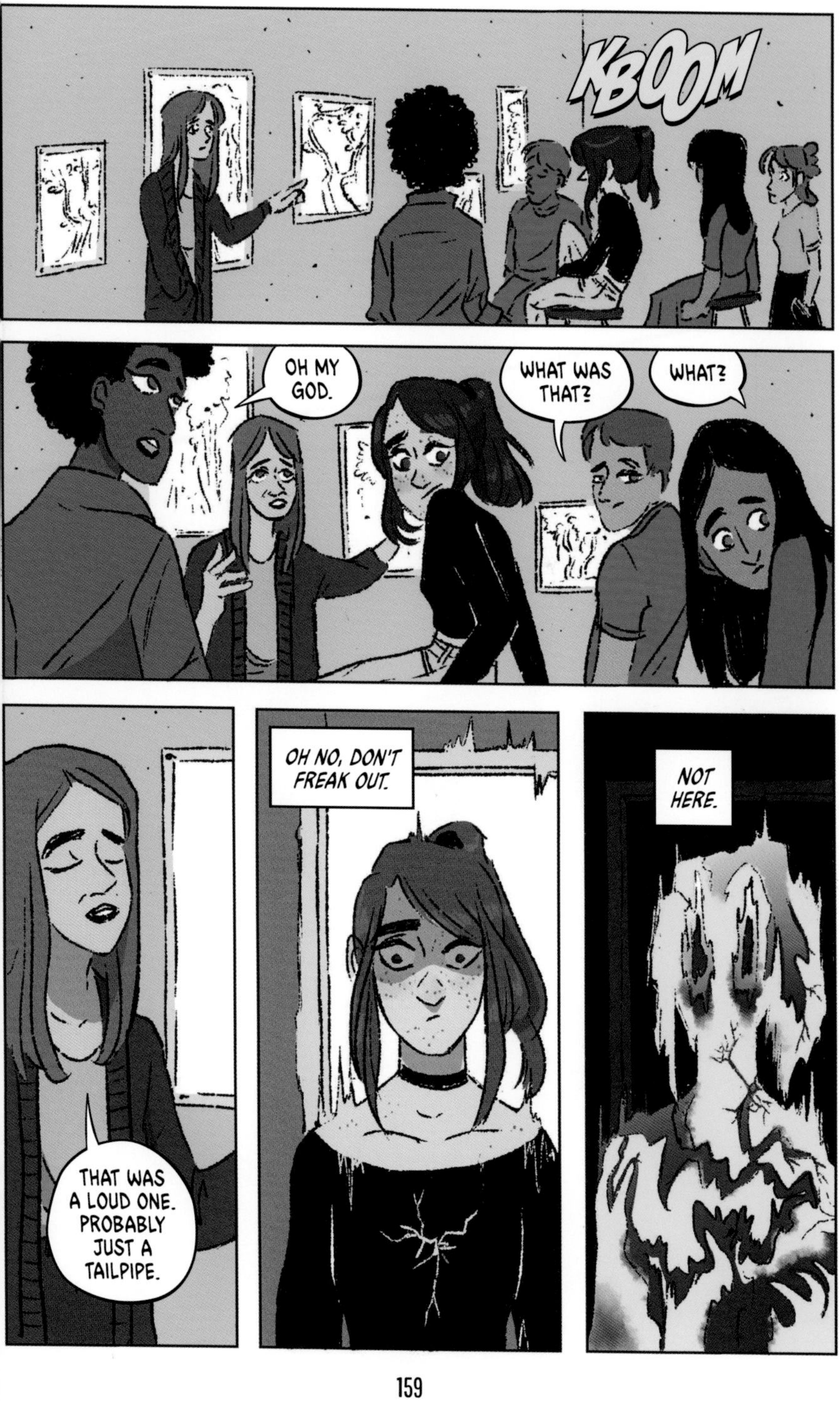
KBOOM
OH MY GOD.
WHAT WAS THAT?
WHAT?
THAT WAS A LOUD ONE. PROBABLY JUST A TAILPIPE.
OH NO, DON'T FREAK OUT.
NOT HERE.

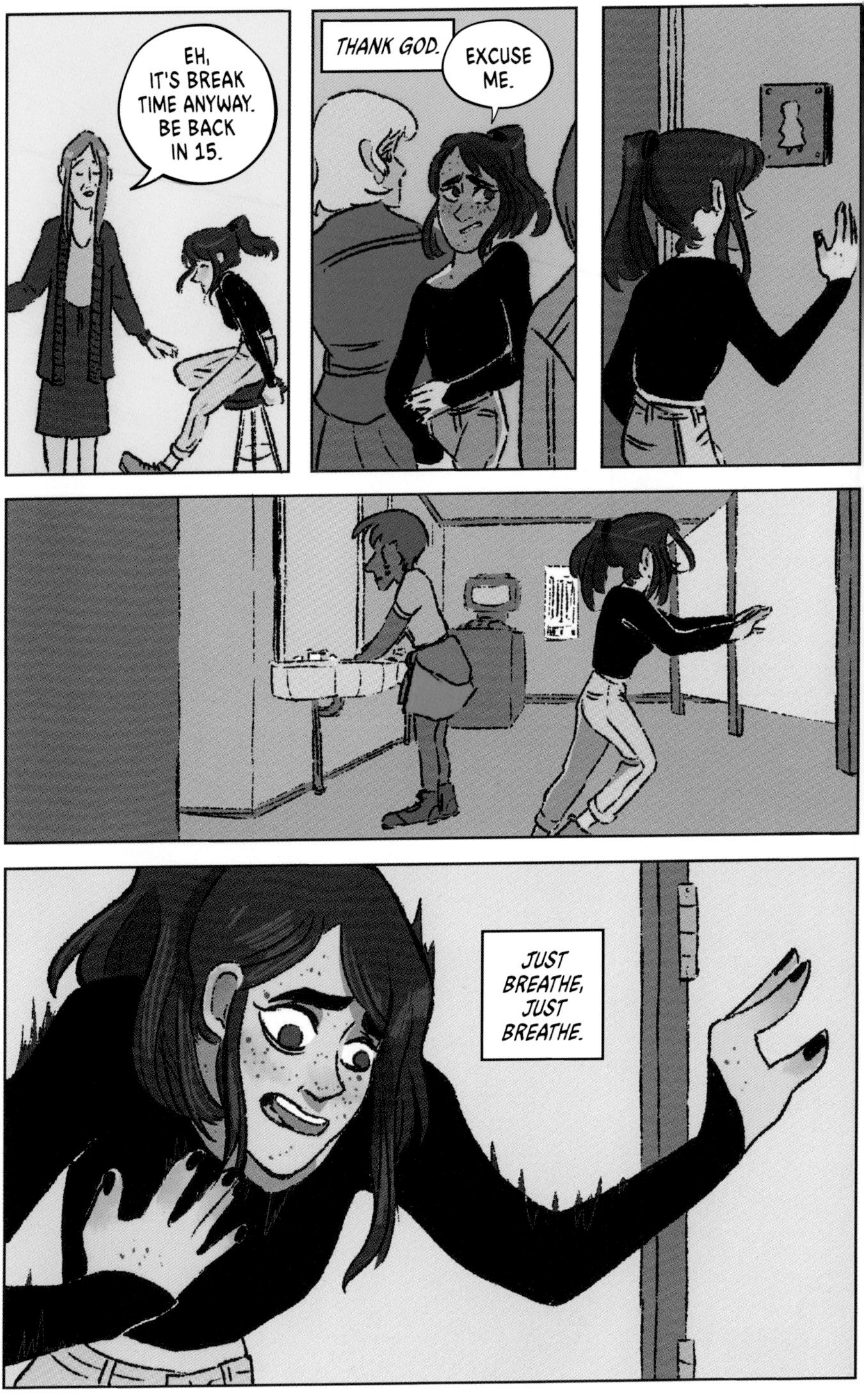
EH, IT'S BREAK TIME ANYWAY. BE BACK IN 15.
THANK GOD.
EXCUSE ME.
JUST BREATHE, JUST BREATHE.

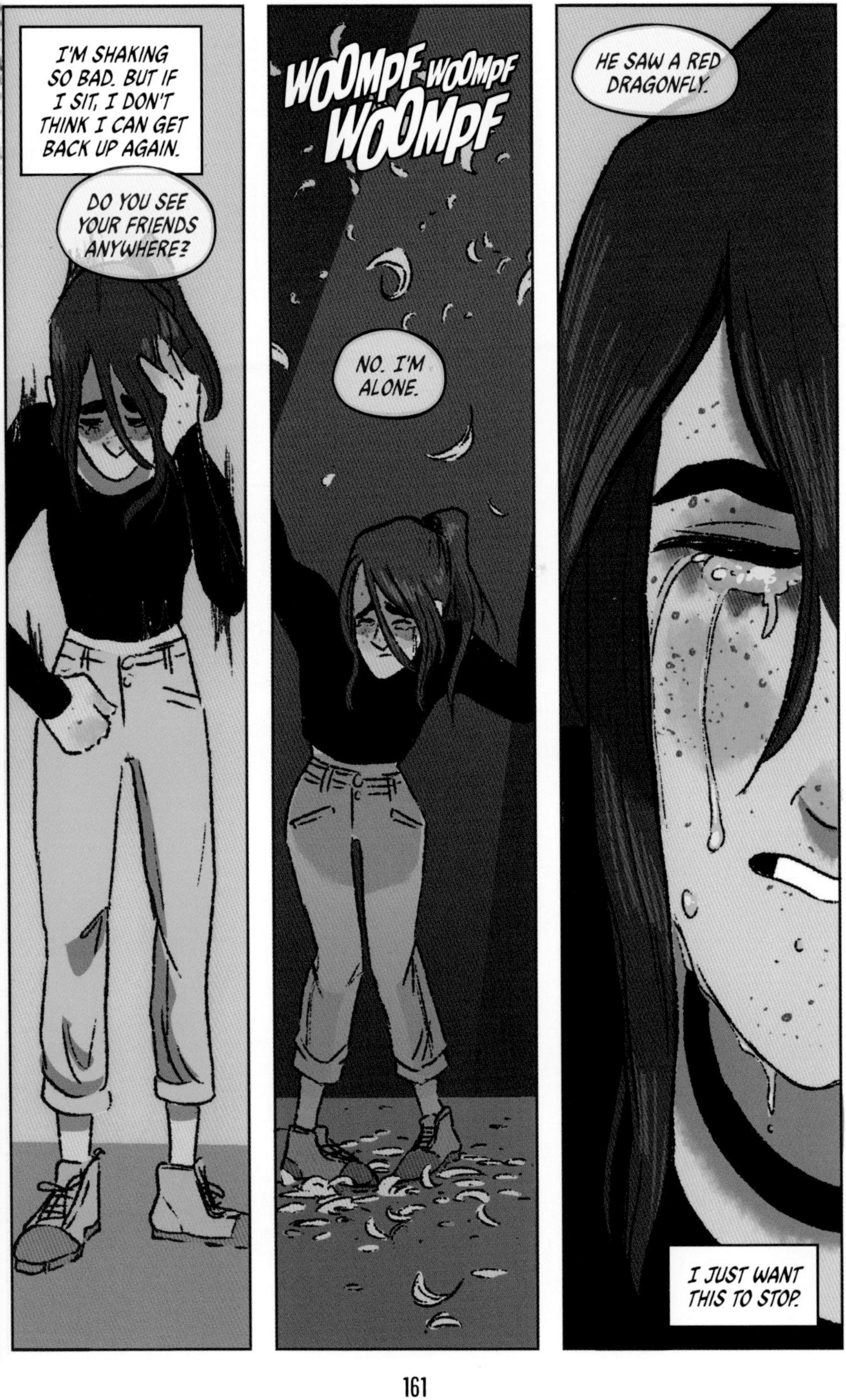
I'M SHAKING SO BAD. BUT IF I SIT, I DON'T THINK I CAN GET BACK UP AGAIN.
DO YOU SEE YOUR FRIENDS ANYWHERE?
WOOMPF WOOMPF WOOMPF
NO. I'M ALONE.
HE SAW A RED DRAGONFLY.
I JUST WANT THIS TO STOP.

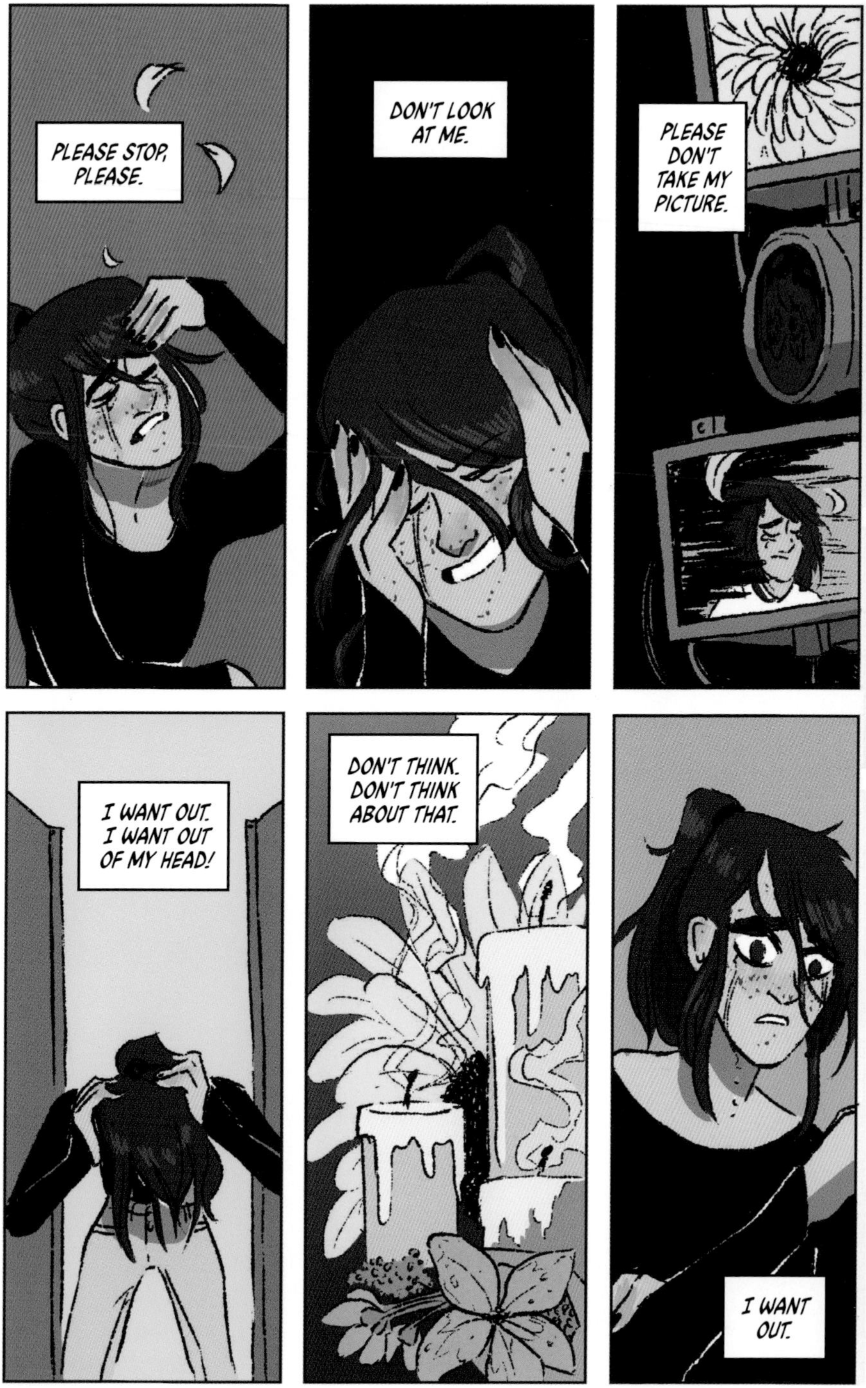
PLEASE STOP, PLEASE.
DON'T LOOK AT ME.
PLEASE DON'T TAKE MY PICTURE.
I WANT OUT. I WANT OUT OF MY HEAD!
DON'T THINK. DON'T THINK ABOUT THAT.
I WANT OUT.

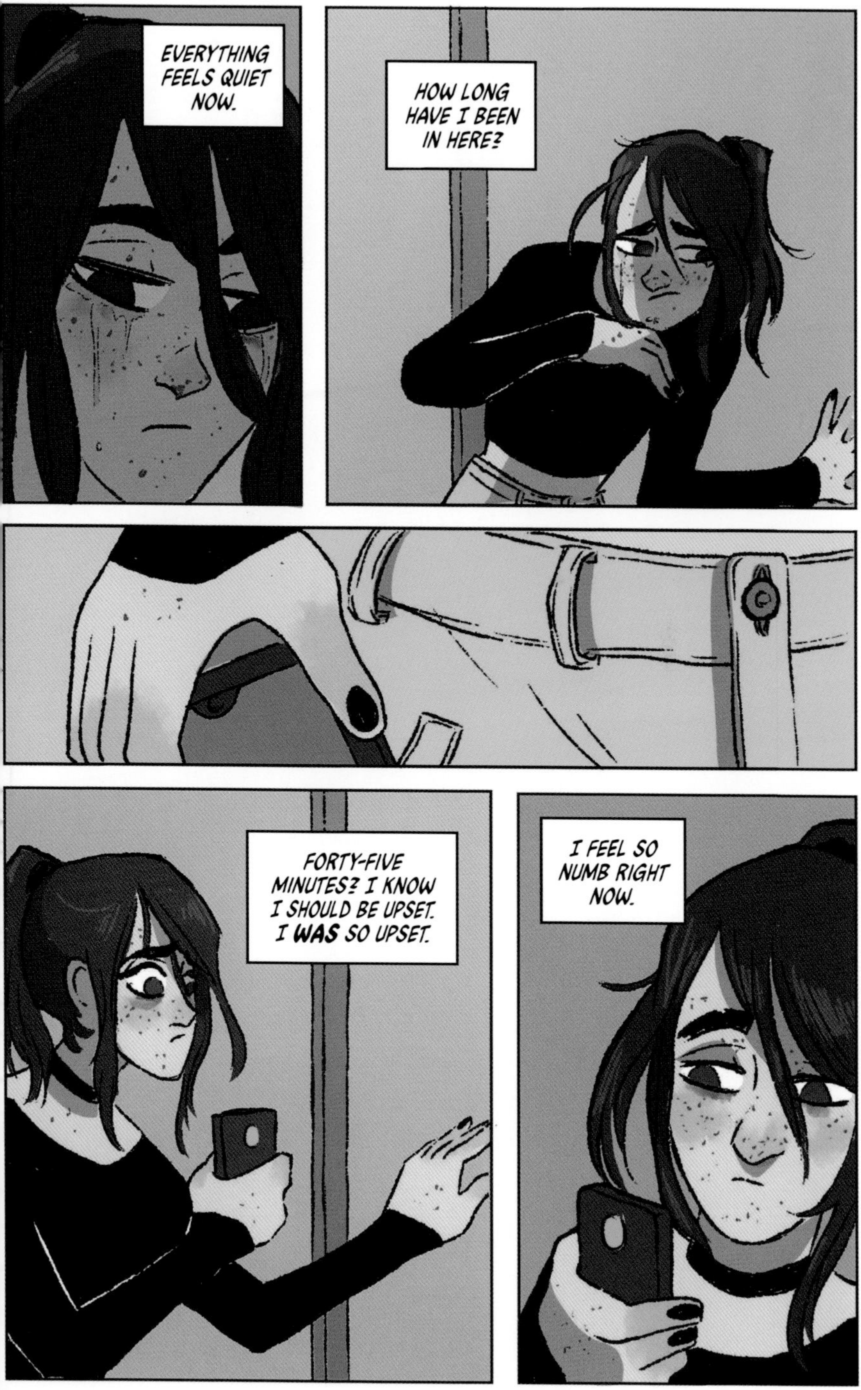
EVERYTHING FEELS QUIET NOW.
HOW LONG HAVE I BEEN IN HERE?
FORTY-FIVE MINUTES? I KNOW I SHOULD BE UPSET. I **WAS** SO UPSET.
I FEEL SO NUMB RIGHT NOW.

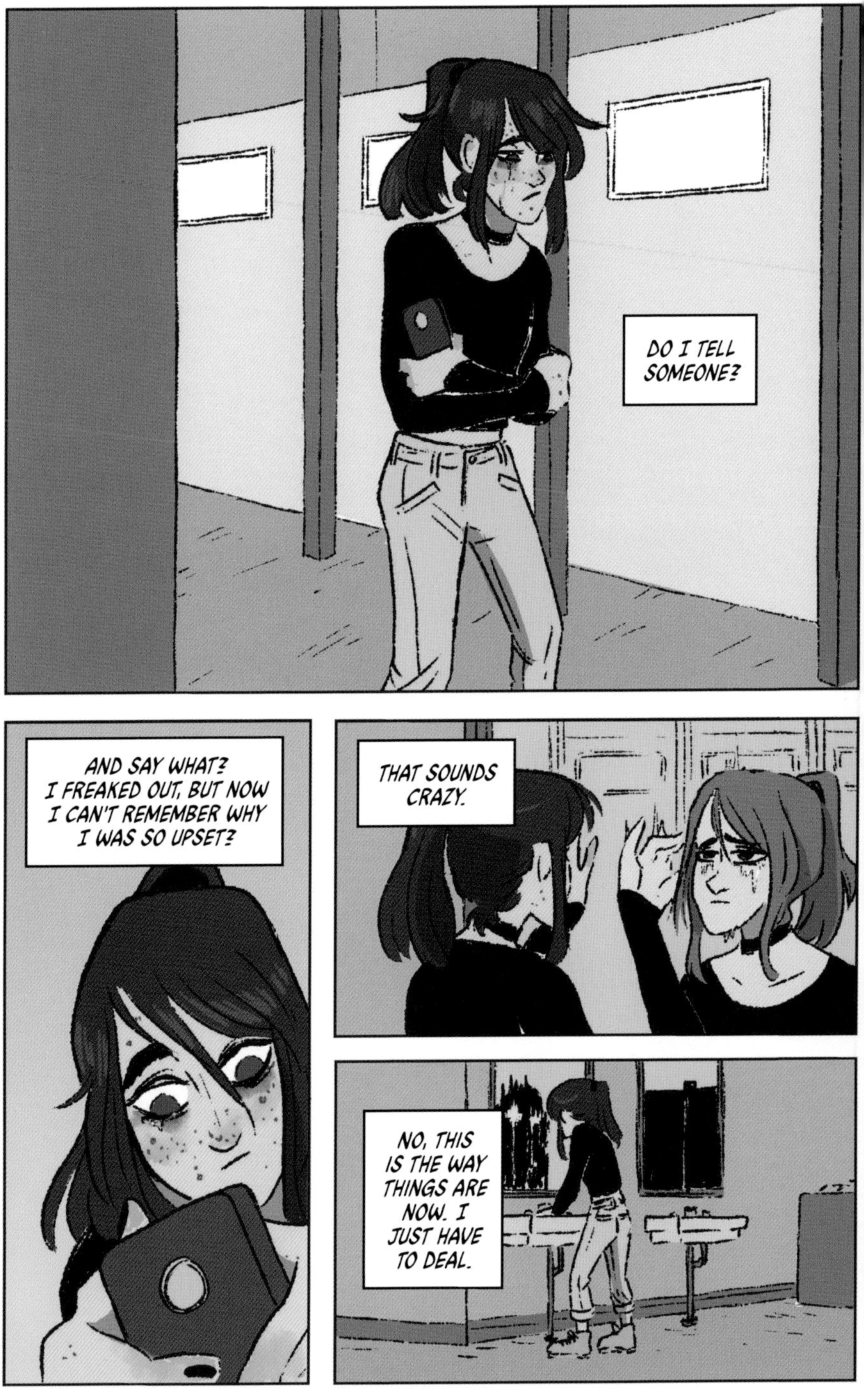
DO I TELL SOMEONE?
AND SAY WHAT? I FREAKED OUT, BUT NOW I CAN'T REMEMBER WHY I WAS SO UPSET?
THAT SOUNDS CRAZY.
NO, THIS IS THE WAY THINGS ARE NOW. I JUST HAVE TO DEAL.

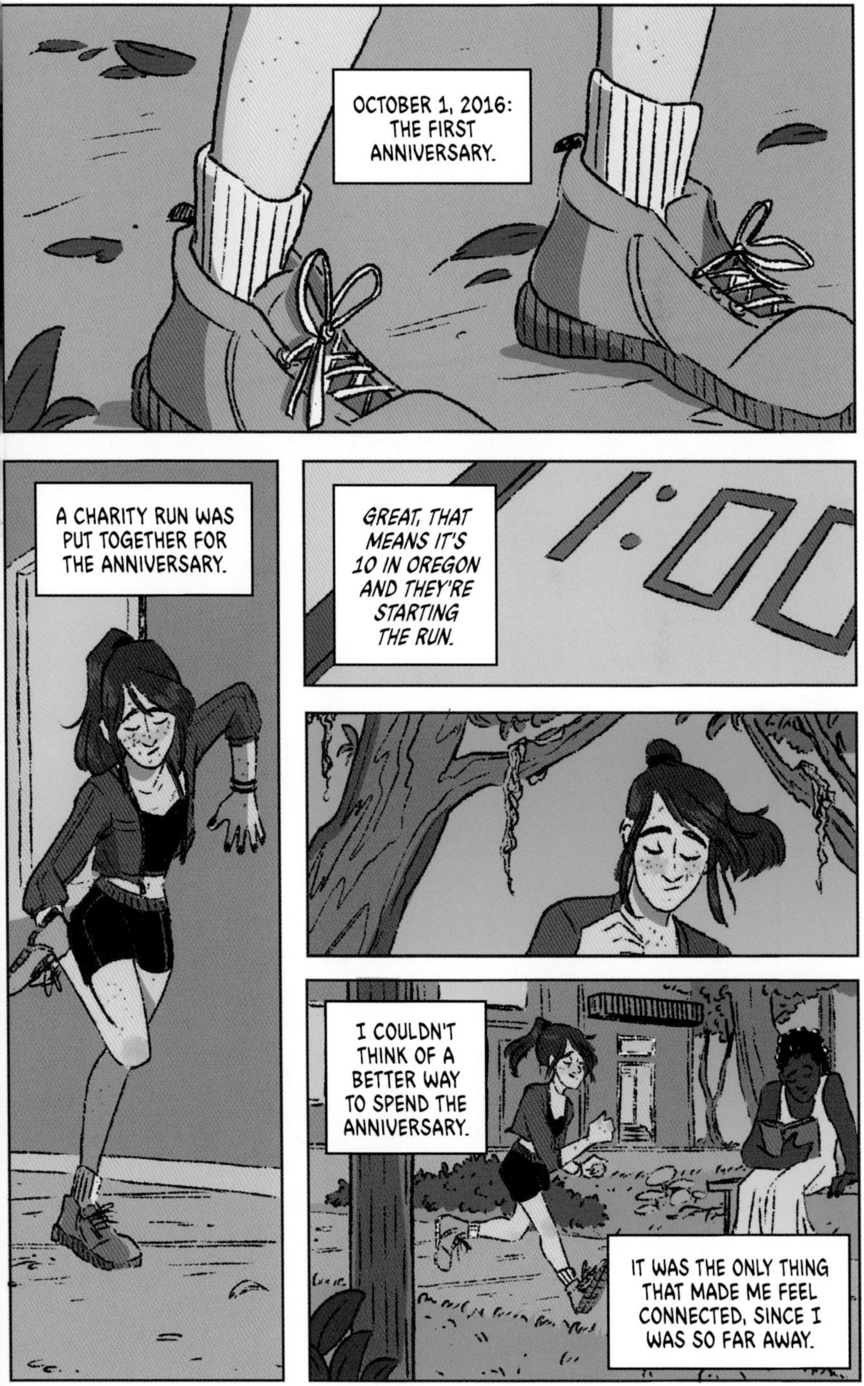
OCTOBER 1, 2016: THE FIRST ANNIVERSARY.
A CHARITY RUN WAS PUT TOGETHER FOR THE ANNIVERSARY.
GREAT, THAT MEANS IT'S 10 IN OREGON AND THEY'RE STARTING THE RUN.
1:00
I COULDN'T THINK OF A BETTER WAY TO SPEND THE ANNIVERSARY.
IT WAS THE ONLY THING THAT MADE ME FEEL CONNECTED, SINCE I WAS SO FAR AWAY.

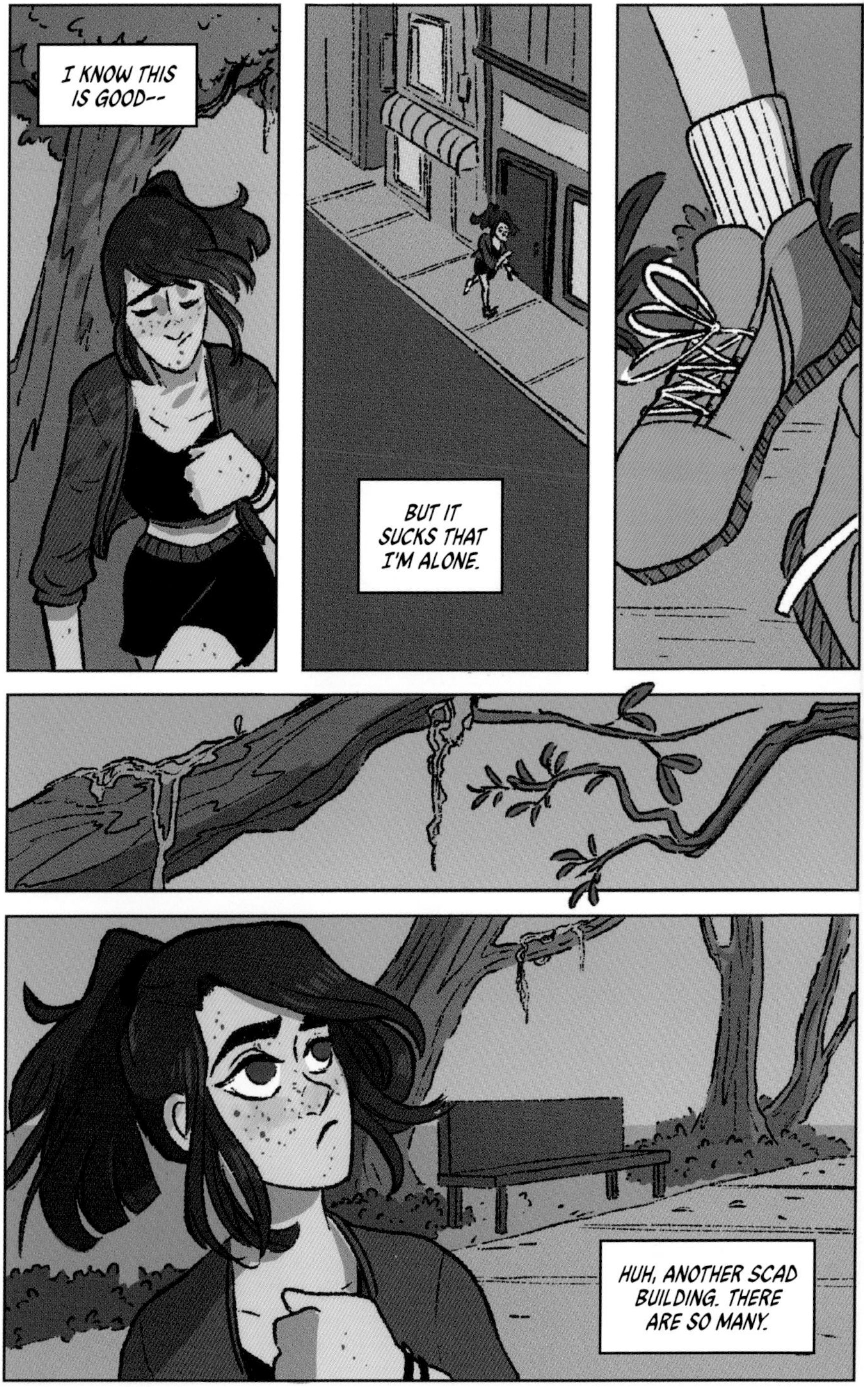
I KNOW THIS IS GOOD--
BUT IT SUCKS THAT I'M ALONE.
HUH, ANOTHER SCAD BUILDING. THERE ARE SO MANY.

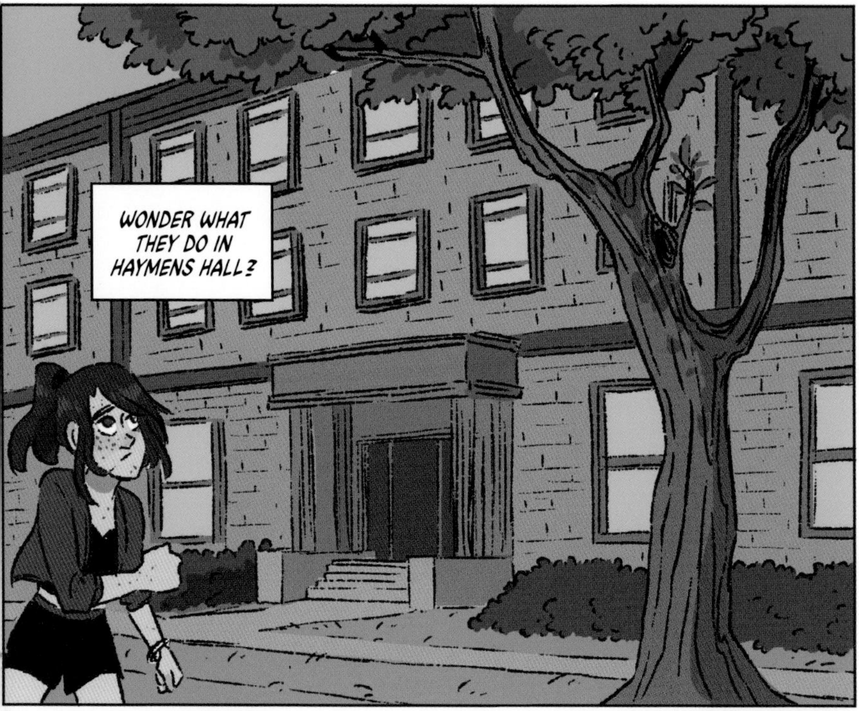
WONDER WHAT THEY DO IN HAYMENS HALL?

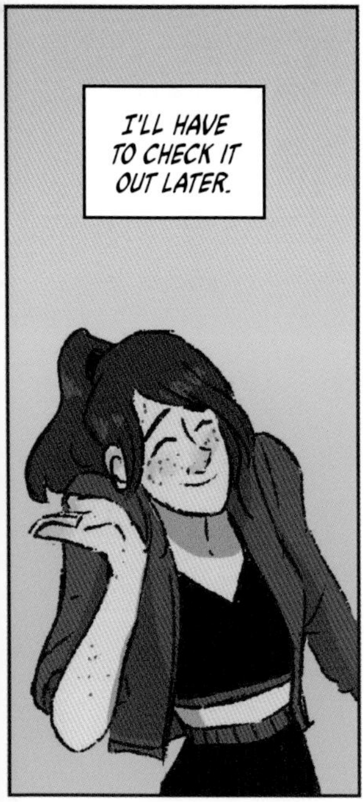
I'LL HAVE TO CHECK IT OUT LATER.

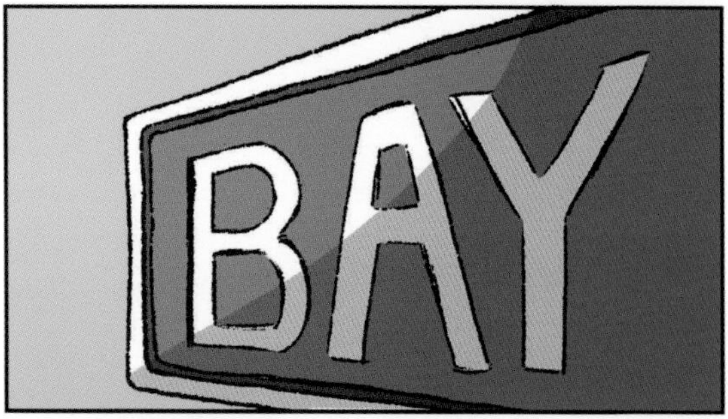
BAY

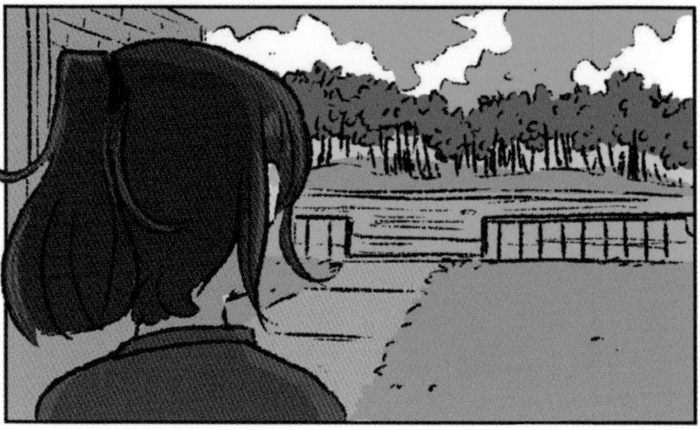

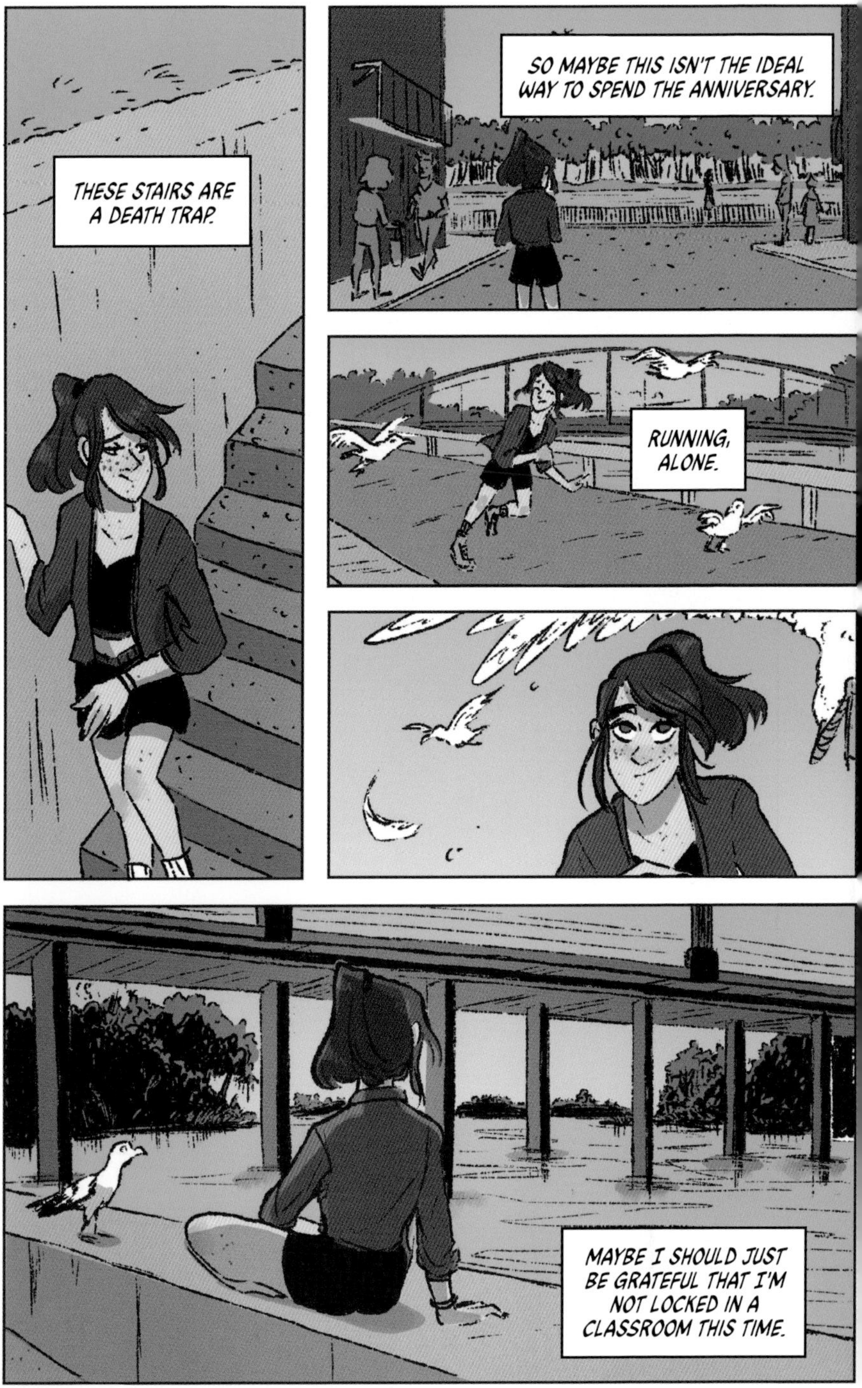
THESE STAIRS ARE A DEATH TRAP.
SO MAYBE THIS ISN'T THE IDEAL WAY TO SPEND THE ANNIVERSARY.
RUNNING, ALONE.
MAYBE I SHOULD JUST BE GRATEFUL THAT I'M NOT LOCKED IN A CLASSROOM THIS TIME.

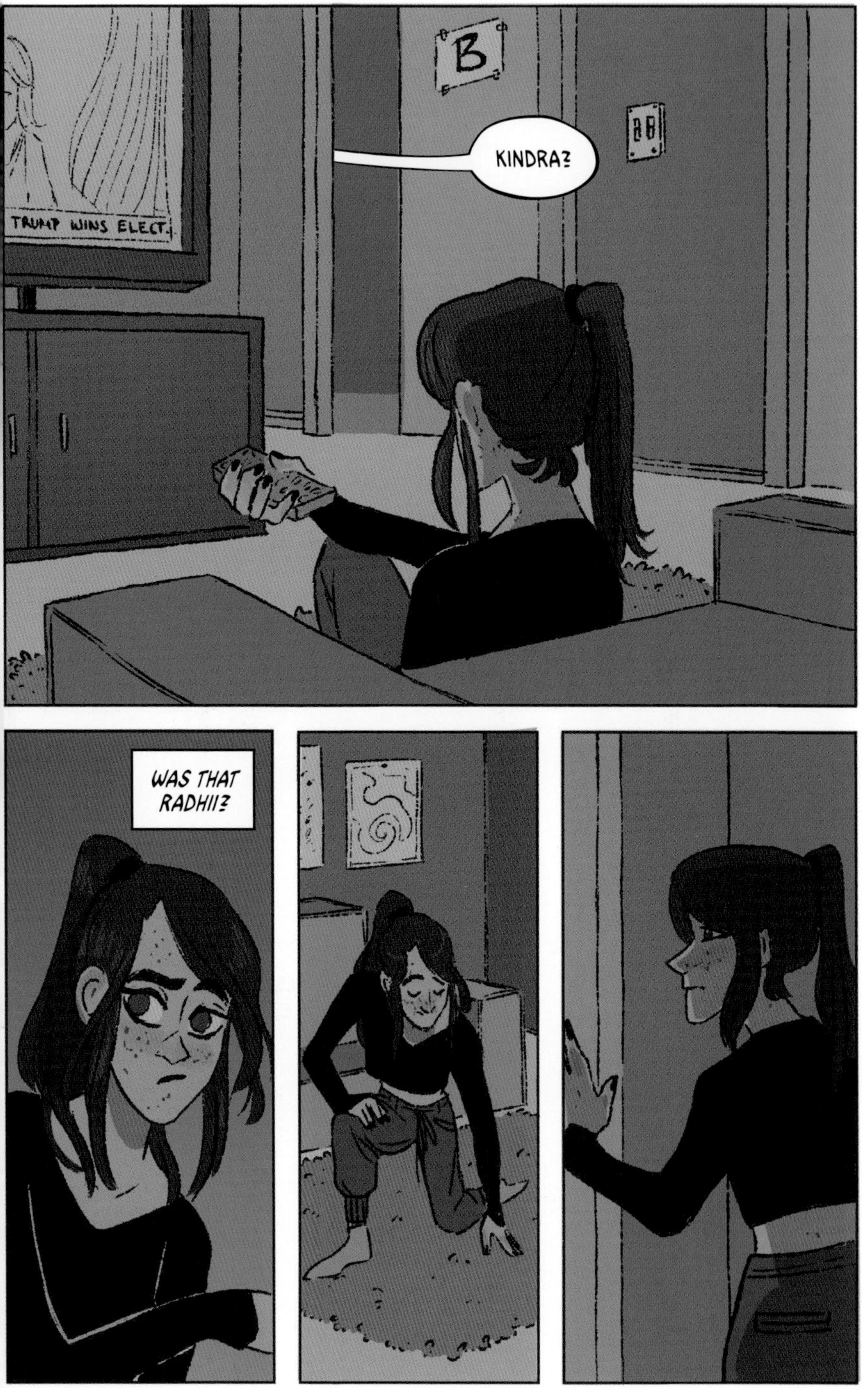
TRUMP WINS ELECT
B
KINDRA?
WAS THAT RADHII?

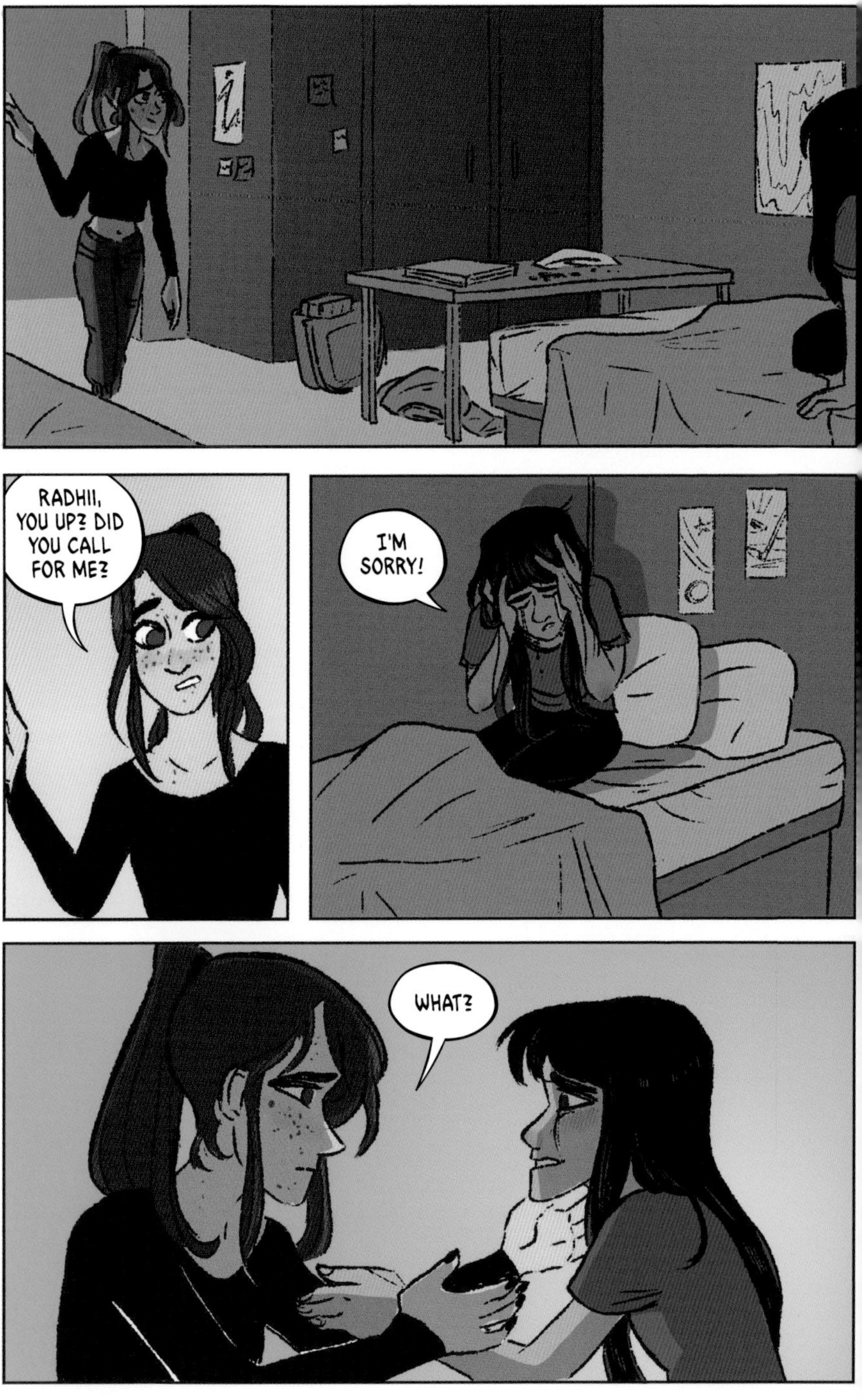
RADHII, YOU UP? DID YOU CALL FOR ME?
I'M SORRY!
WHAT?

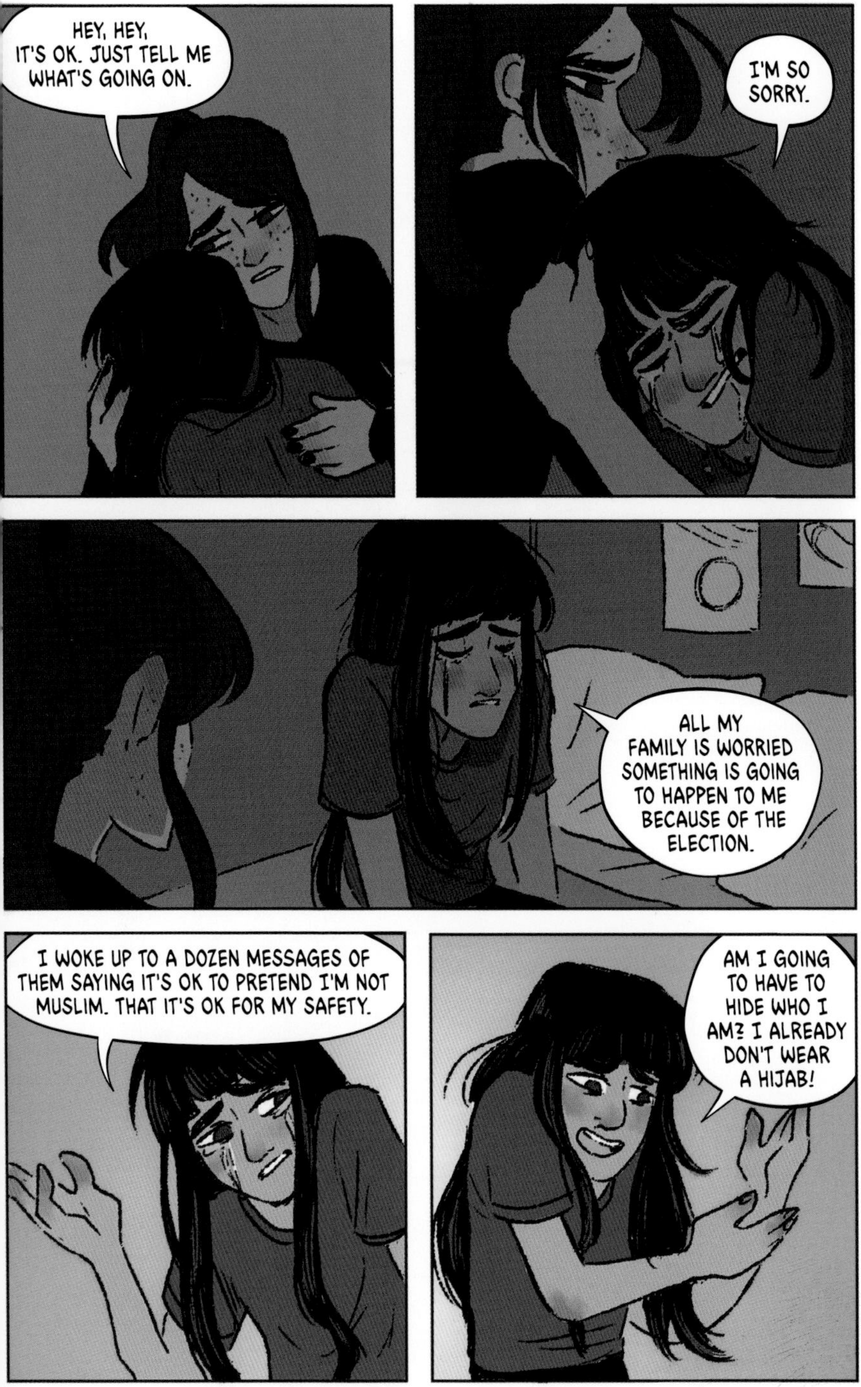
HEY, HEY, IT'S OK. JUST TELL ME WHAT'S GOING ON.
I'M SO SORRY.
ALL MY FAMILY IS WORRIED SOMETHING IS GOING TO HAPPEN TO ME BECAUSE OF THE ELECTION.
I WOKE UP TO A DOZEN MESSAGES OF THEM SAYING IT'S OK TO PRETEND I'M NOT MUSLIM. THAT IT'S OK FOR MY SAFETY.
AM I GOING TO HAVE TO HIDE WHO I AM? I ALREADY DON'T WEAR A HIJAB!

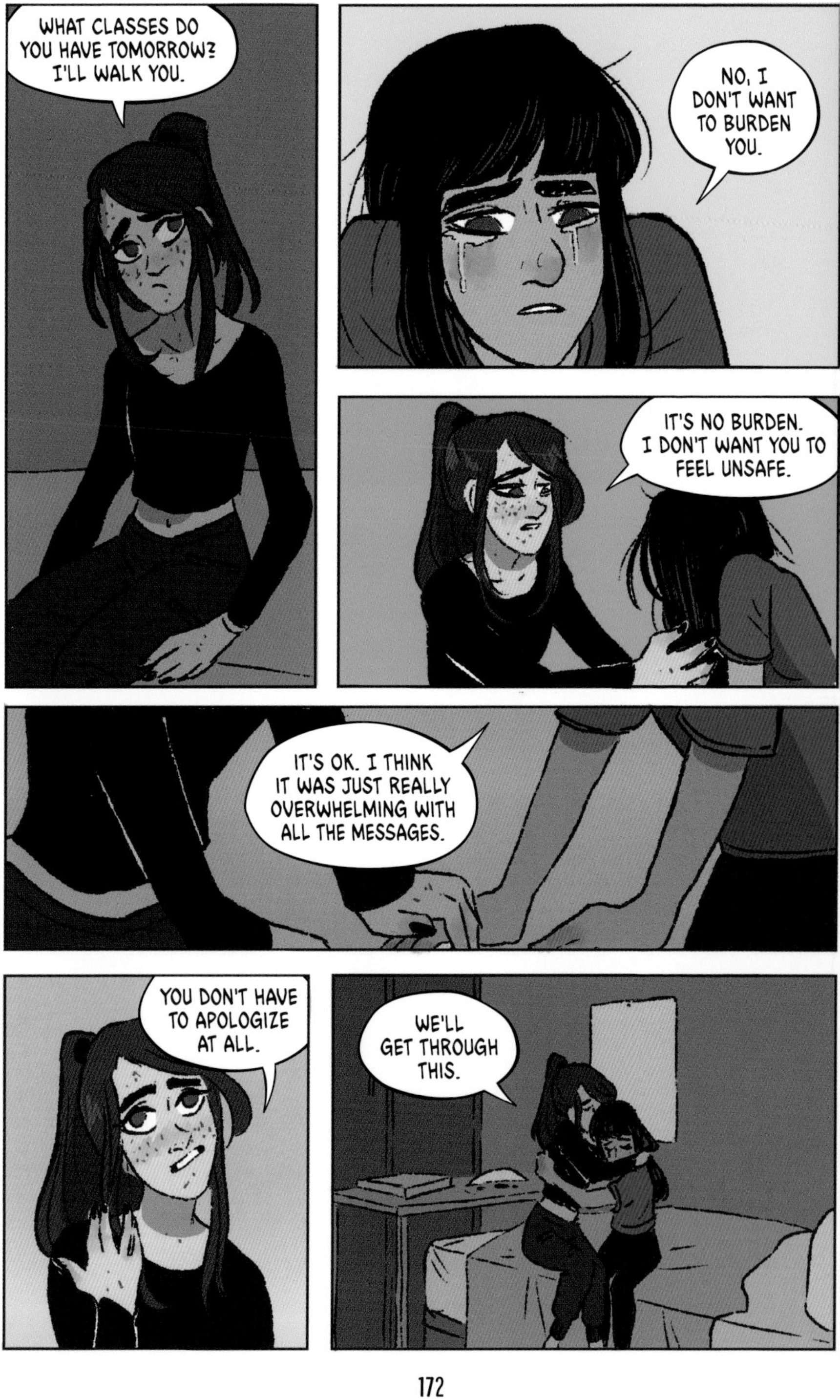
WHAT CLASSES DO YOU HAVE TOMORROW? I'LL WALK YOU.
NO, I DON'T WANT TO BURDEN YOU.
IT'S NO BURDEN. I DON'T WANT YOU TO FEEL UNSAFE.
IT'S OK. I THINK IT WAS JUST REALLY OVERWHELMING WITH ALL THE MESSAGES.
YOU DON'T HAVE TO APOLOGIZE AT ALL.
WE'LL GET THROUGH THIS.

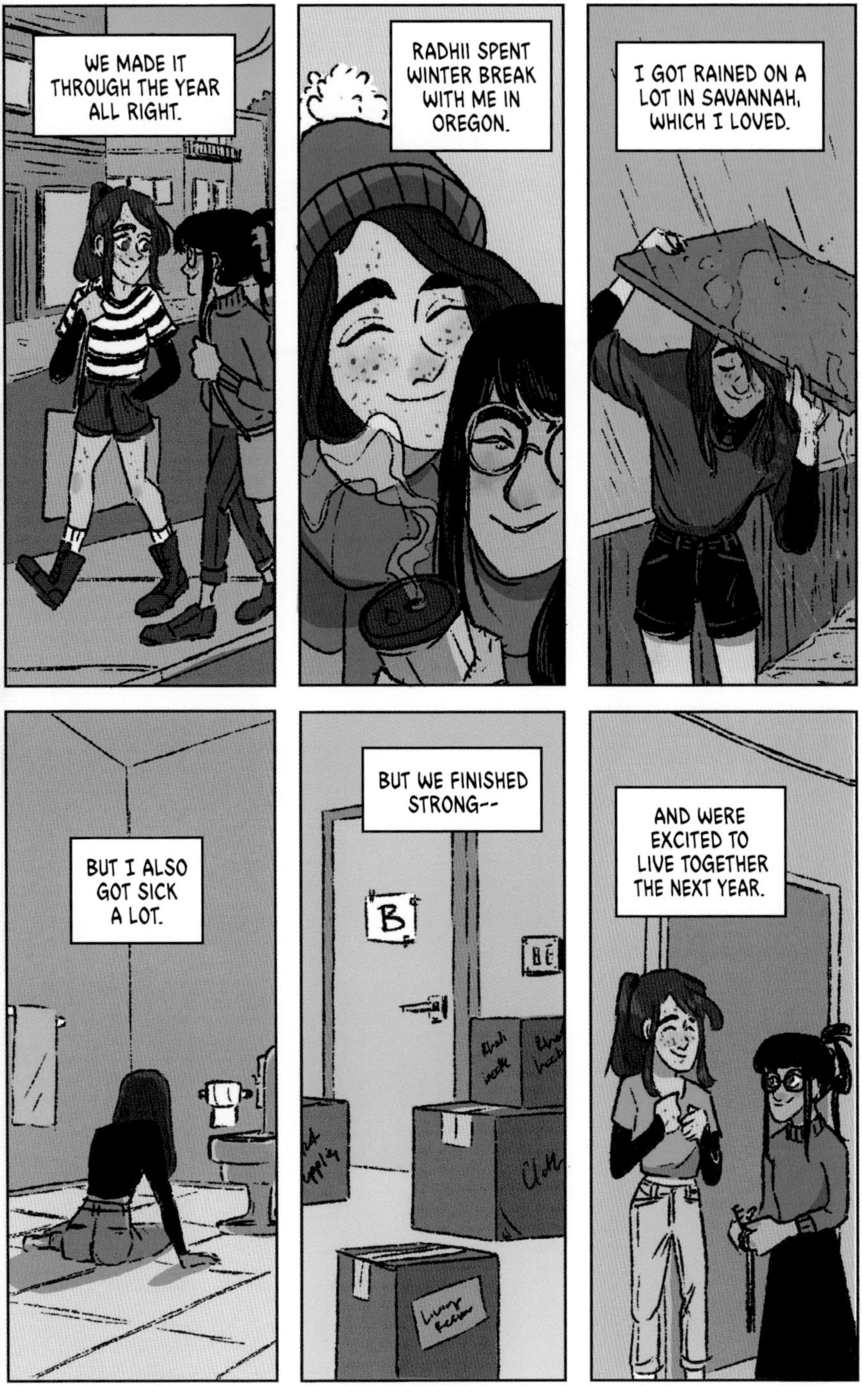
WE MADE IT THROUGH THE YEAR ALL RIGHT.
RADHII SPENT WINTER BREAK WITH ME IN OREGON.
I GOT RAINED ON A LOT IN SAVANNAH, WHICH I LOVED.
BUT I ALSO GOT SICK A LOT.
BUT WE FINISHED STRONG--
B
AND WERE EXCITED TO LIVE TOGETHER THE NEXT YEAR.

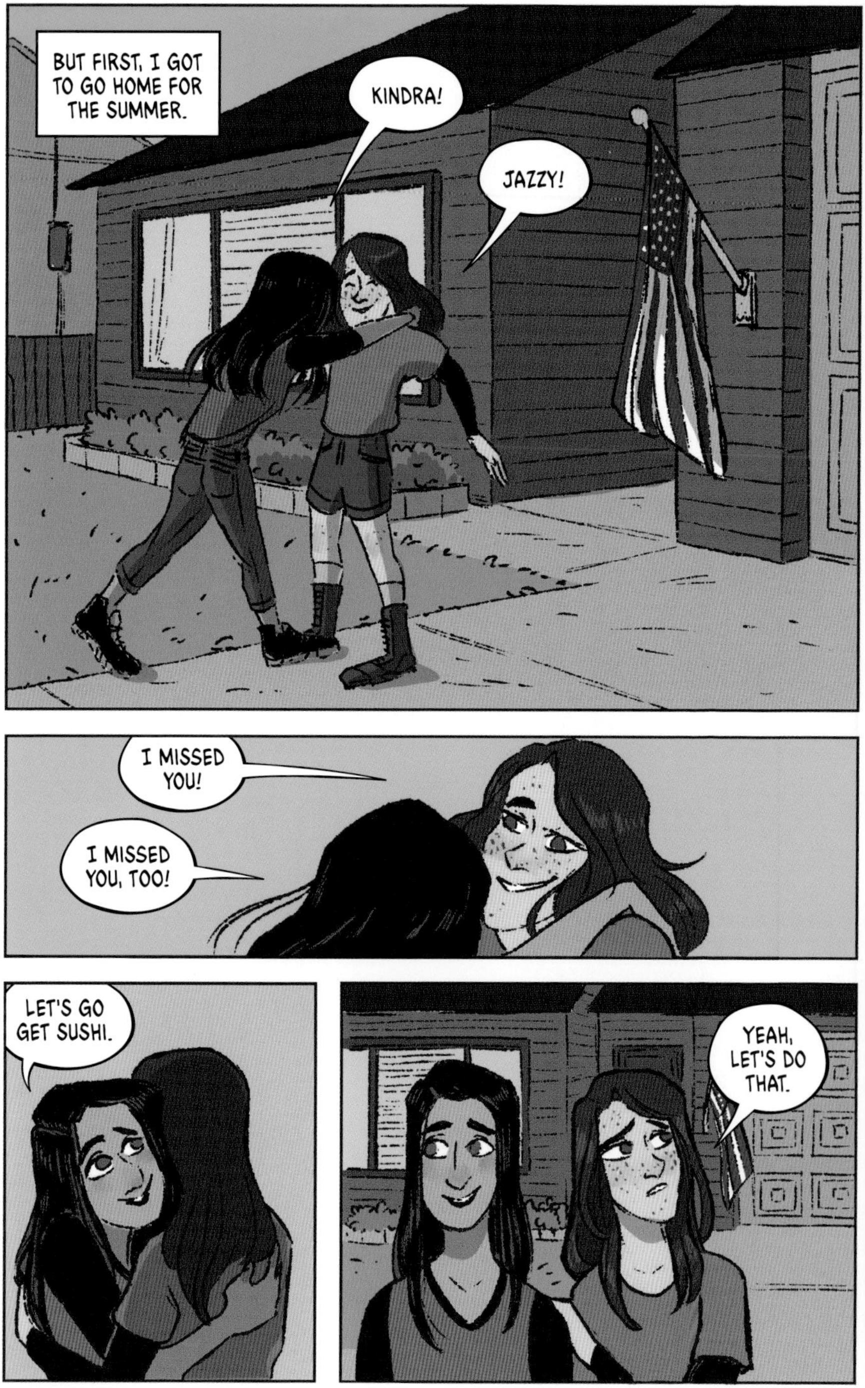
BUT FIRST, I GOT TO GO HOME FOR THE SUMMER.
KINDRA!
JAZZY!
I MISSED YOU!
I MISSED YOU, TOO!
LET'S GO GET SUSHI.
YEAH, LET'S DO THAT.

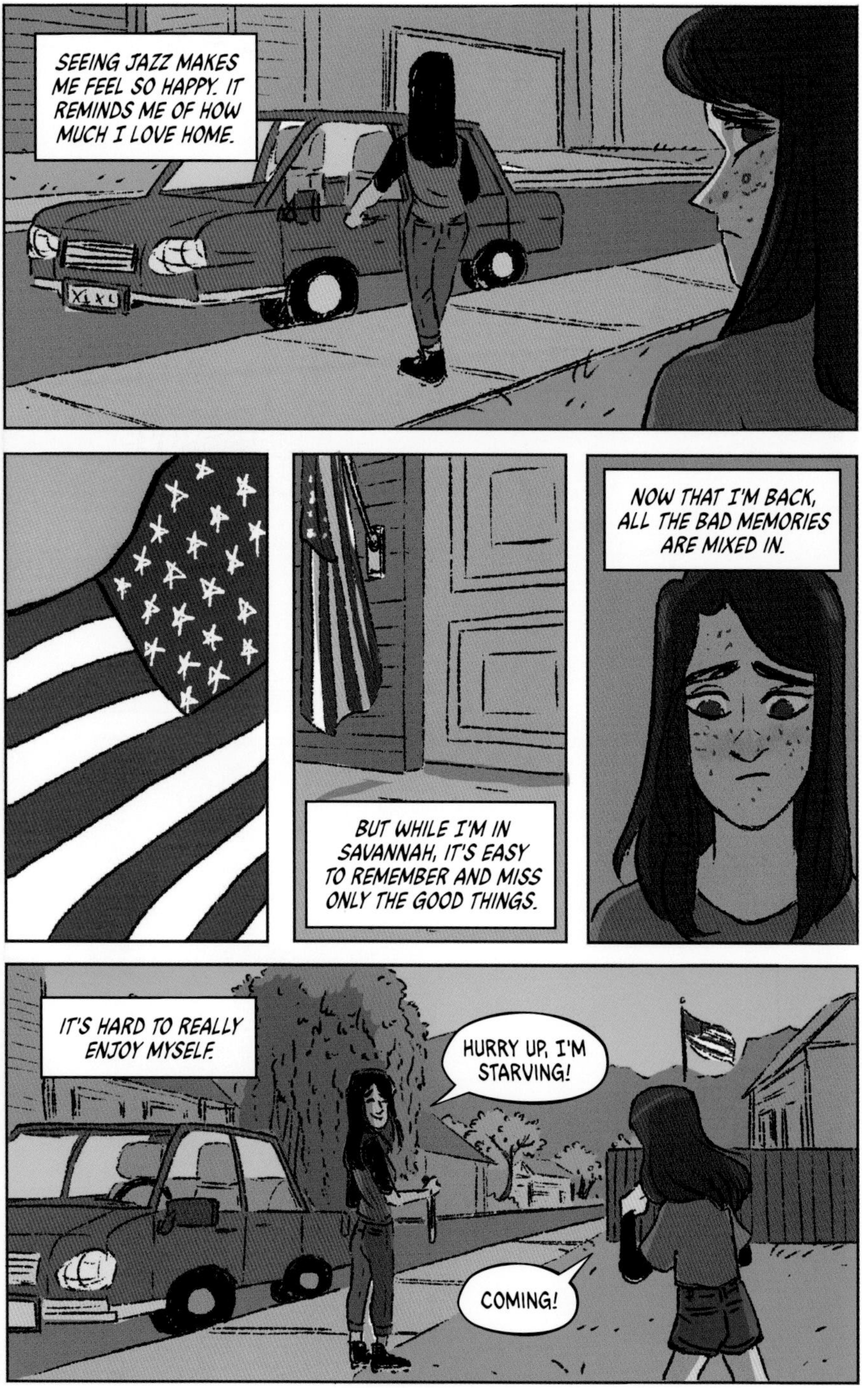
SEEING JAZZ MAKES ME FEEL SO HAPPY. IT REMINDS ME OF HOW MUCH I LOVE HOME.
NOW THAT I'M BACK, ALL THE BAD MEMORIES ARE MIXED IN.
BUT WHILE I'M IN SAVANNAH, IT'S EASY TO REMEMBER AND MISS ONLY THE GOOD THINGS.
IT'S HARD TO REALLY ENJOY MYSELF.
HURRY UP, I'M STARVING!
COMING!

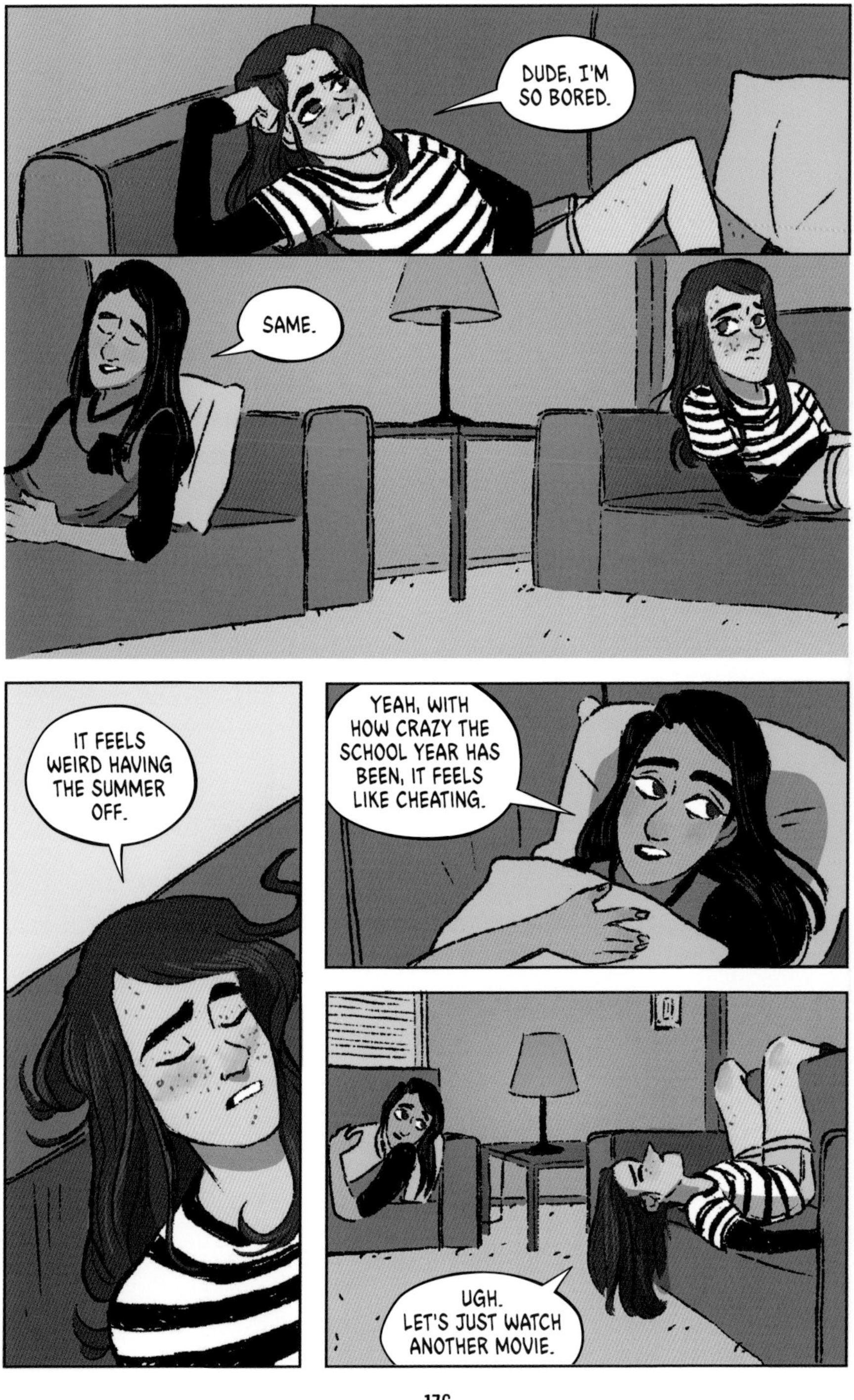
DUDE, I'M SO BORED.
SAME.
IT FEELS WEIRD HAVING THE SUMMER OFF.
YEAH, WITH HOW CRAZY THE SCHOOL YEAR HAS BEEN, IT FEELS LIKE CHEATING.
UGH. LET'S JUST WATCH ANOTHER MOVIE.

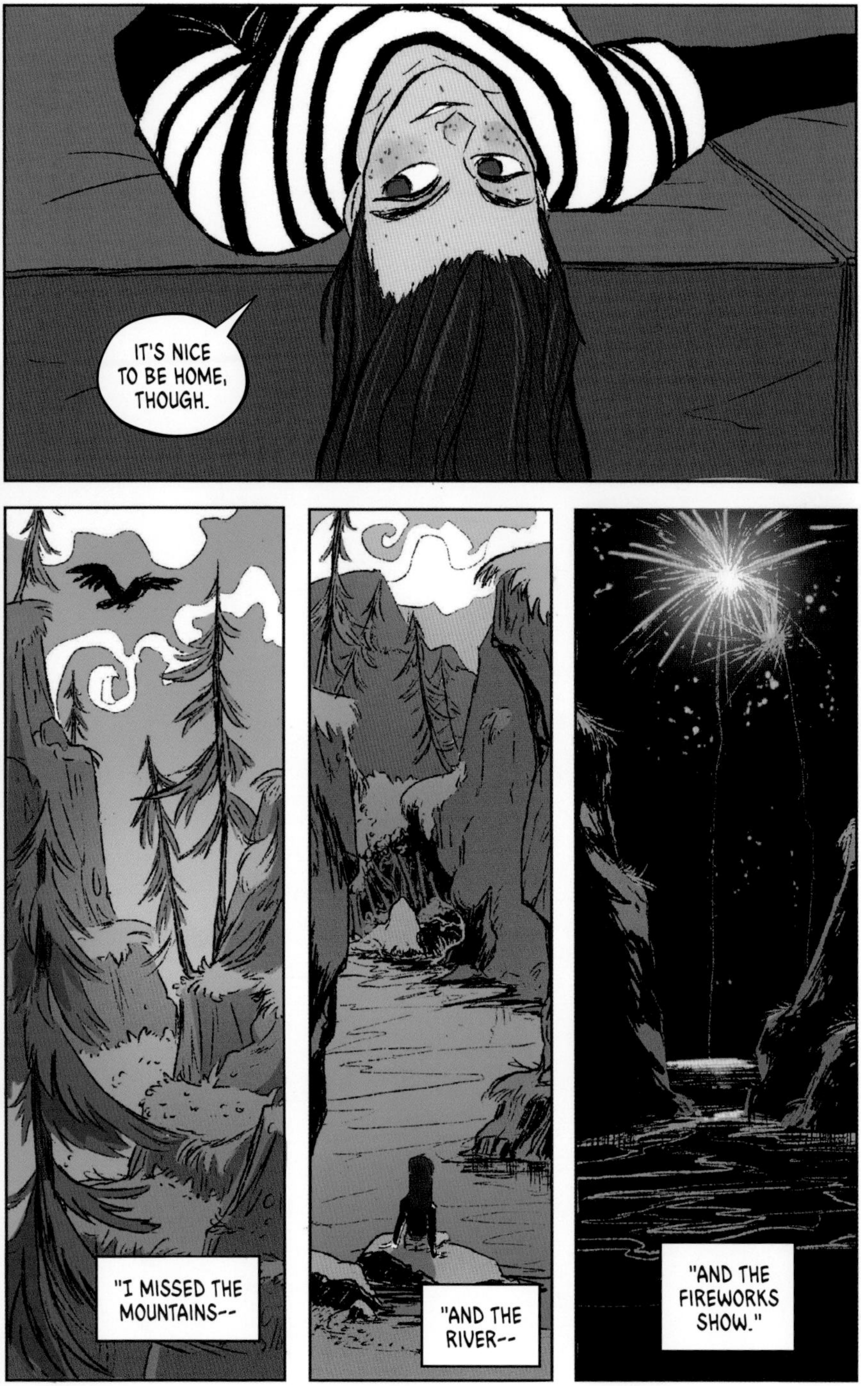
IT'S NICE TO BE HOME, THOUGH.
"I MISSED THE MOUNTAINS--
"AND THE RIVER--
"AND THE FIREWORKS SHOW."

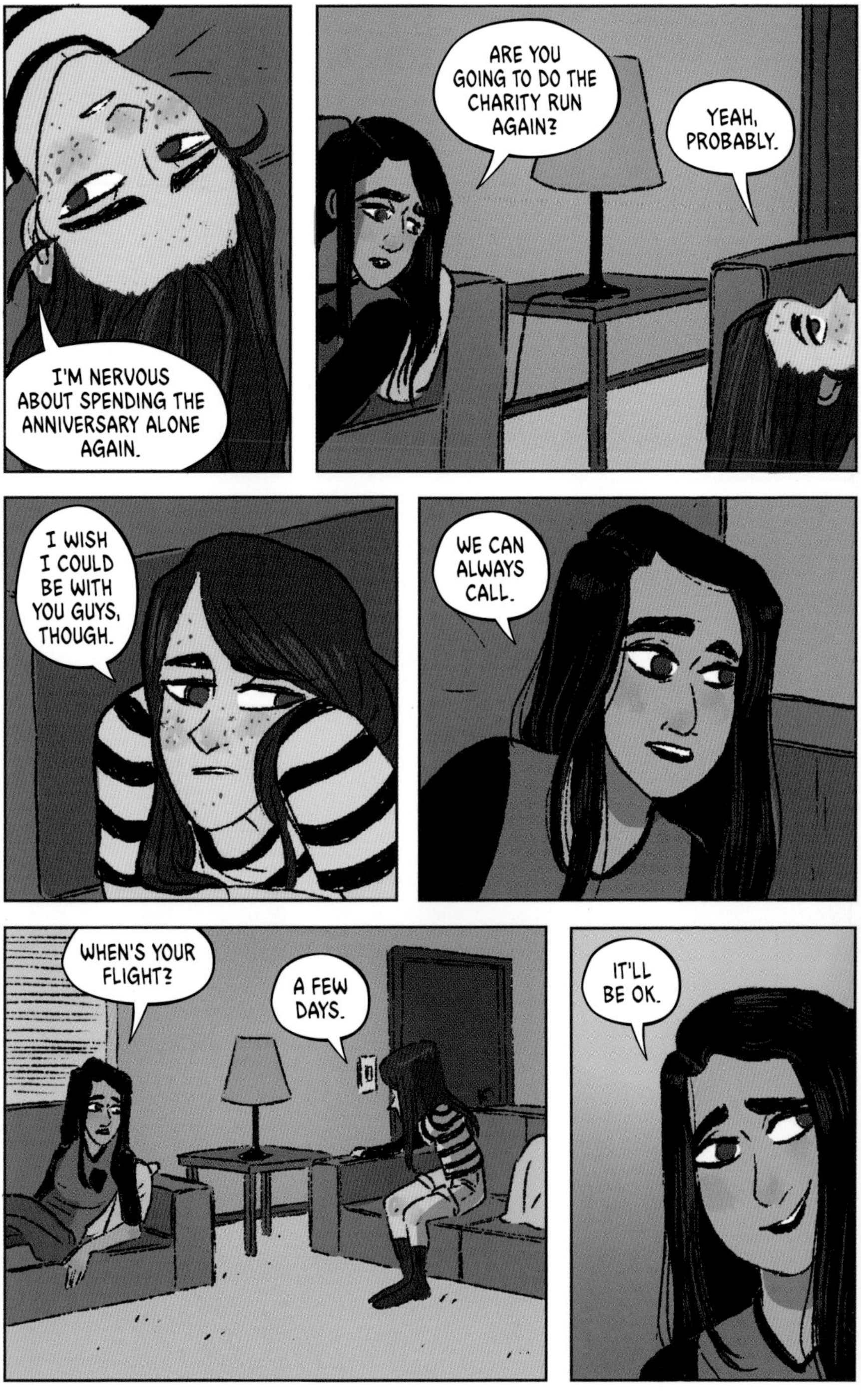

I'M NERVOUS ABOUT SPENDING THE ANNIVERSARY ALONE AGAIN.
ARE YOU GOING TO DO THE CHARITY RUN AGAIN?
YEAH, PROBABLY.
I WISH I COULD BE WITH YOU GUYS, THOUGH.
WE CAN ALWAYS CALL.
WHEN'S YOUR FLIGHT?
A FEW DAYS.
IT'LL BE OK.

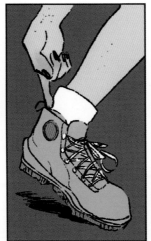

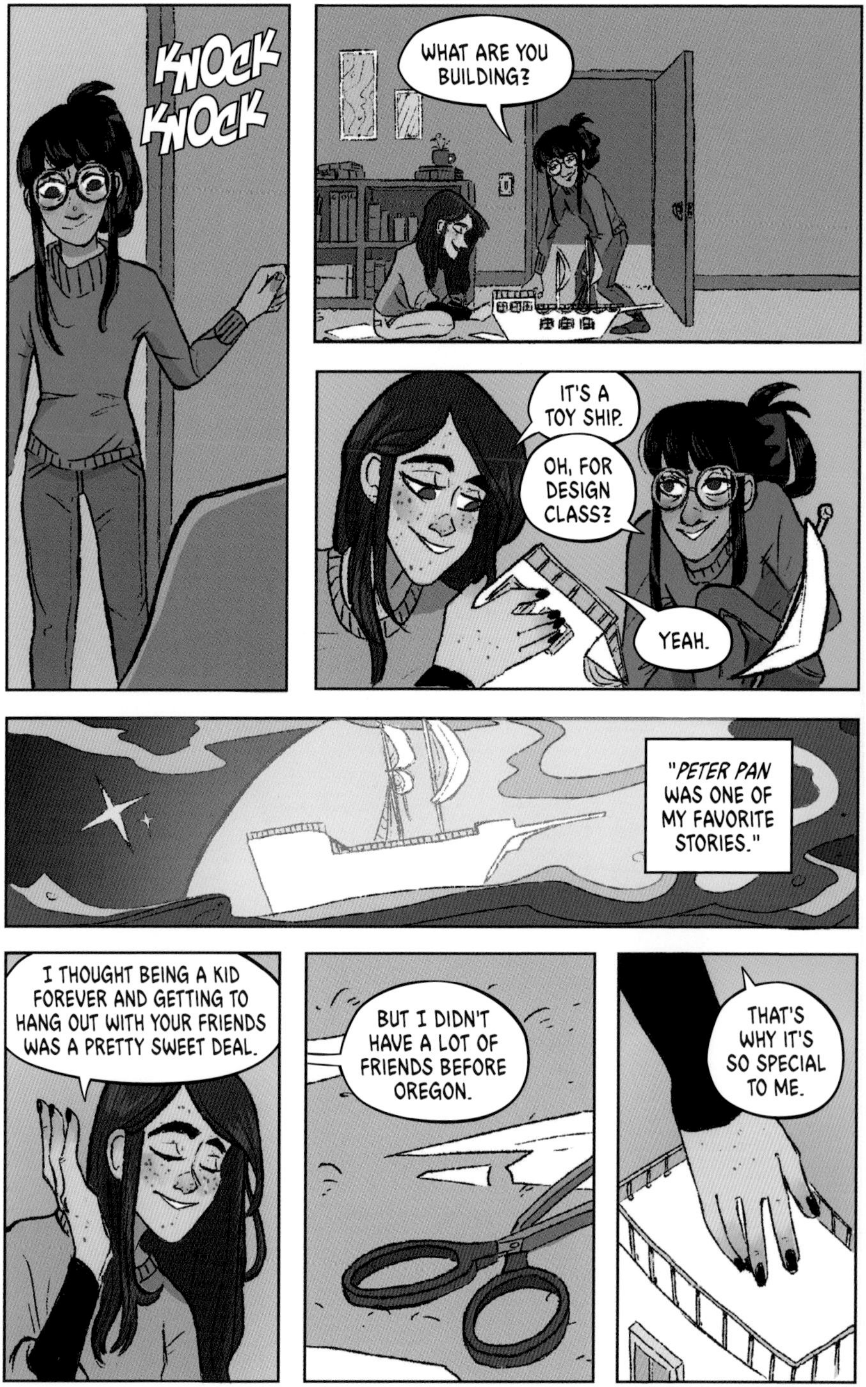
KNOCK KNOCK
WHAT ARE YOU BUILDING?
IT'S A TOY SHIP.
OH, FOR DESIGN CLASS?
YEAH.
"*PETER PAN* WAS ONE OF MY FAVORITE STORIES."
I THOUGHT BEING A KID FOREVER AND GETTING TO HANG OUT WITH YOUR FRIENDS WAS A PRETTY SWEET DEAL.
BUT I DIDN'T HAVE A LOT OF FRIENDS BEFORE OREGON.
THAT'S WHY IT'S SO SPECIAL TO ME.

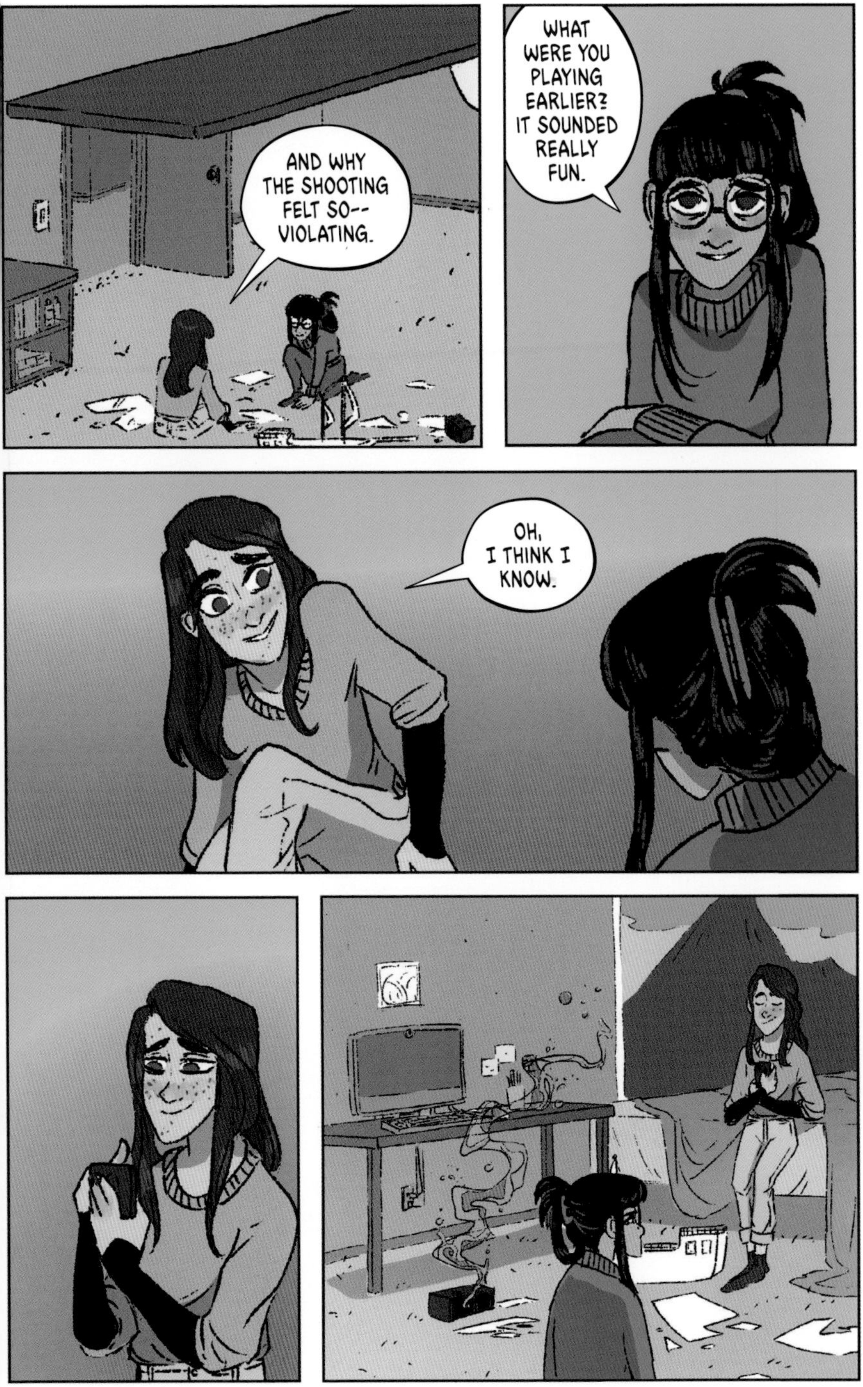
AND WHY THE SHOOTING FELT SO--VIOLATING.
WHAT WERE YOU PLAYING EARLIER? IT SOUNDED REALLY FUN.
OH, I THINK I KNOW.

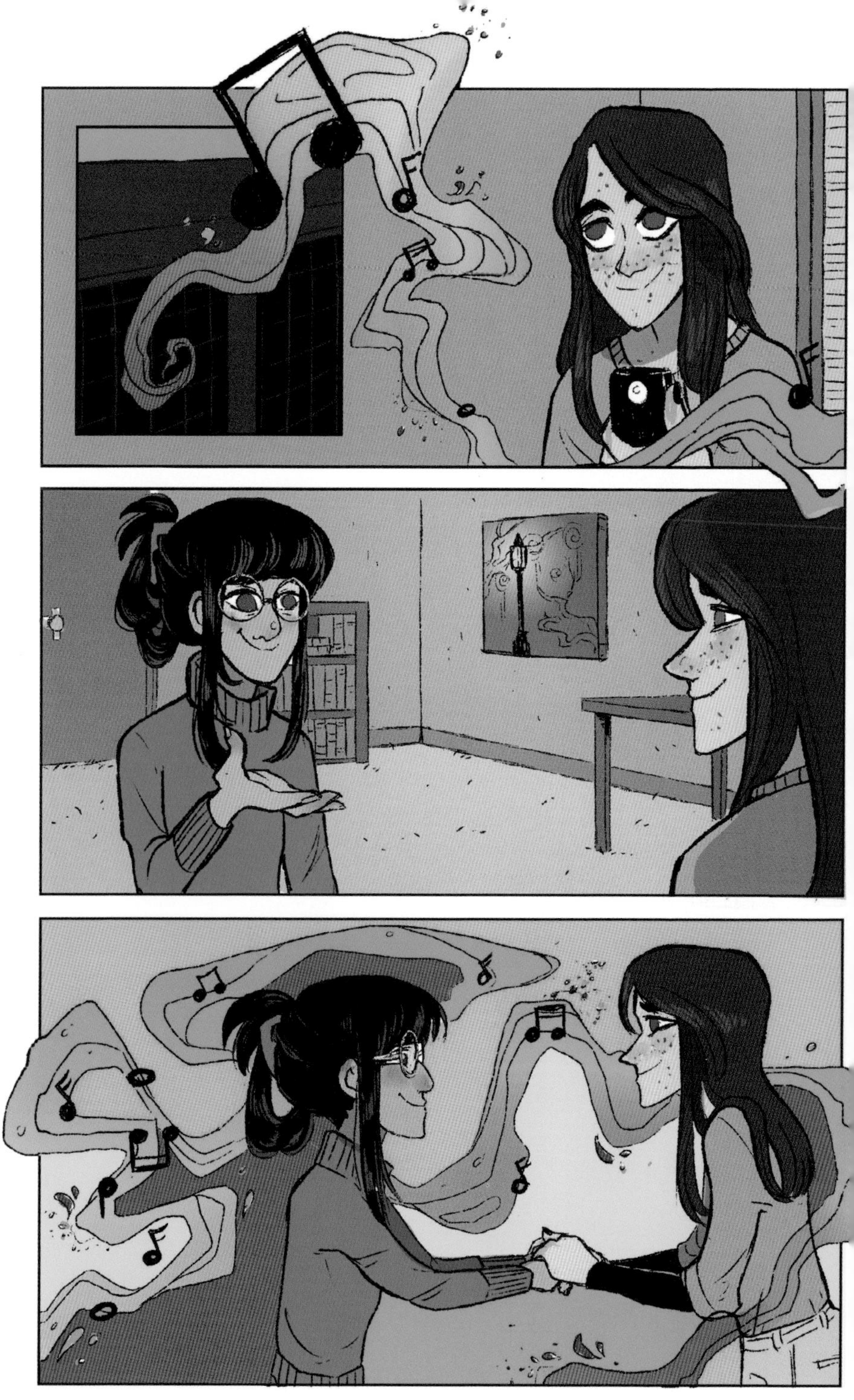

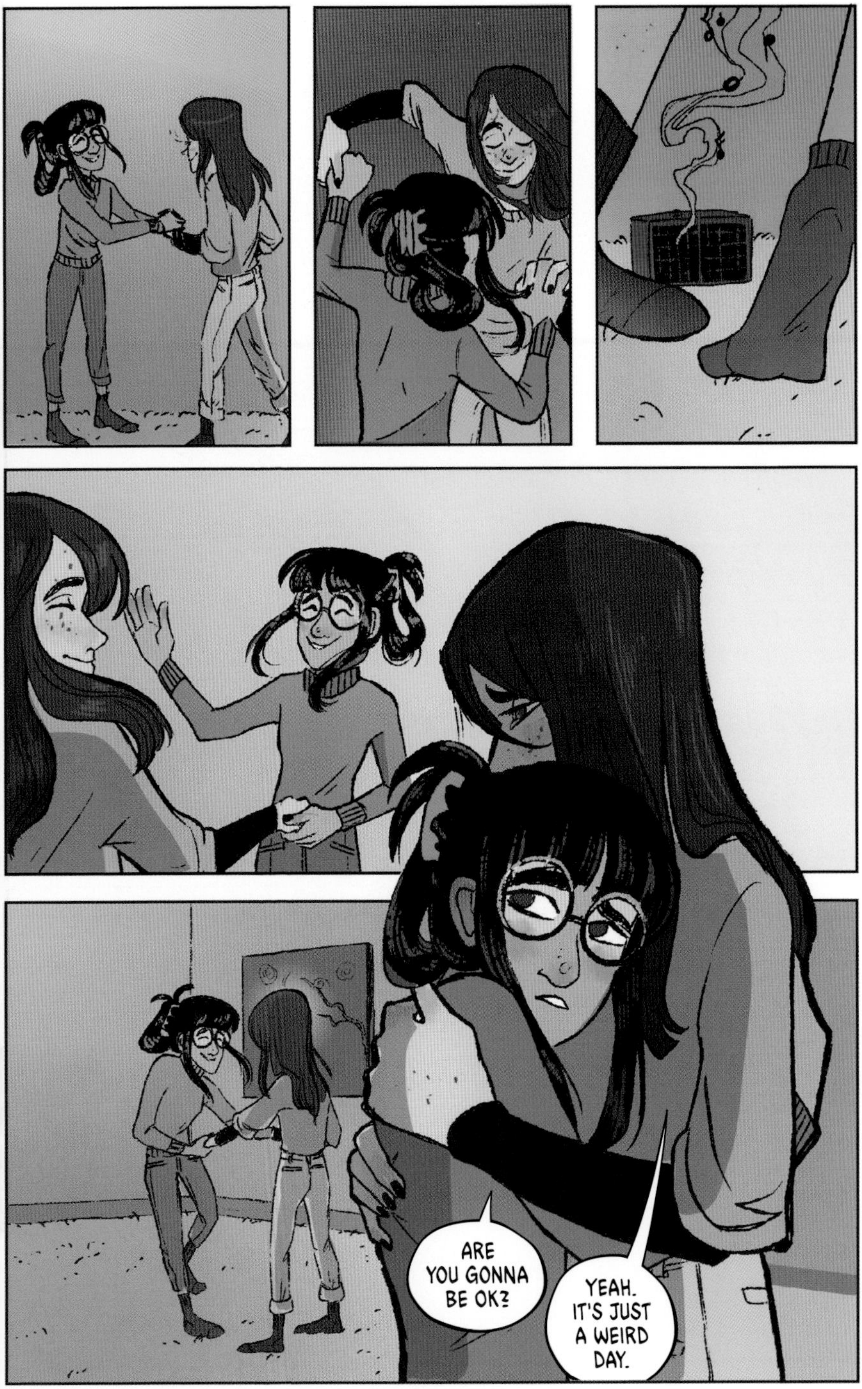
ARE YOU GONNA BE OK?
YEAH. IT'S JUST A WEIRD DAY.

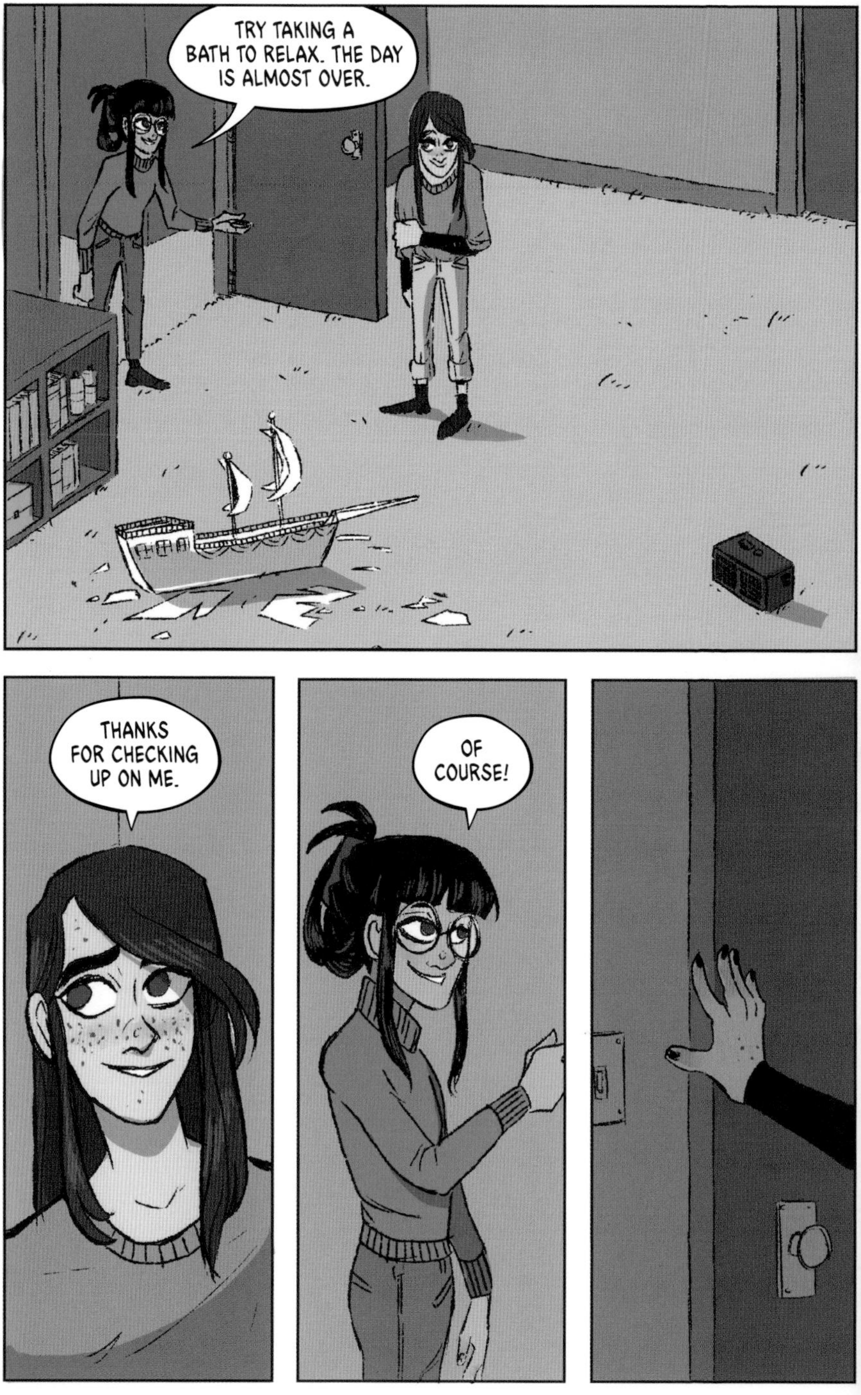
TRY TAKING A BATH TO RELAX. THE DAY IS ALMOST OVER.
THANKS FOR CHECKING UP ON ME.
OF COURSE!

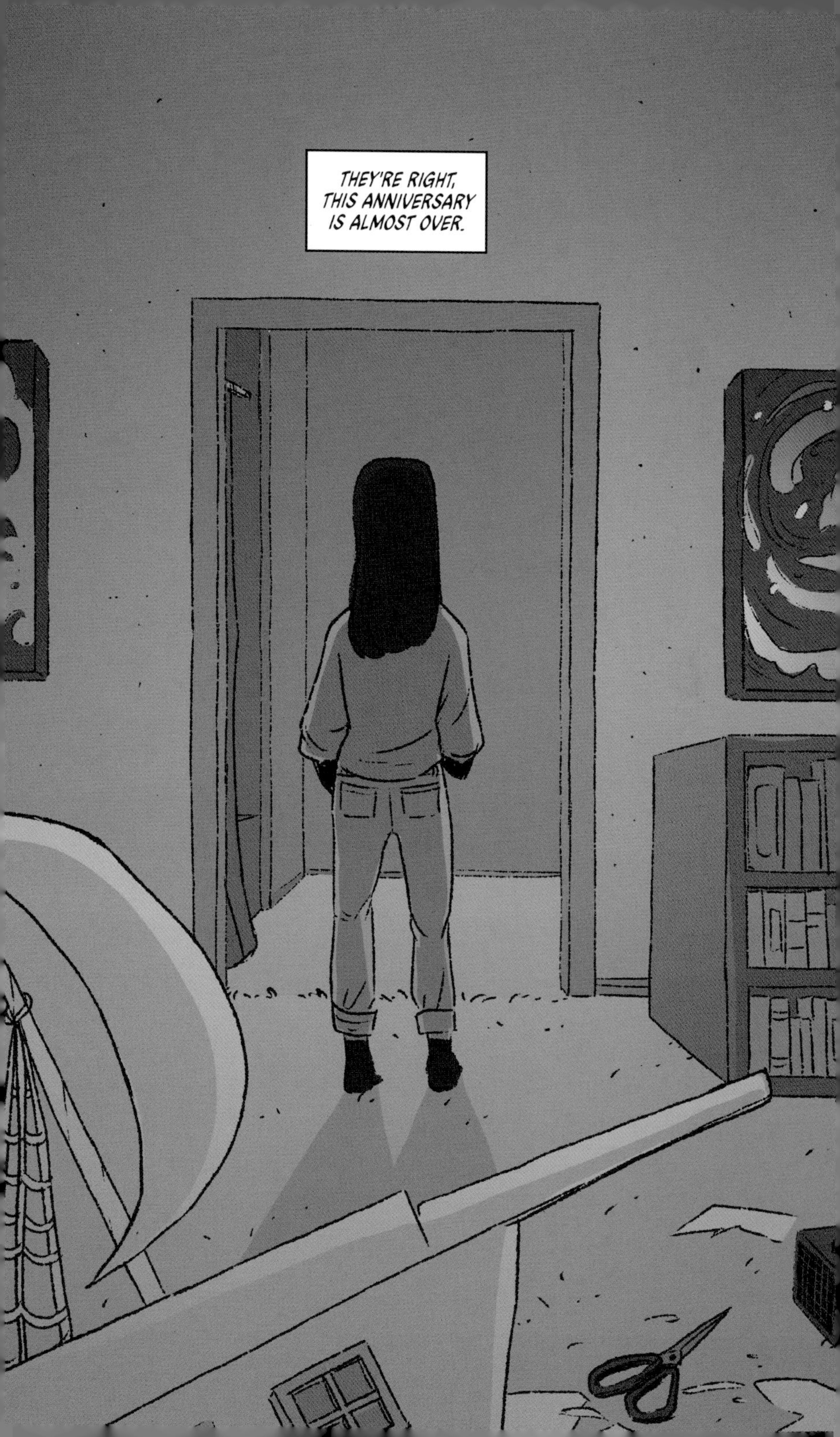
THEY'RE RIGHT, THIS ANNIVERSARY IS ALMOST OVER.

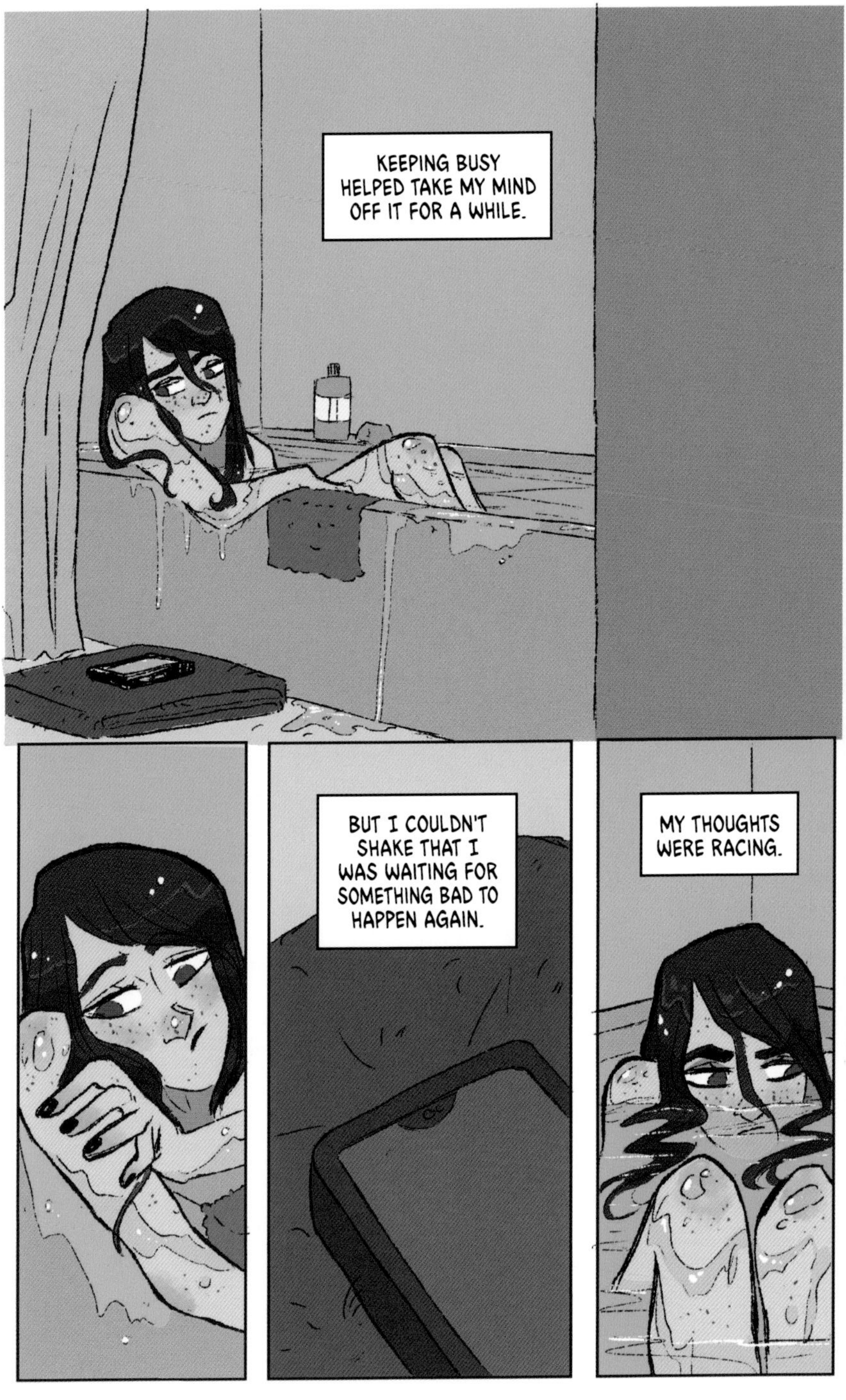
KEEPING BUSY HELPED TAKE MY MIND OFF IT FOR A WHILE.
BUT I COULDN'T SHAKE THAT I WAS WAITING FOR SOMETHING BAD TO HAPPEN AGAIN.
MY THOUGHTS WERE RACING.

I JUST WANTED MY HEAD TO BE QUIET.

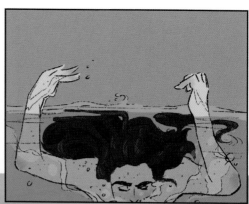

BUT I JUST SLIPPED BACK INTO THAT DAY LIKE IT WAS HAPPENING ALL OVER AGAIN.

WHAT?

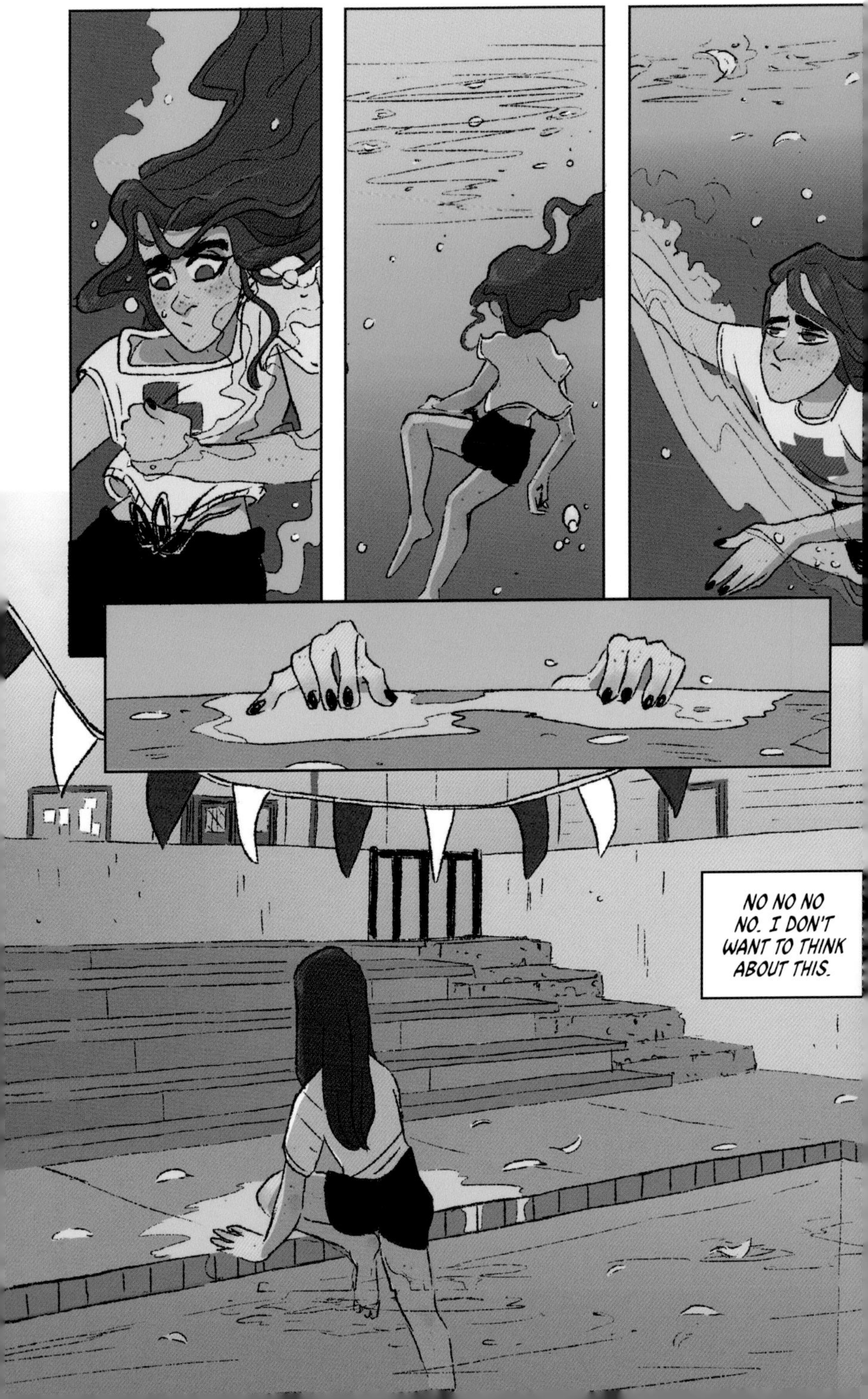
NO NO NO NO. I DON'T WANT TO THINK ABOUT THIS.

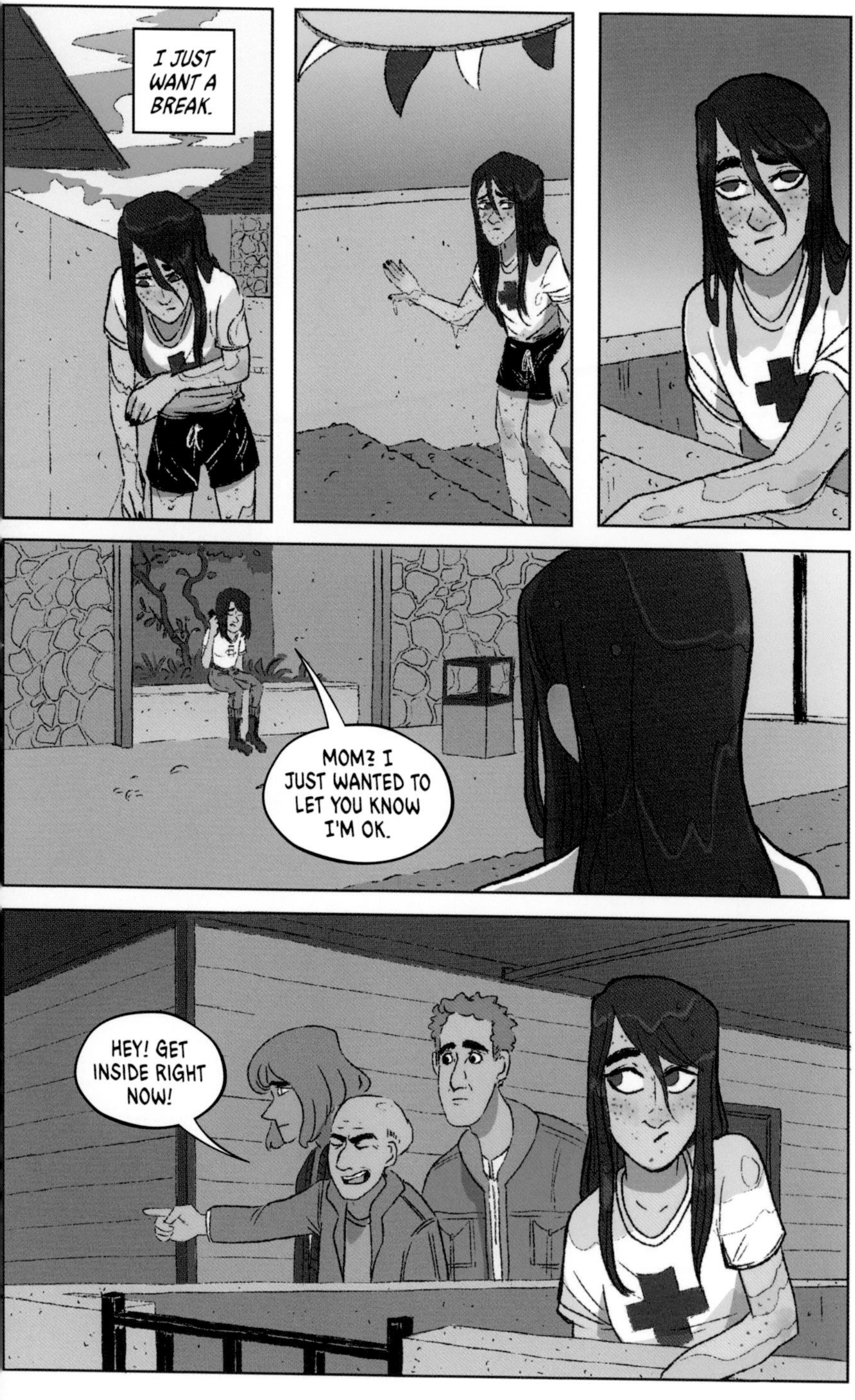
I JUST WANT A BREAK.
MOM? I JUST WANTED TO LET YOU KNOW I'M OK.
HEY! GET INSIDE RIGHT NOW!

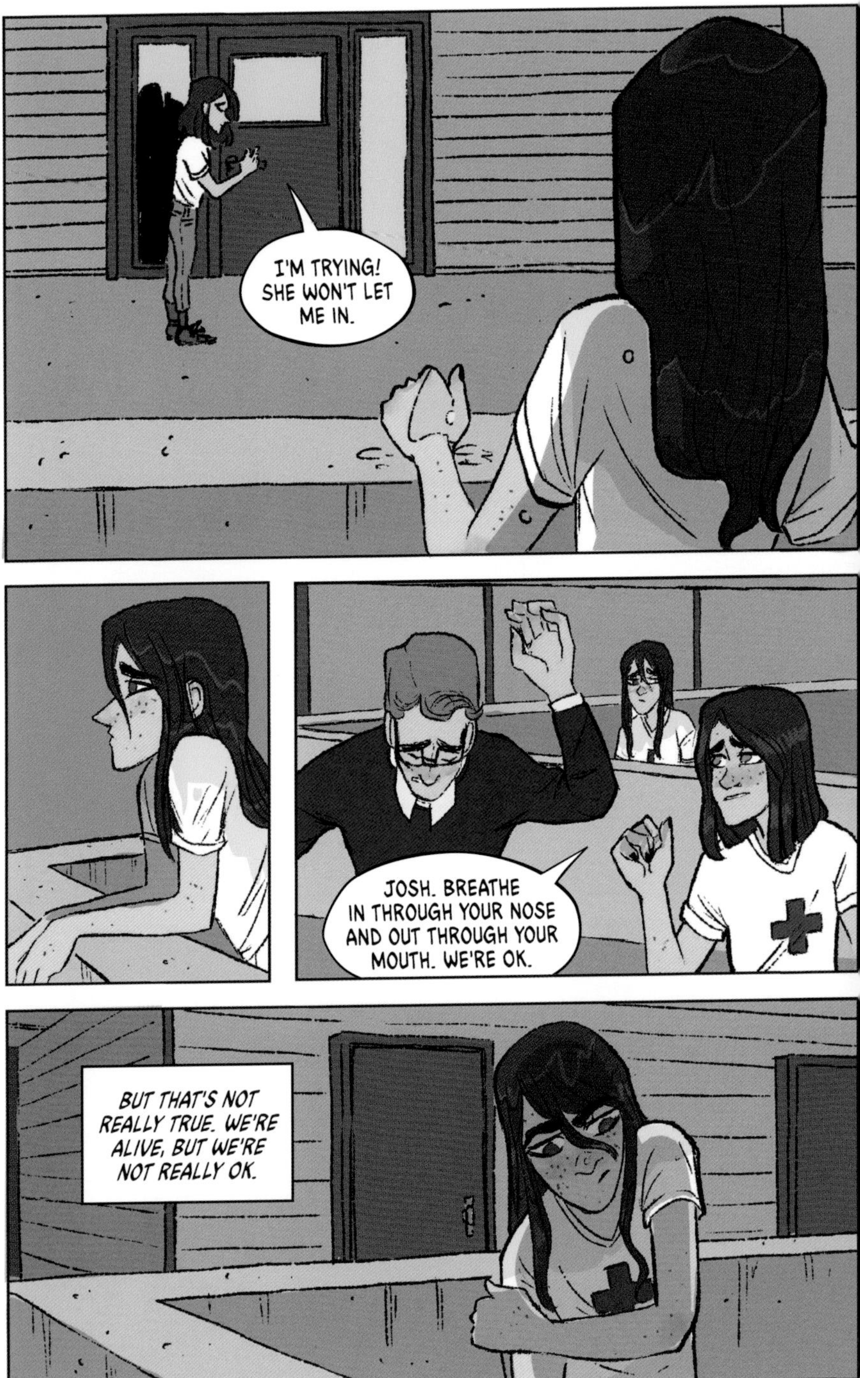
I'M TRYING! SHE WON'T LET ME IN.
JOSH. BREATHE IN THROUGH YOUR NOSE AND OUT THROUGH YOUR MOUTH. WE'RE OK.
BUT THAT'S NOT REALLY TRUE. WE'RE ALIVE, BUT WE'RE NOT REALLY OK.

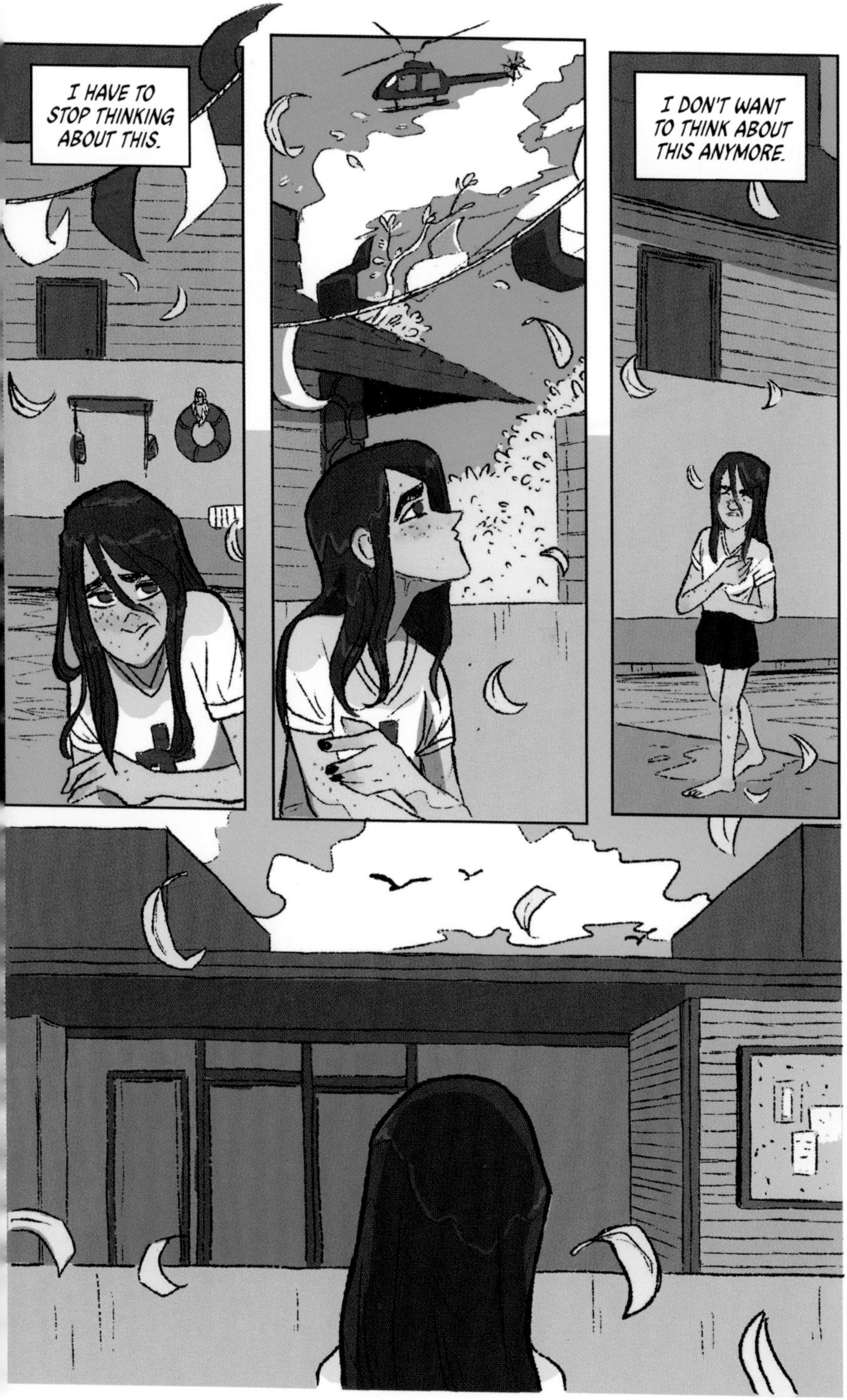
I HAVE TO STOP THINKING ABOUT THIS.
I DON'T WANT TO THINK ABOUT THIS ANYMORE.

I SAID I DON'T WANT TO THINK ABOUT THIS ANYMORE!

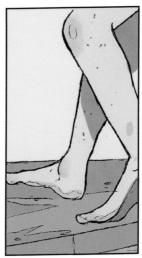

IT'S FINE.
THIS IS FINE.
I'M FINE.

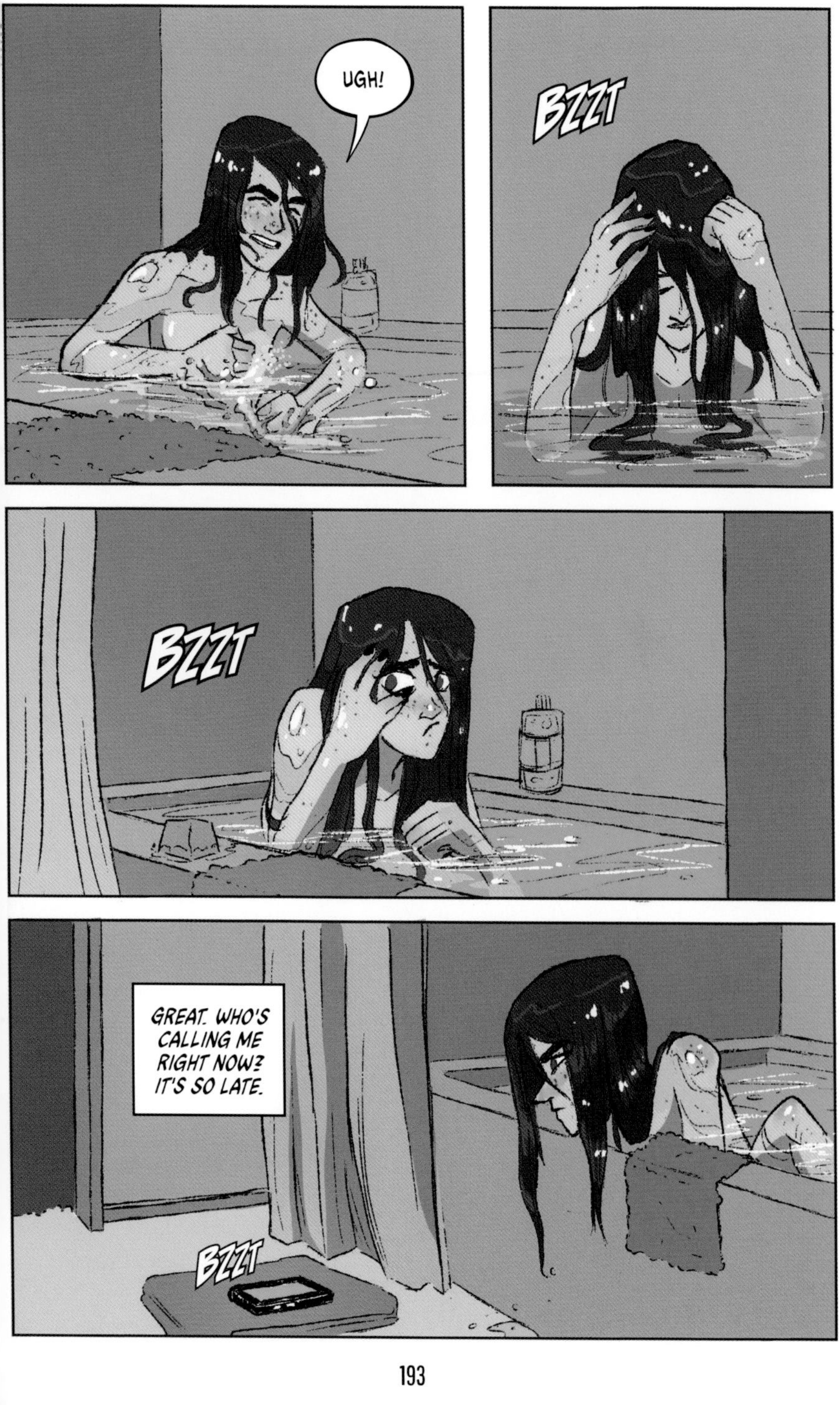
UGH!
BZZT
BZZT
GREAT. WHO'S CALLING ME RIGHT NOW? IT'S SO LATE.
BZZT

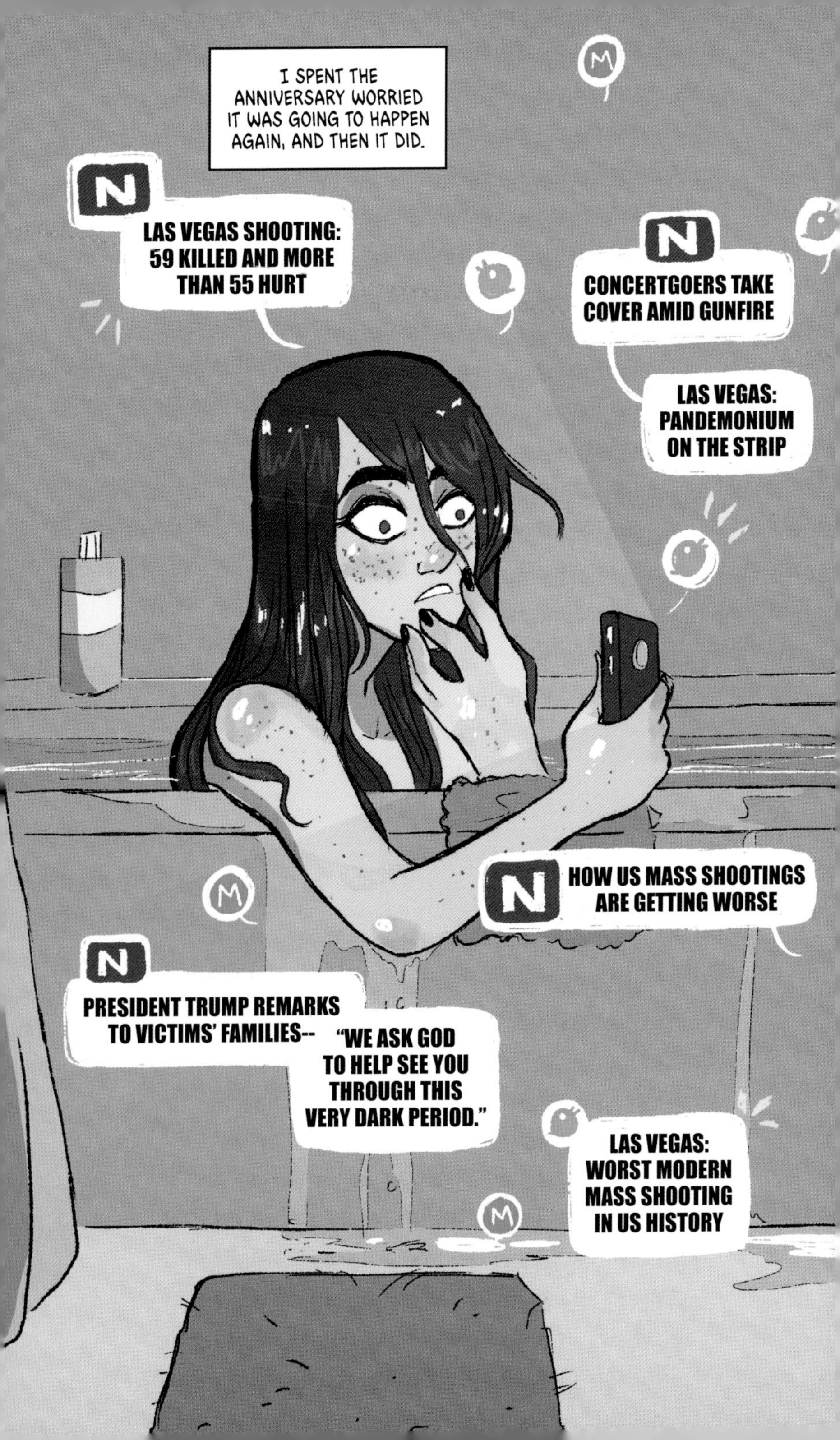
I SPENT THE ANNIVERSARY WORRIED IT WAS GOING TO HAPPEN AGAIN, AND THEN IT DID.
N
LAS VEGAS SHOOTING: 59 KILLED AND MORE THAN 55 HURT
N
CONCERTGOERS TAKE COVER AMID GUNFIRE
LAS VEGAS: PANDEMONIUM ON THE STRIP
N
HOW US MASS SHOOTINGS ARE GETTING WORSE
N
PRESIDENT TRUMP REMARKS TO VICTIMS' FAMILIES--
"WE ASK GOD TO HELP SEE YOU THROUGH THIS VERY DARK PERIOD."
LAS VEGAS: WORST MODERN MASS SHOOTING IN US HISTORY

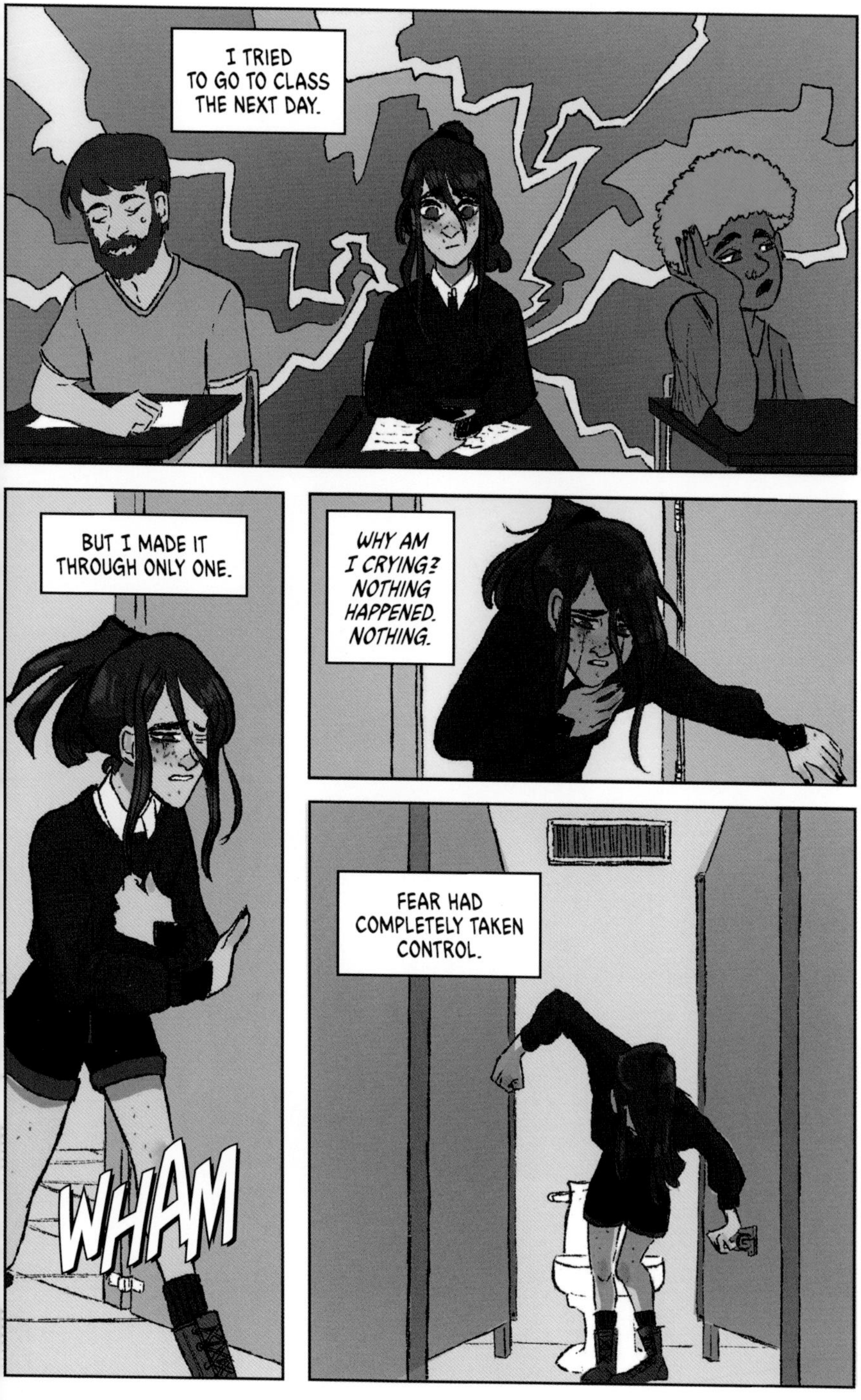
I TRIED TO GO TO CLASS THE NEXT DAY.
BUT I MADE IT THROUGH ONLY ONE.
WHAM
WHY AM I CRYING? NOTHING HAPPENED. NOTHING.
FEAR HAD COMPLETELY TAKEN CONTROL.

IT STARTED AS A VICIOUS CYCLE.

SOMETHING WOULD SCARE ME. IT DIDN'T EVEN HAVE TO BE RELATED TO SHOOTINGS.

I'D GET ANGRY--

THEN SICK--

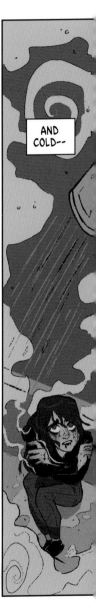

AND COLD--

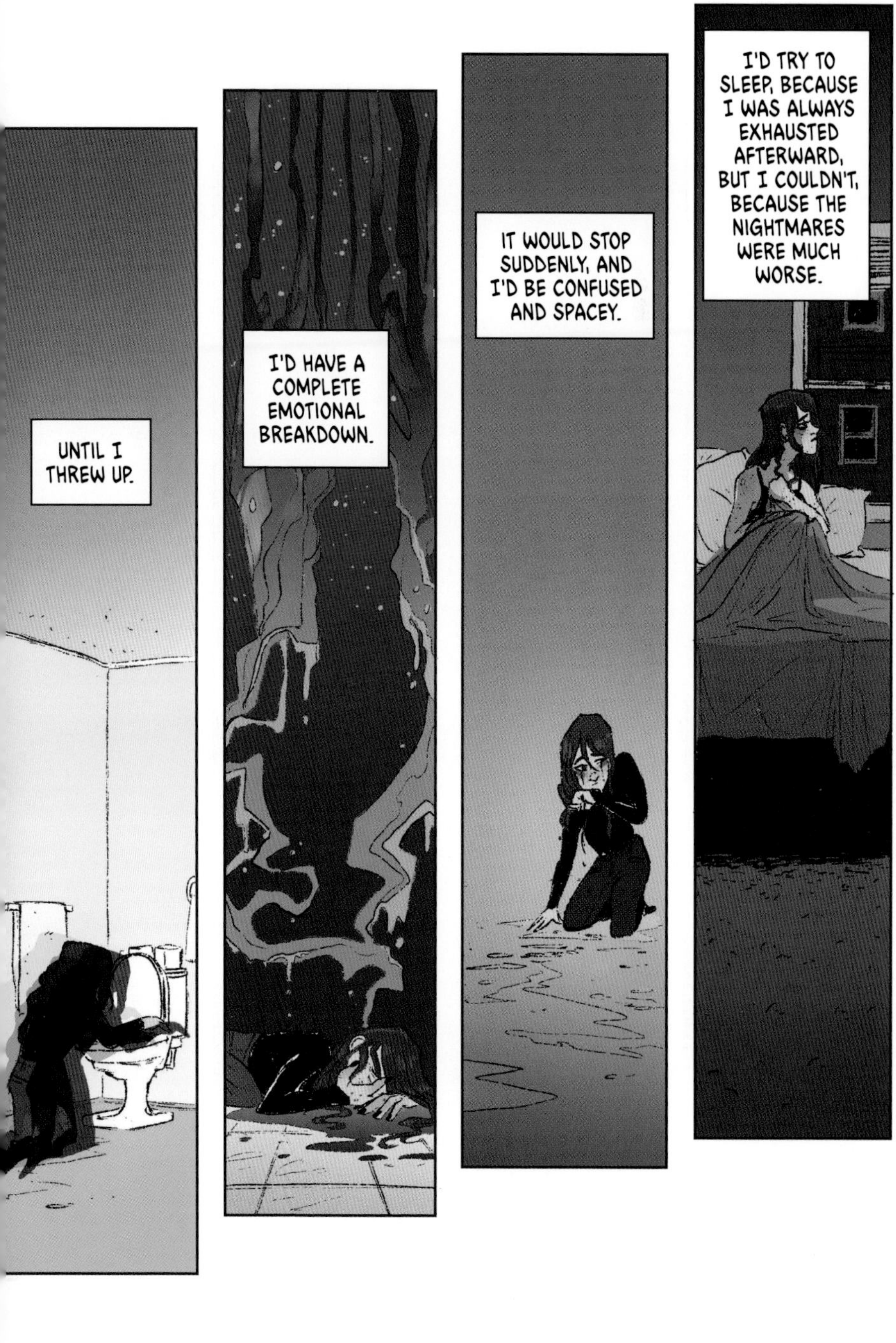
UNTIL I THREW UP.
I'D HAVE A COMPLETE EMOTIONAL BREAKDOWN.
IT WOULD STOP SUDDENLY, AND I'D BE CONFUSED AND SPACEY.
I'D TRY TO SLEEP, BECAUSE I WAS ALWAYS EXHAUSTED AFTERWARD, BUT I COULDN'T, BECAUSE THE NIGHTMARES WERE MUCH WORSE.

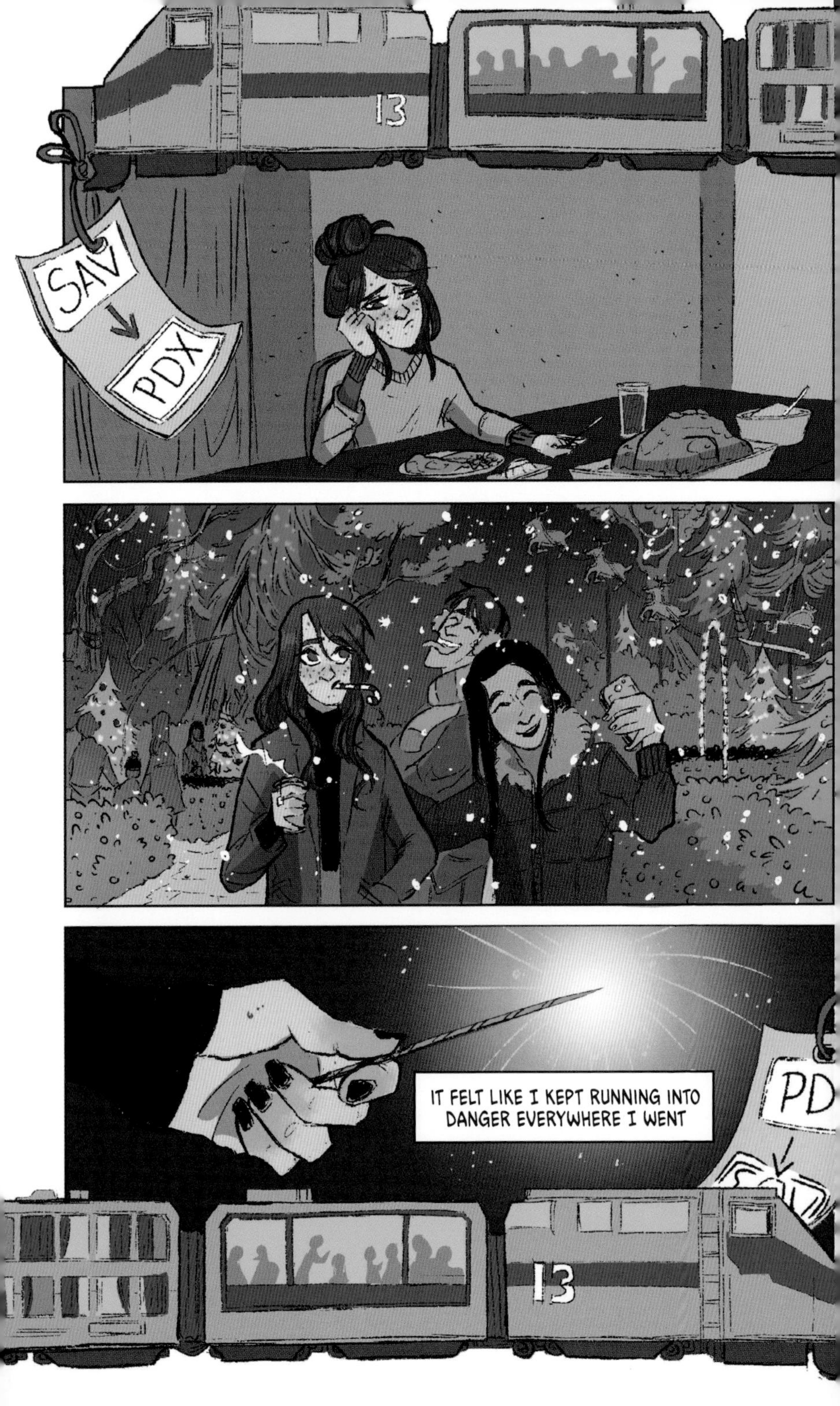
13
SAV
PDX
IT FELT LIKE I KEPT RUNNING INTO DANGER EVERYWHERE I WENT
PD
13

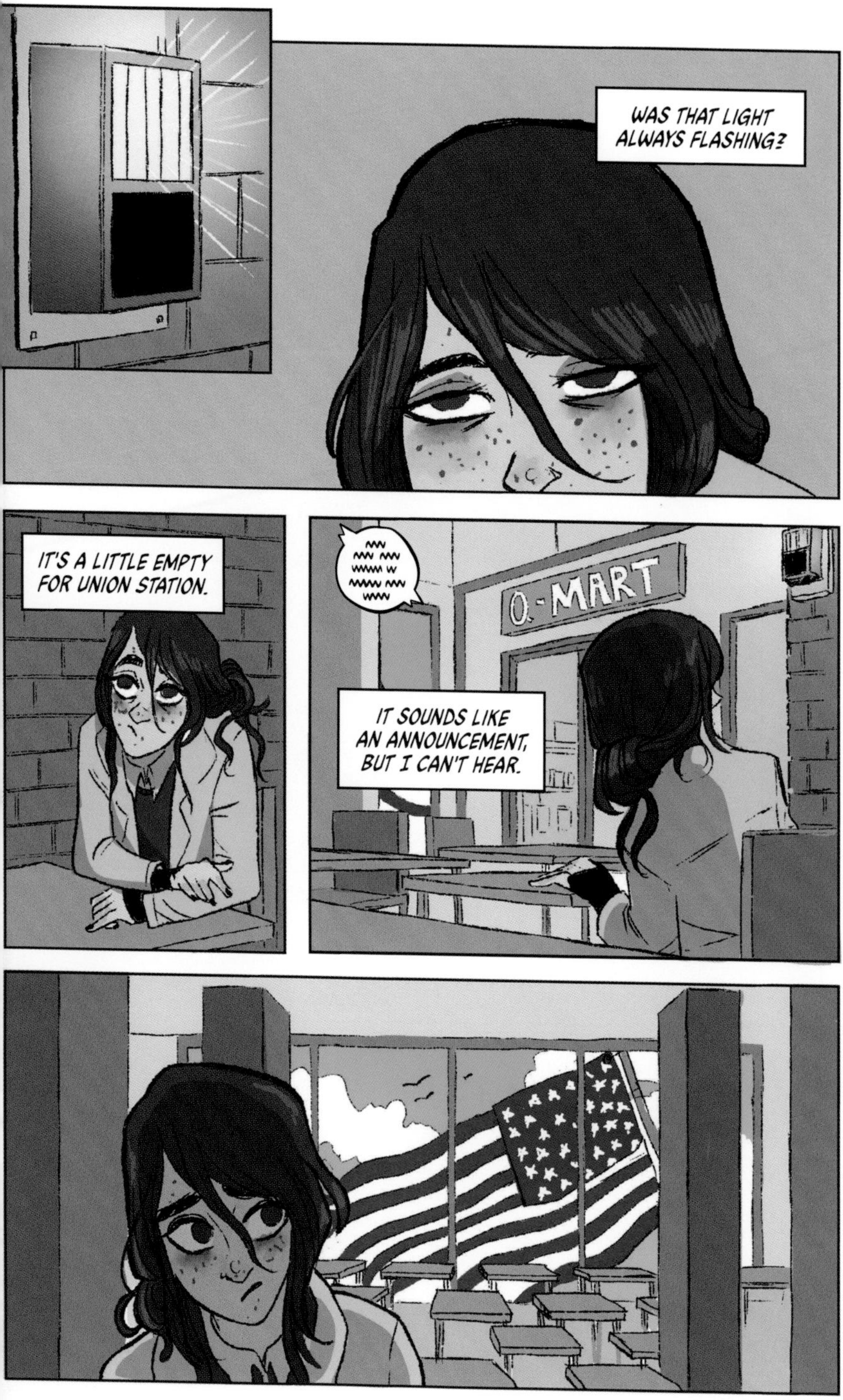
WAS THAT LIGHT ALWAYS FLASHING?
IT'S A LITTLE EMPTY FOR UNION STATION.
Q-MART
IT SOUNDS LIKE AN ANNOUNCEMENT, BUT I CAN'T HEAR.

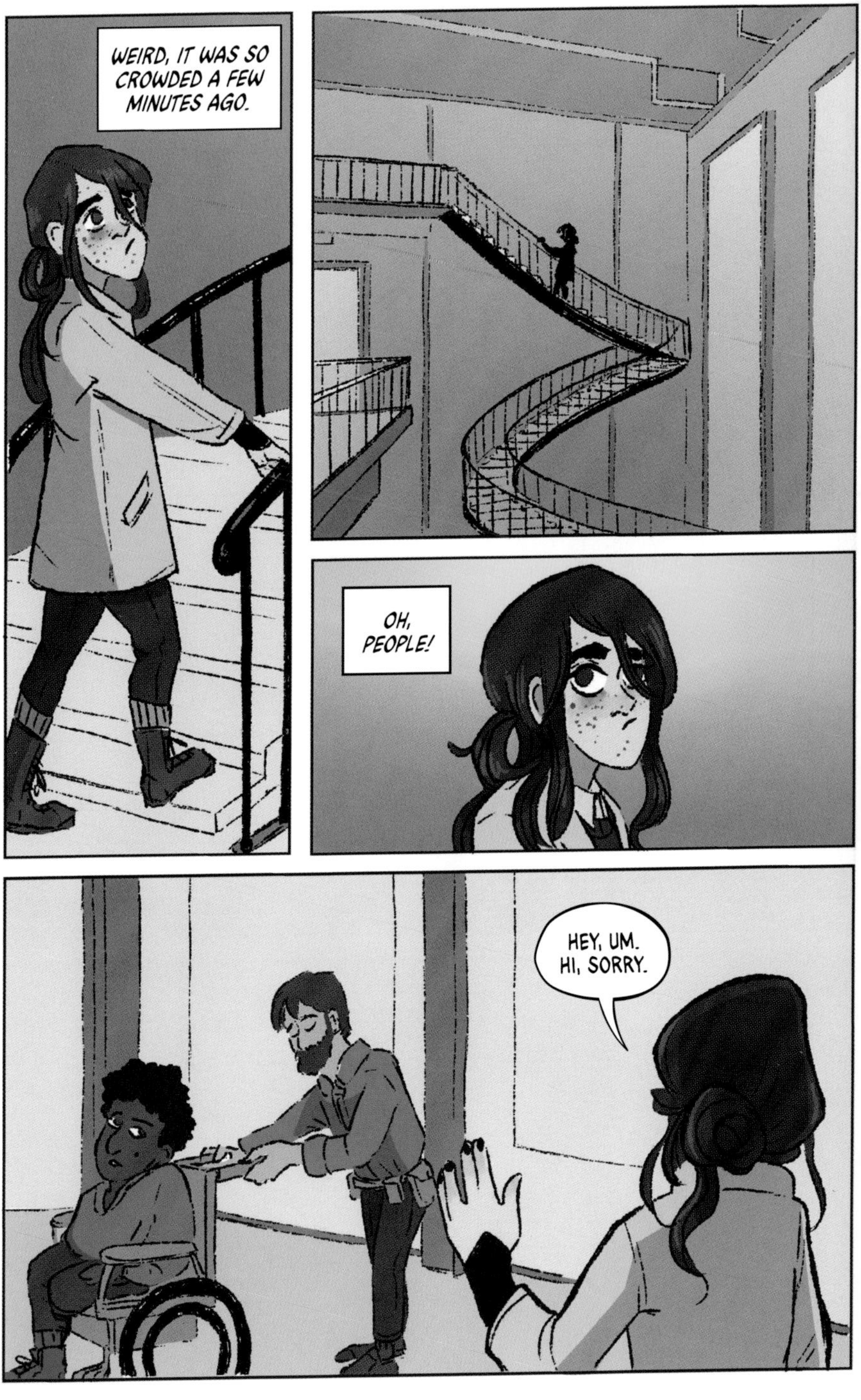
WEIRD, IT WAS SO CROWDED A FEW MINUTES AGO.
OH, PEOPLE!
HEY, UM. HI, SORRY.

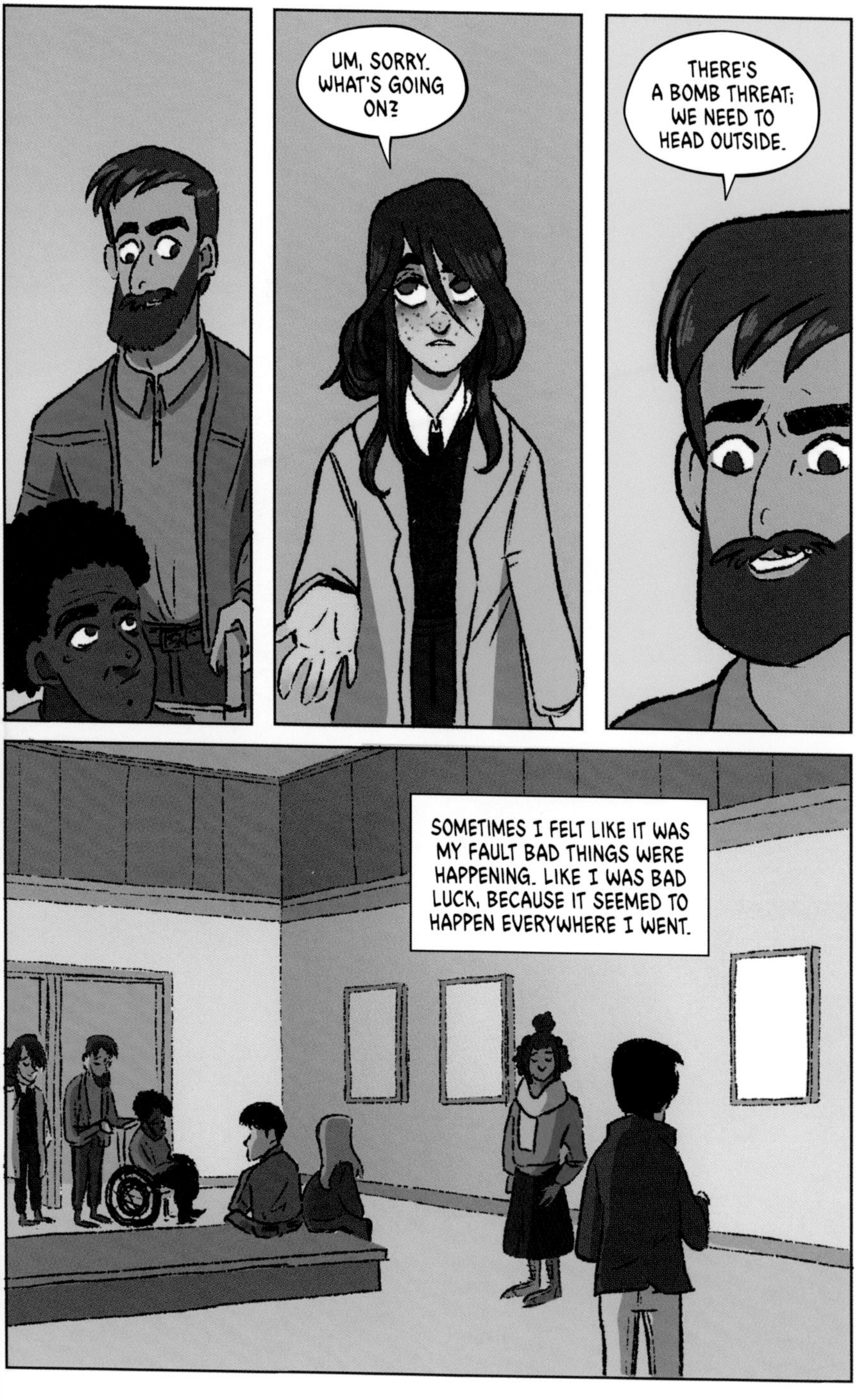
UM, SORRY. WHAT'S GOING ON?
THERE'S A BOMB THREAT; WE NEED TO HEAD OUTSIDE.
SOMETIMES I FELT LIKE IT WAS MY FAULT BAD THINGS WERE HAPPENING. LIKE I WAS BAD LUCK, BECAUSE IT SEEMED TO HAPPEN EVERYWHERE I WENT.

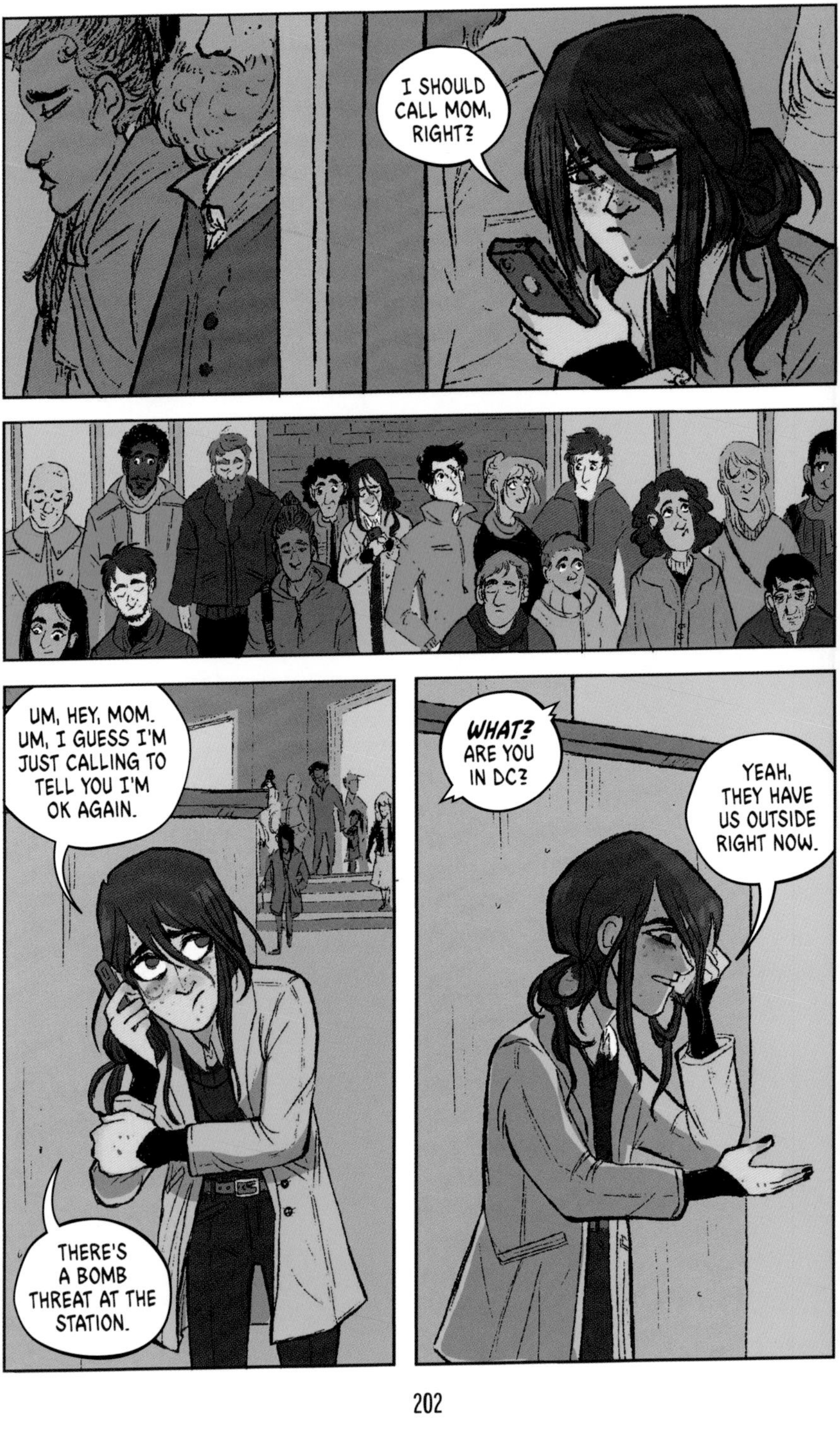
I SHOULD CALL MOM, RIGHT?
UM, HEY, MOM. UM, I GUESS I'M JUST CALLING TO TELL YOU I'M OK AGAIN.
THERE'S A BOMB THREAT AT THE STATION.
WHAT? ARE YOU IN DC?
YEAH, THEY HAVE US OUTSIDE RIGHT NOW.

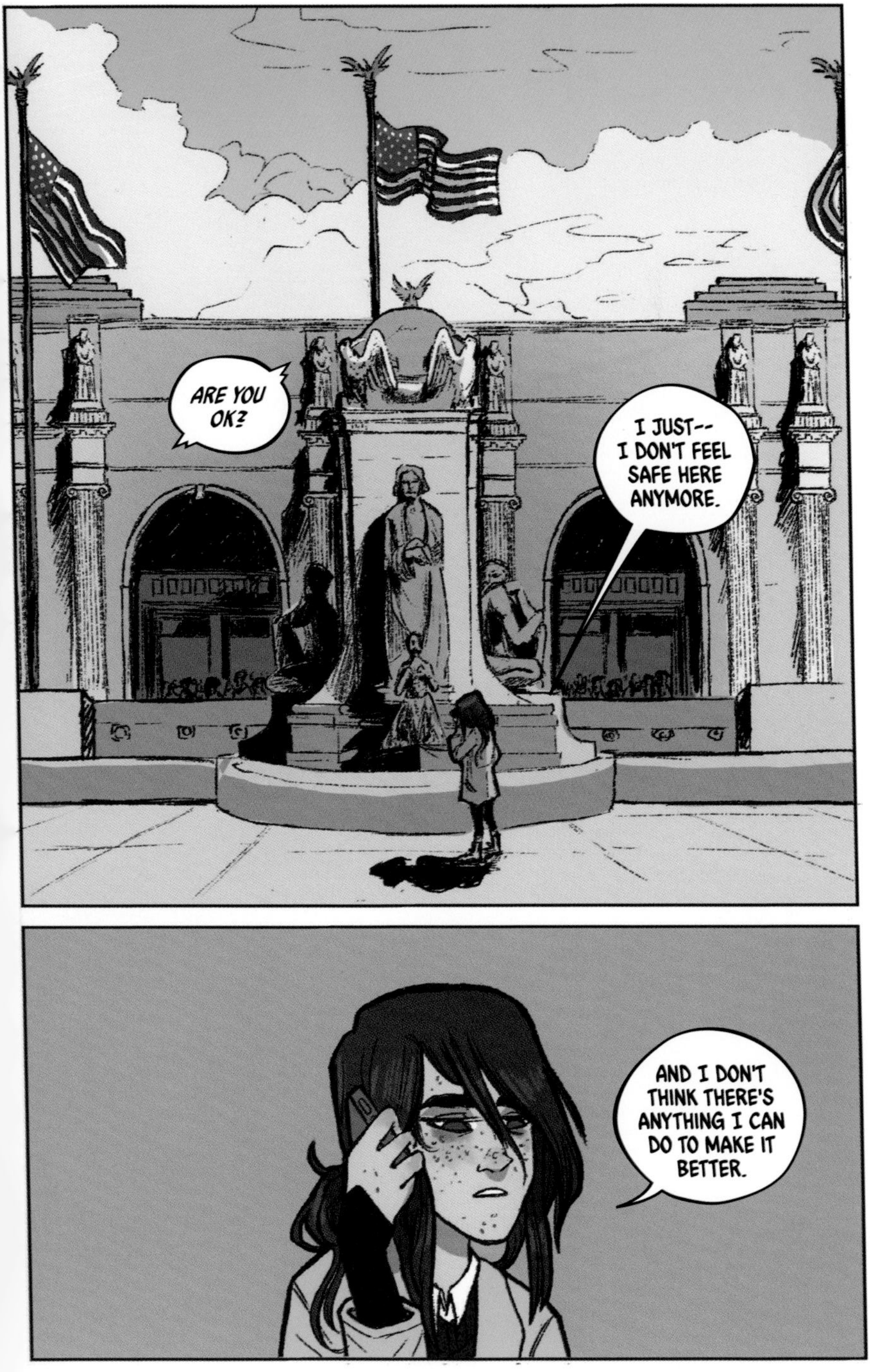
ARE YOU OK?
I JUST-- I DON'T FEEL SAFE HERE ANYMORE.
AND I DON'T THINK THERE'S ANYTHING I CAN DO TO MAKE IT BETTER.

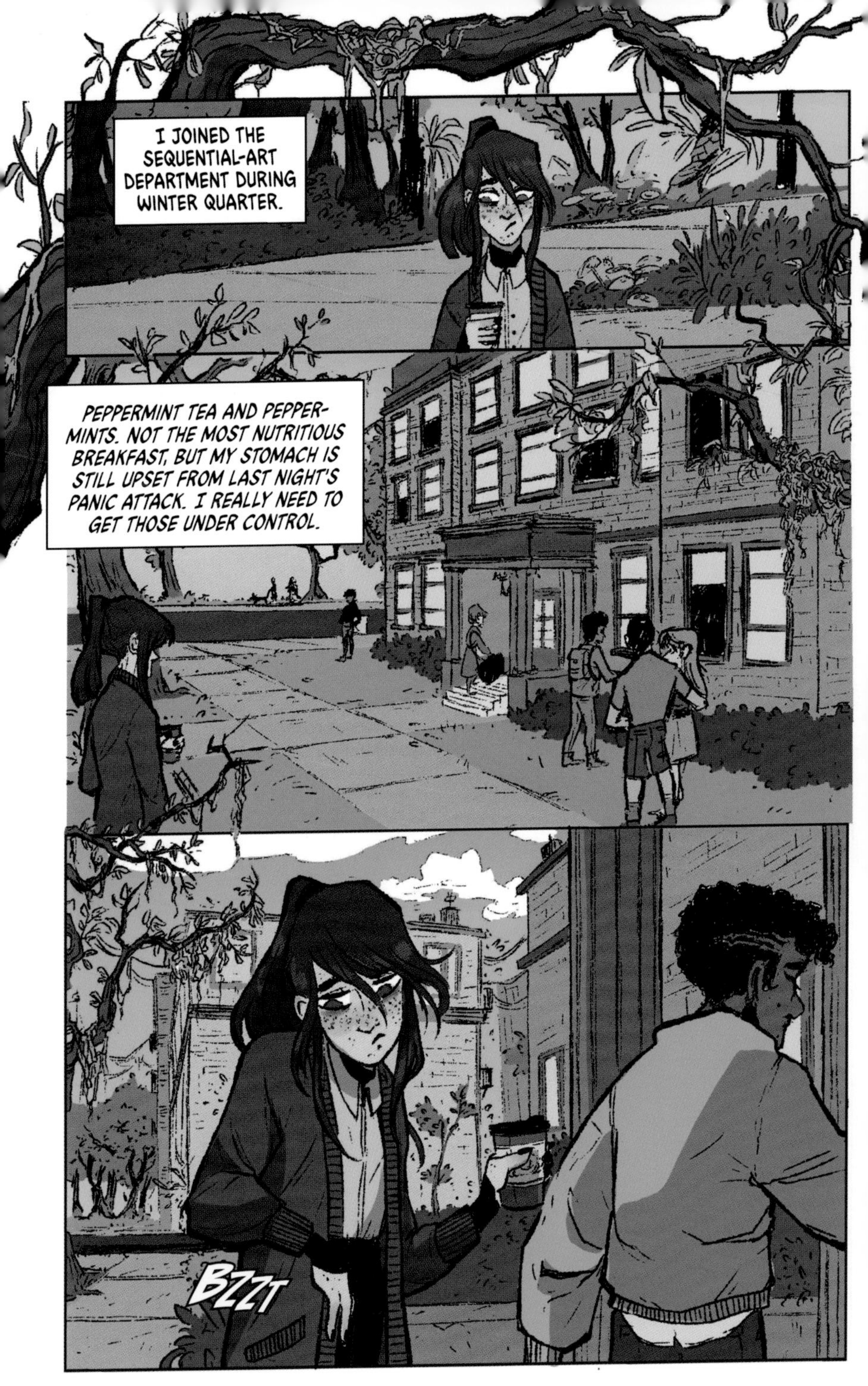
I JOINED THE SEQUENTIAL-ART DEPARTMENT DURING WINTER QUARTER.
PEPPERMINT TEA AND PEPPERMINTS. NOT THE MOST NUTRITIOUS BREAKFAST, BUT MY STOMACH IS STILL UPSET FROM LAST NIGHT'S PANIC ATTACK. I REALLY NEED TO GET THOSE UNDER CONTROL.
BZZT

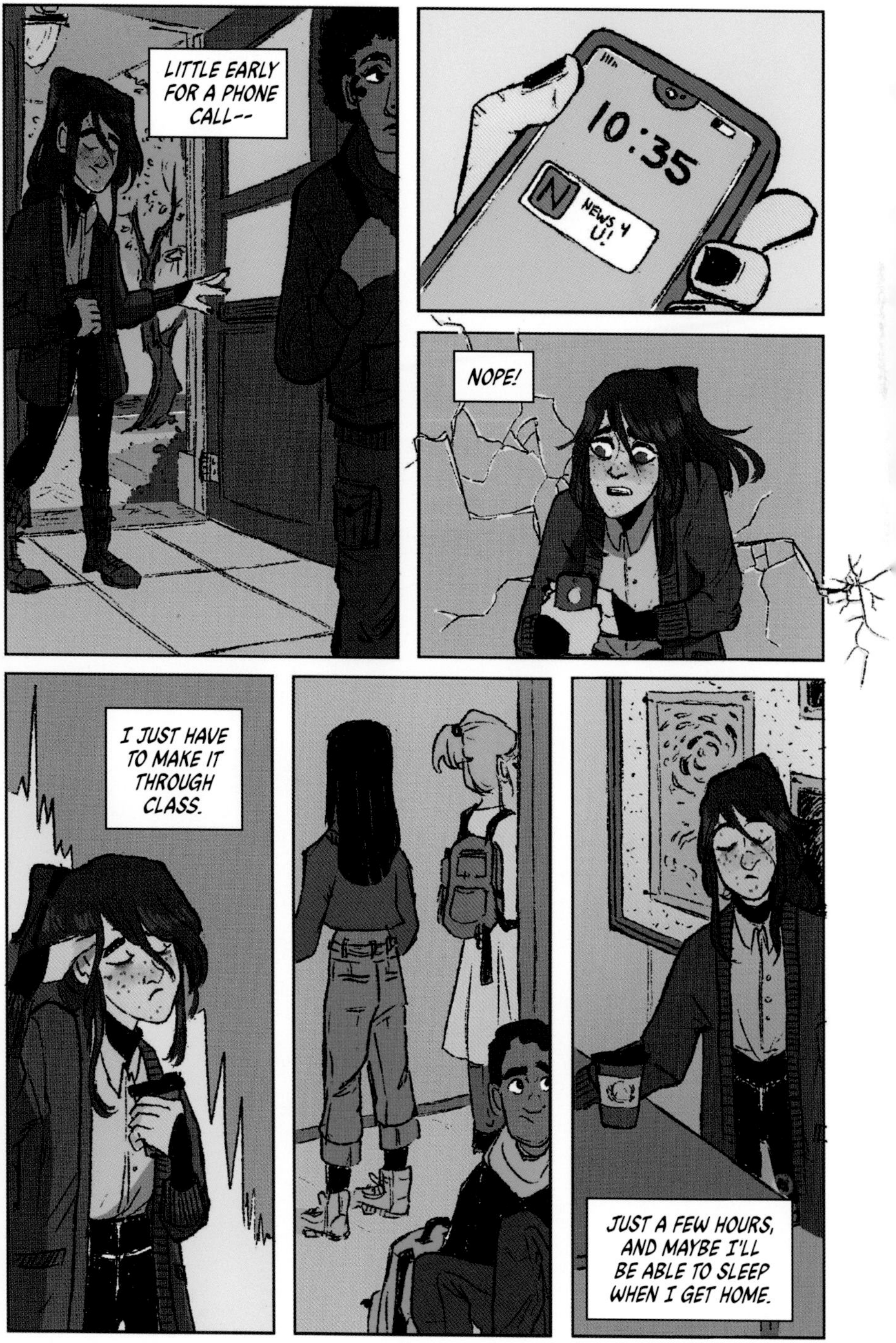
LITTLE EARLY FOR A PHONE CALL--
10:35
N
NEWS 4 U!
NOPE!
I JUST HAVE TO MAKE IT THROUGH CLASS.
JUST A FEW HOURS, AND MAYBE I'LL BE ABLE TO SLEEP WHEN I GET HOME.

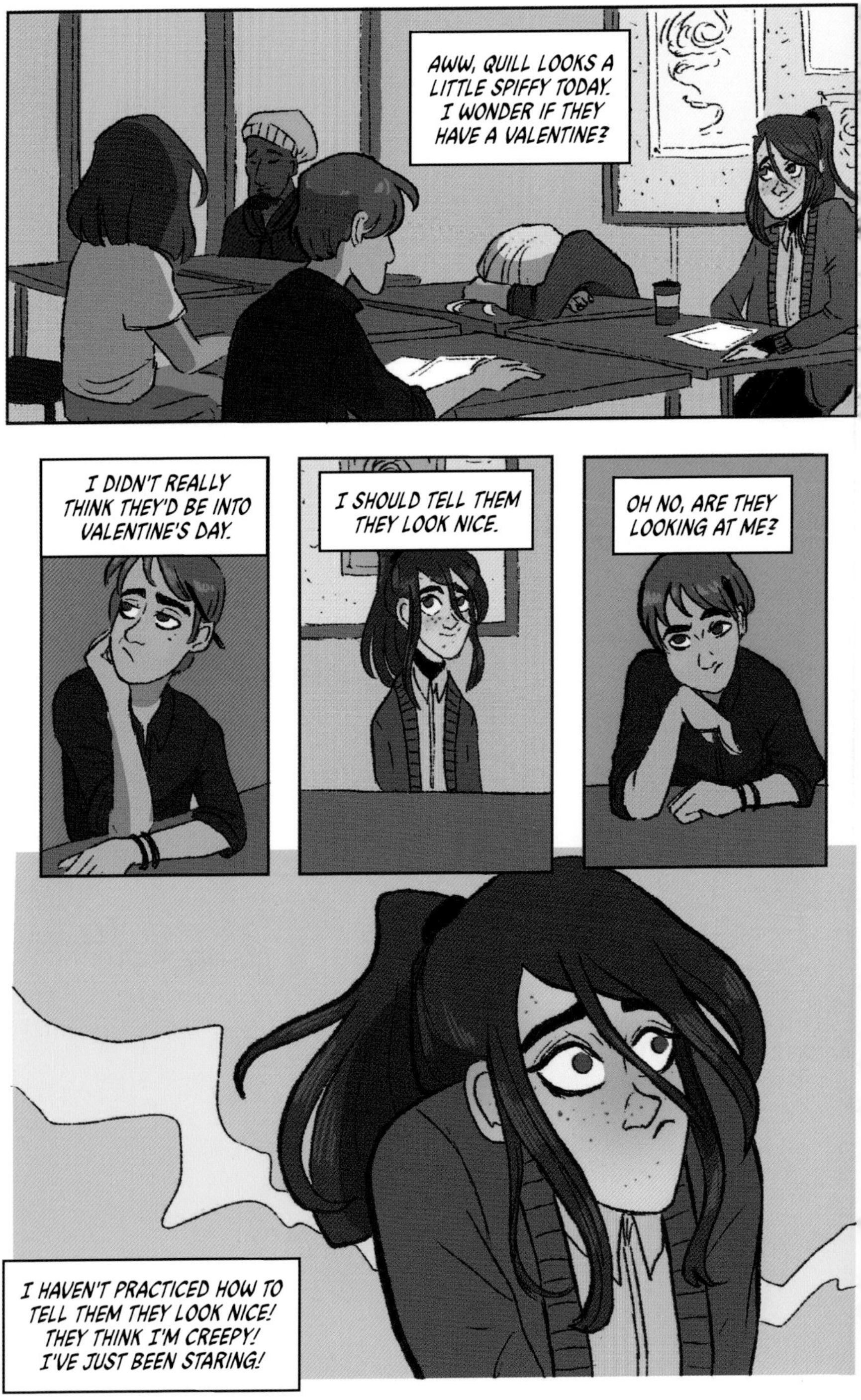
AWW, QUILL LOOKS A LITTLE SPIFFY TODAY. I WONDER IF THEY HAVE A VALENTINE?
I DIDN'T REALLY THINK THEY'D BE INTO VALENTINE'S DAY.
I SHOULD TELL THEM THEY LOOK NICE.
OH NO, ARE THEY LOOKING AT ME?
I HAVEN'T PRACTICED HOW TO TELL THEM THEY LOOK NICE! THEY THINK I'M CREEPY! I'VE JUST BEEN STARING!

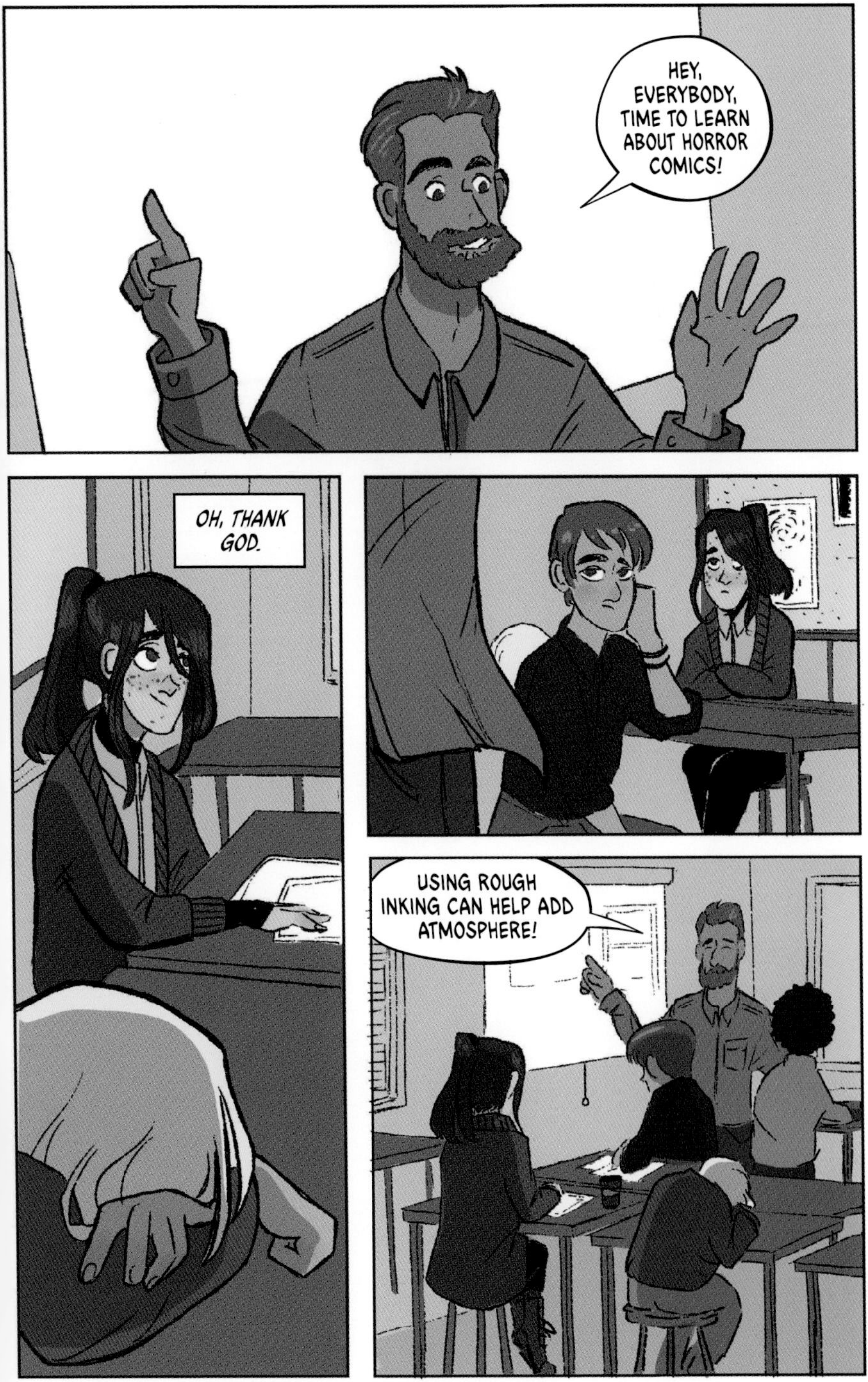
HEY, EVERYBODY, TIME TO LEARN ABOUT HORROR COMICS!
OH, THANK GOD.
USING ROUGH INKING CAN HELP ADD ATMOSPHERE!

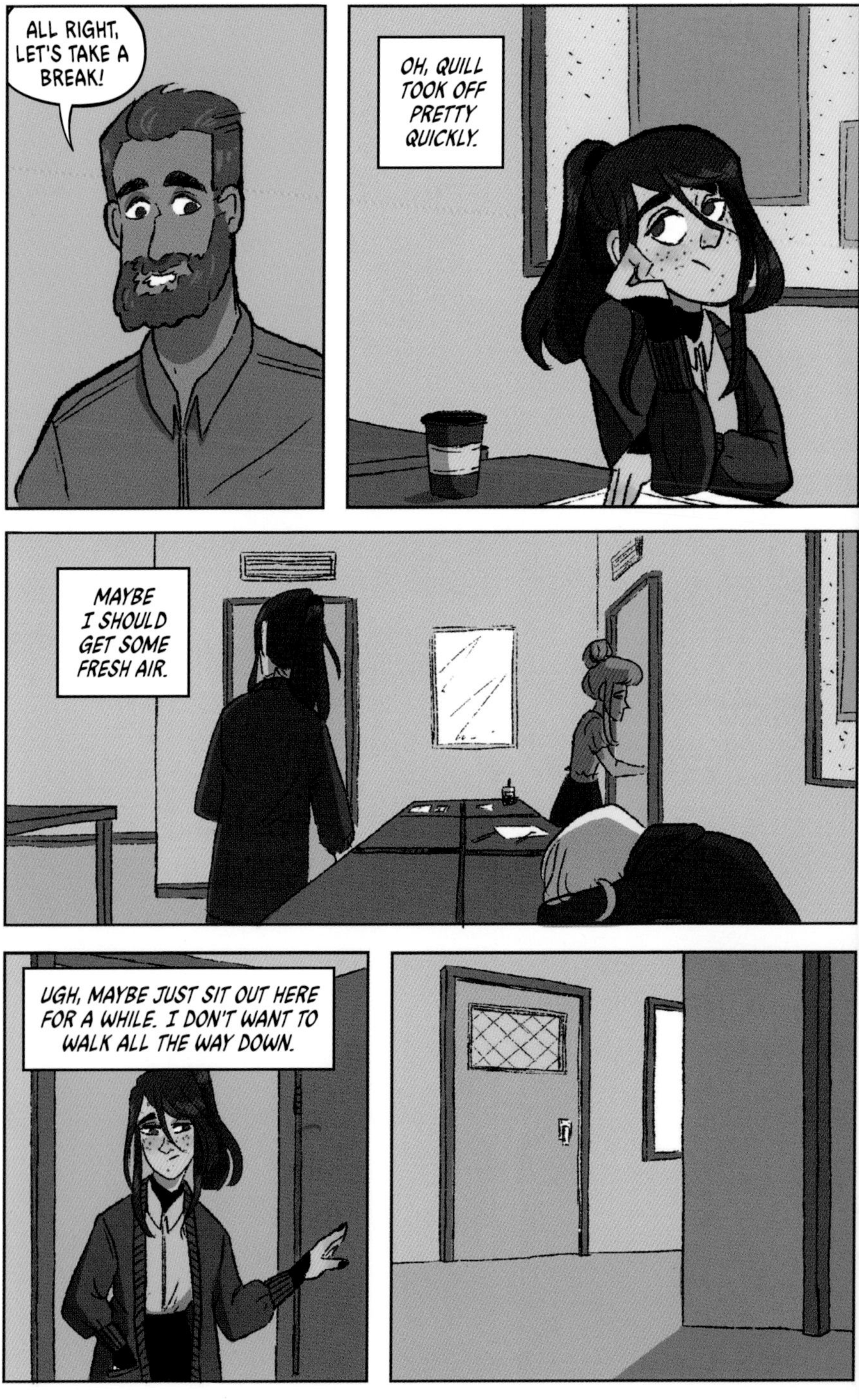

ALL RIGHT, LET'S TAKE A BREAK!
OH, QUILL TOOK OFF PRETTY QUICKLY.
MAYBE I SHOULD GET SOME FRESH AIR.
UGH, MAYBE JUST SIT OUT HERE FOR A WHILE. I DON'T WANT TO WALK ALL THE WAY DOWN.

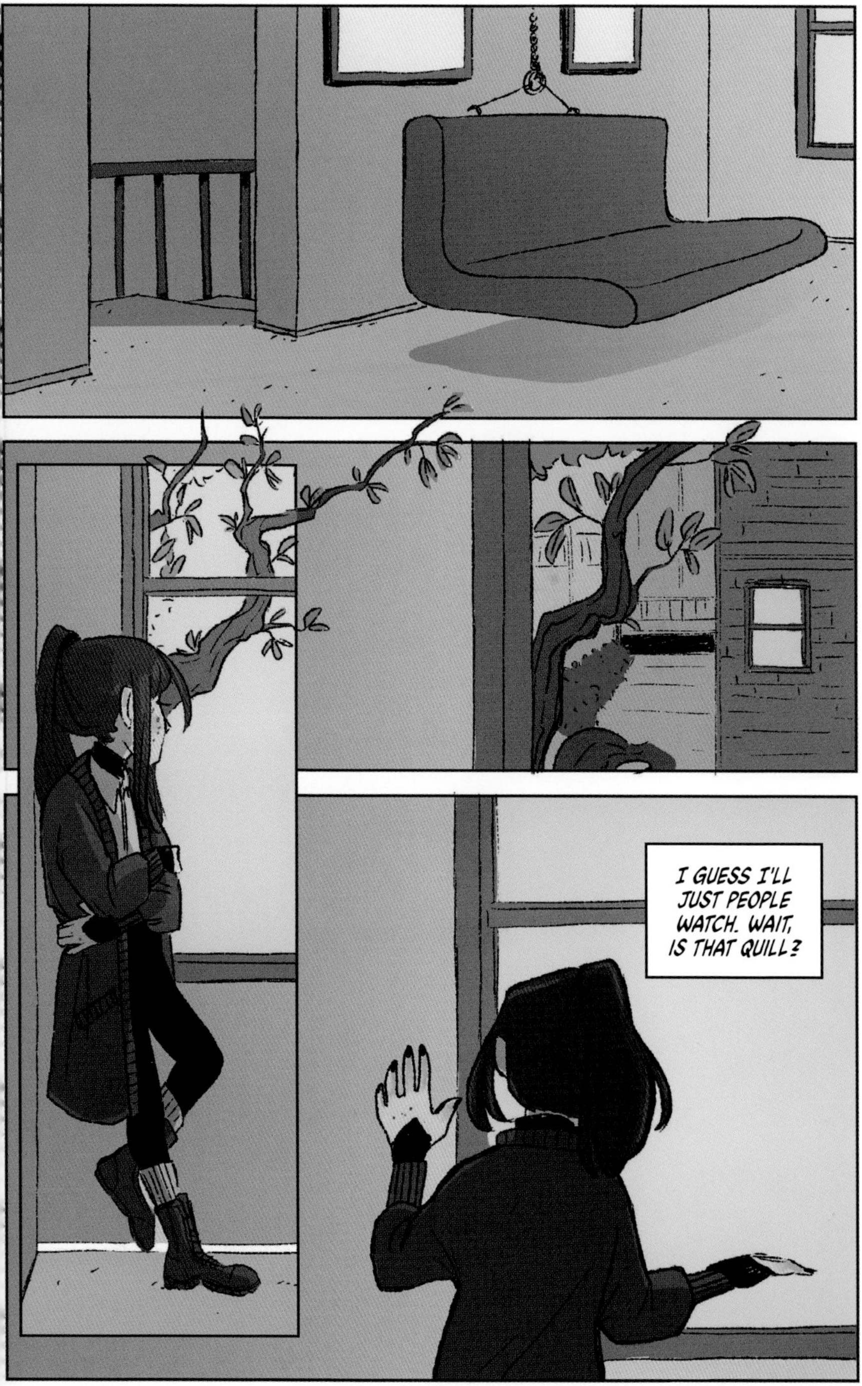
I GUESS I'LL JUST PEOPLE WATCH. WAIT, IS THAT QUILL?

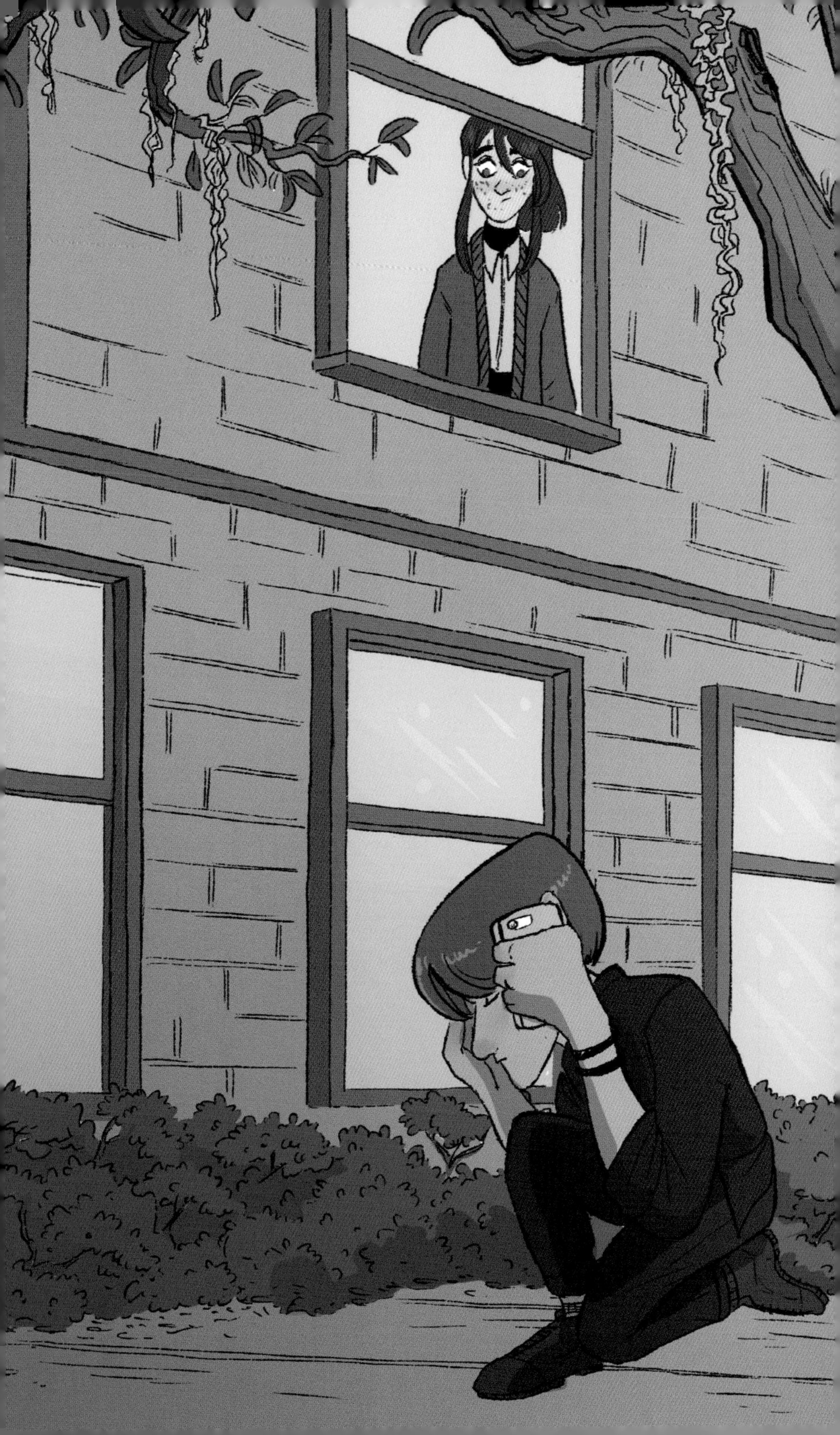

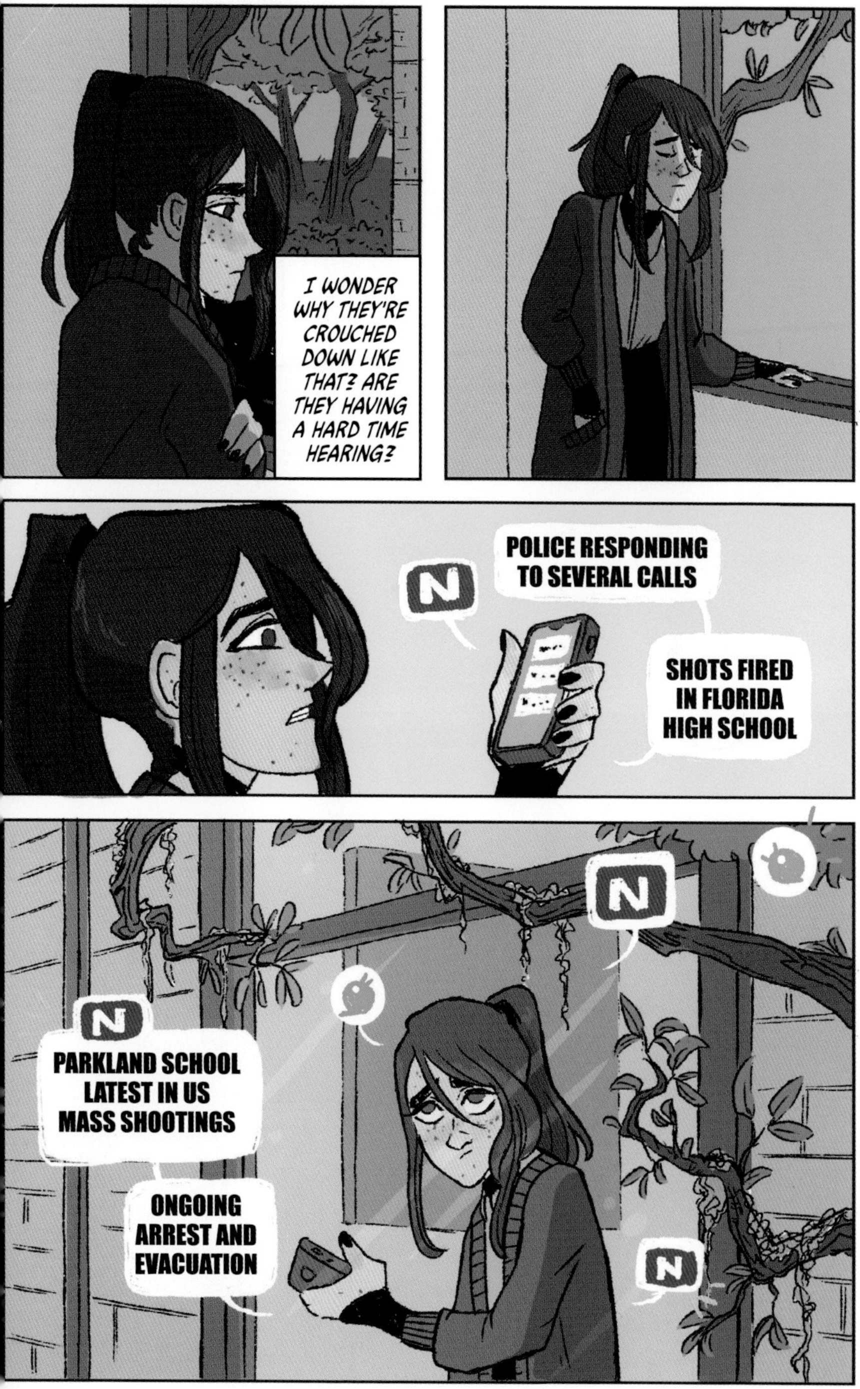
I WONDER WHY THEY'RE CROUCHED DOWN LIKE THAT? ARE THEY HAVING A HARD TIME HEARING?
N
POLICE RESPONDING TO SEVERAL CALLS
SHOTS FIRED IN FLORIDA HIGH SCHOOL
N
N
PARKLAND SCHOOL LATEST IN US MASS SHOOTINGS
ONGOING ARREST AND EVACUATION
N

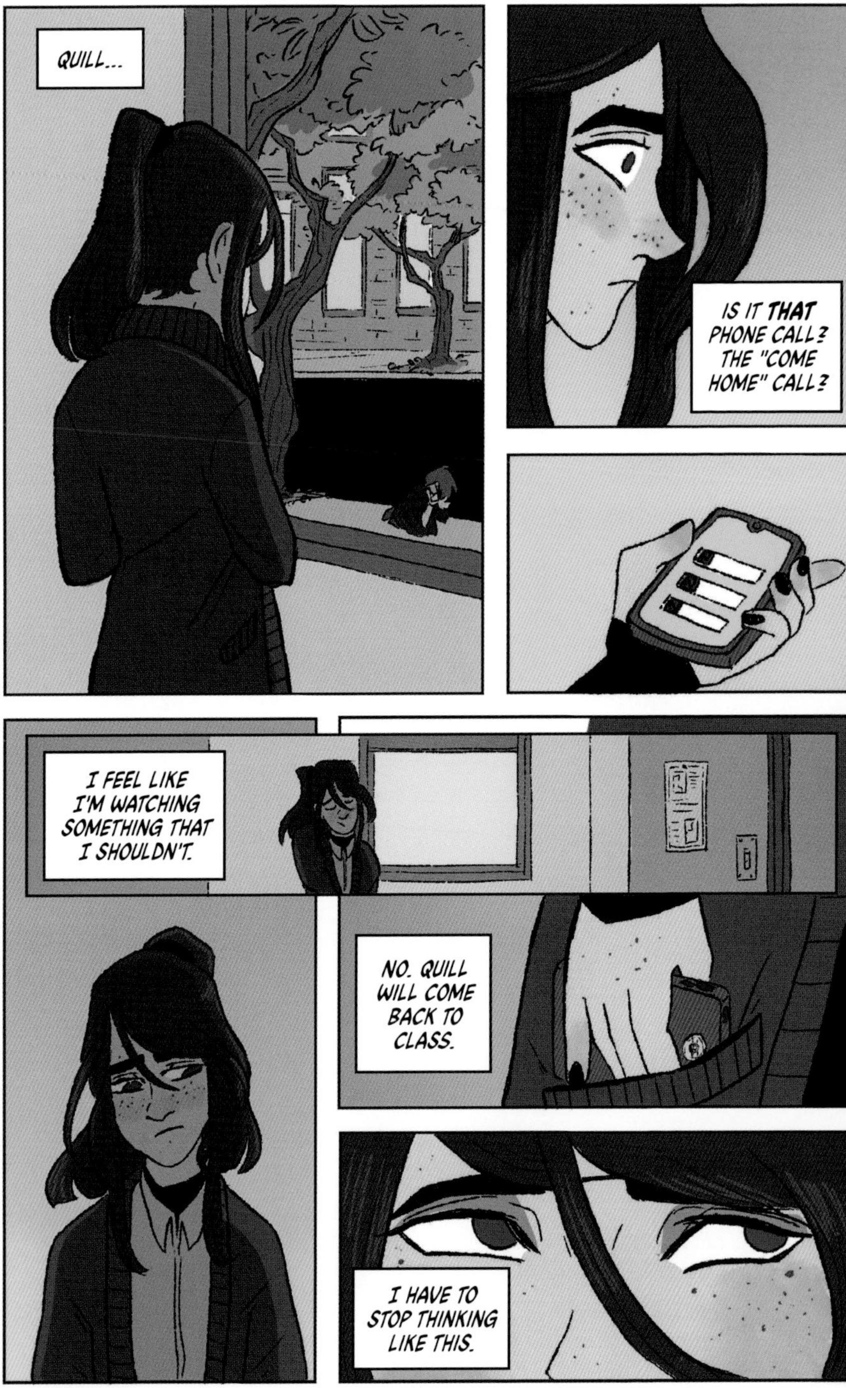
QUILL...
IS IT THAT PHONE CALL? THE "COME HOME" CALL?
I FEEL LIKE I'M WATCHING SOMETHING THAT I SHOULDN'T.
NO. QUILL WILL COME BACK TO CLASS.
I HAVE TO STOP THINKING LIKE THIS.

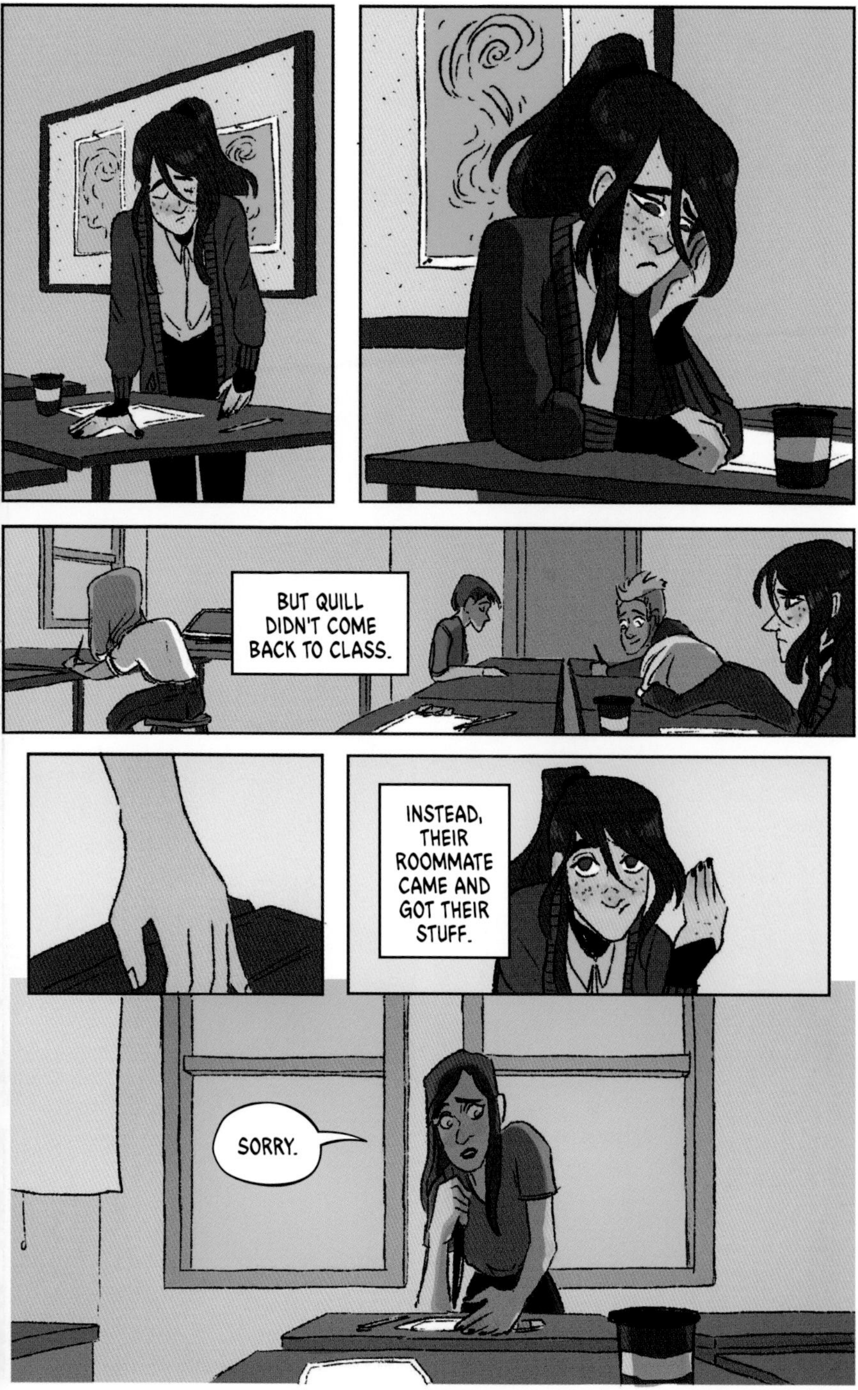
BUT QUILL DIDN'T COME BACK TO CLASS.
INSTEAD, THEIR ROOMMATE CAME AND GOT THEIR STUFF.
SORRY.

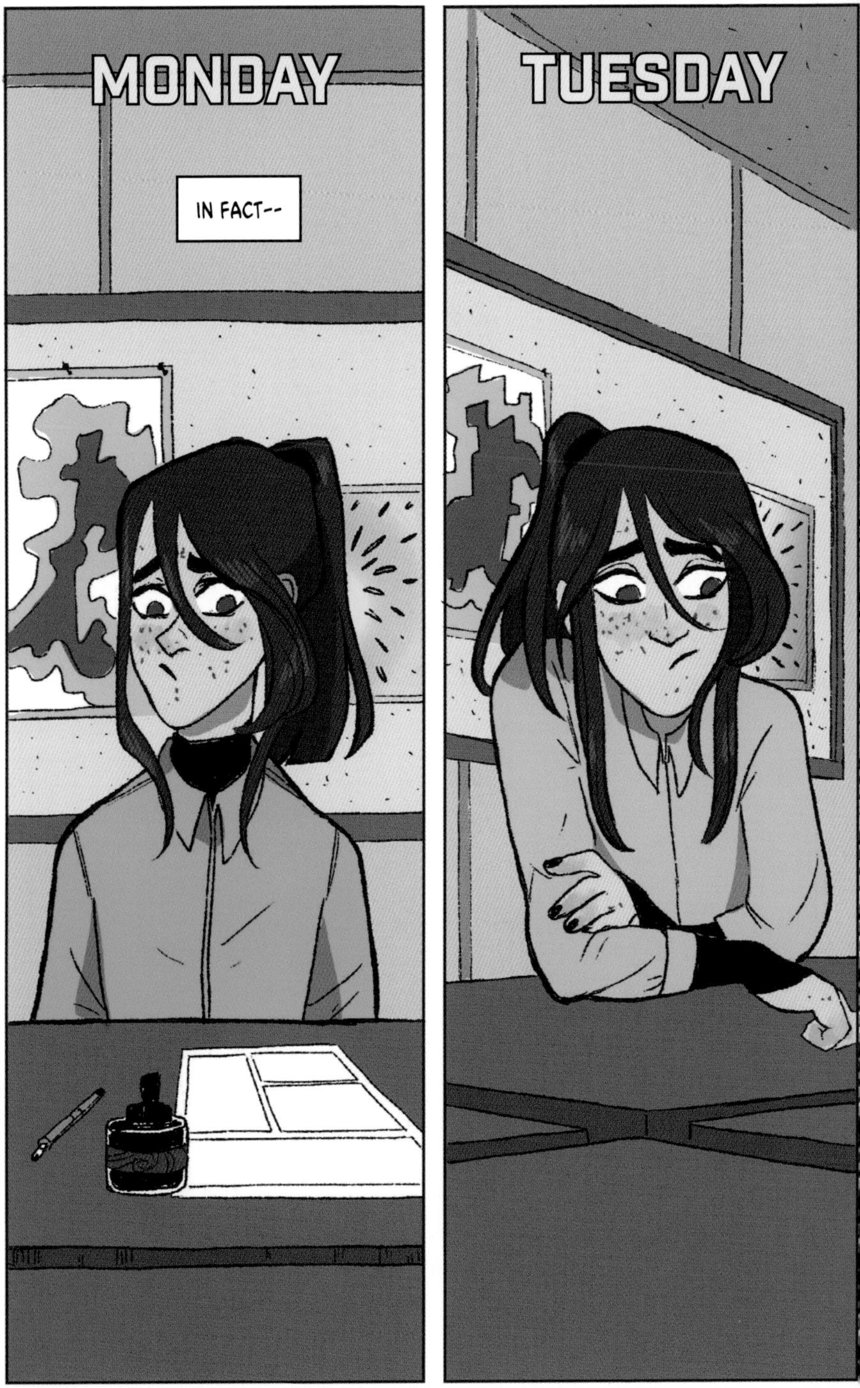
MONDAY
IN FACT--
TUESDAY

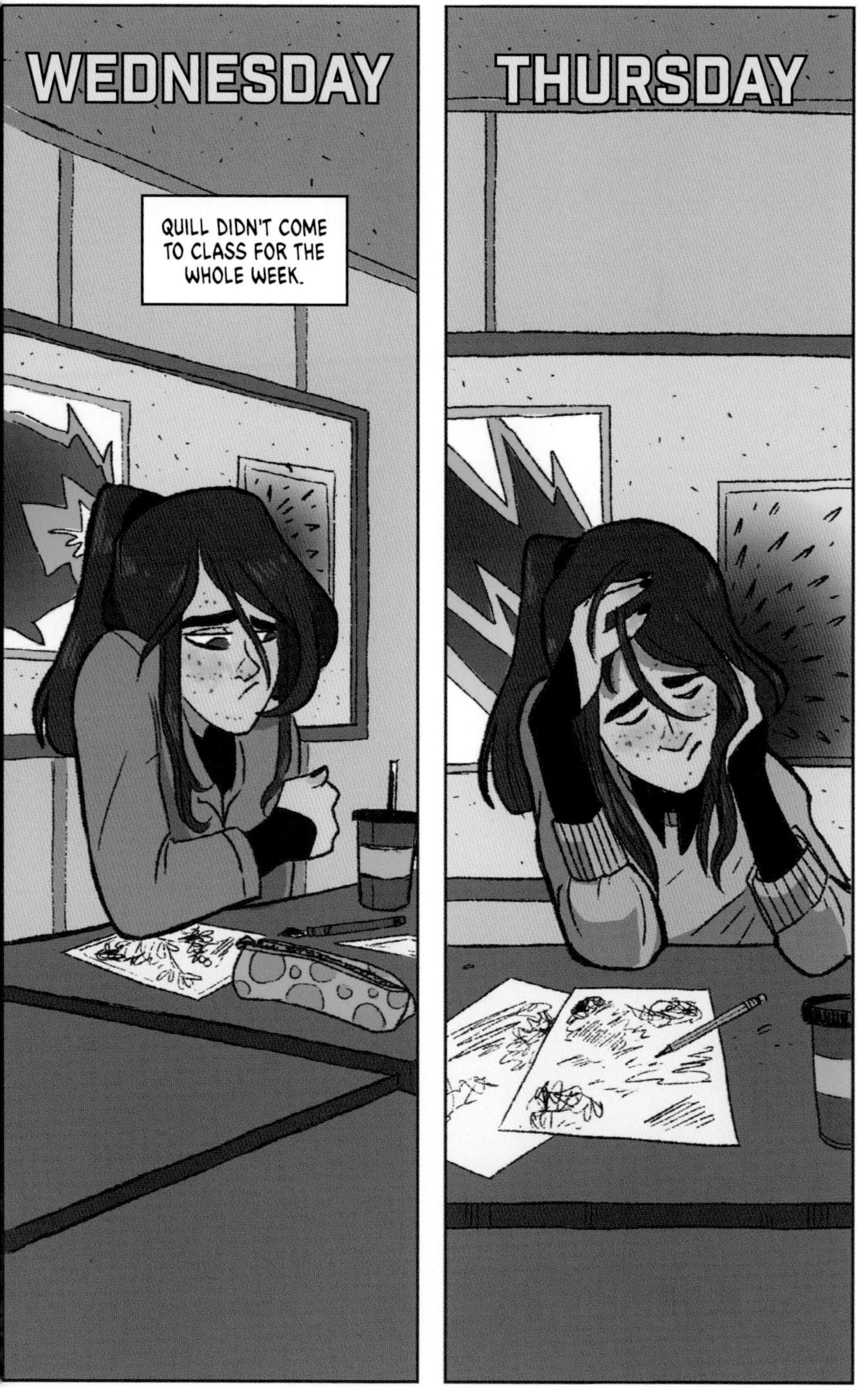
WEDNESDAY
QUILL DIDN'T COME TO CLASS FOR THE WHOLE WEEK.
THURSDAY

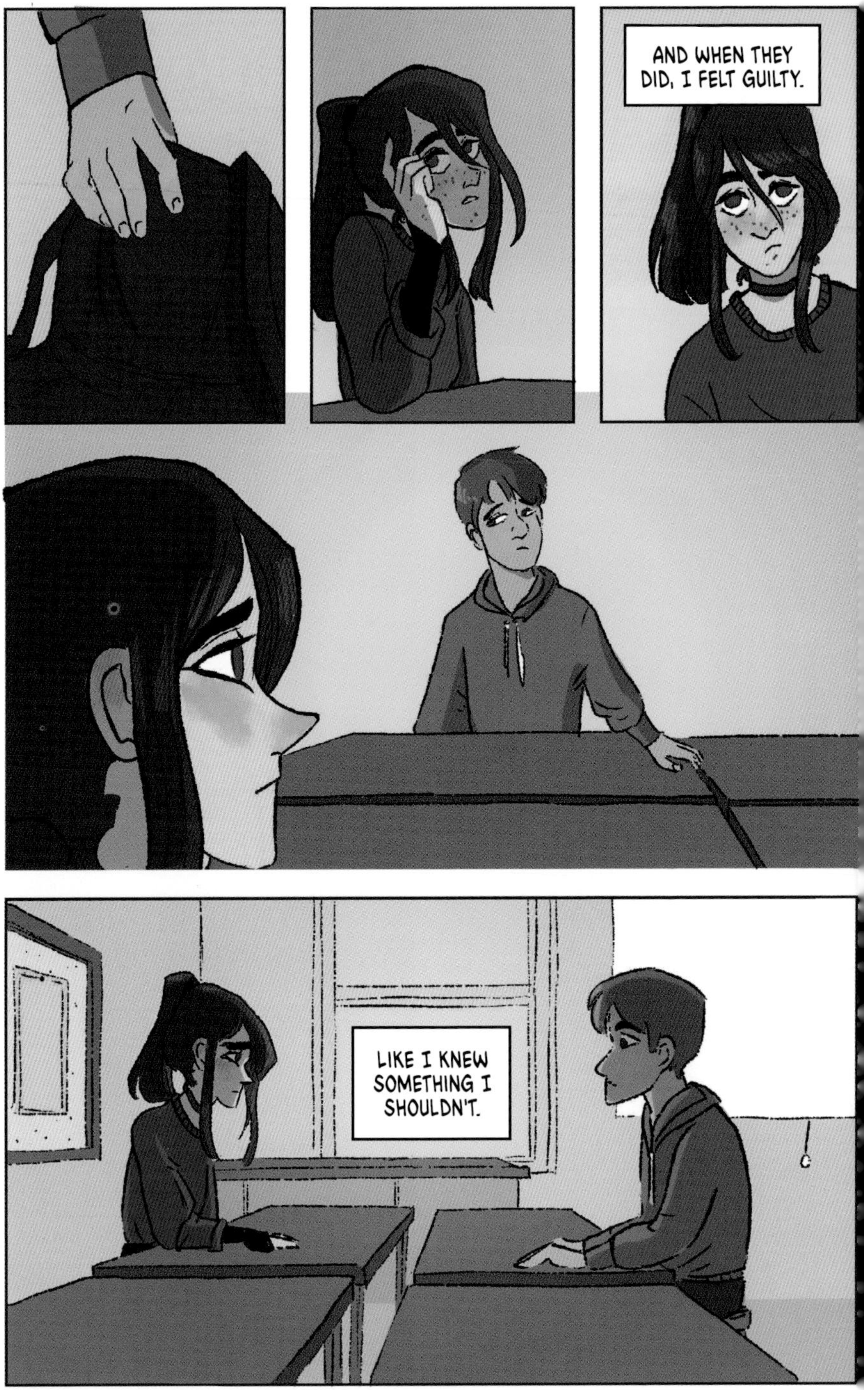
AND WHEN THEY DID, I FELT GUILTY.
LIKE I KNEW SOMETHING I SHOULDN'T.

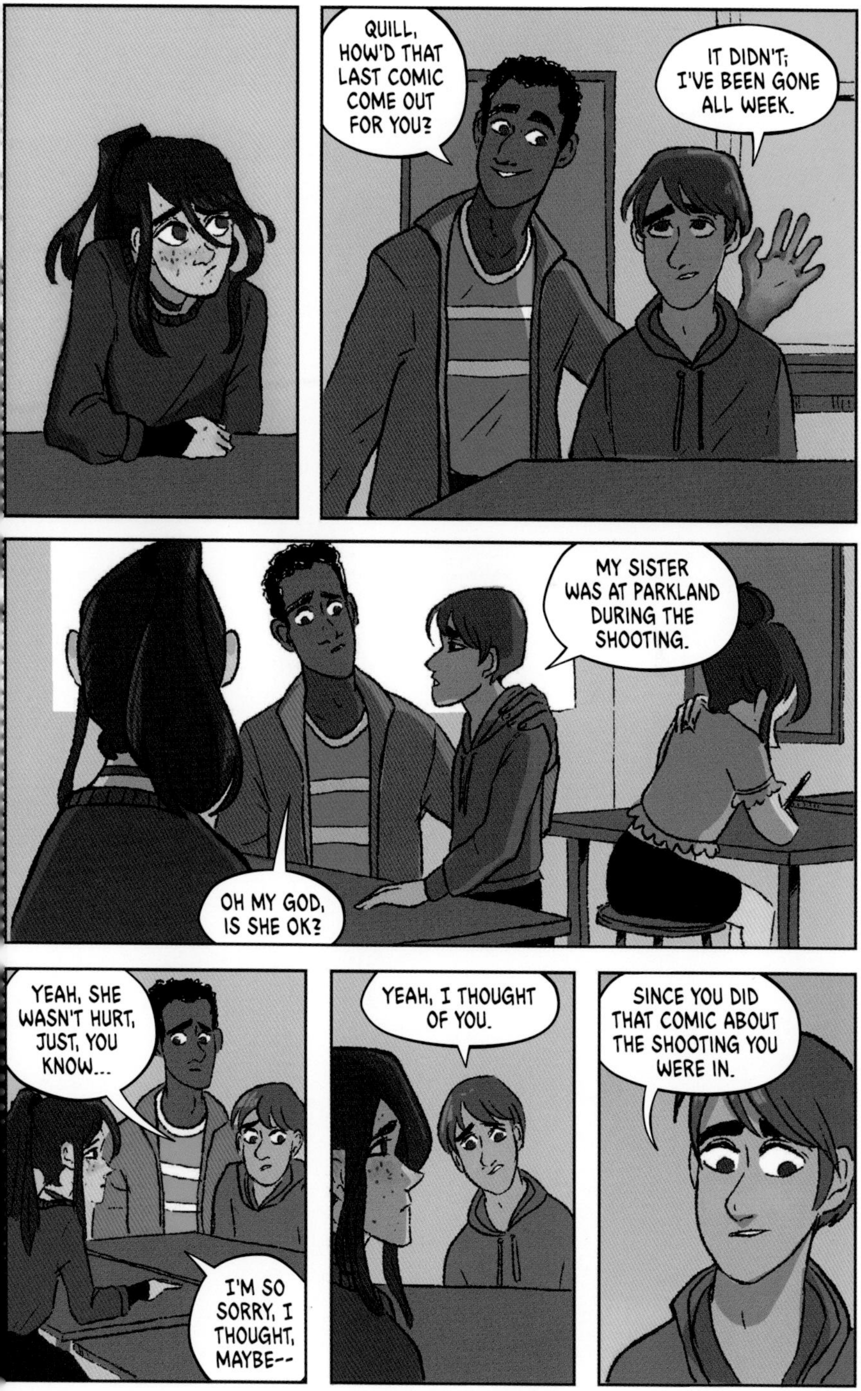
QUILL, HOW'D THAT LAST COMIC COME OUT FOR YOU?
IT DIDN'T; I'VE BEEN GONE ALL WEEK.
MY SISTER WAS AT PARKLAND DURING THE SHOOTING.
OH MY GOD, IS SHE OK?
YEAH, SHE WASN'T HURT, JUST, YOU KNOW...
I'M SO SORRY, I THOUGHT, MAYBE--
YEAH, I THOUGHT OF YOU.
SINCE YOU DID THAT COMIC ABOUT THE SHOOTING YOU WERE IN.

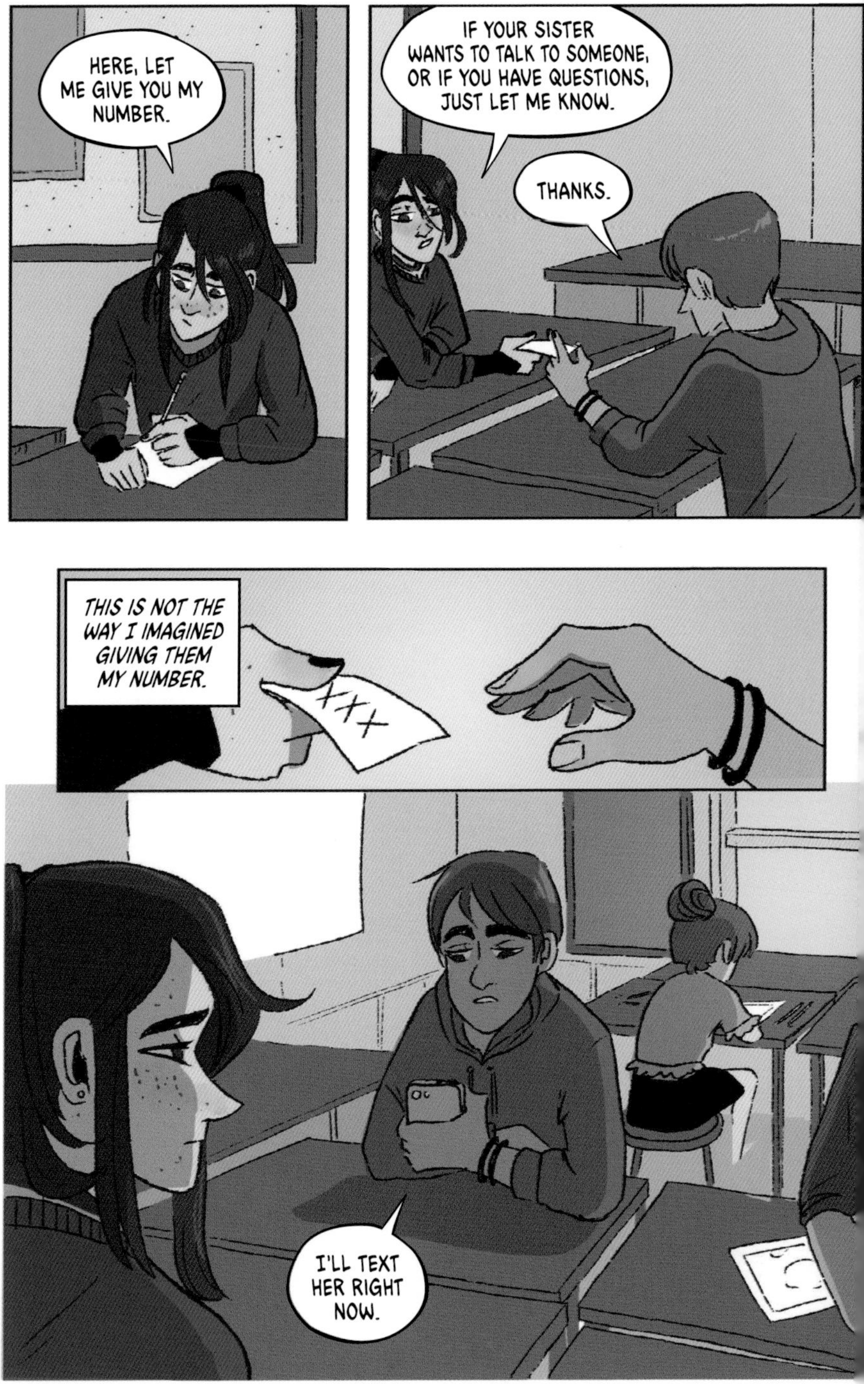
HERE, LET ME GIVE YOU MY NUMBER.
IF YOUR SISTER WANTS TO TALK TO SOMEONE, OR IF YOU HAVE QUESTIONS, JUST LET ME KNOW.
THANKS.
THIS IS NOT THE WAY I IMAGINED GIVING THEM MY NUMBER.
I'LL TEXT HER RIGHT NOW.

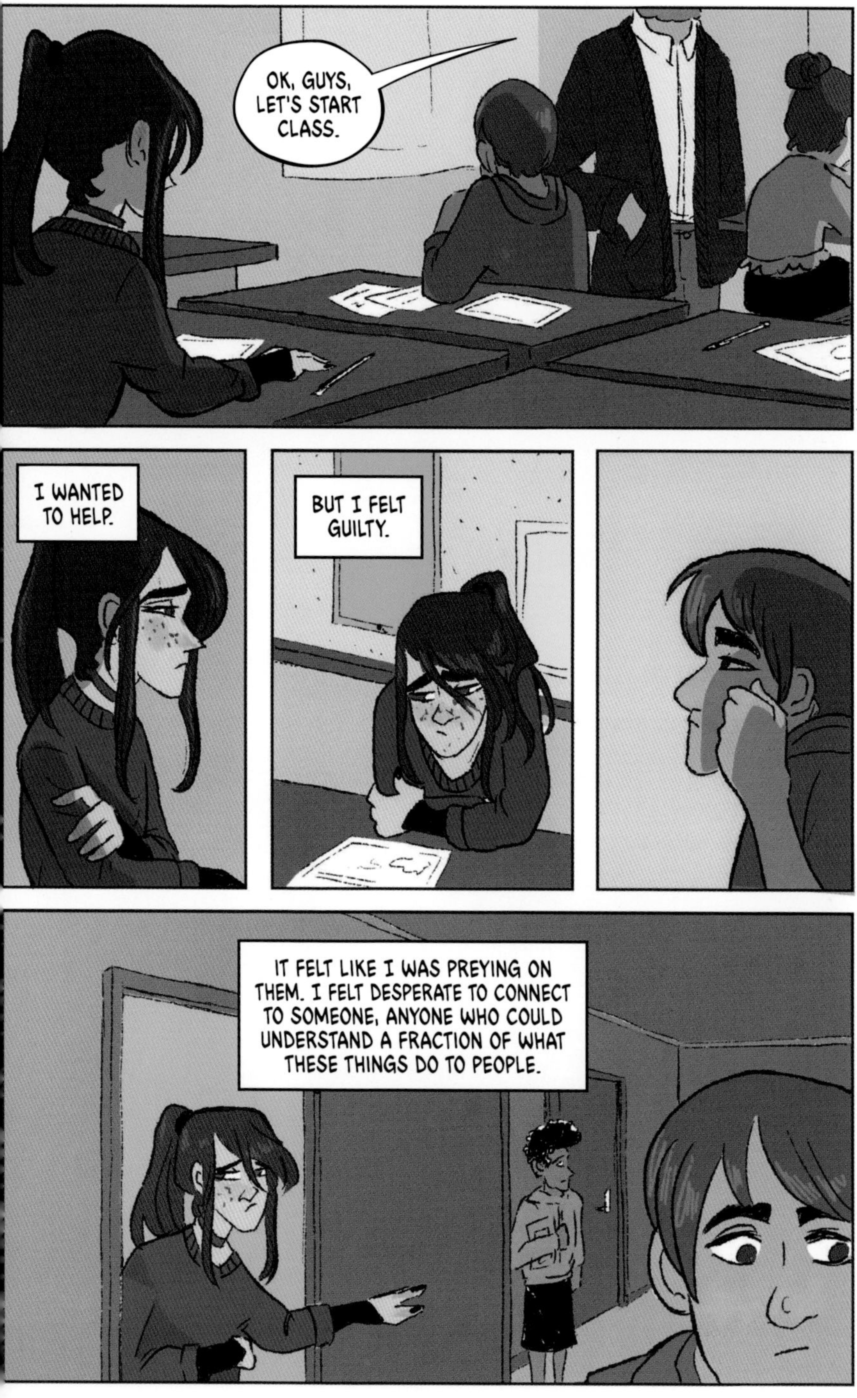
OK, GUYS, LET'S START CLASS.
I WANTED TO HELP.
BUT I FELT GUILTY.
IT FELT LIKE I WAS PREYING ON THEM. I FELT DESPERATE TO CONNECT TO SOMEONE, ANYONE WHO COULD UNDERSTAND A FRACTION OF WHAT THESE THINGS DO TO PEOPLE.

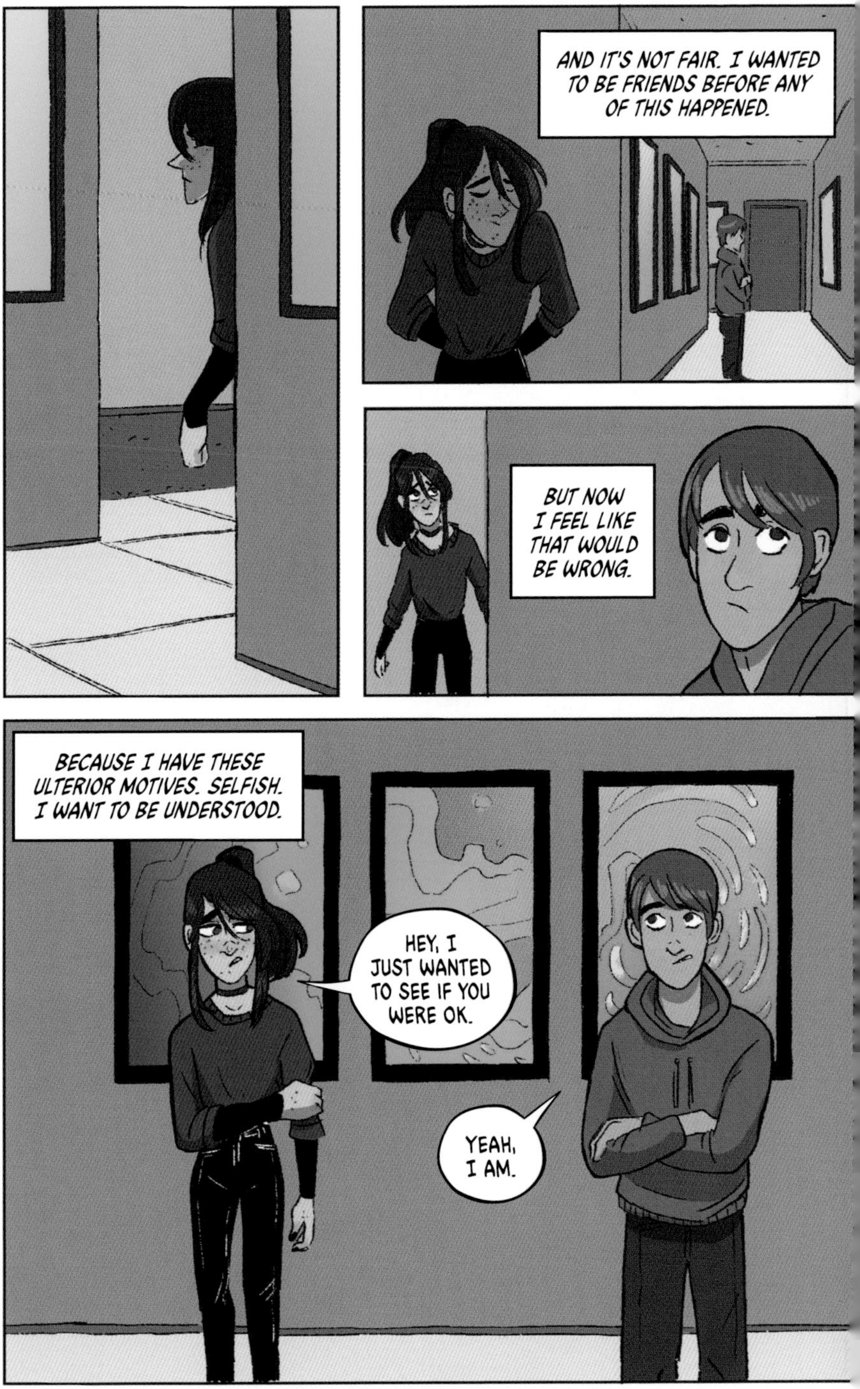
AND IT'S NOT FAIR. I WANTED TO BE FRIENDS BEFORE ANY OF THIS HAPPENED.
BUT NOW I FEEL LIKE THAT WOULD BE WRONG.
BECAUSE I HAVE THESE ULTERIOR MOTIVES. SELFISH. I WANT TO BE UNDERSTOOD.
HEY, I JUST WANTED TO SEE IF YOU WERE OK.
YEAH, I AM.

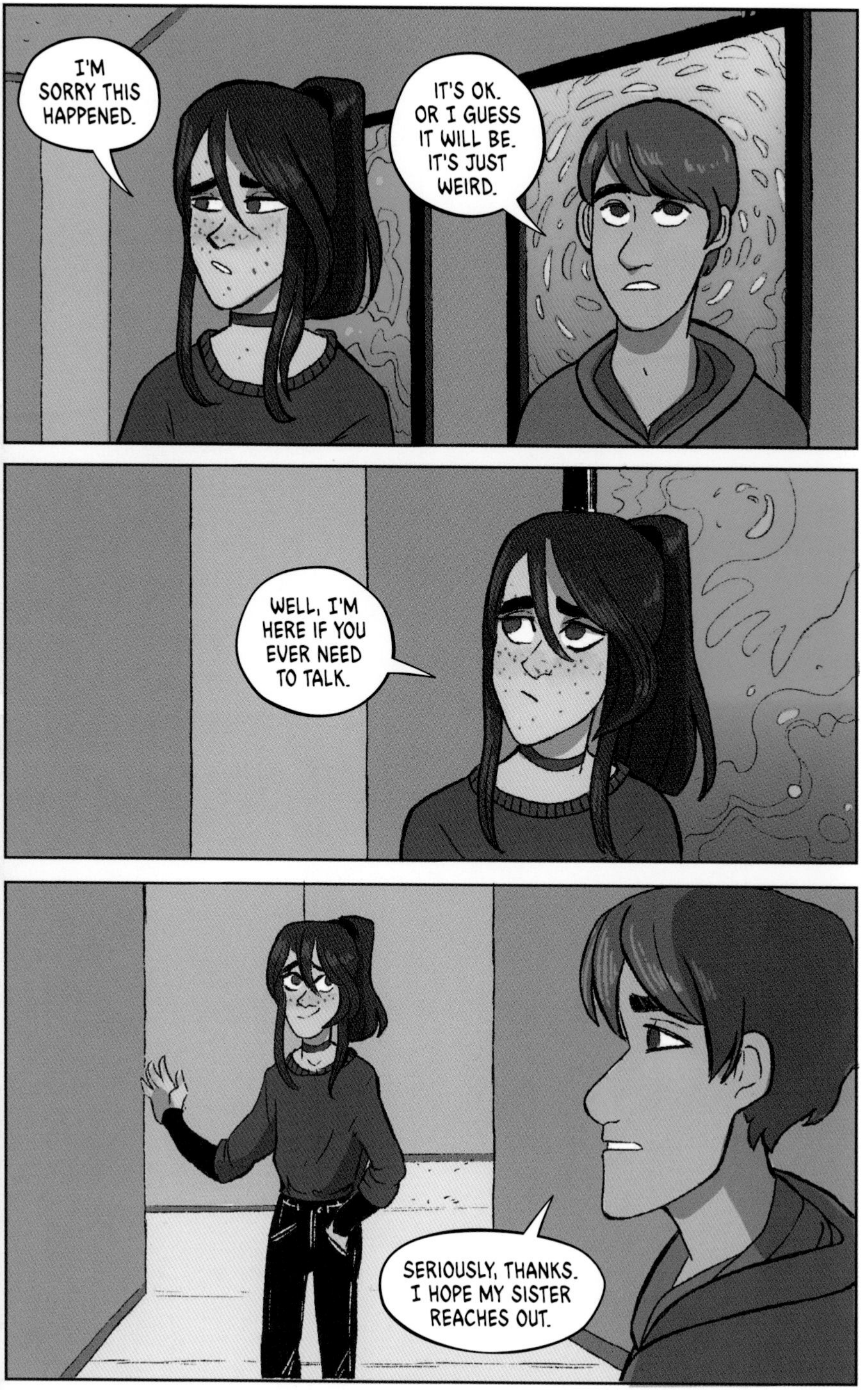
I'M SORRY THIS HAPPENED.
IT'S OK. OR I GUESS IT WILL BE. IT'S JUST WEIRD.
WELL, I'M HERE IF YOU EVER NEED TO TALK.
SERIOUSLY, THANKS. I HOPE MY SISTER REACHES OUT.

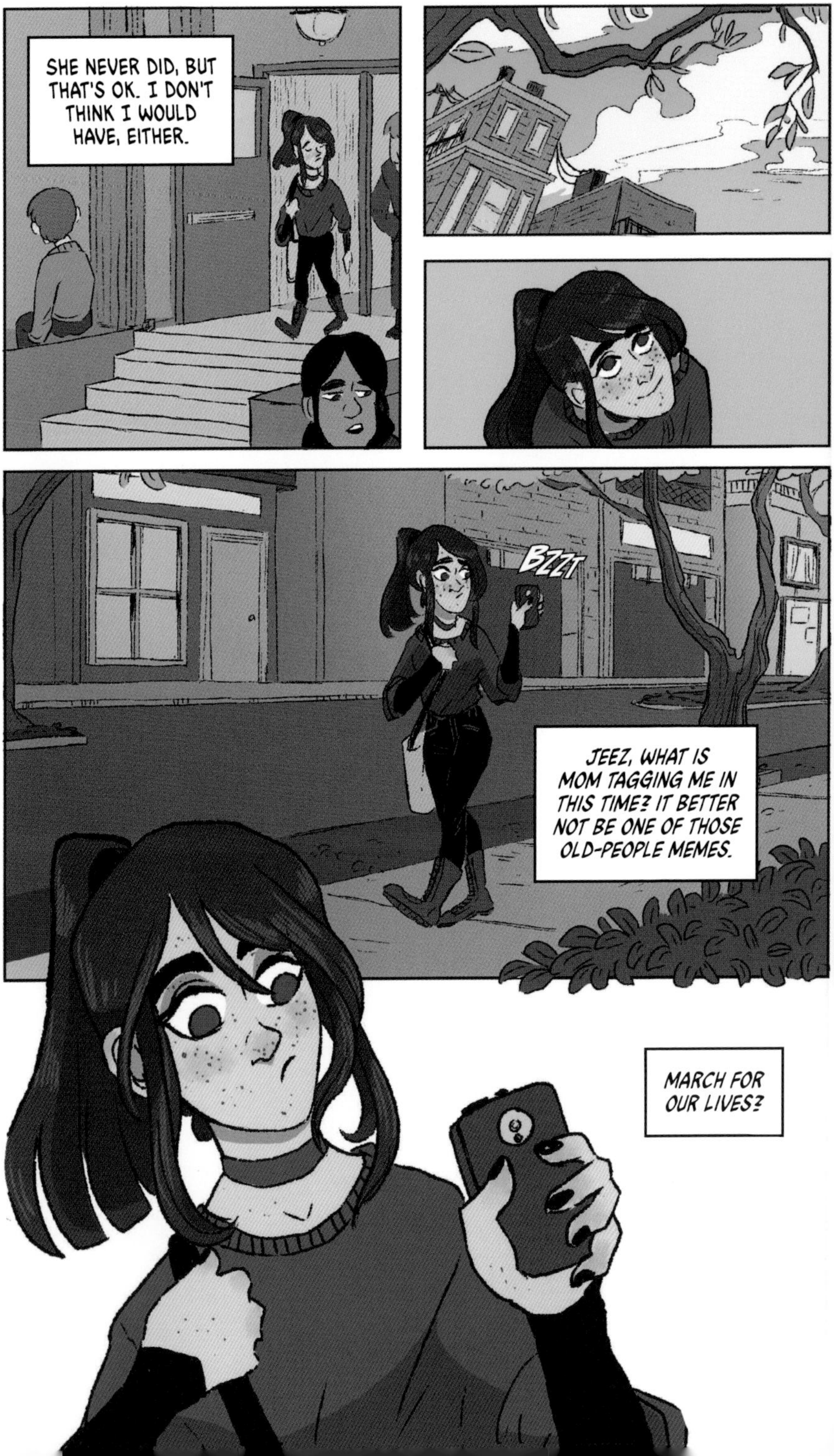
SHE NEVER DID, BUT THAT'S OK. I DON'T THINK I WOULD HAVE, EITHER.
BZZT
JEEZ, WHAT IS MOM TAGGING ME IN THIS TIME? IT BETTER NOT BE ONE OF THOSE OLD-PEOPLE MEMES.
MARCH FOR OUR LIVES?

THE PARKLAND STUDENTS ARE PUTTING IT ON IN DC?
DC
MEET UP
I'LL HAVE TO CHECK IT OUT AS SOON AS I GET BACK TO THE APARTMENT.
HONK
OOPS!
GET OUT OF THE ROAD, YOU IDIOT!

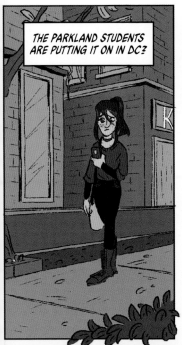

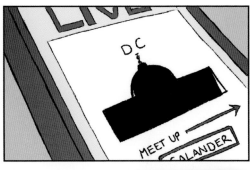

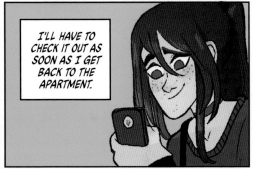

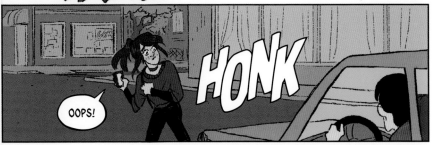

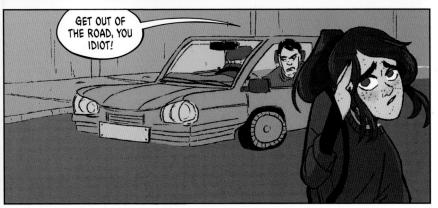

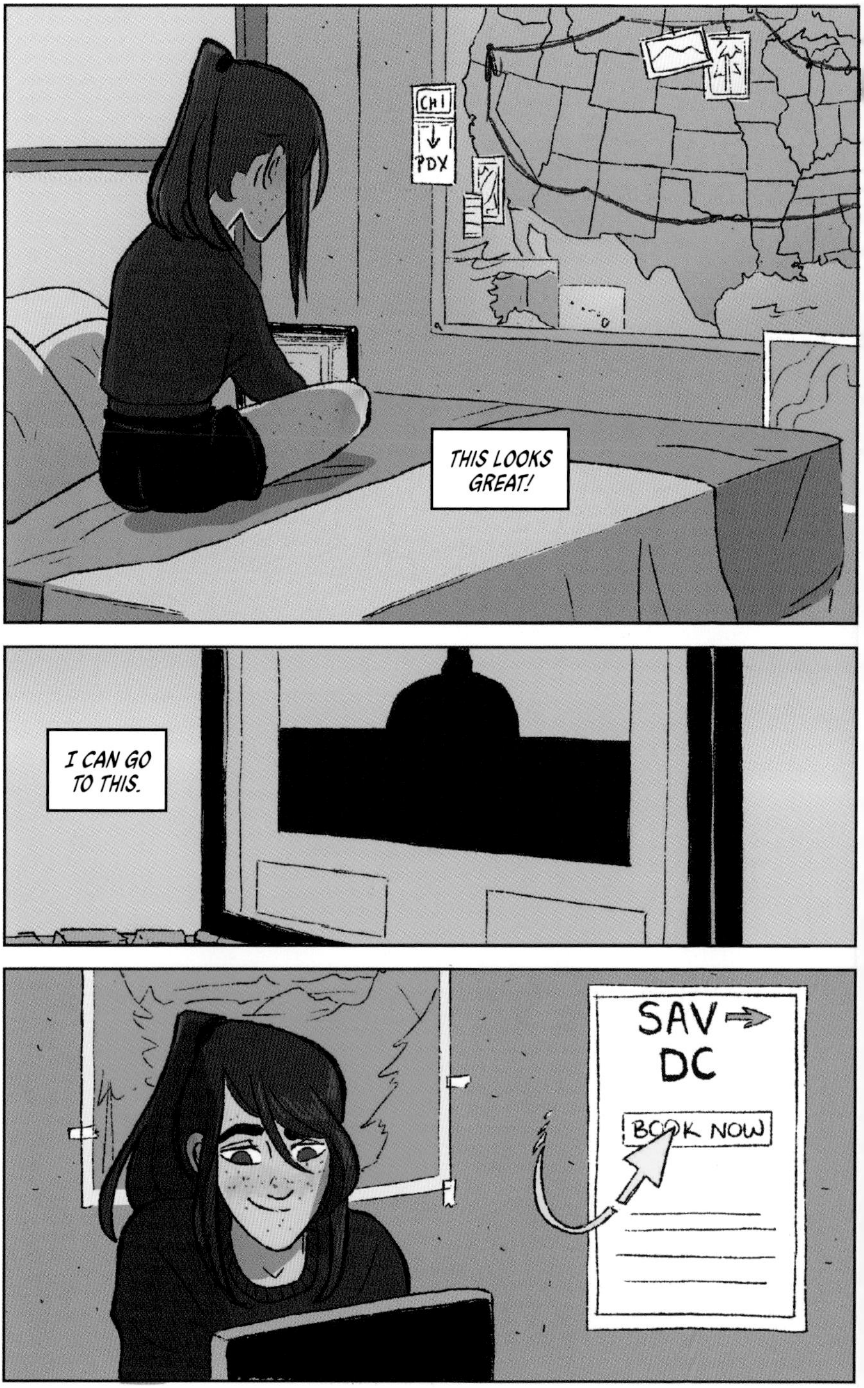
CHI
PDX
THIS LOOKS GREAT!
I CAN GO TO THIS.
SAV
DC
BOOK NOW

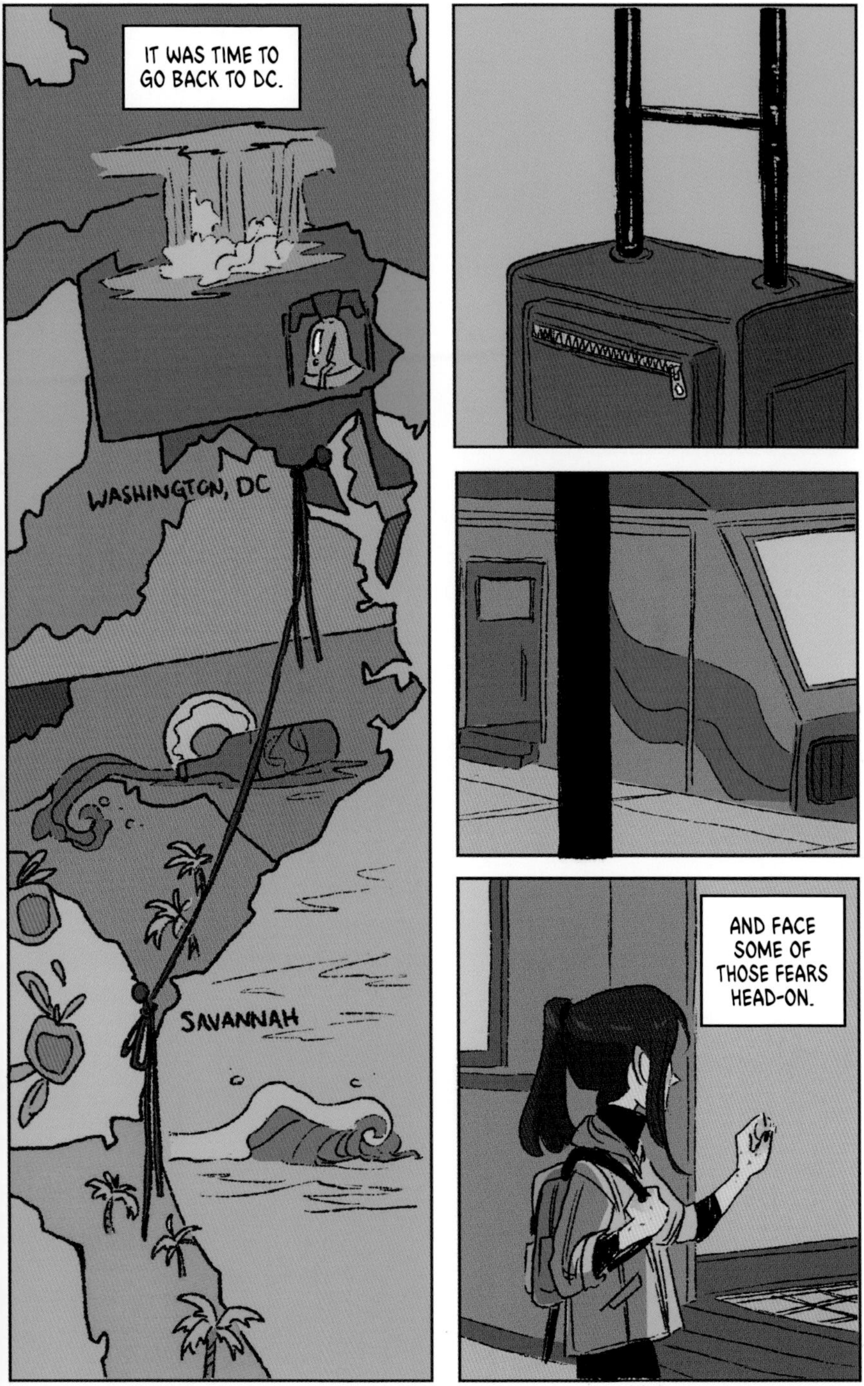
IT WAS TIME TO GO BACK TO DC.
WASHINGTON, DC
SAVANNAH
AND FACE SOME OF THOSE FEARS HEAD-ON.

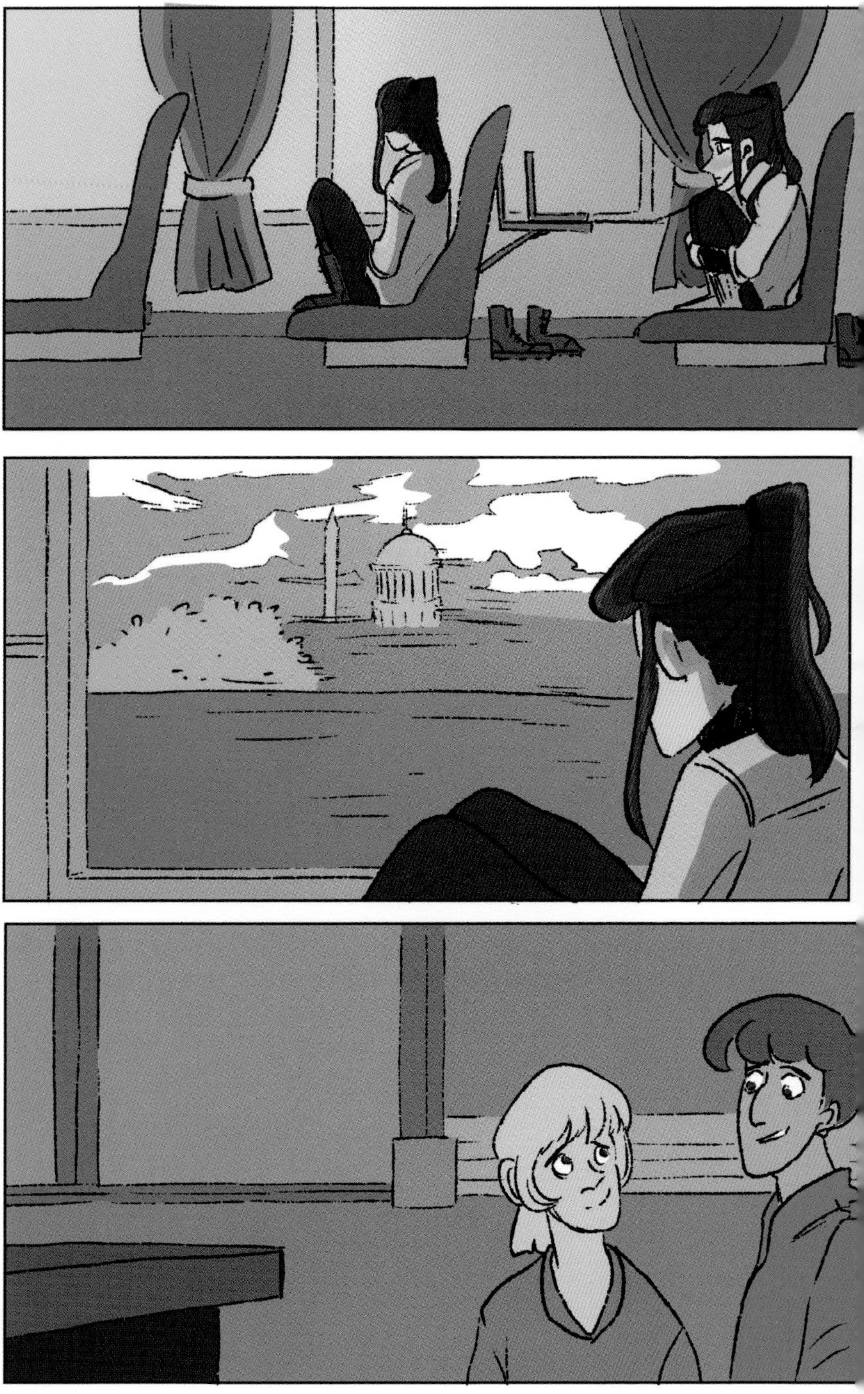

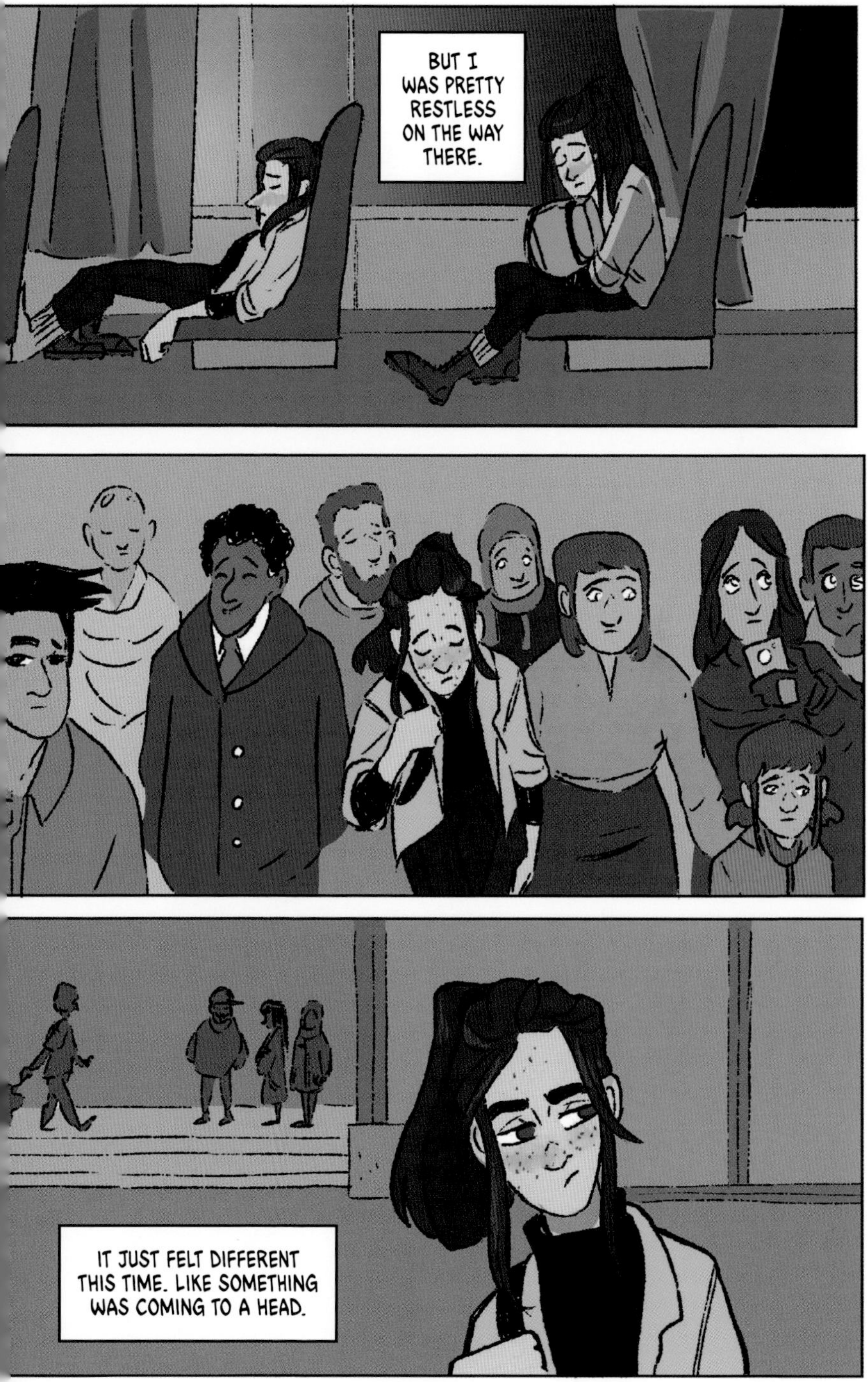
BUT I WAS PRETTY RESTLESS ON THE WAY THERE.
IT JUST FELT DIFFERENT THIS TIME. LIKE SOMETHING WAS COMING TO A HEAD.

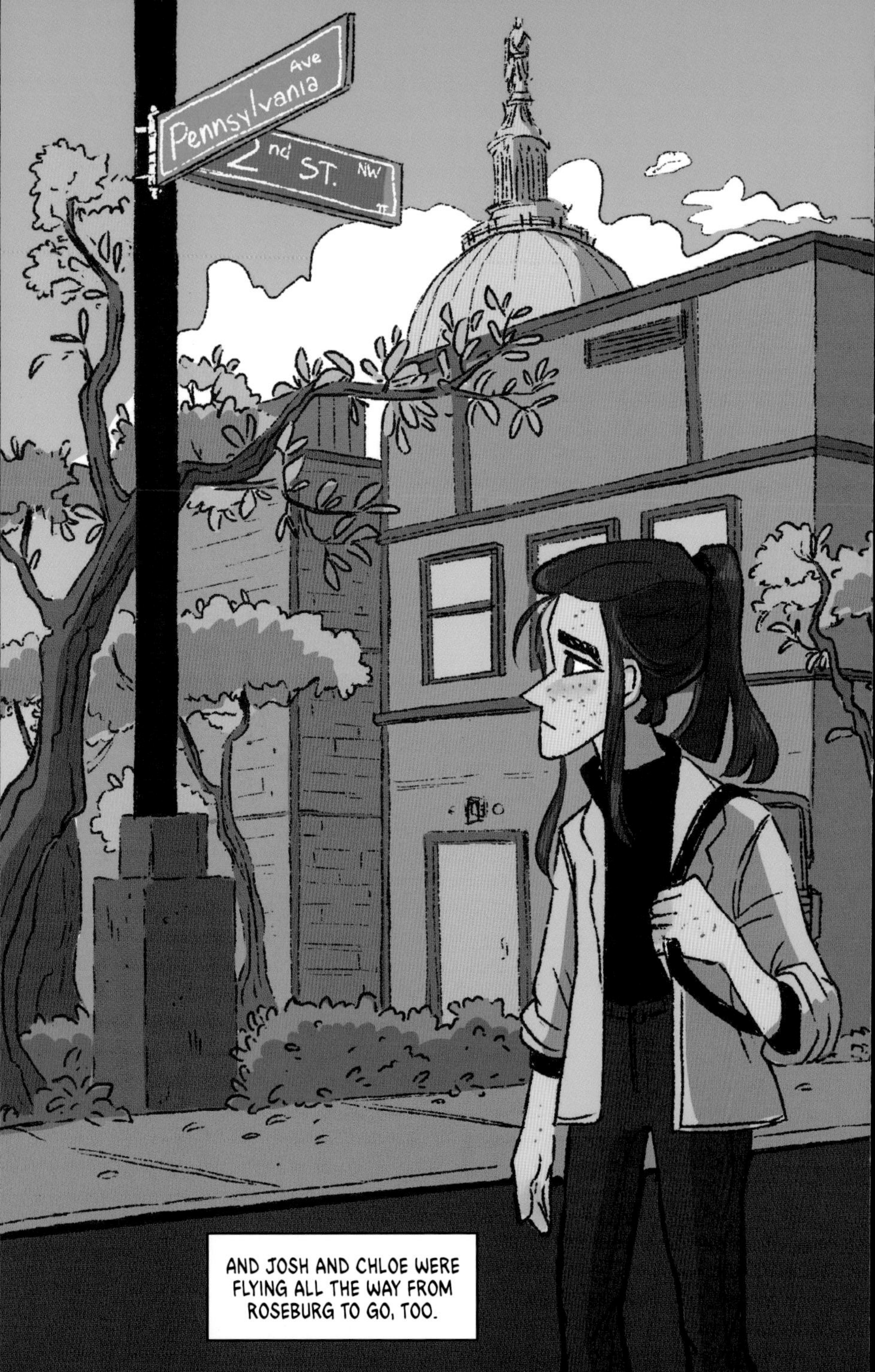
Pennsylvania Ave
2nd ST. NW
AND JOSH AND CHLOE WERE FLYING ALL THE WAY FROM ROSEBURG TO GO, TOO.

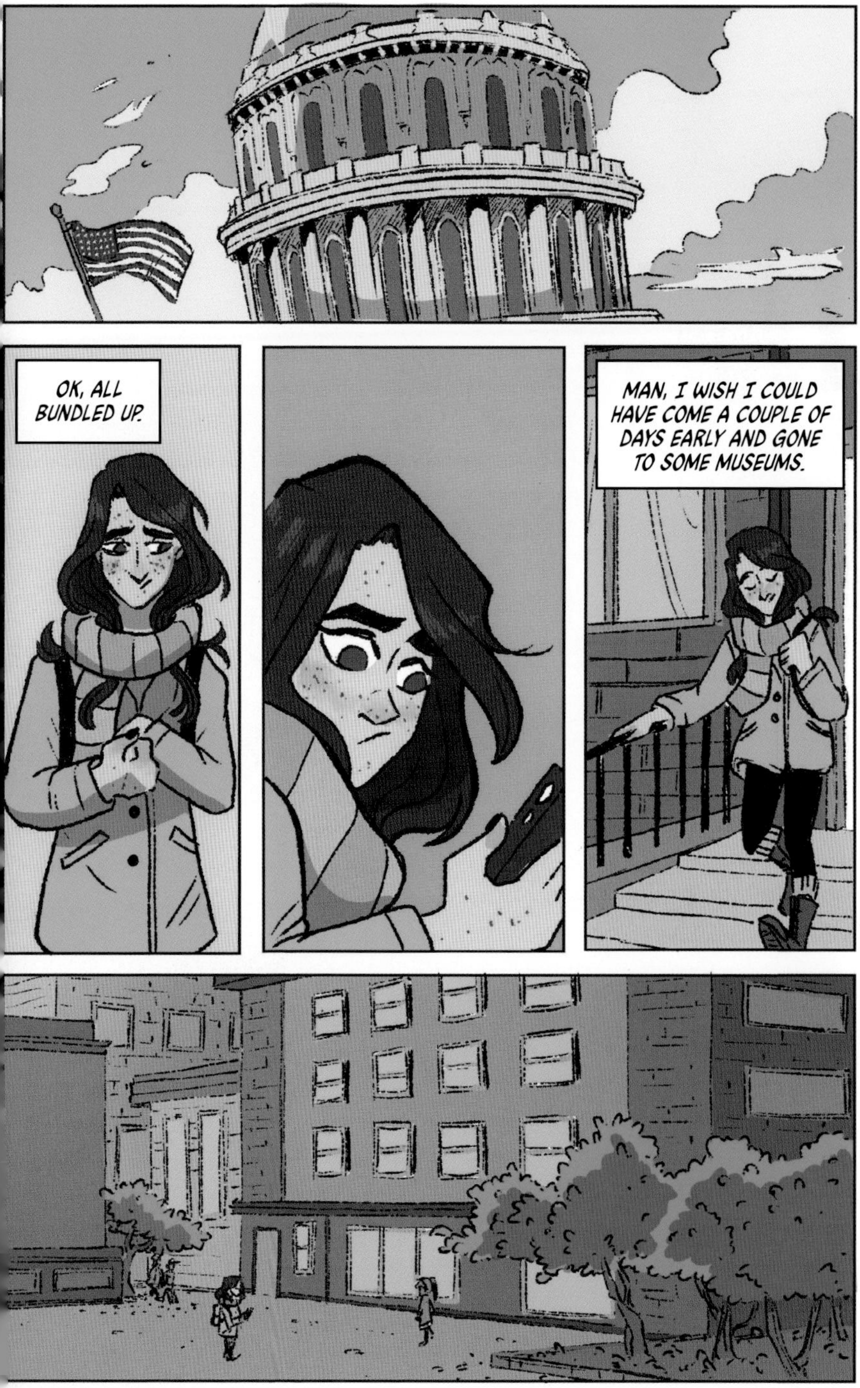
OK, ALL BUNDLED UP.
MAN, I WISH I COULD HAVE COME A COUPLE OF DAYS EARLY AND GONE TO SOME MUSEUMS.

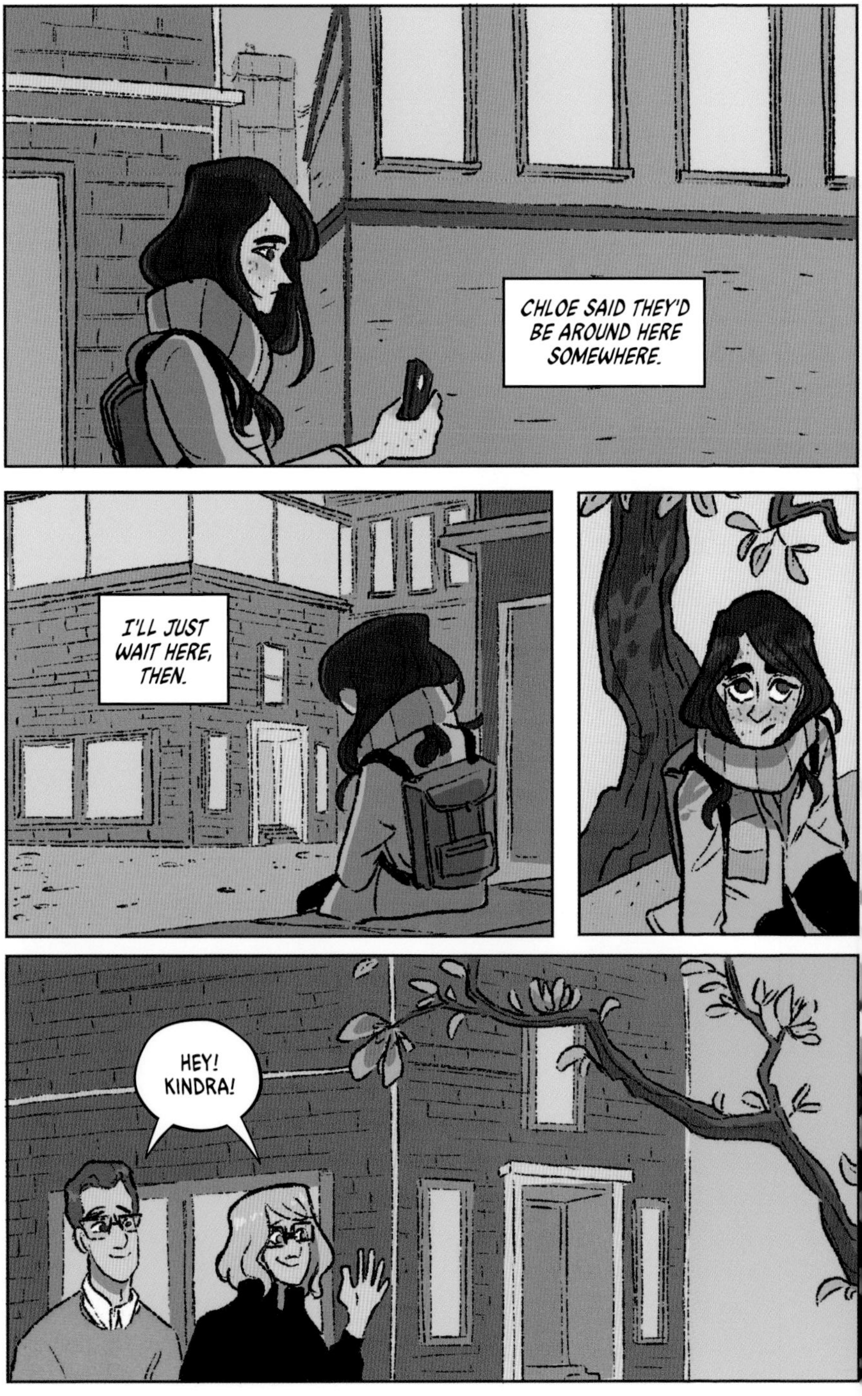
CHLOE SAID THEY'D BE AROUND HERE SOMEWHERE.
I'LL JUST WAIT HERE, THEN.
HEY! KINDRA!

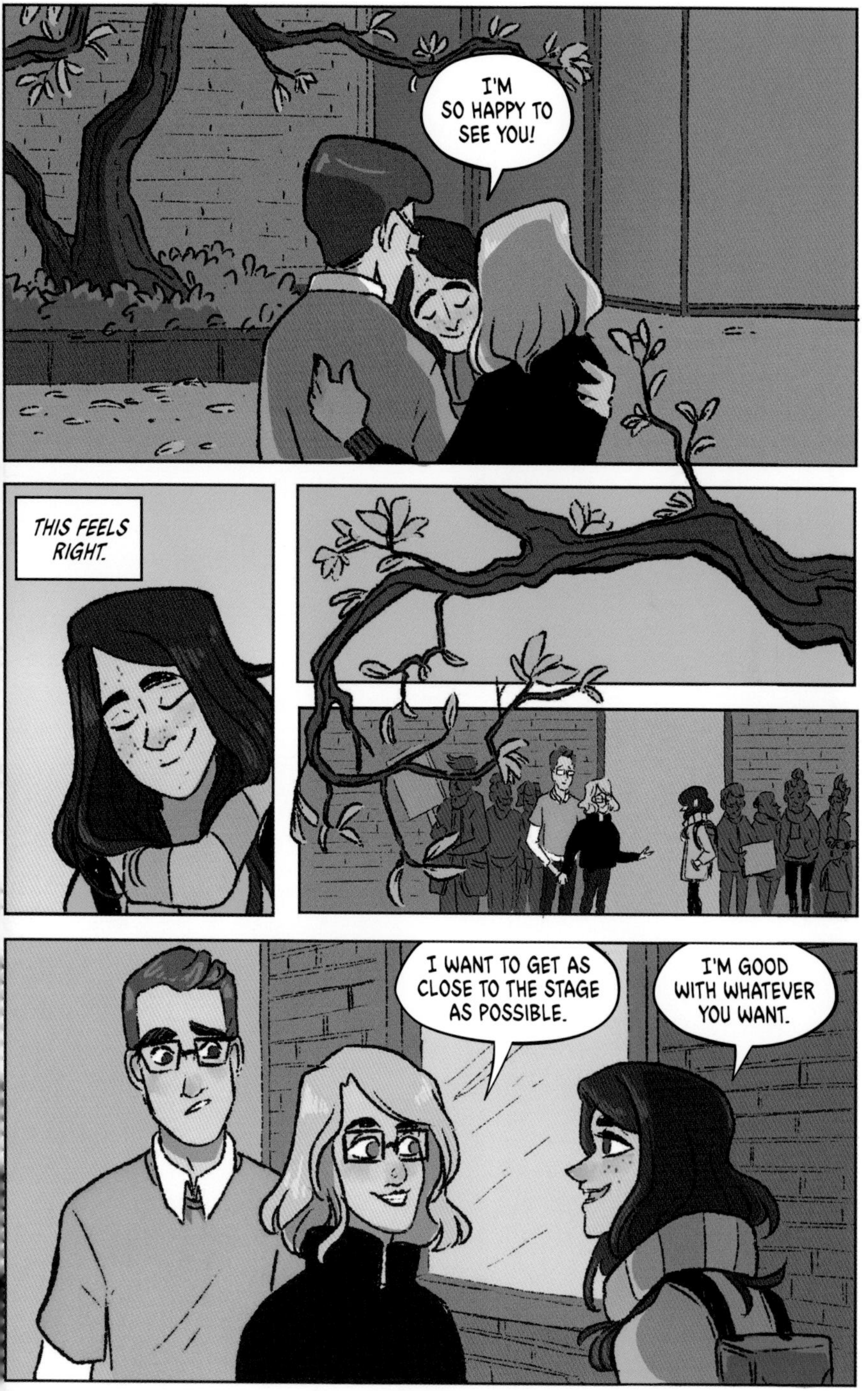
I'M SO HAPPY TO SEE YOU!
THIS FEELS RIGHT.
I WANT TO GET AS CLOSE TO THE STAGE AS POSSIBLE.
I'M GOOD WITH WHATEVER YOU WANT.

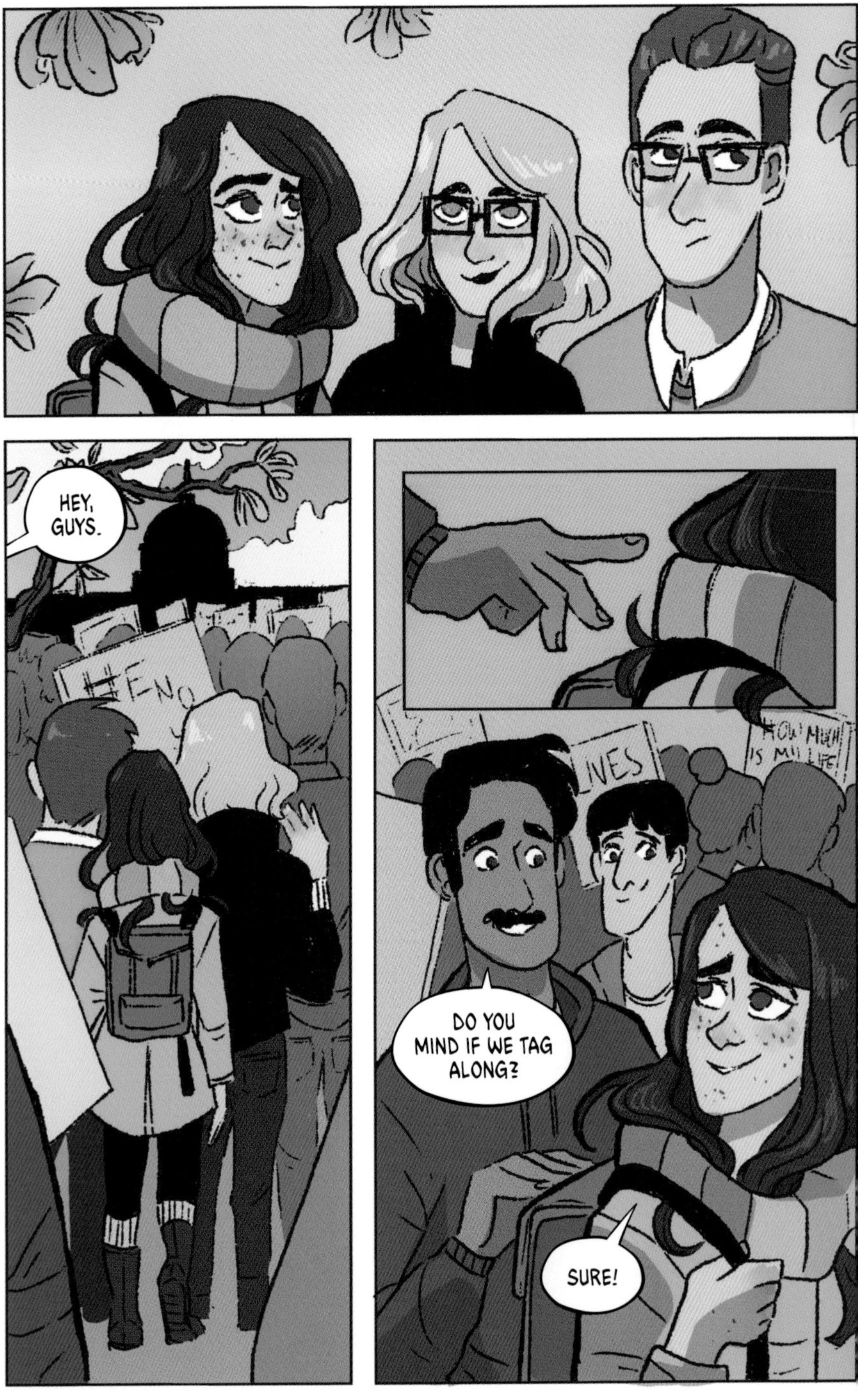
HEY, GUYS.
HENO
HOW MUCH IS MY LIFE
IVES
DO YOU MIND IF WE TAG ALONG?
SURE!

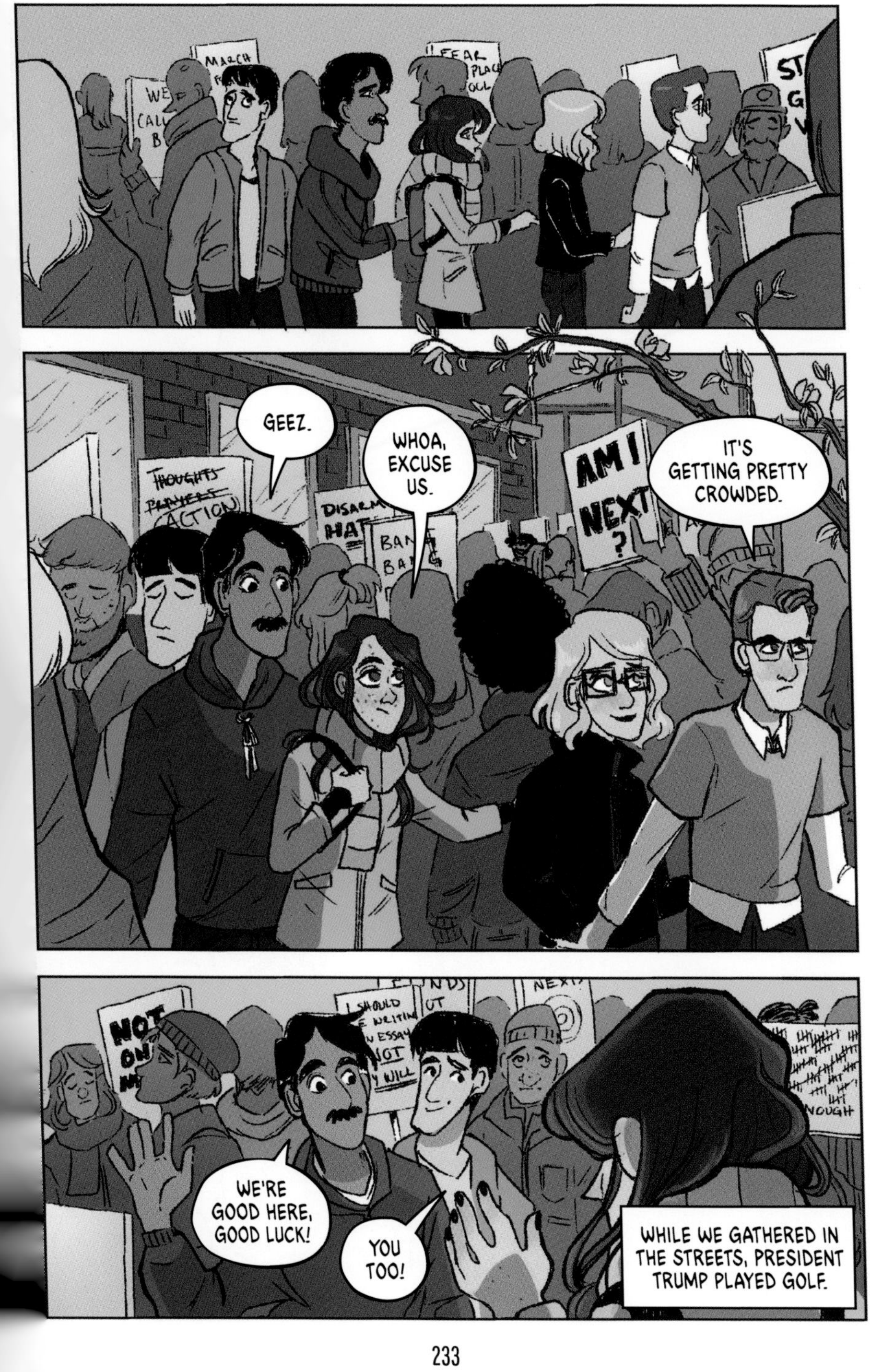
GEEZ.
WHOA, EXCUSE US.
AM I NEXT ?
IT'S GETTING PRETTY CROWDED.
WE'RE GOOD HERE, GOOD LUCK!
YOU TOO!
WHILE WE GATHERED IN THE STREETS, PRESIDENT TRUMP PLAYED GOLF.

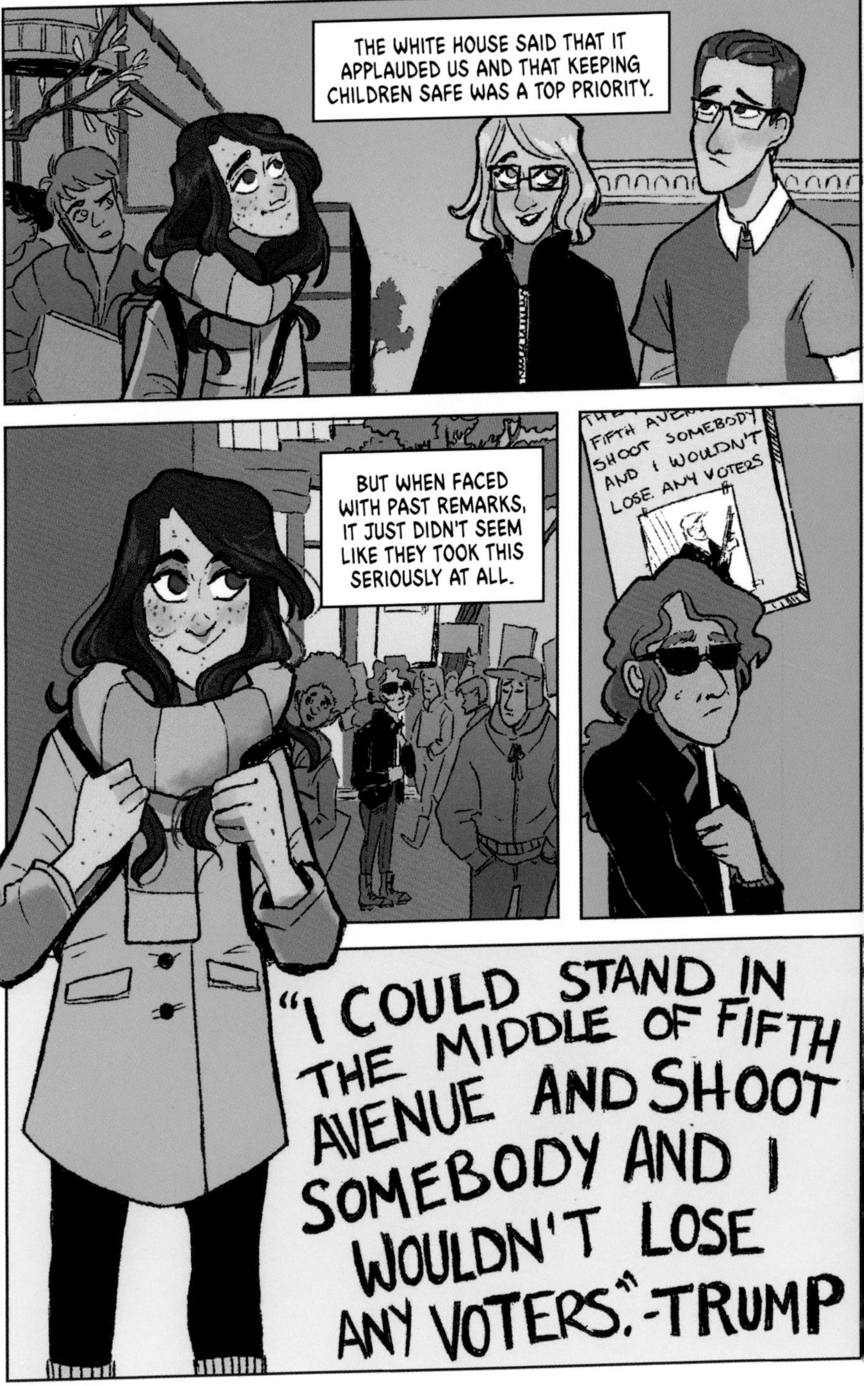
THE WHITE HOUSE SAID THAT IT APPLAUDED US AND THAT KEEPING CHILDREN SAFE WAS A TOP PRIORITY.
BUT WHEN FACED WITH PAST REMARKS, IT JUST DIDN'T SEEM LIKE THEY TOOK THIS SERIOUSLY AT ALL.
SHOOT SOMEBODY
AND I WOULDN'T
LOSE ANY VOTERS
"I COULD STAND IN THE MIDDLE OF FIFTH AVENUE AND SHOOT SOMEBODY AND I WOULDN'T LOSE ANY VOTERS." -TRUMP

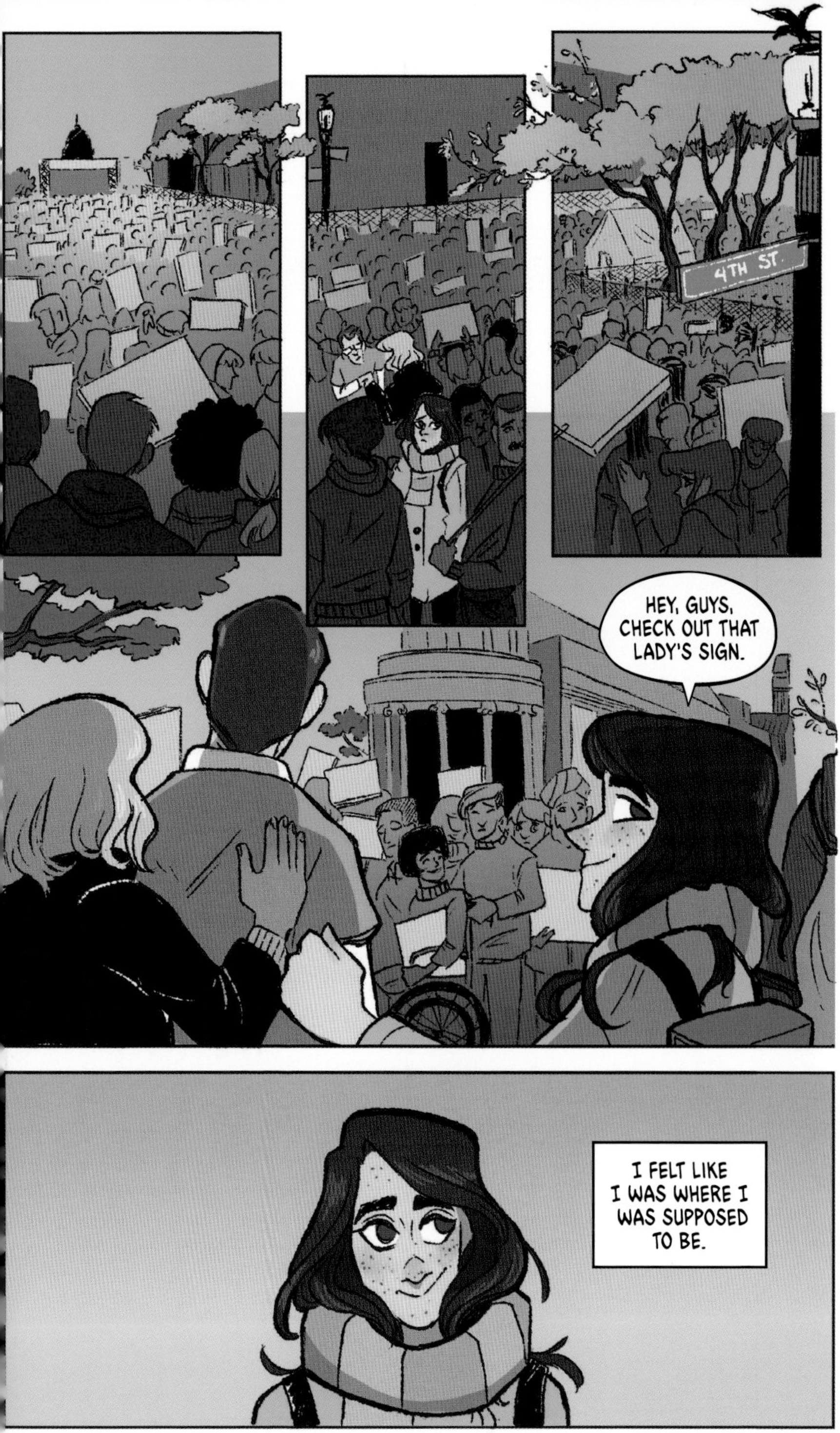
4TH ST.
HEY, GUYS, CHECK OUT THAT LADY'S SIGN.
I FELT LIKE I WAS WHERE I WAS SUPPOSED TO BE.

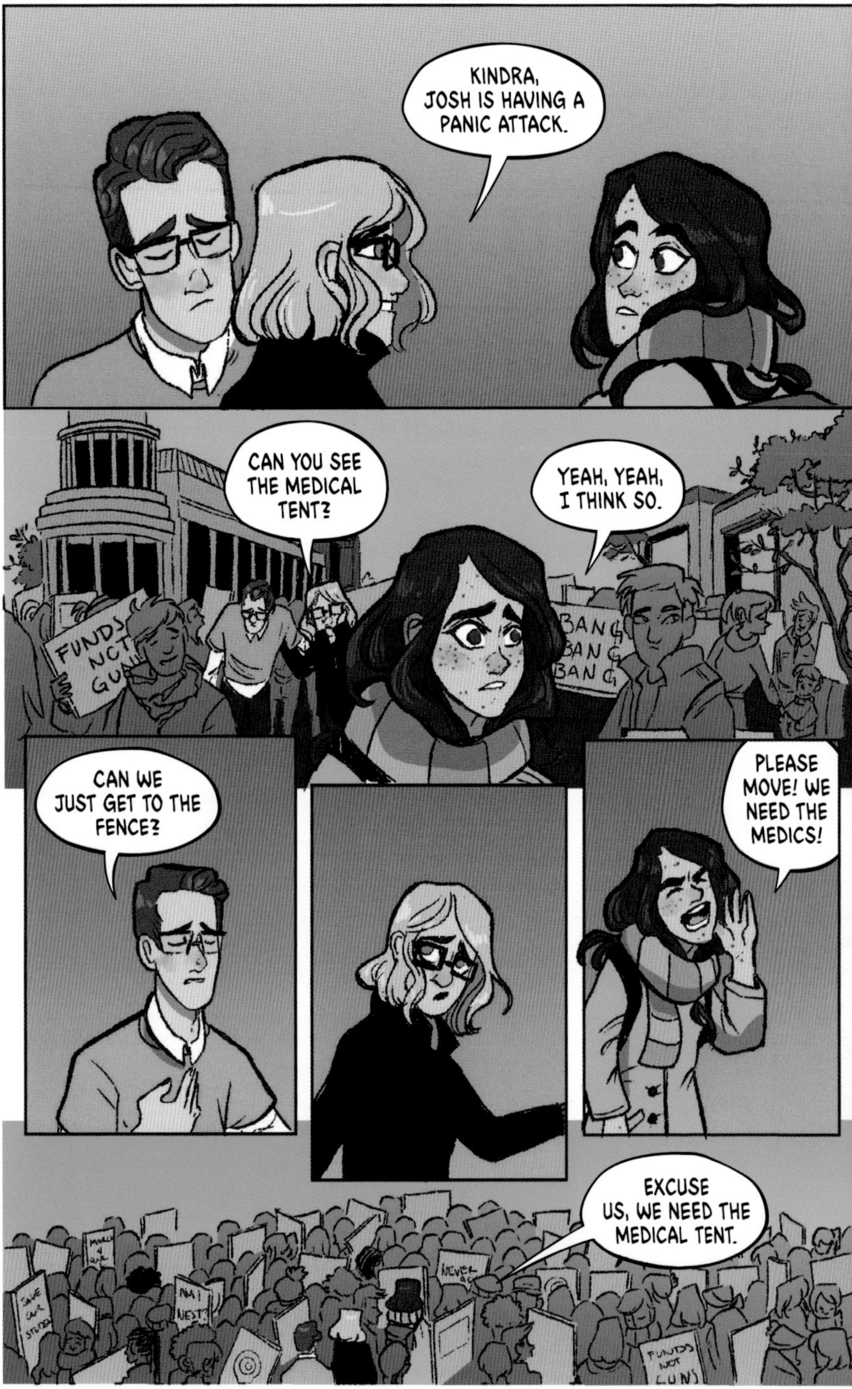
KINDRA, JOSH IS HAVING A PANIC ATTACK.
CAN YOU SEE THE MEDICAL TENT?
YEAH, YEAH, I THINK SO.
FUNDS NOT GUN
BANG BANG BANG
CAN WE JUST GET TO THE FENCE?
PLEASE MOVE! WE NEED THE MEDICS!
EXCUSE US, WE NEED THE MEDICAL TENT.
FUNDS NOT GUNS

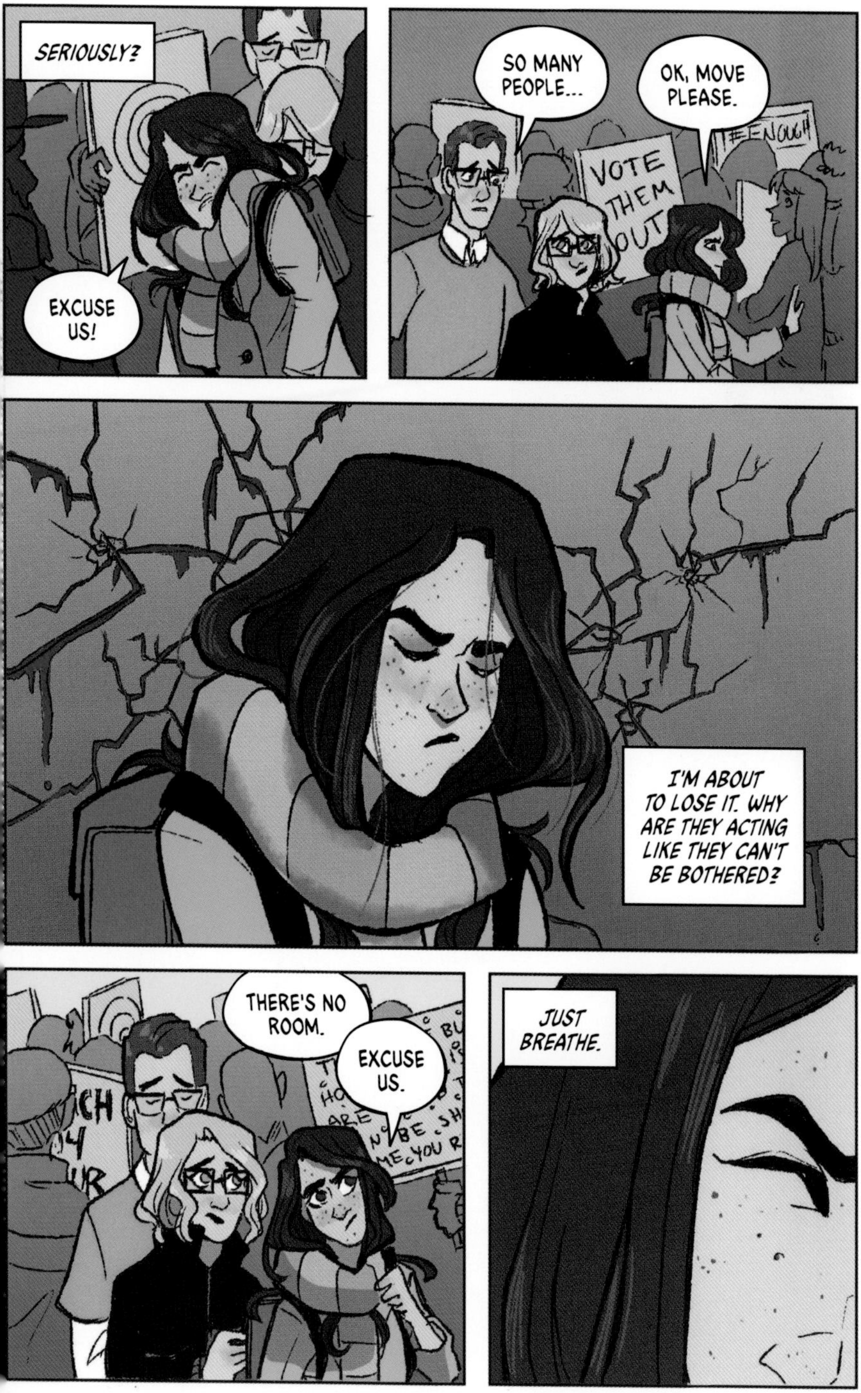
SERIOUSLY?
EXCUSE US!
SO MANY PEOPLE...
OK, MOVE PLEASE.
VOTE THEM OUT
#ENOUGH
I'M ABOUT TO LOSE IT. WHY ARE THEY ACTING LIKE THEY CAN'T BE BOTHERED?
THERE'S NO ROOM.
EXCUSE US.
JUST BREATHE.

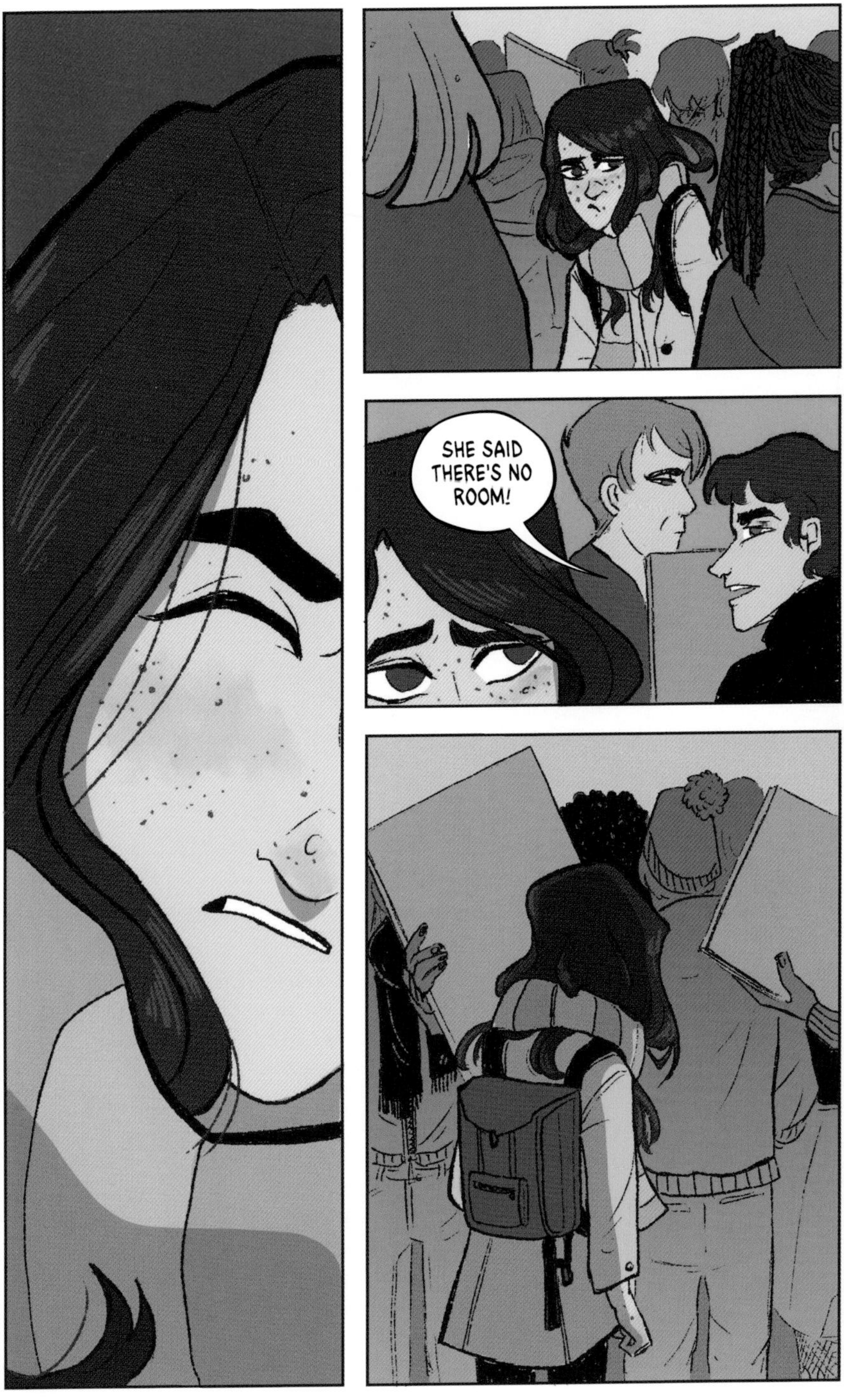
SHE SAID THERE'S NO ROOM!

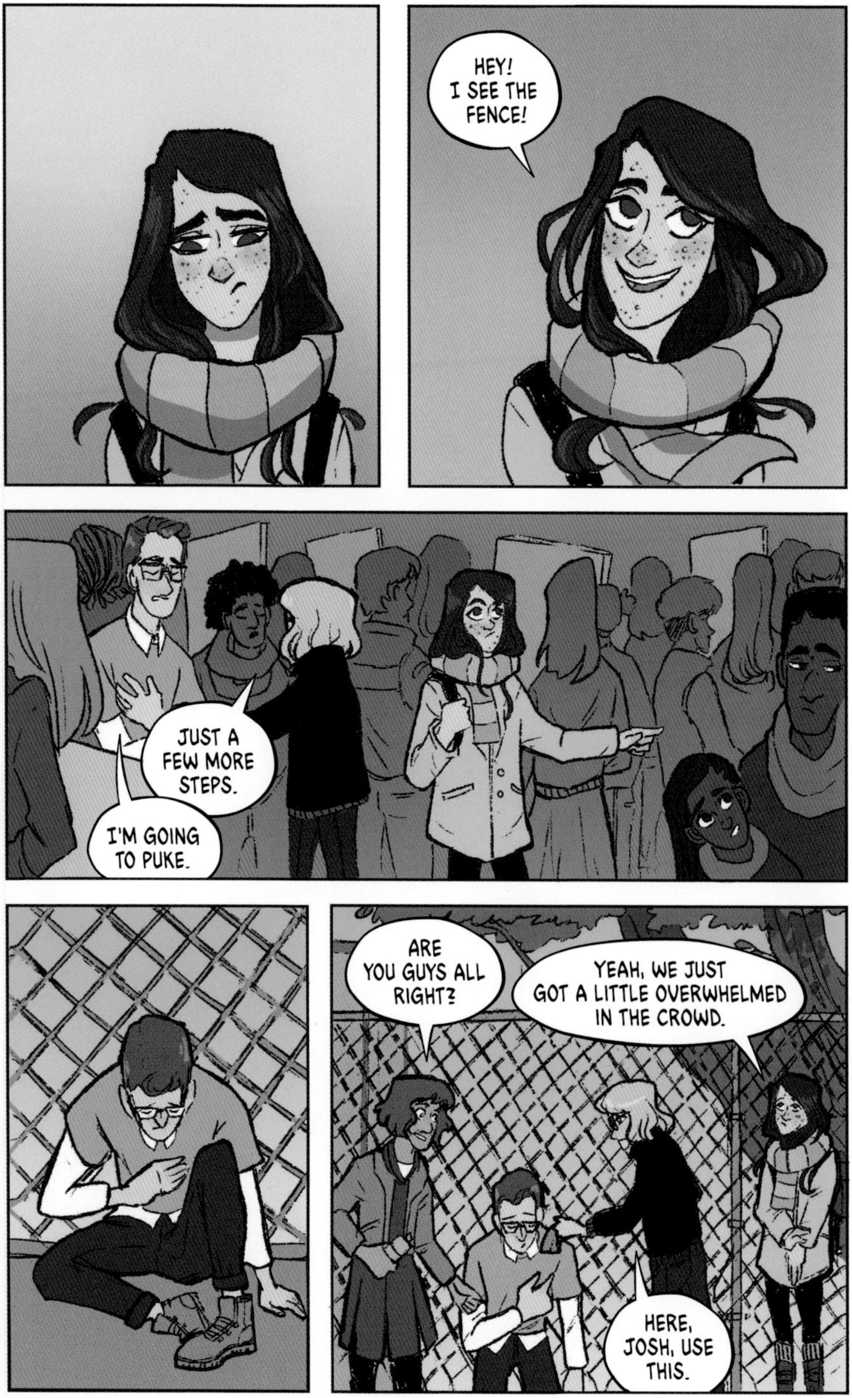
HEY! I SEE THE FENCE!
JUST A FEW MORE STEPS.
I'M GOING TO PUKE.
ARE YOU GUYS ALL RIGHT?
YEAH, WE JUST GOT A LITTLE OVERWHELMED IN THE CROWD.
HERE, JOSH, USE THIS.

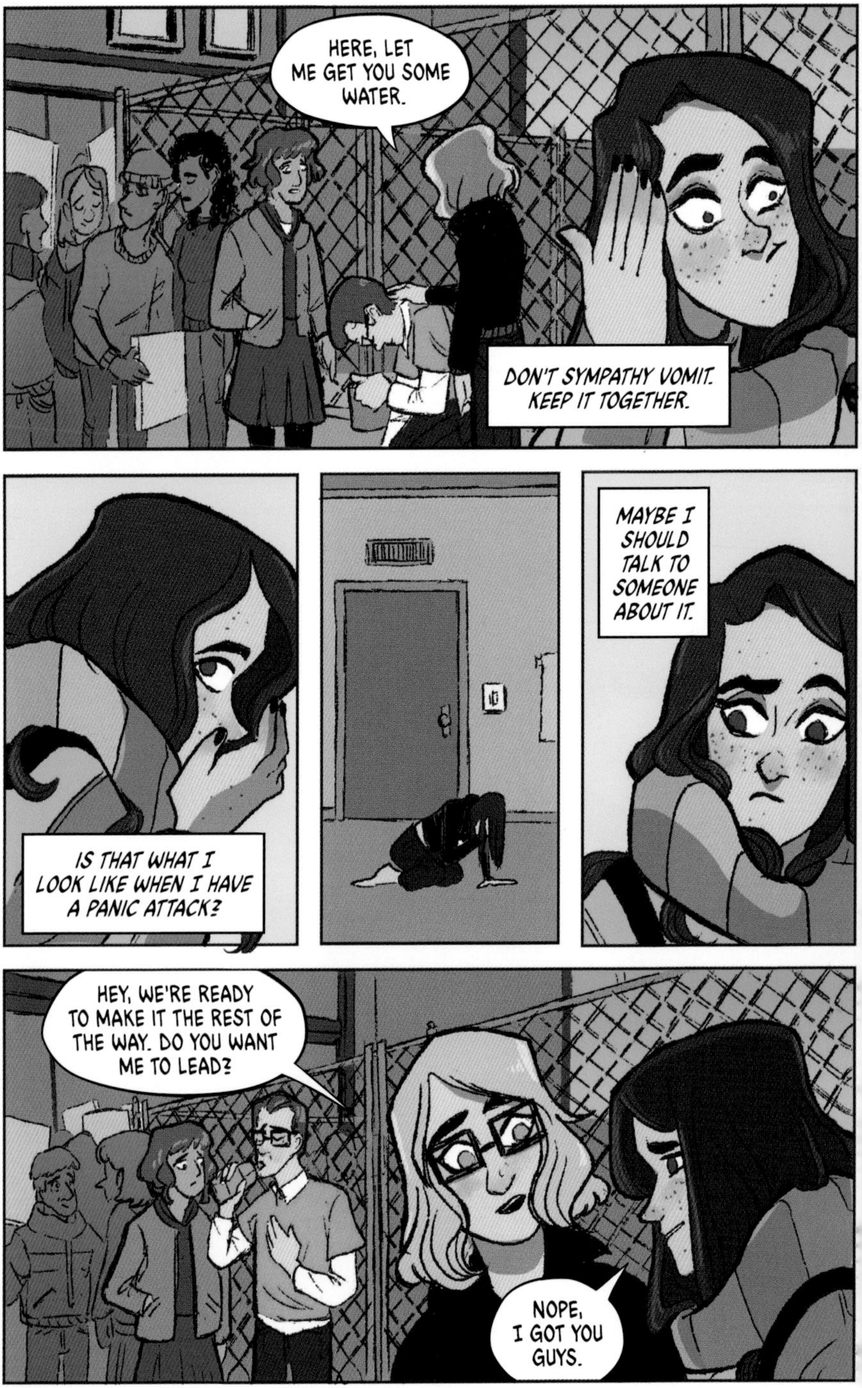

HERE, LET ME GET YOU SOME WATER.
DON'T SYMPATHY VOMIT. KEEP IT TOGETHER.
IS THAT WHAT I LOOK LIKE WHEN I HAVE A PANIC ATTACK?
MAYBE I SHOULD TALK TO SOMEONE ABOUT IT.
HEY, WE'RE READY TO MAKE IT THE REST OF THE WAY. DO YOU WANT ME TO LEAD?
NOPE, I GOT YOU GUYS.

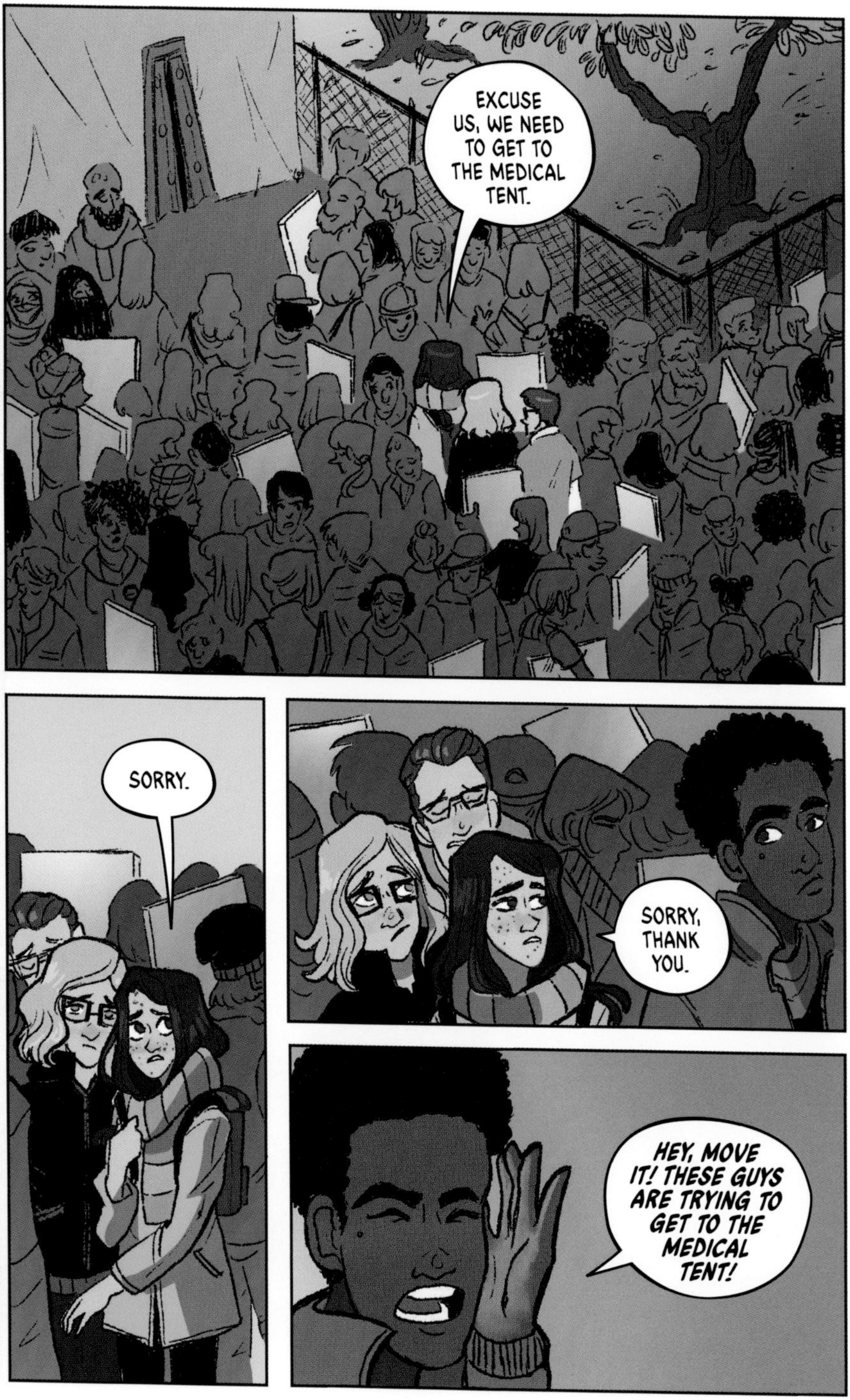
EXCUSE US, WE NEED TO GET TO THE MEDICAL TENT.
SORRY.
SORRY, THANK YOU.
HEY, MOVE IT! THESE GUYS ARE TRYING TO GET TO THE MEDICAL TENT!

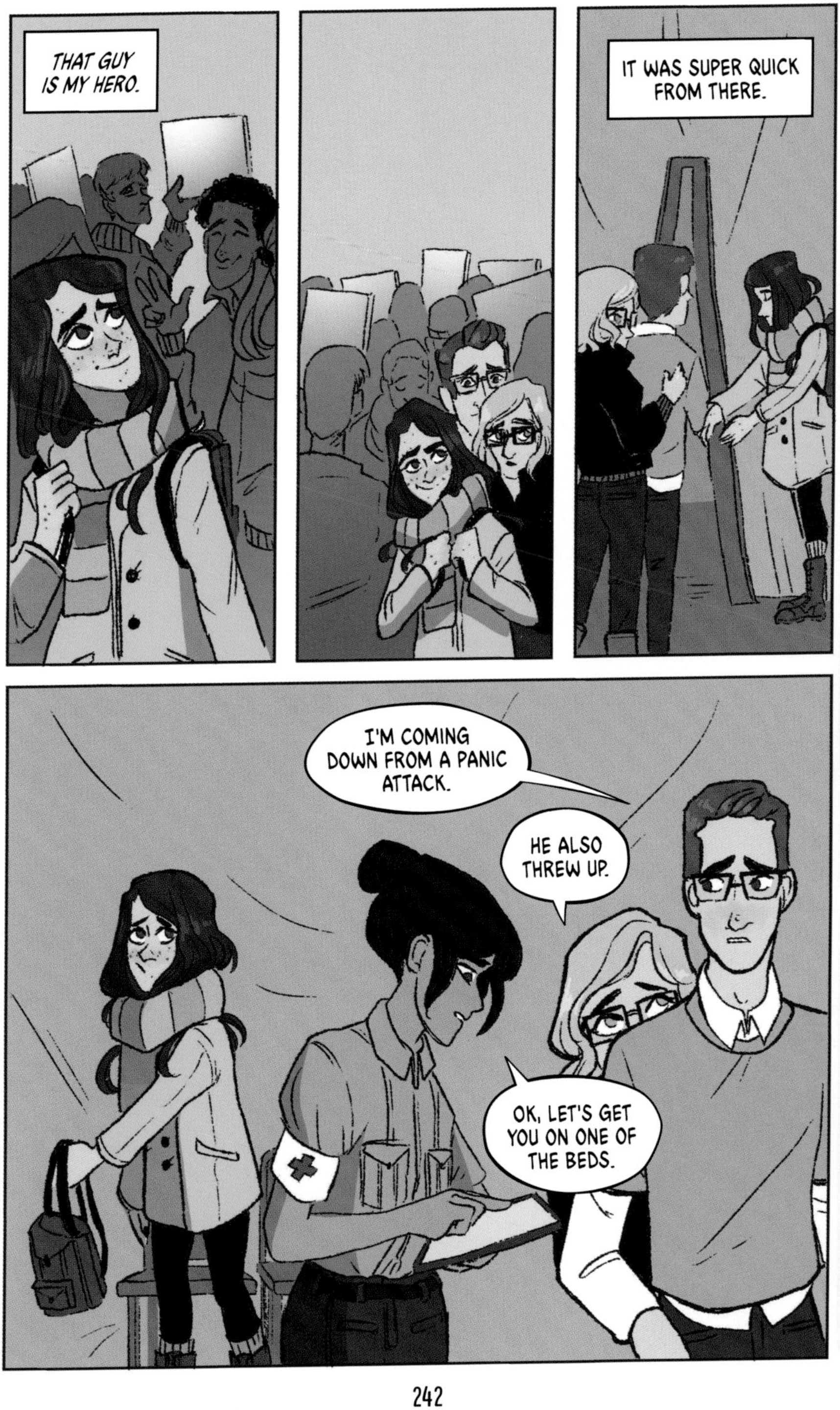
THAT GUY IS MY HERO.
IT WAS SUPER QUICK FROM THERE.
I'M COMING DOWN FROM A PANIC ATTACK.
HE ALSO THREW UP.
OK, LET'S GET YOU ON ONE OF THE BEDS.

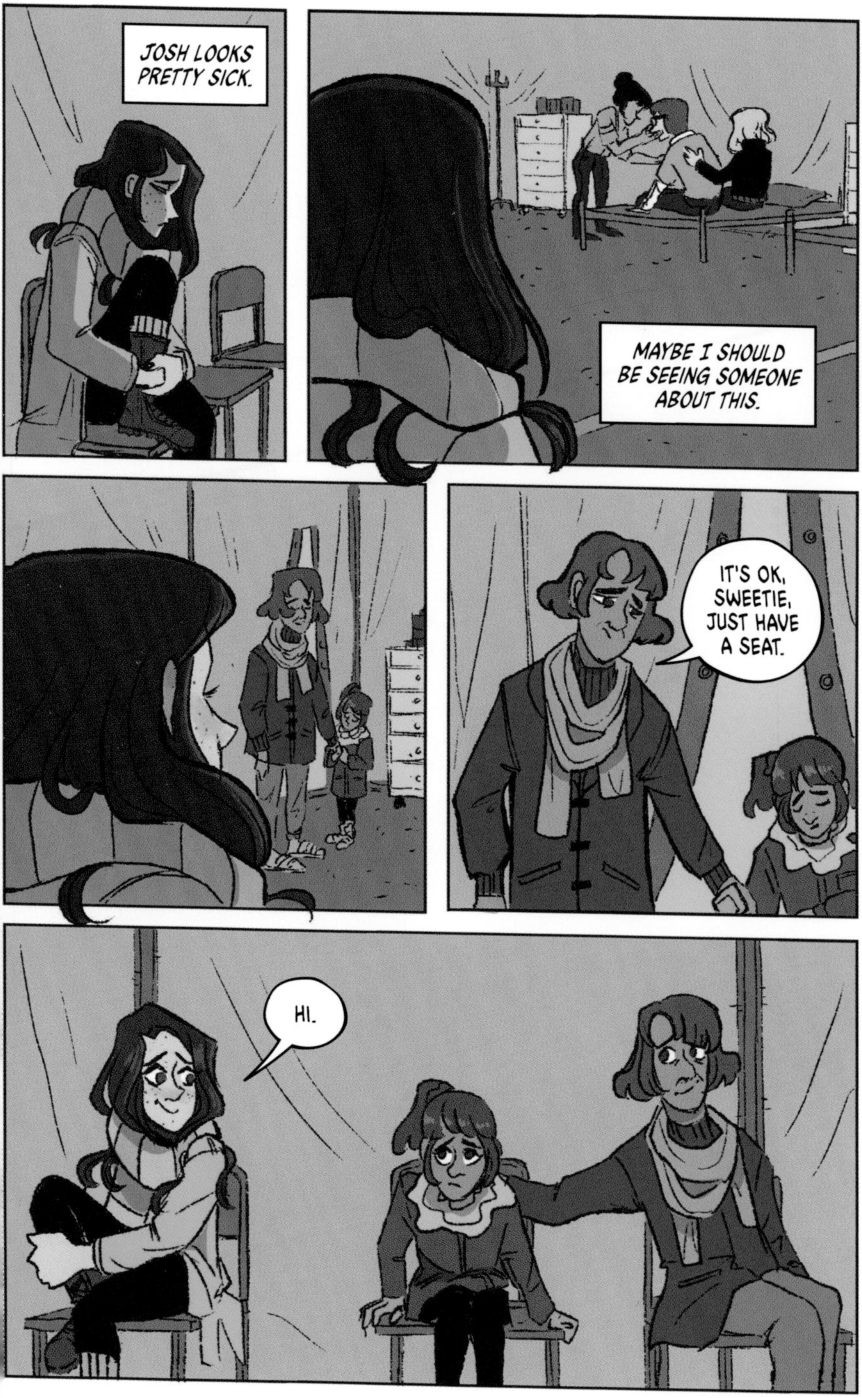
JOSH LOOKS PRETTY SICK.
MAYBE I SHOULD BE SEEING SOMEONE ABOUT THIS.
IT'S OK, SWEETIE, JUST HAVE A SEAT.
HI.

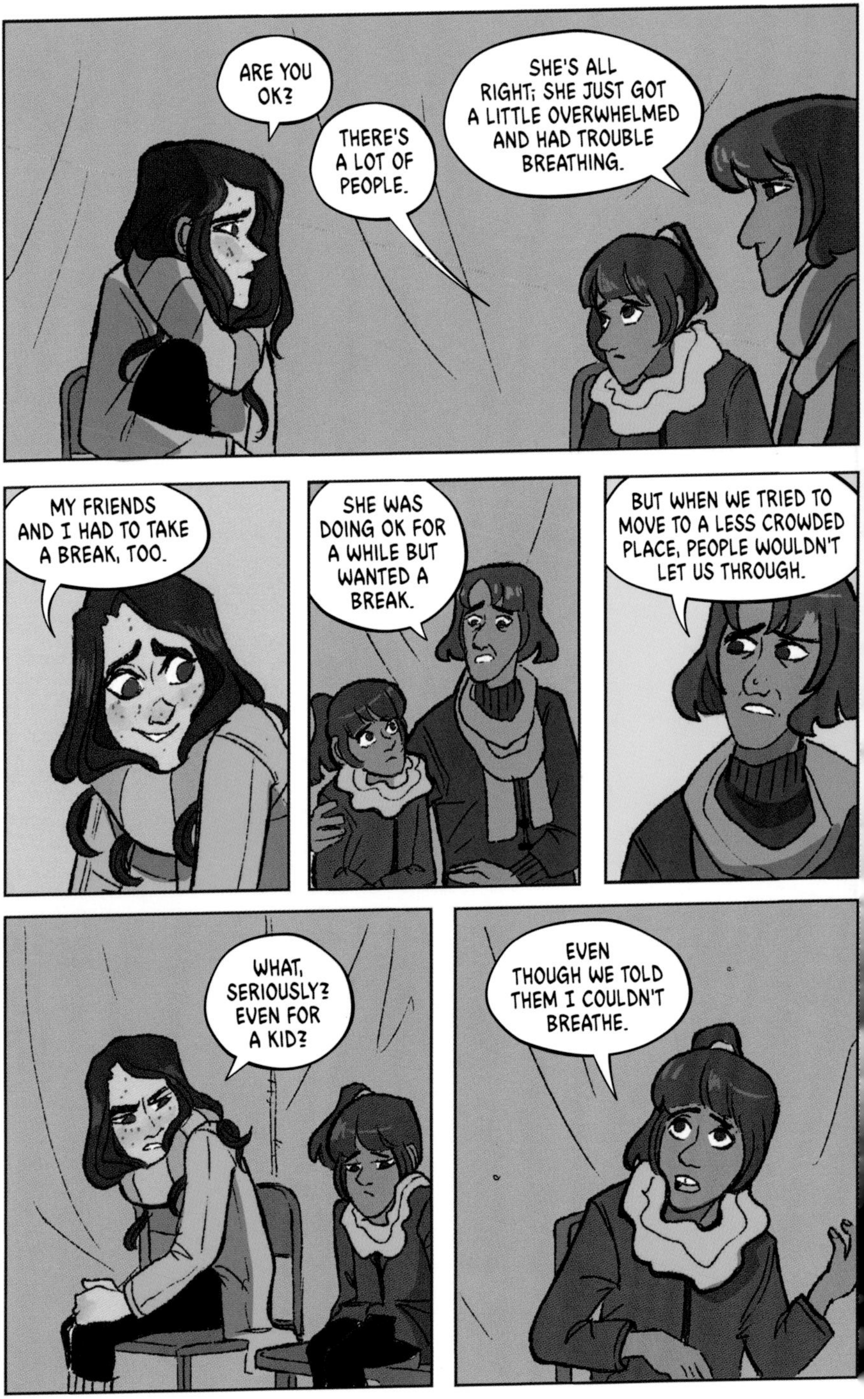
ARE YOU OK?
THERE'S A LOT OF PEOPLE.
SHE'S ALL RIGHT; SHE JUST GOT A LITTLE OVERWHELMED AND HAD TROUBLE BREATHING.
MY FRIENDS AND I HAD TO TAKE A BREAK, TOO.
SHE WAS DOING OK FOR A WHILE BUT WANTED A BREAK.
BUT WHEN WE TRIED TO MOVE TO A LESS CROWDED PLACE, PEOPLE WOULDN'T LET US THROUGH.
WHAT, SERIOUSLY? EVEN FOR A KID?
EVEN THOUGH WE TOLD THEM I COULDN'T BREATHE.

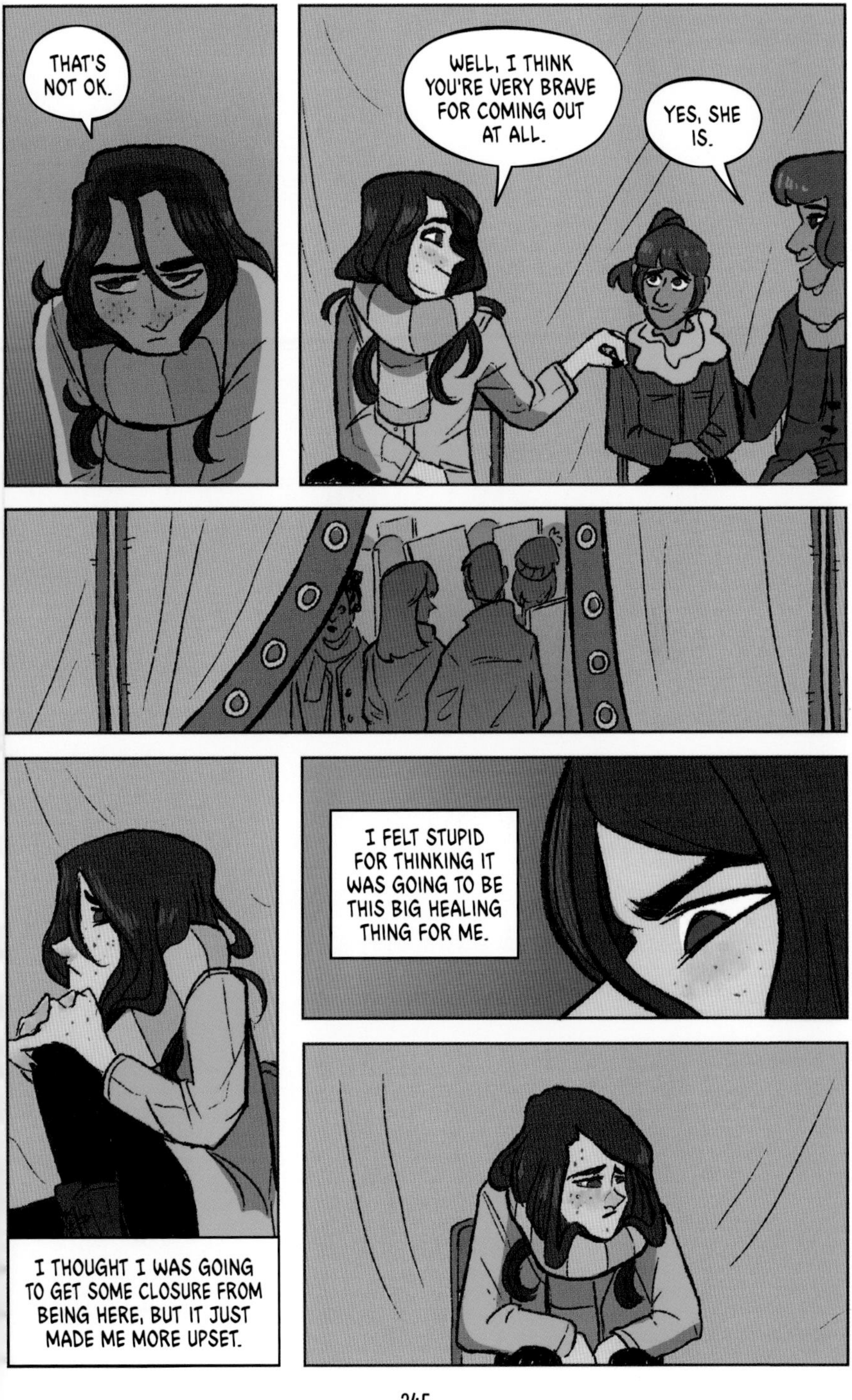
THAT'S NOT OK.
WELL, I THINK YOU'RE VERY BRAVE FOR COMING OUT AT ALL.
YES, SHE IS.
I FELT STUPID FOR THINKING IT WAS GOING TO BE THIS BIG HEALING THING FOR ME.
I THOUGHT I WAS GOING TO GET SOME CLOSURE FROM BEING HERE, BUT IT JUST MADE ME MORE UPSET.

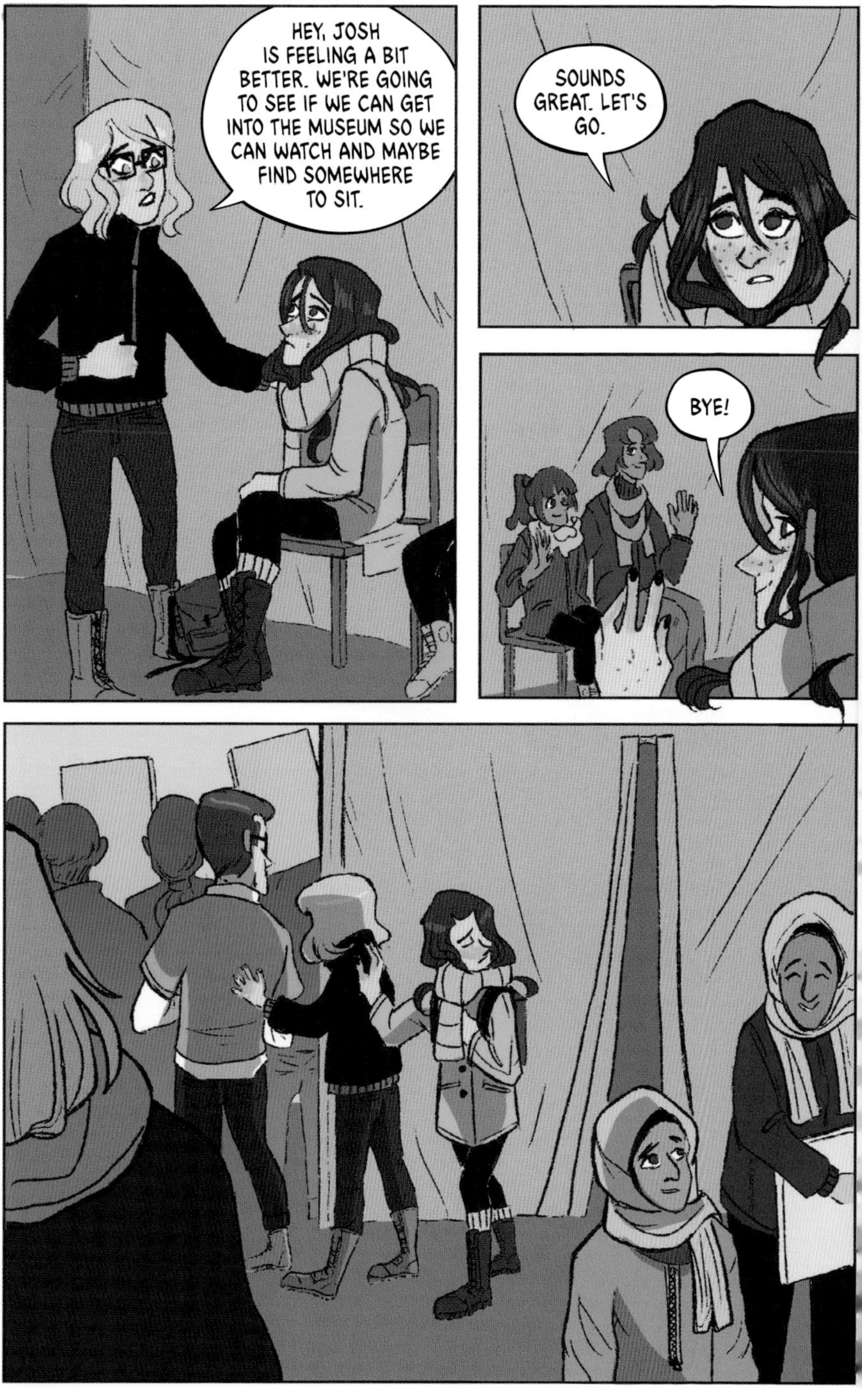
HEY, JOSH IS FEELING A BIT BETTER. WE'RE GOING TO SEE IF WE CAN GET INTO THE MUSEUM SO WE CAN WATCH AND MAYBE FIND SOMEWHERE TO SIT.
SOUNDS GREAT. LET'S GO.
BYE!

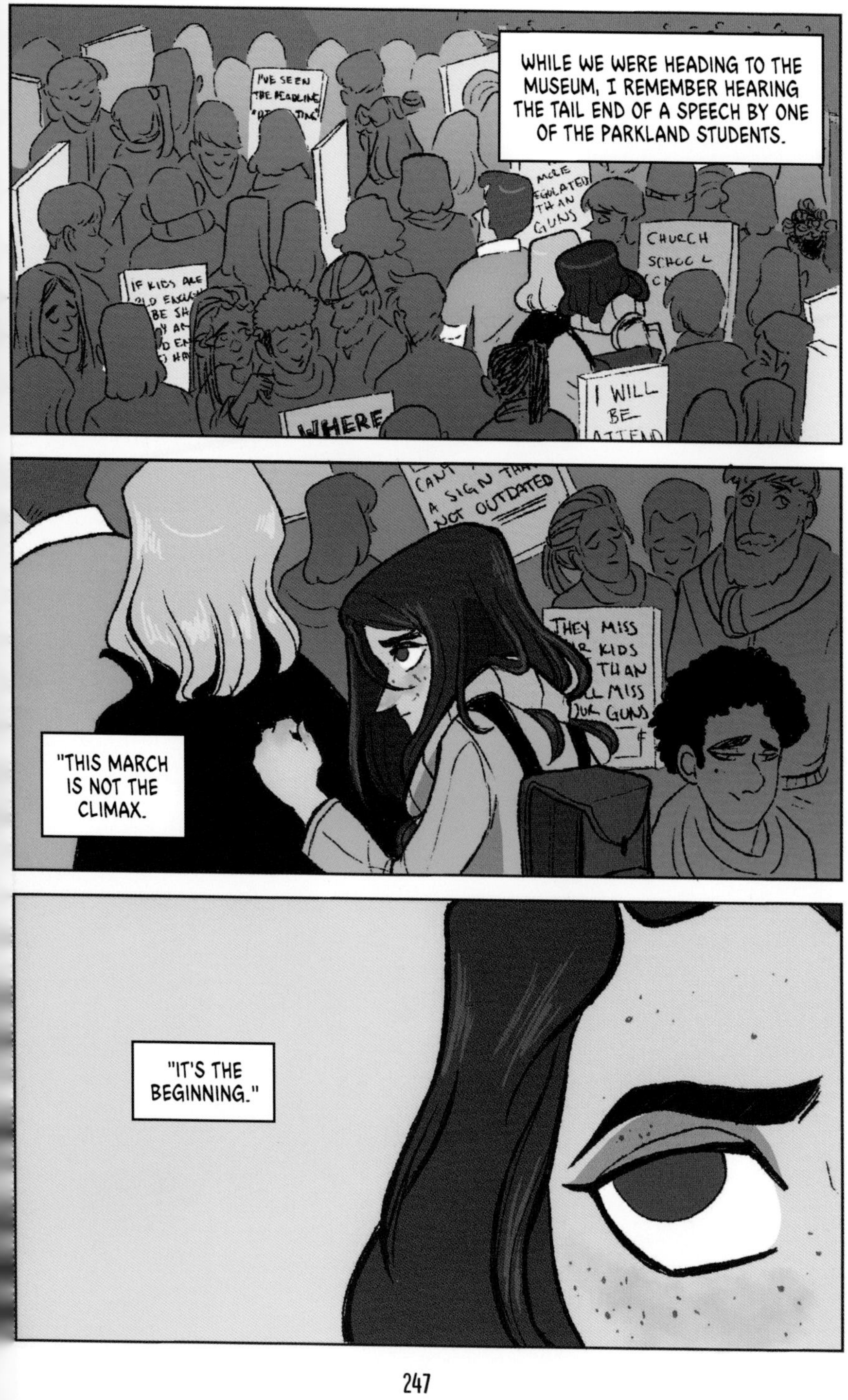
WHILE WE WERE HEADING TO THE MUSEUM, I REMEMBER HEARING THE TAIL END OF A SPEECH BY ONE OF THE PARKLAND STUDENTS.
I'VE SEEN THE HEADLINE
CHURCH
IF KIDS ARE
WHERE
I WILL BE
A SIGN
NOT OUTDATED
THEY MISS
"THIS MARCH IS NOT THE CLIMAX.
"IT'S THE BEGINNING."

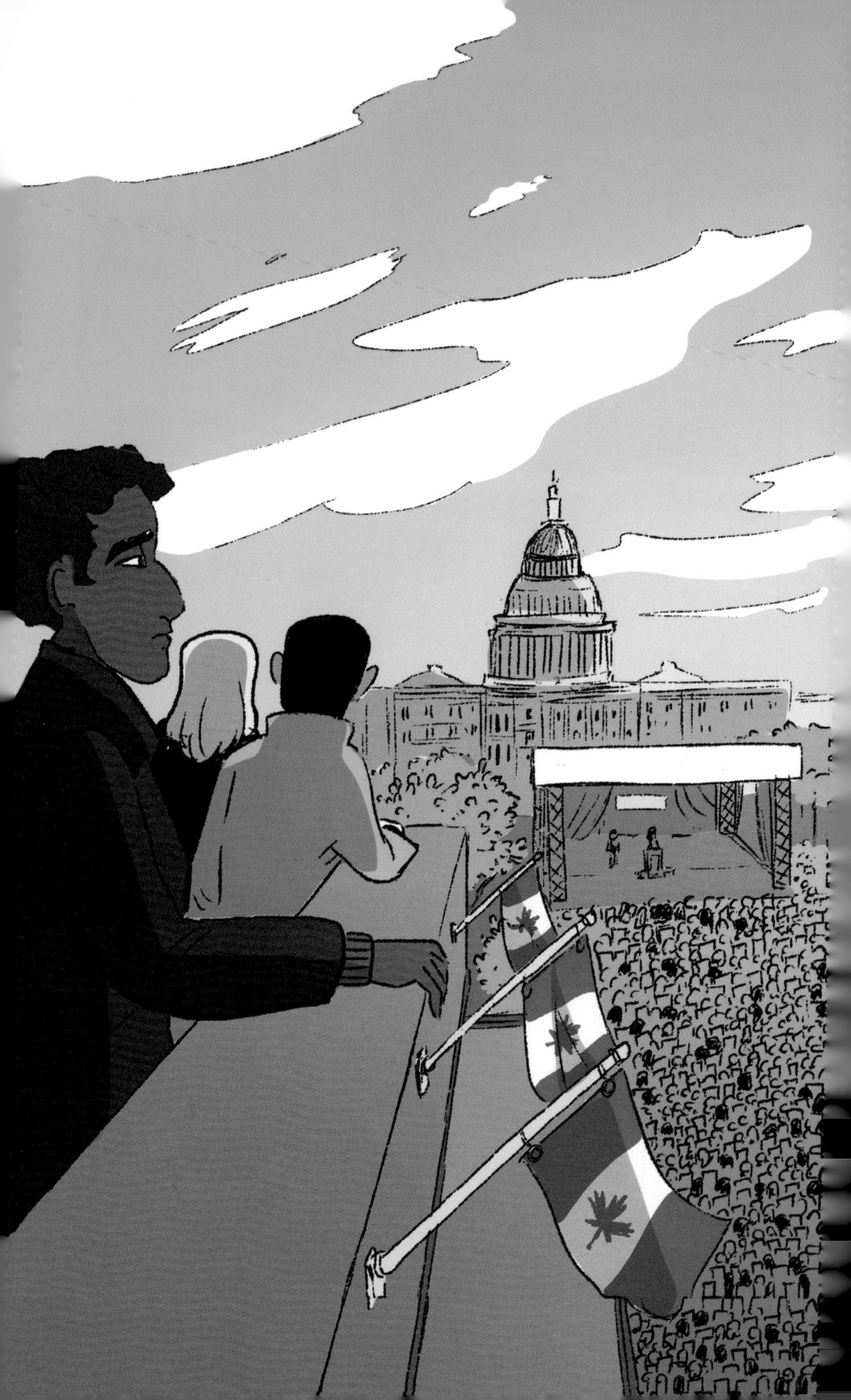

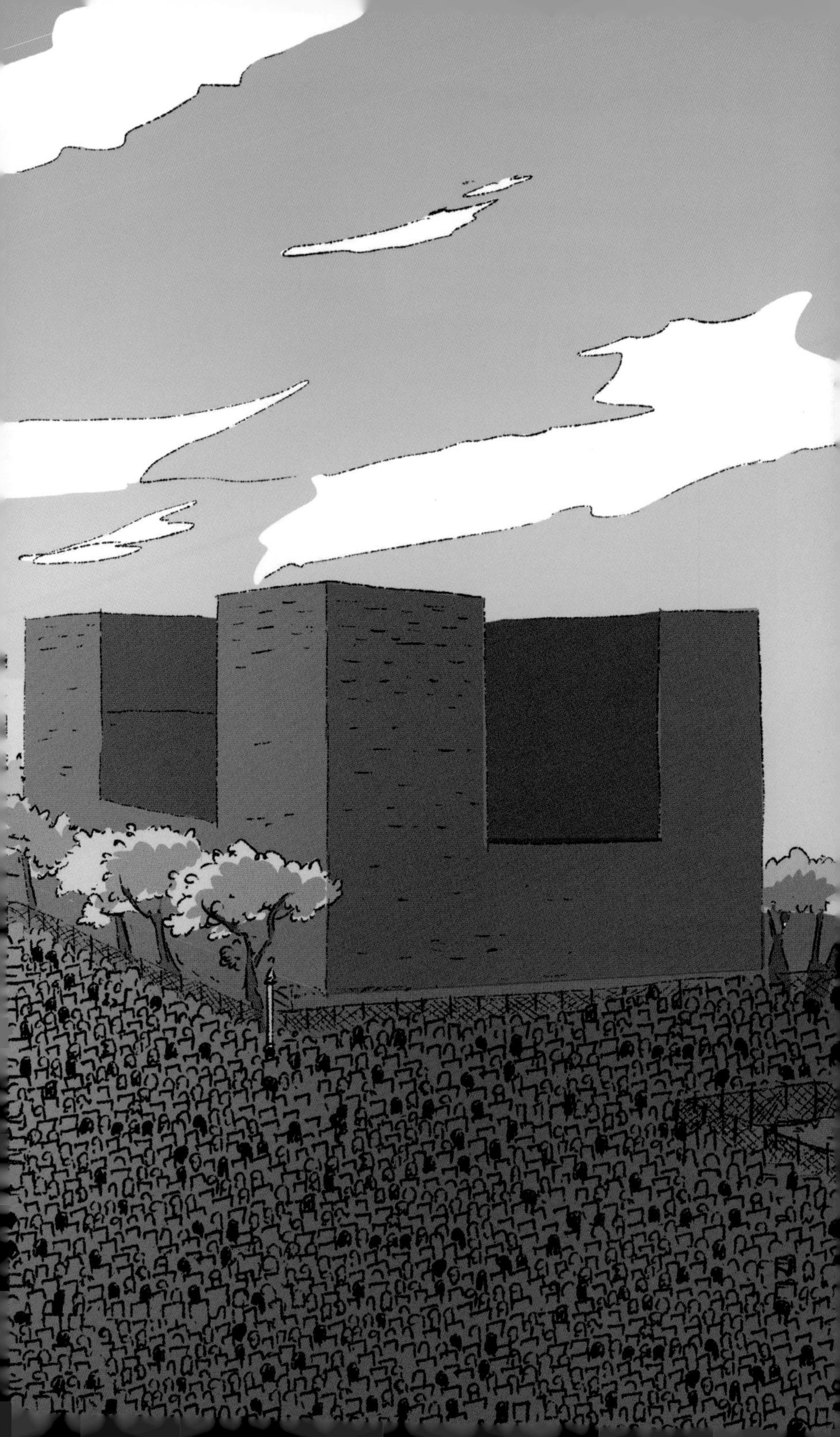

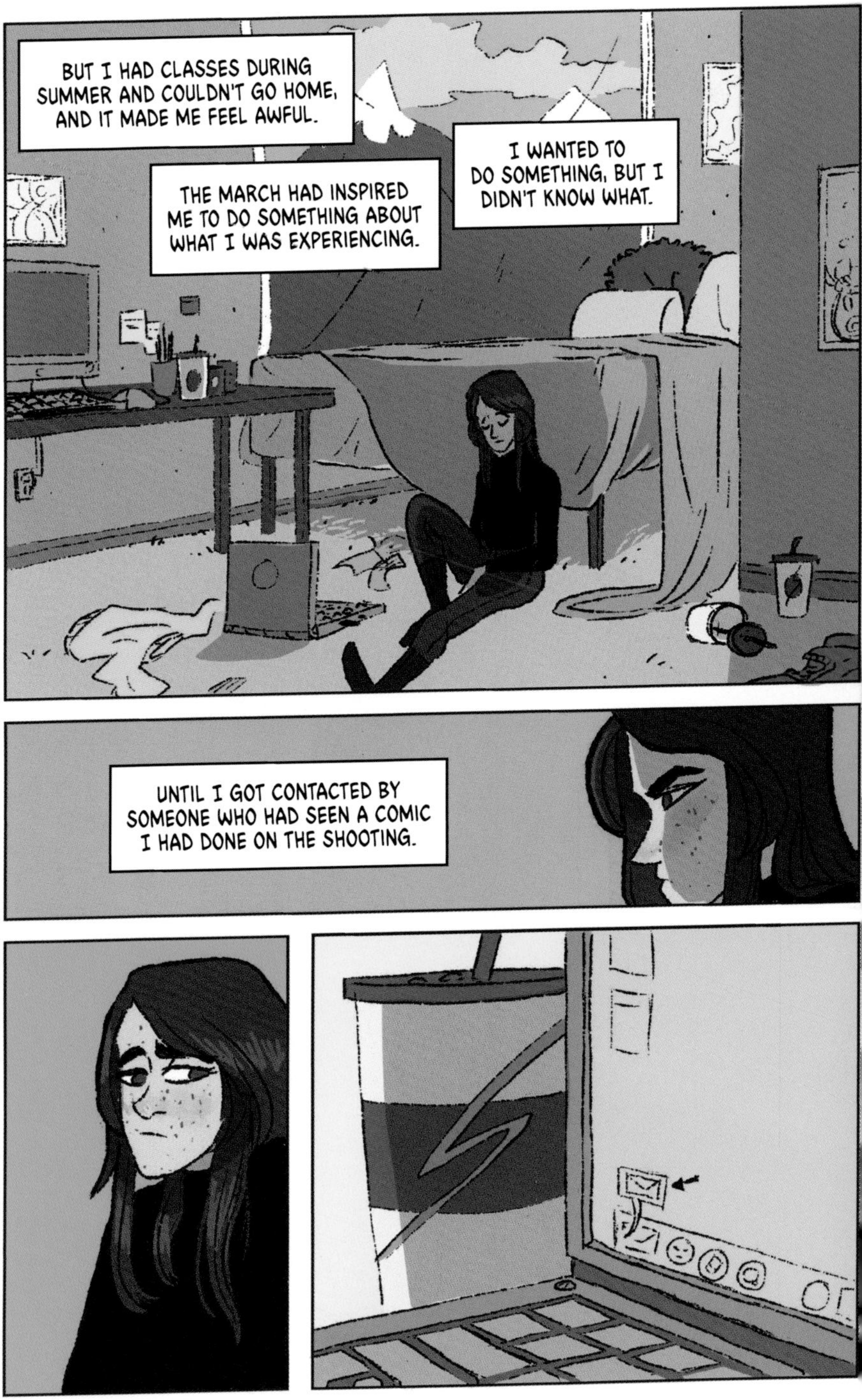
BUT I HAD CLASSES DURING SUMMER AND COULDN'T GO HOME, AND IT MADE ME FEEL AWFUL.
THE MARCH HAD INSPIRED ME TO DO SOMETHING ABOUT WHAT I WAS EXPERIENCING.
I WANTED TO DO SOMETHING, BUT I DIDN'T KNOW WHAT.
UNTIL I GOT CONTACTED BY SOMEONE WHO HAD SEEN A COMIC I HAD DONE ON THE SHOOTING.

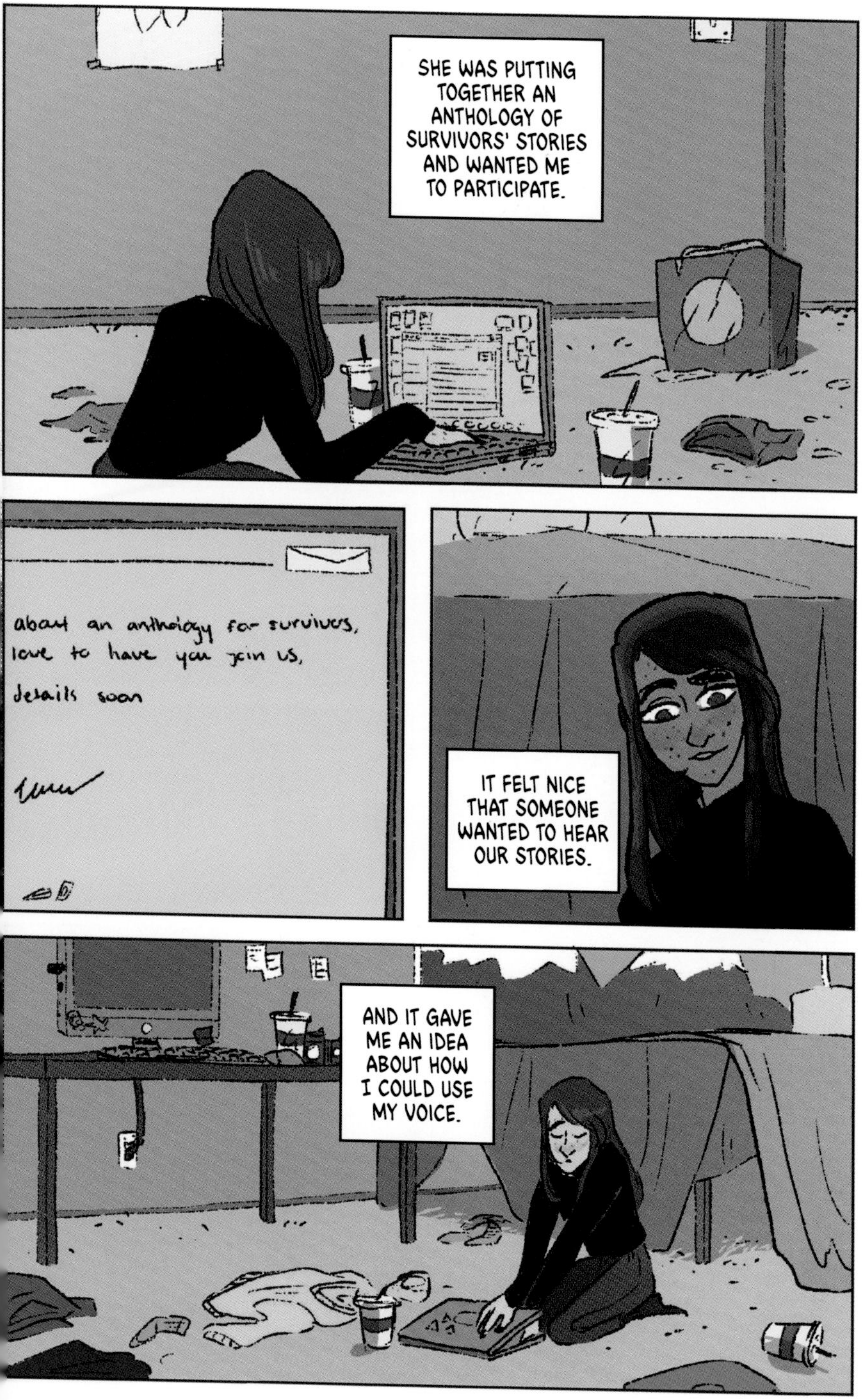
SHE WAS PUTTING TOGETHER AN ANTHOLOGY OF SURVIVORS' STORIES AND WANTED ME TO PARTICIPATE.
about an anthology for survivors,
love to have you join us,
details soon
IT FELT NICE THAT SOMEONE WANTED TO HEAR OUR STORIES.
AND IT GAVE ME AN IDEA ABOUT HOW I COULD USE MY VOICE.

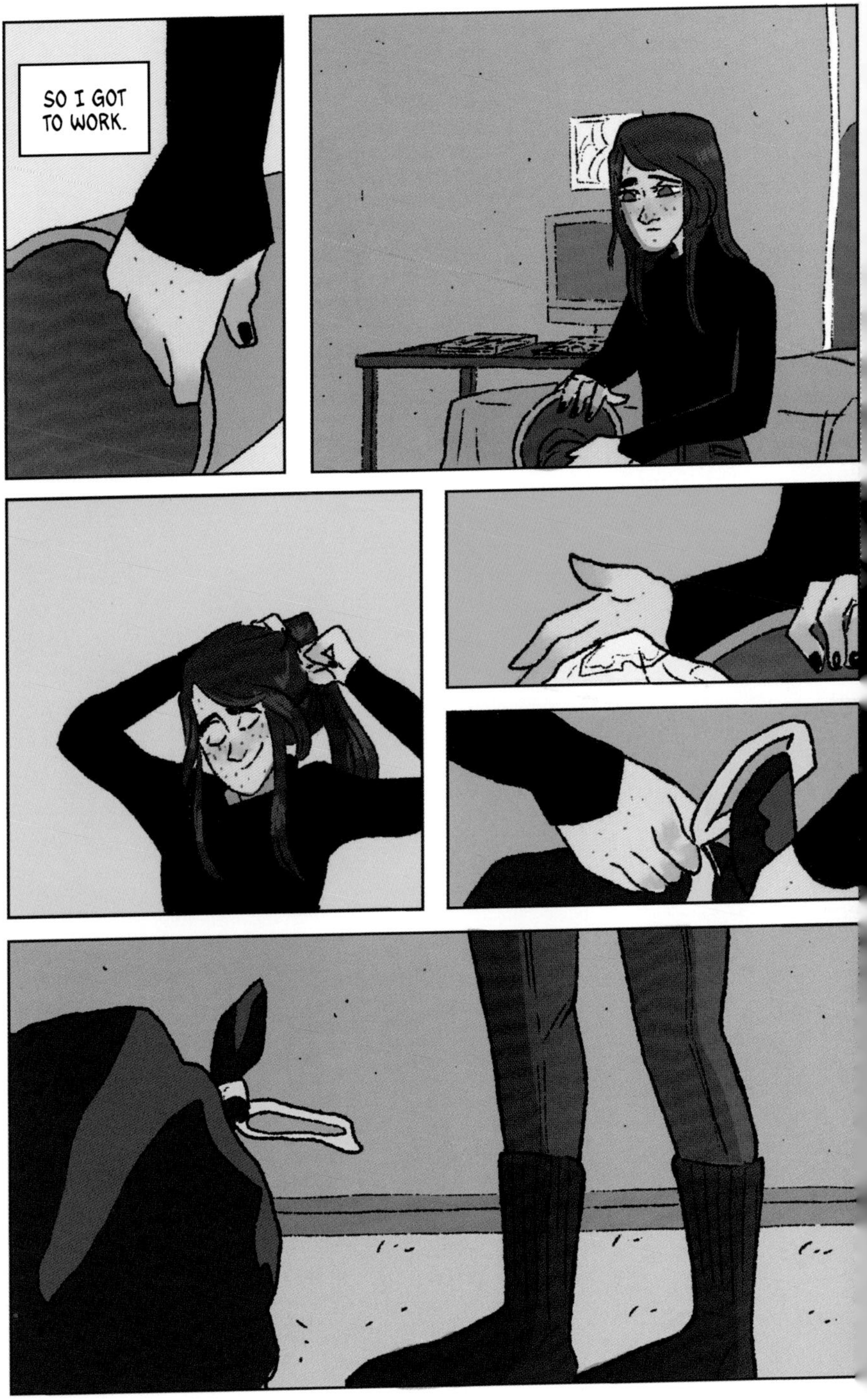
SO I GOT TO WORK.

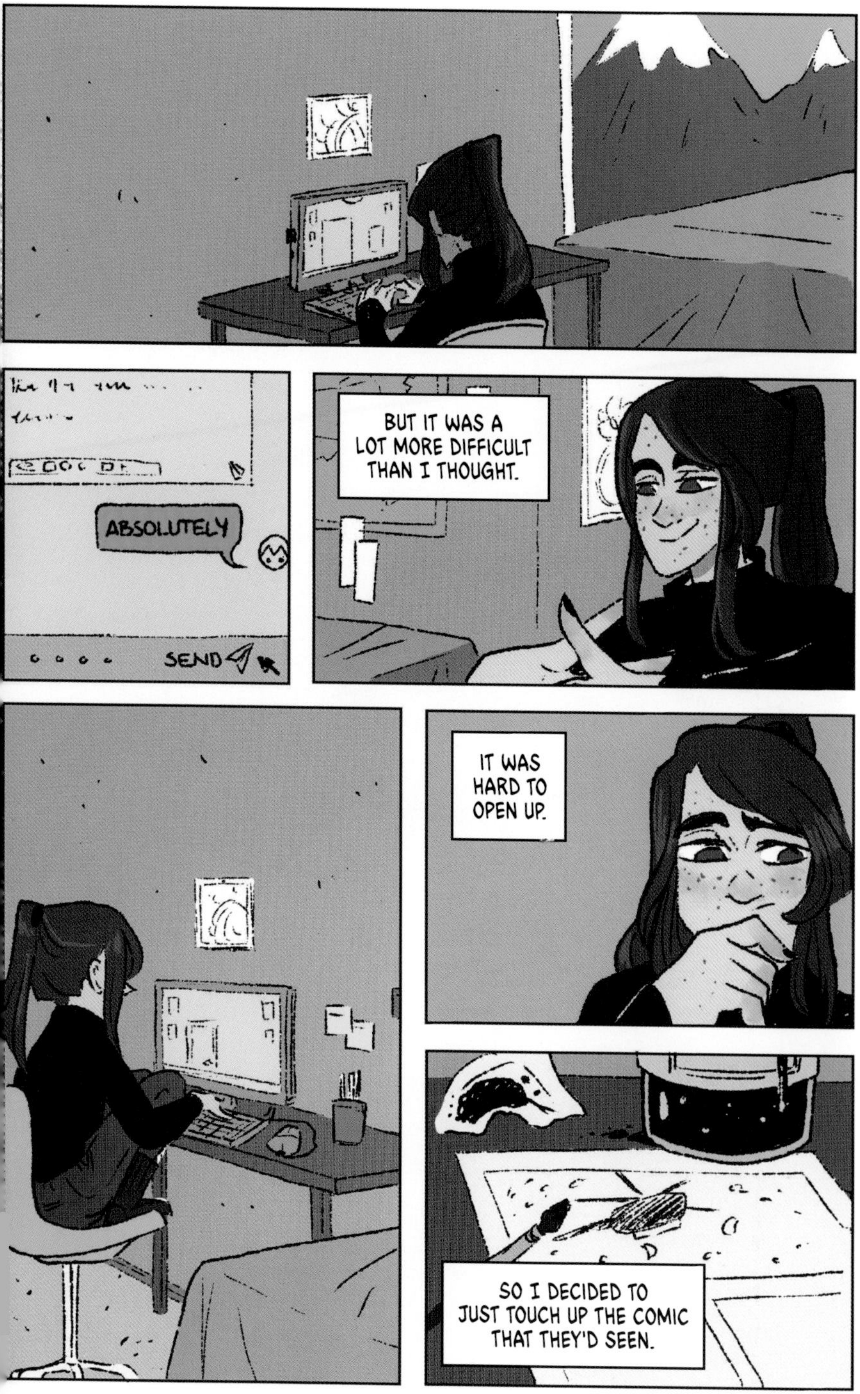
ABSOLUTELY
SEND
BUT IT WAS A LOT MORE DIFFICULT THAN I THOUGHT.
IT WAS HARD TO OPEN UP.
SO I DECIDED TO JUST TOUCH UP THE COMIC THAT THEY'D SEEN.

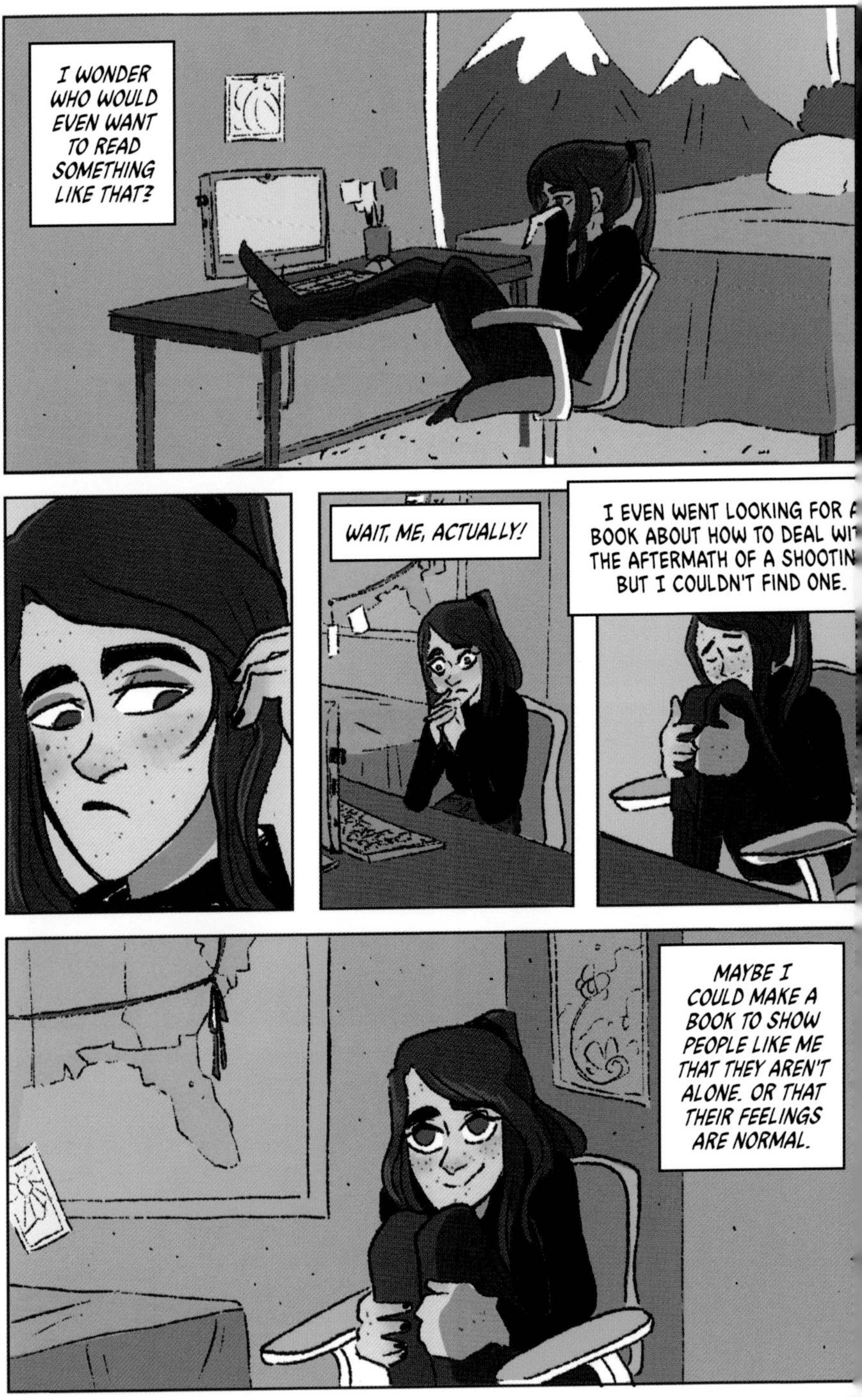
I WONDER WHO WOULD EVEN WANT TO READ SOMETHING LIKE THAT?
WAIT, ME, ACTUALLY!
I EVEN WENT LOOKING FOR A BOOK ABOUT HOW TO DEAL WIT THE AFTERMATH OF A SHOOTIN BUT I COULDN'T FIND ONE.
MAYBE I COULD MAKE A BOOK TO SHOW PEOPLE LIKE ME THAT THEY AREN'T ALONE. OR THAT THEIR FEELINGS ARE NORMAL.

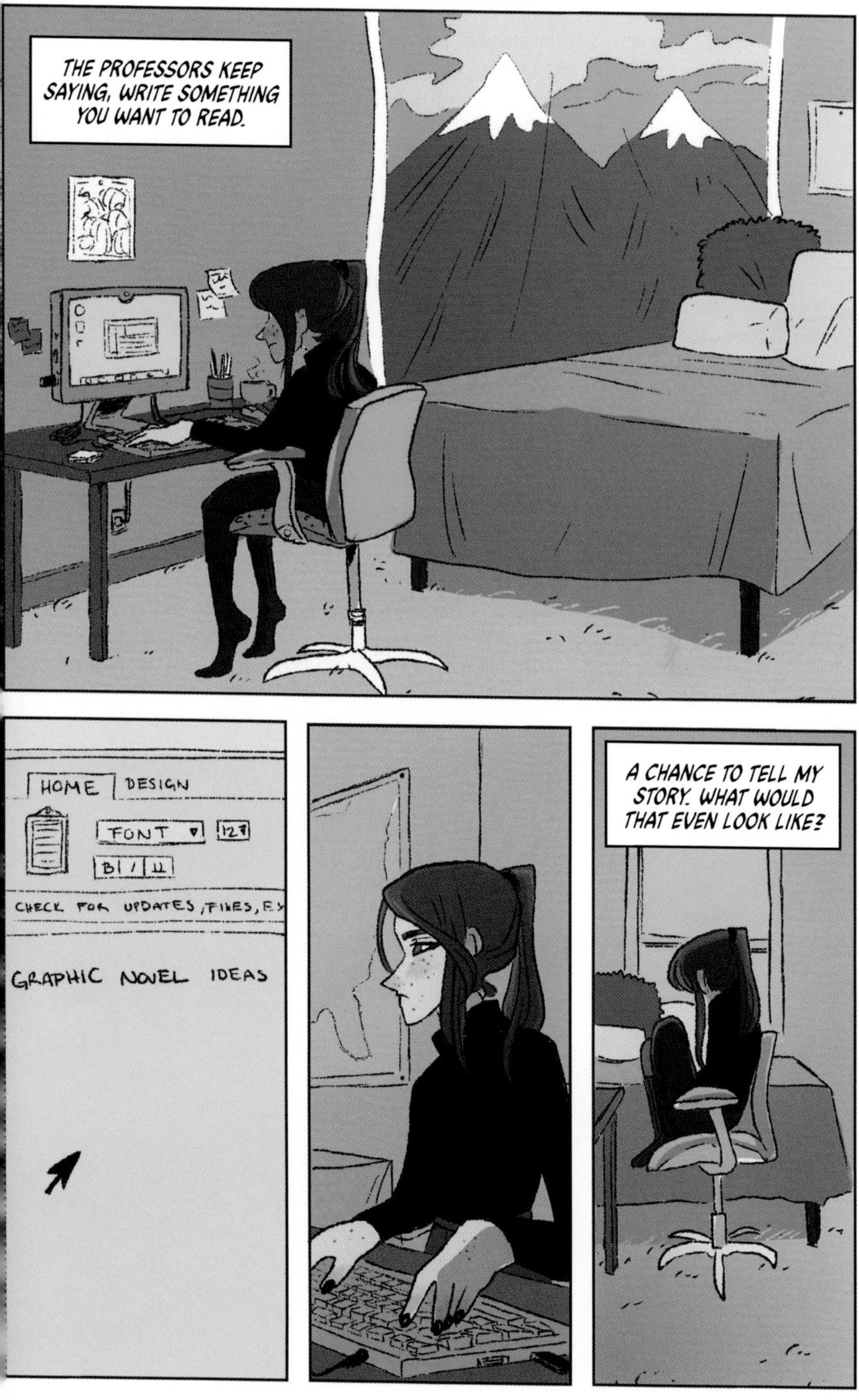
THE PROFESSORS KEEP SAYING, WRITE SOMETHING YOU WANT TO READ.
HOME
DESIGN
FONT
12
B / U
CHECK FOR UPDATES, FILES, E
GRAPHIC NOVEL IDEAS
A CHANCE TO TELL MY STORY. WHAT WOULD THAT EVEN LOOK LIKE?

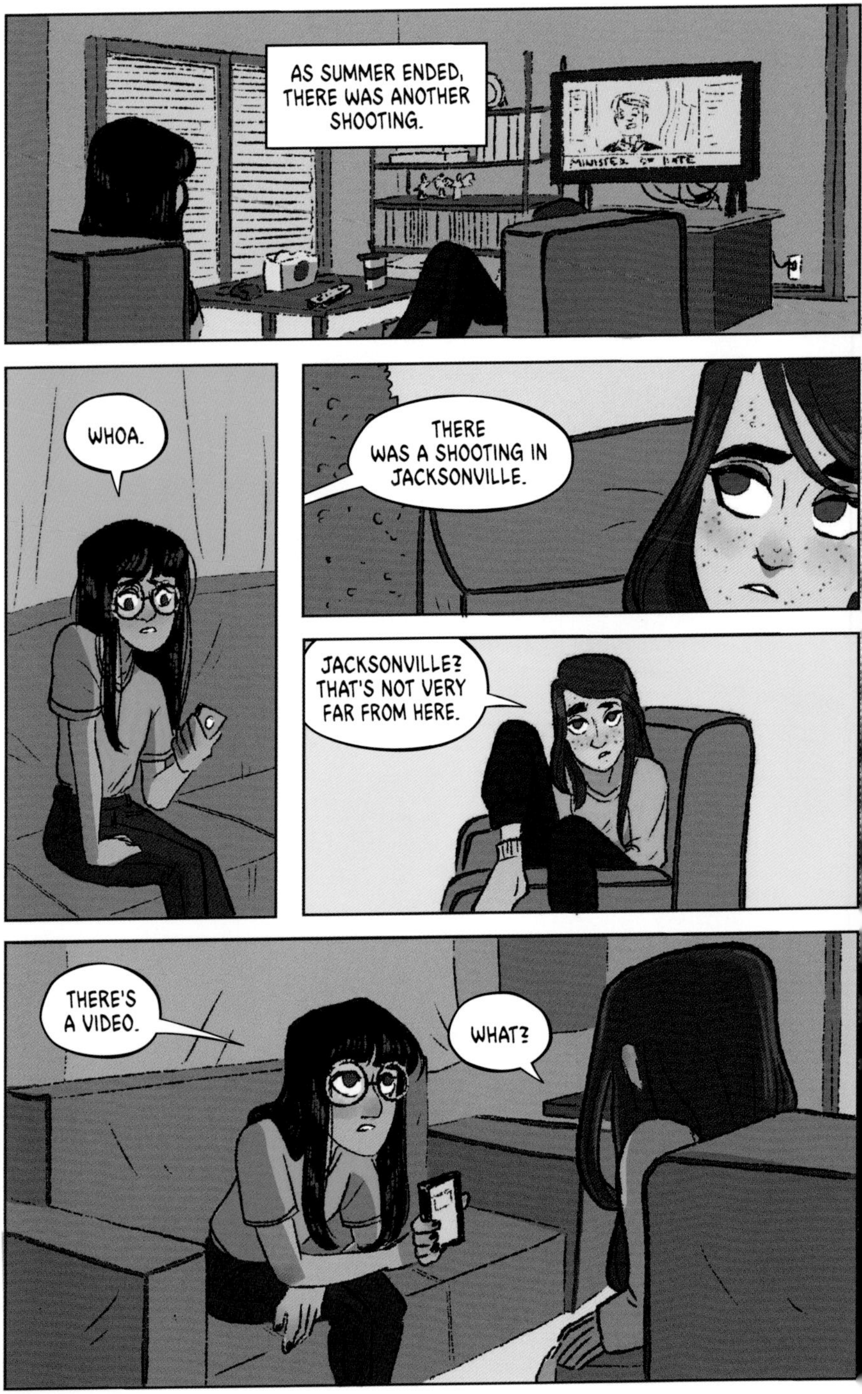
AS SUMMER ENDED, THERE WAS ANOTHER SHOOTING.
WHOA.
THERE WAS A SHOOTING IN JACKSONVILLE.
JACKSONVILLE? THAT'S NOT VERY FAR FROM HERE.
THERE'S A VIDEO.
WHAT?

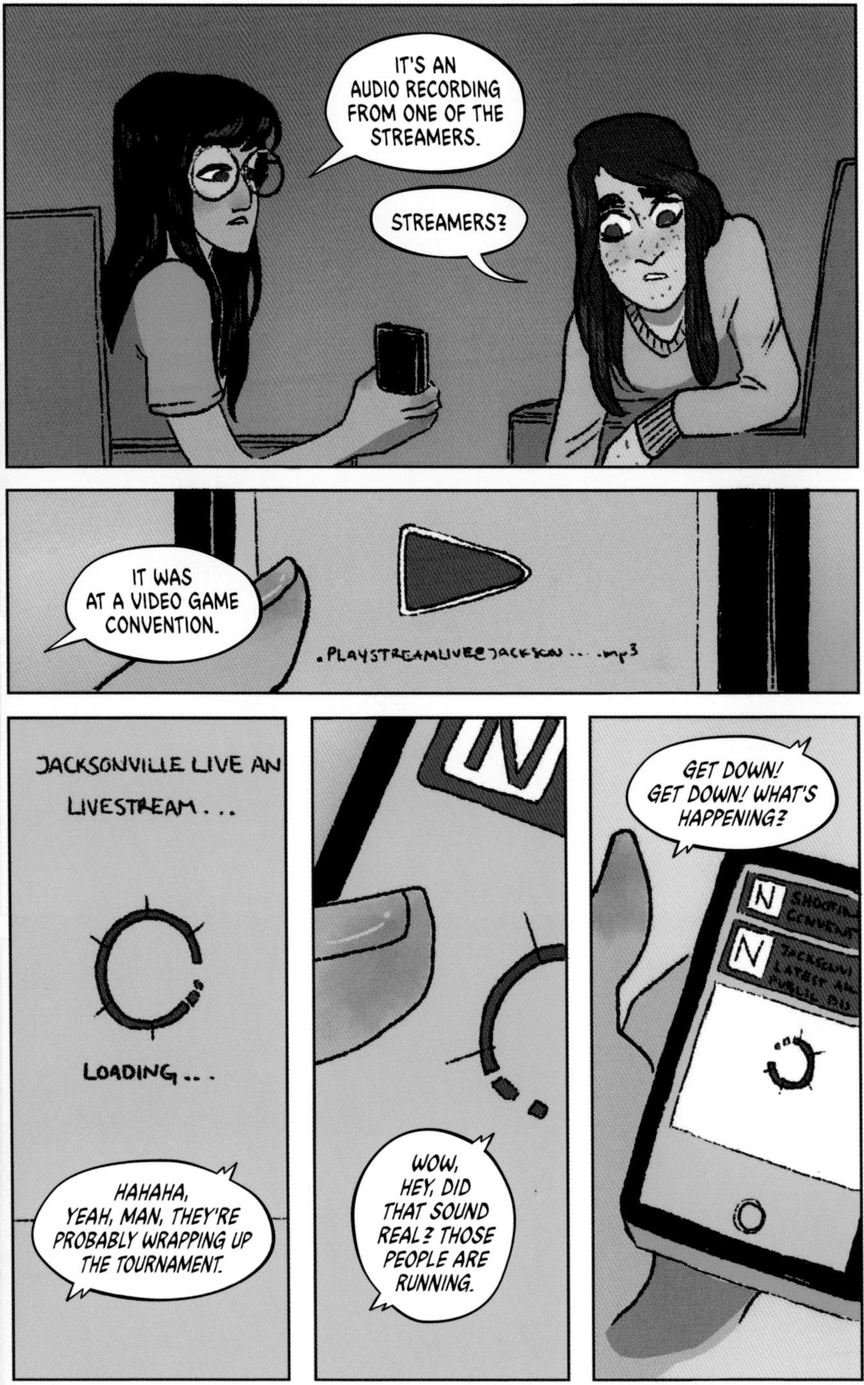
IT'S AN AUDIO RECORDING FROM ONE OF THE STREAMERS.
STREAMERS?
IT WAS AT A VIDEO GAME CONVENTION.
.PLAYSTREAMLIVE@JACKSON mp3
JACKSONVILLE LIVE AN LIVESTREAM . . .
LOADING . . .
HAHAHA, YEAH, MAN, THEY'RE PROBABLY WRAPPING UP THE TOURNAMENT.
WOW, HEY, DID THAT SOUND REAL? THOSE PEOPLE ARE RUNNING.
GET DOWN! GET DOWN! WHAT'S HAPPENING?

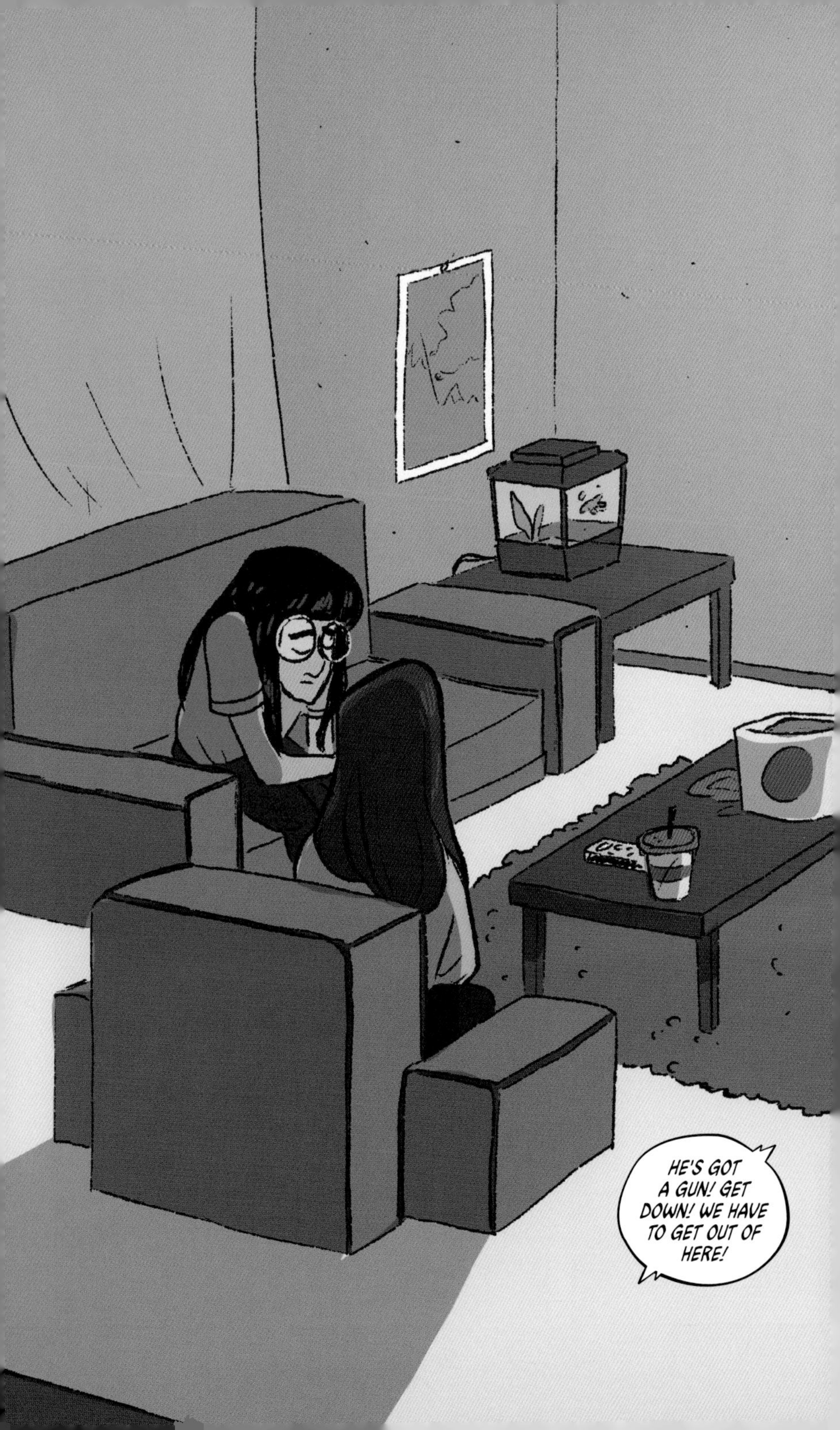
HE'S GOT A GUN! GET DOWN! WE HAVE TO GET OUT OF HERE!

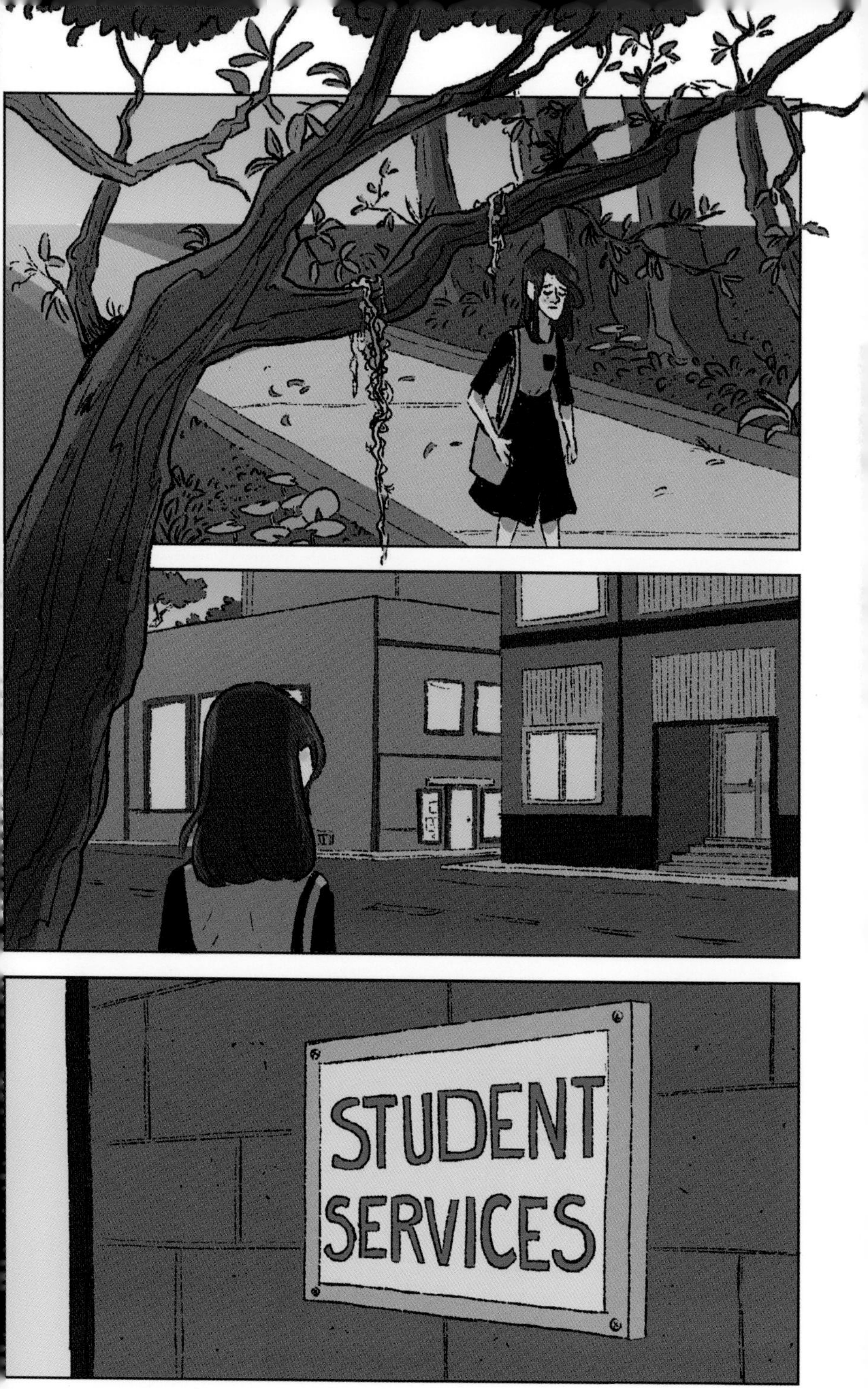
STUDENT
SERVICES

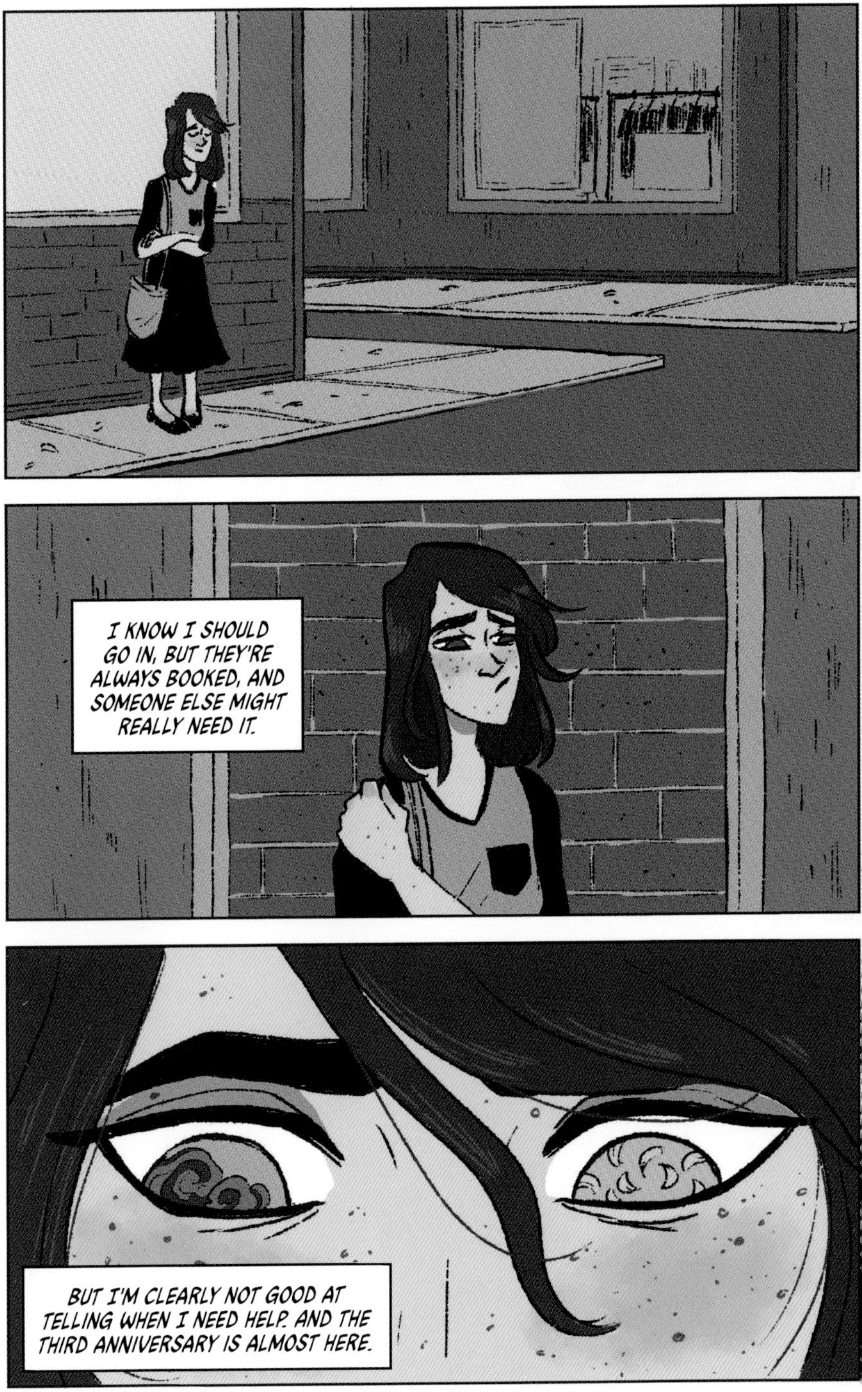
I KNOW I SHOULD GO IN, BUT THEY'RE ALWAYS BOOKED, AND SOMEONE ELSE MIGHT REALLY NEED IT.
BUT I'M CLEARLY NOT GOOD AT TELLING WHEN I NEED HELP. AND THE THIRD ANNIVERSARY IS ALMOST HERE.

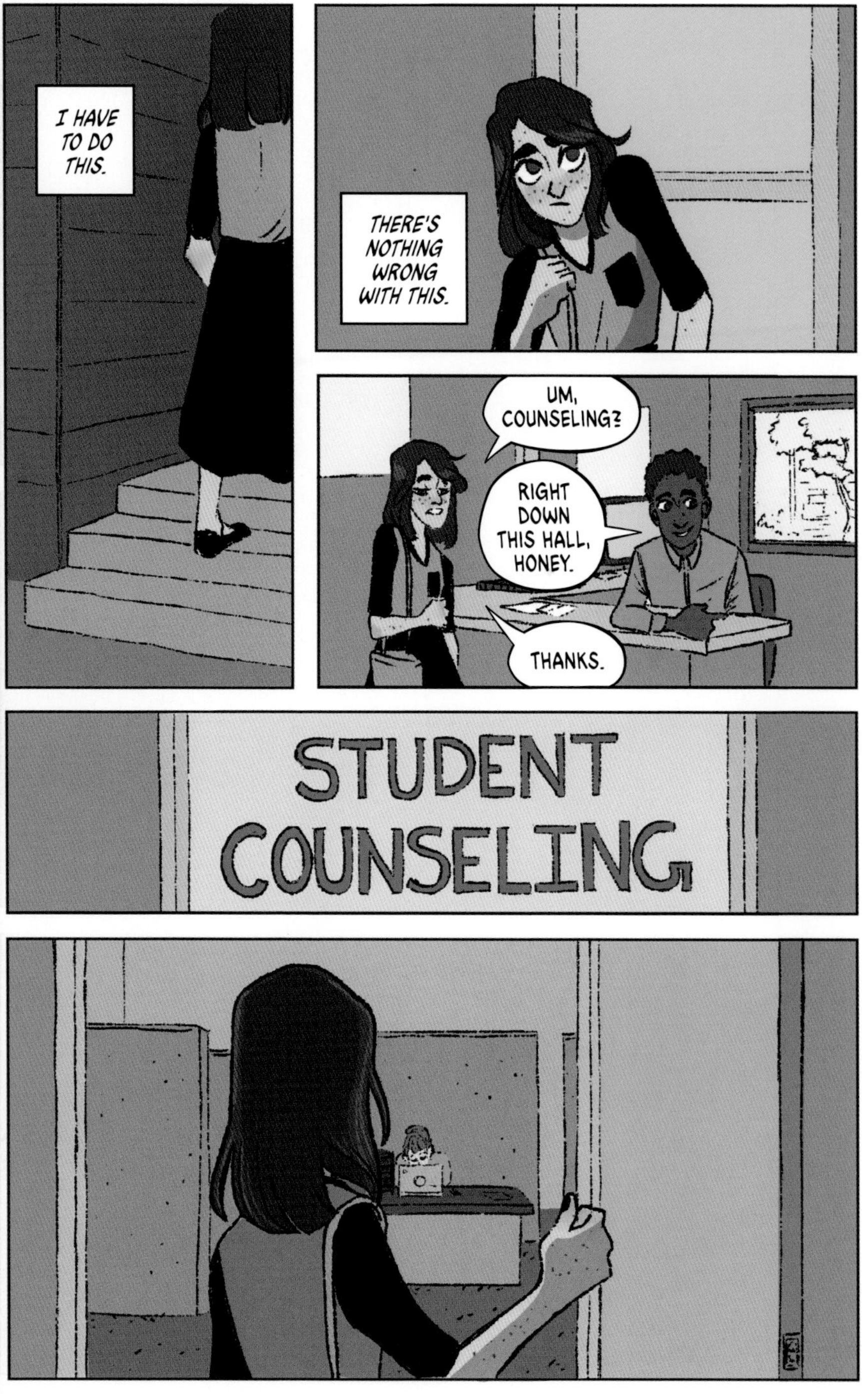
I HAVE TO DO THIS.
THERE'S NOTHING WRONG WITH THIS.
UM, COUNSELING?
RIGHT DOWN THIS HALL, HONEY.
THANKS.
STUDENT COUNSELING

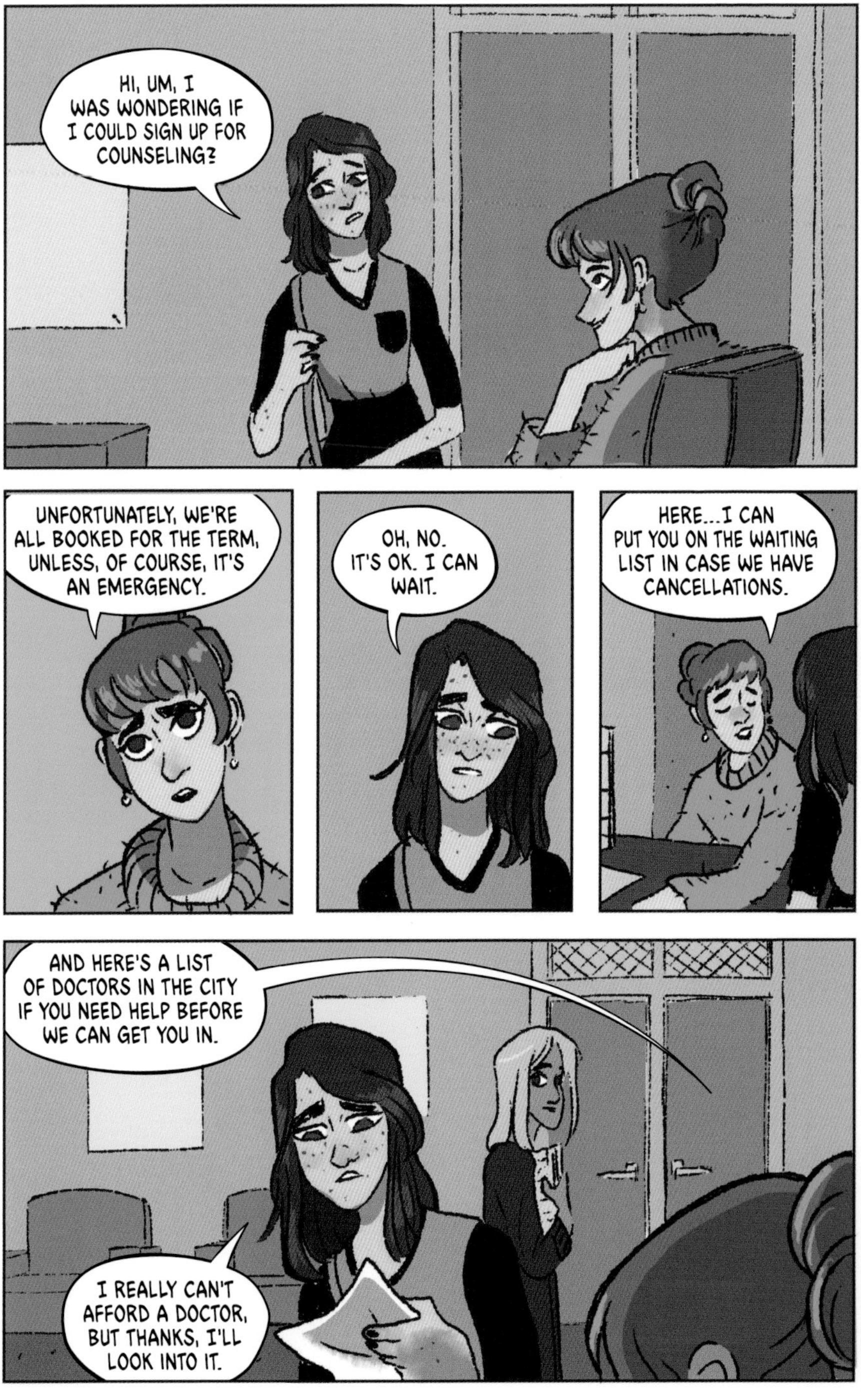
HI, UM, I WAS WONDERING IF I COULD SIGN UP FOR COUNSELING?
UNFORTUNATELY, WE'RE ALL BOOKED FOR THE TERM, UNLESS, OF COURSE, IT'S AN EMERGENCY.
OH, NO. IT'S OK. I CAN WAIT.
HERE...I CAN PUT YOU ON THE WAITING LIST IN CASE WE HAVE CANCELLATIONS.
AND HERE'S A LIST OF DOCTORS IN THE CITY IF YOU NEED HELP BEFORE WE CAN GET YOU IN.
I REALLY CAN'T AFFORD A DOCTOR, BUT THANKS, I'LL LOOK INTO IT.

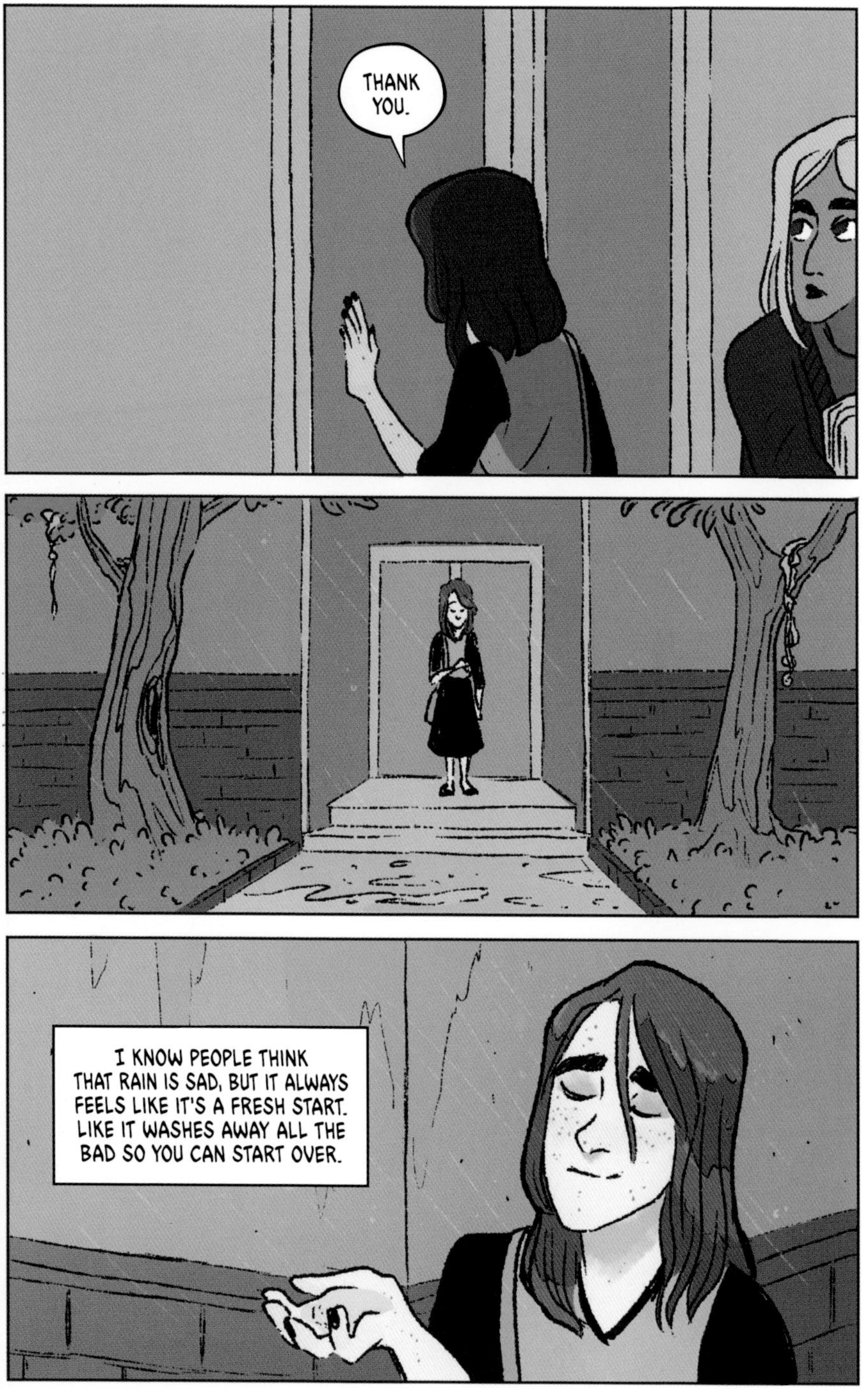
THANK YOU.
I KNOW PEOPLE THINK THAT RAIN IS SAD, BUT IT ALWAYS FEELS LIKE IT'S A FRESH START. LIKE IT WASHES AWAY ALL THE BAD SO YOU CAN START OVER.

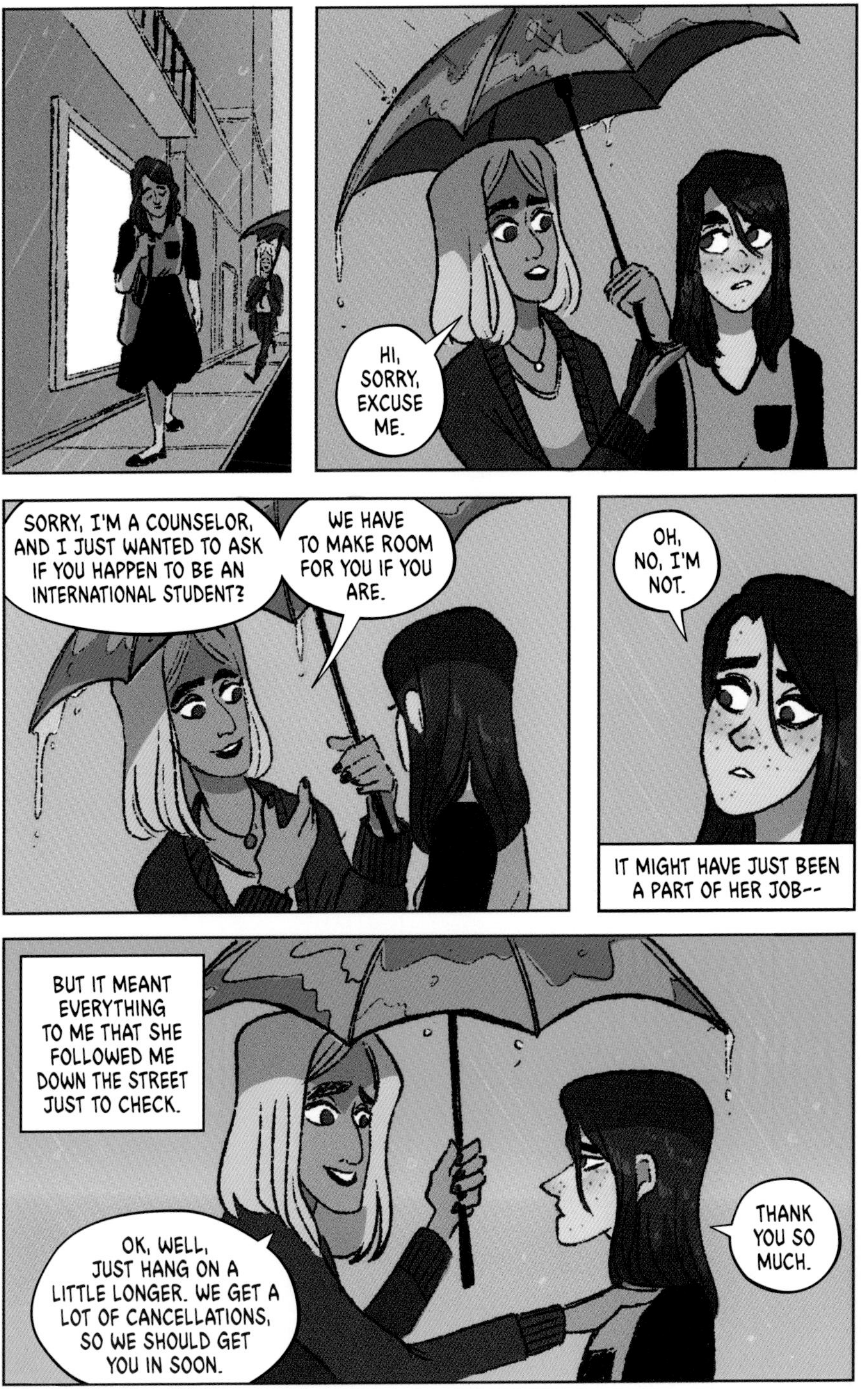
HI, SORRY, EXCUSE ME.
SORRY, I'M A COUNSELOR, AND I JUST WANTED TO ASK IF YOU HAPPEN TO BE AN INTERNATIONAL STUDENT?
WE HAVE TO MAKE ROOM FOR YOU IF YOU ARE.
OH, NO, I'M NOT.
IT MIGHT HAVE JUST BEEN A PART OF HER JOB--
BUT IT MEANT EVERYTHING TO ME THAT SHE FOLLOWED ME DOWN THE STREET JUST TO CHECK.
OK, WELL, JUST HANG ON A LITTLE LONGER. WE GET A LOT OF CANCELLATIONS, SO WE SHOULD GET YOU IN SOON.
THANK YOU SO MUCH.

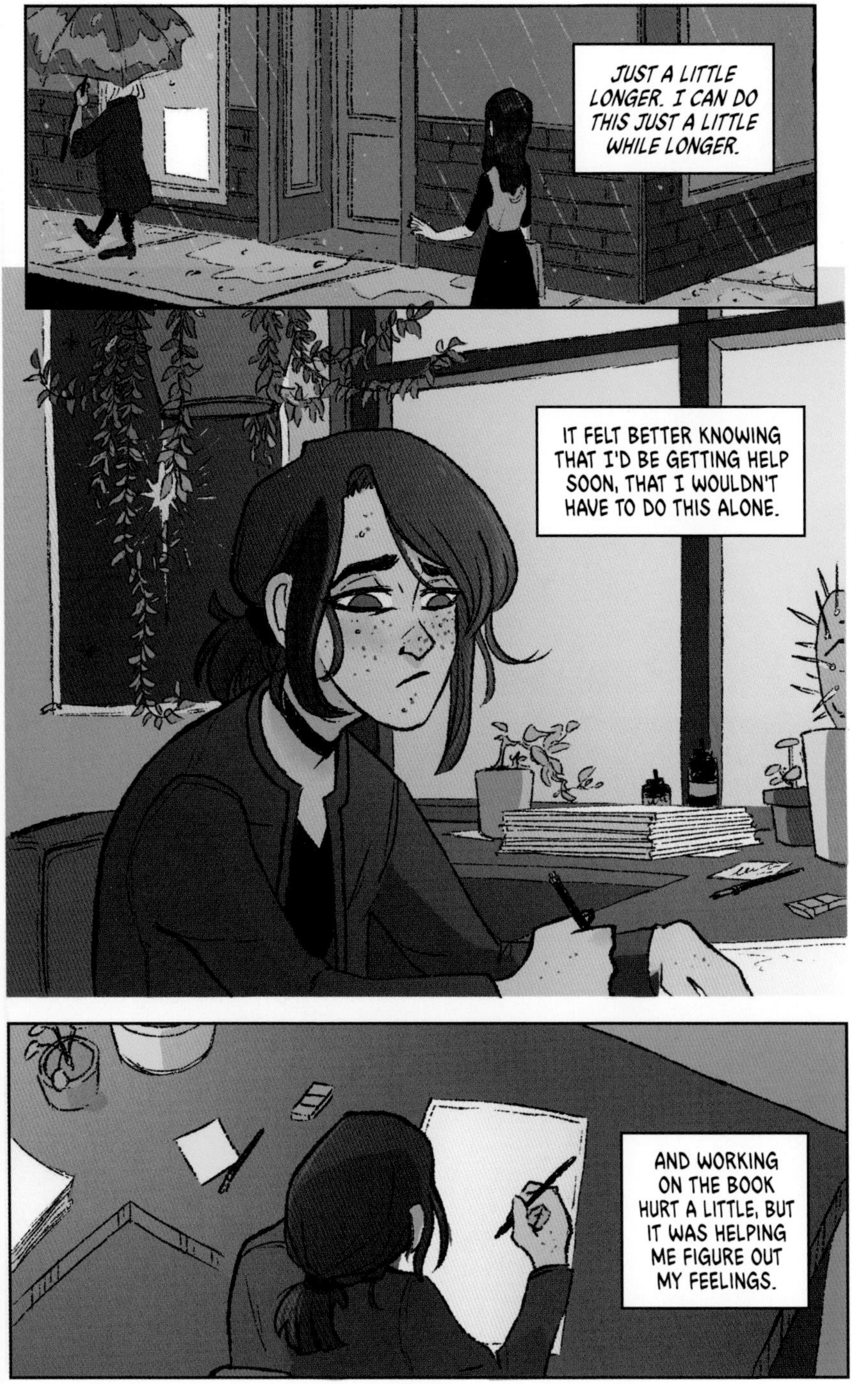
JUST A LITTLE LONGER. I CAN DO THIS JUST A LITTLE WHILE LONGER.
IT FELT BETTER KNOWING THAT I'D BE GETTING HELP SOON, THAT I WOULDN'T HAVE TO DO THIS ALONE.
AND WORKING ON THE BOOK HURT A LITTLE, BUT IT WAS HELPING ME FIGURE OUT MY FEELINGS.

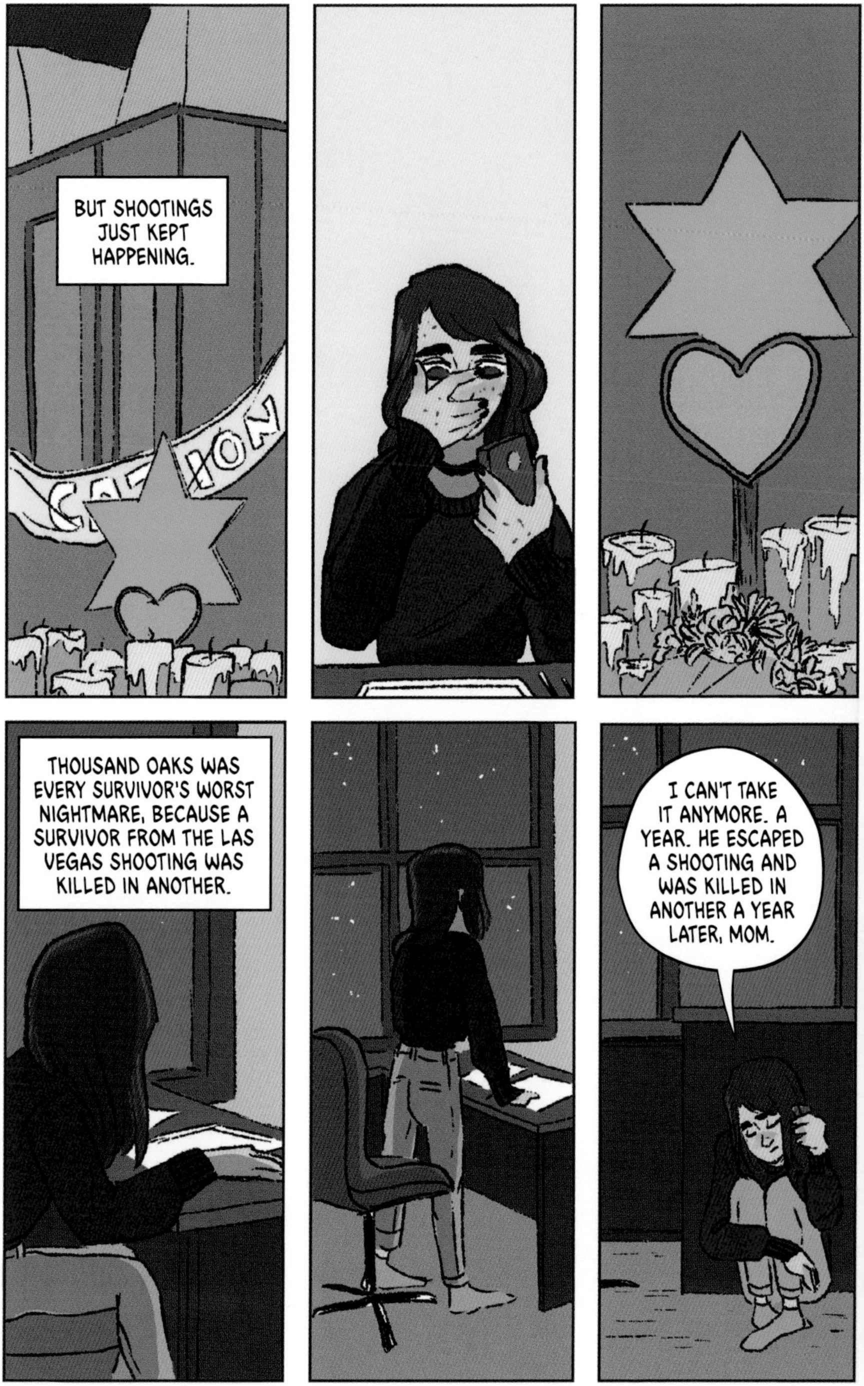
BUT SHOOTINGS JUST KEPT HAPPENING.
THOUSAND OAKS WAS EVERY SURVIVOR'S WORST NIGHTMARE, BECAUSE A SURVIVOR FROM THE LAS VEGAS SHOOTING WAS KILLED IN ANOTHER.
I CAN'T TAKE IT ANYMORE. A YEAR. HE ESCAPED A SHOOTING AND WAS KILLED IN ANOTHER A YEAR LATER, MOM.

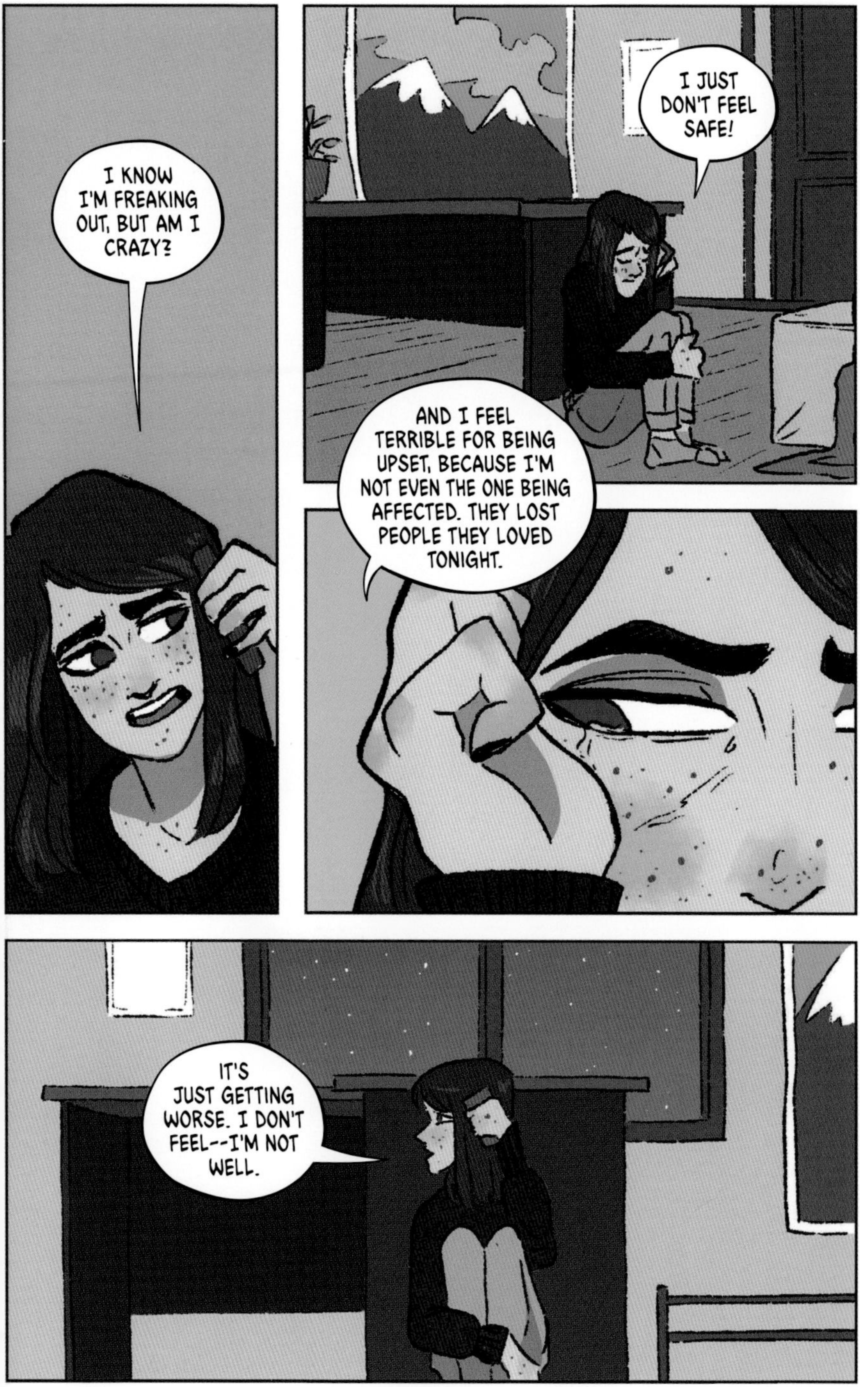
I KNOW I'M FREAKING OUT, BUT AM I CRAZY?
I JUST DON'T FEEL SAFE!
AND I FEEL TERRIBLE FOR BEING UPSET, BECAUSE I'M NOT EVEN THE ONE BEING AFFECTED. THEY LOST PEOPLE THEY LOVED TONIGHT.
IT'S JUST GETTING WORSE. I DON'T FEEL--I'M NOT WELL.

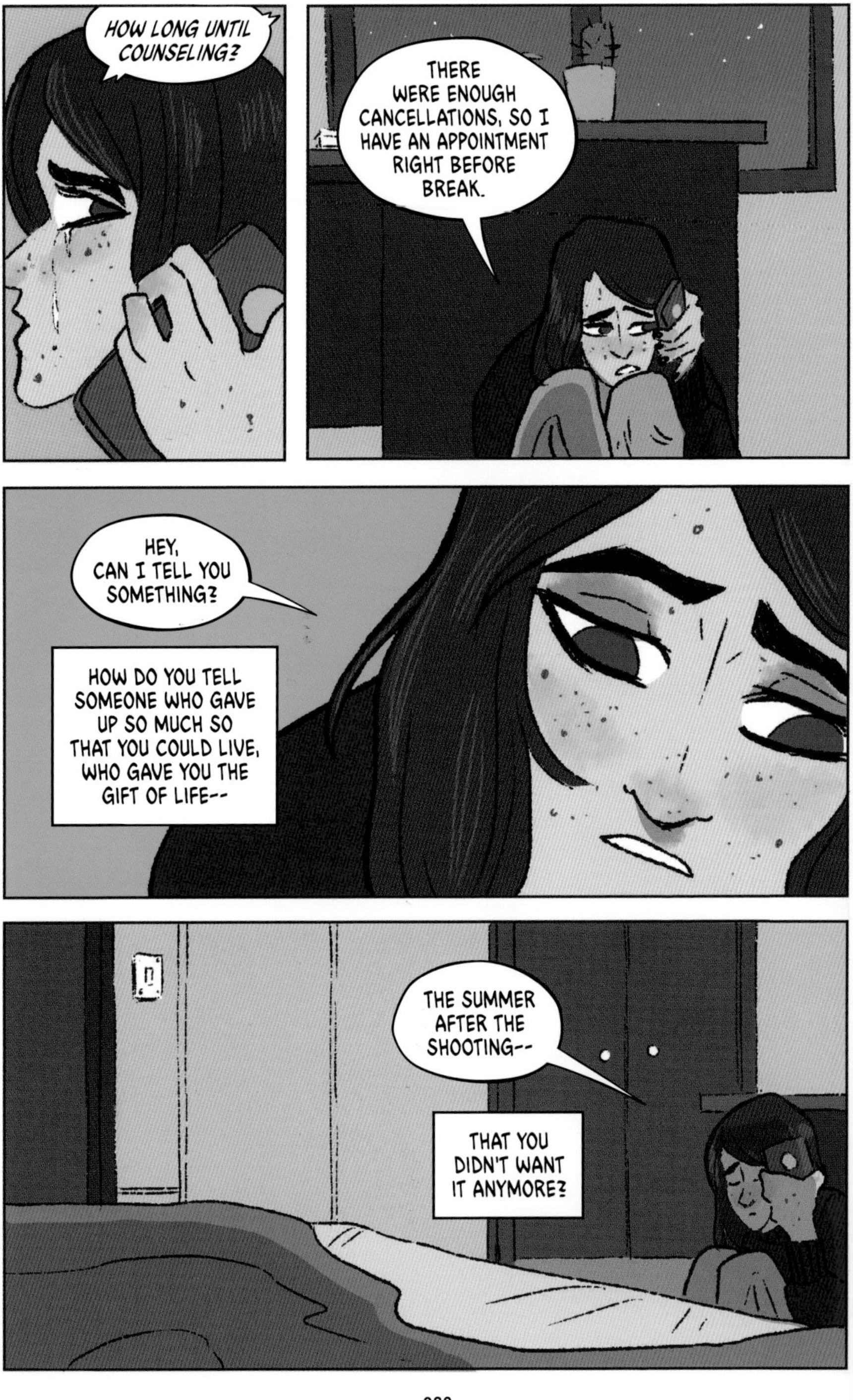
HOW LONG UNTIL COUNSELING?
THERE WERE ENOUGH CANCELLATIONS, SO I HAVE AN APPOINTMENT RIGHT BEFORE BREAK.
HEY, CAN I TELL YOU SOMETHING?
HOW DO YOU TELL SOMEONE WHO GAVE UP SO MUCH SO THAT YOU COULD LIVE, WHO GAVE YOU THE GIFT OF LIFE--
THE SUMMER AFTER THE SHOOTING--
THAT YOU DIDN'T WANT IT ANYMORE?

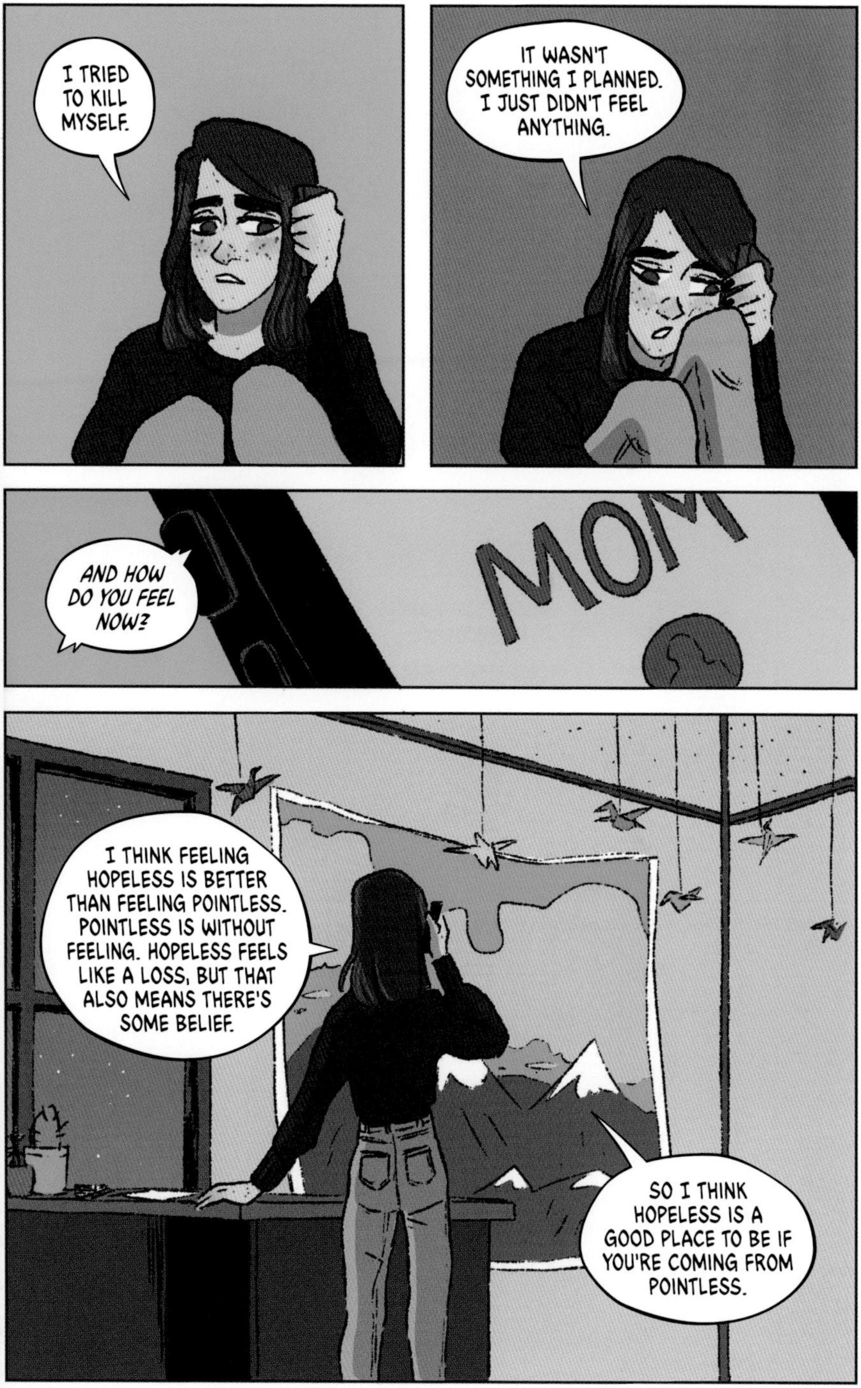
I TRIED TO KILL MYSELF.
IT WASN'T SOMETHING I PLANNED. I JUST DIDN'T FEEL ANYTHING.
MOM
AND HOW DO YOU FEEL NOW?
I THINK FEELING HOPELESS IS BETTER THAN FEELING POINTLESS. POINTLESS IS WITHOUT FEELING. HOPELESS FEELS LIKE A LOSS, BUT THAT ALSO MEANS THERE'S SOME BELIEF.
SO I THINK HOPELESS IS A GOOD PLACE TO BE IF YOU'RE COMING FROM POINTLESS.

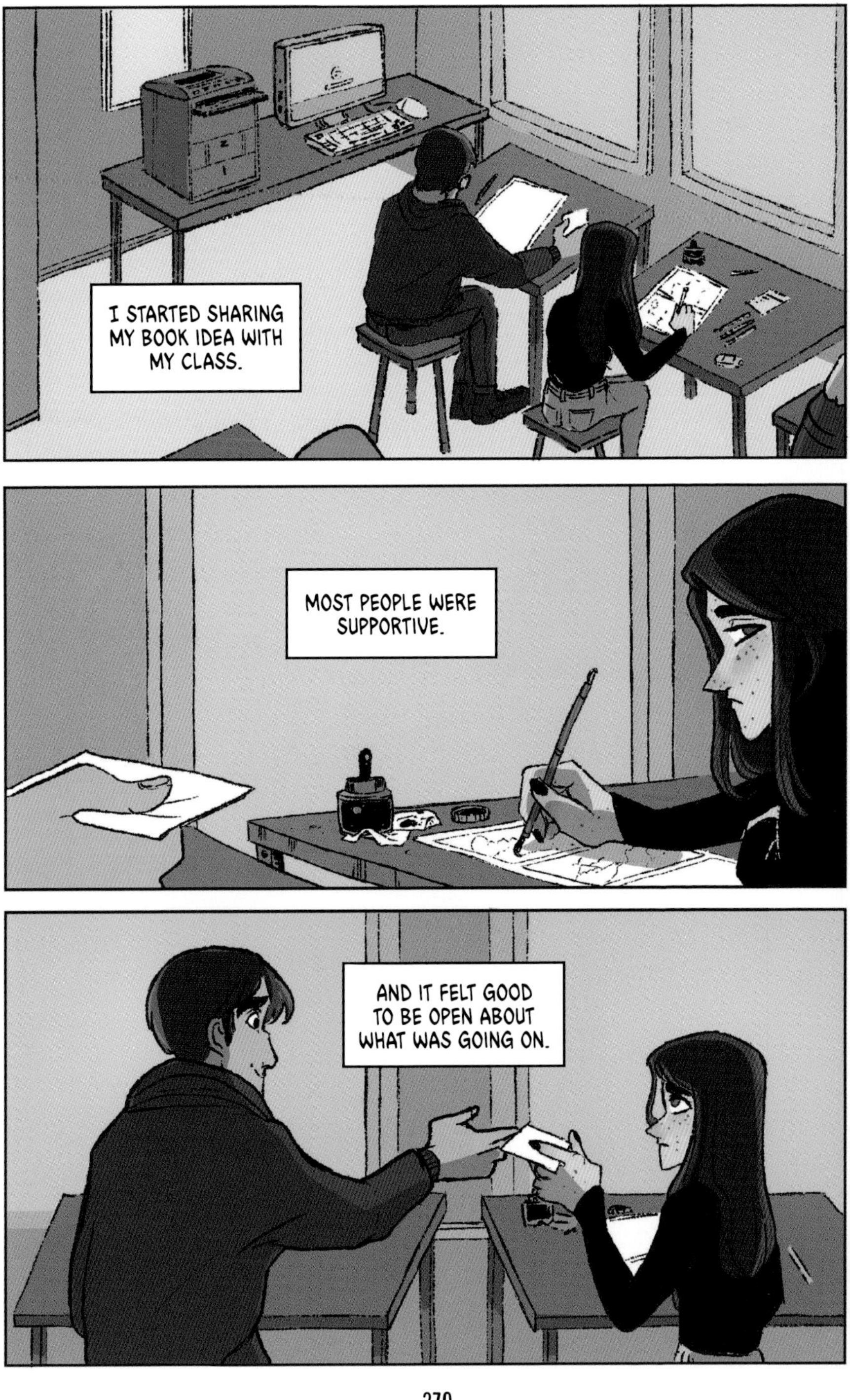
I STARTED SHARING MY BOOK IDEA WITH MY CLASS.
MOST PEOPLE WERE SUPPORTIVE.
AND IT FELT GOOD TO BE OPEN ABOUT WHAT WAS GOING ON.

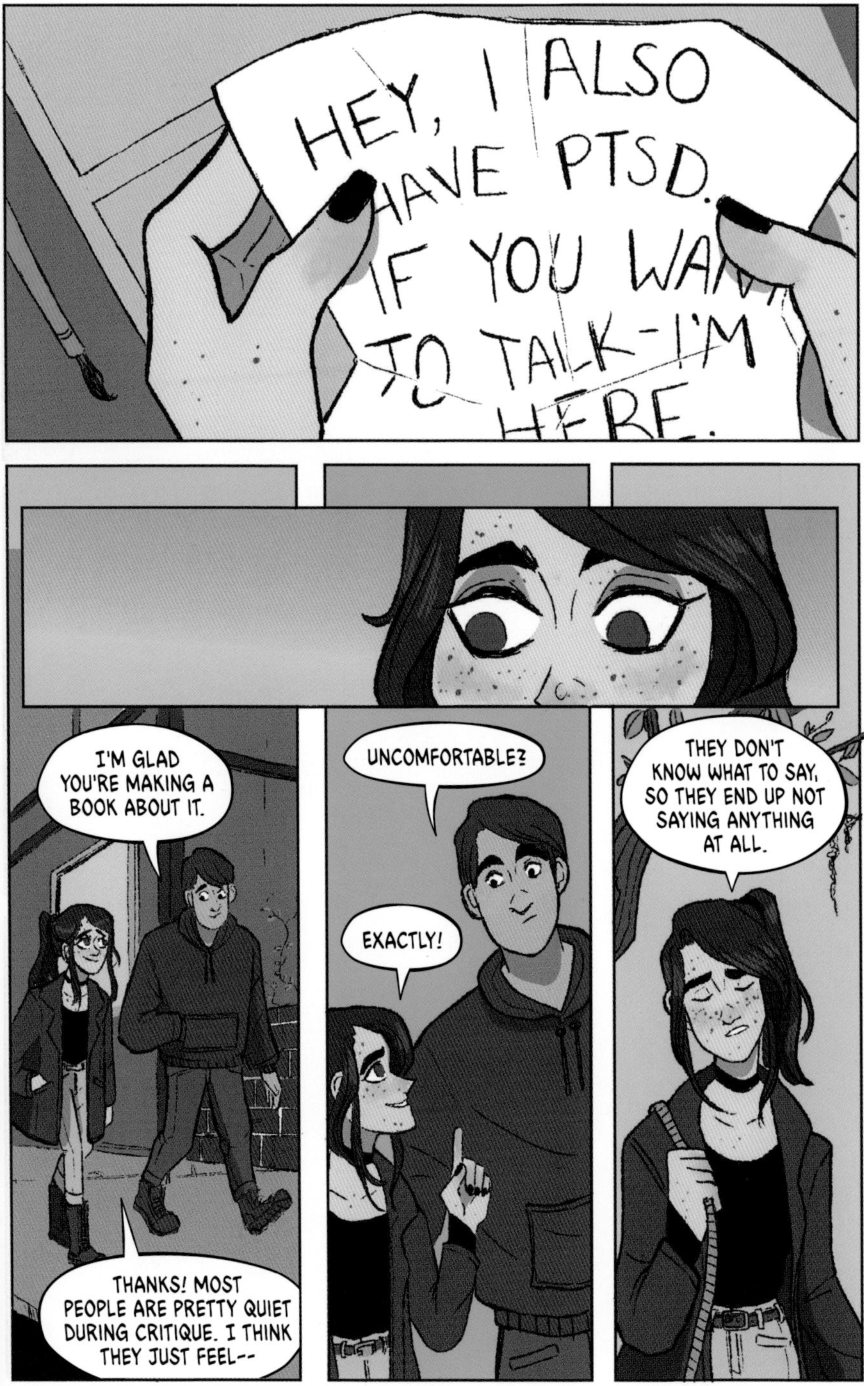
HEY, I ALSO HAVE PTSD. IF YOU WAN TO TALK-I'M HERE.
I'M GLAD YOU'RE MAKING A BOOK ABOUT IT.
THANKS! MOST PEOPLE ARE PRETTY QUIET DURING CRITIQUE. I THINK THEY JUST FEEL--
UNCOMFORTABLE?
EXACTLY!
THEY DON'T KNOW WHAT TO SAY, SO THEY END UP NOT SAYING ANYTHING AT ALL.

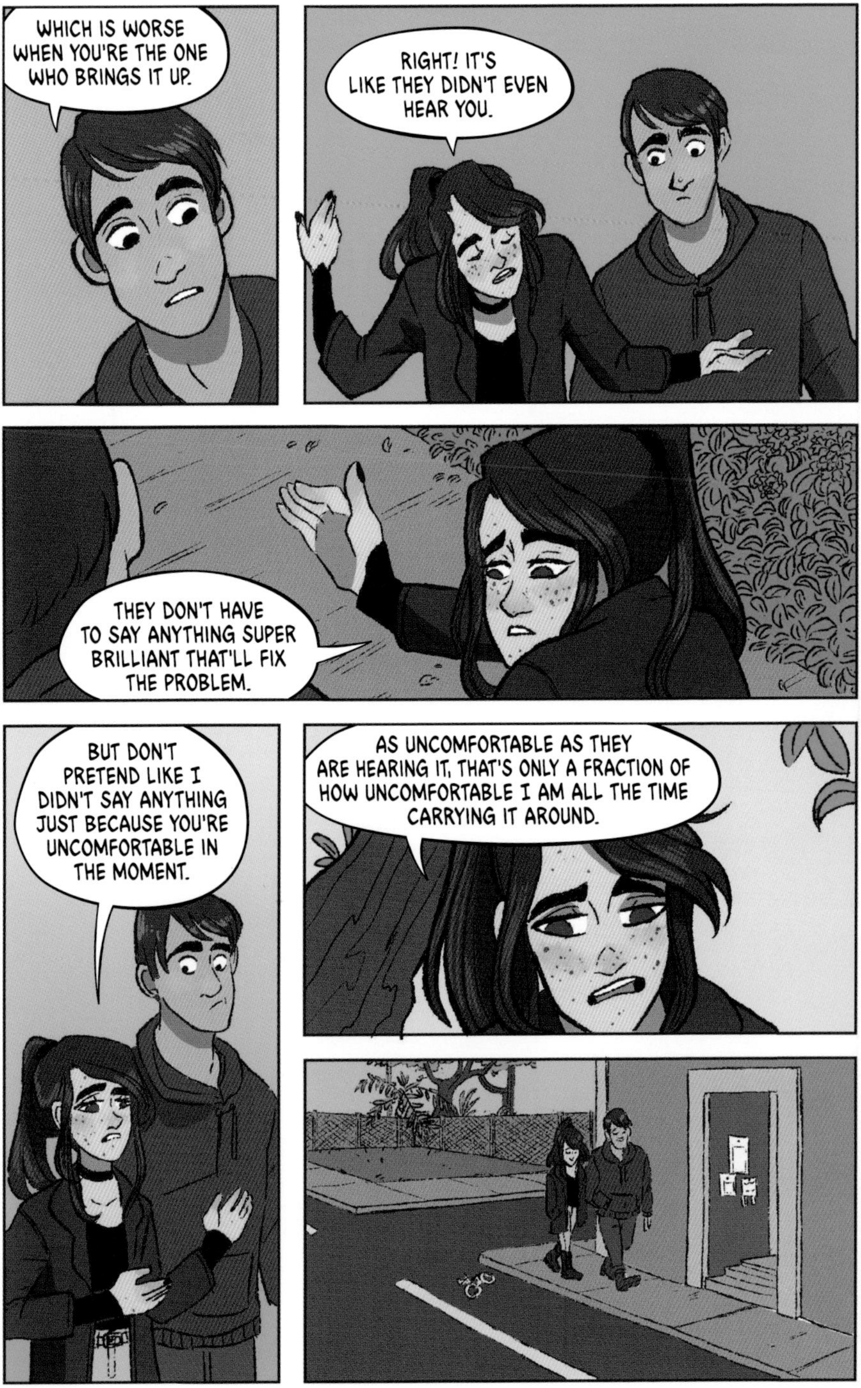
WHICH IS WORSE WHEN YOU'RE THE ONE WHO BRINGS IT UP.
RIGHT! IT'S LIKE THEY DIDN'T EVEN HEAR YOU.
THEY DON'T HAVE TO SAY ANYTHING SUPER BRILLIANT THAT'LL FIX THE PROBLEM.
BUT DON'T PRETEND LIKE I DIDN'T SAY ANYTHING JUST BECAUSE YOU'RE UNCOMFORTABLE IN THE MOMENT.
AS UNCOMFORTABLE AS THEY ARE HEARING IT, THAT'S ONLY A FRACTION OF HOW UNCOMFORTABLE I AM ALL THE TIME CARRYING IT AROUND.

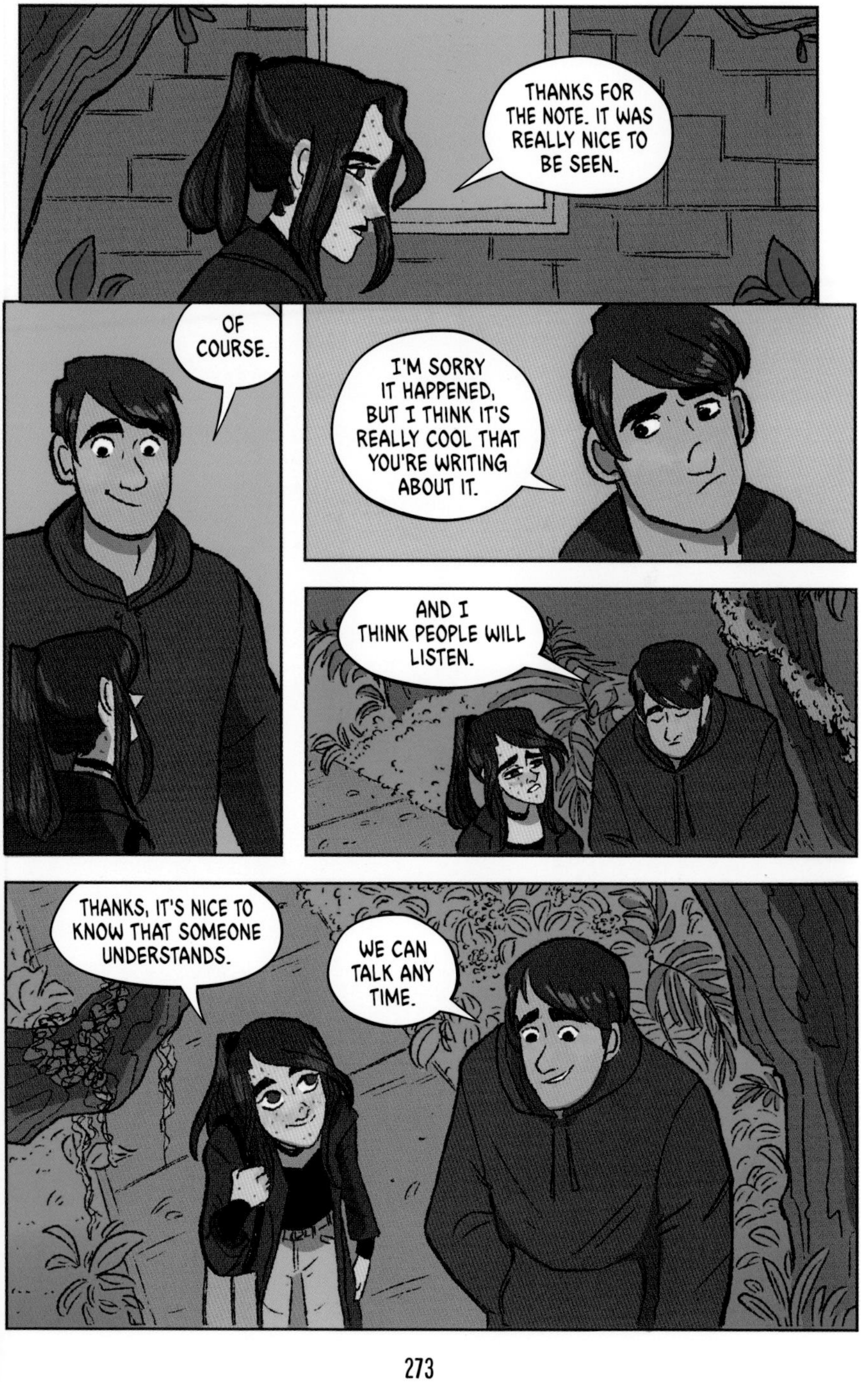
THANKS FOR THE NOTE. IT WAS REALLY NICE TO BE SEEN.
OF COURSE.
I'M SORRY IT HAPPENED, BUT I THINK IT'S REALLY COOL THAT YOU'RE WRITING ABOUT IT.
AND I THINK PEOPLE WILL LISTEN.
THANKS, IT'S NICE TO KNOW THAT SOMEONE UNDERSTANDS.
WE CAN TALK ANY TIME.

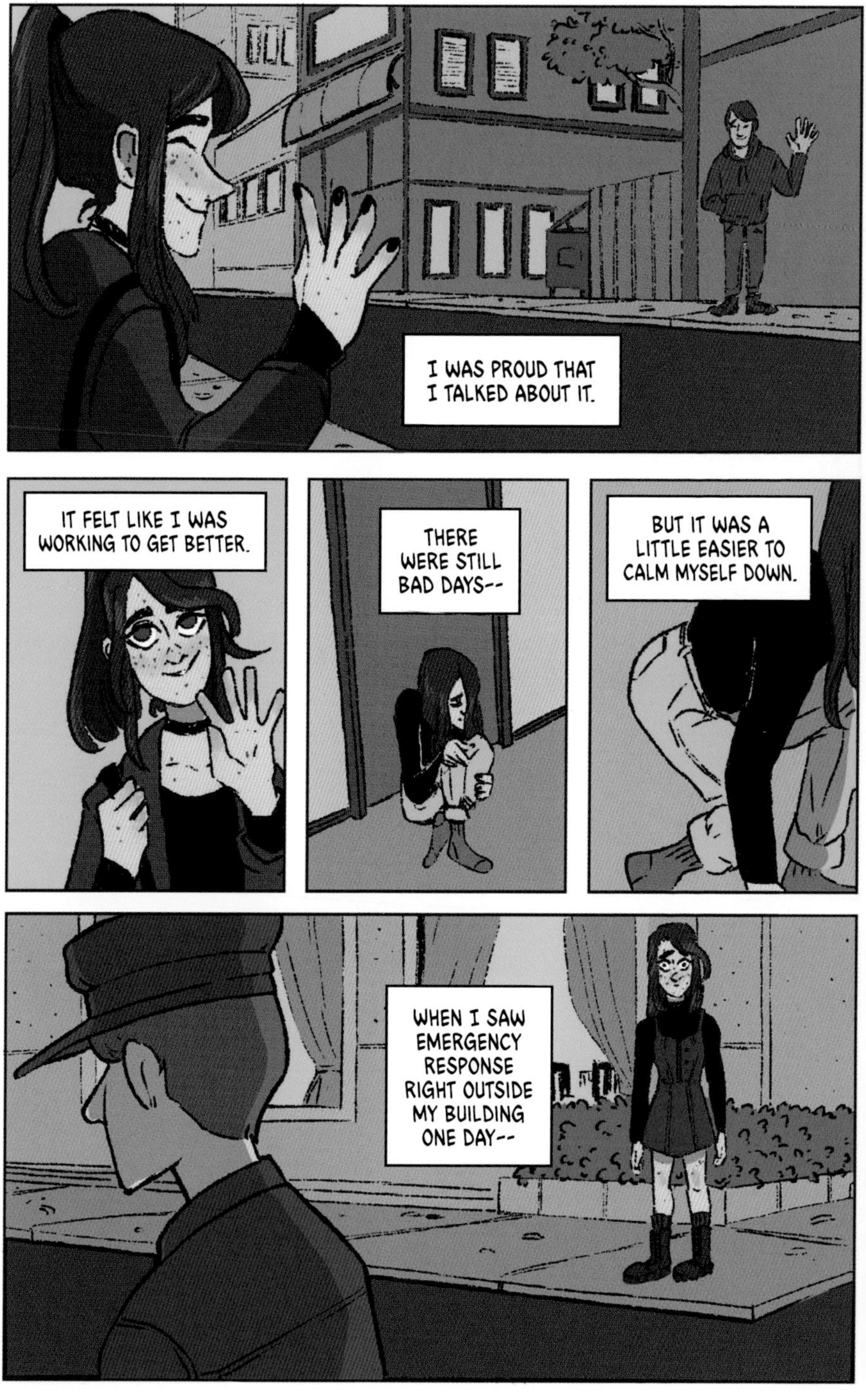
I WAS PROUD THAT I TALKED ABOUT IT.
IT FELT LIKE I WAS WORKING TO GET BETTER.
THERE WERE STILL BAD DAYS--
BUT IT WAS A LITTLE EASIER TO CALM MYSELF DOWN.
WHEN I SAW EMERGENCY RESPONSE RIGHT OUTSIDE MY BUILDING ONE DAY--

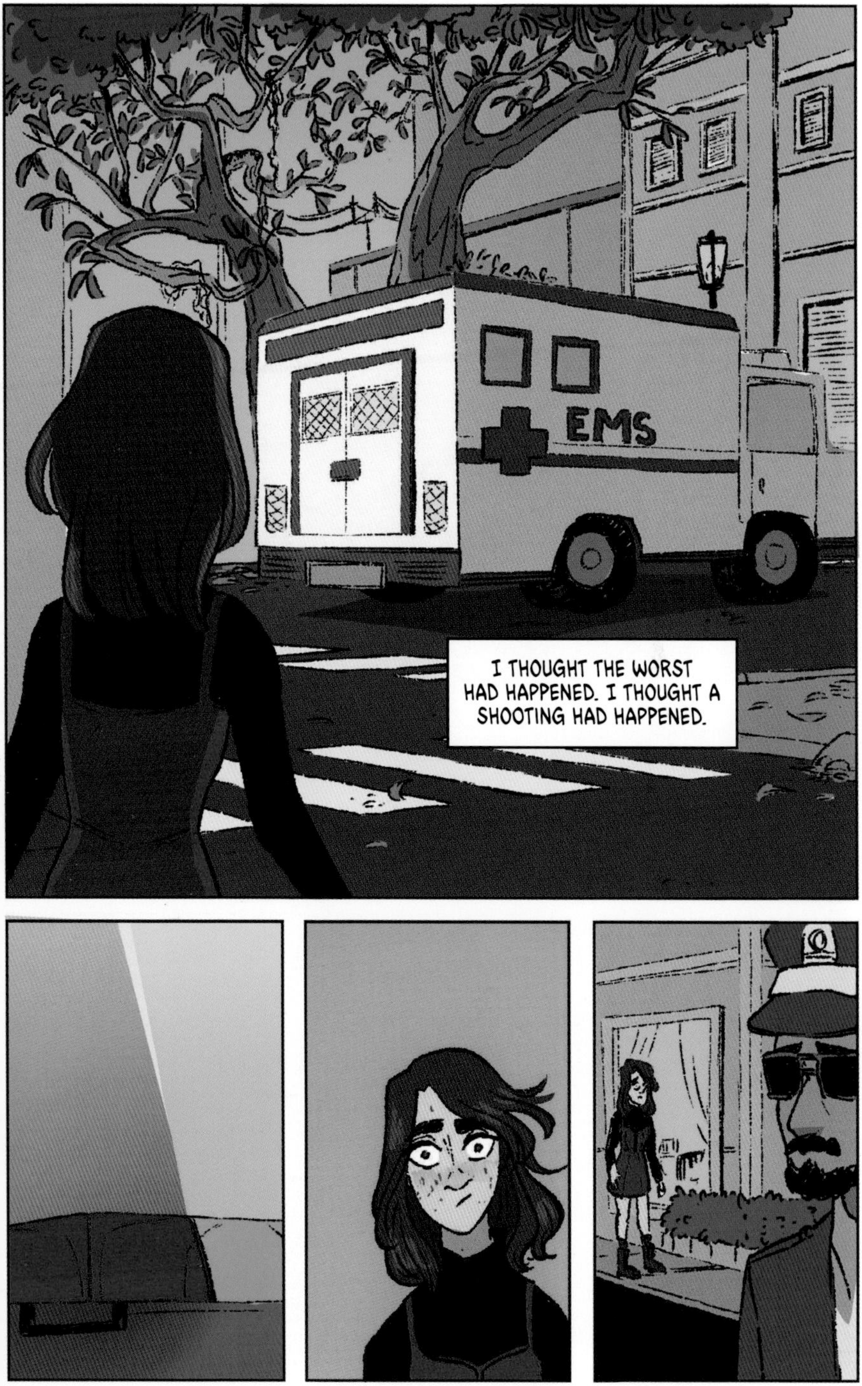

I THOUGHT THE WORST HAD HAPPENED. I THOUGHT A SHOOTING HAD HAPPENED.
EMS

MY HEAD WAS IMMEDIATELY FILLED WITH WHAT-IFS:

WHAT IF MY PROFESSORS WERE KILLED?

WHAT IF PEOPLE TRIED TO RUN BUT DIDN'T MAKE IT PAST THE HALL?

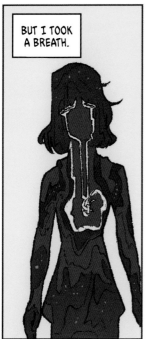

BUT I TOOK A BREATH.

AND IT DIDN'T STOP THE THOUGHTS COMPLETELY--

BUT I WAS ABLE TO STOP THE PANIC ATTACK.

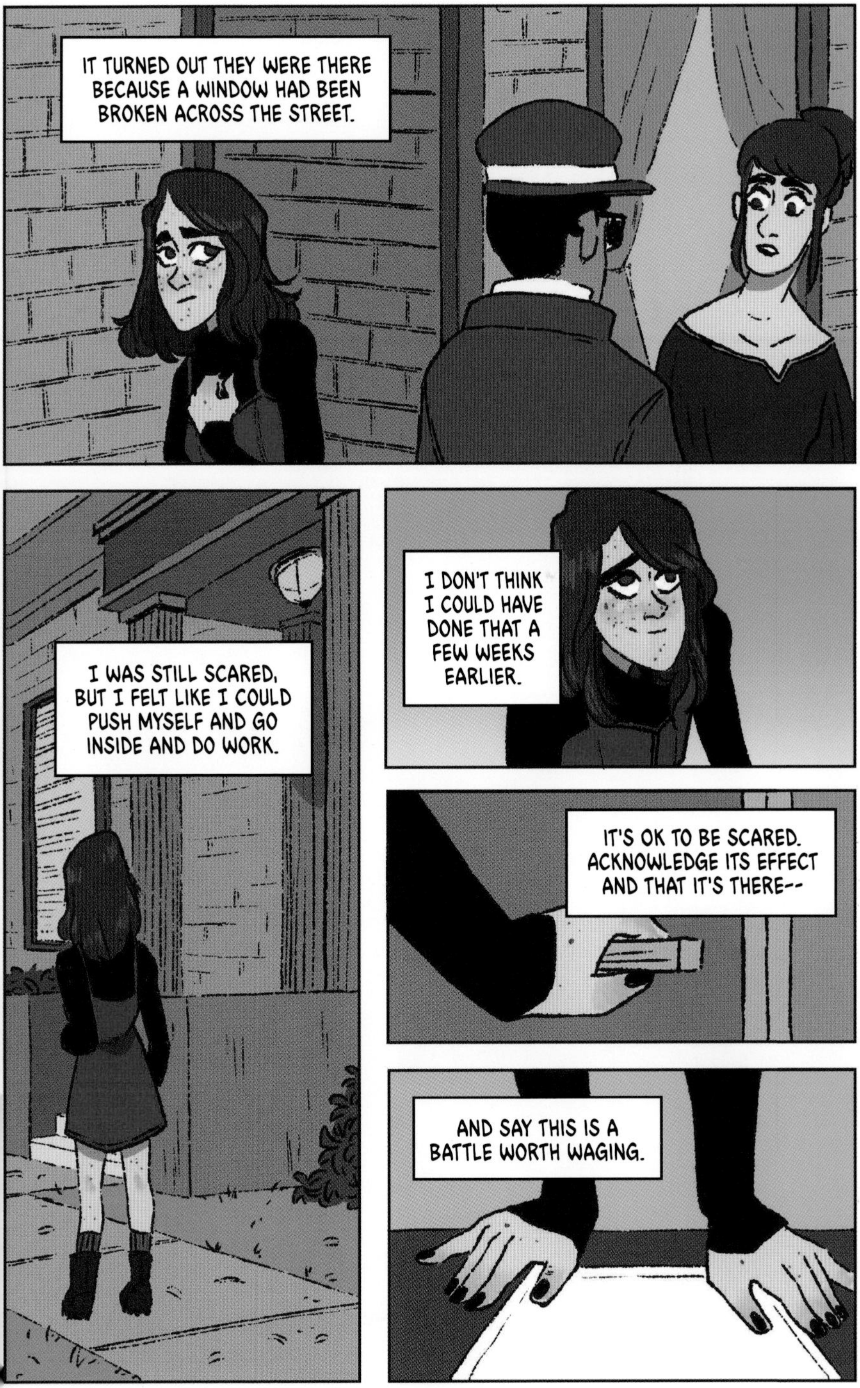

IT TURNED OUT THEY WERE THERE BECAUSE A WINDOW HAD BEEN BROKEN ACROSS THE STREET.
I WAS STILL SCARED, BUT I FELT LIKE I COULD PUSH MYSELF AND GO INSIDE AND DO WORK.
I DON'T THINK I COULD HAVE DONE THAT A FEW WEEKS EARLIER.
IT'S OK TO BE SCARED. ACKNOWLEDGE ITS EFFECT AND THAT IT'S THERE--
AND SAY THIS IS A BATTLE WORTH WAGING.

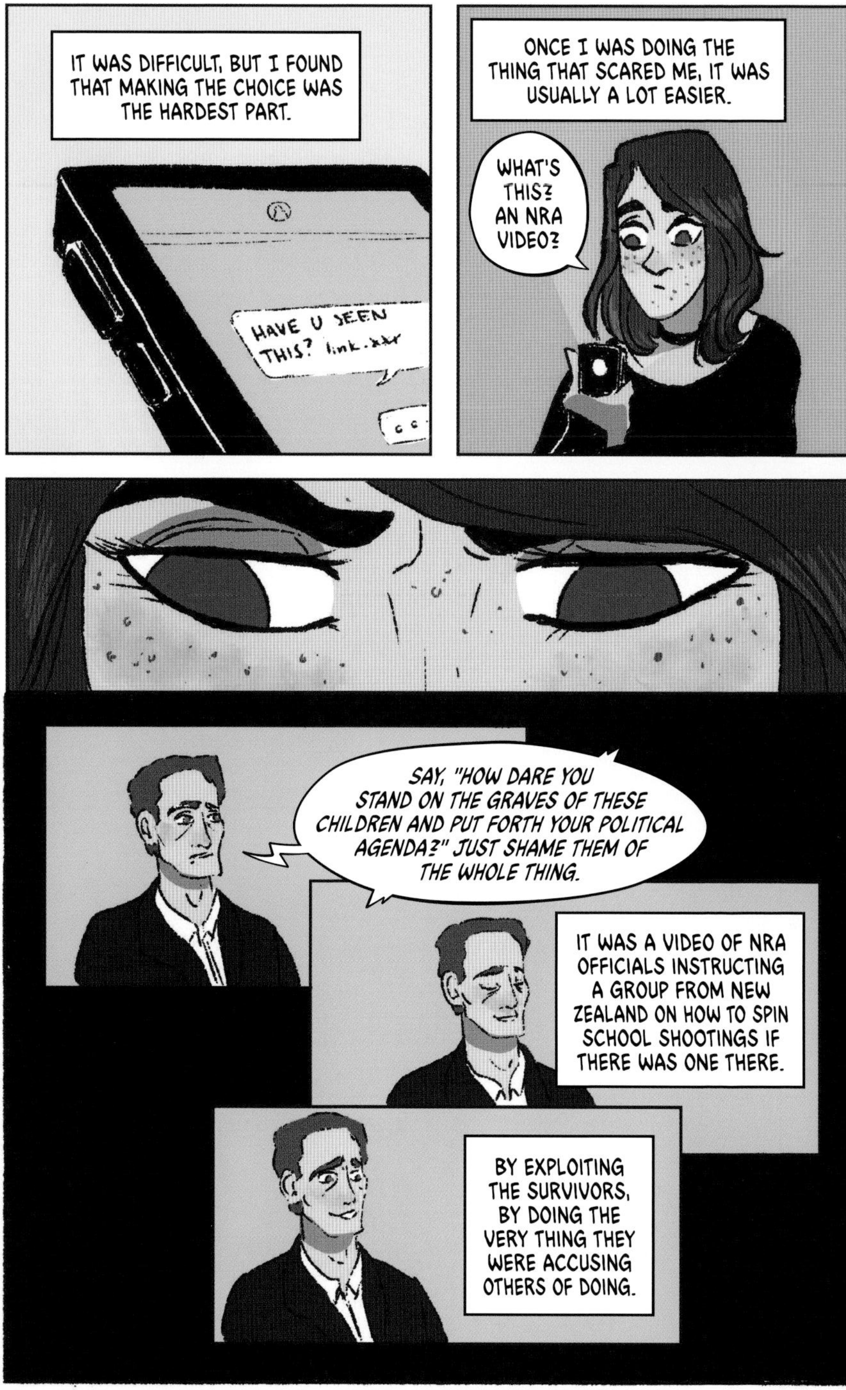
IT WAS DIFFICULT, BUT I FOUND THAT MAKING THE CHOICE WAS THE HARDEST PART.
HAVE U SEEN THIS? link.xxx
ONCE I WAS DOING THE THING THAT SCARED ME, IT WAS USUALLY A LOT EASIER.
WHAT'S THIS? AN NRA VIDEO?
SAY, "HOW DARE YOU STAND ON THE GRAVES OF THESE CHILDREN AND PUT FORTH YOUR POLITICAL AGENDA?" JUST SHAME THEM OF THE WHOLE THING.
IT WAS A VIDEO OF NRA OFFICIALS INSTRUCTING A GROUP FROM NEW ZEALAND ON HOW TO SPIN SCHOOL SHOOTINGS IF THERE WAS ONE THERE.
BY EXPLOITING THE SURVIVORS, BY DOING THE VERY THING THEY WERE ACCUSING OTHERS OF DOING.

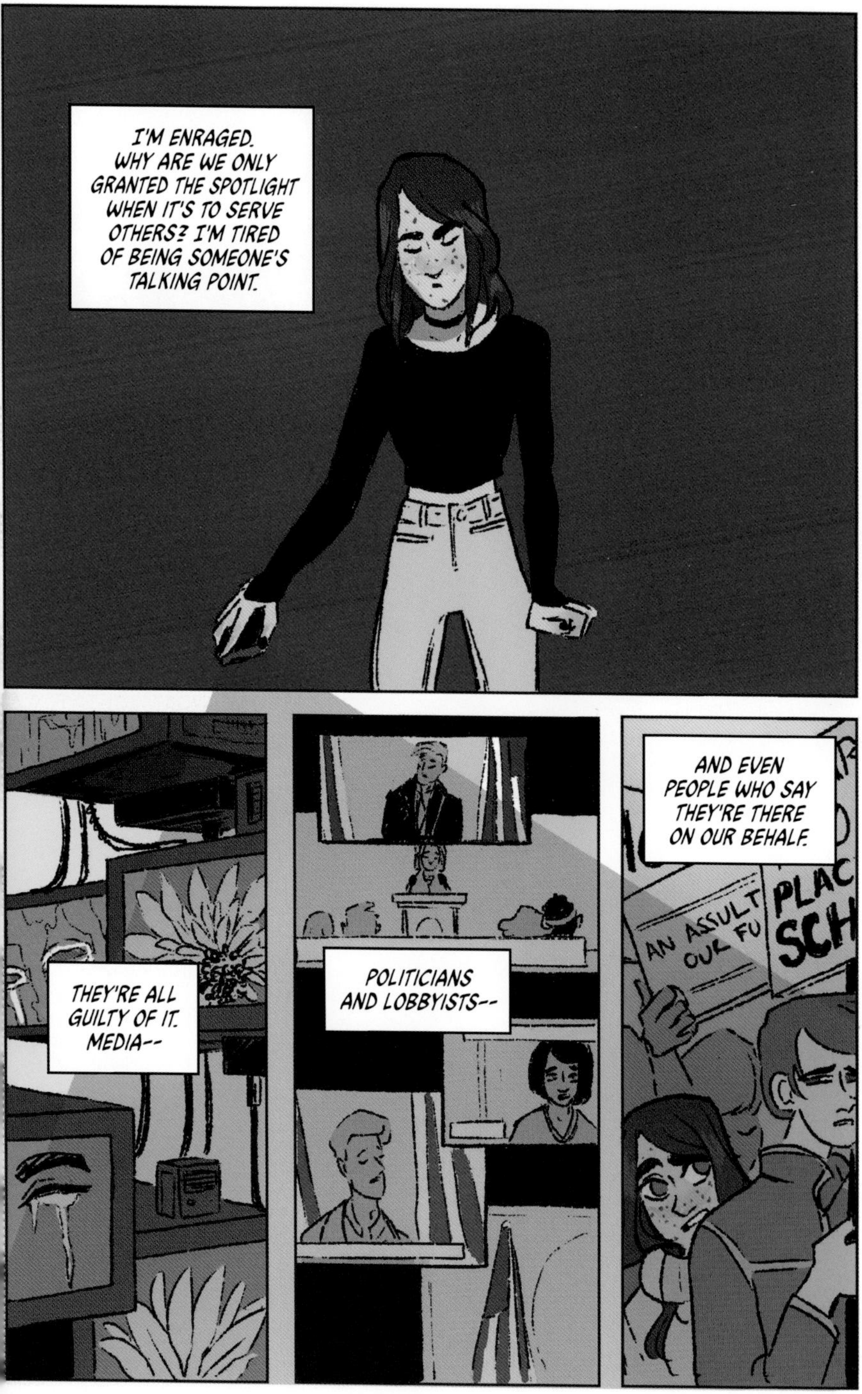
I'M ENRAGED. WHY ARE WE ONLY GRANTED THE SPOTLIGHT WHEN IT'S TO SERVE OTHERS? I'M TIRED OF BEING SOMEONE'S TALKING POINT.
THEY'RE ALL GUILTY OF IT. MEDIA--
POLITICIANS AND LOBBYISTS--
AND EVEN PEOPLE WHO SAY THEY'RE THERE ON OUR BEHALF.
AN ASSULT OUR FU
PLAC SCH

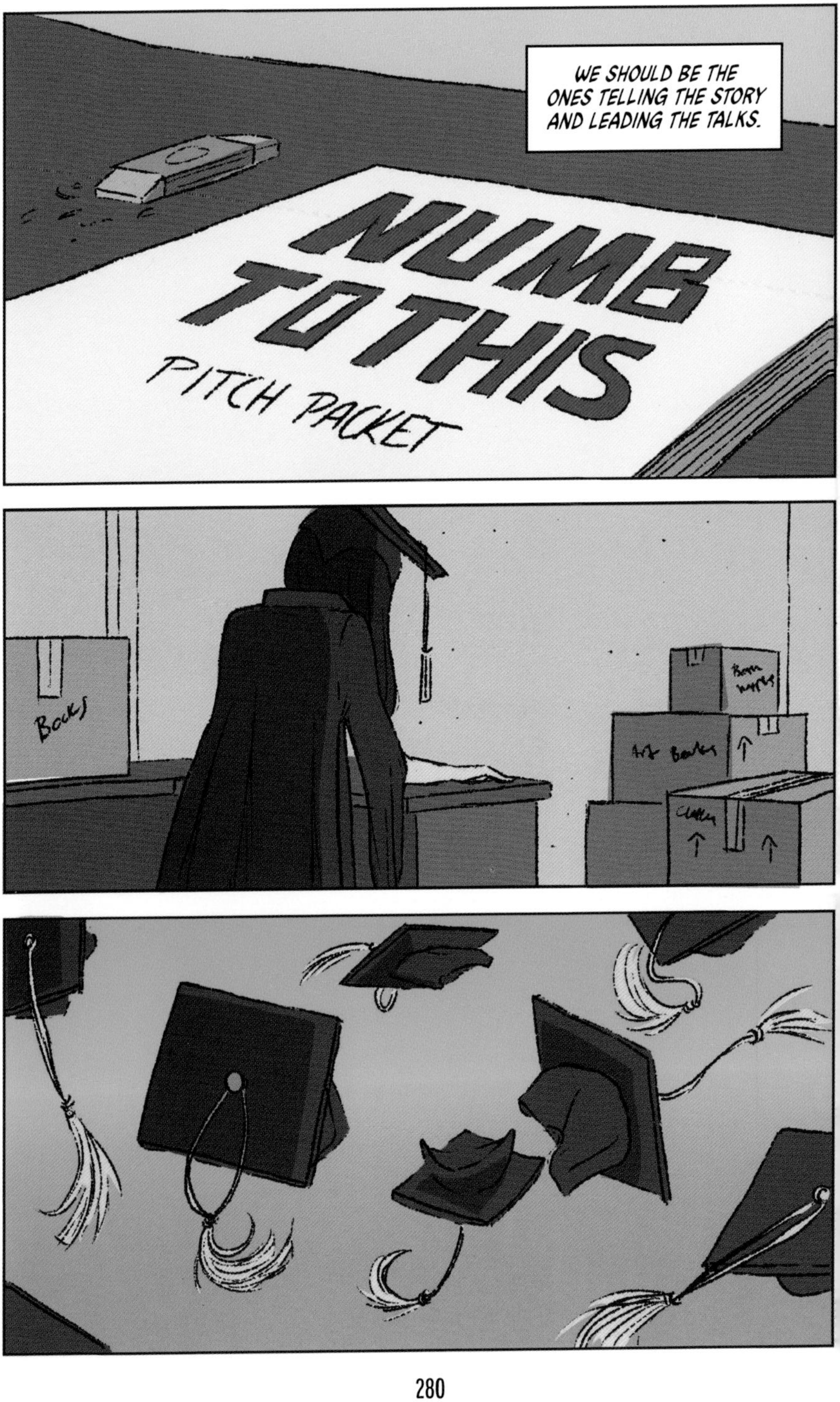
WE SHOULD BE THE ONES TELLING THE STORY AND LEADING THE TALKS.
NUMB TO THIS
PITCH PACKET
Books
Art Books

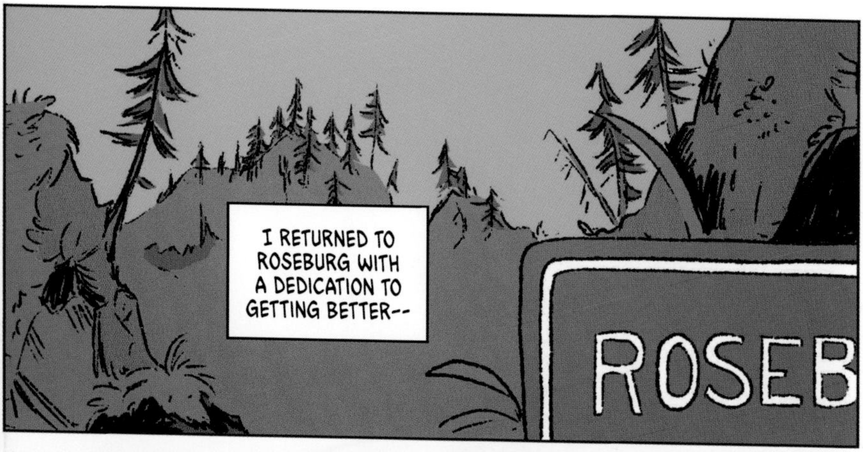
I RETURNED TO ROSEBURG WITH A DEDICATION TO GETTING BETTER--
ROSEB

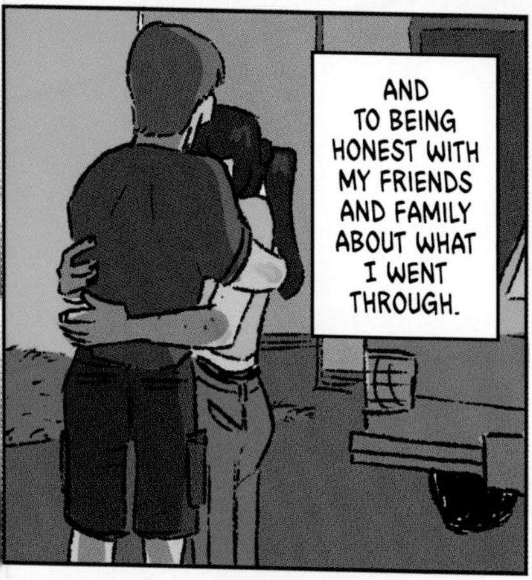
AND TO BEING HONEST WITH MY FRIENDS AND FAMILY ABOUT WHAT I WENT THROUGH.

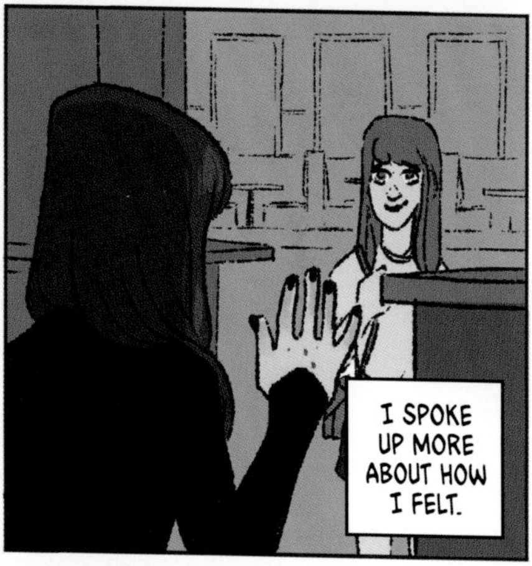
I SPOKE UP MORE ABOUT HOW I FELT.

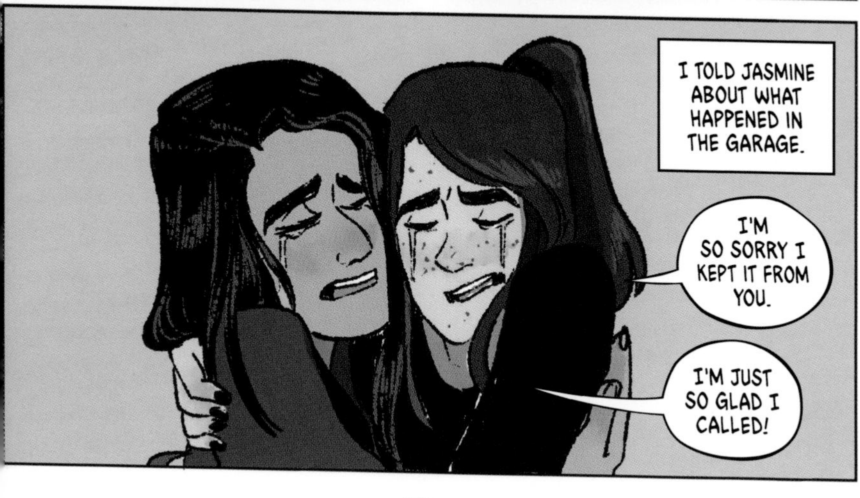
I TOLD JASMINE ABOUT WHAT HAPPENED IN THE GARAGE.
I'M SO SORRY I KEPT IT FROM YOU.
I'M JUST SO GLAD I CALLED!

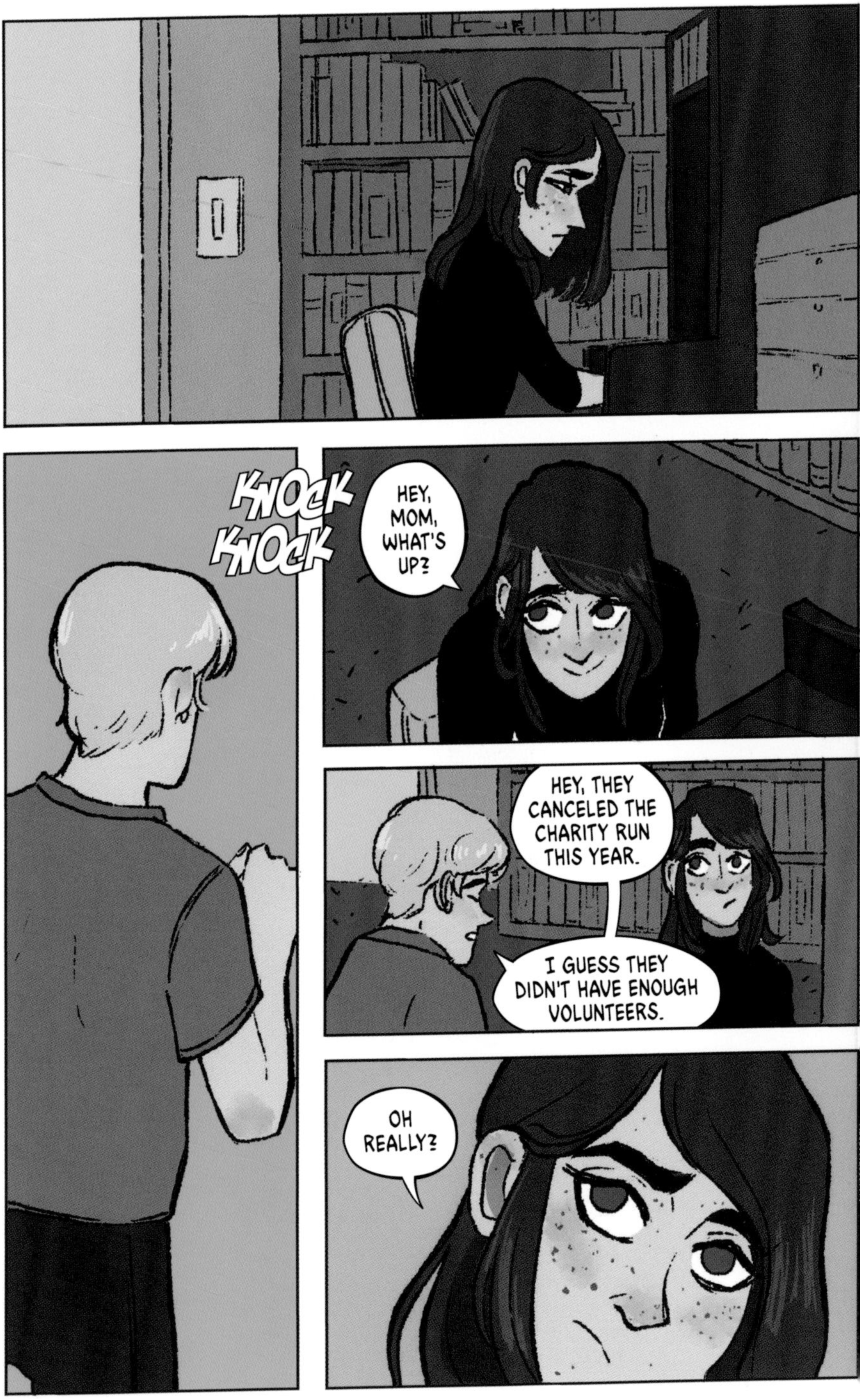
KNOCK KNOCK
HEY, MOM, WHAT'S UP?
HEY, THEY CANCELED THE CHARITY RUN THIS YEAR.
I GUESS THEY DIDN'T HAVE ENOUGH VOLUNTEERS.
OH REALLY?

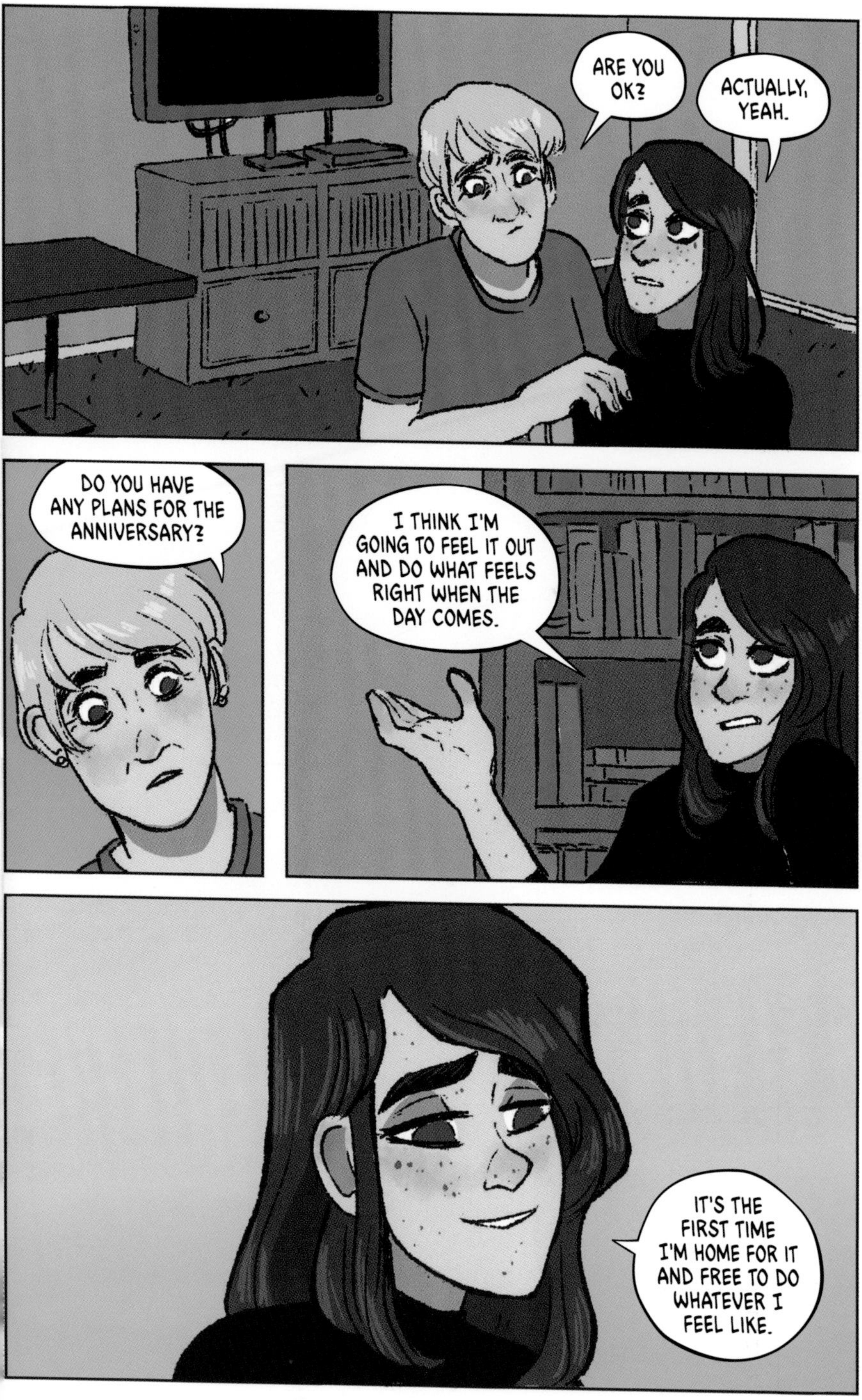
ARE YOU OK?
ACTUALLY, YEAH.
DO YOU HAVE ANY PLANS FOR THE ANNIVERSARY?
I THINK I'M GOING TO FEEL IT OUT AND DO WHAT FEELS RIGHT WHEN THE DAY COMES.
IT'S THE FIRST TIME I'M HOME FOR IT AND FREE TO DO WHATEVER I FEEL LIKE.

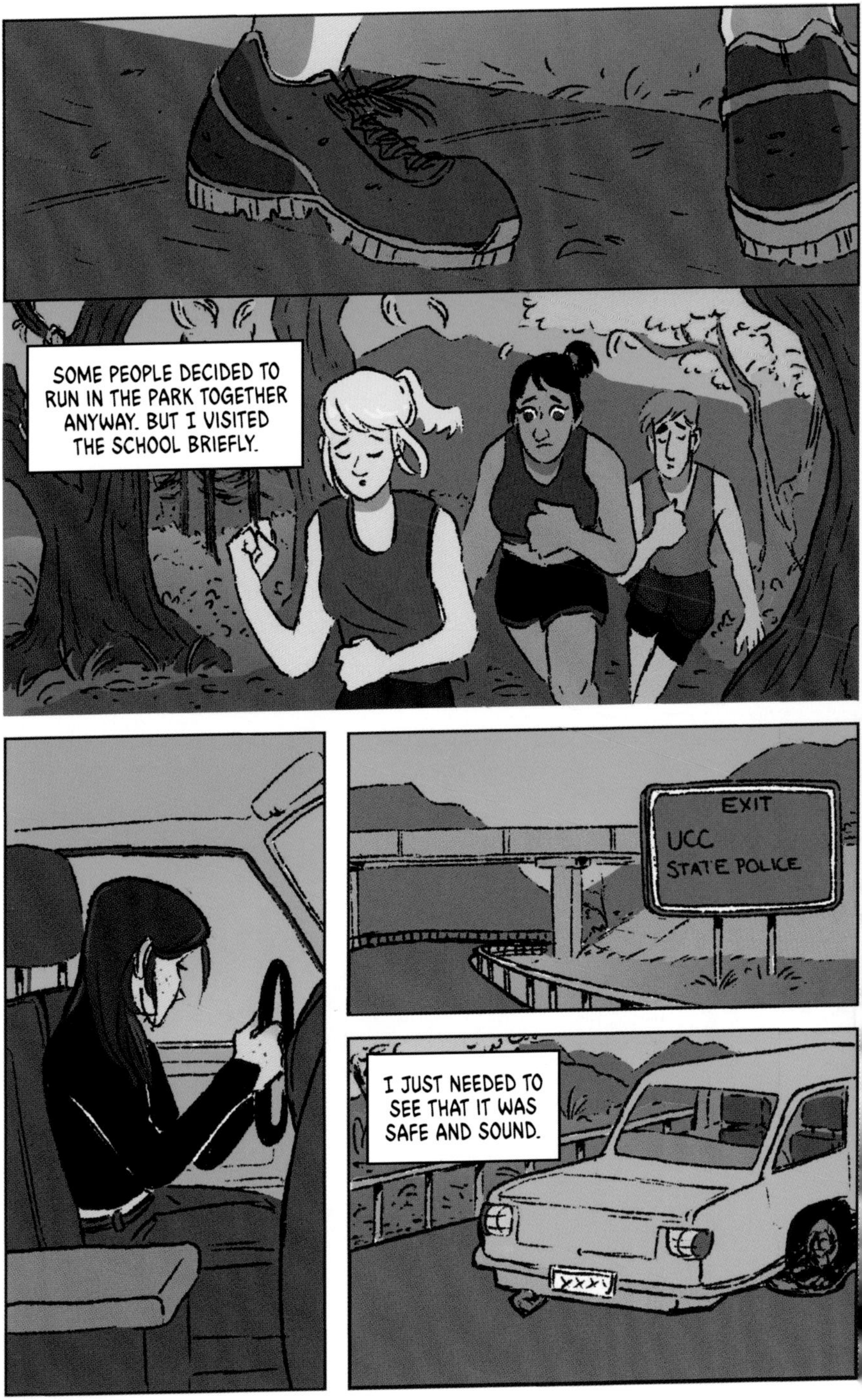
SOME PEOPLE DECIDED TO RUN IN THE PARK TOGETHER ANYWAY. BUT I VISITED THE SCHOOL BRIEFLY.
EXIT
UCC
STATE POLICE
I JUST NEEDED TO SEE THAT IT WAS SAFE AND SOUND.

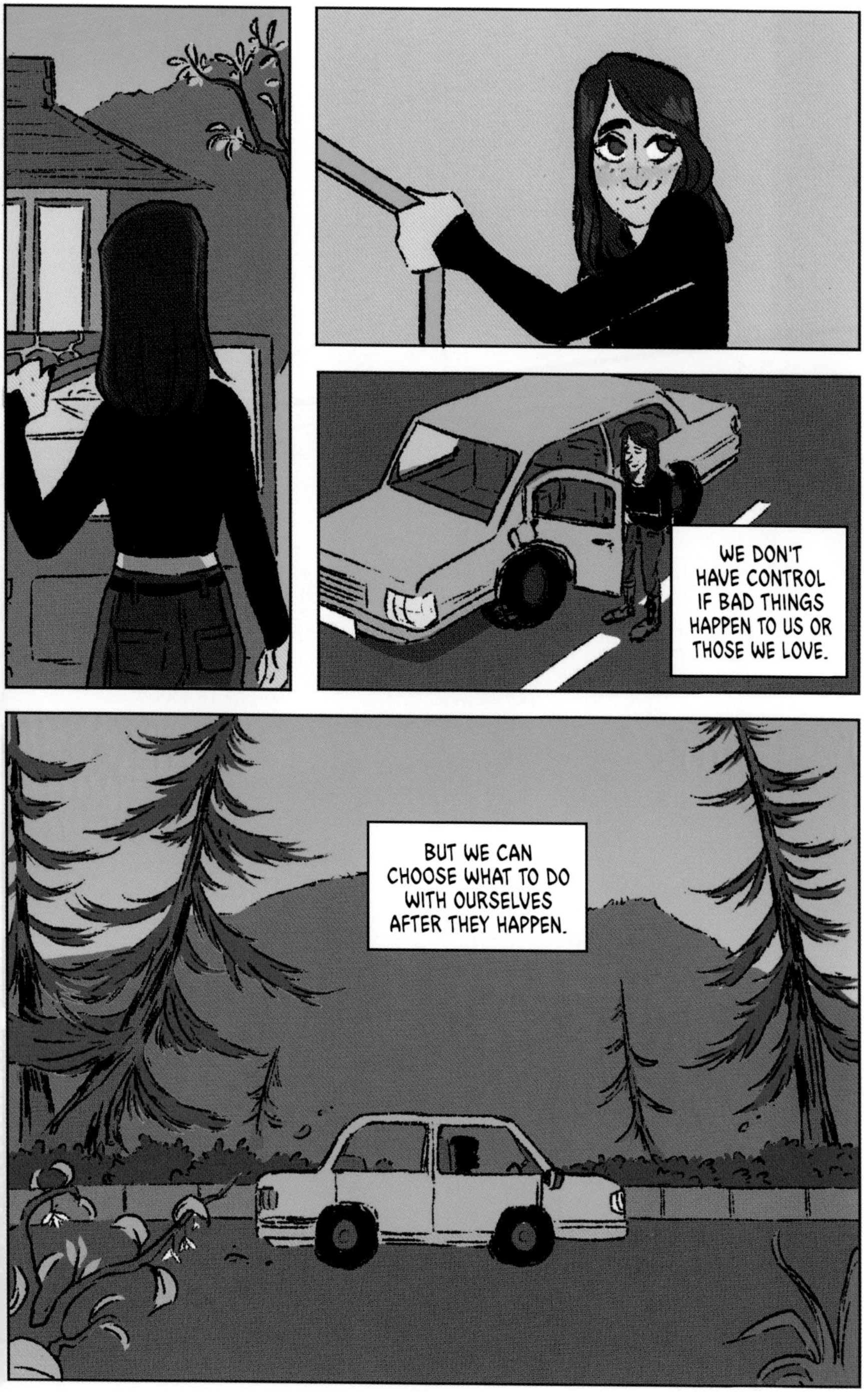
WE DON'T HAVE CONTROL IF BAD THINGS HAPPEN TO US OR THOSE WE LOVE.
BUT WE CAN CHOOSE WHAT TO DO WITH OURSELVES AFTER THEY HAPPEN.

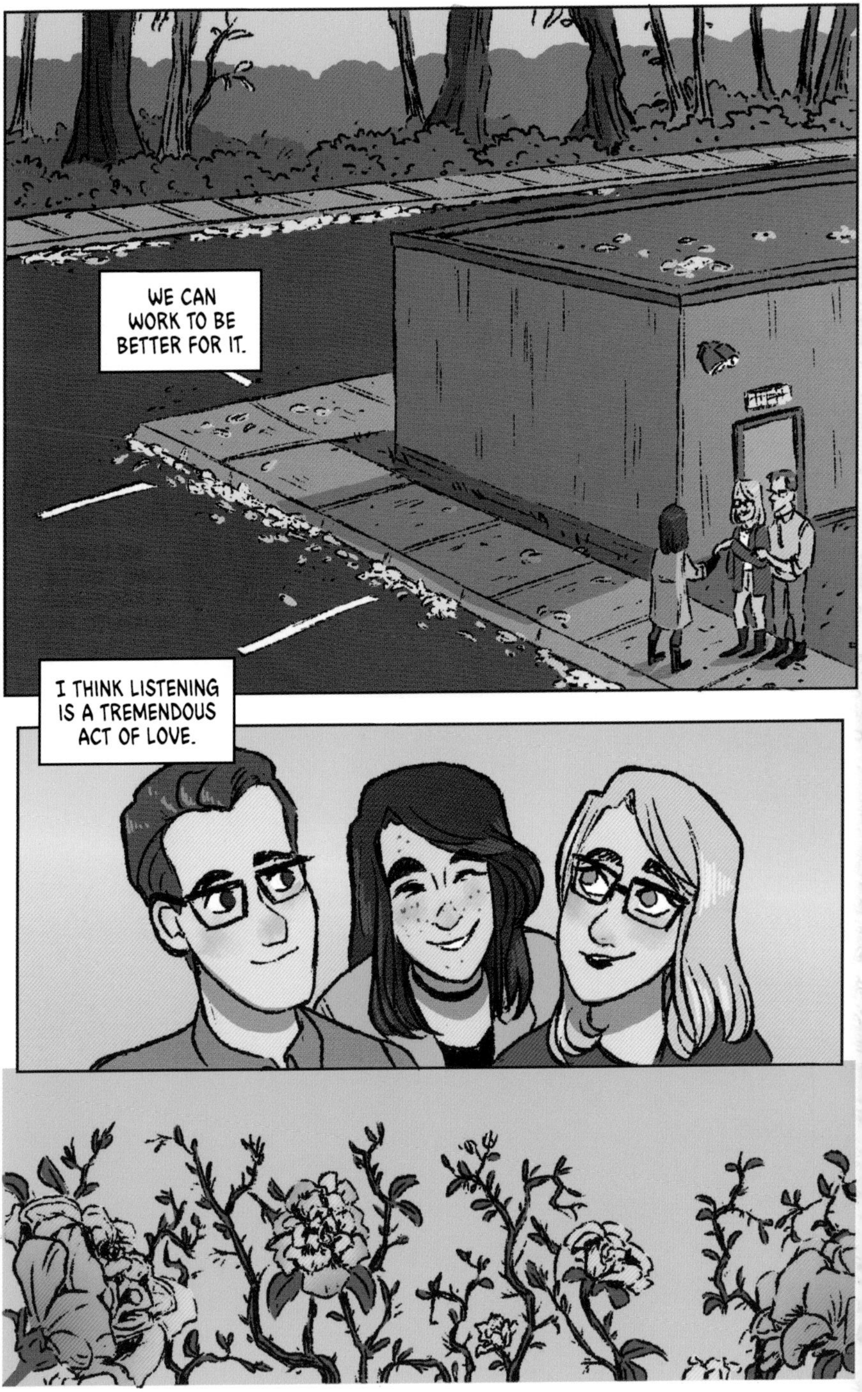
WE CAN WORK TO BE BETTER FOR IT.
I THINK LISTENING IS A TREMENDOUS ACT OF LOVE.

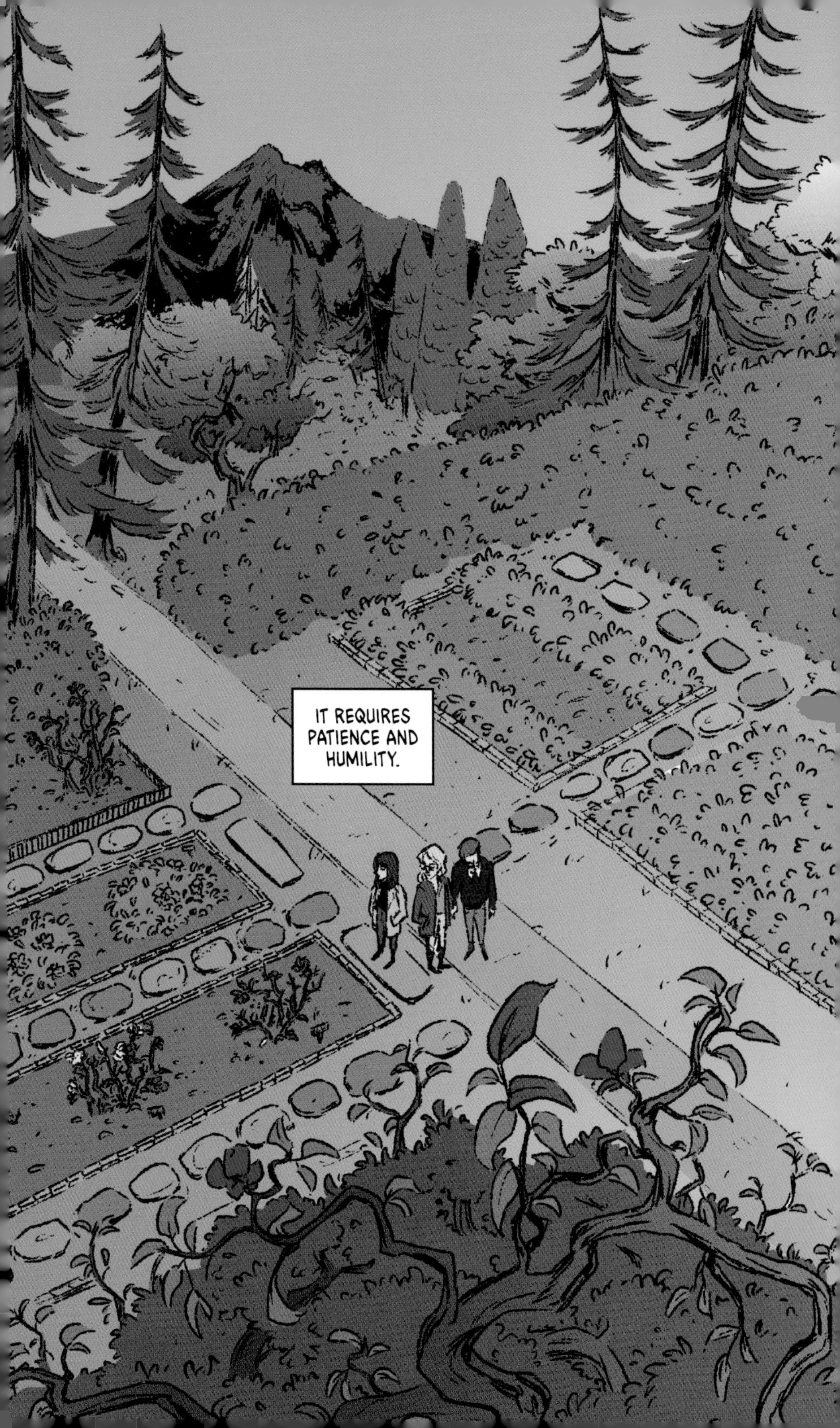
IT REQUIRES PATIENCE AND HUMILITY.

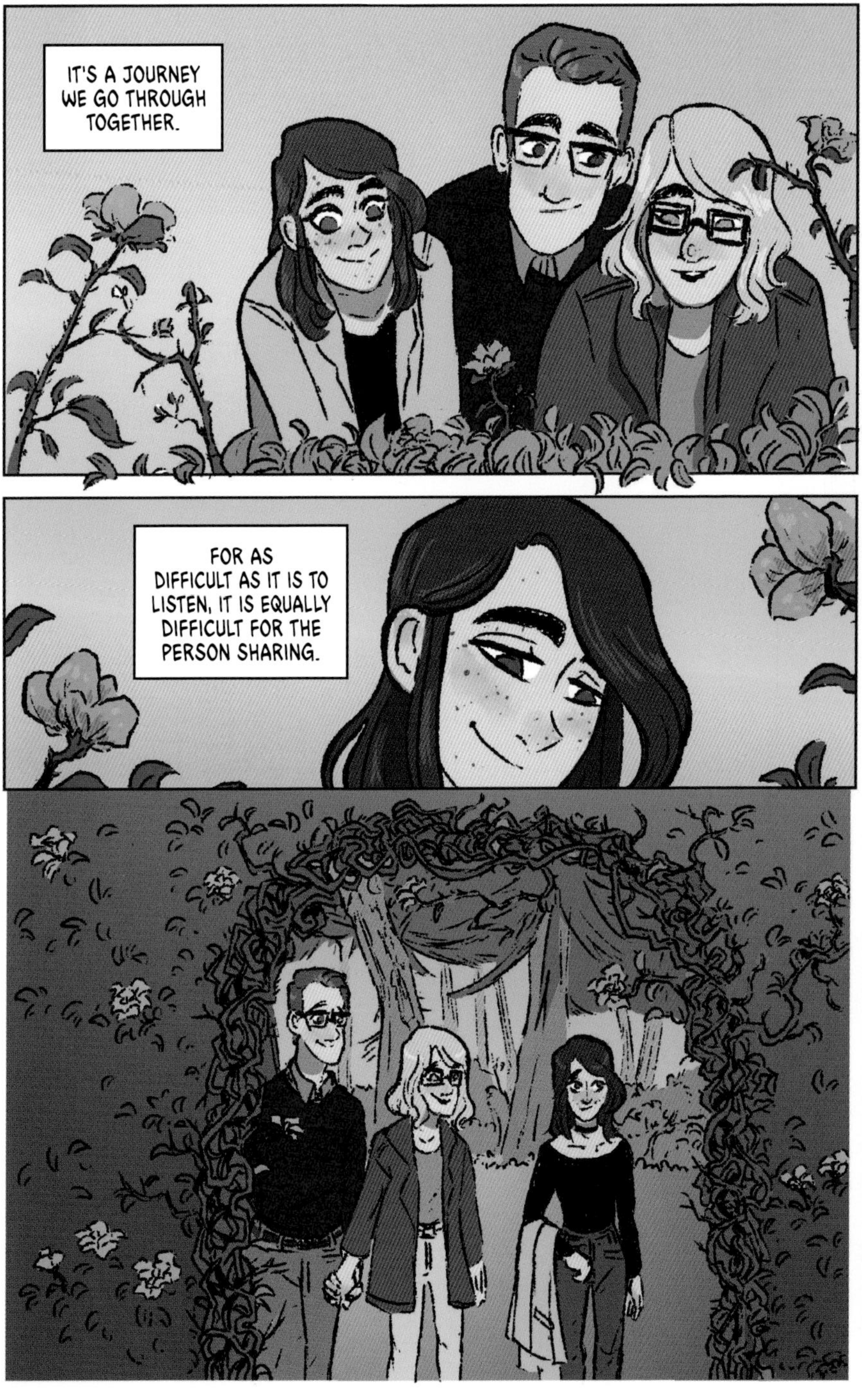
IT'S A JOURNEY WE GO THROUGH TOGETHER.
FOR AS DIFFICULT AS IT IS TO LISTEN, IT IS EQUALLY DIFFICULT FOR THE PERSON SHARING.

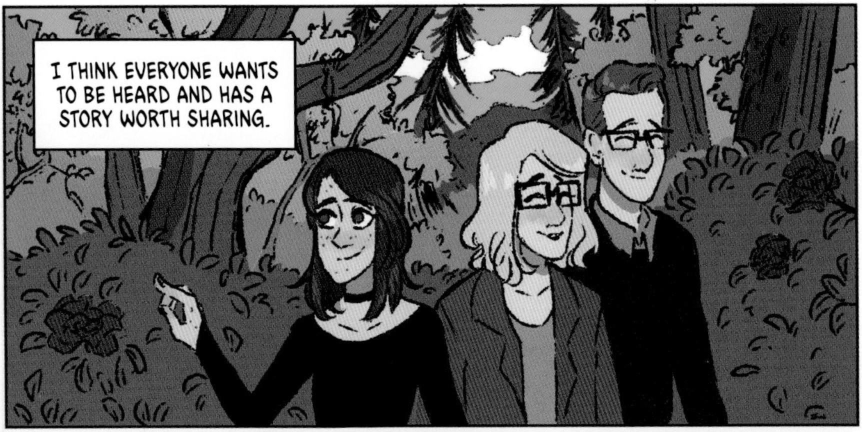
I THINK EVERYONE WANTS TO BE HEARD AND HAS A STORY WORTH SHARING.

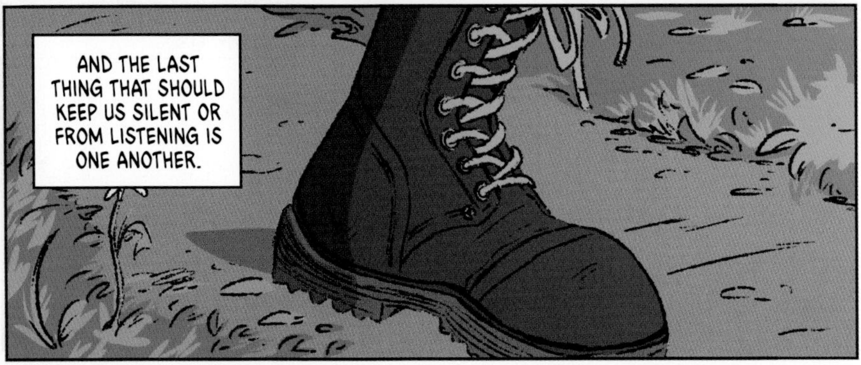
AND THE LAST THING THAT SHOULD KEEP US SILENT OR FROM LISTENING IS ONE ANOTHER.

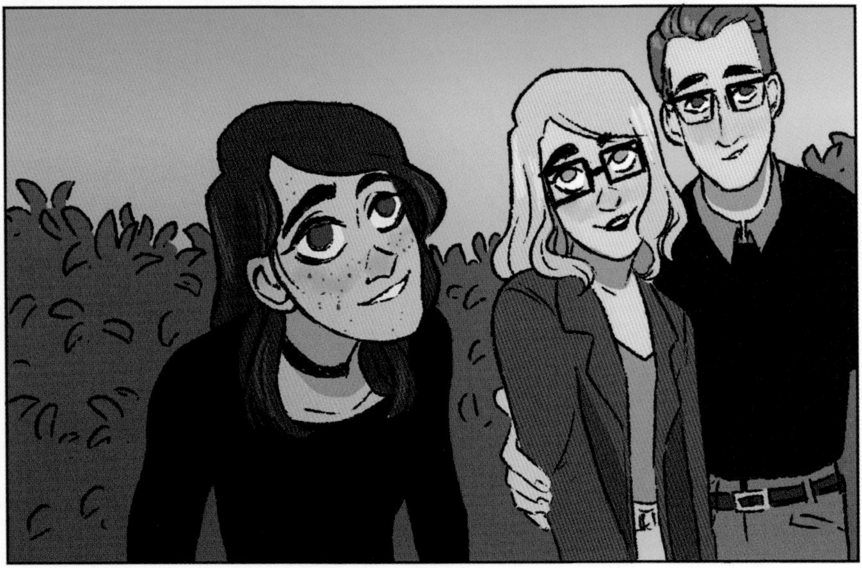

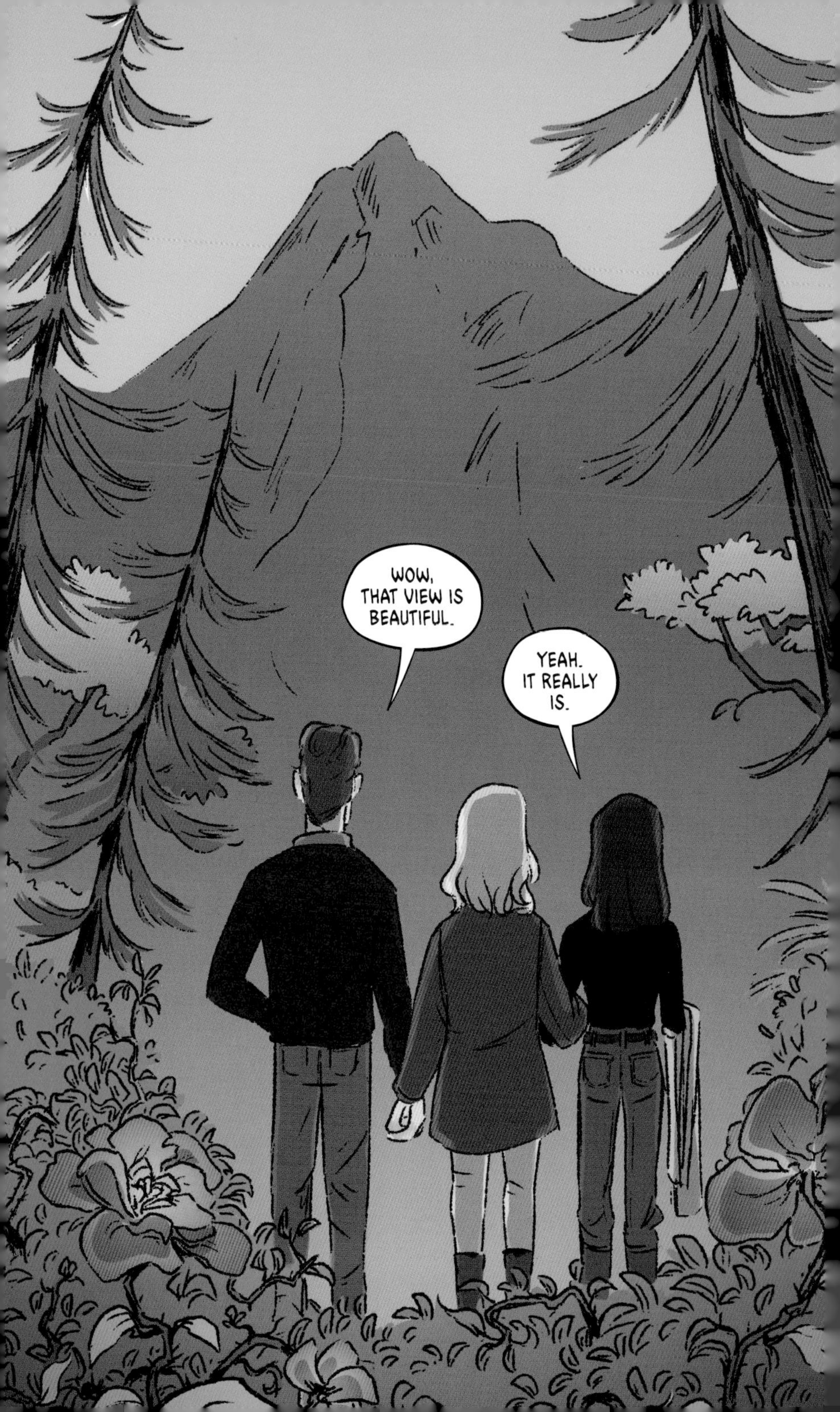
WOW, THAT VIEW IS BEAUTIFUL.
YEAH. IT REALLY IS.

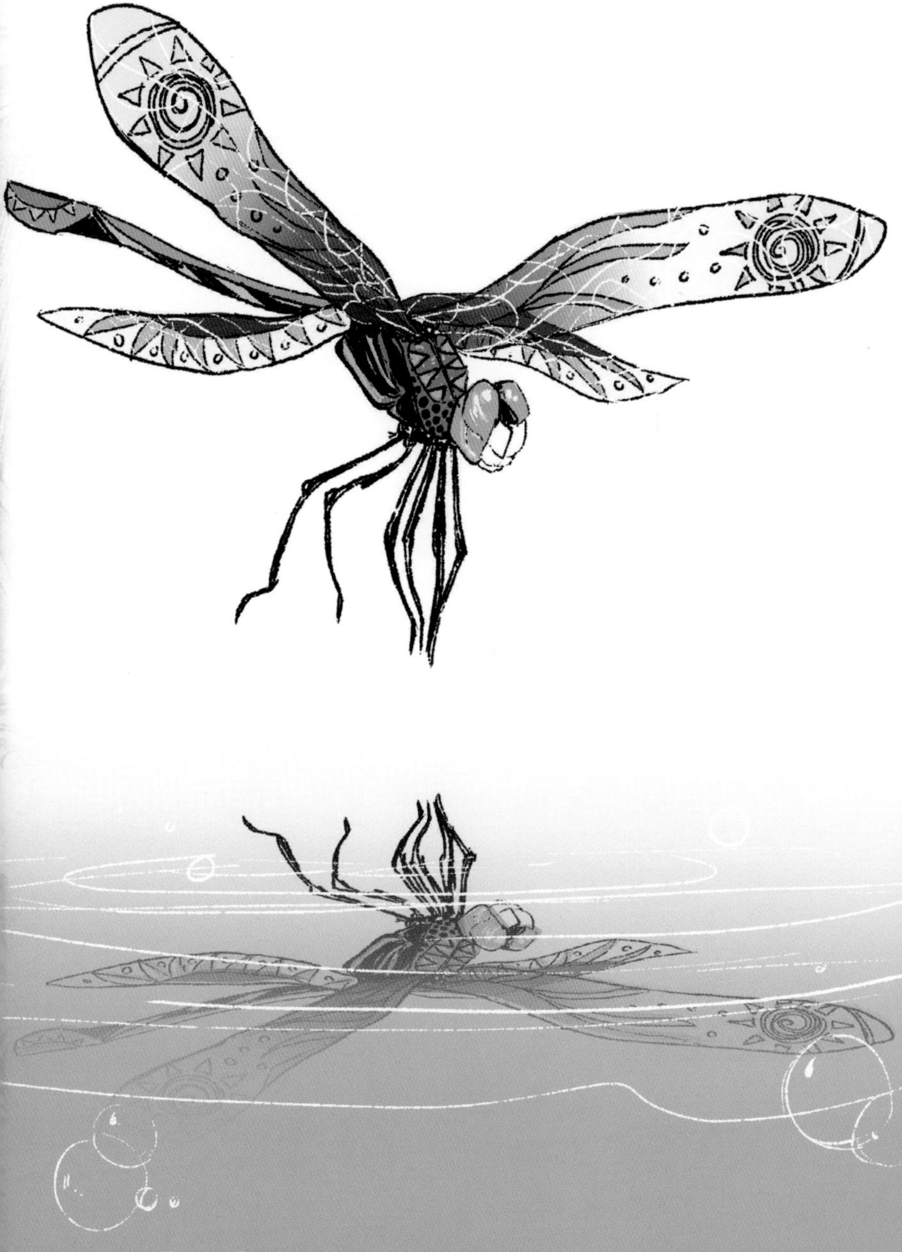

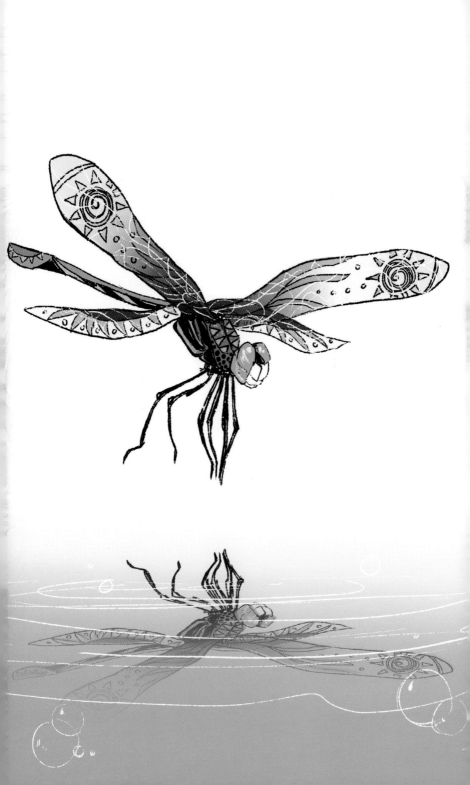

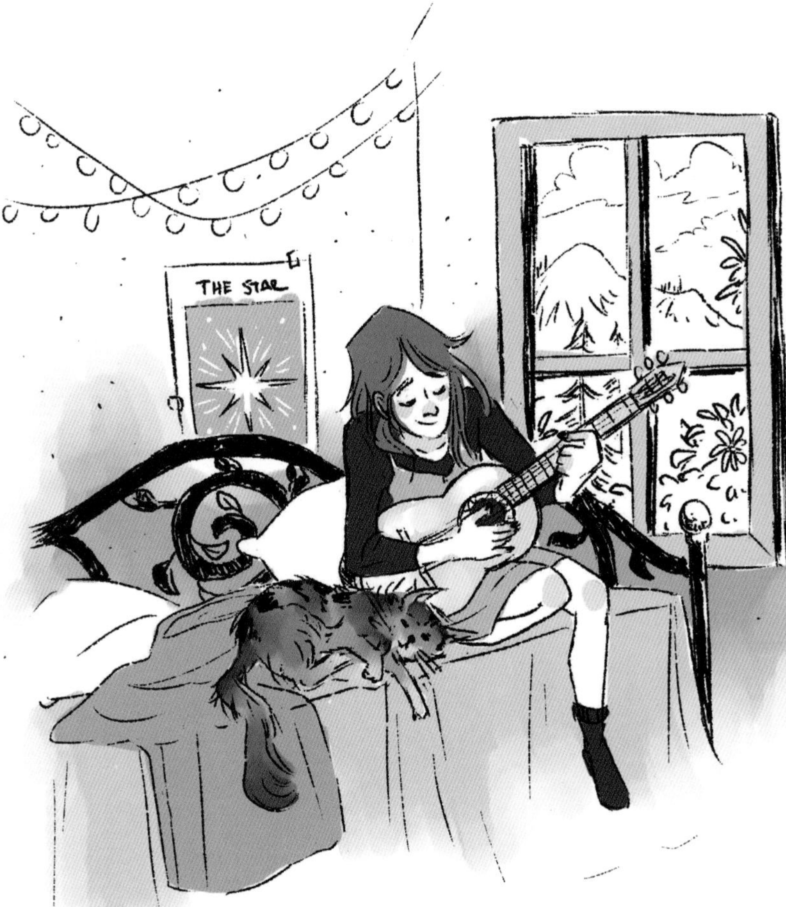
THE STAR

AUTHOR'S NOTE

I'd like to share one more moment with you. A good portion of people who have wanted or attempted to take their lives say that they are glad they didn't. When I first heard this, it almost made me feel even more miserable, because I thought that this feeling would come at major achievements in my life: graduation or a friend's wedding or getting a book deal. I would spend most of these important milestones pacing around and waiting for this euphoric joy I was supposed to feel, and when I didn't, I would be disappointed. I felt a lot of shame for several years for being indifferent toward being alive and for those times when I still struggled with those thoughts.

So here's the moment, about four years after my attempt, when I was truly happy that I was still on this earth. Jasmine has moved down to LA for her work, and I am visiting. This is in the weeks leading up to the pandemic, late January of 2020. Her husband takes me out to go surfing with one of his buddies. They decide to take me the day after it has rained, so the water is all murky and gray from runoff from the city, and it's frigid. I've been surfing a few times, but never in cold water. We've been out there for an hour or so, and I'm not able to stand up on the board. I keep getting tossed under the freezing waves over and over again. I paddle out. I grab a wave. I start to stand. I'm under. Over and over. But there's just something about the moment that the water takes me under. I relax and let it flip me around, and it puts me on my feet. I stick the landing, so to speak, and just walk out of the surf. Eventually, I'm so tired that Jasmine's husband and his friend have to help me get back out over the surf so that I can keep going, but I'm not even trying to stand anymore. I'm just waiting for that moment when the water takes me under.

I get time to myself when the boys are a little way off. I'm sitting out on my board, letting the waves go by, resting, and it hits then. I start crying. Hard. It's not euphoric joy. It's gratitude. Unbelievable, overwhelming gratitude. I could try to intellectualize that moment. I could say something to the effect that the waves were a metaphor for letting go of control, or that water is often symbolic of emotions, but I truly think I was just enjoying myself. It was fun being alive. I liked crashing into the waves. I liked getting tossed around. I liked that it was freezing cold and kind of stinky and a little bit slimy. Most of all, I liked that I kept doing something just because I wanted to.

I've had several more moments like that since then. They're not frequent, and often they're in circumstances that I don't imagine would appeal to many others. The best thing about having them is that when I feel myself struggling again, I can think about them. I'm not worried about having another one of these moments of gratitude. I'm comforted knowing that I have the potential to feel the most alive while playing in dirty water.

RESOURCES

THE REBELS PROJECT

Website: *therebelsproject.org*

Founded by survivors of the Columbine shooting, this supportive group has worked to create a safe environment, specific
resources, and programs to help survivors heal. Involvement
can also include donation, sponsorship, and volunteer service.

I highly encourage anyone that is a part of the survivor community to reach out and take advantage of the thoughtful and
much-needed resources this group provides.

NATIONAL SUICIDE PREVENTION LIFELINE

Website: *suicidepreventionlifeline.org*

Phone: 1-800-273-8255

Available 24/7, they connect you with the nearest crisis center.
Their website also includes education on warning signs, pre-
vention, and other topics surrounding suicide attempts.

MARCH FOR OUR LIVES

Website: *marchforourlives.com*

Gun violence is not random, and March For Our Lives has
numerous programs, events, and resources available to edu-
cate on and help combat this issue. Covering issues like mass
shootings, police brutality, domestic violence, and hate crimes,
this organization is empowering others to vote on policies that
save lives.

You can join a local chapter, donate, or support through merch
and awareness.

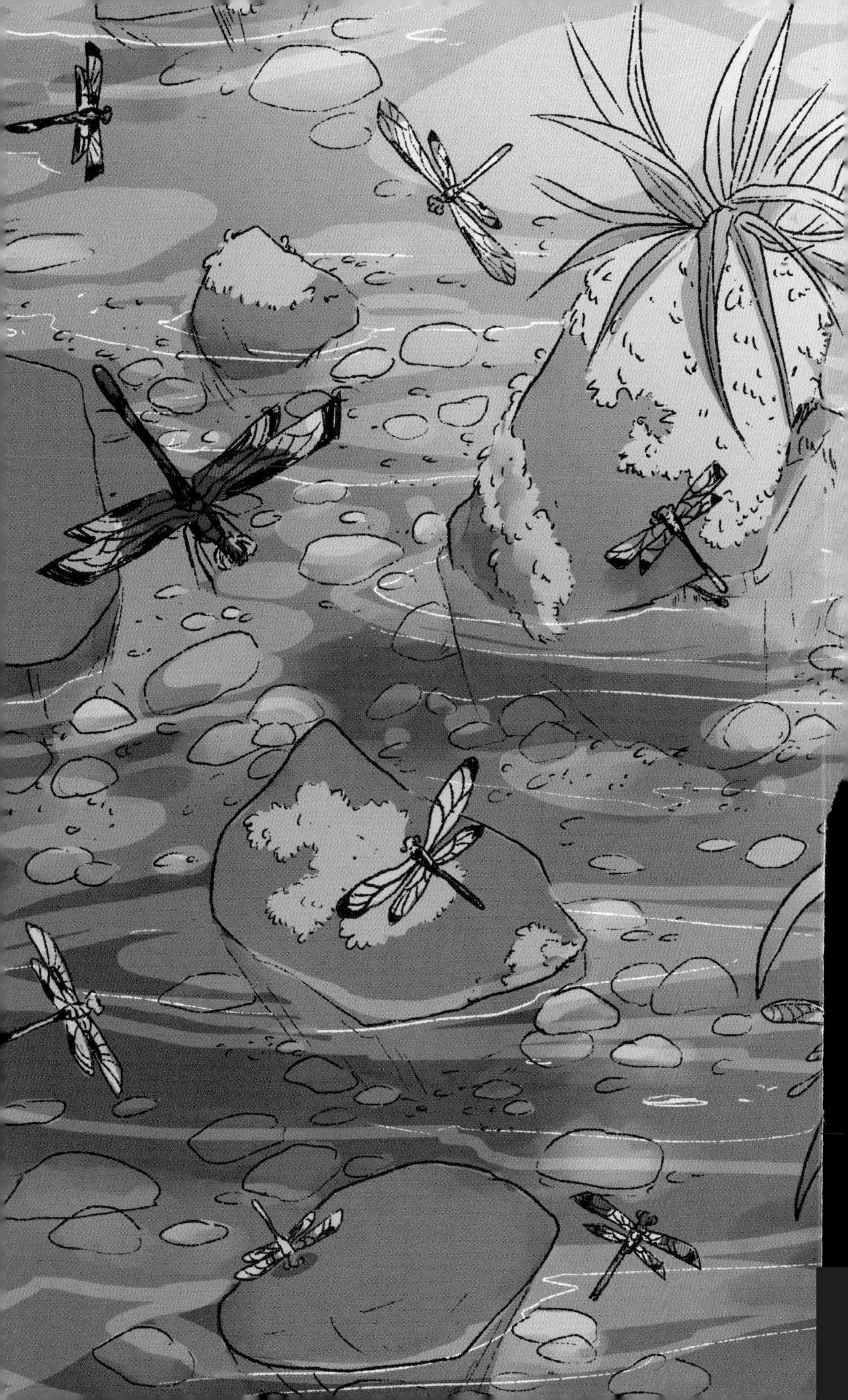

ACKNOWLEDGMENTS

I forgot to thank my mom in a graduation speech in 2016, and she hasn't let me live it down since. So I'd first like to thank my mom for all her support, not only during the making of this book, but in all the events that led up to it and after. I'd also like to thank my aunt Angie and uncle Scott for being incredibly encouraging and supportive of my art education and career.

I have a number of teachers and professors in my life who helped set me on my way. I'd like to thank the entire staff of Umpqua Community College for the absolute best educational experience of my life. Special thanks to the art department, and especially Susan Rochester. I would not have pursued art without you.

Thank you to the professors and staff of the Sequential Art Department at SCAD. You literally made this possible.

Thank you to everyone at Little, Brown who helped shape this book and gave it a place to grow. Thank you to my amazing editor, Andrea Colvin, and art director, Megan McLaughlin. Thank you to Juan Murillo for your amazing work during the coloring.

Lastly, thank you to Jasmine. You and Lexa are the reason I'm here today.

ABOUT THE AUTHOR

Chloe Friedlein

KINDRA NEELY is an artist and writer based in southern Oregon. She took her first drawing class, Drawing Nature, at UCC and still likes to regularly hike the trails to sketch flowers and ferns. *Numb to This* is her debut graphic novel.